SOCIAL INCLUSION: SOCIETAL AND ORGANIZATIONAL IMPLICATIONS FOR INFORMATION SYSTEMS

IFIP – The International Federation for Information Processing

IFIP was founded in 1960 under the auspices of UNESCO, following the First World Computer Congress held in Paris the previous year. An umbrella organization for societies working in information processing, IFIP's aim is two-fold: to support information processing within its member countries and to encourage technology transfer to developing nations. As its mission statement clearly states,

> *IFIP's mission is to be the leading, truly international, apolitical organization which encourages and assists in the development, exploitation and application of information technology for the benefit of all people.*

IFIP is a non-profitmaking organization, run almost solely by 2500 volunteers. It operates through a number of technical committees, which organize events and publications. IFIP's events range from an international congress to local seminars, but the most important are:

• The IFIP World Computer Congress, held every second year;
• Open conferences;
• Working conferences.

The flagship event is the IFIP World Computer Congress, at which both invited and contributed papers are presented. Contributed papers are rigorously refereed and the rejection rate is high.

As with the Congress, participation in the open conferences is open to all and papers may be invited or submitted. Again, submitted papers are stringently refereed.

The working conferences are structured differently. They are usually run by a working group and attendance is small and by invitation only. Their purpose is to create an atmosphere conducive to innovation and development. Refereeing is less rigorous and papers are subjected to extensive group discussion.

Publications arising from IFIP events vary. The papers presented at the IFIP World Computer Congress and at open conferences are published as conference proceedings, while the results of the working conferences are often published as collections of selected and edited papers.

Any national society whose primary activity is in information may apply to become a full member of IFIP, although full membership is restricted to one society per country. Full members are entitled to vote at the annual General Assembly. National societies preferring a less committed involvement may apply for associate or corresponding membership. Associate members enjoy the same benefits as full members, but without voting rights. Corresponding members are not represented in IFIP bodies. Affiliated membership is open to non-national societies, and individual and honorary membership schemes are also offered.

SOCIAL INCLUSION: SOCIETAL AND ORGANIZATIONAL IMPLICATIONS FOR INFORMATION SYSTEMS

IFIP TC8 WG8.2 International Working Conference, July 12-15, 2006, Limerick, Ireland

Edited by

Eileen M. Trauth
The Pennsylvania State University
University Park, PA USA

Debra Howcroft
The University of Manchester
Manchester, UK

Tom Butler
University College Cork
Cork, Ireland

Brian Fitzgerald
University of Limerick
Limerick, Ireland

Janice I. DeGross
University of Minnesota
Minneapolis, MN USA

 Springer

Social Inclusion: Societal and Organizational Implications for Information Systems

Edited by E. Trauth, D. Howcroft, T. Butler, B. Fitzgerald, and J. DeGross

   p. cm. (IFIP International Federation for Information Processing, a Springer Series in Computer Science)

ISSN: 1571-5736 / 1861-2288 (Internet)

eISBN: 10: 0-387-34588-4
Printed on acid-free paper

ISBN: 13: 978-1-4419-4181-7   e-ISBN: 13: 978-0-387-34588-8

9 8 7 6 5 4 3 2 1
springer.com

Contents

Part 4: Demographic Disparities

Part 5: Ethical Issues

Part 6: Technology and its Consequences

Part 7: The Information Systems Profession

PREFACE

This book represents the compilation of papers presented at the IFIP Working Group 8.2 conference entitled "Social Inclusion: Societal and Organizational Implications for Information Systems." The conference took place at the University of Limerick in Ireland on July 12-15, 2006. This conference was truly global in scope. A total of 58 papers were submitted from around the world. Thirteen papers came from North America, 41 from Europe, 2 from Africa, 2 from Asia, and 4 from Oceana (Australia/New Zealand/Polynesia). Papers went through a double-blind review process. The program committee and the additional reviewers enabled us to see the process through to a successful conclusion. Following the review process of the 58 submissions, 24 were accepted for presentation at the conference. In addition, five panel proposals were submitted from which two were accepted. In keeping with the theme of inclusion, a new feature of this year's conference is a poster session. The poster session was established in order to provide a forum for authors of emergent work to receive feedback from the IFIP 8.2 community. Eight papers presented as poster sessions are available on a CD.

We are grateful for the support of the sponsoring and host organizations, whose involvement, endorsement, and financial contribution enabled this conference to come to fruition. We would like to extend our thanks to the following organizations:

- IFIP and in particular Working Group 8.2
- Science Foundation Ireland
- University of Limerick
- University of Manchester
- The Pennsylvania State University

Finally, we would like to acknowledge and thank a few individuals for all the behind the scenes work that they did to make this conference a success. We would like to thank Brian Lake of the University of Limerick for setting up and managing the conference website. We would like to thank Haiyan Huang of Pennsylvania State University for managing program committee recruitment and the submission and review system. Finally, we would like to thank Lorraine Morgan of the University of Limerick for managing all the details associated with local arrangements.

Eileen Trauth
Debra Howcroft
Tom Butler
Brian Fitzgerald
Janice I. DeGross

CONFERENCE CHAIRS

General Chair
Julie Kendall
Rutgers University, U.S.A.

Program Chairs
Eileen M. Trauth
The Pennsylvania State University, U.S.A.

Debra Howcroft
University of Manchester, UK

Organizing Chairs
Tom Butler
University College Cork, Ireland

Brian Fitzgerald
Univerity of Limerick, Ireland

PROGRAM COMMITTEE

ADDITIONAL REVIEWERS

Part 1

Introduction

1 SOCIAL INCLUSION AND THE INFORMATION SYSTEMS FIELD: Why Now?

Eileen M. Trauth
The Pennsylvania State University
University Park, PA U.S.A.

Debra Howcroft
University of Manchester
Manchester, UK

1 INTRODUCTION

The Information Systems field and its research conferences have historically focused their attention on issues associated with the development and diffusion of information systems (IS) and the information and communications technologies (ICTs) upon which they are based. Consideration of the social consequences of new systems and new ICTs has generally been limited to investigations of organizational and managerial impact. Thus, this conference, with its focus on those who are socially excluded, represents a noteworthy expansion in scope for the IFIP 8.2 community. In view of this, one might reasonably ask how this topic came to be chosen as the conference theme at this point in time.

With respect to "why now," perhaps the best answer is that by now, in the early 21st century, we have sufficient confirmation of societal disparities, which could perhaps be ameliorated by the use of ICTs, to know that our community should play a role in addressing them. We have ample evidence that changes in the human condition that have accompanied the pervasiveness of information technology have been both positive and negative, intended and unintended, and that they extend beyond the boundaries of the corporation. These consequences have demonstrated that certain countries and certain regions of the world are not full participants in the so-called information society, that certain parts of every population are underrepresented in and underserved by the IT sector. On a daily basis, the consequences of ICTs are revealed in the individuals who directly experience social exclusion.

Please use the following format when citing this chapter:

Trauth, E.M., and Howcroft, D., 2006, in IFIP International Federation for Information Processing, Volume 208, Social Inclusion: Societal and Organizational Implications for Information Systems, eds. Trauth, E., Howcroft, D., Butler, T., Fitzgerald, B., DeGross, J., (Boston: Springer), pp. 3-12.

In response to this recognition of the need to look at consequences beyond the corporate boundaries, we have chosen *social inclusion* as the theme for the 2006 IFIP 8.2 conference. In recent years, interest in this theme has emanated from many different quarters. It has occurred in European social policy debates and is of central concern within the social science literature. Despite its common currency, however, the concept remains vaguely defined and, as is often the case with concepts that have political salience, it is highly contested. There are a wide variety of national, competing discourses that refer to exclusion in markedly different ways (Levitas 2005), some of which are contradictory.

The term *social exclusion* originated in French social policy to refer to those who were administratively excluded by the state. Over time, the term became more widely adopted in Europe to encompass disaffected youth and isolated individuals (Hills et al. 2002). In North America, meanwhile, the term *digital divide* came into use to refer to people who are cut off in some way from the benefits of mainstream society through lack of adequate access to ICTs. In developing countries, the language of civil and social rights (Cornford and Klecun-Dabrowska 2003) has been used.

Accompanying the political discourse has been that which has come from the academy. Just as competing views are expressed at the political level, academic research has produced differing views regarding the nature of social exclusion. These range from individual behavior and moral values to capitalism and globalization. The concept itself implies a social division between "insiders" (the majority) and "outsiders" (the minority) and places the excluded on the edges of society. An alternative view would look to the inequalities and deprivation that are endemic to society. Conceptualized as the former, the socially excluded are seen as separate rather than understood in relation to the social order as a whole (Byrne 2005). Framed in these terms, a frequently touted solution to the problem is for governments to initiate policy that enables the excluded to cross the boundary in order to become one of the included. Doing so, however, precludes interrogation of structural inequalities. As Fairclough (2000, p. 54) comments, "social exclusion is an outcome rather than a process—it is a condition people are in rather than something that is done to them."

Byrne (2005), drawing on the work of Veit-Wilson (1998), brings to our attention the distinction between "weak" and "strong" versions of social exclusion. In this construction, weak exclusion focuses on improving the integration of the excluded into broader society, whereas strong exclusion emphasizes the role of those who are engaged in the excluding. Many of the current social policy debates about this topic and consequent initiatives have been concerned with the weaker form of exclusion, instead of challenging the power of the excluders. Focusing on ways of including the excluded reflects an underlying assumption that there is nothing inherently wrong with contemporary society and that government policy in itself can bring about inclusiveness.

Within the information systems field, much has been written in recent years about the ubiquitous nature and pervasiveness of ICTs (for example, the 2005 IFIP 8.2 conference; see Sørensen et al. 2005) as this phenomenon is seen as having the potential to alter how social, political, and economic relations are played out. The concept of exclusion features prominently in the information society discourse where access to and knowledge of ICTs are portrayed as either exacerbating exclusion or seen as a platform to engender inclusiveness. In reality, the ability of ICTs and networks to herald social change and reorganize the economy is far less radical than is often assumed (Thompson 2004). Given this debate, IFIP 8.2 has agreed to consider these issues and expand its focus of study beyond the organizational level in relation to broader concerns affecting citizens more generally.

In the context of ICTs, Castells (1996) argues that social exclusion throughout the world is closely linked with the rise of informational capitalism. He describes it as

> the process by which certain individuals and groups are systematically barred from access to positions that would enable them to an autonomous livelihood within the social standards framed by institutions and values in a given context (p. 71).

This position is quite distinct from the discourse concerned with lack of access to material resources and instead refers to the process of being "shut out" from social, economic, political, or cultural systems, which enable integration into society (Walker and Walker 1997).

This process of social exclusion varies over time. Its shifting trajectory is dependent on education, demographic characteristics, social prejudices, business practices, and public policies. Its affect on people has a spatial manifestation as well. Much of the study of social exclusion focuses on individuals and households (for example, access to mobile phones, PCs, Internet connections) but the spatiality of social exclusion is of equal importance (Madanipour 1998) as entire countries, regions, cities, and neighborhoods are seen as excluded. Different types of social experience are predicated on areas of residence, particularly in core global cities (Perron 2004). Globally, ICT penetration is highly uneven (Norris 2001; Sassen 2002) and, as Castells argues, areas that are of little worth from the perspective of informational capitalism are bypassed by flows of wealth and information and deprived of the basic technological infrastructure that allows people to communicate, innovate, and engage as producers and consumers. As a consequence, a dimension of social exclusion is spatial segregation, which marginalizes large groups of people, while simultaneously linking and strengthening through technology those deemed to be of value in the global networks of power.

For these reasons it is appropriate that IFIP 8.2 contribute its voice to the discourse about the exclusion of individuals—who lack access to technological resources—from various societal processes and services. Thus, the theme of this conference, and of the papers in this book, explores the many dimensions of this exclusion. This issue has been the focus of much debate within the social sciences, yet has largely been under-researched in the IS field, despite our concerns with the social and organizational aspects of technology. To the extent that contemporary debates have identified access to information as a key component of poverty, digital exclusion is seen as the problem. Thus, ICTs are portrayed as either exacerbating exclusion or are presented as the solution to greater inclusion. This conference provides us with the opportunity to build upon our strong tradition of studying technology design and use in organizations, and to expand our field of enquiry to consider the processes that engender social exclusion and the issues that derive from it.

This theme invites consideration of social and organizational constraints that result in the underrepresentation of certain groups and, by implication, certain issues. Likewise, it invites consideration of emerging technologies that have the potential to alter social, political, and economic relations. For these reasons, it is timely to expand our focus and progress the study of IS beyond the organizational level of analysis so that we may consider wider societal concerns affecting all citizens.

The papers in this book consider the use of information technology to reproduce exclusion as well as the consequences of social inclusion in the broadest sense to include economic development and geography, political participation, demographic disparities, ethical issues, the role of new ICTs and, finally, the IS profession. In doing so, this book can facilitate a lively debate that may suggest some alternative paths for future researchers to follow.

2   ECONOMIC DEVELOPMENT AND GEOGRAPHY

We begin with consideration of economic development issues that are grounded in a specific geographic location. Korpela et al. ask the question, "Can information systems development (ISD) in Africa by African IS practitioners contribute to human development in Africa?" In order to answer the question they focus on whether everyday ISD practice in Nigeria can contribute to people's health there by summarizing the results of over 15 years of European–African research collaboration. Implications are drawn for ISD practitioners and methodological lessons identified to IS research in general. In the discussion the view is expanded from Nigeria to other African and developing countries.

Bagchi et al. continue this discussion by investigating the factors that influence growth rates of ICTs in developing countries, and make comparisons with industrialized countries. Four factors are identified: human development, social structure, institutional factors, and national infrastructure. These are considered in relation to the growth rate at which ICT adoption has taken place. The technologies considered are cell phones, PCs, and the Internet. Bagchi et al. argue that their study reveals that developing and industrialized countries have a similar, yet distinct, range of factors that influence the ICT growth rates.

The discussion concludes with a consideration of American discourses about economic development and the digital divide by Tu and Kvasny. They examine how strands of discourse—institutionalized ways of thinking and speaking—shape debate about the digital divide and urban poverty in America. They are particularly interested in how discourses inform scholarly inquiry into urgent social problems. As information and communication technologies (ICT) are increasingly hailed as drivers of industry and commerce, they believe it will be instructive to examine economic development discourse, which strongly informs the case for bridging the digital divide.

Complementary to these papers is a panel on digital inclusion projects in developing countries, led by Madon, Reinhard, Roode, and Walsham. The panel focuses on the social, political, institutional, and cultural contexts which shape people's lack of access to ICTs and the skills to use them effectively. One response to this is the development of a number of digital inclusion projects, which will be discussed in the context of telecentres in rural areas of India and urban areas of the city of São Paulo, Brazil, and a community-based ICT project in a rural township in South Africa. The panel will discuss three key issues in relation to these projects, namely: how these projects can be evaluated; the sustainability of the initiative over time; and the scalability of these projects.

3 POLITICAL PARTICIPATION

The problems and consequences of popular political disengagement are well-documented and the second set of papers considers the role of new information and communication technologies in facilitating or inhibiting political processes. Grönlund et al. present a model for assessing the preconditions for eGovernment in developing countries. Despite the high project failure rate, much attention has been paid to the potential of eGovernment to drive forward the information society agenda; therefore, the authors argue that it is timely to find ways to assess the potential for eGovernment in the hope of avoiding costly failures in the future. A framework is developed which aims to assist the decision-making process before embarking on such a project.

Pieters examines the role of online voting technology in relation to people's experience of democracy. Combining the concept of technological mediation with the political philosophy of John Dewey, Pieters considers the mediating role of online voting technology in the context of developments in the Netherlands, which is one of the first countries to introduce electronic voting on a large scale. It is argued that Internet voting presents new challenges to existing concepts of democracy and that discussing democracy requires reconstruction from the perspective of the new technology.

The focus of the paper by Phang and Kankanhalli is on the participation of youths in electronic democratic processes. Utilizing a survey conducted in Singapore, the authors investigate whether electronic participation forums specifically targeted toward youths have appeal, since this group are increasingly withdrawing from participating in such processes. Drawing on the political science and information systems literature, this study aims to shed light on the issues that contribute to e-participation, highlighting the relevance of offline participation theories to the electronic context.

In a grass roots discussion of political participation, Robinson considers email campaigns as a form of *cybersolidarity*: action at a distance mediated by use of the Internet in support of trade unions or groups of workers. This paper takes the example of a campaign in support of imprisoned Eritrean trade unionists and examines the social organization and information flows underlying such campaigns. These are discussed in the light of the effectiveness of such actions, their capacity to overcome the global digital divide, current debates on the role of the Internet in the remaking of trade unionism, and labor's capacity to remake the spatial relations of capitalism.

The final paper in this section takes a somewhat different view by considering the effectiveness of social policies aimed at providing and improving access to ICTs and information and, thereby, redressing the digital divide. Maldonado et al. investigate ICT policies as a means to inhibit social exclusion in South Africa by examining how ICT policies in that country are being employed to reduce social exclusion. They do this by analyzing telecommunication laws and one of the ICT initiatives of the South African government: Multi-Purpose Community Centers (MPCCs). ICT policies in South

Africa were found to address two of the four forms of social exclusion: production of goods and services and civil engagement, spanning both the redistributionist and social integrationist discourses of social exclusion.

4 DEMOGRAPHIC DISPARITIES

Social exclusion arises from social inequalities and in every population there are groups who remain underrepresented in the information technology profession and underserved by the ICTs it develops. Typical population groups are based upon such demographic characteristics as gender, race, ethnicity, age, and disability. Three papers in this book deal with the topic of gender. The first paper explores female underrepresentation in the ICT sector in the UK by examining the various challenges that women ICT workers face in relation to their age, their "life stage" and their "career stage." Using eight case studies of individual female ICT professionals of different ages, Griffiths et al. explore these experiences in relation to career and caring responsibilities. Based on their interpretations of the empirical study, the authors have adapted and developed Super's career stage theory to theorize age, life stage, and career stage. One of the key contributions of this paper to the theorization of gender rests on the argument that heterogeneity in experiences is based on collective rather than individual identity distinctions, such as age, socio-economic status, and ethnicity.

In the second paper on gender, Richardson draws on a 5-year longitudinal study to discuss the neglected area of domestication of ICTs in UK households. Adopting a critical perspective to frame the study, she places the domestication of ICTs specifically in its social, political, economic, and historical context. The analysis describes how ICTs are embedded into gendered households and how technologies are manifested in the everyday experiences of women, weaving together their use of ICTs for work, study and leisure into everyday domestic family environments.

In the final paper on gender Gillard and Mitev consider ICT inclusion policies in the UK and contrast the rhetoric of these narratives with the reality of the lived experiences by groups who traditionally remain on the margins, such as part-time women workers with childcare responsibilities. Using an example of a network engineer training scheme that is operational in many UK educational institutions, the authors use the narratives of women in this program to highlight the complexities involved. Their study is situated within a broader political economy and shows how inclusion strategies fall short of expectations, as they fail to address more deep-seated, essentialist assumptions about women working in an industry that remains primarily a male preserve.

The paper by Adams and Fitch considers issues of age in the context of two empirical studies of a ubiquitous technology: the mobile phone. One study is primarily based on the 18 to 25 year-old age group; the other mostly on retired people. The studies show clear differences between age groups and gender in adoption and use of the mobile telephone. They observe that social inclusion for mobile access is closely linked to deeply embedded structures within society, such as those traditionally associated with gender. Thus, technology may be changing these structures such that *age* may be the new *gender*. The family or social unit may also be a useful entity to consider in the exclusion debate. Technology is being used to address social exclusion.

However, Adams and Fitch suggest that while some leveling may result, there may also be different social exclusion fronts emerging.

Finally, Adam and Kreps consider the topic of Web accessibility for disabled people. Much of the Web remains inaccessible or difficult to access by people across a spectrum of disabilities and this may have serious implications for the potential use of the Web for increasing social inclusion. The topic of disabled Web access is introduced through a consideration of four discourses: digital divide, social construction of disability, legal, and the Web accessibility. The lack of dialogue between these discourses permits a passive liberal approach toward disability discrimination to prevail and this political position has become inscribed in widely used automatic software tools, resulting in a reinforcement of the view that Web-site accessibility approval may, in many cases, be deemed an empty shell.

5 ETHICAL ISSUES

Two papers in this book consider the ethical dimension of social exclusion. Stahl conducts a critical examination of managing digital divides. He argues that manage-ment is part of the construction of the problem and therefore lacks the detached and objective viewpoint required for rational management. Further, the very concept of responsibility, if taken seriously and applied responsibly (here called *reflective responsibility*) requires a participative approach that contradicts the traditional top-down approach of heroic management. The paper concludes with a discussion of what form of management Information Systems needs to take if it wants to be responsible.

In the second paper, Vaccaro analyzes the ethical perspectives associated with the introduction and use of information and communication technologies in contemporary firms. He presents a three-dimensional ethical model that introduces the transparency concern, and its related impact on the digital divide question, as the new ethical perspec-tive of contemporary business organizations.

6 TECHNOLOGY AND ITS CONSEQUENCES

The use of information and communication technologies can be directly linked with social exclusion, although it is manifested in a variety of different ways. This set of papers deals with three themes related to social exclusion and the use of ICTs. The first three papers consider the innovative uses of new technologies to reduce social exclusion. The fourth considers the unintended exclusion that can result from new ICTs. Finally, two papers consider the implications of nonuse of technologies.

Feller et al. consider the use of open source software as a new model for organi-zational and societal collaboration and community bootstrapping. They present an analysis of 155 research artefacts in the area of open source software in order to identify the kinds of open source project communities that have been researched, the kinds of research questions that have been asked, and the methodologies used by researchers.

Byrne et al. present a case study of an initiative launched by the South African Council for Industrial and Scientific Research to stimulate awareness and promote the use of free and open source software in South Africa and the region. The new open source center made use of an African language metaphor to relate the concept of shared intellectual property in software to traditional communal land management. This paper provides a background as to why such a metaphor was chosen as well as some reflection on its effectiveness.

Silva et al. consider the emergent phenomenon of weblogging, which has recently generated much interest in the media, yet has received little attention by IS academics. They conceptualize weblogs by drawing on the concept of communities of practice and the social theory of learning that it proposes. This was used to illustrate the role of weblogging in organizational communication and the potential cultivation of social inclusion for employees working within these organizations.

In the following paper, Davidson et al. offer a deconstruction of a popular management text on Web services, which are often depicted as a highly desirable IT innovation. The article asserts that the Web service architecture takes "people out of the network," removing the need for human activity, while consolidating and extending the role of already powerful social actors in the IT sector, such as large IT vendors and firms. This text is an example of how an IT innovation is promoted in the literature in a progressive way, despite the absence of any consideration of social context and the implications for human actors. Its critical reading raises questions about the social consequences of the dominant organizing vision and the potential for inclusion and exclusion of different groups involved with and affected by IT.

Despite the evidence of the use of ICTs to reduce societal disparities, there remains evidence of the rejection and nonuse of technology. Crump presents a case study of a community computing center that was established in late 2001 in a city council high-rise apartment block in Wellington, New Zealand. The center was part of a project aimed at reducing unequal access to ICT. However, after 4 years of operation, the center was closed. Further analysis revealed that low social capital and the inadequate support of social resources were key factors in the closure of this initiative. Recommendations are made for implementing future projects.

Cushman and Klecun describe findings from a study that explored how nonuse affects individuals' inclusion or exclusion from society and how they can learn to use ICTs to meet their personal goals. The authors argue the need to focus on engagement with technology rather than simple adoption. Since ICTs in general—and Internet use in particular—are experienced technologies, perceived usefulness and perceived ease of use need to be reformulated to recognize limitations on people's ability to construct plans for future action.

7 THE INFORMATION SYSTEMS PROFESSION

Issues of inclusion and exclusion are pertinent to the IS profession as well. Three papers and one panel deal with the topic of social inclusion in the information systems community. Elisberg and Baskerville use the theoretical tools of Bourdieu and the concept of capital to show how the mechanism of social inclusion and exclusion operates at the group level in organizational settings. The focus is on communities of practice in a systems development organization and pays consideration to the struggles within social practices that occur before groups can gain acceptance among their peers. Elisberg and Baskerville demonstrate how formal organizational structures do not necessarily cater for integration and that communities of practice establish threshold events that organizational peers must satisfy before they are deemed worthy of inclusion within this particular community of practice.

Mayasandra et al. apply postcolonial theory to the development and use of ICTs in developing countries. The authors argue that this theory enables us to view ICTs in developing countries within a broader context, given the long-standing historical relationship of colonialism, neocolonialism, and postcolonialism of the West to the developing world. Using an empirical example of an outsourcing vendor in India, the paper discusses the challenges confronting this firm in its attempt to move away from its previous role as a provider of routine outsourcing jobs and transform itself into a leading global IT consultancy firm. From the perspective of postcolonial theory, it is argued that the global outsourcing phenomenon can be seen as the latest manifestation of colonialism.

Sawyer and Annabi argue that software development methods represent theories on how best to engage the impressively complex and inherently sociotechnical activity of making software. To help illustrate their points, they draw on examples of three software methods: the waterfall approach, package software development, and free/libre and open source software development. In doing this, they highlight the fact that software development methods reflect—too often implicitly—theories of how individuals and groups should behave, the tasks that people should do, and the tools needed to achieve these tasks.

Finally, in their panel, Pliskin, Levy, Heart, O'Flaherty, and O'Dea discuss the corporate digital divide between smaller and larger firms. Large organizations invest heavily in ICTs. The situation is somewhat different for small or medium-sized enterprises (SMEs) that invest a much smaller proportion of their revenue. As a consequence, there is evidence that SMEs are unable to employ ICTs strategically, placing them at a disadvantage in relation to larger firms. This panel will present the case for a corporate digital divide between larger and smaller enterprises, arguing that SMEs form an underprivileged sector in terms of ICT usage.

8 CONCLUSION

This conference, with its theme of social inclusion, builds upon the debates that have taken place within the IFIP 8.2 community over the past several years. As information and communications technology, and the information systems based upon them, become ever more pervasive, the human impacts—both positive and negative—and the associated societal disparities will continue to arise. It is our hope that the topics discussed at this conference will be considered mainstream in the future.

References

Byrne, D. *Social Exclusion*, Maidenhead, UK: Open University Press, 2005.
Castells, M. *The Rise of the Network Society*, Oxford, UK: Blackwells, 1996.

Cornford, T., and Klecun-Dabrowska, E. "Social Exclusion and Information Systems in Community Healthcare," in M. Korpela, R. Monteallegre, and A. Poulymenakou (eds.), *Organizational Information Systems in the Context of Globalization*, Boston: Kluwer Academic Publishers, 2003, pp. 291-306.

Fairclough, N. *New Labour: New Language*, London: Routledge, 2000.

Hills, J., Le Grand, J., and Piachaud, D. *Understanding Social Exclusion*, Oxford, UK: Oxford University Press, 2002.

Levitas, R. *The Inclusive Society? Social Exclusion and New Labour*, Basingstoke, UK: Palgrave MacMillan, 2005.

Madanipour, A., Cars, G., and Allen, J. (eds.). *Social Exclusion in European Cities: Processes, Experiences and Responses*, London: Jessica Kingsley Publishers Ltd., 1998.

Norris, P. *Digital Divide: Civic Engagement, Information Poverty, and the Internet Worldwide*, Cambridge, UK: Cambridge University Press, 2001.

Perron, D. *Globalization and Social Change*, London: Routledge, 2004.

Sassen, S. *Global Networks, Linked Cities*, London: Routledge, 2002.

Sørensen, C., Yoo, Y., Lyytinen, K., and DeGross, J. I. *Designing Ubiquitous Information Environments: Socio-Technical Issues and Challenges*, New York: Springer, 2005.

Thompson, G. "Getting to Know the Knowledge Economy: ICTs, Networks and Governance," *Economy and Society* (33:4), 2004, pp. 562-581.

Veit-Wilson, J. *Setting Adequacy Standards*, Bristol, UK: Policy Press, 1998.

Walker, A., and Walker, C. (eds.). *Britain Divided*, London: Child Poverty Action Group, 1997.

About the Authors

Eileen M. Trauth is a professor of Information Sciences and Technology and Director of the Center for the Information Society at The Pennsylvania State University. Her research is concerned with societal, cultural and organizational influences on information technology and the information technology professions with a special focus on the role of diversity within the field. As a Fulbright Scholar in Ireland, Eileen undertook a multi-year investigation of socio-cultural influences on the emergence of Ireland's information economy. Her book, *The Culture of an Information Economy: Influences and Impacts in the Republic of Ireland*, was published in 2000. She has continued that research by investigating cultural, economic, infrastructure, and public policy influences on the development of information technology occupational clusters in the United States. In 2000, Eileen began an investigation of the underrepresentation of women in the information technology professions by researching women in Australia and New Zealand. She has continued that research with grants from the National Science Foundation and Science Foundation Ireland. She is editor of the *Encyclopedia of Gender and Information Technology*, published in 2006. Eileen has also published papers and books on qualitative research methods, global informatics, information policy, information management, and information systems skills. She is author or editor of 9 books and over 100 research papers. She is an associate editor for *Information and Organization* and serves on the editorial boards of several international journals. Eileen received her Ph.D. and Master's degrees in information science from the University of Pittsburgh and her Bachelor's degree in education from the University of Dayton. She can be reached at egrauth@ist.psu.edu.

Debra Howcroft is a senior lecturer in the Accounting and Finance group at Manchester Business School, the University of Manchester. Her research interests focus on technology and organizations within a global context. Debra can be reached at debra.howcroft@mbs.ac.uk.

Part 2

Economic Development and Geography

2 INFORMATION SYSTEMS PRACTICE FOR DEVELOPMENT IN AFRICA: Results from INDEHELA

Mikko Korpela
Anja Mursu
University of Kuopio
Kuopio, Finland

H. Abimbola Soriyan
Obafemi Awolowo University
Ile-Ife, Nigeria

Retha de la Harpe
Cape Peninsula University of Technology
Cape Town, South Africa

Esselina Macome
Eduardo Mondlane University
Maputo City, Mozambique

Abstract   *In this paper we search for answers to the question: Can information systems development (ISD) in Africa by African IS practitioners contribute to human development in Africa? More specifically, we ask if everyday ISD practice in Nigeria can contribute to people's health in Nigeria. We summarize the results of European–African research collaboration spanning more than 15 years. A spectrum of research methods was used from 1998 through 2001, including a survey on software industry (N = 103), a survey on IS education in universities (N = 26), five case studies in industry, and reflection on action in a university-based project. An industry profile of software companies and their ISD practice is presented and contrasted with the education available. Implications are drawn for ISD practitioners and methodological lessons identified for IS research in general. In the discussion, the view is expanded from Nigeria to other African and developing countries.*

Keywords   Systems development, Africa, Nigeria, research methods, activity theory, healthcare, context, sustainability

Please use the following format when citing this chapter:

Korpela, M., Mursu, A., Soriyan, H.A., de la Harpe, R., and Macome, E., 2006, in IFIP International Federation for Information Processing, Volume 208, Social Inclusion: Societal and Organizational Implications for Information Systems, eds. Trauth, E., Howcroft, D., Butler, T., Fitzgerald, B., DeGross, J., (Boston: Springer), pp. 15-35.

1   INTRODUCTION: ENDOGENOUS SYSTEMS DEVELOPMENT AND HEALTHCARE IN NIGERIA

The ultimate challenge of this conference can be squeezed into the question: How can we make a better world with ICTs? In defining the *better world*, we rely on Sen, the only Nobel prize winner in development economics, who argues that "development can be seen as a process of expanding the real freedoms that people enjoy" (1999, p. 20). If ICTs are to have a significant role in human development, in Sen's terms—not just economic development—the real test is to see if ICTs can have a role in the least economically and technologically "developed" region in the world today, Sub-Saharan Africa (UNDP 2001). It is in parts of the world like Africa that stand to gain the most from the promise of ICTs, but Sub-Saharan Africa faces the greatest challenges in achieving the gains and is the least studied region in Information Systems (Mbarika et al. 2005). The potential for ICTs to affect human development is most strikingly seen in Africa, but deeper understanding gained there can enlighten socially concerned information systems researchers and practitioners in North America and Europe as well.

The relation between a better world and an appropriate technology was defined more than a quarter-century ago as follows:

> Technology should be considered "appropriate" when its introduction into a community creates a self-reinforcing process internal to the same community, which supports the growth of the local activities and the development of indigenous capabilities as decided by the community itself (Pellegrini 1980, p. 1).

Studies on the relation between ICTs and development in Africa mainly focus on national economic development and transfer of technology (e.g., Mbarika et al. 2005, Musa et al. 2005). While our interest is on *human* development, the main emphasis should be on endogenous processes by people in Africa in appropriating ICTs to support the expansion of their real freedoms. Exogenous processes of technology transfer by external actors can and do have a role, but they should also be assessed from the viewpoint of how well they support the processes internal to Africa and developing countries in general.

The definition above of appropriate technology does not refer to any static characteristics of a technology, but to the process of its introduction to a community. In discussing ICTs, the introduction of computer-based technologies into organizations and other social settings is understood in Information Systems as information systems development (ISD); that is, the development of organizational systems comprising people, computer-based and other technologies, and processes (Avison 1997; Walsham 1993). It is thus important to study the endogenous processes of ISD in developing countries and Africa in particular.

In this paper we summarize the results of over 15 years of European–African research collaboration focusing on the practice of ISD in Sub-Saharan Africa. While the bulk of the research was conducted in Nigeria, the discussion is based on experience from Africa in general and Mozambique and South Africa in particular. Nigeria is by far the most populous country in Africa, with about 120 million people and a gross domestic product of US$ 860 per capita in 2002, ranking the 151st of 177 countries in the Human Development Index (UNDP 2004). In terms of the human development index, Nigeria is an average Sub-Saharan African country, but it has huge human and natural resources.

In the Nigerian context, endogenous processes of information systems development emerged initially from the 1960s as in-house development in government ministries, universities, the oil industry, and banks, but by 1988 there were 200 companies offering computer-related services (Korpela 1994; Nwachuku 1989). To study endogenous information systems development, we focused on companies in Nigeria that have software-related activities. While health is one of the most fundamental elements of the basic freedom to survive (Sen 1999), we had a special focus on how information systems practice is related to improving health care (Berg et al. 2003). Our research thus initially aimed at searching for answers to the question: *Can ISD in Nigeria by Nigerians con-tribute to human development, specifically to people's health, in Nigeria?*

In the rest of the paper we first elaborate on the origins, objectives, units of analysis, and design of the research conducted in Nigeria, followed by the spectrum of methods applied. The next sections summarize the status of ISD in Nigeria and the implications that can be drawn for ISD practitioners. In the discussion section, we identify methodo-logical lessons for IS research in general and expand the view from Nigeria to other African and developing countries. Finally, we conclude by summarizing the contri-butions.

2 OBJECTIVES OF THE INDEHELA RESEARCH PROGRAM

2.1 The Origins and Actors

The research presented in this paper had its origins in 1989, when a doctoral student from the University of Kuopio in Finland stayed as a visiting researcher at the Obafemi Awolowo University in Nigeria. A very rudimentary hospital information system, running on a stand-alone PC, was then jointly developed (Daini et al. 1992). This gave rise to regular research collaboration between the two universities. The group was then authorized to organize the first Health Informatics in Africa (HELINA) conference in 1993 (Mandil et al. 1993). Several participants felt that ICT could be used more broadly to facilitate healthcare in Africa if appropriate software applications were developed specifically for that purpose.

In the following 3 years, a group of activists from Finland and Norway in Europe and Nigeria, South Africa, Ghana, Senegal, and Zimbabwe in Africa tried to raise funding for a large research and development initiative under the name Informatics Development for Health in Africa (INDEHELA 1995/2006). When this proved to be too difficult, the Norwegian and South African partners embarked on district-level information management (Braa et al. 2004), while the Finnish and Nigerian partners continued work on the hospital information system. In 1998, the latter partners received Finnish funding for academic research on Methods for Informatics Development for Health in Africa (INDEHELA-Methods). This paper reflects on what was achieved.

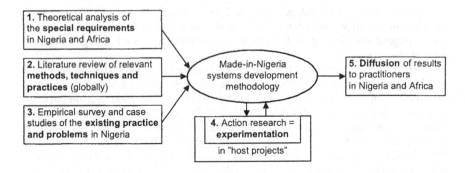

Figure 1. The overall research design in 1998-2001 (from 1997 research proposal, INDEHELA 1995/2006).

2.2 Research Objectives, Units, and Design: 1998-2001

The objective of INDEHELA-Methods in Nigeria was to produce an information systems development methodology appropriate for the special requirements of the Sub-Saharan African context, particularly in the health sector. The required outcome was later characterized as ISD methodologies for severely constrained conditions. In order to produce that outcome, the research design, depicted in Figure 1 was specified (INDEHELA 1995/2006).

Three inputs were identified. First, the general requirements for the methodology had to be specified through theoretical analysis of the specific conditions. Second, the relevant raw materials of methods, techniques, and practices developed for other conditions needed to be identified through literature review. Third, more empirical information was needed on how ISD was currently practiced in Nigeria, so that the outcome would be based on actually perceived needs.

The fourth part of the design was to experiment with ideas gathered from the three inputs in practice, to gradually construct an improved methodology (which was seen as a collection of guidelines, practices, and methods rather than a strict formalism). Action research in a pilot case setting was suggested for that purpose. The final part, after the research project, was to find out how the methodology could be diffused back to everyday use.

The literature surveys in part 1 of the design drew mainly from the conferences of IFIP Working Group 9.4, Social Implications of Computers in Developing Countries, and from the two journals that focus on IS in developing countries. Part 2 drew mainly from IFIP WG8.2, Information Systems and Organizations, from participatory design and activity theory conferences, and related journals. This laid the foundation for the empirical parts 3 and 4, which are described in more detail below.

Research in IS can focus on units of analysis on four integrative levels of increasingly widening scopes: individual, group, organization and society (Korpela et al. 2001; Walsham 2000). INDEHELA-Methods operated on all but the individual level.

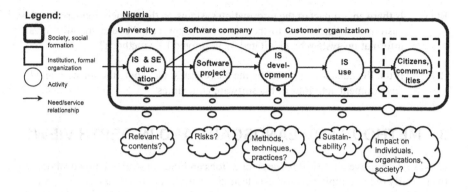

Figure 2. The Core Research Framework: Research Context, Objects, and Questions

Figure 2 depicts the units of analysis as generic concepts (legend) and in specific terms (Korpela et al. 2000). The main emphasis was on the group level. Activity theory (Engeström 1987; Korpela et al. 2004) emerged as the analytical tool on that level, since it provided a practicable theory on the structure of a group activity like ISD (Korpela 1994; see Figure 4). The core chain of activities around ISD from university education and software development to the use of ICT in everyday practice was included.

It was intuitively considered important to study the activities within their organizational contexts of universities, software companies, and customer organizations (rectangular boxes in Figure 2). Finally, Nigeria as a country was included as the broadest unit of analysis.

2.3 Research Questions: 1998–2001

Very broad research questions were identified, since no prior research existed on ISD practice in Africa (Figure 2). A Nigerian and a Finnish Ph.D. student embarked on a number of basic (RQ1–3) and specific (RQ4–6) research questions (Soriyan 2004; Mursu 2002).

RQ1: What kinds of software companies are there in Nigeria? What is the size of the software industry? What human resources, skills, infrastructure, and so on, do they have?

RQ2: What kinds of customers do the software companies have? How does IS benefit them?

RQ3: How many universities provide IS education? What kind of IS education do they provide, and what are their resources?

RQ4: What are the methods, techniques, and practices used in ISD by the software companies and the customer organizations? How can risks in software projects be identified, monitored, and mitigated?

RQ5:   Is there any impact of the information systems on the services rendered by the customer organizations to their clients? How can the sustainability of an information system be facilitated by improved ISD methods?

RQ6:   Is the IS education provided by the universities relevant to the software and IS development activities of the software companies?

3 METHODS FOR LANDSCAPE AND IN-DEPTH VIEWS

The descriptive empirical research questions and the constructive practical objectives clearly did not imply a hypothesis-testing, positivist approach, but an interpretive and critical stand on the phenomena under study (Orlikowski and Baroudi 1991). A combination of methods was selected for getting both a "landscape view" and an "in-depth view," as depicted in Figure 3 (modified from Mursu [2002] and Soriyan [2004]).

3.1 Getting an Insight: Reflecting on Action in Real-Life ISD

The initial purpose was to involve practitioners from one or two software companies in analyzing their current ISD practices and then proceed to experimenting with modified practices, developed by collaborative action by the practitioners and the researchers in the mood of developmental work research (Engeström 1987). It was soon realized, however, that action research in the true sense of the concept (Checkland 1991) was not feasible in companies until after much foundation-laying.

Action research is the research method through which researchers can get the most tangible insight into ISD. Since none of the researchers had initially any significant experience in ISD in Nigeria, the joint hospital information system activities of the two universities and the local teaching hospital in Nigeria was taken as the second-best option for experimenting with ISD methods in practice (lower center of Figure 3).

The initial system from 1989 was modernized and expanded by the Department of Computer Science and Engineering in the late 1990s, named MINPHIS (Made In Nigeria Primary-care and Hospital Information System) and later installed in a few new hospitals. However, the research and the practical development did not proceed at the same pace, so there was not much experimentation in or feedback from MINPHIS during INDEHELA-Methods. Reflecting on the researchers' experience in MINPHIS was still important to their insight.

3.2 In-Depth View from Case Studies Analyzed through Activity Theory

The main method for acquiring an in-depth view of ISD in Nigeria was exploratory case studies (Myers 1997/2005; Yin 1994). Semi-structured, open-ended interviews were conducted in five software companies (lower right-hand side of Figure 3), focusing

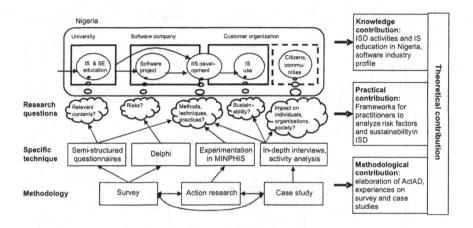

Figure 3. Research Methods and Intended Contributions in 1998-2001

on one current or recently ended ISD project in each case. Three of the companies were selected as good representatives of different types of companies—local and foreign ownership, big and small, package and tailoring oriented (Mursu 2002). The other two were the only ones with healthcare organizations as customers. Customer organizations of the software companies were also interviewed. The MINPHIS project was analyzed as the sixth case. (Soriyan 2004)

Most companies were visited three times from November 1999 to spring 2001—first to collect basic information, then to get feedback to the researchers' interpretation and finally to clarify details. Two researchers attended each interview. The interviews were conducted in English and tape recorded. The average time for an interview was 3 hours.

To analyze the cases, the structural model of an activity used in developmental work research was further developed into a version named Activity Analysis and Development (ActAD). A framework of elements and their relations was used as a checklist during interviews and as a lens in analyzing the case projects (Korpela et al. 2004).

During the first interviews, an imaginary ISD project, illustrated in Figure 4 was described to the interviewees to explain what we were interested in. It was based on the theoretical view of ISD as a border-crossing activity which was developed earlier (Korpela et al. 2001). All the interviewees grasped our intentions well.

The results from the first interviews were mapped to the model of activities and activity networks, which was modified to accommodate the increased understanding. In the second interviews, we used wall graphs to guide discussions.

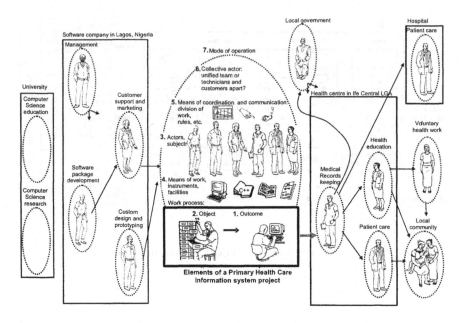

Figure 4. An Illustrated Imaginary ISD Project Used in the Interviews

3.3 Landscape View through Surveys

Since there was no prior research on ISD or software companies in Nigeria, we had to combine the insight from the cases with a shallower but wider landscape view and gather basic information through surveys (Gable 1994). Three surveys were conducted (lower left-hand side of Figure 3).

The most fundamental survey aimed at producing an industry profile of the companies with software-related activities. A fully structured and mostly guided questionnaire contained 45 questions in six parts. Ranges were used instead of exact figures to make it fast and easy to respond. It would not have been feasible to conduct the survey by mail in Nigeria, so students were trained to gather the responses by interviews. The Computer Association of Nigeria and the chartered association Computer Professionals of Nigeria provided an initial list of companies, which was updated from advertisements, roadside notices, and all possible sources. The researchers conducted the first interviews, after which the students traveled to all 37 states of Nigeria to contact as many companies as possible. (Soriyan 2004)

Another questionnaire-based survey focusing on systems analysis and design education was conducted using semi-structured interviews in all Nigerian universities offering Computer Science. This survey was conducted by the Nigerian researcher in person. (Soriyan 2004)

The third survey focused on the risk factors of software projects, as identified by project managers. The idea was to repeat an earlier study conducted in the United

States, Hong Kong, and Finland as precisely as possible to get comparative information. The Delphi method was used in three phases, with a two-round third phase. A subset of 11 software companies in Lagos was initially selected, representing big and small companies, indigenous and foreign-owned. Interviews were conducted mainly by Nigerian research assistants from late 1998 to May 2000. The number of respondents decreased from 39 to 6, and it was concluded that consensus was not achieved in Nigeria. (Mursu et al. 2003)

4 EMPIRICAL RESULTS: THE PROFILE OF SYSTEMS DEVELOPMENT IN NIGERIA

In the following subsections, we briefly summarize the responses to five of the six research questions. The empirical research did not provide sufficient data on the current situation regarding RQ5 about the impact on clients and sustainability.

4.1 Software Industry in Nigeria (RQ1, RQ2)

Altogether, 103 software companies were included in the survey, meaning companies that develop their own software or provide information systems services. We estimate that the total number of software companies in Nigeria might be between 150 and 200 (i.e., about one company per one million people). This does not include hardware vendors, training companies, etc. The software companies are located mostly (80 percent) in the southern part of Nigeria, with 49 percent in metropolitan Lagos State alone. They are mostly (96 percent) Nigerian owned. (Soriyan 2004)

A typical (46 percent) software company's staff strength is in the range of 11 to 50 people, while 34 percent had between 1 and 10 employees. Very few companies had more than 250 employees. An average (44 percent) software company had between 1 and 5 IT professionals, while 27 percent had between 6 and 15, and only 6 percent more than 50 IT professionals. The IT workforce was relatively young, mostly within the age brackets 20–29 and 30–39 years. Mostly they had at least a Bachelors degree. The average work experience was in the range of 1 to 5 years. (Soriyan 2004)

The customers' main business focus was studied using the international trade classification. The biggest customer sector was "private sector services," where 59 percent of the software companies had customers. Thirty percent of the companies had 1 to 10 customers, 49 percent had 11 to 50 customers. Almost all companies (87 percent) used fourth generation programming tools (43 percent along with a lower level programming language).

Most (75 percent) companies offered an imported package among their services (25 percent as the only option, among them 15 percent without local adjustments), but a majority (75 percent) also offered self-made software (25 percent as the only option), with 55 percent offered tailoring from scratch (5 percent as the only option). (Soriyan 2004)

In summary, the software industry in Nigeria consists mostly of small local companies, few of them planning to export to other countries. Foreign software packages

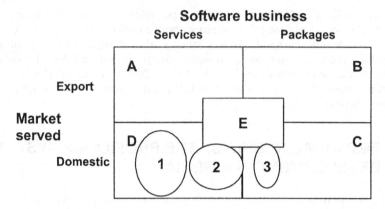

Figure 5. The Current Position of Nigerian Software Industry Within the Heeks Model

predominate, and the software industry provides services including adjustment of these packages to local requirements, installation, configuration, and maintenance. The industry also provides local package development and tailor-made software. Customization is more common than software packaging.

Richard Heeks (1999) presented a model for the strategic positions occupied by the software industry in various countries (see Figure 5). Companies in quadrant A export software services (e.g., programming) to foreign countries, those in B export software packages, those in D provide services to domestic markets, those in C produce packages for domestic consumption, and those in E take a little of each. The ovals in Figure 5 present clusters of Nigerian software industry. Companies in cluster 1 provide services based on an imported package, those in 2 provide services like consultancy and tailoring without a package base, and those in 3 develop and customize packages by themselves for local use. The sizes of the ovals give an idea of the sizes of the respective markets.

4.2 Systems Development Practice in Nigeria (RQ4)

ISD projects are usually quite small (average team size was within the range of 1 to 5 IT staff in 68 percent of companies) and short (48 percent last for up to 6 months, 31 percent about a year). For analysis and design, most (65 percent) companies had an in-house developed formal methodology in use (48 percent as the only option), 36 percent had a text-book methodology in use, while 31 percent had an informal methodology in use and 2 percent had no methodology. (Soriyan 2004)

In the five case studies, the research focused on the relation between the software company and a customer (Figure 6) and on the inner structure of the ISD activity. All cases were professionally ambitious and advanced. Contextual problems were also the same for all of the companies, maybe less for the foreign-owned big companies. The main differences were in the size, user relationships, organization, and formality of activities. The cases and the surveys supported each other quite well. (Mursu 2002; Soriyan 2004)

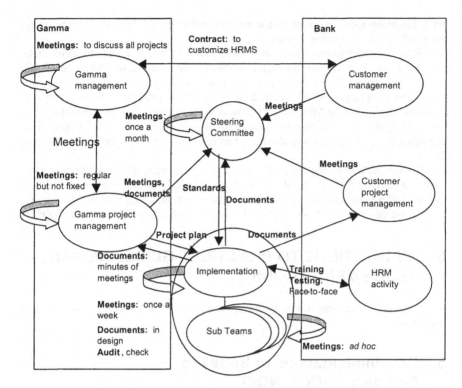

Figure 6. A Sample Analysis of Activity Networks and Means of Networking Around ISD in Software Company Gamma and its Customer (a Bank)

The history of the MINPHIS project since 1989 was analyzed in the same manner. It was realized that the project had gone through four phases from in-house development to a national scope with several customers, each phase characterized by a different network of activities. Despite an experiment in community involvement (Korpela et al. 1998), system development focused first on administrative and then on clinical benefits within the hospital. The development personnel changed several times and remained very few, resulting in mainly *ad hoc* methodologies. (Soriyan 2004)

4.3 Systems Development Education in Nigeria (RQ3, RQ6)

There were 47 universities in Nigeria at the time of the survey (24 federal, 18 state-level. and 4 private). Only 26 offered courses in Computer Science. None of them had the number of academic staff required by the Nigeria Universities Council (NUC) stipulations. None of the universities had up to 50 percent of the required hardware and software tools and almost none had a software engineering laboratory mandated by the

NUC minimum requirement; in fact some universities did not have any computers for their software development courses.

Software development education in Nigeria was within the Computer Science departments. The NUC defined the minimum curriculum standard, which was mandatory for the universities. There were a few variations introduced by the individual universities. The minimum standard provided by the NUC was intended to be reviewed after 10 years, although in practice individual universities review their curriculum every 2 years. Only the waterfall model was taught in the universities. Software management excluding risk management was also taught within software engineering (SE). (Soriyan 2004)

System analysis and design (SAD) as taught in the universities was closely related to SE. It covered the software development life cycle from software requirements to design. ISD was not mentioned in all the responses, although SE, SAD, and some topics in database design and management dealt with some issues in ISD. (Soriyan 2004)

5   IMPLICATIONS TO PRACTICE: GUIDELINES AND RECOMMENDATIONS

In the following subsections, we draw practical implications regarding the research questions.

5.1 Recommendations to Software Companies (RQ1, RQ2)

Originally we had no intention to obtain business policy implications from software companies, only to gather basic information about them. However, analyzing the data produced the following recommendations as an extra outcome.

Good knowledge of market needs and good personal connections are the strengths of Nigerian software companies over foreign competition. It is, therefore, reasonable for them to focus on local markets. In Figure 7, the lower half of the Heeks model (i.e., the local market-oriented positions) is further elaborated (Soriyan 2004; Soriyan and Heeks 2004). It is divided into two rows, for private and public sector markets. The service quadrant D is divided into three columns, D1 denoting services based on foreign packages, D2 services that are not based on packages, and D3 tailoring applications from scratch. The package quadrant C is divided into two columns, C1 being parallel versions for each customer and C2 actual configurable packages.

In our analysis, columns D1 and D2 are unstable since they are not based on local software development experience. In columns D3, C1, and C2 the companies have more control over their destinies since their services are based on their own products. It is reasonable that companies gain experience and customers in columns D1, D2, and D3, but we recommend that they take steps toward column C2. That movement mainly takes place in the private sector (i.e., row A), where there is more market demand.

This recommendation is problematic from the perspective of the healthcare sector which resides mainly on row B. In the software industry survey, only two companies were in position $D3_B$ in the healthcare sector, and the MINPHIS project is in $C2_B$.

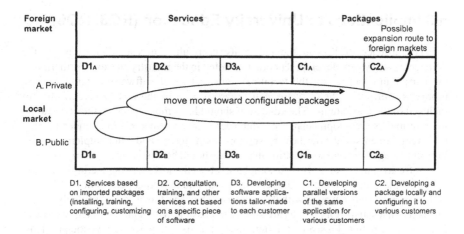

Figure 7. The Proposed Strategic Position for the Nigerian Software Industry

5.2 Recommendations on ISD: Participation, Risk, and Sustainability (RQ4, RQ5)

The industry survey, case studies, and action experience confirmed that user participation in ISD is important and possible even in the severely constrained conditions of a developing country, contrary to some earlier doubts (Avgerou and Land 1996). It is, however, also important to note that there is very little that would apply universally, and the specific promoters and inhibitors of participation vary even from organization to organization (Puri et al. 2004). Thus methods developed within participatory development (Kensing and Blomberg 1998) should be adapted to local needs in specific contexts.

The Delphi study resulted in a list of the most common risk factors in software projects in Nigeria. The most notable differences compared to the risk factors in the United States, Hong Kong, and Finland dealt with the socio-economic context of the country, infrastructure, and relationships with inexperienced users. Only a few items on the list deal with the technical aspects of software development (Mursu et al. 2003). The checklist of risk factors can guide less experienced Nigerian software project managers to address them early enough. However, the international risk study was limited to software projects only, and did not cover the introduction or use of ICT in organizations.

The case studies corroborated our initial assumption that the sustainability of information systems in organizations is an important issue. We then developed a model for sustainability analysis by combining literature on sustainable and appropriate technology (Oyomno 1996; Pellegrini 1980) with the activity network model (Mursu et al. 2005). The model would help project managers to design and implement information systems that are sustainable. The model needs to be developed into an easily applicable form before it can be tried in practice.

5.3 Implications to University Education (RQ3, RQ6)

The absence of ISD in the university curriculum may explain some of the deficiencies in system development practice noted in the industry survey. Furthermore, the curriculum focuses on the technical construction of software systems, but the problems confronting the software industry as revealed by the survey were mostly not included in the curriculum. The education should have more focus on the activities at the early and late development phases which deal with customer relations, understanding their requirements and how best to support them during and after implementation. Project management and social skills in general should be emphasized. (Soriyan 2004)

Software practitioners also had complaints about the software engineering education being behind today's reality. Universities should address this persistent problem by getting more closely engaged with the industry. The departments are so severely under-resourced that satisfactory results are simply impossible without increased government funding. International research relations should be used to partly relieve the problems of outdated contents and dearth of resources.

6   DISCUSSION: IMPLICATIONS TO RESEARCH

In the following subsections, we discuss the methodological and theoretical implications.

6.1 Studying Information Systems in Context

Our experience strongly supports the use of a combination of methods for getting a landscape view and insight in parallel in a situation where even basic topics have not been studied before. This situation is not uncommon in many developing countries. Routinely used methods and research designs from industrialized countries can be unfeasible in developing countries; for example, posted questionnaires could not work in our research, and the scope of the international software project risk study was too narrow to capture essential aspects of the software business in Nigeria (Mursu et al. 2003).

The study in Nigeria operated on three levels. The activity level and research methodology on that level received most of the attention. The ActAD framework and the generic model of ISD as an activity were operationalized into usable checklists without losing touch with the complexity of human activity as a real-life phenomenon. The aspects of ActAD that could not be sufficiently put to practice were historical analysis and proceeding into a phase of work development in software companies.

Unlike the activity level, the organizational level of analysis was not supported by a theoretical framework. In hindsight, empirical research on this level suffered from lack of methodological guidance, and produced a rather superficial understanding based on *ad hoc* frameworks. Neo-institutional theory (Nielsen and Koch 2004) might be a good candidate of an organizational-level social theory that could inform design and share activity theory's emphasis on history and contradictions. To maintain the integrative nature of the levels of analysis (Tobach 1999), activities need to be included as elements in the institutional framework, without reducing institutional phenomena to activities.

The societal level of analysis was not bound to a specific theoretical framework, either. Structuration theory (Giddens 1984; Walsham 1993) has been the most commonly used framework on that level in IS recently, but it is so generic that it is not easy to study the relations between micro and macro level phenomena with it (Macome 2003).

6.2 Nigeria Versus Africa Versus Developing Countries

Starting from 2004, INDEHELA has continued with a new phase, INDEHELA-Context, and research groups from Mozambique and South Africa have joined. Lessons from the first phase have been used in elaborating on the research design. Contextual and impact issues, which were understudied in the first phase, are now in focus.

The same basic chain of activities around ISD is still studied in each country, but the domain of application is now explicitly healthcare (Figure 8; compare with Figure 2). Local companies are no longer the only form of software organizations studied, while in Mozambique nongovernmental organizations (NGOs) have a major role in healthcare information systems (Braa et al. 2004). Small, private medical practices provide an important part of primary healthcare services in South Africa, for instance, so both the public and private sector must be studied (de la Harpe et al. 2005).

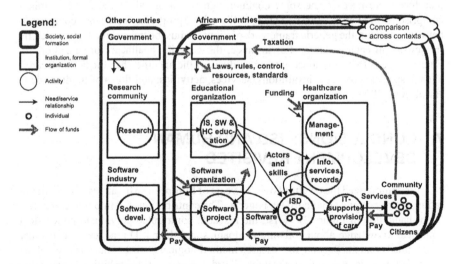

Figure 8. The Expanded Research Framework of 2004-2007

Local software activities by NGOs can collaborate with open source developers within a global network, while commercial companies often have other types of foreign liaisons. Educational activities in universities have international research liaisons, too. It is thus justifiable to include international linkages into the set of research objects, as indicated in a generic form in Figure 8.

Another factor that was missing in INDEHELA-Methods is the government. Particularly in healthcare, the government has the power to provide much control and guidance on whether and what kind of information systems are introduced in organizations. Healthcare and education are also mostly funded by the government, and financial relations (examples of them depicted by wide arrows in Figure 8) are indeed among the most important additions to the research framework. Financial viability is one of the elements of long-term sustainability, and affordability is a critical issue when money is scarce.

It has also become necessary to zoom in from activities to individuals (small circles in Figure 8). At least when studying the impact of IS in healthcare on the services provided to citizens, it is necessary to study if the impact is equal or not on different groups of individuals. Similarly, different professional, ethnic, or gender groups can have different roles in and experience the consequences of ISD differently (de la Harpe et al. 2005). Geographic and other communities (depicted by a small rounded box in Figure 8), including communities of practice (Wenger 1998), need to be studied as social formations different from activities and formal organizations.

Having three different Sub-Saharan African countries in the research network, we are now able to accumulate empirical research results from different organizational, societal, cultural, and political contexts. This will enable us to draw at least hypotheses on how contextual differences affect phenomena of ISD at the activity level. However, this implies that the specific contexts need to be recorded in each empirical study, and therefore there needs to be some common agreement on what "the context" might comprise (Mursu et al. 2005). This is still work in progress. To enable comparison between contexts, the generic framework of Figure 8 must be transformed into a specific framework in each country. For instance, the generic "healthcare organization" in Figure 8 needs to be expanded into an analysis of the specific "healthcare landscape" in each specific country—institutions, services, activities, and flows of funding (de la Harpe et al. 2005).

7 CONCLUSIONS: ISD AND HUMAN DEVELOPMENT REVISITED

We summarized the results of over 15 years of European–African research collaboration, mainly on and around ISD in Nigeria. The contributions fall into four categories (right-hand side of Figure 3). First, the research contributed previously nonexistent empirical knowledge about software companies and their ISD practice in a severely constrained context. Second, the research methodological contribution was to combine methods for landscape view and insight. Third, the practical contribution consisted of tentative recommendations for software companies regarding strategic orientation (unintended contribution) and methods for risk and sustainability analysis, as well as recommendations for universities regarding the relevance of the education they provide. Fourth, theoretical contributions to Information Systems were frameworks for analyzing activities, particularly ISD, in institutional and societal contexts. The recommendations and frameworks are further tested and developed in the new phase.

In the beginning we asked: *Can ISD in Nigeria by Nigerians contribute to human development, specifically to people's health, in Nigeria?* The following subquestions spiral toward the ultimate answer:

- *Can ICTs contribute to socio-economic development in Nigeria/Africa?* Yes, there has been no doubt about this among researchers for the past decade, although the relation is not automatic. Some uses of ICTs can be a waste, some beneficial, as anywhere.

- *Can ISD in Nigeria/Africa be practiced in such a way that it contributes to human development as defined by Sen, particularly people's health?* This is a more challenging question. An organizational information system in a private clinic can contribute to the financial viability of the enterprise without improving health services. Experiments in community involvement in MINPHIS and South Africa indicate that it is actually quite difficult to introduce organizational information systems in healthcare in such a way that the impact on people's health is directly addressed. However, the experiments show that it is not impossible.

- *Are ISD practitioners in Nigeria capable of practicing ISD in such a way?* According to our surveys and case studies, software professionals in local companies in Nigeria are technically quite capable, understand the importance of user involvement, and have good knowledge of the local needs.

- *Do ISD practitioners in Nigeria currently contribute to people's health?* Only two software companies out of 103 had anything to do with healthcare, and even those two focus on administrative and financial benefits. So, in practice, Nigerian ISD practitioners do *not* significantly contribute to people's health.

- *Why is this so?* According to our surveys, there is a dearth of human resources, particularly nontechnical skills of project management, and practicable methods for sustainability and impact analysis, communication, and participation, which are required to ensure that ICT does not become a white elephant. Even more importantly, as our analysis of the strategic position of Nigerian software companies points out, it is not profitable to contribute to people's health or to the "real freedoms that people enjoy" in general.

- *What should be done?* ISD education should be strengthened and expanded, as we recommended earlier. However, the results of INDEHELA-Methods do not tell if and how the need for financial profitability of software organizations can be combined with the unprofitable need to develop information systems that contribute to health. More research in the second phase is needed to address this ultimate question.

These questions referred specifically to Nigeria or Africa. However, in any country any information systems practitioner can ask the same question: *Does information systems practice in my country and by me contribute to the real freedoms that people enjoy, in my country and in my world?*

Acknowledgments

This paper is based on research funded by the Academy of Finland grants no. 39187 (INDEHELA—Methods,1998—2001), 201397, and 104776 (INDEHELA—Context, 2003, 2004—2007).

References

Avgerou, C., and Land, F. "Examining the Appropriateness of Information Technology," in S. C. Bhatnagar and M. Odedra (eds.), *Social Implications of Computers in Developing Countries*, New Delhi: Tata McGraw-Hill, 1992, pp. 26–41.
Avison, D. E. "The 'Discipline' of Information Systems: Teaching, Research and Practice," in J. Mingers and F. Stowell (eds.), *Information Systems: An Emerging Discipline*, Berkeley, CA: McGraw-Hill, 1997, pp. 113-136.
Berg, M., Aarts, J., and van der Lei, J. "ICT in Health Care: Sociotechnical Approaches," *Methods of Information in Medicine* (42:4), 2003, pp. 297-330.
Braa, J., Monteiro, E., and Sahay, S. "Networks of Actions: Sustainable Health Information Systems Across Developing Countries," *MIS Quarterly* (28:3), 2004, pp. 337-362.
Checkland, P. "From Framework through Experience to Learning: The Essential Nature of Action Research," H. E. Nissen, H. K. Klein, and R. Hirschheim (eds.), in *Information Systems Research: Contemporary Approaches and Emergent Traditions*, Amsterdam: Elsevier, 1991, pp. 397-403.
Daini, O. A., Korpela, M., Ojo, J. O., and Soriyan, H. A. "The Computer in a Nigerian Teaching Hospital: First-Year Experiences," in K. C. Lun, P. Degoulet, T. E. Piemme, and O. Rienhoff (eds.), *MEDINFO'92: Proceedings of the Seventh World Congress on Medical Informatics*, Amsterdam: Elsevier, 1992, pp. 230-235.
de la Harpe, R., Korpela, M., and Kamanga, E. "The Potential of Community Informatics in Small Private Medical Practice in South Africa," in G. Erwin, W. Taylor, A. Bytheway, and C. Strumpher (eds.), *Proceedings of the 2nd Annual Conference of the Community Informatics Research Network*, Cape Town, South Africa, August 23-26, 2005, pp. 101-117.
Engeström Y. *Learning by Expanding: An Activity-Theoretical Approach to Developmental Research*, Helsinki: Orienta-Konsultit, 1987.
Gable, G. "Integrating Case Study and Survey Research Methods: An Example in Information Systems," *European Journal of Information Systems* (3:2), 1994, pp. 112-126.
Giddens, A. *The Constitution of Society: Outline of the Theory of Structuration*, Cambridge, UK: Polity Press, 1984.
Heeks, R. "Software Strategies in Developing Countries," *Communications of the ACM* (42:6), 1999, pp. 15-20.
INDEHELA. Project web site and archive from 1995 (available online at http://www.uku.fi/tike/his/indehela).
Kensing, F., and Blomberg, J. "Participatory Design: Issues and Concerns," *Computer Supported Cooperative Work* (7), 1998, pp. 167-185.
Korpela, M. *Nigerian Practice in Computer Systems Development*, Reports TKO-A31, Helsinki University of Technology, Espoo, Finland, 1994.

Korpela, M., Mursu, A., and Soriyan, H. A. "Information Systems Development as an Activity," *Computer Supported Cooperative Work* (11), 2002, pp. 111-128.

Korpela, M., Mursu, A., and Soriyan, H. A. "Two Times Four Integrative Levels of Analysis: A Framework," in N. L. Russo, B. Fitzgerald, and J. I. DeGross (eds.), *Realigning Research and Practice in Information Systems Development: The Social and Organizational Perspective,* Boston: Kluwer Academic Publishers, 2001, pp. 367-377.

Korpela, M., Mursu, A., Soriyan, A., Eerola, A., Häkkinen, H., and Toivanen, M. "IS Research and Development by Activity Analysis and Development: Dead Horse or the Next Wave?," in B. Kaplan, D. P. Truex, D. Wastell, A. T. Wood-Harper, and J. I. DeGross (eds.), *Information Systems Research: Relevant Theory and Informed Practice, IFIP TC8/WG8.2 20th Year Retrospective,* Boston: Kluwer Academic Publishers, 2004, pp. 453-470.

Korpela, M., Soriyan, H. A., Olufokunbi, K. C., and Mursu, A. "Made-in-Nigeria Systems Development Methodologies: An Action Research Project in the Health Sector," in C. Avgerou and G. Walsham (eds.), *Information Technology in Context: Studies from the Perspective of Developing Countries,* Aldershot, UK: Ashgate, 2000, pp. 134-152.

Korpela, M., Soriyan, H. A., Olufokunbi, K. C., Onayade, A. A., Davies-Adetugbo, A., and Adesanmi, D. "Community Participation in Health Informatics in Africa: An Experiment in Tripartite Partnership in Ile-Ife, Nigeria," *Computer Supported Cooperative Work* (7:3-4), 1998, pp. 339-358.

Macome, E. *The Dynamics of the Adoption and Use of ICT-Based Initiatives for Development: Results of a Field Study in Mozambique,* unpublished doctoral dissertation, University of Pretoria, South Africa, 2003 (available online at http://upetd.up.ac.za/thesis/available/etd-02192003-161649/).

Mandil, S. H., Moidu, K., Korpela, M., Byass, P., and Forster, D. (eds.). *Health Informatics in Africa—HELINA 93: Proceedings of the First International Conference,* Amsterdam: Elsevier, 1993.

Mbarika, V. W. A., Okoli, C., Byrd, T. A., and Datta, P. "The Neglected Continent of IS Research: A Research Agenda for Sub-Saharan Africa," *Journal of the Association for Information Systems* (6:5), 2005, pp. 130-170.

Mursu, A. *Information Systems Development in Developing Countries. Risk Management and Sustainability Analysis in Nigerian Software Companies,* Jyväskylä Studies in Computing 21, University of Jyväskylä, Jyväskylä, Finland, 2002.

Mursu, A., Lyytinen, K., Soriyan, H. A., and Korpela, M. "Identifying Software Project Risks in Nigeria: An International Comparative Study," *European Journal of Information Systems* (12), 2003, pp. 182-194.

Mursu, A., Tiihonen, T., and Korpela, M. "Contextual Issues Impacting the Appropriateness of ICT: Setting the Stage for Socio-Technical Research in Africa," in A. O. Bada and A. Okunoye (eds.), *Proceedings of the Eighth International Working Conference of IFIP WG 9.4. Enhancing Human Resource Development through ICT,* Nigeria, May 26-28, 2005, pp. 348-358.

Musa, P. F., Meso, P., and Mbarika, V. W. "Toward Sustainable Adoption of Technologies for Human Development in Sub-Saharan Africa: Precursors, Diagnostics, and Prescriptions," *Communications of the Association for Information Systems* (15), 2005, pp. 592-608.

Myers, M. D. "Qualitative Research in Information Systems," *MIS Quarterly* (21:2), 1997, pp. 241-242 (*MISQ Discovery* archival version, June 1997, available online at http://www.misq.org/discovery/MISQD_isworld/; last modified: July 26, 2005, www.qual.auckland.ac.nz).

Nielsen, K., and Koch C. A. (eds.). *Institutionalism in Economics and Sociology: Variety, Dialogue and Future Challenges,* Cheltenham, UK: Edward Elgar, 2004.

Nwachuku, M. A. *Computers for Industrial Management in Africa: The Case of Nigeria,* United Nations Industrial Development Organization, V.89-57624, PPD.126, United Nations, 1989.

Orlikowski, W. J., and Baroudi, J. J. "Studying Information Technology in Organizations: Research Approaches and Assumptions," *Information System Research* (2:1), 1991, pp. 128.

Oyomno, G. "Sustainability of Governmental Use of Microcomputer-Based Information Technology in Kenya," in M. Odedra-Straub (ed.), *Global Information Technology and Socio-Economic Development*, Nashua, NH: Ivy League Publishing, 1996, pp. 19-34.

Pellegrini, U. "The Problem of Appropriate Technology," in A. De Giorgio and C. Roveda (eds.), *Criteria for Selecting Appropriate Technologies under Different Cultural, Technical and Social Conditions: Proceedings of the IFAC Symposium*, Oxford, UK: Pergamon Press, 1980, pp. 1-5.

Puri, S. K., Byrne, E., Nhampossa, J. L., and Quraishi, Z. B. "Contextuality of Participation in IS design: A Developing Country Perspective," in *Artful Integration: Interweaving Media, Materials and Practices—PDC 2004, Proceedings of the Participatory Design Conference*, Toronto, Canada, July 27-31, 2004, pp. 42-52.

Sen, A. *Development as Freedom*, Westminster, MD: Alfred A. Knopf, 1999.

Soriyan, H. A. *A Conceptual Framework for Information System Development Methodology for Educational and Industrial Sectors in Nigeria*, unpublished doctoral dissertation, Obafemi Awolowo University, Ile-Ife, Nigeria, 2004.

Soriyan, H. A., and Heeks, R. "A Profile of Nigeria's Software Industry," Working Paper No.21/2004, Institute for Development Policy and Management, University of Manchester, Manchester, UK, 2004 (available online at http://www.sed.manchester.ac.uk/idpm/publications/wp/di/di_wp21.pdf).

Tobach, E. "Activity Theory and the Concept of Integrative Levels," in Y. Engeström, R. Miettinen, and R. Punamäki (eds.), *Perspectives on Activity Theory*, Cambridge, UK: Cambridge University Press, 1999, pp. 133-146.

UNDP. *Human Development Report 2001: Making New Technologies Work for Human Development*, United Nations Development Program, New York: Oxford University Press, 2001 (available online at http://hdr.undp.org/reports/global/2001/en/).

UNDP. *Human Development Report 2004: Cultural Liberty in Today's Diverse World*, United Nations Development Program, New York: Oxford University Press, 2004 (available online at http://hdr.undp.org/reports/global/2004/).

Walsham, G. "Globalization and IT: Agenda for Research," in R. Baskerville, J. Stage and J. I. DeGross (eds.), *Organizational and Social Perspectives on Information Technology*, Boston: Kluwer Academic Publishers, 2000, pp. 196-210.

Walsham, G. *Interpreting Information Systems in Organizations*, Cambridge, UK: John Wiley & Sons, 1993.

Wenger, E. *Communities of Practice: Learning, Meaning, and Identity*, New York: Cambridge University Press, 1998.

Yin, R. *Case Study Research: Design and Methods* (2nd ed.), Beverly Hills, CA: Sage Publishing, 1994.

About the Authors

Mikko Korpela is Research Director of the Healthcare Information Systems R&D Unit, University of Kuopio, Finland, and an adjunct professor at the Department of Computer Science at the same university. He received his D.Tech. degree in Information Systems at the Helsinki University of Technology in 1994. He is a member of IFIP WG 8.2 and founding secretary of IFIP WG 9.4, a member of IMIA WG HIS and IMIA WG Health Informatics for Development, the founding organizing chair of HELINA, and Health Commission Co-Chair of IFIP World IT Forum 2007. Mikko can be reached at mikko.korpela@uku.fi. For more information on his work, visit his homepage at www.uku.fi/~korpela.

Anja Mursu is a research director in the Department of Computer Science at the University of Kuopio, Finland. She received her Ph.D. in Information Systems in 2002 at the University of Jyväskylä, Finland. Her research interests include information systems development, sustainability and usability of information systems, and ICT for development in developing countries. For more information on her work, visit her homepage at http://www.cs.uku.fi/~amursu/. Anja can be reached at anja.mursu@uku.fi.

H. Abimbola Soriyan is a senior lecturer in the Computer Science and Engineering Department at Obafemi Awolowo University in Ife-Ife, Nigeria. She is the coordinator of the Hospital Information System Unit at the Obafemi Awolowo University. Abimbola received her M.Sc. in Computer Science in 1997 and her Ph.D. (2004) from Computer Science and Engineering Department of Obafemi Awolowo University. Her research interests are in the areas of computer-based hospital and health care information systems, ICTs and development, and cognitive and social issues in the design and use of computer systems. Currently a visiting scholar at Cornell University, Abimbola is working on the deployment of virtual classroom for higher education and investigating the impact of ICT tools on development focusing on education and gender. She is a member if IFIP 9.4. She can be reached at hasoriyan@yahoo.com, hsoriyan@oauife.edu, or has38@cornell.edu.

Retha de la Harpe is a senior lecturer at the Cape Peninsula University of Technology in Cape Town, South Africa. She is currently busy with her Ph.D., titled "The Organisational Implications of Data Quality in a Developing Country: An Actor-Network Theory Perspective." She is a NRF (National Research Foundation) grant holder and most of the research projects investigate information issues in private healthcare and contribute toward an improved understanding of the healthcare landscape in South Africa. She can be reached at delaharper@cput.ac.za.

Esselina Macome is professor of Information Systems at the Eduardo Mondlane University, Maputo City, Mozambique. She was born in Maputo, Mozambique, and in 1992 achieved her M.Sc. in Information Systems at the University of London (LSE). She received her Ph.D. in Information Technology from the University of Pretoria, South Africa, in 2003. She is a member of IFIP WG 9.4 and HISP (Health Information System Programme). Her research interests include ICT governance, and organizational and social aspects of ICT/IS. Since June 2005, she is one of the general managers at the Central Bank in Mozambique. She can be reached by e-mail at esselina.macome.uem.mz or taila.uffo@tvcabo.co.mz.

3   A COMPARISON OF FACTORS IMPACTING ICT GROWTH RATES IN DEVELOPING AND INDUSTRIALIZED COUNTRIES

Kallol Bagchi
Peeter Kirs
Godwin Udo
University of Texas at El Paso
El Paso, TX U.S.A.

Abstract   *In this paper we investigate the factors that impact ICT growth rates in developing countries and compare those with factors affecting industrialized countries. Four categories of factors, human development, social structure, institutional factors, and national infrastructure, were considered with respect to their impact on three ICTs: cell phones, PCs, and the Internet. ICT infrastructure influenced ICT growth rates in all nations, but the impacts of human development, institutional index, and urbanization varied between industrialized countries and developing countries.*

1   INTRODUCTION

Information and communication technology (ICT) adoption in industrialized countries (IC) has received extensive attention. Most empirical studies on ICT acceptance have been based in North America using American subjects (Straub 1994). This can be a serious shortcoming, since an important concern in scientific research is external validity, and an international focus is a major component of external validity (Anandarajan et al. 2000). Additionally, many ICT manufacturers of one nation try to expand their business by looking at markets of other nations. Also, policy makers of a nation want to find out the recipe of success in ICT adoption of a nation. Thus national-level ICT adoption or growth studies are important. Looking from another angle, Galbraith (1973) considered organizations as information processing systems. Organizations do not exist in a vacuum but have to operate within the frameworks of a

Please use the following format when citing this chapter:

Bagchi, K., Kirs, P., and Udo, G., 2006, in IFIP International Federation for Information Processing, Volume 208, Social Inclusion: Societal and Organizational Implications for Information Systems, eds. Trauth, E., Howcroft, D., Butler, T., Fitzgerald, B., DeGross, J., (Boston: Springer), pp. 37-50.

national boundary and frequently in the international arena. Thus the study of ICT adoption at a national level becomes all the more significant. A national-level analysis is important (especially in the light of technology transfer and the recent debate on globalization) as this kind of analysis can examine the possible influences of widely varying, country-specific characteristics such as government regulations and institutions, national culture, national economy and infrastructure on ICT adoption.

The body of literature which looks at developing countries (DC) tends to be limited in quantity, scope, and time period of investigation. Most of these studies have either considered a single technology in a single DC (e.g., Cheong (2002) investigated Internet adoption only in Macao), factors influencing ICT adoption in a single DC (e.g., Anandarajan et al. (2000) found that social pressure is an important factor affecting technology acceptance in Nigeria), single or multiple ICT adoptions in a small subset of DCs (e.g., Garcia-Murillo (2003) looked at ICT adoption in Latin America), or considered a single component of technology adoption (e.g., Mbarika et al. (2003) investigated infrastructure growth in DCs). The present study attempts to overcome these shortcomings by considering many factors over a large number of nations and over a period of years.

Our dependent variable of interest is the growth rate at which ICT adoptions have taken place. Growth rate refers to the average yearly change in growth level, in terms of users per 1,000 inhabitants, over some period of time and is an indicator of the speed at which penetration is taking place. While early adoption of technology leads to the establishment of niches in the mass market from which the early adopters can expand and further distance themselves from later adopters (Moore 1991), later adoption offers opportunities to DCs to catch-up at a fraction of the cost which the ICs have invested over many years of ICT evolution (Gerschenkron 1962). The more backward the economy is, the higher the productivity growth rate (within reason). ICs may have passed their peak and slowed down in later years (Barro and Sala-i-Martin 1998). As a consequence, a "leapfrogging" effect (Davidson et al. 2000) implies that DCs will have a greater growth rate than ICs (everything else being equal) by applying an investment-based growth strategy (Acemoglu et al. 2002).

In this paper we follow the Organisation for Economic Co-operation and Development (OECD) classification scheme of nations. Data is available for 34 industrialized countries and 74 developing countries (108 in total).

The complete set of nations used in this paper, by category, is given in Table 1.

The purpose of this study is to investigate the factors that impact ICT growth rates in developing countries and compare those with factors affecting industrialized countries. There are some limitations, however. As a consequence of paucity of data, we have selected only the most important factors based on a literature review to be tested in this study.

1.1 Dependent Variables

Since adoption growth rates are affected by the age of the technology, three ICTs (dependent variables) were considered.

Table 1. Nation Classifications

Industrialized Countries		Developing Countries			
Australia	Kuwait	Albania	Czech	Malaysia	Romania
Austria	Luxembourg	Algeria	Ecuador	Mali	Russia
Bahrain	Malta	Argentina	Egypt	Mauritius	South Africa
Belgium	Mexico	Bangladesh	El Salvador	Morocco	Senegal
Canada	Netherlands	Barbados	Estonia	Myanmar	Slovenia
Cyprus	New Zealand	Belize	Fiji	Namibia	Sri Lanka
Denmark	Norway	Benin	Ghana	Nepal	Tanzania
Finland	Portugal	Bolivia	Guatemala	Nicaragua	Thailand
France	South Korea	Botswana	Guyana	Niger	Togo
Gabon	Singapore	Brazil	Honduras	Nigeria	Tunisia
Germany	Spain	Bulgaria	India	Oman	Turkey
Greece	Sweden	Burundi	Indonesia	Pakistan	United Arab
Hong Kong	Switzerland	Cameroon	Jamaica	Panama	Emirates
Hungary	United	Chad	Jordan	Paraguay	Uganda
Iceland	Kingdom	Chile	Kenya	Peru	Ukraine
Ireland	United States	China	Latvia	Philippines	Uruguay
Israel		Colombia	Lithuania	Papua New	Venezuela
Italy		Costa Rica	Madagascar	Guinea	Zambia
Japan		Croatia	Malawi	Poland	Zimbabwe

- Cell phones. The oldest of the ICTs, the first cell phone call was placed on April 3, 1973, although it must be noted that adoption did not really take off until late in the 1990s in most nations.

- PCs. The MITS Altair was first introduced in January, 1975, and the first viable PCs were the Apple II in 1977 and IBM's PC in 1981, with general acceptance a few years later.

- The Internet. The first Internet website appeared on August 6, 1991.

Sample diffusion growth rates for ICs and DCs are given in Table 2. We limit our examination to four major types of national factors which have been found to impact, or have been suggested as impacting, ICT diffusion growth rates: *human development, social structure, institutional factors,* and *national infrastructure.*

1.2 Independent Variables

1.2.1 Human Development

National wealth, typically measured as gross domestic product (GDP), has long been used as a measure of a country's well-being. While Kraemer et al. (1992) found a direct relationship between the level of development and computing expenditures in

Part 2: Economic Development and Geography

Table 2. Sample Dependent Variable Data

	Growth Rates		
	Cell Phone	**PC**	**Internet**
Industrialized Countries			
Sweden	0.264	0.160	0.413
Netherlands	0.510	0.143	0.342
United States	0.299	0.097	0.287
Australia	0.405	0.117	0.504
United Kingdom	0.369	0.117	0.561
Developing Countries			
Senegal	1.865	0.190	1.829
Benin	1.076	0.218	1.727
Tanzania	1.482	0.202	1.266
Zambia	0.853	0.049	0.771
Nigeria	0.744	0.067	0.821
Chile	0.649	0.236	0.826
Lithuania	0.996	0.458	0.941
India	0.288	0.297	0.791
Ghana	0.550	0.438	2.009
Bangladesh	1.275	0.694	1.854
Nepal	0.552	0.139	1.310
Myanmar	0.592	0.663	2.583

Notes: Adoption values in 2002 per 1,000 population
Growth Rates of PC, Cell Phone, and Internet from 1990/1995–2002.

the Asia-Pacific region, economic developmental growth theory states that industrial countries differ from developing countries by much more than their level of capital or even their human capital (Hoff and Stiglitz 2000). Development is no longer seen primarily as a process of capital accumulation but rather as a process of organizational change, since industrialized and developing countries are believed to be organized in different ways. Development does not occur just by infusing more capital or by removing government imposed inefficiencies. National development occurs because of the role of institutions and the presence of income inequality, among other things. Stiglitz (2003) proposed that factors such as human capital development, innovation, infrastructure, and level of strategic cooperation between academia, industry, and government are important catalysts for DCs to close the gap with more developed countries.

Investment in human capital involves both education and training. Illiteracy has been suggested as a significant factor hindering the adoption of ICT (Madon 2000). Quibria et al. (2003) have identified education, among other factors, as a key ICT adoption determinant in Asia. Mbarika et al. (2003) cite the acute shortage of ICT technicians as one the factors that inhibits ICT adoption in Sub-Saharan African.

To obtain precise human development (HD) profiles for countries, the United Nations Development Programme (UNDP) industrialized the human development index (HDI) in 1990 (UNDP 1990). The HDI is based on three primary indicators, with each indicator given equal weight: longevity (as measured by life expectancy at birth); education attainment (as measured by the combination of adult literacy and combined primary, secondary, and tertiary enrollment ratios), and standard of living (as measured by real gross domestic product).

1.2.2   Social Structure

GDP does not necessarily reflect an individual's well-being, since national wealth does not reflect income distribution patterns. Various economic growth studies have pointed out that income inequality is also one of the factors that can also affect the economic growth of a nation (Banerjee and Newman 1998). In global ICT adoption studies, it has been shown that income inequality may play a role in ICT growth. A wide disparity in wealth distribution may mean that some individuals will have enough wealth to buy ICTs to increase their skill levels. Others who do not have enough wealth will not be able to buy ICTs to increase their skill set, thus increasing the differences in ICT adoption levels.

Disparities in wealth can be measured using the GINI Index (Deininger and Squire 1989), which measures the extent to which income among individuals or households within a country deviates from a perfectly equal distribution.

1.2.3   Institutional Factors

There are many reasons to expect that free economies will grow more rapidly than those that are less free. The economic freedom of the world (EFW) index contains 38 components designed to measure the degree to which a nation's institutions and policies are consistent with voluntary exchange, protection of property rights, open markets, and minimal regulation of economic activity (Gwartney and Lawson 2003). EFW data provides ratings in five major areas: (1) size of government, (2) legal structure and security of property rights, (3) access to sound money, (4) exchange with foreigners, and (5) regulation of capital, labor, and business.

Because of its international focus, the EFW index has been used extensively to examine cross-country differences in income levels (Grubel 1998), growth rates (Wu and Davis 1999), and other indicators of economic performance (de Vanssay and Spindler 1996). The relationship between the EFW and ICT growth has also been considered. Green et al. (2002) found that freedom alone is important for technological diffusion and, after accounting for the effects of economic freedom, human capital does not affect technological diffusion. With respect to developing countries, Bate and Montgomery (2004) assert that lack of economic freedom is an important factor hindering improved standards of living in developing countries, in part because a lack of economic freedom is also a major obstacle that hinders technology transfer.

The EFW index uses a scale from 0 to 10, where the country achieving the best results in a given indicator is assigned the value 10 and the country with the worst result receives a 0; other countries are assigned values between 0 and 10 for a given indicator. The EFW index provides current ratings for 123 countries and is the only index for which data were available for the entire period of study.

1.2.4   National Infrastructure: ICT Infrastructure and Urbanization

By definition, infrastructure is the underlying base or foundation system, including the basic facilities, services, and installations needed for the functioning of a community or society. A nation's infrastructure includes such components as transportation networks, utilities, commodities distribution networks, and communications networks, and determines how it functions and how flexible it is to meet future requirements. Davis et al. (1989), Toussea-Oulai and Ura (1991), and Mwesige (2003), have all emphasized that poor basic infrastructures are a barrier to ICT adoption in DCs. To properly adopt and use ICTs, basic infrastructure requirements of electricity, trained technical workers, and communication networks, as well as commitment from the government and other policy makers, should be put in place.

Unfortunately, there are no composite measures of national infrastructure. For our purposes, we use ICT infrastructure as a direct measure of existing technical foundation and urbanization as a proxy measure of general infrastructure.

ICT Infrastructure: A modern, reliable, and rapidly expanding telecommuni-cations infrastructure is assumed to contribute to the promotion of a variety of economic expansion activities (World Bank 1991). The level of a country's telecommunications infrastructure has been associated with its teledensity (Saunders et al. 1994), defined as the relationship between a country's population and the number of main telephone lines (International Telecommunications Union 1999). Cronin et al. (1991) found that for the United States, the sum of the output of all industries and the annual GDP were related to the annual amount of U.S. telecommunications investment. In a follow-up study, Cronin et al. (1993) showed that investment in telecommunications infrastructure (represented by teledensity) was a reliable predictor of national productivity. Ein-Dor et al. (1997) found that small developed countries may have an advantage over larger developed nations if they have a well developed infrastructure and the human skills needed. Dewan and Kraemer (2002) found that the returns from IT capital investments are positive and statistically significant for developed countries, but nonsignificant for developing countries.

Accordingly, our ICT infrastructure measure is the number of mainline telephone installations per 1,000 in a nation.

Urbanization: In 1880, only 3 percent of the world's population lived in urban areas while by 1950, it was 29 percent, and shortly after the year 2000, it was greater than 50 percent of the world's population. United Nations projections are that 80 percent of the growth in population over the coming decade will be urban, not rural (Perlman 1993). It is generally acknowledged that urban areas play a vital role in education, culture, and productivity. Consumers living in a country's major metropoli-tan areas tend to be more cosmopolitan (Hannerz 1990), and diffusion research has documented a positive relationship between cosmopolitanism and the tendency to innovate (Gatignon et al. 1989). Metropolises also tend to have a denser retail infrastructure, thus making it easier for consumers to acquire a new product. Regions with dense concentrations of firms engaged in the same production process are also likely to be information-rich (Marshall 1920).

With respect to DCs, Loboda (1974) has shown that the diffusion of televisions in Poland predominately took place in the richest and the most urban parts of the country.

Proenza (2001)notes that the use of ICTs has grown rapidly only in the most urban areas in Africa. Shakeel et al. (2001) found that telecenters, locations which facilitate and encourage a wide variety of public and private information-based goods and services, are primarily found in urban areas.

2 THE RESEARCH MODEL AND HYPOTHESES

The general research model consists of five independent variables and three dependent variables, each analyzed independently for each set of nation groupings (see Figure 1). In accordance with the tenets that ICs may have passed their peak and slowed down in later years (Mahajan and Peterson 1985) and that DCs are experiencing a leapfrogging effect (Davidson et al. 2000), we expect that ICT growth rates will be negatively impacted by all of the independent variables, with the exception of social structure, which is measured using an inverse scale.

3 DATA AND METHODS

While the basic focus of this research is on developing countries, we first ran regressions using all countries (ACs), providing us with baseline indicators, and then, in order to provide a contrast, industrialized and developing countries were compared. Nine ordinary least squares (OLS) regressions were conducted, three for each ICT growth rate technology for each of the three groups of countries (AC, IC, DC). The regressions were checked for possible multicollinearity, autocorrelations, etc. (Netter et al. 1996).

Typically, diffusion growth modeling studies try to explain patterns of diffusion of technology, usually over time and across a population of potential adopters. Observations of adoption or percentages of adoption are put in the form of a time series and fitted to some functional form (Fichman 1992; Mahajan and Peterson 1985). The functional form of the logistic model used to calculate the growth rate is given by

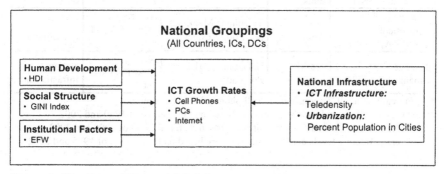

Figure 1. The General Research Model

$$Y = 1 / (1/u + (b_0 * b_1'))$$

Where: u is the upper boundary value and
        b_0 and b_1 are parameters to be estimated

We specify the upper boundary value as 1000 in the regression equation. It can be mentioned that the logistic model is a standard and popular one which has been used in many previous growth studies (Mahajan and Peterson 1985). The maximum penetration rate is achieved at .50u, where u is the limit of penetration. The model is symmetric in nature.

Each of the dependent and independent variables used in the regressions are described in Table 3. As mentioned above, our data are secondary in nature and are collected from various reliable databases. Combining data from more than one source may create problems. However, this method has been used in traditional macro economic and marketing literature research studies (Dekimpe et al. 1994; Gatignon et al. 1989).

Table 3. Summary of Variables, Sources and Representation

Variables	Source	Representation	Years	Factor
Dependent Variables				
Average ICT Adoption Level*	World Bank	Adoption Level per 1,000 Residents	See Below**	Adoption Level
ICT Adoption Rate*	Calculated (see below)	ICT Diffusion over time	See Below**	Growth rate
Independent Variables				
Average Human Development Index (HDI)	UNDP	National Human Development	Average of 1990/1995 and 2002	Human Development
Average Economic Free World (EFW) Index	Fraser Institute	National growth in free economies	Average of 1990/1995 and 2002	Institutional Factors
National Distribution of Wealth (GINI)	World Bank	GINI Index	Average of 1980 and 2002	Social Structure
Average ICT Infrastructure (ITINFRA)	World Bank	Telephone Mainlines per 1,000 Residents	Average of 1990/1995 and 2002	ICT Infrastructure
Average Urbanization (URB)	World Bank	% National Urban Population	Average of 1990/1995 and 2002	National Infrastructure

*   For each of the ICTs considered: cell phones, PCs, and Internet
**   Average cell phone levels and rates are based on the average of 1990 and 2002
     Average PC levels and rates and rates are based on the average of 1990 and 2002
     Average Internet levels and rates and rates are based on the average of 1995 and 2002

Table 4. Growth Rate Regression (Beta Values) Results

Technology	All Nations (AC)	Industrialized Nations (IC)	Developing Nations (DC)
Cell			
HDI	-0.14	0.86*	-0.59*
ICT Infrastructure	0.25	-0.68	0.89***
Urbanization	-0.25	-0.45*	-0.21
EFW Index	-0.40*	-0.35	-0.26*
GINI Index	0.23*	0.16	0.30*
Adj R²	0.28	0.35	0.30
N	69	21	48
PC			
HDI	0.89***	-1.24***	0.90***
ICT Infrastructure	-0.97***	0.16	0.10
Urbanization	-0.48***	-0.17*	-0.86***
EFW Index	0.11	0.27*	0.05
GINI Index	-0.01	-0.17	0.07
Adj R²	0.32	0.76	0.31
N	69	27	41
Internet			
HDI	-0.27	-0.02	-0.05*
ICT Infrastructure	-0.54***	-0.31	-0.55
Urbanization	-0.08	0.26**	-0.14
EFW Index	0.01	-0.60***	-0.02
GINI Index	-0.06	0.16	-0.10
Adj R²	0.62	0.68	0.40
N	83	28	54

Notes: ***p < .000;   **p < .01;   *p < .10

4   RESULTS

Table 4 presents the results of regressions on ICT diffusion growth rates for each of the three ICTs considered, using the five dependent variables for each of the groupings of countries.

The predictive power of the growth rate model varied across technologies. For ACs, the adjusted R^2 ranged between 0.28 (cell phones) to 0.62 (Internet). For each of the other national groupings, the adjusted R^2 values ranged between 0.30 (cell phone growth rates in DCs) to 0.76 (PC growth rates in ICs). No single factor was significant across all groupings, although ICT infrastructure was significant for two of the three groups for Internet growth rate. Human development (HDI), EFW, and income inequality (GINI) indices were significant for two of the three groups for cell phone growth, although again not always in the direction hypothesized.

Table 5. Significant Factors/Combinations of Factors Affecting Growth Rates

Factors	All (AC)	IC	DC
Cell Phone			
HDI		X	X
ICT Infrastructure			X
Urbanization		X	
EFW Index	X		X
GINI Index	X		X
PC			
HDI	X	X	X
ICT Infrastructure	X		
Urbanization	X	X	X
EFW		X	
Internet			
ICT Infrastructure	X		X
Urbanization		X	
EFW Index		X	

With respect to the PC growth rate, HDI (three of three cases), ICT infrastructure (one out of three cases), and urbanization (three out of three cases) were significant for all groupings. Institutional factors were mostly significant for industrialized countries, but not for developing countries in general. Internet growth rate was most impacted by ICT infrastructure, except for ICs (largest value of betas). IC Internet growth rate was impacted by urbanization and institutional factors. For the cell phone rate model, HDI, ICT infrastructures, income inequality index (GINI index), and institutional factor (EFW index) became significant in the DC regression. Table 5 summaries the significant results for the growth rate analysis.

The results in terms of growth rate factors are discussed next. With respect to the growth rate of ICTs in general, ICT infrastructure tends to be one of the most significant factors for all nations and DCs in general and not for ICs. It was significant for both cell phones and Internet growth rates for all DCs. It was not significant for PC growth in DCs. Institutional factors also had a high impact on growth rates. For ACs, its significant impact on cell phone growth rates was noteworthy.

Human development was an important factor on growth rate, especially with respect to cell phones and PCs. The relationship between cell phone rates and the HDI index is positive for ICs and the relationship between cell phone rates and the HDI is negative for DCs. The relationship is just the opposite in case of PC growth rate and ICs/DCs. The cell phone is a new technology and so wealthier nations are still adopting it in large numbers. For developing nations, leapfrogging is taking place. Poorer nations are skipping the traditional adoption path of first telephones and then cell phones. This is possible also because of comparative low costs of installing cell phones in developing nations. The PC is an older technology and relative to cell phones, PCs are more expensive and require more education to operate (two major components of the HDI). Among ICs, richer nations may have reached a peak in PC adoption and so the relation is reverse. In DCs, because of costs and education involved, PCs are getting adopted in comparatively educated and richer nations. HDI was not a factor in Internet growth rate, perhaps because Internet growth rate does not depend on GDP or education and can flourish in less affluent countries.

The GINI index of income inequality was not significant for any nation cluster as far as Internet and PC growth rates were concerned. Urbanization did impact growth rate, especially in ICs. This finding offers some support for Gatignon et al.'s (1989) assertions of the relationship between cosmopolitanism and the tendency to innovate, and Marshall's (1920) finding that regions with dense concentrations of firms engaged in the same production process are likely to be information-rich since, for the most part, urbanization is more pronounced in ICs.

5 CONCLUSIONS

Technologies were initially developed in wealthier countries and then percolated down to developing countries (Walsham 2001). The present study examined the antecedents of ICT growth rate. It was motivated by the need to extract the rate factors that technologies seem to have in common for DCs and ICs and provide us with an overall picture. Our study indicates that factors impacting growth rates differ for DCs and ICs.

The study results show that traditional growth theory can not adequately explain the phenomena of ICT growth in developing countries. This conforms to developmental theories which posit that developmental and gender-related variables, institutional and cultural factors can all play a role in ICT developments in DCs (Walsham 2001). Managers and policy makers should be aware that if technology transfers are to be encouraged, developmental and institutional changes need to be promoted accordingly.

The study offers many contributions. First, the study contributes to the IS developmental research by identifying factors that are responsible for ICT diffusion in ICs and DCs. Previous studies are lacking in this respect. Too often, few countries are grouped together and attempts are made to generalize the conclusions. Specifically, our contribution lies in (1) identifying a set of indicators for ICT growth, (2) including as many countries as possible in the study, subject to the data availability (our major constraint) to generalize the results, and (3) observing that ACs, ICs and DCs have a similar yet distinct set of influencing factors for ICT diffusion rates.

This study has some limitations. Many researchers have previously noted the problems of cross-country research (Barro and Sala-i-Martin,1998; Gibbs 1995). Data sets are often incomplete, data availability is limited, and data can contain errors. This problem was summarized by Gibbs (1995) when he noted that the problem with research on developing countries is not in the laboratory, but in the library. This problem is exacerbated when attempting to conduct longitudinal studies on DCs. Whereas recent data are generally available, it is difficult to find data from 10 years earlier. For example, by 2001 (and after), HDI data was available for 177 countries. In 1995, data was available for only 145 countries, and in 1985 HDI data was available for only 120 countries. Combining incomplete data for various variables further reduces the data set to a common denominator set.

Future research should investigate additional factors, such as culture and trust, all of which have been shown to affect some ICT adoptions in previous studies (Bagchi et al 2004; Boudreau et al. 1998; Walsham 2001; Walsham and Sahay 1999). Our continuing research efforts are in these directions.

References

Acemoglu, D., Aghion, P., and Zilibotti, F. "Distance to Frontier, Selection, and Economic Growth," NBER Working Paper 9066, National Bureau of Economic Research, Cambridge, MA, 2002.

Anandarajan, M., Igbaria, M., and Anakwe, U. P. "IT Acceptance in a Less-Industrialized Country: A Motivational Factor Perspective," *International Journal of Information Management* (22 :1), 2000, pp. 47–65.

Bagchi, K., Hart, P., and Peterson, M. IT Product Adoption and the Influence of National Culture," *Journal of Global Information Technology Management* (7:4), Special Issue on Cross-Cultural IS Research, October 2004, pp. 29-46.

Banerjee, A. V., and Newman, A. F. "Information, the Dual Economy, and Development," *Review of Economic Studies* (65), October 1998, pp. 631-653.

Barro, R., and Sala-i-Martin, X. *Economic Growth*, Cambridge, MA: MIT Press, 1998.

Bate, R., and Montgomery, D. "Beyond Kyoto: Real Solutions to Greenhouse Emissions from Developing Countries," *Environmental Policy Outlook*, July-August 2004, pp. 1-13 (available online at http://www.aei.org/publications/pubID.20982/pub_detail.asp).

Boudreau, M.-C., Loch, K. D., Robey, D., and Straub, D. "Going Global: Using Information Technology to Advance the Competitiveness of the Virtual Transnational Organization," *The Academy of Management Executive* (12 :4), 1998, pp. 120-128.

Cheong, W. H. "Internet Adoption in Macao," *Journal Computer-Mediated Communication* (7:2), 2002 (available online at http://jcmc.indiana.edu/vol7/issue2/macao.html).

Cronin, F. J., Colleran, E. K., Herber, P. L., and Lewitzky S. "Telecommunications and Growth: The Contribution of Telecommunications Infrastructure Investment to Aggregate and Sectoral Productivity," *Telecommunications Policy* (17:9), 1993, pp. 677-690.

Cronin, F. J., Parker, E. B., Colleran, E. K., and Gold, M. A. "Telecommunications Infrastructure and Economic Growth: An Analysis of Causality," *Telecommunications Policy* (15:6), 1991, pp. 529-535.

Davidson, R., Vogel, D., Harris, R., and Jones, N. "Technology Leapfrogging in Developing Countries: An Inevitable Luxury," *Electronic Journal on Information Systems in Developing Countries* (1:5), 2000, pp. 1-10 (available online at http://www.is.cityu.edu.hk/research/ejisdc/vol1/v1d5.pdf).

Davis, F. D., Bagozzi, R., and Warshaw, P. R. "User Acceptance of Computer Technology: A Comparison of Two Theoretical Models," *Management Science* (35:8), 1989, pp. 982-1003.

Deininger, K., and Squire, L. "Economic Growth and Income Inequality: Reexamining the Links," *Finance and Development* (34:1), March 1997, pp. 38-41.

Dekimpe, M. G., Parker, P. M., and Sarvary, M. "Modeling Global Diffusion," Working Paper 94/72/MKT 31, INSEAD, Fontainebleau, France, 1994.

Dewan, S., and Kraemer, K. K. "Information Technology and Productivity: Evidence from Country-Level Data," *Management Science* (46:4), 2000, pp. 548-562.

de Vanssay, X., and Spindler, Z. A. "Constitutions, Institutions and Economic Convergence: An International Comparison," *Journal for Studies in Economics and Econometrics* (20:3), 1996, pp. 1-19.

Ein-Dor, P., Myers, M. D., and Raman, K. S. "Information Technology in Three Small Developed Countries," *Journal of Management Information Systems* (13:4), 1997, pp. 61-89.

Fichman, R. G. "Information Technology Diffusion: A Review of Empirical Research," in J. I. DeGross, J. D. Becker, and J. J. Elam (eds.), *Proceedings of the 13th International Conference on Information Systems*, Dallas, TX, 1992, pp. 195-206.

Galbraith, J. R. *Designing Complex Organizations*, Reading, MA: Addison-Wesley, 1973.

Garcia-Murillo, M. "Patchwork Adoption of ICTs in Latin America," *The Electronic Journal on Information Systems in Developing Countries* (15:1), 2003, pp. 1-9.

Gatignon, H., Eliashberg, J., and Robertson, T. S. "Modeling Multinational Diffusion Patterns: An Efficient Methodology," *Marketing Science* (8:3), 1989, pp. 231-247.

Gerschenkron, A. *Economic Backwardness in Historical Perspective*, Cambridge, MA: Belknap Press, 1962.

Gibbs, W. W. "Lost Science in the Third World," *Scientific American*, August 1995, pp. 92-99.

Green, S., Melnyk, A., and Powers, D. "Is Economic Freedom Necessary for Technology Diffusion?," *Applied Economics Letters* (9:14), 2002, pp. 907-910.

Grubel, H. G. "Economic Freedom and Human Welfare: Some Empirical Findings," *Cato Journal* (18:2), 1998, pp. 287-304.

Gwartney, J., and Lawson, R. "Economic Freedom of the World: 2003 Annual Report," The Fraser Institute, Vancouver, 2003.

Hannerz, U. "Cosmopolitans and Locals in World Culture," *Theory, Culture & Society* (7:2/3), 1990, pp. 237-251.

Hoff, K., and Stiglitz, J. E. "Modern Economic Theory and Development," in G. Meier and J. Stiglitz (eds.), *Frontiers of Development Economics: The Future in Perspective*, Oxford, England: Oxford University Press, 2000, pp. 389-459.

Hofstede, G. *Cultures and Organizations: Software of the Mind: Intercultural Cooperation and its Importance for Survival*, Cambridge, England: McGraw-Hill, 1991.

International Telecommunications Union (ITU). *Telecommunications Indicators Handbook*, Geneva: ITU, 1999.

Kraemer, K. L., Gurbaxani, V., and King, J. L. "Economic Development, Government Policy, and the Diffusion of Computing in Asia-Pacific Countries," *Public Administration* Review (52:2), 1992, pp. 146-156.

Loboda, J. "The Diffusion of Television in Poland," *Economic Geography* (50:1), 1974, pp.70-82.

Mbarika, V. W., Kah, M. M. O., Musa, P. F., Meso, P., and Warren, J. " Predictors of Growth of Teledensity in Developing Countries: A Focus on Middle and Low-Income Countries," *The Electronic Journal on Information Systems in Developing Countries* (12:1), 2003, pp. 1-16.

Madon, S. "The Internet and Socio-Economic Development: Exploring the Interaction," *Information technology and People* (13:2), 2000, pp. 85-101.

Mahajan, V., and Peterson, R. *Models for Innovation Diffusion* (2nd ed.), Beverly Hills, CA: Sage Publications, 1985.

Marshall, A. *Principles of Economics* (8th ed.), London: MacMillan, 1920.

Moore, G. A. *Crossing the Chasm: Marketing and Selling High-Tech Goods to Mainstream Customers*, New York: HarperBusiness, 1991.

Mwesige, P. G. "Cyber Elites: A Survey of Internet Cafe Users in Uganda," *Telematcs & Informatics* (21), 2003, pp. 83-101.

Neter, J., Kutner, M., Nachtsheim, C., and Wasserman, W. *Applied Linear Statistical Models*, Chicago: Irwin Press, 1996.

Perlman, J. E. "Global Urbanization: Challenges and Opportunities," Publication MCP-013, The Mega-Cities Project, 1993 (http://www.megacitiesproject.org).

Proenza, F. J. "Telecenter Sustainability: Myths and Opportunities," *The Journal of Development Communication* (12:2), 2001, pp. 94-109.

Quibria, M. G., Ahmed, S. N., Tschang, T., and Reyes-Macasaquit, M. "Digital Divide: Determinants and Policies with Special Reference to Asia," *Journal of Asian Economics* (13), 2003, pp. 811-825.

Saunders, R. J., Warford, J. I., and Wellenius, B. *Telecommunications and Economic Development* (2nd ed.), Baltimore, MD: John Hopkins University Press, 1994.

Shakeel, H., Best, M., Miller, B., and Weber, S. "Comparing Urban and Rural Telecenters Costs," *The Electronic Journal on Information Systems in Developing Countries* (4:2), 2001, pp. 1-13.

Straub, D. W. "The Effect of Culture on IT Diffusion: E-mail and Fax in Japan and the US," *Information Systems Research* (5), 1994, pp. 23-47.

Stiglitz, J. "Globalization and Growth in Emerging Markets and the New Economy," *Journal of Policy Modeling* (25), 2003, pp. 505-524.

Toussea-Oulai, A., and Ura, S. "Information Technology Transfer: Problems Facing African Developing Nations," *International Journal of Human-Computer Interaction* (3:1), 1991, pp. 79-93.

UNDP. "World Development Report 1990," United Nations Development Programme, Oxford, England, 1990.

Walsham, G. *Making a World of Difference: IT in a Global Context*, Chichester, England: Wiley, 2001.

World Bank. *World Bank Telecommunications Sector Reports,* Washington, DC, 1991.

World Bank. "Country Classifications," 2005 (available online at http://www.worldbank.org/data/countryclass/classgroups.htm).

Wu, W., and Davis, O. A. "The Two Freedoms, Economic Growth and Development: An Empirical Study," *Public Choice* (100), 1999, pp. 39-64.

About the Authors

Kallol Bagchi is an assistant professor in the Department of Information and Decision Sciences in the College of Business at the University of Texas at El Paso. He can be reached at kbagchi@utep.edu.

Peeter Kirs is an associate professor in the Department of Information and Decision Sciences in the College of Business at the University of Texas at El Paso. He can be reached at pkirs@utep.edu.

Godwin Udo is a full professor in the Department of Information and Decision Sciences in the College of Business at the University of Texas at El Paso. He can be reached at gudo@utep.edu.

4 AMERICAN DISCOURSES OF THE DIGITAL DIVIDE AND ECONOMIC DEVELOPMENT: A Sisyphean[1] Order to Catch Up?

Leslie Tu
Lynette Kvasny
Pennsylvania State University
University Park, PA U.S.A.

Abstract   *Discourses about technology and its role in development have been constant themes within IFIP Working Group 8.2 (see the Barcelona proceedings— Wynn et al. 2002). In this paper, we examine how strands of discourse— institutionalized ways of thinking and speaking—shape debate about the digital divide and urban poverty in America. As research is widely esteemed as a wellspring of new ideas, we are especially interested in how discourses inform scholarly inquiry into urgent social problems. As information and communication technologies (ICTs) are increasingly hailed as drivers of industry and commerce, we believe that it will be instructive to examine economic development discourse, which strongly informs the case for bridging the digital divide.*

First, using Fairclough's three-level framework for critical discourse analysis (CDA), we reveal that the discursive hegemony of economic development alarmingly constrains approaches to urban revitalization. Linking economic development to the digital divide, we show how the ongoing evolution of ICTs has become tightly linked to economic development. Both are discourses of equality in which those who lack money and technology are

---

[1] In Greek mythology, Sisyphus was a bold, crafty king of Corinth who angered Zeus by speaking unfavorably of him. The king of the gods became bent on his death, and sent his reaper to haul Sisyphus off to Tartarus. Twice, shrewd Sisyphus cheated death and returned among the living, until at last Zeus devised a special punishment for his impiety: In Tartarus, Sisyphus would have to roll an enormous rock up a hill; just as he would reach the summit, the rock would roll back down, and the laborious task would begin again. The insolent king was condemned to this toil for all eternity.

Please use the following format when citing this chapter:

Tu, L., and Kvasny, L., 2006, in IFIP International Federation for Information Processing, Volume 208, Social Inclusion: Societal and Organizational Implications for Information Systems, eds. Trauth, E., Howcroft, D., Butler, T., Fitzgerald, B., DeGross, J., (Boston: Springer), pp. 51-65.

cast as needy problem sectors that will be left behind, failing to reap a host of benefits. Hence, there is an urgent call for these "have-nots" to catch up to models of prosperity embodied by the wealthy or technology savvy. We find fault with this discourse because it narrowly privileges money and technology, and raises alarm at their mere absence, while obscuring substantive needs— hunger, homelessness, ill health—of actual consequence. We propose that, in order truly to realize the potential of ICT, we must first reinvent discourse— discarding the mantra of catching up—and set in motion efforts to address self-determined needs, supported by ICT.

1 INTRODUCTION

Information and communication technologies (ICTs) are rapidly assuming importance in myriad domains, especially those concerned with economic advancement. Well endowed sectors are overwhelmingly optimistic, touting novel opportunities for business in a global, digital economy.

But, as vast resources are readily committed to improving information tools for the technology savvy, underserved Americans[2] seem only to be gaining from these developments a new claim to exclusion. Long before ICT had acquired mainstream prevalence, the complex problems of poverty and social exclusion had even the most astute scholars and policymakers at a loss. Today, we remain far from having resolved the grave needs of hunger, homelessness, educational deficits, and crime that hold basic life chances beyond the reach of many inner city residents. The rhetoric that celebrates a burgeoning information economy and revolutionary technological advances rings hollow in economically depressed neighborhoods where local residents must contend with more immediate obstacles such as social marginalization and financial hardship.

Because economic development has become the default remedy for poverty, and since ICTs are seen as a cornerstone of economic development (e.g., Thompson 2002; White House 2004), the digital divide has attracted intense interest. The digital divide projects a new form of inequality, whereby society is split between "haves," who enjoy access to ICTs and their benefits, and "have-nots," who somehow lack the means or desire to use them. Increasingly, the discourse that calls for bridging the technological gap draws urgency from the broader debate concerning economic development. Nonusers of ICT, experts commonly warn, risk exclusion from the new economy and other emerging opportunities introduced by these tools.

In what follows, we offer our understanding of discourse and how influential social agents and institutions employ discursive practices designed to garner the complicity of others. We then take up economic development, a prominent discourse that rarely meets

---

[2]By historically underserved Americans, we mean those who have systematically been marginalized in a host of spheres that affect their life chances. This includes Americans with disabilities, low incomes, and limited formal education. It also includes immigrants, racial and ethnic minorities, as well as inner city and urban communities. For decades, these are the people who have been disadvantaged in a host of domains that largely determine social mobility and inclusion.

opposition as a necessary, even laudable strategy for alleviating urban poverty. Using Fairclough's three-level framework for critical discourse analysis (CDA), and guided by Thompson's (2002) critical study of ICT and third world development discourse, we examine the ideas and assumptions underlying academic inquiry into economic distress in American inner cities. Noting how dominant discourses pervade even the province of scholars—long regarded as free-thinking innovators—we then ask how this very hegemony of economic development is steering campaigns for bridging the digital divide. In our analysis we adopt a critical stance, troubled by (1) a dominant economic development discourse that privileges money while failing to inform substantive improvement and (2) what we observe as economic development both shaping and being co-opted to validate the case for bridging the digital divide. We are skeptical of this association because such a bridge is narrowly constructed, removed from substantive needs, and, without a shift in thinking, never to see completion. Like Sisyphus—who time and again seemed to be reaching the end of his toil, only to have the rock roll down and his labor begin all over—as long as the poor are locked into a discourse of catching up, their race will never end. We conclude by offering alternative ways to conceptualize the digital divide discourse—alternatives that encourage the underserved to express their own experiences, leverage their cultural competencies and social networks, and ultimately use ICT creatively to fulfill self-determined needs.

2 DEFINING DISCOURSE

Popular understandings about the digital divide and economic development are profoundly shaped by their proponents' highly selective language. Foucault describes discourse as "a sets of statements that make up a language for discussing a certain topic at some historical moment" (Foucault cited in Kvasny and Sawyer 2002). It constrains the way in which we can meaningfully reason and talk about a topic and, often, assumptions imposed by a discourse are hardly contested or interrogated—with the result that they seem reasonable or inevitable. For example, in a critical study of information systems development practices in developing countries, Avgerou (2000), noting the heavy influence of Western rationalities, concluded that information systems practices and research are often privy to a capitalist, techno-scientific view that "assumes that technology is deployed in the context of an enterprise striving for competitiveness in a free market economy." Escobar (1995) observed a systematic adherence to free market rationality in third world development projects since the 1940s. This mentality, coupled with stubborn confidence in scientific methods and technology, routinely constrained what courses of action were considered useful and possible. Escobar noted that these development conventions constituted a discourse—"a space of thought and action within which only certain things can be said, done, or imagined" (Escobar cited in Avgerou 2000). Discourse shapes our thinking in every context and domain—from the paradigms of social inquiry, to reporting styles in news media, to what qualities merit the distinction of art (Fairclough 1995; Mauws 2000; van Dijk 1996).

Discursive hegemony refers to a state in which a dominant discourse goes uncontested, assuming the weight of common sense. Recipients who neglect to question such a discourse tend to accept its dictates as fact, as their socially constructed nature becomes obscured (Fairclough 1995). Meanwhile, alternative discourses and, perhaps worse, the very liberty to select a favorable discourse from among multiple options become foregone considerations and the dominant view persists, safe from scrutiny. Discourse is inherently associated with power and, as with other valued social resources (e.g., money, work, status), exclusive access to discourse confers an edge in wielding respect, influence, and control (van Dijk 1996). The ability to manipulate structures of text and talk, thus achieving influence over recipients' knowledge, attitudes, and mental models, is a subtle instrument for advancing one's own agenda. Herman and Chomsky (1988) call this kind of manipulation "manufacturing the consent" of others.

2.1 Discourse and the Social Sciences: The Problem with Neutrality

Social scientists often set out seeking knowledge that is neutral, unbiased, objective, and value-free. Such intentions seem a stretch, however, when we note that the language, conventions, and instruments of every such inquiry are all socially constructed. Much as the researcher may strive to contribute unbiased parcels of insight to a body of knowledge that is equally pure, the fact is that strands of discourse will always inform his or her inquiries, approaches, and lines of reasoning. The potential downfall of social science is by no means the sacrifice of neutrality. Rather, it is the obfuscation of their socially constructed, *non*-neutral character that would undermine social studies. We can learn valuable things from openly subjective modes of inquiry, but it is crucial first to understand the values-laden, contextualized nature of our scholarly output (Yapa 1996).

Objects of social science do not have naïvely given properties that are just there to be described by social scientists. One convention that faultily encourages this assumption is the tacit delineation of a subject–object binary, whereby "the social-science investigator (the subject) stands outside the object employing a neutral discourse that studies the object" (Yapa 1996). Yet these perceived counterparts are, in fact, mutually constituted and inseparably linked in the space of the discourse. Failure to recognize the role of discourse in scientific inquiry makes researchers unwittingly compliant with dominant ways of thinking—and whatever stock remedies the discourse prescribes. Such compliance is particularly troubling because research is widely regarded as an important source of novel ideas.

Our analysis has two aims: (1) to grasp how a dominant economic development discourse informs academic research on inner city poverty; and (2) to understand the links between this economic development discourse and the digital divide. As we have adopted a critical stance, our discussion then proceeds to highlight why such a discursive hegemony among scholars is worrisome, and to explain why we are troubled by a tight coupling of the economic development and digital divide discourses. Finally, in light of our findings, we offer an alternative discourse for understanding the digital divide.

2.2 Methodology

Critical Discourse Analysis (CDA): Academic Research Publications. Widely esteemed as subject experts, academics hold unmatched access to research and its constituent discourses such as economic development and the digital divide. It should be instructive, therefore, to examine research journals—an important venue for scholarly reporting and discussion—as telling records of favored discourse among researchers. Our analysis takes up seven academic publications that address economic distress in American inner cities, including a work that has ascended to prominence in the field (Porter 1995); various responses to that work; and additional studies that offer distinct perspectives and approaches to inner city poverty.

Fairclough's Three-Level CDA Framework and Thompson's Discursive Types. Fairclough (1995) observed that texts constitute a major source of evidence for grounding claims about social structures, relations, and processes. Although connections between language use and the exercise of power are generally invisible, he maintains that close examinations of speech and writing can bring to light concealed mechanisms of domination.

In his three-level CDA framework, Fairclough positions discursive practice as the mediating layer between works of micro-level text production and macro-level socio-cultural practice. The mediating processes of text production channel macro-level structures (e.g., ideologies, power relations) down into the micro-level text, leaving traces in the rendered product. Markings in the text, then, reproduce and reinforce their macro-level influences. The interpretive process extracts underlying meanings by probing these textual cues. CDA is critical for exposing connections between micro-level texts and macro-level power structures.

In Fairclough's framework, an order of discourse is defined by certain discursive practices associated with an institutionalized set of ideas (e.g., Third World development, inner city poverty) and the relations between them. Discursive types are thematic constructs that are vertically identifiable with a particular order of discourse. Thompson (2002), for example, identified *technocracy, corporatism*, and *technological optimism* as recurring discursive types in the World Bank's development order of discourse.[3]

Our approach was heavily informed by Thompson's analysis of a speech by former World Bank president James D. Wolfensohn, addressed to a Cambridge University audience in 2000 (see Table 1). Using Thompson's set of discursive types as a sensitizing framework, we roughly reverse his ground-up interpretation process (see Table 2 for an example). Rather than identify constructs anew from our readings of these texts, we began by considering how Thompson's constructs compare to studies of inner city poverty in the United States Where we recognize similar lines of reasoning and argument, we note the parallels (see Table 3); where the ideas of a particular paper strain the given template, we add new constructs (e.g., social capital, local needs), in a sense growing the original space of discourse.

---

[3]Another concept in Fairclough, *speech genre* refers generically to a style of language use, as employed horizontally across various orders of discourse, to achieve a certain response—e.g., interview, humor, persuasion (Thompson 2002). Because the style conventions of academic writing often discourage their (overt, liberal) use, we do not examine speech genres in this analysis.

Table 1. Discursive types (adapted from Thompson 2002)

Discursive Type	Description
Technocracy	Assertion of expertise.
Legitimacy	Appeal to a higher order need for intervention.
Neutrality	Projecting ICT as a neutral force in development; unproblematic neutrality, projecting status as independent . *We take the term as regards the way of thinking and strategies/ideas advocated (i.e., discourse itself).*
Corporatism	The deployment, hence ownership of elements of dominant corporate discourse, such as leveraging, empowering, objectives, and knowledge.
Tech(nological) optimism	The unproblematic linking of ICT to opportunity; bordering on determinism. *Technology here refers to mainstream economic models and associated notions.*
Pragmatism	Show of ICT pragmatic use on the ground, thus ensuring results. *In place of ICT specifically, we consider any technology, strategy, or idea whose demonstrated utility is cited*

Table 2. Comparison of CDA Notes: Thompson's Discursive Types

Discursive Type	CDA Notes*
Technocracy	Asserts private sector expertise; thus, firms must lead revitalization of inner cities.
Legitimacy	Economic distress of U.S. Inner cities are perhaps the most pressing issue facing the nation.
Neutrality	(1) Inner cities should be subject to same economic principles as are other areas. (2) Rules of marketplace assume weight of law—charity distorts these forces.
Corporatism	Inner cities must aspire to find competitive advantage; exploit market opportunities.
Technological optimism	Once private sector firms are allowed to take over, inner city revitalization will have genuine momentum.
Pragmatism	Inner cities need a radically different approach after years of failed social models.

*From M. Porter, "The Competitive Advantage of the Inner City," *Harvard Business Review*, May-June 1995.

2.3 CDA: Discussion/Implications

Although space constraints do not permit a full discussion here, our analysis of academic publications highlighted two important concerns. First, much of academic research omits explicit considerations of the role of discourse—and, hence, theory, research questions and responsive actions—in its studies of inner city poverty. A neutrality discourse, as described by Yapa (1996), continues to obscure the socially constructed nature of research, while automatically consigning knowledge, resources, and agency to the realm of scholars, private sector firms, and government bodies. Meanwhile the object—economic have-nots—is implicated as the needy other in need of development, the embodiment of a problem, examined and done-to, holding no insight or agency. But if subject, object, and discourse are mutually constituted and inextricably linked, such a distinction is impossibly distorted. Moreover, this discursive practice sanctions a highly unbalanced distribution of authority and wherewithal that empowers the subject while stifling the object.

Second, we found that many of Thompson's discursive types are prominently echoed in a majority of texts that address inner city economic distress. While a few papers did expand significantly on this space of discourse informed by corporatism, technocracy, neutrality, etc., much of the debate languishes within those boundaries described by Thompson.

3 LINKING ECONOMIC DEVELOPMENT AND THE DIGITAL DIVIDE THROUGH DISCOURSE

In this section, we examine more closely the linkages between the economic development and digital divide discourses, and how these discourses similarly seek to manufacture the consent of others. These linkages are presented in Table 3, and will be discussed in turn.

3.1 Alleged Motivation: Equality

Gillis and Mitchell (2002), focusing on persistent deprivation within the have-not sector, link uneven ICT access with social exclusion. They argue for bridging the divide against a regrettable scenario of unrealized potential economic and human development which cannot be excused. On an individual basis, this forgone development activity translates into higher rates of poverty, poorer health, lower literacy and quality of life than is necessary. Thus, an aptitude with ICT has become not merely useful, but more or less requisite, for effective democratic participation and economic development. Similarly, Fors and Moreno (2002) write that in our contemporary world, having access to information and knowledge plays a crucial role in advancing economic and social well-being. With the growing prevalence of ICT in prominent domains such as business, education, and government, these technologies are no longer the edge that confers an advantage to the savvy specialist. ICT competence is acquiring the status of a basic commodity that must be in place before any meaningful or productive activity can occur (Kvasny and Truex 2001).

Table 3. Comparison of Discourses: Economic Development and the Digital Divide

Aspect of Discourse	Economic Development	Digital Divide
Alleged Motivation: Equality	Eradication of poverty in inner cities	Bridging the divide, i.e., universal connectivity
Framing the Problem Space	• Statistical construction of a poverty sector based on income • Correlation with factors such as race, educational attainment, unemployment, dysfunctional social behaviors	• Statistical construction of have/have-not sectors based on access • Correlation with factors such as race, age, gender, income, educational attainment, employment, location
Informing Questions	How to inject money, jobs, corporate investment into poor areas	How to supply hardware, connections to those who lack access
Measure of Problem/ Progress	Figures for median income, unemployment, educational attainment, home ownership	• Statistics profiling ICT access (computer ownership, Internet connectivity), and usage • Global divide: national e-readiness assessments; counted tallies of phone lines, servers, web sites, etc.
Favored Policy Strategies	Court private sector firms; increase investment, create job opportunities	Establish public access centers; equip schools, libraries
Authors of Discourse (subject–object)	Government (Census Bureau); private sector; international aid organizations (UN Development, World Bank); academic research	Government (NTIA); private sector; international aid organizations (DOT Force [G8], UN, World Bank); NGOs (Pew Internet, DD Network, bridges.org); academic research

The digital divide pretends to be a problem of inequality—an access gap that separates information haves from Internet-deprived have-nots. The digital divide rapidly ascended to high-priority status in the agenda of national governments, nonprofit groups, and international development organizations (e.g., bridges.org 2001; NTIA 2004; World Bank 2001). In support of efforts to bridge the divide, it is commonly argued that the economic, political and social well-being of all groups is contingent on access to ICT (e.g., Fors and Moreno 2002; Gillis and Mitchell 2002; NTIA 2004). Lack of access to ICT raises all manner of alarms: opportunities in the new economy are at stake;

participation in modern democracy will require a mastery of ICT (Klein 1999; Yu 2002); untold educational benefits are lost without them (NTIA 2004). The obvious solution, by this understanding, is to furnish access to those who lack it. By connecting disadvantaged groups to ICT, we are extending to them the leading edge of innovation, the means to succeed in the new economy. With ICT access representing limitless resources and opportunity, underserved Americans can be molded by rhetoric into new markets, and positioned for empowerment in the digital age (Kvasny and Truex 2001). Thus, digital divide discourse claims legitimacy by its blameless will to level the playing field, and apparent promises to erase the inequities that have long stood in the way of underserved groups.

Similarly, economic development pretends equality because it strives to wipe out economic disparities. Porter (1995) called the crushing cycles of poverty, drug abuse, and crime one of the most pressing issues facing the nation. Bates (1997) referred to disinvestment in inner cities as a symptom of America's urban racial crisis. Loukaitou-Sideris (2000) painted an image of inner city strips so broken and desperate that no one could have questioned the need for responsive action. We are made to believe that these many complex ills are symptomatic of inequality—namely, that of economic wealth. Hence, the strategies of injecting wealth, private sector influence, and jobs into areas that lack them seem straightforward. It is a discourse that emphasizes poverty—a lack of money—as the heart of the problem, and urges catching up as the response.

3.2 Framing the Problem Space, Informing Questions, Measuring Progress, and Favored Solutions

In the economic development discourse premised on economic inequality, have/have-not dichotomies are devised through the statistical construction of a poverty sector—typically that set of households whose earnings fall short of a designated income threshold. In this way, a lack of *money* is the implied emergency, which begs the question, how can people increase their earnings? This statistical construct reinforces an already assumed subject–object binary, and becomes central in the formulation of strategies for understanding and addressing the problem of poverty.

The official approach to alleviating poverty consists of three steps: first, data are collected on the extent and geographical location of poverty; second, information is gathered on "causative" variables such as race, gender, and employment that may be correlated with poverty; third, information on the incidence of poverty and correlated variables is used in models to help formulate appropriate policy and action. (Yapa 1996, p. 712)

Although Yapa was writing about third world poverty and development in a global context, many of these same approaches have been applied similarly to economic development in America. Instruments such as the U.S. Census report have become standard tools for assessing the extent of poverty in the United States.

Initial studies of the digital divide proceeded similarly in the statistical profiling of a technology-deprived have-not sector. As households are considered economically poor for failing to make an official threshold income, individuals are singled out as information-poor if they do not make use of online content, or lack access to an Internet connection.

Statistical profiling is also routinely used to measure progress both at a national and global level. The increasingly worldwide participation of countries in campaigns to bridge the digital divide has led to a barrage of statistical studies whose findings ultimately pit each nation against all others in comparative ICT ratings (much the way nations are ranked economically by GDP, export volumes, etc.). In this context of global competition, access rankings often spur the perverse, short-sighted pursuit of leading statistics. In a 2004 address to the U.S. Department of Commerce, the U.S. President expressed his disappointment in the nation's current tenth place ranking in broadband connectivity worldwide (White House 2004). "That's not good enough," Bush protested, "We don't like to be ranked tenth in anything. The goal is to be ranked first when it comes to per capita use of broadband technology. It's in our nation's interest. It's good for our economy."

Modern development paradigms endorsed by high-profile organizations such as the United Nations and the World Bank now consistently feature e-readiness as a cornerstone of national economic development capacity (bridges.org 2001; Thompson 2002; World Bank 2001. As Thompson pointed out, the two discourses are becoming more and more inseparable, with campaigns to bridge the digital divide aligning their aims with those of economic development. Economic development is rarely contested as the dominant solution to poverty—where poverty implies a root problem of savage deficits and deep social inequities. As ICTs are positioned as key to combating deprivation, even as they otherwise introduce another aspect of lack, this whole discursive package of economic development and bridging the digital divide becomes doubly infused with the legitimacy associated with the pursuit of social equality (Thompson 2002).

3.3 Authoring Discourse (Subject–Object)

Yapa (1996) points out that the study of economics is premised on a situation of scarcity, in which supposedly unlimited wants encounter an inevitably limited stock of resources. Hence the problem: How do we allocate scarce resources in the most equitable, beneficial way, across these endless wants? Since capitalist economies thrive while demand is strong, and while the powers of production command supply, a certain way to stoke the economy is to keep up the endless construction of need. The wealthy, generally beyond the concerns of material subsistence already, must be induced to tap into their surpluses for novel or status/luxury goods. The growth of the economy is largely based upon the inducement of new cravings that spur and magnify consumption. In turn, manufactured wants among the wealthy spread the appeal of status and novelty, via discourse, to the broader population who, though they may be ill-equipped to afford (and in little actual need of) them, are made to believe that they must likewise seek these same goods in order to catch up. Newer, more modern lifestyles are continually invented and marketed while existing ways are phased out as obsolete and inadequate.

Recalling van Dijk (1996), access to discourse is a form of power that can amount to control over the public mind. The information wealthy exercise nearly exclusive command over the production and evolution of ICT; thus, they hold charge of its marketing as well. That is, information haves monopolize ICT discourse in addition to technological innovation. As the leading experts of these technologies, they establish precedents, and determine and market, via discourse, what products and standards are desirable, effective, and up-to-date. Moss (2002) highlights need formation as an important component of what he calls influence. Such influence is especially pro-nounced in top–down development models, in which external specialists define the needs of disadvantaged societies and individuals, whose own self-determination is thereby greatly reduced. Essentially, Moss' concept of need formation is an element of discourse, and influence here is allocated in line with a subject–object binary that privileges the expertise of the wealthy/developed to envision what the marginalized must become.

As long as the lot of the wealthy is accepted as the standard vision of prosperity, genuine equality will remain unattainable. The seemingly higher-order imperative to strive for equality is actually a prescription for permanent *in*equality because its terms are defined and imposed by the wealthy and powerful, who control access to the dominant discourse. By extolling their own ideals as what the marginalized must become, subjects lock their objects into an endless race to catch up while they remain ahead themselves, continually raising the bar (Kvasny and Truex 2001). As first movers, proponents of bridging the divide continue to pioneer new uses for ICT, and gain exponential benefits from their unmatched command of these technologies. Meanwhile, newcomers must contend with the pains of basic adoption, with no control over what standards and architecture have been laid in place by first movers (bridges.org 2001; Yu 2002). True digital equality will demand that newcomers not only gain access to ICT, but also become content producers and designers, exercising creativity at the forefront of innovation *and* discourse (Gurstein 2003).

4   MOVING BEYOND CATCHING UP

Having discussed the limitations of the existing discourse, and possible ways to revise it, we now begin to propose a more hopeful alternative—one that privileges the needs and resources of poor communities. The mainstream discourses that currently define economic development and the digital divide hold out predetermined notions of success to the underserved, urging them to catch up. Bent on the pursuit of a singular course of action—toward official prosperity, toward universal connectivity—these models crowd out other ways of thinking that would allow marginalized groups to pursue alternate strategies for addressing their needs. The abstract ends of *eradicating poverty* and, now, *bridging the digital divide* may have merit, but they bind people to a stock set of solutions that appease an imposed vision; such solutions lack the flexibility to take advantage of particular resources and knowledge which new users may hold. Nor have these stock fixes been shown to accomplish constructive, lasting change (e.g., Lazarus and Mora 2000).

However, we can revise the problem of inequality (with its futile logic of catching up) into more pragmatic, substantive questions of how people can meet their needs. Internet access *per se* is no remedy for our most pressing social problems, such as poor

Table 4. Alternative Discourses

Discursive Type	Alternative Discourse*
Technocracy	Authors do not assert own expertise; do not privilege expertise of outside specialists in creating development framework
Legitimacy	Detailed profile of official poverty area demands attention; local community involvement gives legitimacy to research projects
Neutrality	Not a concern of authors to appear neutral; positions clearly stated as such, theories constructed rather than asserted as fact
Corporatism	Authors reject mainstream corporate discourse, citing examples of its failure to help Belmont (e.g., funding shortages stalled development efforts)
Technological optimism	Argue against notion that economics/IT alone will improve inner city situation
Pragmatism	Projects shaped by substantive questions based on concrete needs; utilize available resources

*From L. Kvasny and L. Yapa, "Rethinking Urban Poverty: Forms of Capital, Information Technology, and Enterprise Management," *Handbook of Information Systems Research: Critical Perspectives on Information Systems Design and Use*, 2005.

public school systems, high unemployment, poor nutrition, and ill health (Kvasny and Sawyer 2002). But perhaps ICTs can support novel strategies for helping underserved Americans address their needs. As an instructive starting point, we revisit our discourse analysis—this time considering those insights that strained and rejected the economic development model (Table 4).

4.1 Sketching an Alternative Discourse

Kvasny and Yapa (2005) suggest that a lack of economic capital need not stop the underserved from seeking alternative strategies for meeting their needs. They draw ideas from Bourdieu's theory of capital, which maintains that social and cultural assets are forms of capital that, like money (economic capital), are of value in business and community building. Moreover, these three forms of capital are convertible, so there is no way to privilege any certain one. Loukaitou-Sideris (2000) and Harrison and Glasmeier (1997) likewise affirmed that tremendous business advantage often flows from intangible social capital. These authors recognized how certain groups were able to accomplish much more when empowered by professional network connections and collective action. Addressing tangible, locally determined needs can give meaning to the abstract challenges labeled as economic development and bridging the digital divide. Context helps to shift the main challenge away from making income or gaining access to ICT, to addressing particular, concrete needs. Moreover, in focusing on local communities, their unique assets and histories invite consideration, possibly offering rich resources and knowledge to the search for new solutions.

Gurstein (2003) reflected that, where there have been useful ends to accomplish with ICT, people have sought out ways to gain access. This time, access itself is not the aim. Instead, we consider needs first, and explore how access to ICT can help in the pursuit of economic development with the following example.

Loukaitou-Sideris reported that merchants in inner city Los Angeles struggled in lackluster local sales, generally scraping by on meager profits. Similar struggles characterize retail efforts in inner city neighborhoods of West Philadelphia (Kvasny and Yapa 2005). Customers in the immediate geographic area have little collective buying power, while more affluent residents who drive down the business corridor, deterred by safety concerns, habitually do not stop to shop. The physical environment is no longer inviting due to criminal activity, unattractive storefronts which have fallen into disrepair, rubble strewn vacant lots, and abandoned structures interspersed among the active businesses. Can the Internet be of service to struggling small businesses in such a setting? What if these merchants could peddle their goods to a much broader customer base *online*? If their market of possible buyers spanned the entire Internet user community rather than just a few miles' radius, then merchants might well enjoy increased sales, especially if many of those online shoppers could better afford to purchase their goods, while also acquiring meaningful ICT skills and business acumen.

A number of small business owners in West Philadelphia have learned how to magnify their sales volumes by seeking far larger markets. A local eBay specialist there has instructed small business owners on how to use the Web's largest auction site to advertise their products to a worldwide audience. Especially for small businesses in rural or inner city communities, the advantages of increased visibility and removed geographical boundaries may vastly improve sales where the local market is limited.

4.2 Conclusion

Our analysis in the preceding sections examined the often unseen influence of discourse in academic conversations about economic development and the digital divide. In failing to contend with institutional discursive practices, social science researchers effectively abandon creativity for one dominant model, whereby economic and technological determinism constrain all solutions to the set of profit-maximizing transactions. Such strategies are objectionable because they have yet to prove themselves tractable or effective. Moreover, these solutions place the greater part of ability and material means in the domain of scholars, private sector firms, and government, leaving underserved groups—whose lives are the most affected by this discussion—with stiflingly little agency.

Where subjects do come to gain a knowing awareness of discourse, they maintain a clarity and command over the questions, theories, and research designs that both constrain learning and are the means to push it further. If we are mindful of the many perspectives, ideologies, and techniques that shape research and knowledge, and critically examine their effects, then we can regard situations with improved clarity and flexibility, while retaining access to a fertile host of alternative views and possibilities.

Acknowledgements

This material is based upon work supported by the National Science Foundation under Grant No. 0238009. Any opinions, findings, and conclusions or recommendations expressed in this material are those of the authors and do not necessarily reflect the views of the National Science Foundation.

References

Avgerou, C. "Recognising Alternative Rationalities in the Deployment of Information System," *Electronic Journal of Information Systems in Developing Countries* (3:7), 2000, pp. 1-15. (available online at http://www.ejisdc.org/ojs/).

Bates, T. "Response: Michael Porter's Conservative Urban Agenda Will Not Revitalize America's Inner Cities: What Will?," *Economic Development Quarterly* (11:1), 1997, pp. 39-44.

bridges.org. "Spanning the Digital Divide: Understanding and Tackling the Issues," May 2001 (available online at http://www.bridges.org/spanning/index.html).

Fairclough, N. *Critical Discourse Analysis: The Critical Study of Language*, Harlow, England: Pearson Education Limited, 1995.

Escobar, A. *Encountering Development: The Making and Unmaking of the Third World*, Princeton, NJ: Princeton University Press, 1995.

Fors, M., and Moreno, A. "The Benefits and Obstacles of Implementing ICT Strategies for Development from a Bottom-Up Approach," *Aslib Proceedings* (54:3), 2002, pp. 198-206.

Foucault, M. *The Politics of Truth*, Cambridge, MA: Semiotext(e) (MIT Press), 1997.

Gillis, B., and Mitchell, M. "Can ICT Stimulate Economic Development?," *Digital Divide Network*, August 2002 (available online at http://www.digitaldividenetwork.org).

Gurstein, M. "Effective Use: A Community Informatics Strategy Beyond the Digital Divide," *First Monday* (8:12), 2003, (available online at http://firstmonday.org/issues/issue8_12/gurstein/index.html).

Harrison, B., and Glasmeier, A. "Response: Why Business Alone Won't Redevelop the Inner City: A Friendly Critique of Michael Porter's Approach to Urban Revitalization," *Economic Development Quarterly* (11:1), 1997, pp. p. 28-38.

Herman, E., and Chomsky, N. *Manufacturing Consent*, New York: Pantheon Books, 1988.

Klein, H. K. "Tocqueville in Cyberspace: Using the Internet for Citizen Associations," *The Information Society* (15), 1999, pp. 213-220.

Kvasny, L., and Sawyer, S. "Reproduction of Inequality through Information Technology," *Proceedings of the Shaping the Network Society Symposium*, Seattle, Washington, May 5-8, 2002, pp. 170-174.

Kvasny, L., and Truex, D. "Defining Away the Digital Divide: A Content Analysis of Institutional Influences on Popular Representations of Technology," in N. Russo, B. Fitzgerald, and J. I. DeGross (eds.), *Realigning Research and Practice in IS Development: The Social and Organizational Perspective*, Boston: Kluwer Academic Publishers, 2001, pp. 399-414.

Kvasny, L., and Yapa, L. "Rethinking Urban Poverty: Forms of Capital, Information Technology, and Enterprise Development," in D. Howcroft and E. Trauth (eds.), *Handbook of Information Systems Research: Critical Perspectives on Information Systems Design, Implementation and Use*, London: Kluwer, 2005, pp. 350-364.

Lazarus, W., and Mora, F. "Online Content for Low-Income and Underserved Americans: The Digital Divide's New Frontier," The Children's Partnership, Santa Monica, CA, 2000 (available online from http://www.childrenspartnership.org/).

Loukaitou-Sideris, A. "Revisiting Inner-City Strips: A Framework for Community and Economic Development," *Economic Development Quarterly* (14:2), 2000, pp. 165-181.

Mauws, M. "But Is it Art? Decision Making and Discursive Resources in the Field of Cultural Production," *Journal of Applied Behavioral Science* (36:2), 2000, pp. 229-244.

Moss, J. "Power and the Digital Divide," *Ethics and Information Technology* (4), 2002, pp. 159-165.

NTIA. "A Nation Online: Entering the Broadband Age, National Telecommunications and Information Administration," U.S. Department of Commerce, Washington, DC, 2004 (available online at http://www.ntia.doc.gov/reports/anol/NationOnlineBroadband04.htm).

Porter, M. "The Competitive Advantage of the Inner City," *Harvard Business Review* (73:3), 1995, pp. 55-71.

Thompson, M. "ICT, Power, and Developmental Discourse: A Critical Analysis," in E. Wynne, E. Whitley, M. Myers, and J. I. DeGross (eds.), *Global and Organizational Discourse About Information Technology*, Boston: Kluwer Academic Publishers, 2002, pp. 347-374.

van Dijk, T. A. "Discourse, Power and Access," in C. R. Caldas-Coulthard and M. Coulthard (eds.), *Texts and Practices: Readings in Critical Discourse Analysis*, London: Routledge, 1996, pp. 84-106.

White House. "President Bush: High Tech Improving Economy, Health Care, Education," U. S. Department of Commerce, Washington, DC, June 24, 2004 (available online at www.whitehouse.gov/news/releases/2004/06/20040624-7.html).

World Bank. "World Development Indicators 2001," 2001 (available online at http://www.worldbank.org/data/wdi2001/pdfs/tab5_10.pdf).

Wynn, E., Whitley, E., Myers, M., and DeGross, J. I. (eds.). *Global and Organizational Discourse About Information Technology*, Boston: Kluwer Academic Publishers, 2002.

Yapa, L. "What Causes Poverty? A Postmodern View," *Annals of the Association of American Geographers* (86:4), 1996, pp. 707-728.

Yu, P. K. "Bridging the Digital Divide: Equality in the Information Age," *Cardozo Arts & Entertainment Law Journal* (20:1), 2002, pp. 1-52.

About the Authors

Leslie Tu holds a BS in classic studies from Wellesley College. She earned an MS in Information Sciences and Technology at the Pennsylvania State University. Her research examines language and information technology. Leslie can be reached at lct109@psu.edu.

Lynette Kvasny is an assistant professor of Information Sciences and Technology, and a founding member of the Center for the Information Society at the Pennsylvania State University. She earned a Ph.D. in Computer Information Systems at Georgia State University. She is the recipient of the National Science Foundation's CAREER award. Her research examines historically underserved groups and their adoption and use of information technology. Her work has appeared in the *Data Base for Advances in Information Systems, Journal of Computer Mediated Communication, International Journal of Technology, and Human Interaction,* and *Information, Communication and Society*. Kvasny can be reached at lkvasny@ist.psu.edu.

5 DIGITAL INCLUSION PROJECTS IN DEVELOPING COUNTRIES: Value, Sustainability, and Scalability

Shirin Madon
London School of Economics
London, U.K.

Nicolau Reinhard
University of São Paulo
São Paulo, Brazil

Dewald Roode
University of Pretoria and
University of Cape Town
Pretoria/Cape Town, South Africa

Geoff Walsham
University of Cambridge
Cambridge, U.K.

1   INTRODUCTION

It is increasingly recognized that the so-called digital divide is not just a matter of unavailability of information and communication technologies (ICTs), but also of the social, political, institutional, and cultural contexts that shape people's lack of access to ICTs, or their inability to use them effectively (e.g., Warschauer 2003). These problems apply to the socially excluded in all countries of the world, the "Fourth World" in the language of Castells (1998). However, it can be argued they are particularly acute in the developing countries, where large numbers of people do not have access to technology, nor the educational background or support to develop their skills in using technology to improve their own lives, or the lives of the communities within which they live.

One response to the above over the last decade or so has been a variety of digital inclusion projects in a wide range of contexts and countries. These projects normally

Please use the following format when citing this chapter:

Madon, S., Reinhard, N., Roode, D., and Walsham, G., 2006, in IFIP International Federation for Information Processing, Volume 208, Social Inclusion: Societal and Organizational Implications for Information Systems, eds. Trauth, E., Howcroft, D., Butler, T., Fitzgerald, B., DeGross, J., (Boston: Springer), pp. 67-70.

aim not only to deliver ICT access to particular targeted groups, but also to provide various types of support for learning and capacity building. In this panel, we will draw on experiences from digital inclusion projects in three different countries and contexts. These involve telecenters in rural areas of India and urban areas of the city of São Paulo in Brazil, and a community-based ICT project in a rural township in South Africa.

We will address three particular questions during the panel. First, what has been the *value* of these projects? It is well-known in the IS field that the evaluation of the costs and benefits of technology is problematic, and this certainly applies to digital inclusion projects (see, for example, Reilly and Gómez 2001). Who has benefited from the projects and in what ways? How can we assess these benefits? One concern, for example, is that digital inclusion projects may miss the least-advantaged groups in the communities that they aim to serve and thus, ironically, produce a local form of digital divide within these communities.

Even if we can be reassured that a digital inclusion project is delivering value, a second key issue is the *sustainability* of the initiative over time. For example, most projects are started with funding from local or central government, aid agencies, or NGOs. However, long-term financial sustainability implies the need to develop indigenous funding sources and sustainable revenue streams. Sustainability is not just a matter of money, but also of the development of institutional arrangements for the continuity of staffing levels, and the long-term cultural and political support for the initiative from government officials, politicians, and the community itself.

Individual projects may deliver value and be sustainable, but the scope of such projects is often limited. A crucial issue for developing countries is *scalability*. Sahay and Walsham (2005) define scaling as the approach through which a product or process is taken from one setting and expanded in size and scope within that same setting and/or also incorporated in other settings. The unfortunate word replication is sometimes used for this process, which implies the copying of an initiative in a straightforward way. However, scaling of digital inclusion projects is not a simple matter of repeating a formula elsewhere, but a much more complex problem involving the development of a heterogeneous network constituted of technology, people, processes, and the institutional context.

2   PANEL CONTENT AND ORGANIZATION

Geoff Walsham will chair the panel session, and he will start the panel with an introduction to the context and purpose of digital inclusion projects in developing countries, as outlined above. He will then ask each of the other panelists to describe a particular project with which they have been involved. In particular, in addition to a brief description of the project, he will ask them to focus on issues of value, sustainability, and scalability related to their project. Each of the four panelists, including the chair, will talk for no longer than 15 minutes, allowing at least half an hour for audience participation and contribution.

Shirin Madon will describe her research work on the Akshaya telecenter project, which was launched as a pilot in Malapurram district of North Kerala, India, in November 2002. Within one year, the project was deemed a success as Malapurram was the first district in India to achieve 100 percent family e-literacy. However, measuring the value of the project in terms of e-literacy became less relevant as other implementation issues gained importance. Evaluation of Akshaya should be seen to consist of a process linked with organizational and institutional reform and long-term sustainability of the project. The presentation will discuss Akshaya's survival in terms of its ability to generate commercial activity and local content in key economic sectors such as health and agriculture. The presentation will also describe the roll-out phase of the project to seven other districts in Kerala. [Reference: Madon 2005]

Nicolau Reinhard will describe his research work on digital inclusion projects in the city of São Paulo, Brazil, a mega-city of 17 million people. The projects have involved the setting up of telecenters in poor areas of the city. The first telecenter was established in 2001, but the number of such centres is now into the hundreds. Additional telecenter initiatives have taken place at the state and federal levels. Despite this success in establishing a large number of working telecenters, there are serious concerns in terms of the difficulty of demonstrating effectiveness and long-term sustainability. On the other hand, the projects are seen to be an important political issue, for example at times of elections, but further problems arise when administrations change. [Reference: Macadar and Reinhard 2002]

Dewald Roode will describe his involvement in, and lessons learned from, a socio-economic development project at the rural community of Siyabuswa in South Africa, which included provision of ICTs. In particular, he will focus on the problems experienced when this project was scaled-up to four other deep-rural communities. He will analyze his experiences through the concept of the "socio-techno divide," and will argue that it is this divide that has to be addressed—not the digital divide. The socio-techno divide describes the gap between governmental, political, and technological attempts to achieve "development" objectives by providing access to digital communication technologies, and approaches where the focus is on people and their developmental needs. [Reference: Roode et al. 2004]

3 ABOUT THE PANELISTS

Shirin Madon is a senior lecturer in Information Systems at the London School of Economics. She is currently responsible for teaching a Master's course on IT and Development. Her research focuses on IT and governance reform in developing countries. She has had a long-term involvement in fieldwork in India, studying both back-end systems for development planning and administration, as well as front-end e-services and telecenter applications. Shirin can be reached at s.madon@lse.ac.uk.

Nicolau Reinhard is a professor in the Business Department of the University of São Paulo, Brazil, from where he also received his Ph.D. His publications, research, and consulting interests are related to the use of ICTs in public administration, and the impacts of ICTs on organizations. He serves on the editorial board of several IT/IS journals, and on the program committees of IT management conferences. In conjunction with his doctoral students and other research collaborators, he has carried out research work for several years on telecenters in Brazil. Nicolau can be reached at reinhard@usp.br.

Dewald Roode was director of the School of Information Technology at the University of Pretoria, South Africa, until his early retirement at the end of 2001. He now holds positions as visiting professor at several South African universities, where he focuses mainly on supervisory work of doctoral students. For the last decade, his research group has centered on the use of ICTs to achieve sustainable socio-economic development in rural communities in South Africa. He chairs IFIP's TC8 on Information Systems, was a member of the Steering Committee of IFIP's World Technology Forum in 2003 and 2005, and the program chair of WITFOR 2005. Dewald can be reached at jdr@inbekon.com.

Geoff Walsham is a professor of Management Studies at Judge Business School, University of Cambridge, UK. His teaching and research is centered on the development, management, and use of information and communication technologies, and the relationship of ICTs to stability and change in organizations and societies. He has field experience in many different countries, including a number of developing countries in Asia, Africa, and Latin America. His publications include *Interpreting Information Systems in Organizations* (Wiley 1993), and *Making a World of Difference: IT in a Global Context* (Wiley 2001). Geoff can be reached at g.walsham@jbs.cam.ac.uk.

References

Castells, M. *End of Millennium*, Oxford, UK: Blackwell, 1998.

Macadar, M. A., and Reinhard, N. "Telecentros comunitários possibilitando a inclusão digital: um estudo de caso comparativo de iniciativas brasileiras," in *Proceedings of the 26th ANPAD Meeting* (Associação Nacional dos Programas de Pós-Graduação em Administração), Information Systems Track (ADI), Salvador-BA-Brasil, September 22-25, 2002.

Madon, S. "Evaluating the Developmental Impact of e-Governance Initiatives: An Exploratory Framework," *Electronic Journal of Information Systems in Developing Countries* (20:5), 2005, pp. 1-13.

Reilly, K.,and Gómez, R. "Comparing Approaches: Telecenter Evaluation Experiences in Asia and Latin America," *Electronic Journal of Information Systems in Developing Countries* (4:3), 2001, 1-17.

Roode, D., Speight, H., Pollock, M., and Webber, R. "It's Not the Digital Divide, it's the Socio-Techno Divide!," in *Proceedings of the 12th European Conference on Information Systems,* Turku, Finland, 2004.

Sahay, S., and Walsham, G. 'Scaling of Health Information Systems in India: Challenges and Approaches," in A. O. Bada and A. Okunoye (eds.), *Proceedings of the 8th International Working Conference of IFIP WG9.4,* Abuja, Nigeria, May 26-28, 2005, pp. 41-52.

Warschauer, M. "Dissecting the 'Digital Divide': A Case Study of Egypt," *The Information Society* (19:4), 2003, pp. 297-304.

Part 3

Political
Participation

6   RIGHT ON TIME: Understanding eGovernment in Developing Countries

Åke Grönlund
Annika Andersson
Karin Hedström
Örebro University
Örebro, Sweden

Abstract   *Many, if not most, developing countries today engage in electronic govern-ment (eGovernment) projects. There are big hopes, not just for modernizing government and making it more effective and efficient; eGovernment is also expected to drive the general development toward the information society, both by examples of good practice and by major investment. However, many sources claim that the project failure rate is high. Reasons are found in many places, but it is reasonable to summarize them by saying that project goals are too ambitious given existing production capacity. Hence there is need to find ways of choosing and defining projects so that they meet the conditions in the country and sector where they are going to be implemented. To do so, this paper presents two tools, a checklist and a maturity model, for assessing the preconditions for eGovernment projects in developing countries. The under-lying data sources are threefold: eGovernment readiness indexes, project experiences, and assessments of social and political conditions. The checklist matches requirements for successful eGovernment against supply and demand side factors, hence providing a guide in choosing which projects to initiate and which to avoid. The maturity model supports mapping projects on a wider development agenda, hence helping avoiding dead ends such as investing in unused technology, or supporting dysfunctional processes with ICT (information and communication technology) instead of first redesigning them and then putting in ICT that support the new and better processes. In particular, the tools show the close relation between eGovernment and other development agendas, for example education, investment policies, or telecom (de)regulation. Without alignment with such programs, eGovernment is likely to fail. The two tools help make factors pertinent to success and failure more explicit and hence improve decision making.*

Please use the following format when citing this chapter:

Grönlund, Å., Andersson, A., and Hedström, K., 2006, in IFIP International Federation for Information Processing, Volume 208, Social Inclusion: Societal and Organizational Implications for Information Systems, eds. Trauth, E., Howcroft, D., Butler, T., Fitzgerald, B., DeGross, J., (Boston: Springer), pp. 73-87.

1   INTRODUCTION

Electronic government (eGovernment) is about applying information and information technology to all aspects of a government's business. One of the targets set during the Geneva summit was that all public centers and governments should have an online system of administration by 2015[1] and the UNDP (United Nations Development Programme) has made information communication technologies (ICT) one of its six priority areas.[2] ICT is generally considered to be a key ingredient for economic growth and for making businesses more efficient and competitive. eGovernment is seen as a trigger for a wider development. First, the major investments by government will help support, or initiate, a local ICT industry and stimulate foreign investments, such as telecom operators. Second, the government would set a good example by reforming government operation and governance structures. Governance is a wider term, indicating that not only government institutions are involved in government operations.

For the public sector, the mission is not only to make the organizations' internal operations more efficient but also to provide the citizens with information by facilitating greater transparency and responsiveness on the part of governments. It is believed that eGovernance in the developing world will improve the effectiveness of public service delivery and to ensure transparency and accountability of government operations.[3] However, the World Bank (WB) has estimated that 85 percent of all eGovernment projects in developing countries are total or partial failures (Sify 2004). An obvious problem, then, is how to know which projects to start and which to avoid. Clearly just copying projects from the developed world is problematic, as many of these rely on a relatively high level of administrative maturity and a comprehensive electronic infrastructure. Also, as governments are different in different countries, so must eGovernment be (Ciborra and Navarra 2003). Given the large amount of failures reported, there is clearly a need for more accurate project definitions, setup, and management. Our aim is, therefore, to provide usable guidance for project managers to better assess success potential and risks early on in eGovernment projects in developing countries. For this purpose, our research question is: *what factors need to be understood to decide how a country should embark on an eGovernment project?*

The paper proceeds as follows. After the method section, we provide a brief literature review of the eGovernment project situation in developing countries. After that we review literature from three types of sources to investigate "readiness" criteria at both micro and macro levels, which we condense into a checklist. We then construct a maturity model based on the criteria and partially validate the model by examples of success and failure. We conclude by discussing the potential application of the two tools.

---

[1]"World Summit on the Information Society," 2005 (http://www.itu.int/wsis/).

[2]UNDP "Information & Communication Technologies for Development," 2005 (http://sdnhq.undp.org/it4dev).

[3]UNDP Global Sub-practice Workshop on e-Governance, "Action Reflection Note Template for Global E-Governance Workshop," Senegal, September 1-3, 2005 (http://www.sdnp.undp.org/egov/arns/Mozambique-arn.pdf).

2 METHOD

The approach is a literature study complemented with discussions with people in aid organizations and experiences from development projects collected from case descriptions, analyses, and assessments. The literature study covers factors for success and failure and various maturity models. The literature covers theoretical as well as model-based factors, provided normatively by, for example, development organizations and empirical accounts of project experiences and evaluations. Literature was found by a "snowball" model. We started with global actors engaged in development, such as the UN and the WB and researchers and research centers concerned with the topic. These have comprehensive Web sites listing literature, including project examples and stories, project evaluations, assessment methods, and indices measuring aspects of development and success or failure.

In parallel with the literature study we visited some countries in Africa—Egypt, Uganda, and South Africa—and discussed ICT and development issues with people from universities and government, and people involved with ICT4D (ICT for development) projects. We also had discussions with university people in Indonesia and Bangladesh, as well as SIDA (Swedish International Development Organization) project officers and project leaders in conjunction with ICT4D projects there. Further, we attended, and took part in, a WB conference concerning eGovernment examples, assessment, and assessment methods.

The checklist and the maturity model presented below were then presented to and discussed with eGovernment experts at the WB, including consultants from the developing world. They have provided considerable feedback on, in particular, the checklist, which has been revised accordingly. These individuals wish to be anony-mous, as this model is not a WB product and they cannot in their capacity of being employees endorse tools produced elsewhere.

Finally, we have tested the model by using it to evaluate eGovernment maturity in a number of countries. The results are published in a report (Grönlund et al. 2005), presented and discussed at a SIDA project conference in June 2005.

3 BACKGROUND: eGOVERNMENT DEFINITIONS AND FINDINGS

3.1 eGovernment

The term *eGovernment* emerged in 1999, but the activities to which it refers are much older and parallel the computing history in business organizations. What all recent definitions by major actors share is that they (1) acknowledge the need for organizational reform to go hand in hand with technology implementation, and (2) focus on the role of government in society, that is, governance. According to the WB,

E-Government refers to the use by government agencies of information technologies that have the ability to *transform relations* with citizens, businesses, and other arms of government. These technologies can serve a variety of different ends: *better delivery* of government services to citizens, *improved interactions* with business and industry, *citizen empowerment* through access to information, or *more efficient government management*. The resulting benefits can be *less corruption*, increased *transparency*, greater *convenience*, *revenue* growth, and/or *cost reductions* (WB 2006, emphasis added).

Although focusing on different types of countries (developed and developing), definitions of eGovernment are unanimously socio-technical: organizational change, skills, and technology are *together* the key to success.

3.2 eGovernment in the Developing World

eGovernment projects target a wide range of topics, including infrastructure development, the legal environment surrounding eGovernment development, policies (national, regional, local), digital divide issues, literacy, education, accessibility, trust (in technology as well as in government), transparency, interoperability (among government agencies), managing records, sustainability, public-private cooperation and partnerships, cost structures, and incentives. While most of these topics are found in developed as well as in developing countries, in the latter more attention is paid to issues like telecommunications liberalization, ICT sector development and investment, trade promotion, local software and content generation, satellite technology, telemedicine and healthcare, and local development through, for example, development of telecenters.[4]

From these projects, and associated as well as independent research, a number of critical issues have emerged, which have been found crucial for success and problematic to overcome. These include political commitment, project design and leadership, implementation, financing, local development, and sustainability. Sustainability here means the ability of an effort to be sustained beyond the period of project funding. Today it is common wisdom that focus should be on engaging, "embedding," user communities in the area of concern as sustainability is the key. Sustainability is hence implicitly defined as adopted in actor–networks' regular operations. Hence, today considerable attention is paid to involving local communities. A UNESCO report from 2004 concludes that championship and responsive organization are crucial:

> ICT and media initiatives…must be as responsive, creative and innovative as the users have shown themselves to be…organizations [must be] responsive on the basis of sensitive, location-specific knowledge (research and experience) both of local media use and of the local structures, dynamics and meanings of poverty in their community….these connections are diverse and often unpredictable; they need to be identified in the actual processes of project development rather than derived from general and abstract models of the

---

[4]African Information Society Initiative, "Africa's Digital Agenda," 2004 (http://www.uneca.org/aisi).

properties of technologies or of poverty or of the connections between them. (UNESCO 2004, p. 93).

The report points to the risk of old mistakes being repeated; there is a need for methods well adapted to local conditions. There is an obvious risk that developing countries are in for much the same failures as have occurred in countries a step ahead in eGovernment development. For this reason, aid organizations are today focusing more on support from and relevance for local communities and less on central governments. The focus is also more on partnerships than on a donor-recipient relation.

In addition to the abundance of projects, there are many attempts to assess eGovernment development. These cover various geographical areas as well as various topics. Many of these studies are showcases or directories, but there are also studies attempting analysis. Many are qualitative detailed case studies of successful eGovernment projects (Devadoss et al. 2002; Golden et al. 2003).

There are a number of more or less recurrent *benchmarking studies* covering various areas, the European Union, the United States, and worldwide (e.g., Accenture 2005). These cover various issues ranging from implementation of services to multidimensional "e-readiness" indexes.[5]

There are also *critical studies* focusing on how and when to measure success (De 2004), and on the connection between eGovernment development in the service area and economic and/or democratic development (Accenture 2005; Bertelsman Foundation 2002).

Different studies use different measures of eGovernment activity, as they focus on different aspects. We now continue to review the attempts to systematically measure the readiness for eGovernment.

4   A CHECKLIST FOR eGOVERNMENT IN DEVELOPING COUNTRIES

The brief review above suggests that, given the diversity of the literature, there is reason to look for factors critical to success or failure in three types of sources. The first is national statistics and derivatives from these, such as e-readiness and eGovernment readiness indexes. A second source is project experiences, roadmaps and handbooks. A third and final source is assessments of social and political developments critical to eGovernment.

National statistics include records on Internet users, the infrastructure, etc. Sources used are the CIA World Fact Book, the Economist Intelligence Unit, and the

---

[5]Examples are the Economic Intelligence Unit's 2004 e-readiness rankings (http:// graphics.eiu.com/files/ad_pdfs/ERR2004.pdf), the World Economic Forum's networked readiness index report for 2003-2004 (http://www.weforum.org/pdf/Gcr/GITR_2003_2004/ Framework_ Chapter.pdf), and the study by Steyaert (2004).

World Economic Forum.[6] E-readiness and eGovernment readiness indexes are derived from national statistics presented in the UN Global EGovernment Readiness Report, in the Economist Intelligence Unit e-readiness rankings, and as the Networked Readiness Index.[7] These indexes are based on factors such as the number of telephone lines, the business environment, and maturity of IT industry in the country.

Experiences from eGovernment projects have been another source for finding important factors critical for the success of eGovernment projects. There are several lists on project benchmarking including success and failure stories.[8] and several handbooks on project experience.[9] Typical factors found here have to do with management structure, organizational culture, user acceptance and requirements, etc. Stories of what happened and how problems were solved, make up vivid pictures of the nuts and bolts of ICT projects in developing countries.

Assessments of the social and political development critical to eGovernment are made by national and international donor agencies and nongovernment organizations (NGOs) and typically focus on the context in which eGovernment projects take place. They stress the importance of the socio-political situation (the level and nature of democracy, of corruption, etc.), social networks, local users, local organizations, partner organizations, social and financial sustainability, goals and visions of the government.[10]

We have combined these criteria to create a tool to be used for assessing candidate projects. We have combined known success factors and established measures into a checklist to be used by practitioners to overview the situation. The point is that the checklist will give the practitioner an overview of the problems to be addressed, and where to look for the information required to assess the size and nature of the details of these problems.

As discussed above, much information needs to be validated using perspectives from several kinds of sources. For example, statistical figures on Internet subscriptions need to be complemented with knowledge of cultural patterns, such as collective or individual access. The latter can be found in social accounts, but need to be complemented with experiences on what are the practical keys to enabling ICT to make use of cultural patterns, something to which handbooks are a guide. The checklist consists of

---

[6]CIA World Fact Book (http://www.cia.gov/cia/publications/factbook/index.html), Economist Intelligence Unit (http://www.eiu.com/), and World Economic Forum (http://www.weforum.org/).

[7]Economist Intelligence Unit (http://www.eiu.com/), Transparency International (http://www.transparency.org/), Human Development Reports (http://hdr.undp.org/statistics), and World Economic Forum (http://www.weforum.org/).

[8]Europe's Information Society (http://europa.eu.int/information_society/activities/atwork/index_en.htm), Information for Development (i4d) (http://www.i4donline.net/feb05/contentimg.asp), and the Heeks (2002) report.

[9]For instance, the CDT and *infoDEV* "E-Government Handbook" (http://www.cdt.org/egov/handbook/).

[10]African Information Society Initiative, "Africa's Digital Agenda," 2004 (http://www.uneca.org/aisi); Amnesty International's 2005 report (http://www.amnesty.org/); the SIDA (Swedish International Development Cooperation Agency) development cooperation projects (http://www.sida.se/Sida/jsp/polopoly.jsp?d=352); and the UNESCO report by Slater and Tacchi (2004).

important aspects concerning the demand side and the supply side. An earlier report (Grönlund et al. 2005) presents our checklist in more detail.

Now we turn our attention to the checklist, divided into supply side factors and demand side factors, with examples of information for each type of factor. As the strategy and political foundation factors show, eGovernment must be integrated with other agendas to be successful. For example, wiring schools without educating teachers and revising curricula is likely to be less successful. The checklist can be used as an information gathering tool for assessing a specific country's technological and administrative maturity (see the maturity model presented later).

- **Demand side factors**
  - o Infrastructure (e.g., broadband access, number of phone lines, availability of mobile phones, internet hosts, costs as well as quality)
  - o Users (level of education, skills, motivation etc.)
  - o Partners (ICT business sector structure, local business culture, etc.)
  - o Consumer and business adoption of e-services (business environment, legal and policy environment, reasons for Internet use, etc.)
  - o Time available (plans and investments for infrastructure, project management, organizational culture, etc.)
- **Supply side factors**
  - o Strategy and political foundation
    - – Government goals (e.g. investments, government culture, democracy)
    - – Political leadership (political organization, political culture, degree of control, etc.)
    - – Government decision making system (e.g., departmental structure, communities of practices, corruption)
    - – Strategic plans (investments, projects, strategies and policies, etc.)
    - – Government communication policies
    - – Other policies (investments in related fields, thrusts of policies, etc.)
    - – Regulatory system/legal framework (cyberlaws, information laws, regulations, etc.)
  - o Organizational preconditions
    - – Government organization (departmentalization, practices, developments, etc.)
    - – Organizational culture (bureaucratic instructions, incentives, etc.)
    - – Administrative maturity (government functions, professionalism, etc.)
    - – Staff skill (education level, experiences and attitudes, etc.)
    - – Staff cost (salary, efficiency of staff, ethical assessments, etc.)
    - – Government on-line presence (eGovernment) readiness indexes, quality of on-line systems, access, etc.)
  - o Business setup
    - – Partnership (national ICT business structure and volume, professionalism, market requirements for the ICT sector)
    - – Balance between cooperation and competition (telecommunications deregulations, local entrepreneurial culture, requirements in rural areas, etc.)

- ○ Economy
  - – Funding (e.g., financing and budget allocation, savings, cost sharing)
  - – Monitoring and evaluating framework (development goals, audit practice, project assessments and tools, user/social requirements, etc.)
- ○ Technical environment
  - – ICT infrastructure (national infrastructure measurements, social/political assessments, etc.)
  - – Supporting e-services (e.g., ICT business sector structure and volume, capacity and competence)

5   CHARTING EGOVERNMENT PROGRESS: THE MATURITY MODEL

In this section we present a maturity model based on the criteria related to strategy and political foundation, organizational preconditions, and technical environment presented in the checklist in the previous section. As will be seen in the examples, the model can be applied not only to nations as a whole, but also to individual sectors. Hence, one purpose with the model is to complement the checklist with a general roadmap of the path toward increased administrative maturity. This is clearly not a reflection of the whole set of criteria we discussed above. For example, the demand side is omitted. This is because the model focuses on what can be done. Whether or not there is demand for a service does not matter much if you can not provide it. Clearly demand for public e-services is important, but it is more difficult to assess as it tends to grow with supply; for example, public demand for social services has a bigger and louder voice in Sweden than in Bangladesh, and this is not because the need is greater. Also, while in Western countries, slow eGovernment uptake has been seen as "failure," the high failure rate refers mainly to limited production capacity, such as budget overruns, lack of skill, poor ICT communication, etc. A problem with eGovernment is not only to assess individual projects, but also to create a good mix of projects so that, together, they contribute reasonably well to general development, something which the model also can help assess.

eGovernment is a comprehensive term covering a maturity process of public administration becoming well-structured and hence better able to serve citizens and to become more transparent (see the definitions in section 3). This process can start anywhere, something the talk of "joined-up," "24/7" government might conceal as the terms are often used to allude to a relatively mature administration with a high level of ICT penetration. Figure 1 illustrates the process, from low administrative maturity and low technological sophistication toward high administrative maturity and high technological sophistication. By "e-infrastructure," we mean a coherent set of working procedures across the whole government. This includes technical standards making all media interoperable (technical infrastructure), standardized or compatible data definitions, well-organized metadata definitions (information infrastructure), and well-defined business procedures implemented in the electronic medium. Other terms, such as enterprise architecture, may be used.

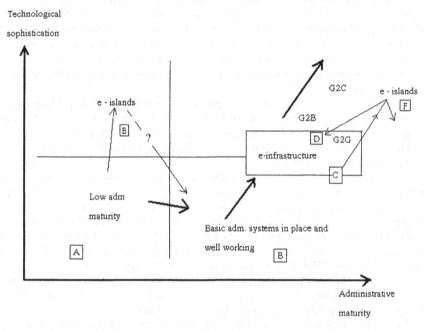

Figure 1. Different Opportunities at Different Development Levels
(Technological sophistication is the degree of informatization and technical inter-operability in government. Administrative maturity is the equivalent as concerns the basic design and availability of data and procedures.)

Below we will describe some of the archetypical positions in Figure 1 and at the same time give examples of how our analysis was created, thus illustrating how the checklist and the maturity model can be used. Factors from the check-list are italicized.

Level A: This is where many developing countries are. Administration is primarily manual, and standardization is low. Assessed at the country level, Uganda, Rwanda, and Indonesia belong here, although some government sectors may be in other positions.

The example of Uganda: Uganda was classified as an A-level country because of its lack of *key technologies* and shortage of *standardization* in the administrative units. The importance of considering the factors *administrative informatization/computeri-zation* is illustrated by several examples of donated and abandoned computers given to rural areas that lack the infrastructure required to deliver anything apart from rudi-mentary eGovernment services.[11] Not many local government offices at the A-level

---

[11]See the eGovernment for Development Design-Reality Gap Case Study No. 5,"An Integrated Information System for Defence Force Management in the Middle East," January 2003 (http://www.e-devexchange.org/eGov/defenceiis.htm) and the Women of Uganda Network's "ICT Policy Issues in Uganda" (http://www.wougnet.org/ICTpolicy/ug/ugictpolicy.html).

have electricity and the institutions *with power access* often have old and rarely *networked computers*. In Uganda, the government is pursuing a *decentralization policy*. But when comparing the *service delivery* of rural and urban local governments, we find that rural areas are less attractive to *qualified staff* and that elected members are less likely to be well *educated*. This also illustrates the importance of *staff skills*.

A-level countries typically strive to move into the B-level but short-cuts are sometimes taken to level E.

Level E: This is the technological opportunity in combination with political hopes. There are many opportunities to take over working systems tried elsewhere. This may be good and bad. It is good if the systems brought in this way can later be integrated as components in the maturing administrative and technical infrastructure. It may be a costly mistake if they cannot.

The example of Indonesia: In Indonesia, the government is in the process of introducing a rather ambitious *national program* to improve governance through eGovernment, with the aim of giving *public access* to *government services* via the Internet. Considering the not fully formed *administration* and the *deficiency of technology*, the plans for eGovernment have so far been too ambitious. What has happened (while waiting for this national program) is that 369 government offices have *published* their own Web sites. This is all very good but, unfortunately, only 85 of them are running (Abhiseka 2003). On the other hand one, does not know what benefits may come from these abandoned Web pages; they may not be a total waste as the projects that produced them may have lead to other positive effects.

Level B: This is where some developing countries are. Administration is relatively well organized in some government sectors, however it is still mainly built on manual procedures. Some records may be computerized but standardization of data definitions may be low and hence preconditions for interoperability may be a concern. Assessed at the country level, Bangladesh belongs to a B-level, although some government sectors may be in other positions, including levels A and F.

The example of Bangladesh: When assessed on the basis of our factors, we found Bangladesh scoring low on their *availability of key technologies* but with a higher degree of *administrative maturity* than Uganda and Indonesia which motivates the "B." Bangladesh's *government on-line presence* is emerging even though they generally only offer *static information* about the organization (Ahmed 2003). Bangladesh has one of the lowest *telephone penetration rates* in the world but there is a remarkable growth in the *use of mobile phones*. The *business adoption of e-services* is growing where the business actors use WAP to enable use of the Internet through mobile phones. One factor that slows down development is the lack of *laws covering the Internet* (Hasan 2003). Other influencing factors to consider are *user aspects* such as *literacy* and *homogeneity*. As a part of introducing e-governance, the Ministry of Communication in Bangladesh launched several Web sites to enable citizen access to government information. These sites only provided information in English (Ahmed 2003) which is unsatisfactory considering that 95 percent of the population speaks Bengali. Another factor that has a great impact in Bangladesh is the *political leadership*. As for local governments, Bangladesh has a long historical tradition of *decentralized administration*, but local governance in Bangladesh is subject to domination by the central government. It does not really muster *local resources* and has a lack of participation by the rural poor in the decentralized units.

Level C: This is where most eGovernment projects in developed countries started. These countries had well functioning administrative systems in place, they were mostly computerized (the lower end of the e-infrastructure box), but not connected and not Web-enabled (which infrastructures in the upper part of the box are). Over the past decade, these countries have spent enormous efforts connecting these systems to the Web, which is the easy part and by now more or less completed, and making them interoperable, which is the hard part and only well developed in some niches (e.g., procurement, police, and customs systems). Assessed at country level, Egypt belongs here, although there is some development in "D," and some in "B" and "F" (see the example of the government portal below). South Africa also mainly belongs here, although some government sectors are venturing into the "D" position.

The example of Egypt: Egypt has a reasonably modern *telephone system*; *Internet access* and *mobile services* are available in most parts of the country and there has been a tremendous improvement of the *infrastructure*. The Egyptian government is issuing a new *E-signature law* because they want to provide faster and cheaper public services at any time (Hassanin 2003). Egypt has taken a great step in *coordination and integrating government information* and services and in 2004 they launched their *one-stop eGovernment services portal* containing 700 services. The portal is in both English and Arabic and includes services from requesting a birth certificate to paying your electricity bill on line.

In countries starting from level C we often find "e-islands" as described below.

Level F: When the World Wide Web was invented, organizations rushed to put information online, starting from level C, which means the e-infrastructure was not sufficiently in place to support the integration of these new services with back-office operations. The result was many closed projects and many obsolete Web pages, but at the same time the effort spent on this unleashed much creativity in finding new opportunities, and certainly a sufficiently high amount of these efforts succeeded well enough to put pressure on the government to enhance the infrastructure necessary to take these services further.

This is what has happened with the *government portal* in Egypt. It has taken over 3 years to build this portal and *the time it takes* to integrate all government sectors has been seriously underestimated. The integration between other government sites has actually not worked, so there is no link to the site from any other Web site; *"The site simply could not be found or accessed by going online to other government Web sites - a user would have to have prior knowledge of the portal itself"* (UN 2004). It also illustrates the importance of looking into the *Government decision making system* because we found that there is a need for a *leading agency*, both at the political level and at the operational, that can both implement policy and allow developments based on emerging technologies and local initiatives.

Level D: This is the position many developed countries are now approaching by "joining up" their information infrastructure. This has required a lot of work on standards and converging processes. The first step is technical integration, using compatible technologies. This is helped by the ICT industry, which has a keen interest in their products being compatible with Web technologies. The more critical part is data integration and metadata definitions. To be interoperable without loss of data quality data definitions themselves must be standardized or convertible.

We have not classified any country as entirely level D. However, there are sectors in both Egypt and South Africa which belong here.

The example of South Africa: South Africa is a *middle-income* country and *technical environment* is relatively well developed.[12] The *government on-line presence* is *networked* with consolidated information and services across departments. South Africa has come far regarding *regulatory system* and *legal framework* (Accenture 2005) and they also have an *eGovernment policy* outlining a 10 year implementation plan for implementing eGovernment (Trusler 2003). South Africa's e-readiness is very high from the perspective of a developing country, The problem we identified is the uneven *access to telecommunications*. The *cost of using the Internet* is high and as the South African government puts more and more *services on-line* there is a risk that users who are without access are likely to be left behind. Disparities are severe and related to the level of income and the *general education level* (UN 2004). eGovernment solutions in South Africa are both initiated and implemented by the government and/or its agencies (*government decision making system*). Although it is important and has strong support from the government, there is a risk of a *top-down-approach* where solutions are built on governmental needs and the government's ideas about their citizens' needs.

6 SUMMARY

From the above examples, we have found support for our maturity model. A few points to be made here are the following:

1. Given a certain diagnosis on a country's position in the figure, there are possibilities and difficulties. But however long, the road toward "e-[countryName]"—a concerted development toward eGovernment—can be embarked on at any point, and the sooner the better, as avoiding it will likely lead to more disparate developments and as a consequence later setbacks.

2. Basically the "main route" should be followed, starting with improving administrative maturity, but this is typically helped by introducing some ICT components, as doing so enforces standards thinking. This means level B is not a goal; rather, level C should be aimed at directly. That is, maturity efforts should in most cases be combined with introducing ICT with a view of building an e-infrastructure, even if that ultimate goal may be far away. Today, certainly technical standards can be well defined as technology and business practices are converging. The harder part is data standards. In some sectors, such as international trade, these exist, but in other areas concerned with internal administration there is greater variation.

3. There is sometimes a trade-off between strictly following the long and boring route and introducing some "level E" factor as this may give some impetus, visibility, and

---

[12]SIDA (Swedish International Development Cooperation Agency) development cooperation projects (http://www.sida.se/Sida/jsp/polopoly.jsp?d=352).

spark more efforts along the maturity route. However, any such effort must be carefully considered in terms of future compatibility with the maturing administrative and technical infrastructure. Experience has shown many such initiatives to fail.

4. Although there are similarities between levels E and F, there are also significant differences. The differences have to do not only with the e-infrastructure but also with education and familiarity with technology. Although both may come out more negative in developing countries than in developed, there is in all countries at least a proportion of the population that is familiar with ICT. These are typically the younger generations, and therefore the demands from these groups will increase rapidly. Further, to be integrated in the world economy, being reasonably up-to-date in some sectors where ICT is becoming a basic precondition, like international trade, or where human resources are concerned, such as basic education, is increasingly a must for any country.

7 CONCLUSION

We have reviewed a number of indexes for e-readiness and eGovernment readiness, with roadmaps and handbooks giving advice based on project experiences or based on policy, together with assessments of social and political developments. There are quite a number of more or less comprehensive and in-depth models of analysis. These typically include a number of similar factors but use different ways of measuring, ranging from interviews with key people to complex models calculating indexes from national statistics. We have chosen to create a checklist to be used for assessing candidate projects, and a maturity model to map projects onto a development map. This means we have combined known success factors and established measures into a checklist to be used by practitioners to overview the situation. The factors are established, but the combination and the checklist format is innovative and, judging from the great number of failures in eGovernment projects, much needed. Many projects fail because goals were not realistic or well specified, or methods were inappropriate. Clearly, the checklist and the model require good judgement to be used well. However, the two make up a tool that still lacks the ability to combine the disparate knowledge in the field into a comprehensive model that can, at least, be used to create a common perspective and so facilitate development and investment discussions.

References

Abhiseka, A. "E-Government to be Launched to Promote Good Governance," *The Jakarta Post.com*, Business and Investment section, March 29, 2006 (available at http://www.thejakartapost.com/yesterdaydetail.asp?fileid=20030115.B01).

Accenture. *Leadership in Customer Service: New Expectations, New Experiences*, The Government Executive Series, Accenture, April 2005 (available online at http://www.accenture.com/xdoc/ca/locations/canada/insights/studies/leadership_ cust.pdf).

Ahmed, M. "Publishing Bangladesh Government Information via the Web," *eTransparency Case Study No. 5*, eGovernment for Development, December 2003 (http://www.egov4dev.org/banglaweb.htm).

Bertelsmann Foundation. "E-Government: Connecting Efficient Administration and Responsive Democracy," *Balanced E-Government*, March 2002 (available online at http://www.begix.de/en/studie/studie.pdf).

Ciborra, C., and Navarra, D. D. "Good Governance and Development Aid: Risks and Challenges in E-Government in Jordan," in *Organizational Information Systems in the Context of Globalization*, M. Korpela, R. Montealegre, and A. Poulymenakou (eds.), Boston: Kluwer Academic Publishers, 2003, Chapter 48.

De, R. "E-Government Systems in Developing Countries: Some Research Issues," paper presented at the Workshop on eGovernment, Washington, DC, December 12, 2004.

Devadoss, P. R., Pan, S. L., and Huang, J. C. "Structurational Analysis of e-Government Initiatives: A Case Study of SCO," *Decision Support Systems* (34), 2002, pp. 253-269.

Golden, W., Hughes, M., and Scott, M. "The Role of Process Evolution in Achieving Citizen-Centered E-Government," in *Proceedings of the 9th Americas Conference on Information Systems*, J. Ross and D. Galletta (eds.), Tampa, FL, August 4-5, 2003, pp. 801-810.

Grölund, Å., Andersson, A., and Hedström, K. "NextStep eGovernment in Developing Countries," Report D1, Örebro University, Mah 15, 2005 (available online at http://www.spider-center.org/upl/filer/507.pdf).

Hasan, S. "Introducing EGovernment in Bangladesh: Problems and Prospects.," *International Social Science Review* (78:3/4), 2003, pp. 111-122.

Hassanin, L. "Africa ICT Policy Monitor Project: Egypt ICT Country Report," report to the Association of Progressive Communications, April 2003 (available online at http://africa.rights.apc.org/research_reports/egypt.pdf).

Heeks, R. "eGovernment in Africa: Promise and Practice," iGovernment Working Paper No. 13, Institute for Development Policy and Manaement, University of Manchester, 2002 (available online at http://unpan1.un.org/intradoc/groups/public/documents/NISPAcee/UNPAN015486.pdf).

Sify Business. "Most e-Governance Projects Fail," November 5, 2004, (available online at http://sify.com/finance/fullstory.php?id=13605188).

Slater, D., and Tacchi, J. *RESEARCH: ICT Innovations for Poverty Reduction*, United Nations Educational, Scientific and Cultural Organisation, UNESCO New Delhi, New Delhi, 2004 (available online at http://unesdoc.unesco.org/images/ 0013/001361/136121e.pdf).

Steyaert, J. C. "Measuring the Performance of Electronic Government Services" *Information and Management* (41:3), 2004, pp. 369-375.

Trusler, J. "South African EGovernment Policy and Practices: A Framework to Close the Gap," paper presented at the EGov 2003 Conference (DEXA 2003), Prague, Czech Republic, September 1-5, 2003.

UN. "UN Global E-Government Readiness Report 2004," UPAN Virtual Library, 2004 (available online at http://www.unpan.org/egovernment4.asp).

West, D. M. "Global E-Government, 2003," Center for Public Policy, Brown University, September 2003 (available online at http://www.insidepolitics.org/ egovt03int.pdf).

World Bank (WB). World Bank E-Government Website, 2006 (http://www1.worldbank.org/publicsector/egov/).

About the Authors

Åke Grönlund is Professor of Informatics at Örebro University, Örebro, Sweden, and one of the pioneers in the field of electronic government. Electronic government and e-democracy are currently his two most prominent research fields. Current publications in those fields include the books *Electronic Government—Design, Applications and Management* and *Managing Electronic Services*, two special sections of leading academic journals, and three books in

Swedish. Åke is the chair of AIS Special Interest Group on Electronic Government. He can be reached at ake.gronlund@esi.oru.se.

Annika Andersson is a Ph.D. student in the field of Electronic Government at Örebro University. She is currently working on a SIDA-sponsored project called SPIDER (The Swedish Program for ICT in Developing Regions), focusing on distance education in Bangladesh. Other fields of interest are accessibility for the disabled and digital divides. Annika is coordinator for SIG eGov (Special Interest Group on eGovernment). She can be reached at annika.andersson@esi.oru.se.

Karin Hedström is an assistant professor in Informatics at Örebro University. She has studied how values become incorporated in and influence the use of information systems, especially applications in the areas of elderly care and the use of information systems. She is member of the research network VITS (www.vits.org) and affiliated to the research school Health, Care, and Values at Örebro University (http://www.oru.se/templates/oruExtNormal___28994.aspx [Note: there are four underline spaces in this address]). She can be reached at karin.hedstrom@esi.oru.se.

7 INTERNET VOTING: A Conceptual Challenge to Democracy

Wolter Pieters
Radboud University Nijmegen
Nijmegen, The Netherlands

Abstract   *In this paper, we discuss the implications for social inclusion of the advent of Internet voting. Although the issue of social exclusion or social inclusion with regard to technological developments in the voting process is often approached as a matter of either security or turnout, we will take a broader view. Using the philosophical concept of technological mediation, as developed by Don Ihde and Peter-Paul Verbeek, we claim that Internet voting may change our experience of democracy, and transform the way we act as citizens in the democratic system. We argue that the mediating role of voting technology requires reconstruction of concepts used in discussing democracy. Our approach of reconstruction departs from the political philosophy of John Dewey. Based on his work, we can describe the political process in a democracy in terms of intellectual reconstruction and institutional reconstruction. Combining the concept of technological mediation and Dewey's political philosophy, we use the mediating role of online voting technology as input to the intellectual reconstruction of the discussion on voting and democracy. Based on the developments in the Netherlands, we present some challenges that the mediating role of online voting technology offers to existing concepts in democracy, and evaluate the benefits for social inclusion of reconstructing these concepts with respect to the new possibilities.*

1   INTRODUCTION

Throughout history, philosophers as well as citizens have often lamented the status of democracy. While John Dewey complained about the "eclipse of the public" in 1927, the Dutch said there was a feeling of *onbehagen* or discomfort concerning politics in the period of the rise and fall of the populist party of Pim Fortuyn in 2002. The "diseases"

Please use the following format when citing this chapter:

Pieters, W., 2006, in IFIP International Federation for Information Processing, Volume 208, Social Inclusion: Societal and Organizational Implications for Information Systems, eds. Trauth, E., Howcroft, D., Butler, T., Fitzgerald, B., DeGross, J., (Boston: Springer), pp. 89-103.

that are diagnosed are often considered a threat to social inclusion[1] in terms of participation in the democratic process. If people are alienated from politics, it is said, representative democracies cannot function properly. Many cures to these alleged diseases have been proposed. Meanwhile, new democracies are being established in countries with different levels of development all over the world.

Since the early 1990s, however, democracy has been changed by something other than political and social developments. The rise of the information and network society, and the accompanying technologies, did not leave democracy untouched. This is especially true in elections. Although mechanical voting machines have been in use for a long time, the impact of the information and network society on the voting process is and will be far more profound. The introduction of electronic voting machines has already shown this.[2]

Today, we are looking ahead to the option of online voting.[3] People tend to do more and more of their transactions online, and the mere existence of these other technologies makes them sensitive to the trouble that casting a vote still brings, in the act of going to the polling station. In the Netherlands, two Internet surveys showed that, depending on the context of the question, between 62 and 79 percent of the Dutch citizens using the Internet would like to vote online.[4] Meanwhile, relatively new democracies such as Estonia are eager to become the early adopters of such modern forms of voting (Dreschler 2003; National Election Committee 2004).

Of course, the issue whether it is desirable to make voting easier for certain groups of people, namely those who have Internet access at home or at work, is a topic of discussion from the point of view of social inclusion itself, in terms of turnout among different groups (Alvarez and Hall 2004, Chapter 3). In developing countries, an infrastructure of physical, digital, human, and social resources is needed to be able to provide online democracy at all (Warschauer 2004, p. 47). Also, many people have pointed out security threats to online voting systems, or electronic voting systems in general, that may be a threat to social inclusion, especially hacking and manipulation by insiders (Jefferson et al. 2004; Kohno et al. 2004; Phillips and Von Spakovsky 2001; Weinstein 2000).

In this paper, however, we focus on the role of online voting technology in people's experience of democracy. Even if Internet voting can be implemented in a secure way based on technical, organizational, and legal measures, and even if we do not consider

---

[1]Warschauer (2004) defines social inclusion as "the extent that individuals, families and communities are able to fully participate in society and control their own destinies, taking into account a variety of factors related to economic resources, employment, health, education, housing, recreation, culture and *civic engagement*" (p. 8, emphasis added).

[2]See the Commission on Electronic Voting (www.cev.ie) and Kohno et al 2004. We will not discuss electronic voting machines and the associated security issues in this paper.

[3]In this paper, we will use the terms "Internet voting" and "online voting" synonymously, in the sense of remote Internet voting (from any computer connected to the Internet). We do not discuss other forms of Internet voting that use access restrictions (Alvarez and Hall 2004, p. 4).

[4]Burger@overheid publiekspanel: stemmen via internet (Citizen@government public's panel: Voting via Internet), www.burger.overheid.nl/publiekspanel/?id=25, November 1, 2004, and www.burger.overheid.nl/publiekspanel/?id=628, September 23, 2004 (in Dutch).

the possible shift in turnout among different groups a problem, there are still many aspects in which it may have unexpected effects. The role of technology in changes in societal life has been shown in many other cases, and voting will not be an exception. This is not to say that technology is autonomous (see Winner 1977) and we follow blindly. But technology is not neutral either, and if we do not take the issue into account, it will be an implicit force in future decisions on voting and democracy.

Democracy is not a static system, and many different theories about its form and function exist (See Cunningham 2002; Held 1997). The discussion on the supposed problems of current democratic institutions cannot be intelligently conducted without knowledge of the impact of new voting technology, especially Internet voting, on the democratic process. An attempt to include technology in the debate is necessary to prevent technology from changing democracy without well-founded political discussion, which would be a serious case of social exclusion in its own right (for a discussion of similar issues, see Harbers 1996). Although voting technologies do receive increased attention in the scientific community, a general framework that can be used in connecting scientific and political discourses is needed. We aim at providing such a framework in this paper.

This paper is organized as follows. First, we discuss our methodology for including technology in the debate on the future of democracy, which is based on the political philosophy of John Dewey and the postphenomenological approach in philosophy of technology. Then, we introduce the possibilities of online voting via a description of the situation in the Netherlands. In section 4, "Challenges to Democracy," we present some results of our methodology by identifying challenges that Internet voting brings to democracy, based on the situation in the Netherlands. These results can be extended by applying our methodology to other cases. In the final section, we present our conclusions and recommendations.

Our conclusions regarding the methodology we develop in this paper do not depend on our choice for the Netherlands as a setting. However, we certainly do not claim completeness of the list of challenges to democracy that is presented, and more (possibly comparative) case studies may yield additional results. Interesting developments to study are found in the United Kingdom (BBC News 2003), the United States (Jefferson et al. 2004), Switzerland,[5] and Estonia (Drechsler 2003; National Election Committee 2004).

2   THE ROLE OF TECHNOLOGY IN DEMOCRACY

In this section, we present the philosophical theories we use in our attempt to include voting technology in the discussion on voting and democracy. Our methodological view is based on the philosophy of John Dewey, whose views on ethics and democracy have been excellently investigated in the Dutch work by Louis Logister (2004). According to Dewey, institutional changes in a democracy are achieved by a process of *reconstruction*. We describe the role of technology in this reconstruction in

---

[5]Official l'Etat de Genève Web page, "E-voting," http://www.geneve.ch/evoting.

terms of *mediation*, a concept developed by the postphenomenological approach of Don Ihde (1990) and Peter-Paul Verbeek (2005).

2.1 John Dewey's Notion of Democracy

John Dewey is a well-known philosopher from the United States, who considers himself an instrumentalist. A more widely known term for the movement that he belongs to is pragmatism. In this section, we will briefly introduce his views on the role of reconstruction in democracy. We cannot cover his theory in depth here, but we will provide references for further reading.

Dewey considers everything, including theories, norms, and values, as tools that function in the context of experience, where experience means continuous interaction between a human being and her environment. "To Dewey, experience is not a mental storage place for empirical sensations, as proposed by traditional correspondence theories, but a complex integrated activity that is characterized by goal-directedness, prospectivism and growth of meaning" (Logister 2004, p. 76, my translation). Dewey's naturalist concept of experience necessarily contains something active and something passive, trying and perceiving.

In the context of experience, Dewey frequently uses the concept of *habit*. This is an acquired tendency to act in a certain way in certain situations (Logister 2004, p. 91, referring to Dewey's *Human Nature and Conduct*). Since they are acquired, habits are *socially transmitted*. If a habit is common within a certain society, this common mode of action is called a *custom*. Habits are reflected in the *institutions* in a society. The most efficient way to change habits is by starting to change the institutions.

Based on these points of departure, Dewey develops his ethical and political theories. Dewey's ethics refrains from posing specific goals, and states that "growth itself is the only moral 'end'" (1948, p. 175) By growth, he means increasing ability to solve problems that hinder the continuous stream of experience. Politics concerns decisions on how to rearrange institutions such that growth in society becomes possible. The best way to do this is a democratic one, since it provides the best capacity for mobilizing the existing problem-solving resources in a society, especially if it is arranged in a participative way (not only votes, but also direct input from the people in political discussion). "Democracy is a name for a life of free and enriching com-munion....It will have its consummation when free social inquiry is indissolubly wedded to the art of full and moving communication" (Dewey 1991, p. 184).

Logister (2004) argues that the idea of social reconstruction (i.e., the reconstruction of the institutions in a society in order to enable growth) is at the heart of Dewey's political philosophy. He refers to the work of James Campbell (1995) in order to further clarify the idea of social reconstruction, which remains rather implicit in Dewey's own work (Logister 2004, pp. 220-226). Following Campbell, he distinguishes two aspects of Dewey's social reconstruction: intellectual reconstruction and institutional recon-struction. In democracy, intellectual reconstruction precedes institutional reconstruction. Intellectual reconstruction consists of formulating the problems that a society faces, and suggesting solutions to these problems. An important part of this task is the recon-struction of the conceptual meaning of political terms. Institutional reconstruction means evaluating the proposed concepts and solutions, and adapting existing institutions based on this evaluation. Whereas institutional reconstruction requires political discussion and should be based on democratic decisions, intellectual reconstruction is the task of philosophers and scientists.

Dewey's ideas on the role of experience and habits in society thus lead to a particular vision on how society can and should be changed. Science does the intellectual reconstruction, politics does the institutional reconstruction. We think that this separation of concerns can be fruitful for both. Moreover, the concept of intellectual reconstruction itself, as provided by Campbell and Logister based on Dewey's work, can serve as the basis for a particular way of analyzing technological developments in society, namely in relation to the reconstruction of our conceptual framework.

2.2 Technological Mediation

How can we understand the challenges that technological developments bring to our conceptual framework, for example the mobile phone? The mobile phone is not just a neutral means of solving a communication problem. Although it is effective with regard to its purpose, communication at non-fixed places and during travel, it has also completely changed the way in which people experience each other's presence and the way in which people arrange their schedules and meetings. "I'll call you when the train leaves the station; pick me up half an hour later." This also requires people to be reachable by mobile phone. The few people who don't have one by now may even run the risk of becoming socially excluded.

Several philosophers have described such developments from what is called the empirical turn in philosophy of technology (Achterhuis 2001). Whereas traditional philosophy of technology had often analyzed "technology" as a phenomenon in itself, these movements argue that we should analyze the role of concrete technological artifacts in our lives in order to understand what technology is all about. These approaches have been inspired by empirical studies into such developments.

One theory on the role of technology in our experience of our world and in the way in which we realize our existence has been described based on notions of the philosophical movement of phenomenology. Especially *intentionality*, the directedness of people toward their environment, has been used as a concept in describing changes in the lifeworld invoked by technological developments. It is said that technology can *mediate* our relation to our world by forcing itself into the intentional relation. Thereby, it may amplify as well as reduce certain aspects of our experience.

The work by Ihde (1990) focuses on these forms of mediation. In the mobile phone example, we can state that this technology amplifies the interpretation of known people as directly available for contact, whereas the presence of people we do not know in our direct environment (e.g., in a train) is reduced. Verbeek (2005) takes one step further in the theory of mediation, and states that technology can not only change our experience, but also the way in which we act, by invitation and inhibition of certain actions. A mobile phone invites calling people when it is not strictly necessary ("I caught the train I said I would catch"), and this may even become a social norm. At the same time, it inhibits talking to people in the train.

In the same sense, Internet voting is not only a means to make it easier to vote. It can profoundly change the relation between people and their environment, in this case the political world of democracy. Interpretations of what democracy is can be shifted, and Internet voting will invite different voting behavior. We therefore think that the phenomenological approach can be a fruitful starting point for a description of the possible changes that Internet voting brings to democracy, which can then serve as a basis for an intellectual reconstruction of the concept of voting in the network age.

2.3 Our Approach

Pragmatism is an especially helpful philosophical approach in cases where the conceptual framework is not fixed. Because of the mediating role of technology, introduction of new technologies is precisely such an issue. In this paper, we perform the intellectual reconstruction of the concept of voting based on the technological developments in the information society. We investigate the mediating role of voting technology in society, and reconstruct the discussion on voting and democracy based on the challenges that technology brings. Thus, our approach applies the theory of mediation of human experience and existence by technology, not only after the fact, but as an input to the political discussions that will guide the introduction of the new technology. This can be seen as a special approach to constructive technology assessment (Schot and Rip 1997).

3   INTERNET VOTING IN ACTION

We will introduce the application of our methodology to online voting by describing the developments around online voting in the Netherlands. Next to the fact that we are most familiar with the Dutch situation, we think that the Netherlands provide an interesting case study for the following reasons. First, the Netherlands were one of the first countries to introduce electronic voting machines on a large scale, which yields an interesting setting for online developments. Second, the Dutch Ministry of Domestic Affairs is very open about the development of new technologies, and cooperates intensively with the scientific community. Third, the typical Dutch phenomenon of local water management authorities (*waterschappen*) offers a particularly fruitful niche for online voting to develop (Weber et al. 1999).

In the Netherlands, several experiments have been performed with voting via the Internet. During the European elections in 2004, Dutch citizens living abroad were allowed to vote online. Moreover, elections for two local water management authorities combined postal ballots with Internet voting in the fall of 2004, with a total of 120,000 actual online voters. Although one of the main reasons to start such experiments, increasing turnout, does not seem to be based on empirical evidence,[6] people either tend

---

[6]See Oostveen and Van den Besselaar (2004). Also, the first elections using the RIES system, to be discussed later, showed decreased turnout.

to be enthusiastic about it for other reasons, or argue that turnout *will* be increased when Internet voting is used in more appealing elections.

The first of the two experiments in the Netherlands was initiated by the Ministry of Domestic Affairs. They decided that citizens living abroad, who could already vote by postal ballot, should be given the opportunity to vote via Internet or phone. For this purpose, the KOA system was developed,[7] and a law regulating the experiment was passed through parliament. The experiment took place during the European elections in 2004. A follow-up trial is planned for the national elections in 2007.

A more sophisticated system was developed with far less money by the local water management authorities of Rijnland[8] together with two companies cooperating under the name TTPI.[9] This system, called RIES, uses cryptographic operations to protect votes and at the same time offers good transparency. It is possible for voters to verify their vote after the elections, and for independent institutions to do a full recount of the results. The Radboud University Nijmegen did such a recount, and confirmed the official result.[10]

Because the water management authorities are not bound by Dutch election law, they are relatively free in their means of voting. In 2008, all local water management authorities will use the RIES system in their combined elections. We expect that RIES or similar systems will find their way into more official elections at local level soon.[11] This makes the issue of incorporating technological developments in discussions on democracy pressing.

We present some challenges that Internet voting brings to the discussion on voting and democracy next. We use features of the Dutch RIES system to illustrate our points.

4 CHALLENGES TO DEMOCRACY

The advent of Internet voting is not just a matter of changing the means of attaining certain ends. By introducing new technologies, the relation between people and their environment can be changed, in terms of experience and action. In this section, we try to intellectually reconstruct the concept of voting, based on the challenges that the mediating role of Internet voting offers to traditional conceptions of and discussions on democracy. These issues can serve as a starting point for the institutional reconstruction that Internet voting requires. We do not strive for completeness here, but we show the most important issues we identified based on our knowledge of and experience with

---

[7]Ministerie van Binnenlandse Zaken en Koninkrijksrelaties (2004), see also www.minbzk.nl/grondwet_en/kiezen_op_afstand (Remote Voting) (in Dutch).

[8]Hoogheemraadschap van Rijnland (Public Water Management Authorities of Rijnland) (www.rijnland.net and www.rijnlandkiest.nl, in Dutch).

[9]TTP Internetstemmen (TTPI Internet Voting) (www.ttpi.nl, in Dutch).

[10]More information about RIES is available in Hubbers et al. (2005).

[11]The Beverwijk local authorities announced that they wished to use a new system in the 2006 local elections (www.beverwijk.nl/websites/beverwijk/website/default.asp?Path=1731, in Dutch). However, the Ministry did not approve their proposal, officially because the law could not be adapted in time.

online voting systems in the Netherlands. Neither do we take an exclusively positive or negative point of view here. The challenges that we identify can work out either way, depending on how we handle them.

4.1 A Challenge to Individual Rational Choice

In common sense, democracy means one man, one vote. People are assumed to make their choices individually, based on rational deliberation. This is an individualistic vision, related to the common economic conceptions of individual desires and choices.[12] However, psychological research has indicated that people are not as individual as Enlightenment philosophers might first have thought. Dewey already noticed this, and his concept of habits can be thought of as a way to criticize individualistic theories.

Dewey indicates that by the implicit assumptions of liberalism and individualism, people are assumed to be free, whereas they are at the same time unconsciously suppressed by the very values of these "isms." By stressing too much the individual capacities as opposed to social structures, traditional social ties fall apart and people become easy prey for manipulation, such as by mass media. The irony is that by focusing too much on the freedom of the individual, freedom and political discussion seem to be inhibited.

The continuation of the process of individualization in the last century also has implications for elections. Whereas people tended to vote for the party connected to the social group they belonged to before, they are now free to vote how they want. At the same time, it becomes more interesting to persuade voters. This is one of the reasons why elections tend to become more and more of a media circus.

Although many alternative visions on democracy are readily available in (scientific) literature, existing institutions and technologies play an important role in maintaining the status quo. Using current election systems, it is hard to think of a different way of collecting votes that would introduce a less individualistic conception of voting and more consciousness of the alternatives that are available to the view that the media offer. In the online case, however, things may have a more flexible nature.

First of all, it becomes more interesting to use different methods of tallying, like weighted voting, where one can mark more than one candidate in a chosen order. Whereas the design of paper ballots or dedicated voting machines does not offer much flexibility,[13] voting via a web site allows for all the flexibility that is needed to implement different voting schemes.[14] A user can be taken through different screens,

---

[12]Dewey (1991, p. 86). Dewey further states, "The utilitarian economic theory was such an important factor in developing the theory, as distinct from the practice, of democratic government that it is worth while to expound it in outline" (p. 91)

[13]Many people remember the Florida "butterfly ballots" in the 2000 U.S. presidential election. Due to bad design, many people are suspected to have chosen the wrong candidate. If designing ballots for the one man, one vote system is already hard, there is no way of integrating different methods of tallying into the old-fashioned election system.

[14]This is also true for non-remote forms of Internet voting, where people cast their vote on a protected PC located in a polling station, for example.

where confirmation can be asked at each point, and—by consistency checking—overvoting or undervoting can be reduced to practically zero, even in case of complicated ballots (see Alvarez and Hall 2004, p. 40). This makes it quite relevant to discuss the benefits of different voting schemes again, and this can be fruitful for our consciousness of alternatives in the democratic process, since we may be allowed to select more than one candidate. When it becomes possible to cast more than one vote, some of the rational benefit analysis is challenged, since it is no longer required to weigh, for example, national nature preservation against foreign policy in the choice for one party. One can choose both by casting two votes. The concept of voting is subject to reconstruction here.

An even more interesting feature of the RIES system is that it is impossible[15] to create valid votes without the appropriate access token (e.g., a password or a chipcard). In our current election system, votes are created and collected in a safe place, and never leave the safe environment until they get counted. If creating false votes is impossible, this is not necessary anymore. Anyone may collect votes for her own purpose, and send them to the central counting facility later. For example, political parties may get the opportunity to collect their own votes. Also, interest groups may allow citizens who visit their site to cast a vote for the candidate that the interest group prefers (see Alvarez and Hall 2004, p. 59). One can then give a vote to an organization for which one feels sympathy, or that one trusts, instead of weighing party views on different issues. The experience of the group character of politics is amplified here, and the individual "rational" aspects are reduced.

Whether this is desirable should be subject to political discussion. People may be more conscious of the alternative options that they have in their participation in democracy. This would be a good thing for social inclusion in terms of the amount of choices available to voters and in the reduced distance between them and the organization to which they give their vote. On the other hand, this may lead to the advent of so-called "one-issue" parties. For example, a nature protection organization may collect votes for a political party or candidate that mainly focuses on nature, and does not have a clear opinion on immigration policy.

These options must be considered, however, since the advent of Internet voting makes them feasible, and may mediate people's experience in such a way that these possibilities are amplified in their interpretation of voting. In the same sense in which the mobile phone morphed itself from a seemingly purely instrumental business device into a social device with extensive implications for the way in which people stay in touch, Internet voting may lead to profound changes in voting practices. By mediating the practice of voting, Internet elections may raise the public's sensitivity to different voting methods. Although people cannot decide themselves how to vote, understanding of the possibilities may increase pressure on the government, and may in the long run change the entire system.

---

[15]"Impossible" here means computationally infeasible. Although this is not an absolute guarantee, the probability of being able to guess the correct values in bounded time is negligible.

4.2 A Challenge to the Secret Ballot

Because Internet voting does not allow for government control over the voting environment, guaranteeing secrecy of the ballot is impossible (Jefferson et al. 2004). People can always watch over your shoulder if you cast your vote at home.[16] In this sense, accepting Internet voting as the technology for casting votes will change the election system. Moreover, the mediating role of the technology will change the experience of voting, and will reduce the aspect of secrecy in the experience of the voter. If people vote at home, they may be more inclined to accept that their vote is not secret. This means that the introduction of Internet voting may lead to a whole new idea about secrecy in elections. Why is this a challenge?

The secret ballot can be important for two reasons: as instrumental to the prevention of vote buying and coercion and as an intrinsic value in democracy. In the first case, it relates to social inclusion in the sense that nobody loses her vote by either being forced or selling it. In the second case, it is related to the view that nobody needs to justify her choice in an election. We discuss both reasons in relation to the loss of secrecy in the case of remote voting.

Forced voting is already possible on a small scale in the current Dutch system, since there are limited possibilities for authorizing others to vote for you.[17] One can force someone else to sign such an authorization.[18] For the same reason, there is already limited opportunity for vote buying and selling. The question is what will happen if these limits on the "vote market" are abandoned. Measures should be taken to regulate this market, such that the actual number of illegal transactions remains low. If manipulation is reported anyway, secret elections may be the only remedy, but experiments need to tell if people even try. Possible measures include

- allowing voters to vote more than once, but only for different parties; this reduces the chance of one party gaining absolute majority by buying votes

- using criminal law to make vote buying and selling less attractive

- creating a good infrastructure for reporting misuse (e.g., pay double the price a buyer would pay if the potential seller reports it)

- making it more difficult to transfer access tokens (e.g., biometric authentication instead of passwords)

---

[16]This is also known as "family voting." Of course, this also holds for postal ballots, which have been used in various countries to various extents (Alvarez and Hall 2004, Chapter 6). We do not discuss postal ballots further in this paper.

[17]"*Stemmen bij volmacht*" (voting by authorization) was introduced in the Netherlands in 1928. The possibilities for authorization have been restricted over time, because, especially in local elections, there had been cases of active vote gathering; currently, you are allowed to have only two authorizations (Art. L 4 Dutch Election Law).

[18]Interestingly, the abandonment of the obligation to vote in 1970 increased the possibilities for manipulation: one can now force someone else to stay home, without anybody noticing.

Internet voting seems to force the market out into the open. Whereas small scale vote buying was possible in the old Dutch system as well (due to limited possibilities for authorization), the opportunities now become clear. This also requires thinking about measures to prevent force (stealing) and sale. In the old days, people were unconsciously "forced" to vote for the party everyone in their social group voted for. There was not much contact between different social groups. Vote secrecy was necessary to protect the nonconformists within the groups. Nowadays, social ties are much looser. Is vote secrecy still the solution? Or should everything be open? Some research suggests that vote buying may "survive the secret ballot" (Brusco et al. 2004), thus making the value of the secret ballot as an instrument to prevent vote buying debatable. In the same sense, one may wonder if the secret ballot helps against coercion.[19]

When secrecy is considered an intrinsic value, different arguments apply. Not being required to justify one's choice can be helpful if one has a nonconformist opinion. Even the idea that one's vote may not be secret may lead to more conformist voting (Oostveen and Van den Besselaar 2005). Therefore, secrecy may be considered essential in order to allow people to express their "real" choice. However, secrecy may also be a source of social exclusion. Is it not true that people will have better chances of being included in the public debate if they openly present their choice? Is it not fruitful for democracy if people debate their choices in public? These questions will need renewed deliberation if we wish to implement online voting.

In the RIES system, the sacrifice of secrecy is compensated for by a new option: it is possible to verify your vote in the results after the elections. This can only be done if your vote is not completely secret, since you need some information about your vote to be able to do the verification procedure afterward. There is no guarantee that others may not obtain this information from you in some way. However, the verification procedure presents a completely new dimension of elections. People will be less inclined to tacitly accept the results. The technology invites people to be more active in the counting procedure, which may be a good thing for social inclusion in terms of participation in the election procedures, or at least a replacement for the involvement of people in election management at polling stations in current systems. Again, this feature of the specific technology used may influence people's interpretation of elections.

4.3 A Challenge to the Relation Between Voting and Democracy

The last challenge we identified is that Internet voting may bring to democracy a shift in the place of voting within the democratic framework. Whereas voting is done in complete isolation nowadays, it may become more related to other political activities if the Internet is used, for example via links to other websites. The fact that people vote

---

[19]Does a wife vote against the will of her husband, even if she is threatened and beaten regularly? Social science research into these issues would be useful, although we are not aware of any such work.

via the Internet can "link" the voting environment in their experience to all kinds of other options for exercising influence (such as discussion forums). When I vote in a polling station, there is no link at all to my contribution to a discussion on immigration policy in a forum. When I vote at home, I might have both windows, voting and forum, open at the same time.

The technology may mediate the relation between people and democracy in such a way that the experience of different possibilities of participation is amplified, and active participation is invited, instead of isolating voting from the rest of the lifeworld by means of a polling booth. However, this is not necessarily a benefit. If voters do not have the skills to use these additional possibilities appropriately, it may increase their dependence on opinions articulated by others (e.g., in a forum). On the other hand, if voters do have the skills, it may lead to a new "e-democracy," in which social inclusion in different democratic processes becomes more common. Again, the institutional reconstruction requires political discussion.

5 CONCLUSIONS AND RECOMMENDATIONS

Following John Dewey, we described the political process in a democracy in terms of intellectual reconstruction and institutional reconstruction. We think that it is important to consider technological developments in the process of intellectual reconstruction, to prevent technology from becoming an unconscious force that changes our world unexpectedly by processes of mediation. In this case, we focused on the role of Internet voting in reconstructing the concepts involved in discussing elections. Based on this analysis, we argue that there is much more to social inclusion in Internet voting than turnout or security threats.

There are two types of conclusions to draw: conclusions regarding our methodology and conclusions regarding the results of this methodology in this (limited) study. We start with the methodology, which we think is fruitful for the following reasons. First, it provides a way to reflect on the mediating role of technology before it is actually introduced, analogous to constructive technology assessment. Second, it connects technological developments with developments in our conceptual framework, or cultural categories (Smits 2002a, 2002b), in a pro-active way. This approach, therefore, has the potential to explicate challenges on a conceptual level before they present themselves in the real world. We think the results of this paper regarding Internet voting illustrate the benefits.

The results of our methodology in this paper consist of three challenges that Internet voting brings to democracy, which require intellectual reconstruction of the involved concepts. These results are based on the situation in the Netherlands, and further case studies may provide additional challenges.

First, Internet voting may require reconstruction of our idea of voting as a completely *individual rational choice*. Internet voting may, by the extremely flexible nature of its user interface, make us more conscious of the different election systems that are possible, ranging from different tallying methods to completely new ways of transferring votes to the central counting facility (e.g., via interest groups). In all of these cases, a shift may occur in the interpretation of voting from the individual weighing of benefits to the collective weighing of alternatives, which may change the way in which social inclusion in democracy is understood and realized.

Second, online voting may require rethinking the concept of vote *secrecy*. The mediating role of the technology will change the experience of voting, and will reduce the aspect of secrecy in the traditional sense. One may argue that this concept stems from a social situation that has been changed profoundly since, and even if Internet voting cannot guarantee complete secrecy in the old meaning, this may not be a problem in our new social situation. The questions that this transition raises are how we wish to protect voters from undue influence exercised by others, and how we wish to balance the benefits of secrecy and the benefits of openness for social inclusion. There are many solutions to these problems, and the traditional idea of vote secrecy combined with voluntary party membership is just one of the options.

Third, online voting requires discussion on the *relation between voting and other aspects of democracy*. Voting may no longer be experienced as an act isolated from other forms of participation. For example, voters may add comments to their votes suggesting improvements to the proposals, or ideas they would like their candidate to implement. Online voting may invite people to participate in other Internet democracy issues as well, whereas polling stations do not invite anything but voting. These features can make democracy more participative, and this may diminish the gap that is felt between citizen and government.

We investigated which concepts used in discussing democracy require reconstruction from the perspective of the new technology of Internet voting. These challenges to democracy are both opportunities and risks, depending on how they are appropriated within the existing democratic system. Additional case studies may yield more challenges than the ones we identified. We hope we have broadened the discussion on social inclusion in Internet elections from security and turnout to social inclusion in technology-mediated democracy in a broad sense; that is, to the aspect of civic engagement that is a vital part of being a full member of society.

One recommendation is to incorporate this broader view into the political discussion on the future of democracy, which may lead to institutional reconstruction based on the concepts sketched here. Whereas—in the Netherlands—the focus in this discussion lies on adoption of the chosen mayor and revision of the election procedures with more focus on regional candidates, new technologies may turn out to be a more important factor in the improvement of social inclusion in democracy. If we do not take these developments seriously, we cannot steer the adoption of the technology in a proper way, which means that we will have the same situation as in the case of the introduction of voting machines: suddenly the technology is there, and nobody knows whether we really wanted it.

6   RELATED WORK

Although this paper deliberately avoids the term *ethics*, it fits within a larger debate on the role of technology assessment and technology ethics (Grunwald 1999). A solution to this problem that is also based on a pragmatist attitude has been presented by Martijntje Smits (2002a, 2002b). Ethical considerations on the use of the Internet in elections have been discussed by Pieters and Becker (2005). A more social science oriented approach is found in the work by Oostveen and Van den Besselaar (2004, 2005).

Acknowledgments

This work is supported by a Pionier grant from NWO, the Netherlands Organisation for Scientific Research. The author further wishes to thank (in alphabetical order) Marcel Becker, Erik Poll, and Martijn Warnier for useful comments on drafts of this paper.

References

Achterhuis, H. "Introduction: American Philosophers of Technology," in H. Achterhuis (ed.), *American Philosophy of Technology: The Empirical Turn*, Bloomington, IN: Indiana University Press, 2001, pp. 1-10.

Alvarez, R. M. and Hall, T. E. *Point, Click & Vote: The Future of Internet Voting*, Washington, DC: Brookings Institution Press, 2004.

BBC News. "E-Voting Fails to Stir the Public," May 2, 2003 (available online at http://news.bbc.co.uk/1/hi/technology/2995493.stm).

Brusco, V., Nazareno, M., and Stokes, S. C. "Vote Buying in Argentina," *Latin American Research Review* (39:2), 2004, pp. 66-88.

Campbell, J. *Understanding John Dewey: Nature and Cooperative Intelligence*, Chicago: Open Court, 1995.

Cunningham, F. *Theories of Democracy: A Critical Introduction*, London: Routledge, 2002.

Dewey, J. *Reconstruction in Philosophy*, Boston: Beacon, 1948.

Dewey, J. *The Public and its Problems*, Athens, OH: Swallow Press, 1991.

Drechsler, W. "The Estonian E-Voting Laws Discourse: Paradigmatic Benchmarking for Central and Eastern Europe," unpublished paper, University of Tartu, Estonia, 2003 (available online, http://unpan1.un.org/intradoc/groups/public/documents/nispacee/unpan009212.pdf).

Grunwald, A. "Technology Assessment or Ethics of Technology?," *Ethical Perspectives* (6:2), 1999, pp. 170-182.

Held, D. *Models of Democracy*, Stanford, CA: Stanford University Press, 1997.

Harbers, H. "Politiek van de technologie" (Politics of Technology), *Kennis en Methode* (20:3), 1996, pp. 308-315.

Hubbers, E., Jacobs, B., and Pieters, W. "RIES: Internet Voting in Action," in R. Bilof (ed.), *Proceedings of the 29th Annual International Computer Software and Applications Conference, COMPSAC'05*, Los Alamitos, CA: IEEE Computer Society Press, 2005, pp. 417-424.

Ihde, D. *Technology and the Lifeworld*, Bloomington, IN: Indiana University Press, 1990.

Jefferson, D., Rubin, A. D, Simons, B., and Wagner, D. "Analyzing Internet Voting Security," *Communications of the ACM* (47:10), 2004, pp. 59-64.

Kohno, T., Stubblefield, A., Rubin, A .D., and Wallach, D. S. "Analysis of an Electronic Voting System," in *IEEE Symposium on Security and Privacy*, Los Alamitos, CA: IEEE Computer Society Press, May 2004 (available online at http://www.avirubin.com/vote.pdf).

Logister, L. *Creatieve democratie: John Dewey's pragmatisme als grondslag voor een democratische samenleving* (Creative Democracy: John Dewey's Pragmatism as Foundation of a Democratic Society), Budel, Netherlands: DAMON, 2004.

Ministerie van Binnenlandse Zaken en Koninkrijksrelaties (Dutch Ministry of Domestic Affairs). *Project Kiezen op Afstand* (Project Remote Voting), report BPR2004/U79957, November 11, 2004.

National Election Committee. "E-Voting System Overview," Tallinn, Estonia, 2005 (available online, http://www.vvk.ee/elektr/docs/Yldkirjeldus-eng.pdf).

Oostveen, A. M., and Van den Besselaar, P. "The Effects of Voting Technologies on Voting Behavior: Issues of Trust and Social Identity," *Social Science Computer Review* (23:3), 2005, pp. 304-311.

Oostveen, A. M., and Van den Besselaar, P. "Internet Voting Technologies and Civic Participation: The Users' Perspective," *The Public* (11:1), 2004, pp. 61-78.

Phillips, D., and Von Spakovsky, H. "Gauging the Risks of Internet Elections," *Communications of the ACM* (44:1), 2001, pp. 72-85.

Pieters, W., and Becker, M. J. "Ethics of E-Voting: An Essay on Requirements and Values in Internet Elections," in P. Brey, F. Grodzinsky, and L. Introna (eds.), *Ethics of New Information Technology: Proceedings of the Sixth International Conference of Computer Ethics: Philosophical Enquiry (CEPE 2005)*, Center for Telematics and Information Technology, Enschede, The Netherlands, July 17-19, 2005, pp. 307-318.

Schot, J., and Rip, A. "The Past and Future of Constructive Technology Assessment," *Technological Forecasting and Social Change* (54), 1997, pp. 251-268.

Smits, M. "Monster Ethics: A Pragmatist Approach to Risk Controversies on New Technology," paper presented at the Research in Ethics and Engineering Conference, University of Delft, The Netherlands, April 25-27, 2002a.

Smits, M. *Monsterbezwering: de culturele domesticatie van nieuwe technologie*, Amsterdam: Boom, 2002b.

Verbeek, P-P. *What Things Do: Philosophical Reflections on Technology, Agency, and Design*, University Park, PA: Pennsylvania State University Press, 2005.

Warschauer, M. *Technology and Social Inclusion: Rethinking the Digital Divide*, Cambridge, MA: MIT Press, 2004.

Weber, M., Hoogma, R., Lane, B., and Schot, J. *Experimenting with Sustainable Transport Innovations: A Workbook for Strategic Niche Management*, Enschede, The Netherlands: University of Twente, 1999.

Weinstein, L. "Risks of Internet Voting," *Communications of the ACM* (43:6), 2000, p. 128.

Winner, L. *Autonomous Technology: Technics-Out-of-Control as a Theme in Political Thought*, Cambridge, MA: MIT Press, 1977.

About the Author

Wolter Pieters is a junior researcher in the Security of Systems group at the Radboud University Nijmegen. He studied computer science and philosophy of science, technology, and society at the University of Twente. The topic of his current research is the conditions under which Internet voting can be acceptable, both from technical and social perspectives. He can be reached at wolterp@cs.ru.nl.

8 ENGAGING YOUTHS VIA E-PARTICIPATION INITIATIVES: An Investigation into the Context of Online Policy Discussion Forums

Chee Wei Phang
Atreyi Kankanhalli
National University of Singapore
Singapore

Abstract   *Advances in information and communication technologies (ICTs) have offered governments new opportunities to enhance citizen participation in democratic processes. The participation opportunities afforded by ICT may be particularly pertinent for youths, who are more likely to be ICT-savvy and yet are reported to show declining participation in politics. The currently increasing exclusion of youths from democratic processes has been attributed to their apathy toward politics and a lack of participation channels for them. ICT as a familiar tool for this specific age group may present an opportunity to elicit youths' participation in democratic processes. In this study we examine an e-participation initiative targeted at youths and seek to investigate the factors contributing to their participation in an online discussion forum employed for policy deliberation. We build upon theoretical bases from the political science and information systems literature to construct a research model of participation in online policy discussion forums. As an initial study of youths' e-participation, our survey indicates that collective and selective incentives may positively impact youths' participation intention. In addition, civic skills and political efficacy of individuals may also contribute to their participation. Connectivity with an online policy discussion forum can enhance youths' perceptions of selective process incentives while communality negatively impacts their intention to participate. Overall, our study aims to inform theory by showing that existing participation theories may be applicable to youth's participation in the electronic context. Further, ICT features (connectivity and communality) are found to have both positive and negative effects on participation. The findings may provide insights to practitioners for promoting inclusion of youths in democratic processes via e-participation initiatives.*

Please use the following format when citing this chapter:

Phang, C.W., and Kankanhalli, A., 2006, in IFIP International Federation for Information Processing, Volume 208, Social Inclusion: Societal and Organizational Implications for Information Systems, eds. Trauth, E., Howcroft, D., Butler, T., Fitzgerald, B., DeGross, J., (Boston: Springer), pp. 105-121.

Keywords   E-Participation, inclusion of youths, online policy discussion forum, participation theories, ICT features

1   INTRODUCTION

Governments around the world are tapping into the potential of information and communication technologies (ICT) to enable citizen participation in democratic processes (e.g., Whyte and Macintosh 2002). It is argued that enhanced citizen participation can lead to formulation of policies that are more realistically grounded in citizens' preferences and improved public support for these policies (Aristotle 1987; Irvin and Stansbury 2004). Implementation of citizen participation programs can be traced back as far as 1950s (Day 1997), with the first deployment of ICT to enable participation about two decades later (Hiltz and Turoff 1978). Today e-participation initiatives are exploiting the Internet's capabilities of providing 24/7 accessibility as well as mass transmission and reception of information to facilitate citizen participation.

The use of ICT to enable participation may be particularly relevant to youths. It is seen that youths' participation in politics has been generally declining over the years (e.g., Institute of Politics 2002). Some studies attribute this to youths' apathy toward politics (Bennett 1997). Others find that despite youths' purported interest in political issues, they lack appropriate channels to participate (Institute of Politics 2002). Such a trend suggests a widening exclusion or disengagement of youths from democratic processes. This is troubling because youths are a nation's most valuable future asset. Ensuring the inclusion of youths in democratic processes is important in preparing them to exercise their rights and responsibilities of citizenship and increase their involvement in the future governance of the country. Being a generation that has grown up with ICT, youths today have been found to be more technology savvy (Pew Research 2000) and more ready to embrace new e-Government applications (Thrane et al. 2004) than other age groups. Given that youths are regular users of ICT in their everyday life, they may find the use of ICT for participation appealing. Hence, to policy makers, ICT may present an opportunity to combat the trend and promote inclusion of youths in democratic processes.

While ICT is increasingly being deployed to enable participation, little is known of the factors responsible for e-participation. To address this void, we delve into political science and information systems literatures to identify antecedents of citizen participation, particularly in the context of online discussion forums. The online discussion forum is deemed a low cost, scalable ICT that is particularly suited for policy deliberation (Kumar and Vragov 2005). In this study we use the term online policy discussion forum (henceforth denoted by OPDF) to refer to Web-based forums using bulletin boards employed by governments to engage citizens in policy deliberation. The integration of the relevant participation factors and ICT features form our research model, which is empirically tested through a survey of youths' intention to participate in an OPDF.

2 CONCEPTUAL BACKGROUND AND RESEARCH MODEL

In the political science literature, two widely employed theoretical perspectives that elucidate individual-level participation factors are socio-economic theories and rational choice theories. We describe two specific participation models that are derived from these two theoretical strands: civic voluntarism model (Verba et al. 1995) and general incentives model (Seyd and Whiteley 1992). In addition we also identify two ICT features that are likely to be relevant in the context of e-participation via OPDF.

2.1 Socio-Economic Theories and Civic Voluntarism Model

Socio-economic theories attempt to explain citizen participation in terms of the social circumstances that shape an individual's attitude toward participation (Parry et al. 1992; Verba and Nie 1972). Social circumstances include an individual's age, education level, and financial status. While initial thinking along this perspective held that individuals who are older, better educated, and wealthier are more likely to participate, subsequent research questioned such propositions and the mechanisms behind the effects of socio-economic factors (Verba et al. 1995). Past studies have also shown that the general rise in education level does not necessarily lead to increased electoral parti-cipation (e.g., Lyons and Alexander 2000). These limitations have led to refinements in socio-economic theories in terms of including a more comprehensive set of partici-pation factors and the mechanisms linking social circumstances to participation.

Along this line, Verba et al. (1995) developed the civic voluntarism model (CVM), which aims to specify "in detail how socio-economic position is linked to political activity" (p. 19). Cited as the most widely employed participation theory (Seyd et al. 2001), the model considers resources, motivations, and mobilization as antecedents of participation. *Resources* that include time, money, and civic skills (individual's organi-zational and communications abilities that can facilitate their political participation) bridge the individual's socio-economic status to their participation. In other words, individuals with better socio-economic status are more likely to participate because they possess the resources to do so. *Motivations* are conceptualized as individual and group incentives as well as a sense of political efficacy (Verba et al. 1995). *Political efficacy* refers to the individual's perception that political change is possible, and that the individual citizen can play a part in bringing about this change (Campbell et al. 1954). Last, *mobilization* refers to the extent to which individuals are influenced by people around them to participate.

2.2 Rational Choice Theories and General Incentives Model

Rational choice theories of participation see citizen participation as a rational activity in which the aim is to maximize benefits and minimize costs (Olson 1965). In this light, the individual's decision to participate is essentially an outcome of cost-benefit calculation. The perceived benefits from participation are closely tied to one's political efficacy. However, rational choice theories have been criticized for not being able to explain electoral participation. In an election where many actors are involved, the likely influence that an individual has on the outcome, and thus the potential benefit, is extremely small. Considering the cost required to vote, a truly rational actor may choose not to vote. However, we do see people participating in elections. Explanations have been offered in terms of the sufficiently low cost of voting (Aldrich 1993) and in subsequent refinements to the initial theories.

Arguing that the benefits for participation are too narrowly conceptualized in traditional rational choice theories, Seyd and Whiteley (1992) developed a general incentives model (GIM) that incorporates incentives related to altruistic concerns and social norms. The resulting GIM encompasses five incentives types for participation: collective, selective, group, expressive, and social norms-derived incentives. *Collective* incentives are derived from policy goals that are available for all to enjoy regardless of whether one participates (e.g., tax reduction). This is in contrast to selective incentives that are restricted to participants, which include the gratification obtained during the participating *process* (e.g., enjoying interaction with others) and the privatized *outcomes* from participation (e.g., political career advancement). Group incentives and expressive incentives are related to individuals' attachment to a group (e.g., political party). *Group* incentives have to do with individuals' perception about the efficacy of the group as a whole to bring about desired social change, whereas expressive incentives are grounded in a sense of loyalty and affection to the group. Finally, *social norms-derived* incentives refer to the influence of other people on the individual's willingness to participate, and are similar to the concept of mobilization in the CVM.

2.3 Antecedents of Participation Derived from the Two Models

Based on the above discussion, we integrate the resource and mobilization concepts from the CVM with the incentives from the GIM to develop our model of e-participation. The five incentive types explicated in the GIM may serve as motivations of participation outlined in the CVM. Of the five incentives, we consider collective and selective incentives of particular relevance. Group and expressive incentives are less relevant in the context of the general population where individuals may not be members of political organizations, that is, the two incentive types assume citizens' attachment to a group (e.g., political party). Social norms-derived incentives are captured through the concept of mobilization in CVM.

Collective incentives in the context of participation in OPDF refer to the benefits that are available for all to enjoy whether or not they participate in the OPDF. These incentives can be in the form of improved policies resulting from participation by some individuals in the OPDF, but which will benefit all including nonparticipants (Seyd and Whiteley 1992). Although collective incentives are subject to the "free-rider" problem (Olson 1965), such incentives remain important because people realize that they would not materialize if everyone chooses to stay inactive (Gamson 1975). Consistent with this logic, past studies have shown significant effect of collective incentives on participation (e.g., Scholzman et al. 1995). Therefore, we expect that

H1: *Collective incentives are positively related to intention to participate in OPDF.*

Selective incentives include selective process incentives derived from the process of participating in the OPDF, such as the enjoyment in interacting with others (Seyd and Whiteley 1992). These incentives are found to be salient for participation that involves participant interactions (Scholzman et al. 1995), such as during the policy deliberation process in OPDF. Selective incentives also include selective outcome incentives, defined as privatized outcomes accruing from participating in the OPDF. These incentives can be in the form of furthering one's political career (e.g., becoming a community leader) (Seyd and Whiteley 1992) and fulfillment of civic duties (Verba et al. 1995). To the extent that these privatized outcomes are attractive to an individual, his or her intention to participate is expected to be higher.

H2: *Selective process incentives are positively related to intention to participate in OPDF.*

H3: *Selective outcome incentives are positively related to intention to participate in OPDF.*

Political efficacy (Verba et al. 1995) is expected to be another important motivational factor for participation intention in OPDF. The positive relationship between political efficacy and participation is well documented in the literature (Brady et al. 1995; Rosenstone and Hansen 1993). Previous studies have identified two dimensions of political efficacy, internal and external (Niemi et al. 1991). Internal political efficacy refers to the beliefs about one's own competence to understand and to participate effectively in politics, whereas external political efficacy refers to individual's beliefs about the responsiveness of government authorities to citizen demands (Niemi et al. 1991). The more individuals feel that they are politically competent and that government will respond to their inputs, the higher their intention would be to participate in OPDF.

H4: *Political efficacy is positively related to intention to participate in OPDF.*

In addition to motivations, the CVM emphasizes the role of resource factors in determining an individual's participation. Since participating in OPDF requires formulation and expression of ideas, a salient resource factor may be the civic skills (Brady et al. 1995; Verba et al. 1995). Individuals who possess the requisite organizational and communications capacities, who can speak or write well and feel comfortable taking part in discussions, will find it less daunting to participate in policy deliberation through the OPDF. This will likely translate into their higher intention to participate in the OPDF.

H5: *Civic skills are positively related to intention to participate in OPDF.*

Last, mobilization is also expected to influence participation in OPDF. Mobilization can be seen as a product of social norms, which are pressures to conform to the influence of other people (Whiteley 1995). Mobilization for participation in the OPDF may be in the form of requests that come to individuals from their friends, relatives, acquaintances, or strangers. Being asked to participate by others has been found to be a triggering factor for participation (Rosenstone and Hansen 1993). Therefore we expect that

H6: *Mobilization is positively related to intention to participate in OPDF.*

2.4 ICT Features Pertinent to Participation in OPDF

A number of ICT features have been highlighted with respect to communication and other tasks. However, in the context of e-participation via OPDF, we are concerned with those features of ICT that enhance collective action such as policy deliberation and formulation. Previous literature indicates connectivity and communality as two features of ICT that are relevant in the context of collective action (Fulk et al. 1996).

Connectivity is the feature of ICT that enables individuals who share common goals and interests to easily communicate with each other (Fulk et al. 1996; Kumar and Benbasat 2001). Monge et al. (1998) observe that the connectivity offered by inter-organizational information systems can create benefits of easy collaboration and coordination between members. In an OPDF, messages are structured and displayed according to topic along with the message posters. This allows individuals to easily identify others who share similar interests and goals, and communicate with them by directly replying to their postings. Such connectivity afforded by the OPDF may help amplify the selective process incentives obtainable from participation. If individuals are able to easily reach and communicate with others who share common goals and interests, they are likely to perceive greater enjoyment from such interactions during participation. Connectivity is also expected to have a direct positive impact on participation intention as the feature can facilitate collective deliberation on a policy issue through the OPDF (Kumar and Vragov 2005).

H7a: *Connectivity is positively related to selective process incentives obtainable by participating in OPDF.*

H7b: *Connectivity is positively related to intention to participate in OPDF.*

Communality refers to the availability of a commonly accessible pool of information enabled by ICT to all participants (Fulk et al. 1996; Monge et al. 1998), such as through the OPDF. The fundamental function of communality is to facilitate generalized and productive types of exchange (Cook 1991). Generalized exchange refers to a pattern of social exchange where an individual may contribute to and receive resources from different people. In productive exchange, information is assembled and analyzed to create something new, such as formulation of broad public policy from data gathered (Fulk et al. 1996). The OPDF may serve as a repository containing relevant policy information contributed by policy makers and other participants. Such communality afforded by the OPDF may reduce the cost of a participant's access to a common pool

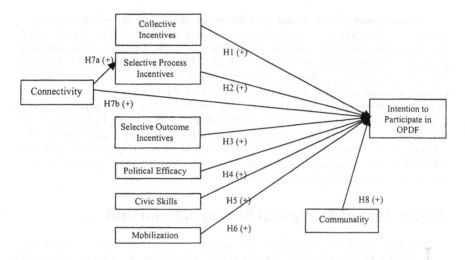

Figure 1. Research Model of Participation in Online Policy Discussion Forum

of relevant policy information (Kumar and Vragov 2005) and make exchange of information easier, thus facilitating participation in policy deliberation. Therefore, we expect that the communality feature would promote intention to participate.

H8:   *Communality is positively related to intention to participate in OPDF.*

The above hypotheses constitute our research model shown in Figure 1.

3   RESEARCH METHODOLOGY

The survey method was employed in this study to aim for better generalizability of results. Given that the study was exploratory and some items were self-developed, a thorough instrument validation exercise was conducted as per procedures prescribed by Moore and Benbasat (1991).

3.1 Construct Operationalization

Where available, constructs were measured using tested items from previous literature to enhance validity. Other items were developed by converting the definition of constructs into questionnaire format.[1]

---

[1]The questionnaire items are available upon request from the authors.

All constructs were modeled as reflective constructs, except selective outcome incentives, political efficacy, and civic skills. Selective outcome incentives are modeled as a formative construct consisting of two dimensions: fulfillment of civic duty and political career advancement (Seyd and Whiteley 1992; Verba et al. 1995). Political efficacy is measured as a formative construct with two dimensions: internal political efficacy and external political efficacy (Niemi et al. 1991). Civic skills are modeled as a second-order formative construct in which individuals' practicing of five relevant skill-acts adapted from Brady et al. (1995) and Verba et al. (1995) in three places where these skill-acts are commonly practiced (i.e., workplace, voluntary organizations, and religious institutions) are measured. Last, mobilization is a single-item measure in which respondents were asked whether they have been requested by people surroudning them to participat ein the OPDF (Verba et al. 1995).

3.2 Context of Study and Survey Administration

The study was conducted in Singapore, which is ranked second for e-participation readiness (UPAN 2005). In conjunction with the Singapore government's growing emphasis on engaging citizens, public consultation was made a requirement for formulation of all government policies starting in 2004 (Chia 2004). A government consultation portal (http://www.feedback.gov.sg) has been launched to solicit citizens' inputs on a range of policy issues. One of the goals of this portal is engage youths, who are observed to be increasingly apathetic about politics (Vinluan et al. 2005). The target e-participation initiative in our study represents one such effort to promote inclusion of youths in consultation through the portal. The initiative invites inputs from youths on the building and designing of a youth community space in the downtown area of Singapore via an OPDF.

We administered the survey to Singaporean undergraduate students across various disciplines at a large public university. Undergraduate students have been typically used as a representative sample in previous studies of youths' involvement (Institute of Politics 2002; Jarvis et al. 2005). The survey was administered after the lecture session of four higher-level undergraduate courses. All students of Singaporean nationality took the survey, amounting to 126 responses received. Participation in the survey was voluntary. Nonetheless, a token payment was given for their participation. Respondents were first directed to the target OPDF before they filled in the survey form. Since only a handful of students had visited the consultation portal before, intention to participate was considered as a suitable dependent variable as compared to actual participation. Respondents were asked to provide their responses with respect to the above-mentioned e-participation initiative. Of the 126 responses received, 5 were dropped due to substantial missing data. This resulted in a total of 121 usable responses for data analysis. Demographic information of our respondents is shown in Table 1.

3.3 Data Analysis and Results

Partial least square (PLS) was used for data analysis due to the formative constructs (selective outcome incentives, political efficacy, and civic skills) in our model. Additionally, PLS can be used for prediction-oriented studies and is appropriate for early

Table 1. Demographic Information of Respondents

	Category	Frequency (n = 121)	Percent
Gender	Male	81	67%
	Female	40	33%
Age	19–21	28	23%
	22–24	85	70%
	25–27	8	7%
Computer Experience	**Mean** = 9.93 years; **Standard Deviation** = 2.73		
Internet Experience	**Mean** = 7.45 years; **Standard Deviation** = 1.75		

stages of theory development (Fornell 1982). Given that this study represents an initial attempt to explore factors influencing intention to participate in OPDF, PLS was deemed appropriate. PLS-Graph v3.00 was used in our analysis.

The measurement model was first assessed followed by the structural model. The strength of the measurement model can be demonstrated by convergent and discriminant validity tests (Hair et al. 1998); that is, items of the same construct being similar and dissimilar from items of other constructs. All reflective constructs in our study exhibited acceptable levels of convergent validity (i.e., in Table 3, Cronbach's Alpha (CA) > 0.7, Composite Reliability (CR) > 0.7, and Average Variance Extracted (AVE) > 0.5 (Fornell and Larcker 1987; Nunnally 1994). The constructs also showed acceptable discriminant validity (i.e., in Table 2, loadings of all items in factor analysis were above the minimum recommended level of 0.5 and no serious cross-loading (> 0.4) was detected). In Table 4, the construct correlations, diagonal elements exceeded other entries in the same row or column (Fornell and Larcker 1987). No multicollinearity problems were detected. Mobilization being a single indicator measure and civic skills being a second-order formative construct were not included in the tests of Tables 2 and 4.

For formative indicators, where the items represent the causes rather than the effects of the construct, the weights rather than loadings are examined (Table 3). Item weights can be interpreted as a beta coefficient in a standard regression. Rather than interpreting the weights in a factor loading sense (i.e., how close the weights are to 1.0), the general approach is to compare the weights of different indicators (Sambamurthy and Chin 1994). In our study, all dimensions of each of the formative constructs (selective outcome incentives, civic skills, and political efficacy) contribute substantially to their respective construct.

Figure 2 and Table 5 present the results of structural model testing with path coefficients estimated by resampling. The results show that collective incentives (H1), selective process incentives (H2), selective outcome incentives (H3), political efficacy (H4), and civic skills (H5) have significant effects on youths' participation intention in the OPDF. Additionally, connectivity has significant effect on selective process incentives (H7a). The model has adequate explanatory power ($R^2 = 0.45$).

Table 2. Results of Factor Analysis

	Component								
	1	**2**	**3**	**4**	**5**	**6**	**7**	**8**	**9**
INT1	0.17	0.26	0.17	-0.02	0.16	0.16	0.05	0.16	**0.77**
INT2	0.30	0.27	0.08	0.11	0.13	0.01	0.21	0.14	**0.73**
COL1	**0.73**	-0.06	0.03	0.34	0.03	-0.02	-0.06	0.15	0.24
COL2	**0.81**	-0.11	0.10	0.21	0.10	0.06	0.07	0.08	0.16
COL3	**0.85**	-0.06	0.04	0.21	0.25	0.06	0.00	0.12	0.00
COL4	**0.83**	-0.06	0.16	0.10	0.12	0.13	-0.08	0.26	0.05
COL5	**0.82**	-0.03	0.12	0.08	0.25	0.14	0.14	-0.01	0.06
SELP1	0.10	0.14	0.15	0.14	0.05	**0.78**	0.08	0.18	-0.22
SELP2	0.07	0.09	0.14	0.25	0.20	**0.82**	0.11	-0.11	0.17
SELP3	0.17	0.09	0.23	0.08	0.11	**0.71**	-0.05	0.08	0.36
SELD1	0.31	0.04	0.14	0.27	0.15	0.08	0.19	**0.82**	0.17
SELD2	0.29	0.07	0.17	0.23	0.18	0.08	0.16	**0.84**	0.16
SELC1	0.14	0.01	0.05	0.00	0.10	0.02	**0.93**	0.11	0.06
SELC2	-0.09	-0.08	0.12	0.06	0.02	0.09	**0.91**	0.11	0.10
IPEF1	-0.10	**0.78**	-0.10	0.02	-0.02	0.15	-0.04	-0.09	0.07
IPEF2	0.02	**0.81**	-0.20	0.09	0.11	0.08	0.07	-0.12	0.24
IPEF3	0.01	**0.87**	0.06	-0.11	0.04	0.01	-0.08	0.11	0.03
IPEF4	-0.09	**0.89**	0.13	-0.02	0.11	0.01	0.02	0.10	0.05
IPEF5	-0.10	**0.91**	0.10	0.02	0.05	0.04	-0.02	0.07	0.08
EPEF1	0.26	0.06	0.06	0.07	**0.85**	0.08	-0.01	0.06	0.07
EPEF2	0.26	0.05	0.04	0.12	**0.86**	0.16	0.05	0.04	0.14
EPEF3	0.09	0.16	0.13	0.12	**0.83**	0.07	0.11	0.16	0.06
CON1	0.06	0.08	**0.90**	0.19	0.08	0.06	0.03	0.13	-0.01
CON2	0.13	0.07	**0.90**	0.21	0.02	0.14	0.09	0.03	0.04
CON3	0.10	-0.07	**0.86**	0.23	0.07	0.18	0.06	0.06	0.12
CON4	0.12	-0.05	**0.89**	0.23	0.10	0.11	0.05	0.07	0.11
COM1	0.17	0.06	0.28	**0.83**	0.06	0.11	-0.03	0.07	0.07
COM2	0.18	-0.08	0.28	**0.83**	0.10	0.11	0.08	0.04	0.09
COM3	0.26	0.04	0.14	**0.81**	0.15	0.15	0.00	0.21	-0.01
COM4	0.23	-0.04	0.26	**0.79**	0.08	0.12	0.05	0.14	-0.05

Table 3. Psychometric Properties of Measures

Construct	Item	Weight	Loading
Intention (INT)	INT1	N. A.	0.90***
CA = 0.79, CR = 0.91, AVE = 0.83	INT2		0.92***
Collective Incentives (COL)	COL1	N. A.	0.83***
CA = 0.92, CR = 0.94, AVE = 0.76	COL2		0.88***
	COL3		0.90***
	COL4		0.88***
	COL5		0.85***
Sel. Process Incentives (SELP)	SELP1	N. A.	0.73***
CA = 0.78, CR = 0.88, AVE = 0.70	SELP2		0.90***
	SELP3		0.88***
Sel. Outcome Incentives (SELO)	SELD	0.71***	N. A.
Formative, consisting of 2 dimensions:	SELC	0.51***	
CA = 0.97, CR = 0.99, AVE = 0.98	SELD1	N. A.	0.99***
Political advancement (SELC)	SELD2		0.99***
CA = 0.88, CR = 0.95, AVE = 0.90	SELC1	N. A.	0.94***
	SELC2		0.95***
Civic Skill (CIVIC)	W.CIV	0.42***	N. A.
Formative, all the items (i.e. individual skill-	V.CIV	0.55***	
acts) are measured with respect to:	R.CIV	0.33*	
Workplace (W.CIV),	W.CIV1	0.44*	N. A.
Voluntary organizations (V.CIV), and	W.CIV2	-0.18	
Religious Institutions (R.CIV)	W.CIV3	0.24	
	W.CIV4	0.32	
	W.CIV5	0.34*	
	V.CIV1	0.34***	N. A.
	V.CIV2	-0.02	
	V.CIV3	0.42***	
	V.CIV4	0.29*	
	V.CIV5	0.12	
	R.CIV1	0.70	N. A.
	R.CIV2	0.11	
	R.CIV3	0.21	
	R.CIV4	0.48	
	R.CIV5	-0.30	
Political Efficacy (PEF)	IPEFF	0.88***	N. A.
Formative, consisting of 2 dimensions:	EPEF	0.34***	
Internal political efficacy (IPEF)	IPEF1	N. A.	0.79***
CA = 0.91, CR = 0.94, AVE = 0.75	IPEF2		0.83***
External political efficacy (EPEF)	IPEF3		0.87***
CA = 0.89, CR = 0.93, AVE = 0.81	IPEF4		0.90***
	IPEF5		0.93***
	EPEF1	N. A.	0.90***
	EPEF2		0.92***
	EPEF3		0.89***

Construct	Item	Weight	Loading
Connectivity (CON)	CON1	N.A.	0.92***
CA = 0.95, CR = 0.97, AVE = 0.88	CON2		0.94***
	CON3		0.94***
	CON4		0.95***
Communality (COM)	COM1	N.A.	0.90***
CA = 0.92, CR = 0.94, AVE = 0.81	COM2		0.87***
	COM3		0.92***
	COM4		0.91***

*p < 0.05; **p < 0.01; ***p < 0.005

Table 4. Correlations between Constructs

	INT	COL	SELP	SELD	SELC	IPEF	EPEF	CON	COM
INT	**0.91**								
COL	0.40	**0.87**							
SELP	0.36	0.31	**0.84**						
SELD	0.45	0.52	0.30	**0.99**					
SELC	0.24	0.11	0.16	0.32	**0.95**				
IPEF	0.37	-0.10	0.21	0.09	-0.20	**0.87**			
EPEF	0.37	0.43	0.36	0.40	0.16	0.18	**0.90**		
CON	0.27	0.29	0.40	0.35	0.18	0.02	0.24	**0.94**	
COM	0.23	0.49	0.40	0.48	0.12	0.01	0.32	0.51	**0.90**

Table 5. Results of Hypothesis Tests

Hypothesis	Coefficient	T-value	Outcome
H1: COL to INT	0.27	3.08***	**Supported**
H2: SELP to INT	0.13	1.70*	**Supported**
H3: SELO to INT	0.25	2.81***	**Supported**
H4: PEF to INT	0.32	4.24***	**Supported**
H5: CIV to INT	0.16	2.44**	**Supported**
H6: MOB to INT	0.04	0.62	Not supported
H7a: CON to SELP	0.40	4.65***	**Supported**
H7b: CON to INT	0.11	1.21	Not supported
H8: COM to INT	-0.15	1.73*	Not supported†

*p < 0.05; **p < 0.01; ***p < 0.005.
†Significant but in opposite direction

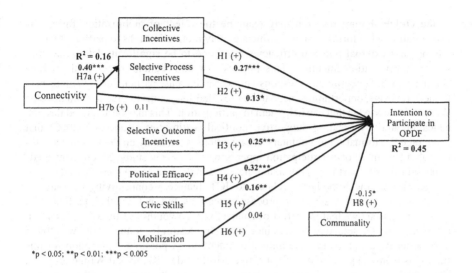

Figure 2. Graphical Summary of Results

4   DISCUSSION, IMPLICATIONS AND CONCLUSION

In a preliminary effort that attempts to integrate relevant work from political science and IS fields in explaining a youths' participation in OPDF, our study shows that existing offline participation theories may be applicable in the electronic context. Additionally, our findings also suggest that ICT can have both positive and negative impacts on a youths' e-participation intention. All motivational factors hypothesized have significant effects on youths' intention to participate in OPDF. Youths' e-participation intention is driven by the collective incentives that can also be enjoyed by nonparticipants and selective incentives derived from both the process and outcomes of participation. Accordingly, e-participation practitioners may convey to youths the potential benefits that can be brought about by the initiative to the broader society. Additionally, efforts can to be invested to make the participation process in OPDF more enjoyable through such means as having moderators to improve the interactivity of discussion (see Edwards 2002). Explicit appreciation of youths' fulfillment of civic duty may be communicated to them, so as to reinforce their emphasis on such incentives. Online networking opportunities can also be provided to youths who are looking to advance their political career by involving prominent political figures from the community in the discussion.

Apart from incentives, civic skills are a significant resource factor that can determine a youths' participation intention. This indicates that youths' lack of abilities to articulate their ideas and to involve in discourse with others may be an important barrier to their participation. Mobilization is not significant in this study probably because there were only a handful of respondents who had received requests from others to participate in the OPDF. Future research may examine the effect of mobilization further by investigating what forms of social influences may motivate youths to participate. Both internal and external political efficacies are found to be significant determinants of youths' participation intention. This implies that both beliefs in personal political competence and government's responsiveness can increase participation. With respect to these findings, opportunities need to be provided for youths to practice and develop skills and knowledge that can help them in participation. This may be achieved through education and by creating supportive political institutions (Rubenson 2000) that encourage the formation of voluntary organizations (e.g., study circles). Since aware-ness about avenues for e-participation appears to be low in our study, government needs to put additional effort into publicizing these channels such as the consultation portal.

Regarding the hypotheses related to ICT features, connectivity is found to significantly influence selective process incentives but not youths' participation intention. This shows that the effect of connectivity on youths' participation intention is mediated by the selective process incentives. Interestingly, communality was found to be a negative significant determinant of intention. A possible explanation for this finding is from the perspective of collective effort model (Karau and Williams 1993). The model posits that people will contribute more to the collective effort if they perceive that their inputs are unique and important, and vice versa. In this light, communality may instead deter individuals' intention to participate because they are uncertain of the uniqueness and importance of their ideas since the policy issue may have been well deliberated by others with the ease of information exchange. The dual impacts of ICT on participation raises the caution that while ICT can in theory provide promising opportunities for enhancing participation, ICT deployment for this purpose needs to be done cautiously. E-participation practitioners can strive to enhance connectivity by designing a forum that offers easy correspondence between two or more participants. For communality, practitioners may attempt to minimize its negative impact while retaining its benefits by employing a forum moderator. The moderator may summarize the discussion and identify the important and unique points covered periodically, so potential participants get an idea of whether their inputs are still valuable and subsequently make the decision to participate (see Edwards 2002).

As an initial attempt to explore the antecedents of youths' participation in OPDF, several limitations need to be recognized when interpreting the results of this study. First, the study was conducted in a single nation. Rubenson (2000) has highlighted the importance of political institutions (e.g., government supportive of civic group formation) in accounting for participation. Future research may be conducted in other countries with different political institutions to further validate our results. Second, the sample was confined to university students. Although studies have shown that factors pertinent to participation of other youths are not substantially different (Jarvis et al. 2005), a validation can be done to verify these results. Third, the sample size can be increased in future studies to obtain better statistical power. Additionally, actual participation behavior of youths can be measured in future studies (although support has been found for intention as a predictor of actual behavior, e.g., Taylor and Todd 1995). Future studies may examine youths' e-participation with respect to issues of a different nature from the current study (e.g., controversial issues with divided views). Individuals may perceive issues as having different importance or salience to them that subsequently influence their participation intention (Nadeau et al. 1995). Since the model has been developed for citizens in general, it can also be used to investigate the differences between youth and other groups. Further, differences between OPDF and other e-participation mechanisms can be studied. Finally, interviews with subjects can be used to supplement the survey questionnaire to obtain better understanding of individuals' e-participation behavior.

As governments around the globe attempt to leverage the potential of e-participation initiatives, studies of this nature can serve to inform theory and practice on how ICT can be employed to enhance citizen participation in democratic processes. Specifically, they may add to the understanding of an important issue facing countries around the world: how inclusion of youths in democratic processes can be promoted to prepare them for future governance.

References

Aldrich, J. H. "National Choice and Turnout," *American Journal of Political Science* (37), 1993, pp. 246-278.

Aristotle. *Politics*, London: Penguin Classics, 1987.

Bennett, S. E. "Why Young Americans Hate Politics, and What We Should Do to About it," *Political Science and Politics* (30:1), 1997, pp. 47-53.

Brady, H. E., Verba, S., and Schlozman, K. L. "Beyond SES: A Resource Model of Political Participation," *American Political Science Review* (89:2), 1995, pp. 271-294.

Campbell, A., Gurin, G., and Milner, W. *The Voter Decides*, Evanston, IL: Row Peterson and Company, 1954.

Chia, S-A. "Public Views Now a Must for All Policies," *The Straits Times* (Singapore), Prime News, November 13, 2004.

Clary, E., Ridge, R., Stukas, A., Snyder, M., Copeland, J., Haugen, J., and Miene, P. "Understanding and Assessing the Motivations of Volunteers: A Functional Approach," *Journal of Personality and Social Psychology* (74:6), 1998, pp. 1516-1530.

Cook, K. S. "The Microfoundations of Social Structure: An Exchange Perspective," in J. Huber (ed.), *Macro-Micro Linkages in Sociology*, Newbury Park, CA: Sage Publicatoins, 1991, pp. 29-45.

Craig, S. C., Niemi, R. G., and Silver, G. E. "Political Efficacy and Trust: A Report on the NES Pilot Study Items," *Political Behavior* (12:3), 1990, pp. 289-314.

Day, D. "Citizen Participation in the Planning Process: An Essentially Contested Concept?," *Journal of Planning Literature* (11:3), 1997, pp. 421-434.

Edwards, A. R. "The Moderator as an Emerging Democratic Intermediary: The Role of the Moderator in Internet Discussion about Public Issues," *Information Polity* (7), 2002, pp. 3-20.

Fornell, C. *A Second Generation of Multivariate Analysis: Methods* (Volume 1), New York: Praeger, 1982.

Fornell, C., and Larcker, D. "Evaluating Structural Equation Models with Unobservable Variables and Measurement Error," *Journal of Marketing Research* (18), 1987, pp. 39-50.

Fulk, J., Flanagin, A. J., Kalman, M. E., Monge, P. R., and Ryan, T. "Connective and Communal Public Goods in Interactive Communication Systems," *Communication Theory* (6:1), 1996, pp. 60-87.

Gamson, W. A. *The Strategy of Social Protest*, Homewood, IL: Dorsey, 1975.

Hair, J. F., Anderson, R. E., Tatham, R. L., and Black, W. C. *Multivariate Data Analysis with Readings* (5th ed.), New York: Macmillan, 1998.

Hiltz, S. R., and Turoff, M. *The Network Nation: Human Communication via Computer*, Cambridge, MA: MIT Press, 1978.

Institute of Politics. "The Institute of Politics Survey of Student Attitudes: A National Survey of College Undergraduates," John F. Kennedy School of Government, Harvard University, 2002 (available online at http://www.iop.harvard.edu/pdfs/survey/2002.pdf).

Irvin, R. A., and Stansbury, J. "Citizen Participation in Decision Making: Is it Worth the Effort?," *Public Administration Review* (64:1), 2004, pp. 55-65.

Jarvis, S. E., Montoya, L., and Mulvoy, E. "The Political Participation of Working Youth and College Students," Circle Working Paper (36), August 2005 (available online at http://www.civicyouth.org/PopUps/WorkingPapers/WP36Jarvis.pdf).

Karau, S., and Williams, K. "Social Loafing: A Meta-Analytic Review and Theoretical Integration," *Journal of Personality and Social Psychology* (65:4), 1993, pp. 681-706.

Kumar, N., and Benbasat, I. "Para-Social Presence and Communication Capabilities of a Web Site," *e-Service Journal* (1:3), 2001, pp. 5-25.

Kumar, N., and Vragov, R. "The Citizen Participation Continuum: Where Does the US Stand?," in *Proceedings of the 11th America's Conference on Information Systems,* Omaha, NE, August 11-14, 2005, pp. 1984-1990.

Lyons, W., and Alexander, R. "A Tale of Two Electorates: Generational Replacement and the Decline of Voting in Presidential Elections," *Journal of Politics* (62), 2000, pp. 1014-1034.

Monge, P., Fulk, J., Kalman, M., Flanagin, A., Parnassa, C., and Rumsey, S. "Production of Collective Action in Alliance-Based Interorganizational Communication and Information Systems," *Organization Science* (9:3), 1998, pp. 411-433.

Moore, G. C., and Benbasat, I. "Development of an Instrument to Measure Perceptions of Adopting an Information Technology Innovation," *Information Systems Research* (2:3), 1991, pp. 192-222.

Nadeau, R., Niemi, R. G., and Amato, T. "Emotions, Issue Importance, and Political Learning," *American Journal of Political Science* 39(3), 1995, pp. 558-574.

Niemi, R. G., Craig, S. C., and Mattei, F. "Measuring Internal Political Efficacy in the 1988 National Election Study," *American Political Science Review* (85:4), 1991, pp. 1407-1413.

Nunnally, J. *Psychometric Theory* (3rd ed.), New York: McGraw-Hill Education, 1994.

Olson, M. *The Logic of Collective Action: Public Goods and the Theory of Groups*, Cambridge, MA: Harvard University Press, 1965.

Parry, G., Moyser, G., and Day, N. *Political Participation and Democracy in Britain*, New York: Cambridge University Press, 1992.

Pattie, C., Seyd, P., and Whiteley, P. "Citizen and Civic Engagement: Attitudes and Behavior in Britain," *Political Studies* (51), 2003, pp. 443-468.

Pew Research Center. "Internet Sapping Broadcast News Audience," June 11, 2000 (available online at http://www.people-press.org/reports/display.php3?ReportID=36).

Rosenstone, S. J., and Hansen, J. M. *Mobilization, Participation, and Democracy in America*, New York: MacMillan, 1993.

Rubenson, D. "Participation and Politics: Social Capital, Civic Voluntarism, and Institutional Context," paper presented at the Political Studies Association-UK 50th Annual Conference, London, April 10-13, 2000.

Sambamurthy, V., and Chin, W. W. "The Effects of Group Attitudes Toward Alternative GDSS Designs on the Decision-Making Performance of Computer-Supported Groups," *Decision Science* (25: 2), 1994, pp. 215-41.

Scholzman, K., Verba, S., and Brady. H. "Participation's Not a Paradox: The View from American Activists," *British Journal of Political Science* (25), 1995, pp. 1-36.

Seyd, P., and Whiteley, P. *Labor Grass Roots: The Politics of Party Membership*, Oxford, UK: Clarendon Press, 1992.

Seyd, P., Whiteley, P., and Pattie, C. "Citizenship in Britain: Attitudes and Behavior," *The Political Quarterly* (72:1), 2001, pp. 141-148.

Taylor, S., and Todd, P. A. "Understanding Information Technology Usage: A Test of Competing Models," *Information Systems Research* (6:2), 1995, pp. 144-176.

Thrane, L. E., Shelley II, M. C., Shulman, S. W., Beisser, S. R., and Larson, T. B. "E-Political Involvement: Age Effects or Attitudinal Barriers?," *Journal of E-Government* (1:4), 2004, pp. 21-37.

UNPAN. *UN Global E-Government Readiness Report*, United Nations, 2005, (available online at http://www.unpan.org/egovernment5.asp).

Verba, S., and Nie, N. *Participation in America: Political Democracy and Social Equality*, New York: Harper and Row, 1972.

Verba, S., Schlozman, K, and Brady, H. *Voice and Equality: Civic Voluntarism in American Politics*, Cambridge, MA: Harvard University Press, 1995.

Vinluan, G., Teo, A., Seah, V., Grewal, H., and Sidek, I. (eds.). *Quarterly Newsletter of the Feedback Unit*, January 2005 (available online at http://www.gov.sg/).

Whiteley, P. "National Choice and Political Participation—Evaluating the Debate," *Political Research Quarterly* (48), 1995, pp. 211-234.

Whyte, A., and Macintosh, A. "Analysis and Evaluation of E-Consultations," *e-Service Journal* (2:1), 2002, pp. 9-34.

About the Authors

Chee Wei Phang is currently a doctoral student in the Department of Information Systems, School of Computing, at the National University of Singapore. His research interests include eGovernment, eParticipation, IT-induced organizational change, IT innovation adoption, and knowledge management. His work has been published or is forthcoming in *IEEE Transactions on Engineering Management* and top-tier information systems conferences such as the International Conference on Information Systems, the European Conference on Information Systems, the Hawaii International Conference on System Sciences, and the Americas Conference on Information Systems. He is a member of the Association for Information Systems. Phang can be reached at phangcw@comp.nus.edu.sg.

Atreyi Kankanhalli is an assistant professor in the Department of Information Systems, School of Computing, at the National University of Singapore. She received her Ph.D. in information systems for the National University of Singapore. Atreyi has been a visiting scholar at the Haas Business School, University of California, Berkeley, and the Indian Institute of Science, Bangalore. Prior to joining NUS, she had considerable experience in industrial research and development, and has consulted for a number of organizations including the World Bank. Atreyi's work has been published in journals such as *MIS Quarterly*, *Journal of the American Society of Information Science and Technology*, *Communications of the ACM*, *Decision Support Systems*, and *International Journal of Information Management*. She has presented research at conferences including the International Conference on Information Systems, the Hawaii International Conference on System Sciences, and the Workshop on Information Technologies and Systems. She has served or is serving on several IS conference committees such as PACIS, ICKM, and IRMA and on the editorial boards of *International Journal of Knowledge Management*, *Journal of Global Information Management*, and *Journal of Information Privacy and Security*. Her research interests include knowledge management, eGovernment, virtual teams, and information systems security. Atreyi can be reached at atreyi@comp.nus.edu.sg.

9   CYBERSOLIDARITY: Internet-Based Campaigning and Trade Union Internationalism

Bruce Robinson
University of Salford
Salford, U.K.

Abstract   *E-mail campaigns are one form of cybersolidarity— action at a distance mediated by use of the Internet in support of trade unions or groups of workers. This paper, taking the example of a campaign in support of imprisoned Eritrean trade unionists, examines the social organization and information flows underlying such campaigns. These are discussed in the light of the effectiveness of such actions, their capacity to overcome the global digital divide, current debates on the role of the Internet in the remaking of trade unionism, and labor's capacity to remake the spatial relations of capitalism.*

1   PROLOGUE: CYBERSOLIDARITY IN ACTION

Three Eritrean trade union leaders were arrested and illegally held on March 30 and April 9, 2005. News of this emerged 6 weeks later via the international trade union federations with which their unions were affiliated. The Geneva-based International Union of Food, Agricultural, Hotel, Restaurant, Catering, Tobacco and Allied Workers' Associations (IUF) made a call to protest to the Eritrean government.

The campaign was picked up by the trade union news service Labour Start from the Web site of the IUF and a link provided among the day's news stories. Another link urged visitors to "Act Now," leading to the text of a letter to the Eritrean government calling for their release that could be dispatched with the addition of some minimal personal information. These letters were forwarded to Eritrean embassies round the world. At the same time, details of the campaign were sent to the 31,000 subscribers to Labour Start's e-list with a link to the "Act Now!" page.

The campaign was taken up by other organizations and over 5,000 e-mails were sent within a week (1,500 in the first 14 hours) through Labour Start and other Web sites

Please use the following format when citing this chapter:

Robinson, B., 2006, in IFIP International Federation for Information Processing, Volume 208, Social Inclusion: Societal and Organizational Implications for Information Systems, eds. Trauth, E., Howcroft, D., Butler, T., Fitzgerald, B., DeGross, J., (Boston: Springer), pp. 123-135.

taking a news feed from it. The U.S. Campaign for Labor Rights and the Stop Killer Coke campaign sent it off to their e-lists—one of those arrested worked at Coca Cola. The UK campaign "No Sweat" picketed the embassy in London. UK Coca Cola workers and their union, the GMB, gave support. The umbrella international union federation, the ICFTU, has now taken up the case with the International Labour Organisation. While it has not led to the freeing of the trade unionists, it has certainly been noticed by Eritrean embassies, one of which phoned to request that no further messages were sent to its fax machine!

While other campaigns may have been more successful in reaching their aims or attracted more participants, the Eritrean campaign throws a spotlight on a number of issues of interest from the viewpoint of both IS researchers and labor activists.

2   INTRODUCTION

This e-mail campaign is one example of what we shall call *cybersolidarity*: Internet-mediated action in support of trade unions or groups of workers involved in disputes with employers or the state. An e-mail campaign is only one form of cyber-solidarity. Others include "info war" or "hacktivism" where the information assets of a target are attacked over the net (Walker 2002), boycott campaigns, and the collection of funds.

This paper will consider the organization and working of e-mail cybersolidarity campaigns and use this analysis to assess their effectiveness and value in trade union action. For reasons outlined below, the analysis will focus on the relationships between, and roles of, participants in the action and the information flows between them. This informational analysis indicates a possible area for IS researchers to contribute to the understanding of and development of social movements.

The material used is largely drawn from documentation publicly available on the World Wide Web or received by the author as a participant in labor-oriented e-lists and e-mail actions since the 1990s. Some of this material is ephemeral in that it is removed from public access as one campaign follows another.[1] Of particular value have been the regular reflections by Eric Lee of Labour Start on the effectiveness of various activities undertaken through that Web site. He has also kindly responded to my questions.

My own participation has enabled me to follow Kendall's (1999) recommendation for Internet researchers to be involved in the online forums they are researching as a means of better understanding the processes at work in the interactions they are describing. This participation reflects a commitment both to the goal of using the Internet to support trade unions as a means of emancipatory action and, at the same time, to reflecting on the nature and effectiveness of these actions as a critical researcher.

This paper examines the operation and effectiveness of campaigns such as the Eritrean and puts them in the context of the broader issues concerning implications of

---

[1]Material relating to the Eritrean campaign can be found at http://www.labourstart.org/ cgi-bin/dbman/db.cgi?db=2005&uid=default&view_records=1&sb=4&so=descend&labstart_ jump=1&keyword=eritrea.

globalization, the Internet, and networked activism for labor. A brief history will first indicate the development of union use of the Internet. E-mail campaigns will then be contextualized in terms of a number of issues raised in the academic literature before more detailed analysis in terms of the social organization and information flows that make them possible.

3   THE PRE-HISTORY OF CYBERSOLIDARITY

The drive toward using the Internet as a vehicle for international trade union solidarity has not, on the whole, come from within the formal structures of trade unions themselves. Rather it has depended on a process of convincing both unions and their members and supporters of its value. Although this continues, the decisive period—in developed countries, at least—can be seen as the mid to late 1990s. Alongside the pressure toward international action from globalization, two factors were particularly important.

The first was advocacy and support from a number of people with a political commitment to the trade union movement who were also enthusiasts for the use of ICTs for these goals. They proselytized for the use of the Internet and began to create institutions ranging from Web sites to training centers that would support this activity. The Labour Telematics Centre in Manchester, U.S. Labornet, which produced a number of internationally affiliated imitators, Labor Tech conferences on use of the new media and ICTs, Eric Lee's book on trade unions and the Internet (1996) (which preceded his own Labour Start site), and the Cyber Picket Line directory all began to encourage and develop trade union interest in the Internet in this period.

Alongside advocacy of technology use, there were a number of high profile industrial disputes which demonstrated the immediate practical value of computer-mediated communications, particularly for winning support across national boundaries. The 1996-1998 Liverpool Dockers' Dispute showed the value of CMC in setting up acts of solidarity across international boundaries, which enabled them to evade the local constraints of strict anti-union laws and organize face-to-face meetings across the world. It also provided the spur to the setting up of UK Labournet (Bailey 1997; Renton 2004). The ICEM's international campaign against the Bridgestone tire company showed how it was possible to mobilize individuals internationally in cyberspace and to use the technology (in this case, the company's Web site) to wage "information warfare" in pursuit of a trade union dispute (Herod 1998a; Walker 2002). The South Korean general strike of 1996-1997 used the Internet to build support around the world.

Activities in this period laid the basis for the growth of "net-internationalism." Cybersolidarity has developed under the enabling power of widened access to the technology and the driving force of globalization and the resistance to it. Some of the pioneers have remained active and continue to play an important role in the creation and maintenance of the infrastructure and information flows required to support cyber-solidarity.

4   THEORIZING CYBERSOLIDARITY: FOUR RESEARCH AREAS

Cybersolidarity is a multifaceted phenomenon: a form of action involving trade unions; a form of cyberactivism and social movement; action across space, potentially on a global scale; and a complex structure of human activity mediated by information flows. This paper, therefore, draws on a number of related and converging areas, each of which throws up questions of relevance to an understanding of cybersolidarity.

4.1 Trade Unions and the Internet

The implications of Internet use can vary widely according to the differing organizational contexts within which it occurs (Bennett, 2003). Thus while pro-labor activism shares many features with broader cyberactivism—most generally, the development of activist networks and the use of ICTs in support of a social movement—it has a number of specific features that are important (Bailey 1999). Trade unions existed long before the Internet and their structures and ideology affect how their members take up new forms of communication (Lucio Martinez and Walker, 2005). Particular "e-forms" (Greene et al. 2003) of established activities result.

The spread of the Internet encountered a trade union movement faced with a crisis. Globalization and the shift in industrial production to countries of the South corresponds to the development of labor movements in those countries, while facing those in the North with decline (Monck 2002). A remaking of trade unionism with an international dimension is consequently widely recognized to be necessary.

The role of the Internet in this is now generally recognized but its precise contribution and potentialities are still the subject of debate. Hodkinson (2001) asks "Will the new union internationalism be a 'net-internationalism'?" His negative response focuses both on political and social obstacles to internationalism per se and on what he sees as the limitations of the Internet, particularly the global digital divide. In contrast, Castells (2000) simply dismisses the potential of labor internationalism because he believes labor is exhausted as an emancipatory force as a result of its "desocialization" and "individuation" (pp. 505-506; see also Waterman 1998). Waterman (2001) and Monck (2002), accept much of Castells' analysis of the network society but dispute his conclusion, arguing that unions themselves should take on the network form typical of Internet activism. Still others believe that ICTs can at best be a useful supplement to more traditional forms of international union solidarity (e.g., Renton 2004).

How much, then, are cybersolidarity actions part of an effective remaking of trade union action in the face of globalization?   How do they support trade union internationalism?

4.2 Trade Union Action and the Global Digital Divide

The impact of the Internet on trade unions is not uniform but reflects broader inequalities. Can these be overcome? The Eritrean campaign spanned the global digital divide. Eritrea comes 149th in the world for Internet users, according to UNCTAD, and was the last country in Africa to be connected to the Internet. While one trade union federation in Eritrea has an e-mail address (one of the 9,500 Internet users in 2003), African unions generally face major problems in exploiting ICTs, mostly endemic to their societies as with the absence of infrastructure and cost; others are more specific to unions such as resources and priorities (Bélanger n.d.). Yet, despite this technological gap, the Eritrean campaign was taken up by individuals and organizations across the globe. How far, then, can activist networks provide a way around the absence of direct access to technology?

4.3 Labor and the Remaking of Spatial Relations

A major theme in critical approaches in geography is the notion that spatial relations are remade through social practices and their relationships to physical and social structures. "Space [is] not merely an inert stage on which social life simply plays itself out, but rather a social product" (Herod 2003, p. 507). Thus space is counterposed to place, in the sense of a physical location. One aspect of this debate concerns the different spatial scales—local, national, regional, and global—at which action should be taken if it is to be successful as a response to globalization.

The notions of space and the making of geographical scale are linked directly to the remaking of trade union internationalism (Waterman and Wills 2001). Two issues arise: first, the relation between the local and the global and whether trade union actions and structures necessarily have to be global to be effective against multinationals; second, whether and how labor can play an active role in the remodeling of spatial relations implied by globalization or whether it merely responds to the remaking of those relations by capital. Can trade unions and their supporters take action to remake the spatial structure in which they operate to their advantage? Herod (2001) has argued that the remaking of space by labor has tended to be downplayed in favor of its dominance by a globalizing capital. He has given a number of examples of this including the use of computer-mediated communication to redefine the spatial scope of action (Herod 1998a, 2001).

Labor solidarity is part of this remaking of spatial relations. For Herod, "the practice of labor solidarity is an inherently geographical one…a process of opening up the landscape and making the connections between workers in different parts of the globe visible" (2003, p. 509). It involves "the manipulation of space by workers and unions [which] is a potent form of social power [which] flows through spatial structures just as it flows through social structures" (Herod 1998b, p. 5). How far then does cybersolidarity actively shift the scale of trade union action? What are its spatial implications?

4.4 Cybersolidarity as Internet Activism

Despite the peculiarities of trade union use of the Internet, cybersolidarity remains a form of cyberactivism (McCaughey and Ayers 2003), dependent on the commitment and participation of individuals who identify with its goals in activist networks.

In summing up the motivations of "Internet-worked social movements" inspired by the consequences of globalization, Langman (2005, p. 52) notes four "mediations between injustice and adversity, which are often far removed from personal experience, and actual participation in a social movement." They are: "(1) information and the way it is framed; (2) a personal identity that is receptive to this information; (3) a structural location that is conducive to activism; (4) linkages or ties with networks of social actors with similar concerns."

The rooting of cybersolidarity in a preexisting trade union movement points to an identity and location that can underpin specific campaigns. However, it is clear that it is the relations between groups of actors as mediated by information that are crucial in forming effective and active networks. Our analysis of e-mail campaigns, therefore, takes the form of identifying the actors involved in different aspects of the action and the information flows between them. The latter link and coordinate the actors in pursuit of an overall goal. Thus the underlying social organization and information flows play important roles in defining the effectiveness and transformational power of campaigns. By examining this structure and its implications we can begin to answer some of the broader issues raised above. Our focus is on Labour Start as the most wide ranging and technologically innovative site.

5   THE SOCIAL AND INFORMATIONAL STRUCTURE OF CYBERSOLIDARITY

There are three major groups of actors necessarily involved in a cybersolidarity action: the protagonists in the labor dispute; the intermediaries concerned with supplying the information about it and setting up and monitoring the action; and the respondents who take part in the action. Each acts in a distinct way in response to an initial triggering event and, although their actions are coordinated to serve a single goal, the differences between them and how these are overcome are central to defining the implications of this form of action.

5.1 The Protagonists

An act of solidarity starts naturally with a triggering event such as the imprisonment of trade unionists in Eritrea. The instigators may be the state, the employer, a union organization, or a group of workers. The triggering event is place-based, although it may occur across a number of physical locations. From the viewpoint of the cybersolidarity action, two groups provide the overall framework through their position in the dispute.

- *The subjects*: Those in whose support the action is taken. They may be those directly calling for the action or the call may come from an organization that represents them (in our case, the IUF). It is worth noting that the subjects of the call may have no direct involvement in it and only become aware that the action has been taken after the fact.

- ***The target***: Those the action seeks to influence, in our case the Eritrean government. This may be more than one organization across a wide range: a company,
  state organization or government, employers' organizations, even sometimes trade
  unionists themselves.[2] They are not necessarily those most immediately involved
  in the dispute. It may, for example, be more effective to urge a multinational to
  intervene with a subcontractor to resolve a dispute than to seek to influence the subcontractor directly. The target will typically be unaware of the action until they
  begin to receive e-mails or faxes.

The protagonists typically enter the cybersolidarity action at its start and its end.
The action is initiated by or on behalf of the subjects through a call for support; the
target receives the flow of information generated by the action and the action ends when
it is felt that it will no longer bring about useful pressure on the target.

5.2 The Intermediaries

The subsequent course of a cybersolidarity action depends crucially on a range of
intermediaries who structure and initiate the information flows that underlie the action
and who define and present the action to those who take part in it.

These intermediaries have several functions which are conceptually separable. In
practice, they may be carried out by the same people.

- ***Information source:*** The first is acting as an information source that provides the
  link between the triggering action and the organizer of the online action. This need
  not be done by those directly involved, which suggests the digital divide need not
  be an obstacle here. It can be an organization to which they belong or which
  supports them; in the case of Eritrea, it was the international union federation to
  which their unions belong.

Other sources include media reports and other activists and some Web sites enlist
volunteers to help. For example, China Labor Report, based in New York, has
sources providing information inside China, which has enabled them to run very
precisely targeted e-mail campaigns. Labour Start has a network of correspondents,
who have volunteered to provide Labour Start with current news stories from
different countries or sectors. Labour Start also provides a means for any user of
the Web site to submit stories or information not found elsewhere on the site.

- ***Information gatherer:*** This role consists of bringing together information and
  making it available for presentation on the Net. This may be an automated process,
  as when Web sites are scanned for items that may relate to trade union issues.
  Alternatively, individuals may have responsibility for covering particular countries
  or industries in order to ensure thorough coverage, as with Labour Start correspondents.

---

[2]Often messages of support are sent to workers in dispute to encourage them in their action
rather than to influence an employer or government.

At this stage, the basic information is available but the call has yet to be presented in a form to which anyone can respond electronically.

- *Networkers:* The next category of intermediaries are those that run the Web sites, e-lists, or other online mechanisms for campaigning. They form the key link between those who request a campaign and those that respond to it. The term networkers, which we borrow from Waterman (see Herod 1998a), does not do justice to the range of functions they undertake, which include

  — Maintaining the infrastructure that enables the dissemination of the information and the campaigning (e.g., Web sites, e-lists).
  — Collating, editing and making the information available in an easily accessible form.
  — Initiating, monitoring, and backing up the campaigns.
  — Building and maintaining a constituency of potential participants in campaigns.

These functions may be distributed among a team with varying emphasis put on each of them by different Web masters. Typically with trade union related sites, the networkers are technically qualified people who have a commitment to the labor movement.

The overall control of cybersolidarity actions is in their hands in that they decide what information to make available through their Net resources and which calls to take up as appeals for action. A number of concerns is involved in these decisions. One is the origin of the call for support and its relationship to the subjects of the action. Labour Start has the position that a call should come from an official trade union organization.[3] Eric Lee goes further: "The best campaigns are the ones run with the full support both of the local union... sister unions in the same sector in different countries, as well as the global union federation" (Lee 2004a). In contrast, Labour Net UK places emphasis on "contributions and reports from rank and file trade unionists, although we also welcome contributions from trade union organizations,"[4] recognizing that workers in dispute may also be in conflict with union structures (as was the case with the Liverpool dockers). This difference is also reflected in the user identity to which they appeal.

Labour Start also tends to select campaigns around issues of workers' rights, rather than privatization or wages, believing that they have a broader appeal (Lee 2004a).

Other considerations emerge from the need to build a constituency that uses a site regularly and is prepared to take part in actions. Alongside concerns about information quality and timeliness are others, including avoiding bombarding readers with appeals they are less likely to read and act upon.

At this stage, the information is presented in a form that both gives the background to the dispute and the *pro forma* letter that, on Labour Start at least, can be edited before being sent.

---

[3]Personal communication with Eric Lee, 2003.
[4]"What is LabourNet" (http://www.labournet.net/whatis.html).

5.3 Respondents

Up to now, our analysis has been concerned with the flows of information and forms of action that enable a cybersolidarity action to take place. We now move to those directly involved in taking the suggested action. Here questions of a personal identity that is receptive to the information and a structural location that is conducive to activism become important in forming the basis for joining a network and responding to calls to take action.

In the case of trade unions, there is a preexisting ethos of solidarity and inter-nationalism and organizational identities as trade unionists to which an appeal can be made. These ideas do not lose their importance as a means of collective identity because of the individualistic nature of Internet use. Rather, users bring their social identities, including such norms, into the virtual collective (Brunsting and Postmes 2002; Kendall 1999).

It is possible for networkers to orient their Web sites to appeal to such preexisting identities and exploit them as an aid to mobilization (Robinson 2003). Labour Start promotes itself as the place where "trade unionists start their day on the Net." The site contains little that seeks to convince people to join a union but rather sees its role as servicing existing trade unionists in terms of information, campaigns, and technology. The identity is not one that emphasizes the differences between general secretaries and rank and file members as with Labour Net UK.

With a couple of mouse clicks, it is possible to find the information and send the letter to a prescribed recipient. Yet, however well a Web site appeals to a collective identity and however easy it is, involvement in online campaigns is ultimately an individual decision. The extent of responses to particular campaigns may vary con-siderably, not always in proportion to the inherent importance of the issue (Lee 2004b).

Greene et al. (2002) see peaks and troughs as characteristic of participation in trade unionism in general. However, some characteristics of cybersolidarity emphasize this. Participants do not necessarily have any incentive to move from one campaign to the next. Rather the very ease of participating means that the campaigning requires less consistent or deep commitment than a more long-term campaign. The incorporation of the individual into the network remains limited and, in deciding whether to participate in a given campaign, he or she may be swayed by other considerations such as time, "compassion fatigue," or the geographical closeness and familiarity of the dispute (Lee 2004b).

5.4 Assessing Campaigns

It is only when respondents act that the flow of information is transformed into a means of pressure on a target and re-enters the arena of the real world dispute that triggered the action. The subsequent impact of cybersolidarity action on the outcome of an industrial dispute is very difficult to assess. There are two measures of success (Lee 2005). The first depends on the impact of the whole action on the dispute. Here some indication of success is dependent on feedback from the direct participants, whether the subjects of the action or the targets. This might not give a true picture of the real impact of the action and it is difficult otherwise to ascribe a precise assessment of its role in the global outcome of a dispute (e.g., winning a strike).

The second measure is a measure of how far the action has served to mobilize respondents to take part in it. This is a quantitative measure in terms of the number of e-mails sent in response to a call. The wide range of responses to different campaigns points to each respondent deciding on every campaign separately and as an individual.

There is no necessary correlation between the two measures of success, a consequence of the structure of cybersolidarity action as outlined. Lee contrasts the Eritrean campaign (high mobilization but so far no result) with a low mobilization, highly focused, but successful campaign for the reinstatement of workers at a hotel in the Bahamas (Lee 2005)—one of several successes at hotels. It is possible that certain types of target (e.g., those concerned with brand reputation or potential consumer reaction) are more susceptible to e-mail campaigns than repressive governments.

6 IMPLICATIONS

The forms of social organization and the mediating information flows implied by the nature of cybersolidarity have implications that enable us to address questions of the digital divide, the remaking of spatial relations, and the possibilities and limitations of Internet-mediated international trade union action.

Such action is in some sense a proxy action. For the respondents who act in it, it is mediated by the form in which the information is presented to them by the Web site or other means of transmission. The subjects of the action are not directly present at this stage and may not, or only minimally, be present in the whole process. This has some advantages: it means that the absence of direct access to the Internet or possession of the technology need not be an obstacle to obtaining support through the Net. To this extent, cybersolidarity can overcome the digital divide. It is also a necessity when, as in our example, the subjects of the action sit in jail or are otherwise unable to act freely.

Nevertheless, there are obvious disadvantages to this. Control of the action is in the hands of the networkers rather than those directly affected by the outcome of the action. Mostly this does not lead to problems as the networkers take steps to keep contact where possible and to ensure that the action corresponds to their wishes, even if expressed indirectly. There is, however, the potential danger of conflicts of interest here. The ability of networkers to choose news and select which campaigns are taken up as actions also lays them open to accusations of favoritism or censorship (as in a claim that Labour Start was insufficiently reporting Palestinian news).

The remoteness of respondents and subjects in the action need not be an obstacle to subsequent face-to-face interaction, as when "No Sweat" organized a trade union delegation to Mexico following a cybersolidarity action undertaken in support of workers on strike at a subcontractor for Puma in 2002. Davies (n.d., p. 4) notes that it is "extremely rare for online campaigning and 'virtual' associations to be entirely divorced from traditional, offline, place-based and face-to-face campaigns."

A cybersolidarity action clearly enables action across spatial scales that were not previously easily accessible to the actors, "opening up the landscape and making the connections between workers in different parts of the globe visible" (Herod 2003, p. 509). This has been the result of the active creation and maintenance of a new form of action.

However there is little evidence that this has resulted in a "spatial fix" (Harvey 1996), a redefinition of the spatial parameters in the relations between capital and labor, such that it has become something generally taken into account in decisions by employers, at least outside certain highly consumer-sensitive industries such as clothing. The place-based legal and social conditions still play a dominant role in industrial disputes, although creative use of the Internet may enable trade unionists to evade local restrictions (see Grieco and Bhopal 2005).

Unless it results—accidentally or deliberately—in damage to the target's information resources or infrastructure, a cybersolidarity action does not have the direct effect on the target that place-based solidarity actions such as a sympathy strike, a human picket line, or a refusal to handle an organization's goods can have. The individual nature of the response means that it does not have the collective cohesion and power of place-based actions. A virtual presence is not a substitute. This is recognized by those who organize Internet actions. Lee (2004a) notes that, "The most successful online campaigns feature strong offline elements as well, including picket lines and other protests. They are not exclusively online." But action in cyberspace can also serve to provide the spark that leads to place-based action too (as with the pickets over Eritrea). The two supplement each other. Cybersolidarity also acts as an indication to the target that there exists a spreading awareness of a dispute and a willingness to exert pressure. This can be important in winning a dispute.

7 CONCLUSIONS

This paper has examined one form of labor-oriented cyberactivism, looking at its impact on the practice of international trade union solidarity through the lens of the social relations and information flows associated with it. This points to both the strengths and weaknesses of e-mail solidarity actions, both as an aid to effective trade union struggles, a response to the global nature of capital, and a means for overcoming the global digital divide.

While Internet-enabled communications have made possible a new range of possibilities for trade union action, perhaps unsurprisingly, e-mail actions do not replace place-based forms of solidarity, although they can remain valuable as a means of support and, in the case of workers facing repression, may be one of the only forms of protest open. They may tip the balance of disputes in certain circumstances and serve to awaken and nurture a feeling of solidarity among those who respond. "Net internationalism" does not replace more traditional forms but becomes a weapon alongside them, through which they can become more effective.

References

Bailey, C. "The Labour Movement and the Internet," AMRC Archive, 1999 (http://www.amrc.org.hk/Arch/3401.htm).

Bailey, C. "Towards a Global Labournet," 1997 (http://lmedia.nodong.net/1997/article/w4-2e.html).

Bélanger, M. *The Digital Development of Labuor Organisations in Africa*, Turin: ILO International Training Centre, n.d.

Bennett, W. L. "Communicating Global Activism," *Information, Communication and Society* (6:2), March 2003, pp. 143-168.

Brunsting, S., and Postmes, T. "Social Movement Participation in the Online Age: Predicting Offline and Online Collective Action," *Small Group Research* (33:5), 2002, pp. 525-554.

Castells, M. *The Rise of the Network Society* (2nd ed.), Oxford, UK: Basil Blackwell, 2000.

Davies, W. *Trade Union Movement and the Internet: Lessons from Civil Society*, London: IPPR, n.d.

Grieco, M., and Bhopal, M. "Globalisation, Collective Action and Counter-Coordination: The Use of the New Information Communication Technology by the Malaysian Labour Movement," *Critical Perspectives on International Business* (1:2/3), pp. 109-122

Greene, A. M., Hogan, J., and Grieco, M. "E-Collectivism: Emergent Opportunities for Renewal," 2002 (http://www.geocities.com/e_collectivism/papers/madrid.html).

Harvey, D. *Justice, Nature and the Geography of Difference*, Oxford, UK: Basil Blackwell, 1996.

Herod, A. "Of Blocs, Flows and Networks: The End of the Cold War, Cyberspace and the Geo-Economics of Organized Labor at the *Fin de Millenaire*," in A. Herod, G. O. Tuathail, and S. M. Roberts (eds.), *An Unruly World? Globalization, Governance and Geography*, London: Routledge, 1998a, pp. 162-194.

Herod, A. "Geographies of Labor Internationalism," *Social Science History* (27:4), 2003, pp. 501-23.

Herod, A. *Labor Geographies: Workers and the Landscapes of Capitalism*, New York: Guilford Press, 2001.

Herod, A. "The Spatiality of Labor Unionism: A Review Essay," in A. Herod (ed.), *Organizing the Landscape: Geographical Perspectives on Labor Unionism*, Minneapolis, MN: University of Minnesota Press, 1998b, pp. 1-36.

Hodkinson, S. "Problems@Labor: Towards a Net-Internationalism?," 2001 (www.globalstudiesassociation.org/conference1papers/Problems1.doc).

Kendall, L. "Recontextualizing 'Cyberspace': Methodological Considerations for On-Line Research," in S. Jones (ed.), *Doing Internet Research*, Thousand Oaks, CA: Sage Publications, 1999, pp. 57-74.

Langman, L. "From Virtual Public Spheres to Global Justice: A Critical Theory of Internetworked Social Movements," *Sociological Theory* (23:1), 1, 2005, pp. 42-74.

Lee, E. "Building International Solidarity, One Campaign at a Time," 2005 (http://www.ericlee.me.uk/archive/000117.html#more).

Lee, E. "How to Win an Online Campaign," 2004a (http://www.ericlee.me.uk/archive/000094.html#more).

Lee, E. *The Labor Movement and the Internet: The New Internationalism*, London: Pluto Press, 1996.

Lee, E. "Why We Don't Give: Online Donations and International Solidarity," 2004b (http://www.ericlee.me.uk/archive/000077.html).

Martinez Lucio, M., and Walker, S. "The Networked Union? The Internet as a Challenge to Trade Union Identity and Roles," *Critical Perspectives on International Business* (1:2/3), 2005, pp. 137-154.

McCaughey, M., and Ayers, M. D. (eds.). *Cyberactivism: Online Activism in Theory and Practice*, London: Routledge, 2003.

Monck, R. *Globalization and Labor: The new "Great Transformation,"* London: Zed Books, 2002.

Renton, D. "The Means to Fight Globalization? Using the Internet to Support Rank-and-File Trade Unionism," 2004 (http://www.dkrenton.co.uk/research/edgepaper.html).

Robinson, B. "Building a Constituency for Online Activism: The Labour Start Experience," paper delivered at the Workshop on Social Movement Informatics, Leeds Metropolitan University, 2003.

Walker, S. "To Picket Just Click It! Social Netwar and Industrial Conflict in a Global Economy," IMRIP 2002-1, Leeds Metropolitan University School of Information Management, 2002.

Waterman, P. "The Brave New World of Manuel Castells: What on Earth (or in the Ether) Is Going On?," Global Solidarity Dialogue, 1998 (www.antenna.nl/~waterman/castells.html).

Waterman, P. "16 Propositions on International Labor (and Other?) Networking," 2001 (http://www.lmu.ac.uk/ies/im/people/swalker/labournetworking/pw16props-31-5-01.htm).

Waterman, P., and Wills, J. *Place, Space and the New Labour Internationalisms*, Oxford, UK: Basil Blackwell, 2001.

About the Author

Bruce Robinson is Honorary Research Fellow in the Informatics Research Institute at the University of Salford, UK. His research interests include the theoretical foundations of critical IS research and the use of ICTs by social movements. He is also active in the anti-sweatshop movement. Bruce can be reached at bruce@dolphy.eclipse.co.uk.

10 ICT POLICIES AS A MEANS TO INHIBIT SOCIAL EXCLUSION: The South African Case

Edgar A. Maldonado
Nicolai A. Pogrebnyakov
Annemijn F. van Gorp
Pennsylvania State University
University Park, PA U.S.A.

Abstract   *Social exclusion is a multi dimensional phenomenon that manifests itself in the exclusion of an individual from one or more of the four following activities: production of goods and services, consumption, civil engagement, and social interaction. Information and communication technologies (ICTs) have been argued to have the potential to reduce these forms of social exclusion. However, the extent to which they deal with these different forms of social exclusion remains unknown. Therefore, in this study we examine how ICT policies in South Africa are being employed to reduce social exclusion. In particular, we analyze which dimensions of social exclusion are targeted in telecommunication laws and one of the ICT initiatives of the South African government, Multi-Purpose Community Centers (MPCCs). Using a framework that portrays the four forms of social exclusion within the discourses used in phenomenon debates (redistributionist, moral underclass, and social integrationist) for analysis, we find that ICT policies in South Africa address two of the four forms of social exclusion: production of goods and services and civil engagement, spanning both the redistributionist and social integrationist discourses of social exclusion.*

Keywords   Social exclusion, information and communication technologies, policy analysis, South Africa

1 INTRODUCTION

Social exclusion entails a multidimensional phenomenon that refers to the exclusion of individuals from full participation in society. It may manifest itself in a variety of

Please use the following format when citing this chapter:

Maldonado, E.A., Pogrebnyakov, N.A., and van Gorp, A.F., 2006, in IFIP International Federation for Information Processing, Volume 208, Social Inclusion: Societal and Organizational Implications for Information Systems, eds. Trauth, E., Howcroft, D., Butler, T., Fitzgerald, B., DeGross, J., (Boston: Springer), pp. 137-150.

forms such as unemployment and lack of quality education. Increased ICT deployment and use are believed by many to have the potential of tackling a wide range of issues resulting from social exclusion such as unemployment, lack of political participation, and limited access to education, as ICTs provide a means for increased access to information and potential for knowledge sharing and learning (Katz and Rice 2002; Kennard 2001; Oden and Rock 2004; Oden and Strover 2002; Tufekcioglu 2003). For this reason, numerous governmental offices around the world have published policies aiming to increase ICT use. However, over the years it has also become clear that the information era in itself has generated and reinforced new forms of inequality and exclusion. A gap is rising between groups of people who can, and who cannot, get access to, and meaningfully use, ICTs. This has also been referred to as the digital divide (Zeitlyn et al. 1998).

Governments have introduced a variety of measures in an attempt to reduce this gap, and efforts have been taken to evaluate the impact of ICT policies. Nevertheless, the implicit conceptualizations of social exclusion in such policies, and hence the way ICT initiatives will inherently affect the digital divide and social exclusion, have not been analyzed thoroughly. Explicating conceptualizations of social exclusion allows insight into exactly which dimensions of social exclusion are targeted through social policies, and may shed light on which aspects need further attention to increase social inclusion.

South Africa constitutes an interesting case with regard to its attempts to increase social inclusion. In spite of being classified as an upper middle-income country,[1] South Africa has one of the greatest income disparities and highest unemployment rates in the world. Reducing inequality and poverty in the post-apartheid environment has been one of the greatest challenges for the government of this country. The economy has grown rapidly since political changes in the 1990s, but unemployment still constituted 31 percent in 2003.[2] While South Africa's telecommunication system is the best developed of the continent, counting more than 4 million fixed line subscribers and already 16 million mobile subscribers, Internet services still reach less than 3 million users that are concentrated in the urban centers of the country.

Hence, in this paper we analyze the extent to which South Africa addresses and handles social exclusion in ICT-related policy documents, and how a specific ICT initiative—the Multi-Purpose Community Centers initiative—deals with the social exclusion phenomenon. We will address the following questions: How do ICT policies address social exclusion in South Africa? How is this further reflected in governmental ICT projects?

The paper is structured as follows: First, we review conceptualizations of social exclusion and their relation to the digital divide. This is followed by a discussion of our methodology. Finally, the results of data analysis are presented and discussed.

---

[1]World Bank country brief for South Africa, 2004, available online through http://www.worldbank.org/.

[2]From the CIA's world factbook for South Africa, 2005; available at http://www.cia.gov/cia/publications/factbook/geos/sf.html.

2   SOCIAL EXCLUSION AND THE DIGITAL DIVIDE

Definitions of social exclusion are abundant. European Union documents define it as a process through which individuals or groups are wholly or partially excluded from full participation in the society in which they live (European Foundation for the Improvement of Living and Working Conditions 1995, p. 4). This definition highlights two aspects of the social exclusion phenomenon: it is a dynamic event and relates to a certain social context. Atkinson (1998) adds a third element, agency, affirming that "exclusion implies an act," thus indicating that a person is either excluded by the society or by his or her own will.

David (2003) discusses various circumstances that may lead to social exclusion: limited knowledge, lack of employment opportunities, low income levels, limited access to state and market services, limited geographical mobility, limited access to education, training and information, discrimination, limited family and community support, and resources. In addition, McDonagh (2006) explains that social exclusion is not only defined by poverty and deprivation, but is part of broader political and structural barriers to opportunities.

The concept of social exclusion used in this paper will be based in the definition of a socially excluded individual as used by Burchardt et al. (1999, p. 229):

An individual is socially excluded if (a) he or she is geographically resident in a society, (b) he or she cannot participate in the normal activities of citizens in that society, and (c) he or she would like to so participate, but is prevented from doing so by factors beyond his or her control.

Normal activities are defined as five types of activity: consumption, generation of savings, production, political, and social (Burchardt et al. 1999).

2.1 Digital Divide

Social exclusion is interwoven in the phenomenon of the digital divide. The digital divide refers to the difference among those with access to information technologies and those without, and has been discussed at three different levels: the global divide, the social divide, and the democratic divide (Norris 2004). The global divide is related to the disparity of access between developed and developing countries. The social divide refers to the divergence of access among social groups in a nation. Finally, the democratic divide refers to the difference among those who use digital tools to engage in civic life and those who do not. The last two aspects are especially important in our discussion as they potentially constitute both cause and effect of social exclusion: both the social and democratic divide describe activities from which individuals are being excluded.

In a report for the European Community, Schienstock (1999) describes how the digital divide can actually lead to social exclusion. The author argues that a lack of technical skills drives people out of the job market, which is one of the first steps to become socially excluded. From this perspective, social exclusion is a consequence of the digital divide phenomenon. Nevertheless, the digital divide per se can be considered a form of social exclusion. In the words of a subject interviewed in Foley's article, whose job was not related to computers: "There is no huge benefit if you learn how to use computers and the Internet. However, if you don learn you are behind socially" (Foley 2004, p. 145). The interviewee did not see the computer as an empowerment tool, but understood that the lack of computer knowledge caused exclusion. Thus, in order to decrease the digital divide, we need to gain a better understanding of one of its basic underlying phenomena, social exclusion, and its many aspects, and bring together these formerly distinct research areas.

2.2 Dimensions of Social Exclusion

Whereas numerous studies have emphasized various aspects of social exclusion, the multidimensionality of the phenomenon has been widely accepted (Bradshaw 2003; Burchardt et al. 1999; Byrne 1999; Percy-Smith 2000; Saunders 2003). For example, Percy-Smith (2000) focused on the political dimension, the neighborhood dimension, the individual dimension, the spatial dimension, and the group dimension. Byrne (1999), citing Madanipour et al. (1998), suggested the following dimensions of the social exclusion phenomenon: political processes, access to employment, integration to the culture, and access to material resources. Although the last factor (access to material resources) could follow from the first three, this does not necessarily have to be the case. Burchardt et al. (1999) take a similar approach and identify five dimensions of social exclusion that are more related with the "normal activities" of a citizen: consumption activities, saving activities, production activities, political activities, and social activities. Finally, Bradshaw (2003) identifies four dimensions of exclusion: consumption, production, political engagement, and social interaction.

In this study we use Bradshaw's description as it integrates both Burchardt et al.'s and Byrne's representations of social exclusion, and additionally defines dimensions of social exclusion that could be addressed by means of ICT deployment. We redefine Bradshaw's third dimension, political engagement, to civil engagement so that it also includes activities where individuals are using governmental services. Table 1 describes the four dimensions.

2.3 Theoretical Framework

The previous section provided a conceptualization of social exclusion, structuring the phenomenon across four dimensions. However, since our goal is to analyze the extent to which South Africa addresses social exclusion in ICT-related policy documents, we need not only understand the manifestations of social exclusion as these dimensions address, but also on which causes of the phenomenon they concentrate.

With this goal in mind, we turn our attention to the academic literature that describes forces that lead an individual to become socially excluded. To this extent, Levitas (1999) categorization provides a comprehensive overview of forces that create social exclusion. Levitas finds that academic literature can be grouped into three major discourses, and lays out how these shape conceptualizations of social exclusion. Levitas

Table 1. Dimensions of Social Exclusion

Dimension	Description	Manifestation
Consumption	"The capacity to purchase goods and services, as constrained by low income relative to need"*	Because of low income people cannot access goods or services
Production	"Lack of participation in economically or socially valued activities"*	Unemployment; people are not able to own businesses
Civil engagement	"Lack of involvement in local or national decision making"* or other activities related to being a citizen	The person does not participate in the political process, or does not have access to government bureaucracy.
Social interaction	" Lacking emotional support or integration with family, friends or community"*	Lack of integration with family or community.

*Saunders 2003, p. 8

categorizes these discourses as redistributionist discourse (RED), moral underclass discourse (MUD), and social integrationist discourse (SID). RED is concerned with poverty and the social processes that cause it. MUD points out how the behavior of those in low-income neighborhoods causes and increases the gravity of their situation. SID perceives absence of paid employment as the principal cause of the social exclusion.

Combining RED, SID, and MUD with the four dimensions explained earlier, we built the conceptual framework showed in Figure 1. The four-dimensional framework will be used to identify the definitions of the phenomenon, which will facilitate the analysis of how policies handle the concept of social exclusion.

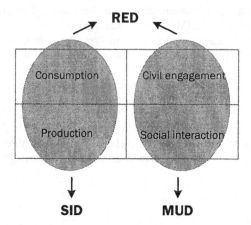

Figure 1. The Four-Dimensional Framework used in the Analysis of ICT Policies in South Africa

3   METHODOLOGY

To answer our research questions, we first identify segments in South Africa's ICT policies that specifically address the concept of social exclusion, and conduct a policy analysis to unravel the conceptualizations of social exclusion. This is followed by an analysis of solutions that the policy offers to that particular problem. To this extent, we analyze one of the government's ICT implementation initiatives, namely the multi-purpose community centers (MPCCs).

The reason for focusing on MPCCs is as follows. Our policy analysis began looking for notions of social exclusion in documents. After first examinations, we decided to narrow the scope of the study and focus on a specific initiative, which was included in the policies. The multipurpose community centers resulted in one that matched our criterion. Established under the auspices of the South African Universal Service Agency (USA), the MPCC initiative was designed as

> the primary approach for the implementation of development communication and information as they can offer a wide range of services that communities can use for their own empowerment.... Providing services and information in an integrated fashion seeks to address particular historical, social and economic factors, which characterized freedom of access to information and citizen participation in South Africa.[3]

This initiative looks to address elements that are related to social exclusion, so the framework could be applied.

Primary data sources for answering the first research question are publicly available government policy documents on the Internet. The definition of social exclusion given earlier was mapped on policy documents in order to search for relevant information in these documents. The study uses documents from three sources: (1) the *Communications* section of the official web site of the South African Government; (2) the *Education* section of the South Africa Government's web site; and (3) the web site of the *Multi-Purpose Community Centers* (MPCC) of South Africa.

The initial set of documents selected for analysis can be divided into two categories: laws and reports regarding the MPCC initiative. The list of these documents is presented in Table 2.

A mix of theory-driven and open coding was used for data analysis, by interpretively reading the data. The concept of social exclusion as laid out above provided a first frame to analyze the documents, which led to the identification of the following high-level concepts that are involved in both ICT and social exclusion: (1) people, (2) government, and (3) technology. These three categories have subsequently been analyzed and iteratively expanded upon through open coding.

---

[3]From the MPCC Initiative web page, http://www.gcis.gov.za/mpcc/initiative/documents/implementation/strategy.htm.

Table 2. Documents Selected for Analysis

Laws	MPCC Documents
Electronic Communications and Transactions Act, 2002 (Presidency of the Republic of South Africa, http://www.internet.org.za/ect_act.html #Objects_of_Act)	MPCC Business Plan (http://www.gcis.gov.za/docs/publications/mppcplan.htm)
Telecommunications Amendment Act, 2001.	Communication Strategy for Government's Multi Purpose Community Center initiative (http://www.gcis.gov.za/mpcc/initiative/documents/implementation/strategy.htm)
Telecommunications Act, 1996 (Presidency of the Republic of South Africa, http://www.polity.org.za/html/govdocs/legislation/1996/act96-103.html)	Draft 2 of the Guideline document on the MPCC Project.
	Correlation of ISRDS nodes and MPCCs (http://www.gcis.gov.za/mpcc/initiative/documents/implementation/correlation.htm)
	Report on the establishment of Government Multi-Purpose Community Centers: Towards an integrated information and service delivery system, by Chief Directorate: Provincial and Local Liaison (http://www.gcis.gov.za/mpcc/initiative/documents/implementation/report.htm)
	Report: Multi Purpose Community Centers/One stop shops as vehicles of a shared service delivery approach (http://www.gcis.gov.za/mpcc/initiative/documents/implementation/servicedelivery.htm)

4 RESULTS

4.1 South Africa's Telecommunications Laws

Policy documents acknowledge the existence of historically disadvantaged groups and encourage ownership and control of telecommunication services by persons from these groups. However, the Telecommunications Act[4] contains only general provisions related to historically disadvantaged groups (e.g., "due regard shall be given to appli-

---

[4]Telecommunications Act, 1996, http://www.polity.org.za/html/govdocs/legislation/1996/act96-103.html.

cations by persons from historically disadvantaged groups" (section 35(3)). The Telecommunications Act does not provide any specific incentives for these groups to become owners of, and gain control over, telecommunication services. However, the laws do provide specific guidelines on what should be done to promote services to areas where such groups live. The Telecommunications Act with the Amendment (2001) establishes the Universal Service Agency (USA) (sections 58 through 64) that promotes universal access to ICT in under served areas. The USA is funded from the state budget and conducts tenders to purchase equipment in order to provide telecommunications services to underserviced areas. In addition, the USA stimulates public awareness of the benefits of telecommunication services. The USA aims at targeting the production and civil engagement dimensions of social exclusion. The production dimension is targeted by establishing computer laboratories in schools and providing them with ICT equipment. Students that have access to such laboratories will have a certain number of computer skills, which will make them more competitive on the job market. By providing equipment and connectivity for e-government services, the Agency targets the civil engagement dimension of social exclusion.

In addition to the USA, the Telecommunications Act established the Universal Service Fund (sections 65 through 68) that is used for subsidizing certain population groups in order to engage them in adoption of technology. Money for the Fund is provided by holders of licenses for telecommunication services (such as cellular operators). The Telecommunications Regulatory Authority determines the categories of persons it provides with assistance from the Fund. Money provided to these persons would be used toward compensating the cost of provision of telecommunication services to them.

However, the Telecommunications Act and the Amendment are targeted at "generic" use of telecommunication services (i.e., they do not specify or imply reasons from any of the four dimensions listed in Table 1 on what issues the adoption of a telecommunication service or technology will resolve). It is through institutions that are established through the policy, including the Universal Service Agency and the Universal Service Fund, that social exclusion on a large scale can be tackled.

The USA created in accordance with provisions of the Telecommunications Act (Chapter VII) has established a network of so-called telecenters across South Africa with the goal of providing access to ICTs to areas with limited or no level of telecommunications access (Telecenter Project Directory 2003[5]). This purpose is achieved in telecenters by providing access to various equipment (e.g., computers, video equipment, etc.) as well as to ICT training services. There are several categories of telecenters, which differ in their purposes (for example, providing IT services in underserviced areas, in schools, etc.). One of these categories is telecenters at MPCCs, which allow, as will be discussed below, use of ICT resources provided by telecenters to facilitate and complement government services provided at MPCCs. However, MPCCs do not just serve as a source for information from the government or a means for citizens to communicate with the government. They also allow people that otherwise do not have access to ICT resources to use those available at the centers. For example,

---

[5]http://www.usa.org.za/TELECENTER%20PROJECT%20DIRECTORY.doc

using these resources allows people to find a job or start their own business. This combination of available information and means for practical application of this information allows MPCCs to promote social inclusion from several perspectives simultaneously, which in turn was the reason for targeting MPCCs in this research.

4.2 Multi-Purpose Community Centers (MPCCs)

The Multi-Purpose Community Center is an initiative that the government of South Africa is pushing to deliver services and information about government resources to remote communities. The Government Communication and Information System (GCIS) works with local governmental offices and the private sector to coordinate the development and management of these centers.

This idea was officially introduced in 1999 in the Cabinet Memorandum 15, dated November 18, 1999. Since the creation of these "one stop" centers, the GCIS has focused its goals on delivery of not only technology, but also services and resources that this tool can provide to communities. Figure 2 shows how GCIS delivers ICT services to communities and thus plays a key role in the development of communities.

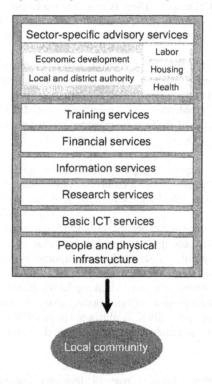

Figure 2. Layered Structure of Information and Service Delivery (adapted from Diagram 3.2of "The MPCC Business Plan," p. 13 [http://www.gcis.gov.za/mpcc/ initiative/documents/ implementation/businessplan.pdf])

The graphic in Figure 2 can be compared with the open system interconnection model (OSI model) in communications. Every layer can operate independently of the other layers but it is necessary for all layers to effectively communicate. In line with this model, the GCIS acknowledges that technology is an important component in the process of development, but it is not sufficient to guarantee it; information, financial and training activities must be offered to allow technology to contribute in an effective way.

The MPCC business plan states that its initiative aims at tackling historical, social, and economic problems of the South Africa population. This document lists some of those problems:

> *poverty, high unemployment, low standards of living (people living below the poverty line), poor access to basic services, remote settlement patterns, lack to access to technology and information, poor health services, insufficient education and skills, poor infrastructure, etc.*[6]

Kapur recommends that developing countries should identify the major constraints in themselves and examine if new technologies can solve these in a fundamental way (2001, p.14), instead of copying models and technologies of the world leaders. That is the case with the MPCC model. There is no reference to any other model or similar development in another country in the entire MPCC business plan document; all ideas expressed in the manuscript come from specific South Africa issues and locally generated solutions.

GCIS regards MPCCs as a tool to focus on socio-economical problems, which goes further than just solving the digital divide issue. In the MPCC Business Plan, the institution acknowledges that providing ICT to communities can be beneficial only if they address real, everyday problems in the communities. An MPCC is a resource that can help to improve the standard of life, but it must be directed to include the citizen in the process:

> *An MPCC aims to empower the poor and disadvantaged by means of access to information, services and resources from governmental and non-governmental source, which can be used for their own development.*[7]

The MPCC business plan document gives specific examples of how MPCCs try to accomplish this. The manuscript describes four scenarios where four potential *clients* use the center to carry out different tasks: a community member, a job seeker, a community organization, and an entrepreneur.

The community member is a woman looking for information (government regulations, medical care, school projects, etc.) to improve an informal cr he in her community. The job seeker is a man using MPCC facilities to create a CV to apply for a job; since he does not have a phone number, MPCC phone and fax numbers are provided as

---

[6]MPCC Business Plan, Chapter 4, page 14 (http://www.gcis.gov.za/docs/publications/mpccplan/chap4.pdf).

[7]MPCC Business Plan, Executive Summary, page 3 (http://www.gcis.gov.za/docs/publications/mpccplan/summary.pdf).

contact information. The community organization is a woman who wants to look for information on governmental initiatives for training community women in sewing and knitting; she obtains this information and brings it to an informal women's organization. The entrepreneur is a worker in the building industry who knows that the offer of bricks in his town is low, and the nearest place to buy them is 30 miles away; he wants to look for guidelines to start a business for manufacturing bricks locally.

These initiatives can be mapped on two out of the four dimensions of social exclusion explained in the data analysis section: production and civil engagement. Lowering unemployment and connecting people with the government are the principal goals that underlie the implementation of the MPCCs. The other two forms of social exclusion are not addressed. MPCC documentation does not propose solutions that stimulate social interaction or consumption. Figure 3 shows the MPCC initiative in the framework exposed in the first part of this document.

In a mental exercise, it is possible to extrapolate the consequences of bringing telecommunication technologies to rural activities. It is possible that the simple act of providing access can stimulate interaction between distant relatives, friends, or communities. But the MPCC policies do not provide direct activities to promote this interaction. The problem of the diversity of languages—South Africa has 11 official languages—for example, is not taken into account.

The same happens with the possibilities of using ICT for purchases or other forms of consumption. These centers could be a vehicle for the distribution of goods that are not available locally in some communities. The documents seem to avoid any association of the centers with commerce or other form of e-business.

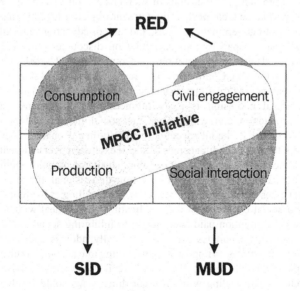

Figure 3. The MPCC Initiative Mapped to the Four Dimensional Framework

Although the GCIS has carefully planned the launch and management of the MPCC (advertisement, costs, and implementation planning), the MPCC business plan document acknowledges the problems that the implementation could face: (1) since the initiative is an effort shared with the private sector, the lack of incentives to the stakeholders can drop their participation and interest; (2) some areas do not have the minimal services required (electricity and water); and (3) the distributed character of the program makes it hard to control.

5   CONCLUSION

Social exclusion is an acute problem for South Africa as the country is recovering from the consequences of apartheid, which had a profound effect on the country's economic and social condition. Information and communication technologies provide a way of tackling some forms of exclusion. This study developed a four-dimensional framework to identify how specific ICT-related actions promoted by South African laws and government initiatives can be considered as social exclusion palliatives.

This paper contributes to research on the digital divide by looking at how social exclusion—a basic phenomenon underlying the digital divide—is addressed through adoption and implementation of ICT policies. We decomposed social exclusion into several dimensions and connected these dimensions with factors that caused them. We found that policy documents do not contain provisions that specifically address reduction of social exclusion. This task is reserved to institutions that have been established as envisioned by these policies. The governmental initiative of MPCCs targets the civil engagement and production dimensions of social exclusion, as can be observed in the MPCC's business plan, which specifically states the objective to reduce unemployment, insufficient access to government services, and lack of education and skills.

These dimensions span two social exclusion discourses: the redistributionist discourse (RED) and the social integrationist discourse (SID). The MUD discourse does not have a place in the MPCC initiative. This result was expected since MUD assumes that the individual, not external factors, is the cause of social exclusion.

Because social exclusion is a multidimensional phenomenon and includes consumption, production, civil engagement, and social interaction dimensions, policy responses should ideally take into account this multidimensionality. While spreading efforts to reduce the different dimensions of social exclusion over different policies and initiatives is a means to take an overall comprehensive approach to inhibiting social exclusion, we recommend the use of this four-dimensional framework in policy generation processes to allow for a more integrative handling of the four dimensions in order to inhibit social exclusion. First, explicating how to deal with all dimensions likely increases the attention paid specifically to inhibiting social exclusion. As we showed, South Africa's policies do not specifically address social exclusion, but nevertheless this constitutes an important issue, taking into account South Africa's large gap between poor and rich. Second, the spread of efforts to reduce social exclusion over different initiatives, all dealing with different dimensions could result in overlap of resources. The spread of efforts requires significant coordination by different agencies in order to align their efforts, and thus is prone to failure.

In addition, we call for greater attention to the phenomenon of social exclusion itself by academics who research the digital divide. This paper, drawing on relevant literature, showed that causes of social exclusion are different depending on the dimension of the latter. As the concepts of digital divide and social exclusion are highly interwoven, specifically addressing the multiple dimensions of social exclusion and how they are both a cause and consequence of the digital divide is of prime importance. More insight on how these dimensions are addressed in policies and ICT projects will provide a way forward to further reduce the global, social, and democratic divide.

References

Atkinson, A. B. "Social Exclusion, Poverty and Unemployment," in A. B. Atkinson and J. Hills (eds.), *Exclusion, Employment and Opportunity, CASE Paper 4*, London: Center for the Analysis of Social exclusion, London School of Economics, 1998.

Bradshaw, J. "How Has the Notion of Social Exclusion Developed in the European Discourse?," paper presented at the Plenary Session, 2003 Australian Social Policy Conference, University of New South Wales, 2003.

Burchardt, T., Le Grand, J., and Piachaud, D. "Social Exclusion in Britain 1991-1995," *Social Policy and Administration* (33:3), 1999, pp. 227-244.

Byrne, D. S. *Social Exclusion*, Philadelphia: Open University Press, 1999.

David, M. "The Politics of Communications: Information Technology, Local Knowledge and Social Exclusion," *Telematics and Informatics* (20), 2003, pp. 235-253.

European Foundation for the Improvement of Living and Working Conditions. *Public Welfare Services and Social Exclusion: The Development of Consumer Oriented Initiatives in the European Union*, Dublin: The Foundation, 1995.

Foley, P. "Does the Internet Help to Overcome Social Exclusion," *Electronic Journal of e-Government* (2:2), 2004, pp. 139-146.

Kapur, S. "Developing Countries in the Network Economy: A Blueprint for Success," paper presented at the International Symposium on Network Economy and Economic Governance, Beijing, China, April 19-20, 2001.

Katz, J., and Rice, R. *Social Consequences of Internet Use*, Cambridge, MA: The MIT Press, 2002.

Kennard, W. "Equality in the Information Age," in B. Compaine (ed.), *The Digital Divide: Facing a Crisis or Creating a Myth*, Cambridge, MA: The MIT Press, 2001.

Levitas, R. "New Labour and Social Exclusion," paper presented at the Political Studies Association Conference, Nottingham, England, 1999.

Madanipour, A., Cars, G., and Allen, J. *Social Exclusion in European Cities*, London: Jessica Kingsley, 1998.

McDonagh, J. "Transport Policy Instruments and Transport-Related Social Exclusion in Rural Republic of Ireland," *Journal of Transport Geography*, 2006 (forthcoming; available online August 11, 2005).

Norris, P. "The Digital Divide," in F. Webster (ed.), *The Information Society Reader*, New York: Routledge, 2004, pp. 273-286.

Oden, M., and Rock, C. "Beyond the Digital Access Divide, Developing Meaningful Measures of Information and Communications Technology Gaps," paper presented at the Fifth Internet Research Conference: Ubiquity?, University of Sussex, UK, September 19-22, 2004.

Oden, M., and Strover, S. "Links to the Future: Information and Telecommunications Technology and Economic Development in the Appalachian Region," report presented to the Appalachian Regional Commission, Washington, DC, 2002.

Percy-Smith, J. "Introduction: The Contours of Social Exclusion," in J. Percy-Smith (ed.), *Policy Responses to Social Exclusion: Towards Inclusion?*, Philadelphia: Open University Press, 2000, pp. 2-22.

Saunders, P. "Can Social Exclusion Provide a New Framewrok for Measuring Poverty?," paper presented at the Measuring Social Inclusion and Exclusion: Dilemmas and Directions, University of Queensland, Australia, July 25, 2003.

Schienstock, G. "Social Exclusion in the Learning Economy," paper presented at the European Socio-Economic Research Conference, Brussels, April 28-30, 1999.

Tufekcioglu, Z. *In Search of Lost Jobs: The Rhetoric and Practice of Computer Skills Training*, unpublished doctoral dissertation, University of Texas, Austin, Texas. 2003.

Zeitlyn, D., Bex, J., and David, M. "Access Denied: The Politics of New Communications Media," *Telematics and Informatics* (15), 1998, pp. 219-230.

About the Authors

Edgar Maldonado is a Ph.D. candidate in the College of Information Sciences and Technology at the Pennsylvania State University . He has an undergraduate degree in Electronic Engineering from Simon Bolivar University in Caracas, Venezuela. Before entering graduate school, Edgar worked as a software support engineer for banking networks, with projects in Venezuela, Trinidad and Tobago, Panama, Guatemala, and Cayman Islands. Edgar's research interests include education policies and their influence in the development of knowledge based societies and economies, and learning theories for information technologies. Edgar can be reached at eam264@psu.edu.

Nicolai Pogrebnyakov is a Ph.D. candidate in the College of Information Sciences and Technology at the Pennsylvania State University. Nicolai holds an undergraduate degree in Informatics from the Belarussian State University for Informatics and Radioelectronics in Minsk, Belarus. Before entering graduate school, he was a software developer. His research interests include the use of information and communication technologies for coordination among relief organizations and mechanisms for acquisition of new technologies by developing countries. Nicolai can be reached at nap151@psu.edu.

Annemijn van Gorp is a Ph.D. candidate in the College of Information Sciences and Technology at the Pennsylvania State University. She has an M.Sc. degree in Systems Engineering, Policy Analysis, and Management from Delft University of Technology in the Netherlands. Annemijn's research interests include the changing roles of national, regional, and international institutions in the provision of telecommunications services, and the effect of policies, market structure, and firm strategies on the provision of advanced communication and Internet access services. Annemijn can be reached at avangorp@ist.psu.edu.

Part 4

Demographic Disparities

11

INCLUSION THROUGH THE AGES?
Gender, ICT Workplaces, and Life
Stage Experiences in England

Marie Griffiths
Claire Keogh
Karenza Moore
Helen J. Richardson
Angela Tattersall
Information Systems Institute
University of Salford
Salford, United Kingdom

Abstract   *This exploratory paper examines the various challenges that women working in information and communications technology (ICT) in England face in relation to their age, their life stage, and their career stage, with these three aspects being at least partially related. We first examine the literature currently available in relation to women, age and ICT work, arguing that age tends to be the forgotten variable in research on women in ICT. Using eight case studies of individual female ICT professionals in their twenties, thirties, forties, and fifties, we explore the nuances of experience these women have in relation to their career and their caring responsibilities. We consider the possibility that women in ICT may have heterogeneous experiences of working in what are often "masculinized" environments related to, but not determined by, their age. Based on our interpretations of our empirical data, we adapt Super's career-stage theory to better frame our subsequent theoretical assertions. To conclude, we suggest that exploring age, life stage, and/or career stage in relation to female ICT professionals' circumstances and experiences means that we can better theorize gender in the field of information systems, and hence develop more relevant gender inclusion strategies.*

Please use the following format when citing this chapter:

Griffiths, M., Keogh, C., Moore, K., Richardson, H.J., and Tattersall, A., 2006, in IFIP International Federation for Information Processing, Volume 208, Social Inclusion: Societal and Organizational Implications for Information Systems, eds. Trauth, E., Howcroft, D., Butler, T., Fitzgerald, B., DeGross, J., (Boston: Springer), pp. 153-168.

1   GENDER, AGE, AND SOCIAL INCLUSION IN INFORMATION SYSTEMS

Gender as an issue has largely been excluded from mainstream IS research. In 2004 Adam, Howcroft, and Richardson highlighted a decade of neglect on gender within Information Systems as a discipline, arguing that gender remains under-theorized in IS, while barely featuring as an issue within published literature.[1] Efforts to incorporate gender as an issue within the academic IS community have included the establishment of the Gender Research in Information Systems (GRIS) group based at the University of Salford, but such efforts face deeply entrenched views of what practices are, and are not, possible within mainstream IS. As Adam et al. highlight, for example, "some authors-well known in the IS world-save their research on gender for a more feminist audience where they may get a more sympathetic hearing" (p. 235).

While gender is only recently being recognized as an issue within the mainstream IS academic community, 30 years of female underrepresentation in the ICT field in more general terms has received more attention from academics, industry, and government agencies alike. Numerous research projects and centers (such as the UK Resource Centre for Women in Science, Engineering and Technology) exist to tackle the under-representation of women in science, engineering, and technology careers, although the figures for women's participation in the ICT sector remain disheartening, with current estimates standing at around 15 percent (EOC 2004). Various innovative initiatives, such as e-Skills' Computer Clubs for Girls, appear to have had little impact on these low female participation rates. Additionally, these and other initiatives have been interpreted as a means to fill the skills gap and "make up the numbers" to boost the UK economy (French and Richardson 2005), resulting in "add more women and stir" solutions to the "problem" of gender in relation to inclusion in IS and ICT (Henwood 1996).

In this context of the neglect of gender issues in mainstream IS, and the continuation of female underrepresentation in the UK ICT sector more generally, it is perhaps unsurprising that IS academics and researchers are reluctant to shift their focus from the ever-important issue of gender to multiple identity affiliations and differences (Cerulo 1997), where gender is one among many considerations. Hence one of the difficulties faced by those working on gender and IS is incorporating possible nuances of gendered experiences according to other identity distinctions including age, class, economic status, ethnicity, disability, sexual orientation, marital status, and geographical location. To offer an example, the interweaving of gender, class, age and nationality have been highlighted in cross-cultural research as important factors in the unfolding of working life biographies (Tulloch and Lupton 2003) and particularly in workers' experiences of labor market insecurity and risk (Mythen 2005). Clearly it is not possible or even desirable to bring in all such concerns when looking at female ICT profes-

---

[1]In an analysis of research papers over a 10 year period (1992-2002) in 10 key IS journals, only 15 papers and one special issue on gender and IS were found. Nine of these papers were quantitative in nature, and Adam et al. (2004) criticize much of this quantitative literature for being essentialist in its theorization of gender as a dichotomy against which differences are measured.

sionals' experiences. However, we suggest that by looking at gender in relation to one or two other identity differences, one may develop a sense in which women's experiences of ICT workplaces are far from homogenous, and in turn answer the call by Adam et al. for a better theorization of gender issues in Information Systems.

In our considerations of female ICT professionals' experiences, we incorporate gender and chronological age with career-stage and life-stage in our analyses of our research participants' circumstances and experiences of working in ICT. Key career stage theorists include Super (1957, 1963, 1980), who developed the "career-stage theory," and Levinson (1978), who developed the "life-span model." Both have fostered a plethora of work on the effects of career stage and age on an individual's performance and job attitudes. Both have also prompted a wide-range of criticisms ranging from the static nature of each "stage" of the models, to criticisms surrounding the dominance of male subjects in studies testing the viability of each model (Smart 1998). It is now generally recognized that modern careers are more fluid and dynamic than allowed for by older models (Hall 1996; Schein 1996). In addition, Adamson et al. (1998) have noted that the concept of a career itself, as encompassing notions of hierarchical progression, has long been undermined by widespread organizational and economic restructuring in Western societies (p. 251).

Most importantly for our purposes, women may progress through careers at different rates and in varied sequences depending on a variety of factors, often unique to women given wider gender relations, such as expectations on women to be the primary care giver. For this very reason, it may be more helpful to use a stage theory that is at least partially independent of age rather than using solely age-based theories. Age-based retirement stages, for example, are premised on the "ideal type" male retiring following a life-long career, while a woman may "retire" from the workforce to carry out caring responsibilities at a variety of stages in her career. It is in this sense that a woman's life stage (e.g., caring responsibilities) may intermesh with her age and career stage to produce a complex and nuanced set of circumstances and experiences that need differentiated strategies to ensure social inclusion throughout her whole life span.

In order to capture these nuances of the relationship between age, life stage, and career stage, we have adapted and developed the aforementioned career-stage work of Super. Super documented what he saw as four linear career-stages, namely *exploration, establishment, maintenance,* and *decline.* In our analysis, we have retained these four stages, but renamed them *exploring, establishing, maintaining/reflecting,* and *restricted freedom.* Adapting and developing Super's model, and undermining the linearity of it by highlighting the fluidity of contemporary career trajectories, has meant we are in a position to better reflect women's heterogeneous circumstances and experiences of the ICT labor market in England.

2 TALKING TO AND LEARNING FROM FEMALE ICT PROFESSIONALS

The empirical material used in this paper is drawn from data generated by on-going research projects, Women in Information Technology (WINIT), funded by the European Social Fund (ESF), and a recently completed research project Women in North West

Information Technology (WINWIT), also funded by the ESF.[2] The research was primarily focused upon women in the ICT industry, or working in ICT in non-ICT organizations, in England and the Northwest of England.[3] The issue of defining the ICT[4] sector is an ongoing complexity within the Information Systems community. Duerden Comeau's (2003) work on defining ICT was used in constructing the research rationale for both the WINIT and WINWIT projects. In framing gender within the ICT sector, the research teams make the assumption that the skills and expertise required from the industry are multidisciplinary and that the work force is generated from within a diverse boundary of disciplines (Cukier et al. 2002).

Drawing on a self-selecting sample of eight female ICT professionals,[5] the stories we present reflect a broad spectrum of career backgrounds, unique family units, and life experiences, with each woman a pioneer in her own right (Czarnaiwska 2005). Such an approach builds on a long tradition of feminist research that aims to take women's stories and accounts of their gendered experiences seriously, using predominately qualitative and ethnographic methods to explore their thoughts and actions (McRobbie 1997).

Our narrative approach falls within a critical research framework with emancipatory ideals of listening to "silenced voices" (Bowen and Blackmon 2003), giving voice to marginalized groups (Cecez-Kecmanovic 2005), and letting stories be heard (Richardson and Howcroft 2006). The process of conducting critical research means disrupting ongoing social reality to question what is ignored or taken for granted and to tell those stories often left untold (Alvesson and Deetz 2000). By attempting to hear silenced and multiple voices and stories through narrative techniques, we can pay better attention to the diversity of women's lives and experiences (Spraque and Kobrynowicz 2004, p. 91) and explore the social experiences of silenced groups (Oakley 1981, p. 89).

The narrative approach we used in our research was chosen in part for its sensitivity to heterogeneity within and across collective experiences, and in part for its sensitivity to the coproduction of knowledge between researcher and the participant. Feminist and critical research positions acknowledge the place of the researcher in producing knowledge, primarily through reflexive thinking (Oakley 2000). Reflexivity is a tool where a researcher recognizes, examines, and tries to understand how her social background, positionality, and assumptions shape the practice of research (Hesse-Biber and Yaiser 2004, p. 115), making this shaping as visible as possible to participants. In research

---

[2]For information on WINIT and WINWIT, please see their websites at http://www.isi.salford.ac.uk/gris/winit and http://www.isi.salford.ac.uk/gris/winit, respectively.

[3]Although many of the women interviewed work in global ICT corporations, the research is inevitably positioned in the context of the English labor market.

[4]The broad convergence of communications with information technology has led to a recent shift of these industries being classified as ICT. For a detailed discussion of the difficulties of defining IT, ICT, and the ICT industry, see Duerden Comeau (2003).

[5]The women included in this study answered a general call for research participants made by the WINIT team through a wide variety of channels. The eight stories in this paper comprise of narrations selected from a series of informal (semi-structured) interviews conducted between March and September 2004. Each interview lasted 90 minutes, and was held either in the participant's office or a mutually convenient venue. Interviews were recorded and transcribed.

terms this meant writing ourselves into the research (Piacentini 2005, p. 204), for example, by telling stories of our own experiences of working in ICT during the interview process and encouraging participants to do the same.

We now construct short summaries of the circumstances and experiences of eight women who were interviewed for the WINIT/WINWIT projects. Each woman has been paired with a woman in the same age range (i.e., twenties, thirties, forties, and fifties) so that we may better compare and contrast their experiences. We suggest that by using in-depth, qualitative material such as interviews to draw out similarities and contradictions apparent between and across women's accounts, we may find ways in which gender can be explored in relation to other issues such as age, career stage, and life stage, while preserving the heterogeneity of experiences which we feel is vital to incorporate in work on social inclusion/exclusion.

3 INCLUSION AND EXCLUSION THROUGH THE AGES AND CAREER-STAGES

3.1 Exploring? Female ICT Professionals in Their Twenties

3.1.1 Beatrice's Story[6]

Neither university educated, nor technically qualified, Beatrice, 26 years of age, owns a computer reselling and distribution business with her partner. Her driving ambition is *"a massive house and a flash car."* Perceiving that in the past she had *"disappointed her father,"* her other source of motivation includes *"determination to succeed and try to prove to him wrong."* Beatrice's ICT sales career started at 17 years of age, having being told *"to get into IT because you will earn loads of money."* She established herself as the *"youngest product manager"* with the *"highest wage"* at 19 in South-East England. Circumstances, including an offer of higher wages, induced a move to Northern England to a company where again she was the *"only girl who worked there apart from the receptionist."* In career-terms, she thrived in this environment, saying, *"they hated me and I pulled all their big accounts."* She was subsequently sacked just before she was meant to collect £100,000 commission. This proved a turning-point in Beatrice's career trajectory. In an example of her determined attitude, she says, *"I said what better opportunity have we got"* and consequently she started her own business with her long-term partner. Two-years later, their reselling and distribution business is an award winning success story. In addition, she recently set up a woman's ICT training forum. Beatrice works seven days a week. In relation to starting a family, she says, *"I would love to have kids and then I think I'd have to have a day off."*

---

[6]Names have been changed to ensure anonymity.

3.1.2 Gayle's Story

Highly qualified, Gayle, a 27-year old business consultant in London, has rapidly climbed the ICT career ladder. Working for a global organisation in a predominantly male environment, she is *"much more visible. I am remembered a lot more."* Essential networking and negotiation skills have also contributed to ensuring her selection in an aggressive internal recruitment market. She is ambitious, has high expectations of herself and her career, and works hard. This combination has enabled her progression from junior software developer to general management status over a 6-year period. Gayle's current role requires longer periods away from home. Extra responsibilities have brought added pressure to Gayle's life, and some uncertainty about the future, *"I have no idea where it will go. I will either get used to it...some days I think why am I doing this."* Involvement in the company's *"ridiculously long-hours"* culture of 12-hour days and attending evening team meetings leaves Gayle little time for life beyond work; *"I barely have time to look after myself."* Secure in a relationship, her partner is in a similar IS role but in the public sector. Gayle says, with regard to having a family in the future, that *"I honestly can't see how I'd do it [the job] with children and spend any time with them."* In the meantime Gayle is happy to spend some of her earnings on her passion: exotic scuba-diving holidays.

3.1.3 Exploratory? Discussion of Women in Their Twenties

From polar opposite starts, these two women have continuously worked hard since their school days. Beatrice left school *"a failure"* without any qualifications or family support, taking only confidence and the determination to succeed and a relentless ambition to make money. Gayle, educated at a selective, independent girls' school, left with five A-levels and a determination to succeed. These alternative groundings have guided these women's approach to their chosen career trajectories and help us understand these women's motivations for working extremely hard, long-hours, leaving them little time for their personal lives. Only 26, Beatrice has had a dynamic 8-year career in the ICT industry, changing roles, changing organizations, and relocating without hesitation. Similarly Gayle, while moving in a relatively linear manner along her chosen career path, has undertaken a number of diverse roles, leading her to specialize in document management and procure a managerial position. Both women have explored the various opportunities available to them in ICT, and are moving into positions in which they can become more established in their careers.

This exploratory stage finds Beatrice working 7 days a week. In comparison, Gayle took a more traditional, university-based route, starting on a graduate training scheme in global ICT consultancy that experienced three mergers within a 6 year period. Staying in one company has enabled Gayle to explore a broad spectrum of project work. These women are not currently prioritizing work–life balance but instead are working hard to achieve job status and related financial rewards. While both women have long-term partners and no dependants, and so in a sense are working without family constraints, they are aware that they may be unable to continue this pace of work if they wish to have a family. When both women contemplated how children would impact upon their current lifestyles, they looked around for female role models, of which there is a scarcity and a need (Faulkner 2004, p. 13). Gayle says, for example, *"People in my position don't have kids, or they are older men with wives at home."* The most recent report by the Department of Trade and Industry on women in the IT industry also addresses this issue, highlighting an "anti-women culture" in many IT organizations that results in a "loss of opportunities when women are of childbearing age" (DTI 2005, p. 19). Here we see how gender, age, career-stage, family choices, work–life balance priorities, the male-domination of ICT workplaces, and wider factors such as the societal expectation for women to be the main care-givers in a family, all combine to shape the ways women at the early stages of their ICT careers.

3.2 Establishing? Female ICT Professionals in Their Thirties

3.2.1 Mary's Story

Mary is a 34-year-old mother of two young children who entered the ICT labor market in an ICT support role. With no formal ICT qualifications, she progressed to the position of Technical Trainer for Europe for a global ICT organization before being made redundant. During her career she often worked long hours, and was extremely career focused and ambitious. She states she has no maternal feelings for her children, *"I am not a mother by any stretch of the imagination, I can't be a mother."* She feels frustrated for not networking and socializing more while employed, saying, *"If I socialized a lot more, I would know a lot more people and I could use that knowledge to network to get back into the industry."* She suspects her previous lack of networking has affected her current ability to find employment. Mary found being made redundant difficult given her previous frantic workload. She says, *"Being in the industry for 13 years and working 60 hours a week, I sat on the sofa not knowing what to do with myself....I literally went through death."* She is eager to return to ICT.

3.2.2 Jasmine's Story

Jasmine is a woman in her thirties who works for a large private organization as a Service Delivery Manager. She is currently single and has no children or care giving responsibilities. After gaining a degree in European Studies, Jasmine entered the ICT labor market by chance in June 2000 as a "temp." A permanent position, a two-year secondment to London, and a promotion, quickly followed. However, she indicates that she does not want to progress to a more senior management position within her organization—*"I don't personally have massive career aspirations anymore"*—after experiencing a number of difficult challenges during her career. She had a particularly incompetent and malevolent senior manager who bullied her, and was working exceptionally long hours away from family and friends. She subsequently became ill and had to take considerable sick leave due to stress. On returning to work with renewed vigor and reevaluating her career options, Jasmine feels she is now more aware of her work–life balance needs. Working in the private sector for a profit-focused organization and gaining a high salary and other financial benefits no longer solely motivates Jasmine. She expressed how she would gladly exchange the cut-throat and long hour's culture of private ICT companies for a position in the public sector, where she believes the stress is reduced.

3.2.3   Establishing? Discussion of Women in Their Thirties

While it may be expected, according to a linear career stage, that women in their thirties would be well established in their career, wider economic and social forces that shape the ICT labor market means the context for such women's careers may change due to redundancy and/or downsizing, outsourcing, geosourcing, and so on. As Mary's story highlights, a sometimes drastic change in circumstances may occur at any point of the career stage, meaning that female ICT professionals of various ages may have to reorientate themselves in relation to their personal and work-centered trajectories. To continue this theme of disruption to a linear career-stage model, the bullying Jasmine was subjected to in her current workplace meant for her a reevaluation of what was formerly a reasonably well-established career. The ICT sector's long-hours culture, higher job demands, "chilly" workplace culture (Faulkner 2004), and lack of work–life balance initiatives (DTI 2004) have contributed to high levels of stress, particularly for Jasmine—contributing to her weakened emotional well-being and increased absence due to illness (Bond 2004). Although Jasmine does not have a partner or children, she is now in her thirties with increased financial responsibilities (such as a mortgage). Hence, she may be less likely to take risks by changing firms, being less mobile at this point in her life stage than those women in their twenties (or those at different life stages) who focus on employability rather than job security (Finegold et al. 2002).

Traditionally, career-ambitious women are often measured against the male norm and successful individuals are described as ruthless with continuous dedication to a career goal rewarded with high salary, progression, and prestige (O'Leary 1997). Although well established in her career this trajectory has been rejected by Jasmine. In comparison, while some may portray non-maternal women as "unnatural" (Christ 2004), Mary is highly ambitious and chose to reject caring responsibilities in favor of career focus. However, reentry to the ICT industry after redundancy has proved problematic, since leaving a senior post without a web of social relations, information and support has limited Mary's reemployment opportunities (Tharenou 1999). In short, both Mary and Jasmine have had to work at reestablishing their careers, a situation that links in with the vagaries of the ICT labor market, and their particular experiences of the *masculinized domain*[7] of many ICT workplaces (Griffiths and Moore 2006).

---

[7]The notion of *masculinized domain* suggests that, within certain spheres of social life, such as ICT workplaces, men tend to dominate proportionately and symbolically.

3.3 Maintaining/Reflecting: Female ICT Professionals in Their Forties

3.3.1 Janine's Story

Janine is in her forties and a mother of two. She is employed by a global ICT organization as Partner, Industry Leader for Computer Systems Integrator Europe, Middle East, and Africa. She moved into ICT via a background in sales where she thrived on achieving and exceeding targets. Janine perceives that her lack of assertiveness in her early career meant she was not offered the same promotion opportunities as her male colleagues. She feels she has worked so hard for the organization that she did not put enough effort into her personal and professional development. She maintains that being based in the North-West of England has been restrictive in career terms, saying, "*I think I would have got to where I am now a good few years earlier had I been more able to liaise and socialize with senior male executives, whereas 200 miles away I am out of sight out of mind.*" She has found managing her career and children problematic. When the children were young, Janine employed a nanny to provide childcare, enabling her to maintain a career focus. She demonstrates some regret with this decision, saying, "*Sometimes I used to think they loved her more than me.*" Janine remains ambitious and is seeking further promotion. However, she is conscious about making the right decision for herself and her family. She concludes, "*I don't want to get divorced and my children become strangers to me.*"

3.3.2 Habibah's Story

Currently Director of ICT and planning to undertake an MBA, Habibah's ICT career began when she became a single mother of three children at the age of 30. Exploring the options available to her, she decided on a career in ICT, gaining 38 qualifications in 5 years while she worked in administrative roles. Strategically not applying for ICT roles until highly qualified, Habibah's career began in earnest with the offer of Head of ICT as her first ICT post. She recounts how she "*went home and cried and cried because I thought, my God, I am never going to be able to do this.*" Her hectic professional life is coupled with an equally eventful domestic life, with a family of five ranging from an 18-year-old to a new-born child. She is supported by an extended family. She admits that 23 hour days are not unusual, and that she has not "*quite got the balance right between my family and my career because my career seems to take precedence at the moment.*" Habibah is currently reflecting on her past experiences and making plans for the future. She aims to publish a technical book, but also wishes to move toward a situation whereby "*work is centered around the family, because I feel I have neglected the family and they have paid the price.*" This dynamic, driven, and honest woman admits that she has not managed to achieve a work-family balance However, now ;that her professional reputation is established, she feels she is better able to contemplate the future of her family, aiming to "*be there, especially for the younger ones.*"

3.3.3   Maintaining/Reflecting? Discussion of Women in Their Forties

Borrowing Howcroft and Wilson's (2003) metaphorical use of the two-headed Janus[8] of the IS/ICT professional who is forced to look two ways (i.e., work and family) enables the exploration of the nuances of the female IS/ICT professionals who are also a parents. Clearly, not all female IS/ICT professionals are parents. However, many are, and such caring responsibilities at diverse stages of a woman's career may have a differential impact upon a her work–life balance, and hence the kinds of inclusion strategies needed. Both Janine and Habibah highlighted the ways in which their careers have taken precedent over the family at various points in their life-stage, a trade-off emphasized by Liff and Ward (2001) in their work on female senior managers. The women in our forties age group have job status, career ambition, and high aspirations *"to move onward and upward,"* as Janine says. Women in their forties, and those women at the maintaining/reflecting stage of their careers, are often maintaining their job status, but also reflecting on their past, present, and possible future experiences (Moore and Griffiths 2005). Work pressures, a "presenteeism"[9] culture within contemporary workplaces (Simpson 1998) and lifestyle preferences predisposed both women to take minimum maternity leave. As Janine says, *"I went back when she was three months old."* The juxtaposition of work–family conflict is a *bidirectional* construct (Posig and Kickul 2004) because these women *"want to be there for my kids and husband"* but are also steadfastly focused upon the next career move. The maintaining/reflecting career stage, for women of any age, is one in which family responsibilities, career choices and pressures, and lifestyle preferences combine to present women with a very particular, and highly gendered, set of conflicts.

3.4 Restricted Freedom? Female ICT Professionals in Their Fifties

3.4.1   Eve's Story

Eve is a woman in her fifties with a working partner and two adult children. She has recently taken voluntary early retirement. She began her career as a punch card operator before moving into COBOL programming. For 16 years, she was employed as a Business Analyst in the public sector. After being internally head hunted to the post of Business Analyst, Eve became disheartened and bored—a situation that reached deadlock when very little new work and few new challenges were presented to her. During her time in the public sector, Eve received no training to update her skills and felt she was not qualified to apply for posts elsewhere. She regrets staying with the same em-

---

[8]Janus was the Roman god of gates and doorways, depicted with two faces looking in opposite directions.

[9]*Presenteeism* can be defined as the social/peer pressure to be seen to be at work beyond the call of duty and beyond contract stipulations, possibly to improve promotion prospects.

ployer for such a long period of time. She feels this has hindered her pay and promotion opportunities. She recommends, based on her experiences, *"changing your employer more often, don't stay at the same place because that's how you get your promotions."* Eve is concentrating on a new career as a horse trainer, her hobby of many years.

3.4.2   Jayne's Story

Jayne is an award winning 57-year-old ICT professional who has reached the peak of her career. She sits on the board of a global legal firm in addition to her entrepreneurial role in management consultancy. A serendipitous career trajectory began in the 1960s as personal assistant to a deputy chairman of one of the UK's largest insurance organizations. She says of her current position, *"If you walk into any firm of [solicitors] and say who do you know in legal technology, I would be stunned if my name is not in the first three."* Jayne's management of process and procedures to *"analyze the way people worked"* created a relationship with IBM where she worked on developing industry specific technology. She recounts how she *"used to go and lecture for IBM all over the world."* A high profile women's networking forum has also been added to Jayne's busy schedule. Her hectic career of long hours, hard work and determination witnesses Jayne getting *"up at 4:50 a.m. to catch the 6:03 a.m....so I hit my desk at 7:10 a.m."* Working 12 hours days, she also *"keeps on top of e-mails of a weekend."* She is happily married but says, *"we didn't have kids so I don't have to make the trade off."* She has caring responsibilities for her sick, elderly parents, although her partner appears to shoulder the bulk of the daily care work involved.

3.4.3   Freedom? Discussion of Women in Their Fifties

The UK labor force in general is being subjected to a profound demographic shift as proportionally the population aged 50 and over is beginning to surpass younger age groups (Platman and Taylor 2004). In accordance to the linear career-stage, these women in their fifties are experiencing a certain amount of freedom and/or restricted freedom. They are free in the sense that they do not have children at home to look after, and free in the sense that they can shape the ways in which they use their time, albeit in very different ways. Eve is pursuing her long-term hobby and moving away from IS/ICT work. Conversely, Jayne is continuing to pursue a very successful career, while diversifying into management consultancy and the design and production of women's forums.

Despite this greater freedom in later career-stages, many women still hold the majority of the responsibility for home, family, and children (Gordon and Whelan-Berry 2004). Eve's interruption to a linear career-stage model and subsequent early departure from the ICT labor market is partly due to her individual characteristics (lack of promotion) and organizational-related factors (lack of training opportunities), leading to her lack of career satisfaction (Armstrong-Stassen and Cameron 2005). It appears that for many years Eve has been "psychologically retired" (O'Neil and Bilimoria 2005). Given her longevity at one organization, she was able to plan and negotiate her transition into retirement. Conversely, Jayne's career has been innovative, exciting, and rewarding.

In contrast to Eve, and in a twist to Super's (1957) fourth and final career-stage, *decline*, Jayne is resisting withdrawing from the work-force. While Jayne's freedom is restricted somewhat in that she has elder care responsibilities, this is presently being undertaken by her spouse. Equally, while Eve has greater freedom by instigating a late life career change, she still has restrictions due to caring responsibilities for her adult children, practically, emotionally and financially. The career stage both women have reached means that they are now in the position, and have the freedom and/or restricted freedom, to reconceptualize, pursue, and achieve new opportunities and challenges (O'Neil and Bilimoria 2005).

4   CONCLUSIONS

Given our concern with gender, age, career-stage, and life-stage, we have adapted Super's career-stage model to help us draw out some of the key themes identified in interviews with our female research participants. Super identifies the key career-stages as follows: *exploration, establishment, maintenance,* and *decline.* We have retained Super's four stages, but renamed them *exploring, establishing, maintaining/reflecting,* and *restricted freedom,* to better reflect women's circumstances and experiences in the ICT labor market, and the fluidity of contemporary career trajectories. We use age as a key difference marker among our sample of women in order to build coherence into our model at this preliminary stage of our research. However, in keeping with our non-deterministic approach, we maintain that women of different ages may move between, or across, these different stages at various points in their lives. A female professional in her thirties, for example, may feel moved to *reflect* on her career choice and decide to leave the ICT industry if she has an unpleasant experience during the *establishing* stage of her career, as was the case with Jasmine.

We suggest that one of our key contributions to the theorization of gender in IS is highlighting the heterogeneity in experiences based on *collective* rather than individual identity distinctions, such as age, class, socio-economic status, and ethnicity. We adapted Super's career-stage model to better theorize lived experiential heterogeneity as coalescing around age and career stage and life stage, these being specific cultural, structural, and relational identity markers of difference. As Cerulo (1997) notes, "The existence of these multiple categories alerts us to the flaws of binary gender concep-tualizations, focusing us instead on the ways in which multiple identity affiliations qualitatively change the nature of human experience" (p. 392).

We acknowledge the limitations of our empirical research and our preliminary theoretical model. The main shortcoming is that our empirical data was gathered from female ICT professionals *in England*, and hence the generalizability of our findings to other countries needs to be investigated through further research. The possibility remains that our theoretical assertions may be limited to the particularities of English society, although equally there is the possibility that our model is appropriate, perhaps following culturally specific adaptation, to female ICT professionals' experiences in other Western societies and beyond.

To conclude, we argue that when developing strategies for social inclusion in the fields of information systems and information communication technologies (see

Faulkner 2004), we need to consider the experiences of women based on their age, their career stage, and any family and domestic responsibilities they may have depending on their life-stage. We suggest that when devising strategies for social inclusion that focus on gender, an awareness of the heterogeneity of female ICT professionals' experiences according to other concerns such as those highlighted in this paper may lead to more robust and positive outcomes. One of our key concerns is that age, and indeed gender, is not taken as an inflexible, deterministic variable, but instead can be used as a sensitizing difference marker in conjunction with concepts such as career stage and life stage. This helps to explore the possibility of a diversification of responses to the continuation of female underrepresentation in the UK ICT sector which remains an important area of research.

References

Adam, A., Richardson, H., and Howcroft, D. "A Decade of Neglect: Reflecting on Gender and IS," *New Technology, Work and Employment* (19:3), 2004, pp. 222-241.

Adamson, S. J., Doherty, N., and Viney, C. "The Meanings of Career Revisited: Implications for Theory and Practice," *British Journal of Management* (9:4), 1998, pp. 251-259.

Alvesson, M., and Deetz, S. *Doing Critical Management Research*, London: Sage Publications, 2000.

Armstrong-Stassen, M., and Cameron, S. "Factors Related to the Career Satisfaction of Older Managerial and Professional Women," *Career Development International* (10:3), May 2005, pp. 203-215.

Bond, S. "Organizational Culture and Work–Life Conflict in the UK," *International Journal of Sociology and Social Policy* (24:12), December 2004, pp. 1-24.

Bowen, F., and Blackmon, K. "Spirals of Silence: The Dynamic Effects of Diversity on Organizational Voice," *Journal of management Studies* (40:6), 2003, pp. 1391-1417.

Cecez-Kecmanovic, D. "Basic Assumptions of the Critical Research Perspective in Information Systems," in D. Howcroft and E. M. Trauth (eds.), *Handbook of Critical Information Systems Research Theory and Application*, Cheltenham, UK: Edward Elgar, 2005.

Cerulo, K. "Identity Construction: New Issues, New Directions," *Annual Review of Sociology* (23), 1997, pp. 385-409.

Christ, C. "Inside the Clockwork of Women's Careers," speech to the European Professional Women's Network, Paris, September 21, 2004.

Cukier, W., Shortt, D., and Devine, I. "Gender and Information Technology: Implications of Definitions," *SICGSE Bulletin* (34:4), 2002, pp. 142-148.

Czarnaiwska, B. "The Thin End of the Wedge," keynote speech presented at the at Gender, Work and Organization Conference, University of Keele, UK, June 22-24, 2005.

Duerden Comeau, T. "Information Technology (IT) Employment: What is IT?," working paper, Workforce Ageing in the New Economy (WANE), University of Western Ontario, 2003 (available online at http://www.wane.ca/PDF/WP1.pdf).

DTI. "Flexible Working in the IT Industry: Long-Hours Cultures and Work Life Balance at the Margins?," report to the Department of Trade and Industry and the Women and IT Forum, March 2004 (http://www.dti.gov.uk/).

DTI. "Women in the IT Industry: Phase 2 Research: How to Retain Women in the IT Industry," Department of Trade and Industry, 2005 (http://www.dti.gov.uk/).

EOC. "Plugging Britain's Skills Gap: Challenging Gender Segregation in Training and Work," report of Equal Opportunities Commission, Manchester, UK, May 2004 (available online from http://www.eoc.org.uk/pdf/phaseone.pdf).

Faulkner, W. "Strategies of Inclusion: Gender and the Information Society," University of Edinburgh/European Commission IST Programme, August 2004 (available online at www.rcss.ed.ac.uk/sigis/public/documents/SIGIS_D08_Final_Public.pdf).

Finegold, D., Mohrman, S., and Spreitzer, G. "Age Effects on the Predictors of Technical Workers' Commitment and Willingness to Turnover," *Journal of Organizational Behavior* (23), February 2002, pp. 655-674.

French, S., and Richardson, H. "Opting Out? Women and On-Line Learning," *Computers and Society* (35:2), June 2005 (available online at http://doi.acm.org/10.1145/1111646.1111648).

Gordon, J. R., and Whelan-Berry, K. S. "It Takes Two to Tango: An Empirical Study of Perceived Spousal/Partner Support for Working Women," *Women in Management Review* (19:5), 2004, pp. 260-273.

Griffiths, M., and Moore, K. "Issues Raised by the WINIT Project," in E. M. Trauth (ed.), *Encyclopedia of Gender and Information Technology*, Hershey, PA: Idea Group Inc., 2006 (forthcoming).

Hall, D. T. *The Career Is Dead, Long Live the Career*, San Francisco: Jossey-Bass Publishers, 1996.

Henwood, F. "WISE Choices? Understanding Occupational Decision-Making in a Climate of Equal Opportunities for Women in Science and Engineering," *Gender and Education* (8:2), 1996, pp. 199-214.

Hesse-Biber, S. N., and Yaiser, M. L. "Difference matters: Studying Across Race, Class, Gender and Sexuality," in S. N. Hesse-Biber and M. L. Yaiser (eds.), *Feminist Perspectives on Social Research*, Oxford, UK: Oxford University Press, 2004, pp. 101-120.

Howcroft, D., and Wilson, M. "Paradoxes of Participatory Practices: The Janus Role of the Systems Developer," *Information and Organization* (13:1), 2003, pp. 1-24.

Levinson, D. *The Seasons of a Man's Life*, New York: Knopf, 1978.

Liff, S., and Ward, K. "Distorted Views through the Glass Ceiling: The Construction of Women's 'Understandings of Promotions and Senior Management Positions," *Gender Work and Organizations* (8:1), 2001, pp. 19-36.

Moore, K., and Griffiths, M. "Gendered Futures? Women, the ICT Workplace, and Stories of the Future," in *Book of Abstracts, 4th Interdisciplinary Conference*, Keele University, Staffordshire, UK, June 22-24, 2005.

McRobbie, A. "The E's and the Anti-E's: New Questions for Feminism and Cultural Studies," in M. Fergusson and P. Golding (eds.), *Cultural Studies in Question*, London: Sage Publications, 1997, pp. 170-186.

Mythen, G. "Employment, Individualization and Insecurity: Rethinking the Risk Society Perspective," *The Sociological Review* (53:1), 2005, pp. 129-149.

Oakley, A. *Experiments in Knowing: Gender and Method in the Social Sciences*, Cambridge, UK: Polity Press, 2000.

Oakley, A. *Subject Women*, Oxford, UK: Martin Robinson, 1981.

O'Leary, J. "Developing a New Mindset: The Career Ambitious Individual," *Women in Management Review* (12:3), 1997, pp. 91-99.

O'Neil, D., and Bilimoria, D. "Women's Career Development Phases: Idealism, Endurance, and Reinvention," *Career Development International* (10:3), May 2005, pp. 168-189.

Piacentini, L. "Cultural Talk and Other Intimate Acquaintances with Russian Prisons," *Crime, Media, Culture* (1:2), 2005, pp. 189-208.

Platman, K., and Taylor, P. "Workforce Ageing in the New Economy: A Comparative Study of Information Technology Employment," University of Cambridge, 2004. (available online at http://www.circa.cam.ac.uk/index.html).

Posig, M., and Kickul, J. "Work-Role Expectations and Work Family Conflict: Gender Differences in Emotional Exhaustion," *Women in Management Review* (19:7), 2004, pp. 373-386.

Richardson, H., and Howcroft, D. "The Contradictions of CRM: A Critical Lens on Call Centres," *Information and Organization* (16:1), Jarnuary 2006, pp. 56-81.

Schein, E. H. "Career Anchors Revisited: Implications for Career Development in the 21st Century," *Academy of Management Executive* (10:4), 1996, pp. 80-89.

Simpson, R. "Presenteeism, Power and Organizational Change: Long Hours as a Career Barrier and the Impact on the Working Lives of Women Managers," *British Journal of Management* (9:Special Issue), 1998, pp. 37-50.

Smart, R. M. "Career Stages in Australian Professional Women: A Test of Super's Model," *Journal of Vocational Behavior* (52), 1998, pp. 379-395.

Sprague, J., and Kobrynowicz, D. "A Feminist Epistemology," in S. N. Hesse-Biber and M. L. Yaiser (eds.), *Feminist Perspectives on Social Research*, Oxford, UK: Oxford University Press, 2004, pp. 78-98.

Super, D. E. "The Definition and Measurement of Early Career Behaviors: A First Formulation," *Personnel and Guidance Journal* (41), 1963, pp. 775-779.

Super, D. E. "A Life Span, Life Space Approach to Career Development," *Journal of Vocational Behavior* (16), 1980, pp. 282-298.

Super, D. E. *The Psychology of Careers: An Introduction to Vocational Development*, New York: Harper, 1957.

Tharenou, P. "Gender Differences in Advancing to the Top," *International Journal of Management Reviews* (2), June 1999, pp. 1-22.

Tulloch, J., and Lupton, D. *Risk and Everyday Life*, London: Sage Publications, 2003.

About the Authors

Marie Griffiths is currently working on Disappearing Women Project: Northwest ICT, researching why women leave the ICT sector for good! Marie initially joined the IS Department at Salford in 2004 to work on the Women in IT (WINIT) project (2004–2006) and closed that project with an international and interdisciplinary conference on Gender, Technology and the ICT workplace (details of which can be found at http://www.winit-salford.com/conference). Marie is due to complete her Ph.D. in the area of organizations, metaphors, and user resistance later this year and she can be contacted at m.griffiths@salford.ac.uk.

Claire Keogh is currently working as a research assistant for the Directing Equal Pay in ICT project Claire graduated with a degree in Information Technology from the University of Salford in 2003. Since graduating, Claire has become a managing director for ARC Business IT Solutions Limited, an organization serving small to medium enterprises in the Northwest. Additionally she is continuing her studies at Salford by exploring the field of gender and information technology. E-mail Claire at c.keogh@salford.ac.uk.

Karenza Moore is currently working on the Disappearing Women Project: Northwest ICT. She joined the IS Department in Salford in 2004 as a research associate on the Women in IT (WINIT) project. Karenza's research interests include gender and IS and future-oriented discourses surrounding new technologies. She also conducts research on clubbing and related recreational drug use in the UK.

Helen J. Richardson is a senior lecturer in Information Systems and joined the University of Salford in 1998 after a varied career including working in the field of social care and running a research and training unit promoting positive action for women at work. She is engaged in critical research in IS including issues of gender in the ICT labor market. Helen can be reached at H.Richardson@salford.ac.uk.

Angela Tattersall is currently working as a research assistant for the Directing Equal Pay in ICT project and undertaking postgraduate study in the area of gender and technology. Angela joined the Information Systems Institute in January 2004 as a research assistant to investigate issues relating to gender and technology. Projects to date include Women In North West IT and the current Directing Equal Pay in ICT. Additionally she was previously employed at Manchester Metropolitan University as a part-time lecturer in the department of Information Communications. E-mail Angela at a.l.tattersall@salford.ac.uk.

12 SPACE INVADERS–TIME RAIDERS: Gendered Technologies in Gendered UK Households

Helen J. Richardson
University of Salford
Salford, U.K.

Abstract   *This paper discusses the domestication of ICTs in the UK, using a critical lens to focus in on ICT use by families and households drawing on a 5 year longitudinal study. Analysis concentrates on how ICTs are embedded into gendered households, how issues of gendered technologies are manifested in the everyday experiences of women, enmeshing ICT use for work, study, and leisure into domestic family life. The social, political, economic, and historical context is that of versions of inclusion in the so-called information society—a debate that wavers between a somber and shining vision.*

Keywords   Domestication of ICTs, gendered technology, gendered family, versions of inclusion

1   INTRODUCTION

Using a critical lens, this paper focuses in on ICT use by families and households in the UK. The household is a complex social, economic, and political space that powerfully affects both the way technologies are used and their significance (Silverstone and Hirsch 1992). We know little about the economic or social context of the use of technologies in the home or how ICTs are appropriated and consumed in households,[1] including the gender dimensions of this and the negotiation involved (Green 2001). A feature of the UK family today is the blurring of the private and public as working at home increases and the importance of the home takes on new significance with what is

---

[1]Although studies are emerging, for example from the EMTEL network (European Media and Technology in Everyday Life, www.emtel2.org).

Please use the following format when citing this chapter:

Richardson, H.J., 2006, in IFIP International Federation for Information Processing, Volume 208, Social Inclusion: Societal and Organizational Implications for Information Systems, eds. Trauth, E., Howcroft, D., Butler, T., Fitzgerald, B., DeGross, J., (Boston: Springer), pp. 169-184.

private and what is public becoming hazy (Huws 2003). In this context, how are ICTs domesticated? Who is using what, why, when, and how in the home? My argument is that even the mundane and everyday reveals complex ideas and struggles and to make sense of home ICT use in gendered households needs a critical analysis that cuts through the myriad of often contradictory notions that shape people's lives, "connecting the ideas with the material world in which people live and think" (Harman 2005, p. 21).

Placing the domestication of ICTs in the UK specifically in its social, political, economic, and historical context has wide relevance in many arenas. There are contending discourses of government, education, ICT manufacturing, and parents in innovation research (Haddon 1992). There are versions of what inclusion in the so-called *information society* means. Brants and Frissen (2003) find that the debate wavers between a somber and shining vision, with the optimists positioning the Internet as an enabling technology, for example leading to empowerment and greater social justice. The pessimists talk about ICTs as intrusive and the domain of inclusion and exclusion—the digital divide—being a development strengthened by existing divides and inequalities with the marginalized being excluded from the information society. As Brants and Frissen point out, both visions seem to be inspired by technological determinism. In this paper, I argue that inclusion strategies cannot happen in a vacuum (Kvasny and Keil 2006) and analyses are limited if the dynamics of family life, and gender and technology relations, are overlooked.

This research fundamentally aims to advance critical research in Information Systems and, to this end, broaden understanding of ICT use in everyday life. To take critical research in IS forward, Howcroft and Trauth (2004) suggest that research should describe the relevant underlying structures of social and material conditions and explain how they shape and determine the nature and content of IS and the ways they mediate work. It should assist in demystifying the myths of technological determinism, enable exposure of taken-for-granted assumptions, provide an insight into the broader social, organizational, and political implications of IS. It should enable both researchers and the researched to see or envision the desired changes. To this end, I draw on a longi-tudinal study of primarily women in seven UK households from 1999 to 2004 and six self-selected in-depth interviews of women known to me to use ICTs in the home and conducted during 2004. I analyze how ICTs are embedded into gendered households, how issues of gendered technologies are manifested, and the everyday experiences of women enmeshing ICT use for work, study, and leisure into everyday domestic family life. In conclusion and comment, I call for an alternative version and vision of the future free from commercial and governmental discourse centering as it does on digital inclusion for the contributions citizens can thus make to economic and social stability. I also call for more research into the neglected area of ICTs and families, households, and everyday lives often rooted as it currently is, in flawed views of technological determinism and gender neutrality.

This paper will proceed by discussing the family and households in the UK and the domestication of technologies, in particular ICTs. From the context of versions of inclusion, I give an overview of examples of research that consider ICT use in domestic settings using the typology of the household, gender, and technology as a critical discursive tool. I then present my research methodology and provide illustrative commentary from my qualitative inquiry.

2 UK HOUSEHOLDS

Considering ICT use in the home, the household becomes the focus of enhanced consumption and so the lens shifts to the family. Many policy makers and commentators decry the "new family" in the "new economy." German (2003) points out that, in the UK, there has been a dramatic increase in single-parent households in the past two decades. However, as she explains, while the family is broken down by the effects of capitalism, it is also maintained and reinforced by capital as the cheapest, most convenient, and most socially stable way of caring for the existing generation of workers and reproducing the next generation. The family is also a gendered institution and is often taken for granted. Wharton (2005) describes how the family is viewed as "somehow functional for society rather than a social construction and changing in relation to history and culture" and she continues to observe that, although family diversity is a social fact, this is "obscured by a set of taken-for-granted beliefs about the family as a social institution" (p. 105). These include myths of the nuclear family, the heterosexual family, women as mothers and caretakers, and men as fathers and breadwinners. However, it is these myths that inform the choices made, including government and employment policies. So in summary, UK domestic households cannot be considered apart from consideration of gender and the role of the family in capitalism today and this includes gendered ways of knowing and being which become an "inextricable part of the intimate details of everyday life" (Silva 2000).

Wajcman (1991) discusses how housework began to be presented as an expression of the housewife's affection for her family. The split between public and private meant that the home was expected to provide a haven from the alienated, stressful technological order of the workplace and was expected to provide entertainment, emotional support, and sexual gratification. The burden of satisfying these needs fell on the housewife (pp. 85-86). The gender politics of the household and sexual division of domestic labor are reflected in surveys of gender and housework today. Kan (2001, p. 6), for example, uses the British panel household survey and analyzes that, in general, women in the UK spend 18.5 hours a week doing housework and men just over 6.

In terms of the domestication of technology, Wajcman (2000) discusses the early debates around domestic technologies, particularly the paradox that despite mechanization of the house this hasn't substantially decreased the amount of time women spent on household tasks. Although in the domestic sphere many technologies are used by women—from the microwave to the washing machine, yet the "world of technology is made to feel remote and overwhelmingly powerful" (Faulkner 2000, p. 80). The notion of "hard" technology—use of industrial machinery, or solitary geeks programming computers—is commonly associated with a masculine world of work, whether or not women are engaged in these occupations. Hard technology implies a dualism of "soft" technology—like domestic technology and ICTs used by women in clerical work, for example. In these terms, the hard–soft dualism factors out those other technologies which we all meet on a daily basis and can in some sense relate to (Faulkner 2000). In conclusion, many changes between the household and economy passed almost unrecorded (Huws 2003), yet without an understanding of these changes it is difficult to grasp the impact of ICTs on the home and everyday life.

3   THE DOMESTICATION OF ICTS IN THE CONTEXT OF INCLUSION

How does the domestication of ICTs fit in here, then? How are ICTs appropriated and consumed in UK households? Green and Adam (1998) have observed the gendered social relation of domesticity that surrounds the use of ICTs. Research such as the Home Net project has shown how home computers are used predominantly for communication by adults in households (Boneva et al. 2001), although PCs are often bought with children's education in mind. In this context, women often view the home computer as a shared family resource. Research indicates that men are much more likely to see the computer as belonging to them and therefore prioritize their access (Richardson and French 2002). Home PC ownership has a strong association with the daily bombardment of digital divide rhetoric as well, demanding an individual commitment and responsibility to self-help. In other words, the message is, embrace the ICT revolution or be a victim of digital "have-not-ness" brought about, it is implied, by personal inadequacy and culpable neglect. Many people in this study are "catching hell" (Kvasny 2004) living busy lives with an overload of domestic and work commitments in the everyday struggle to make ends meet. Use of ICTs in the home in this context is just another thing to be dealt with.

What the discourse about the transformational impact of ICTs (Mandleson 2001) reveals is a burning wish to direct the future, regarded by Wajcman (2000) as symbolic and a highly valued and mythologized activity. Yet there are versions of the future. Moore (2003) describes the corporate versions that seek to produce corporate identities presenting a future that is ultimately knowable through expertise resting on the valued endpoint of competitive advantage. She continues to highlight the inexorable logic of future-orientated technological determinism. Of course the urge to consume ICTs in a domestic setting is inevitably linked to domestication of new media and communication devices and is very attractive to this corporate vision. Ward (2003) notes how discourse surrounding inclusion centers around consumers engaging with the information society with e-commerce being seen as synonymous to this, implying that users need to learn how to consume, not only to participate within but also to construct the information society. In the context of everyday life, it is important to dissect the limits and misunderstandings embedded in the rhetoric of the information society to challenge the presumptions of rationality and efficiency operationalized as they so often are in a discourse of consumer need (Ward 2003). Brants and Frissen (2003, p. 6) observe that there is a strong emphasis in digital divide discourse on quantitative data such as PC ownership and this is correlated to socio-demographic characteristics of potential users, for example the level of education and skill. They continue that while perhaps this is helpful to identify "laggers," marginalized groups are thus often stigmatized and such a perspective tells us little about the skills, capacities, or other highly relevant dimensions of the everyday lives of these stragglers. The specific contexts, dynamics and dimensions of inclusion or exclusion thus remain under researched. The future and what technologies we have and how they are used are not inevitable. Domestication of ICTs in this context highlights a dominant viewpoint of the essentialist assumptions held about technologies and those that consume them.

4 ICTS IN THE HOME: A CRITICAL LITERATURE REVIEW

Steward and Williams (2005, p. 203) concluded that domestication—or appropriation—of technologies (in research) tends to be about where the product is located or how it is incorporated within family routines, but they suggest that a broader view is that domestication is about *taming* the technology—how ICTs are used in unanticipated ways and the integration of ICTs within their particular contexts and purposes.

There are a small but growing number of studies that consider ICTs in the home. These sometimes originate from commercial considerations, for example the research from "BT exact" published in various volumes of British Telecom's *BT Technology Journal* (for example, see volume 17, 1999, and volume 20, 2002). Other studies are concerned with user-centered design and HCI considerations (e.g., Baille et al. 2003; Phillips et al. 2001). These studies focus on "smart homes" characterized as being "intelligent, connected and wireless" (Patel and Pearson 2002, p. 106). Use of technology in the home involves issues such as the extent to which the Internet had an impact on the way interviewees spent their time and how Internet use displaced other activities and as such what can be done to maximize money-making potential (Anderson et al. 2002, p. 15). The driving force of much research is to highlight the benefits of a digital home described as offering flexibility (services available when and where wanted), peace of mind (safety when away, independence for older people, and so on), and saving money, for example, "'time-shifting activities to benefit from cheapest energy supply, monitoring energy use, reducing waste and controlling your home climate" (Rout 2002, p. 103). Other studies discussing technology in the home are more sociologically driven, some taking a feminist approach that, in my view, provides a richer view of the domestication of technologies within dynamic and gendered households. Hynes (2002) also notes that study of consumption of ICTs is often a number-crunching exercise and that quantitative discourse pervades—in other words, trying to profile a typical user buying a particular brand in a technology-driven strategy. Often studies tend to adopt a determinist position with regard to gender, so they also adopt a determinist position with regard to the technology, tending to see it as fixed and inevitable in its introduction and use (Adam et al. 2004). So both gender and technology need to be problematized, to be seen as cultural products rather than as "givens."

When reviewing this literature, it astounded me how little the household itself was analyzed in some of the studies and how gender and technology were not problematized or even considered worthy of any comment. Rather than a "haven or hell" described above, I came away from reading some studies with a view of households as sterile places, neutral and bland. I propose that research wishing to consider how ICTs are appropriated, used, or "tamed" in the domestication process should provide analysis of the household context, the gendered family, and theorize technology. Using this typology, I have summarized some examples of studies that discuss technology in the home in Table 1.

Following this debated version of inclusion, I now introduce my research methodology and analysis, applying the typology utilized above.

Table 1. Summary of Some Examples of Literature Discussing Technology in the Home

Authors	Study	View of the Household	Gender Analysis	View of Technology
Anderson et al. (1999)	Family life in the digital home: how and why people purchase and adapt to ICTs	Consists of individuals within a family structure	A variable	Not considered or theorized
Anderson et al. (2002)	People-centered innovation and strategy	Unproblematic and non-theorized	Not considered	Understanding usage by people important for money making
Baille et al. (2003)	The design of interactive technologies and household settings	Home as living space comprising of social, technological and physical space (from Venkatesh 1996)	Not analyzed	User-centered usability of technological artifacts informs research
Cronberg and Sangregorio (1981) cited in Huws (2003)	Impact of IT on domestic life in Japan	Not theorized or considered	As a result of methodology, subjects were largely women at home; not theorized	Advantageous
Green and Adam (1998)	ICTs and leisure in the home	Contested and gendered social space	Feminist approach; gender necessitates theorization	Socially shaped; gender and technology co-constructed
Habib and Cornford (2002)	Integration of the home PC into domestic spaces	Multigenerational; complex units of values, relationships, symbols, and routines of family life	Gender needs to be theorized and gender differences and divides identified	Technology is gendered
Morley (2000)	Home territories and media, mobility and identity	Symbolic territory; locus of power relations	Space and homes are gendered; gender as a geographical and cultural construct	Non-technological deterministic approach; technologies and their use are contradictory and involve dynamic mutually shaping relations
Patel and Pearson (2002)	Hype and reality in the future home	Unproblematic and non-theorized	Not considered	Advantageous

Authors	Study	View of the Household	Gender Analysis	View of Technology
Phillips et al. (2001)	The domestic space as smart environment	A design space	Not considered	Domestic technologies support personal, group, or public devices and dimensions of control, binding to people and interfaces; not theorized
Rout (2002)	Digital homes and stakeholders	Unproblematic and non-theorized	Not considered	Advantageous
Silva (2002)	Time and emotion in studies of household technologies	Homes centrally involve relationships; households can no longer support an adult as sole career in the home	Dynamic gender division of labor and gender roles	Technologies impact on transforming domestic labor
Silverstone and Hirsch (ed) (1992)	Consuming technologies; media and information in domestic spaces	Social, cultural, and economic unit engaged in the consumption of objects and meanings	Gender as largely a cultural construct	Relational— design, production, use— embodying gender identity
Venkatesh (1996)	Capturing the structure and dynamics of computer adoption in the home	Social organization; main site of technological innovation and development	Not considered	Usage involves socially motivated decisions
Ward (2003)	Ethnographic study of Internet consumption in Ireland	Domestic culture—a symbolic space	Aspect of the family and web of human relations	Intrusive, construed with meanings in definition, function, use, and status

5 Research Methodology

I began this enquiry in 1999 and at the outset I formed a focus group to guide the research and this shaped what is a longitudinal study of seven households and the domestication of ICTs within these households over the 5 year research period. In terms of my research, however, I used focus groups not only as an interviewing technique to gather information about each household and their experiences of the domestication of ICTs but also as a self-focus group to help me as a researcher to clarify and refine concepts, to observe, to place interaction at the center of the research process, and to explore attitudes, opinions, meanings, and definitions in the participant's own terms (Tonkiss 2004).

The seven households representing the focus groups consisted of five households known to me and two that were new to my acquaintance at the start of the study but who were willing volunteers in the research. I attempted to include households with children and without, single households and shared, self-defined as heterosexual and gay— although in the latter instance, there were two households involving lesbian relationships and no gay males were involved. This was important in thinking about the dynamics of households and family life, not taking the "family" for granted, as suggested by Wharton (2005) and discussed earlier. As you may expect, these households did not remain static but participants moved house and joined up with new partners and children grew, babies were born, and domestication of ICTs were shaped by the members in the households and shaped their everyday lives in turn.

The focus group households were involved with the research. We met up on a regular basis and the interviews were transcribed and reflexive stories written but always shown and discussed with the individuals and families concerned. It is important to think about myself as a critical researcher—as a woman with children, working full-time and studying as well, and using ICTs extensively in the home. Clearly the critical research approach in challenging the status quo, questioning assumptions and research practice informed by critical social theory impacted on the research process and the discussions held. Part of critical research is to let voices, often unheard, be heard, and so what follows are the personal stories of the family members in the focus group households and also those from the in-depth interviews. The six in-depth interviewees were women selected by me. They were known to me as women who used ICTs extensively in the home. However, prior to the interviews I had little idea about the extent of their ICT use, the field of study that was their households and family life or their attitudes to and experiences of technology.

All of the homes involved had a myriad of technological gadgets and ICTs. Most members of the households had a mobile phone; there were DVDs, TVs in many rooms, games consoles of every shape and hue, and one or more PCs housed mainly in shared household spaces. The qualitative enquiry in general centered on gaining an understanding of women's experiences with ICTs—in particular with PCs—in the home. In the following, analysis the participants came up with new names to ensure anonymity.

6   ANALYSIS: THE HOUSEHOLD

For the purposes of a critical study of ICT use, clearly an issue is how new technologies have impacted the household generally. The PC has particular significance in the home, often housed in communal space and taking up more physical space. In addition, the PC has a symbolic link embedding a subtext of personal improvement through its reported educative role. What the analysis draws out is that there is a process of domestication (Habib and Cornford 2002) of ICTs.

6.1 ICTs as Space Invaders

Where the PC is situated has an impact on family life. These interjections give an inkling of the dynamics involved. In the households visited, childcare is rarely far away for women in the home. Fran talked about an idealized time before the introduction of the laptop into the home.

We're scattered all around the house now instead of gathered together round the fire. He's [husband] doing his work somewhere. I'm in the front room on this [laptop]. Then at the same time I'm trying to stop the kids playing football against the wall.

Laura and Jed's house was chaotic, with Laura trying to work in the kitchen and Simon, Matthew, and Mark in and out for food, a chat, to borrow money, and so on. Laura pointed to her kitchen table.

There's the PC on the kitchen table surrounded by mountains of paper—I don't know when we last had a family meal on the kitchen table. He [husband] gets annoyed, he says "I can't see the floor or the table." Everything spills out onto the floor. Wires are hanging across the doorway and everyone has to step over them and the dog gets strangled. Then Mark shows me his Irish dancing in the middle of it!

Amanda showed me the PC in her dining room. It felt like a huge imposition on the communal space. She said,

It's here in the dining room—it clashes with everything—the TV, people talking. It's in the way but it's the only option.

6.2 PCs for Work in the Home

Some of the focus group households and in-depth interviewees spend a lot of time working at home and using the PC for that purpose and, for women in particular, this means juggling working time with family life as can be seen with the following observations. Laura was discussing working at home.

My kitchen is my office but the kids come in like a herd of elephants—in, out, in, out—because you're their mum, wherever you are and whatever you're doing.

Wilson and Greenhill (2004) suggest that home-working "magnifies the conflict of roles that women experience in attempting to equalize the work–life balance" (p. 43). One element of this is providing food at the time the family requires, clearly a role that women fulfill, and this can cause conflict with working at home. Laura discussed the impact on mealtimes.

I get so engrossed I forget everything else. I don't eat when I'm working but the kids are sometimes crying "where's my dinner." Family life goes on around me; sometimes I'm oblivious, like when the potatoes boiled dry and the pan went on fire!

Erica also discussed how engrossing work becomes when using the PC.

One example, I put an egg on to boil for my son's tea. Son: "Is my egg ready?" Me: "Yeah in a minute." I'm clacking away on the PC, then 10 minutes have elapsed, another hard boiled egg. Son: "When am I ever going to get a runny egg again?" [Jamie then butted in: "I can do my own eggs now," and Erica responded] Yeah that's one good thing—they're so much more independent now.

6.3 PCs for Study in the Home

Some women face a great deal of domestic pressure when in education and are more likely to have to try to balance study, work, and home responsibilities, and student mothers often felt they had to reassure the family of the minimal repercussions their studies would have on family life in order to get approval (Maynard and Pearsall 1994). On-line courses can exacerbate domestic tensions for women, as Rachel suggests.

You feel guilty because you have to spread yourself between everything. I did spend some time explaining to the children that I was studying and then making it up to them in the holidays—still loads of guilt. After a while, they learn that when you are studying they leave you alone but I don't think husbands understand this.

Mary found using the PC for study was essential but very stressful, in particular fitting it into family life.

I find using the PC very stressful—I've got to go on the PC because of study but at home the cry is "are you on the computer AGAIN!"

The lives of some of the in-depth interviewees were changed beyond recognition through going to study. There was habitually a lot of support from the immediate family but often conflict from the wider family. Criticism centered on husbands, who were deemed to be neglected or let down. Not providing regular meals was often a bone of contention, as Erica described.

Before my access course we all sat down as a family for tea at 5:30 p.m. on the dot—access changed all that. It was a big thing to sit down together, now I couldn't give a [expletive]—it's not important to me anymore.

7   ANALYSIS—GENDER PERSPECTIVES: ICTS AS TIME RAIDERS

As stated earlier, all of the homes in the study housed a myriad of technological gadgets and ICTs. In analysis, it was evident that there was not only competition to use the technologies but also competition for the time that children and partners want and expect from the wife, mother, or female partner in the home, and this conflicted at times with women's use of ICTs. As Brants and Frissen (2003) observe, those who are marginalized in a socio-economic sense may still be well equipped with ICTs.

Women in the family are often leading busy lives and this can result in personal conflicts with a desire to spend time with the family and the pressures from using ICTs at home. The competing demands of labor market and domestic work are associated with a perception of a loss of control over time, often called "time crunch," and research suggests that women with children feel more time crunched than men (Peters and Raaijmakers 1999). Using ICTs in the home makes many feel time squeezed as a result of multiple role conflict and role overload (Peters and Raaijmakers 1999), with a feeling of loss of control over time. *"Time just passes,"* says Erica. *"You never have time for anything,"* Laura notes. Work and home life boundaries blur and time needs to be negotiated.

Guilt is never far away, as can be seen from Erica's comment: *"Sometimes I feel bad because I'm busy—I'm always busy on the computer."* Amanda confirms this: *"It gets too stressful and anyway I get sick of saying 'yeah in a minute.' I want to play, not be on the PC. I feel guilty when the kids want to use it."*

In this analysis of the domestication of ICTs in UK households, women especially feel that they should be doing something else when using ICTs—guilt that spending time on things they want to do should happen after the household chores and family have been taken care of. Analysis indicated that negotiation is required in the relationships between adults in the household. One resource that is competed for is the time of women in the home and this causes stress if using ICTs takes women away from interaction with husbands and partners, as Laura suggests.

When he [husband] comes home from work, he doesn't do anything else and gets cheesed off if I'm working all evening. He says, "Are you coming to bed?" Then he's very annoyed when I get in bed at 2 a.m. with freezing cold feet.

Working or studying at home and using ICTs often interfered with a husband's or partner's view of bedtime. This meant, in some cases, women trying to conceal the fact that they had been working on the PC. Amanda explained,

My PC was in the bedroom—very inconvenient. Sometimes [husband] had to sleep on the sofa if I was working, or I'd work in the dark but he'd complain. [Later she said,] I had to conceal when I went to bed—I'd creep in at 2 a.m. but if he woke up he'd say, "Are you stupid, what are you doing still working?

As Morley (2000, p. 56) has pointed out, "the home as a locus of power relations has often been almost entirely neglected."

Research in the UK suggests that families have the least amount of leisure time (MINTEL 2000). This report goes on to suggest that the pace of leisure has also become more frenetic as "it is squeezed between existing commitments of work and childcare." In this context, women increasingly have to juggle work, time, and money. They have less free time than ever before and the gap between their free time and that of men's is widening: "men retain their ability to do absolutely nothing for longer periods than women" (MINTEL 2000). Leisure is often viewed as a residual category by women but remains an unconditional entitlement for their male partners (Kay 1996). A striking feature of everyday life from my qualitative enquiry is how little leisure time people have or perceive themselves to have. Leisure time also is often taken in snatched and fragmented moments and at times that precludes preplanning. This concurs with Green's (2001) studies of women's leisure, revealing that time synchronization and time fragmentation dominates many women's lives in the UK, leading them to find snatched spaces for leisure and enjoyment rather than undertaking planned activities. In my qualitative enquiry, the question of time and unequal access to leisure featured heavily. In terms of domestic leisure Morley (2000, p. 72) comments that women maintain primary responsibility for the smooth running of the home and for the reproduction of domestic order and comfort. This means, among other things, that domestic leisure remains heavily gendered.

8 ANALYSIS: TECHNOLOGY

In terms of understanding the use of technologies in everyday life, Silverstone (2003, p. 21) has noted how individuals, families, and groups make choices based on their own perceptions of their needs and values, and on the often-unconscious frameworks that guide their actions and interactions. In these terms, technologies do not emerge without active involvement of the consumers and users who have to accept them as relevant and useful in their everyday lives.

A theme raised by the qualitative enquiry relating to the domestication of ICTs is that of technological skill and how this relates to how gender and technology have been theorized. It is important to note the strong link between the notion of skill and masculinity, in particular technical skill, and how something becomes defined as a technical skill. Indeed Wajcman (1991) identifies technical skill and masculinity as mutually constitutive. As Grint and Gill (1995, p. 9) suggest, "'Skill' is not some objectively identifiable quality, but rather is an ideological category, one over which women were (and continue to be) denied the rights of contestation."

There were some interesting tales to tell about the skills of ICT use and maintenance that support and contradict ideas of women and their lack or otherwise of technical ability. Gloria, for example, would constantly say how ignorant she was about computers: *"I know nothing; I don't understand them."* Despite this, through the 5 years of the study, she managed to install software, set up web cam facilities, work out how to scan and send pictures by e-mail, set up e-mail accounts, upgrade hardware, and troubleshoot printer problems. When this was pointed out, she would shrug: *"Well I still don't understand them."*

My qualitative enquiry uncovered no clichéd pattern of male fascination and female avoidance of technology. Gender differences were in the free time available to use ICTs and views on priorities. Although many of the women were more experienced with technology, this didn't always go down well, as Rachel explained.

I've had various situations where men in my company have asked each other questions about the PCs and ignored me completely and they know full well that I have much more knowledge about IT than they do. I've butted in with the answer it really annoys them. Now I take another tack—just let them talk and smugly gloat or laugh to myself. I don't offer until they ask. I get such pleasure out of seeing them struggle.

9 CONCLUSIONS AND COMMENTS

Certain themes have arisen from my qualitative enquiry. The gendered family in this UK-based study involves sexual division of labor and inequality in the share of domestic and household management tasks. Gender is shaping the use and domestication of ICTs. There are unequal time demands and competition for the time of women in the home with ensuing feelings of guilt aroused by role overload. There are conflicting uses of ICTs in the home and competition for these resources. Work and study impact in the home with the public creeping into the private sphere. Domestication of ICTs also reflects changes in household spaces occupied by ICTs and their use. ICT use in the home doesn't match the hype, which is that they will help with the education of kids and others, they will make life easier, and they will encourage inclusion in the digital society. Manufacturing and commercial visions and versions of the future, in terms of ICT use in the home, are contested. It is, therefore, crucial to consider how ICTs are appropriated and consumed in households, including an understanding of how the family and technologies are gendered. Analysis without this leaves gaping holes in understanding the future and yet again fails to appreciate the reality of women's gendered domestic lives. In these terms, Ward (2003, p. 18) emphasizes that the household is a space where technology is adopted, consumed, argued about, and—to varying degrees of success—integrated into domestic culture. Indeed the home is a contested domain – an arena where differing interests struggle to define their own spaces (Morley 2000, Silverstone and Hirsch 1992). Hynes (2002) stresses that the household has such a central role in our lives that there is a great need to document, analyze, and understand changes that are occurring in the ways in which people consume technologies in the domestic setting through their everyday lives. Not to do so is to give in to the corporate version and vision of the future.

My qualitative enquiry of gendered technologies in gendered households in the UK presented in this paper is clearly not exhaustive of the field. Issues of class, age, and ethnicity, for example, have not been deeply analyzed in this study. Yet in relation to taking critical research forward (Howcroft and Trauth 2004), this paper addressed this task set by discussing the political economy of the gendered household and the dynamic relationship and struggle between home and work arenas. It analyses how ICTs are embedded into everyday life and the gender shaping of ICTs, considers how empirical evidence suggests that, in the UK, ICTs in the home are a leisure and communication tool primarily and analyzes this in the light of government and commercial visions. It provides a rich analysis of ICT use in the gendered family and the contested political, social, and gender politics of the household. It challenges the status quo views of the domestication of ICTs in the UK and concludes that further work is clearly needed in this neglected area of research.

References

Adam, A., Howcroft, D., and Richardson, H. "A Decade of Neglect: Reflecting on Gender and IS," *New Technology Work and Employment* (19:3), 2004, pp. 333-352.

Anderson, B., Gale, C., Gower, A. P., France, E. F., Jones, M. L. R., Lacohee, H. V., McWilliam, A., Tracey, K., and Trimby, M. "Digital Living—People Centered Innovation and Strategy," *BT Technology Journal* (20:2), April 2002, pp. 11-29.

Anderson, B., Gale, C., Gower, A. P., France, E. F., Jones, M. L. R., Lacohee, H. V., McWilliam, A., Tracey, K., and Trimby, M. "Family Life in the Digital Home—Domestic Technology at the End of the 20th Century," *BT Technology Journal* (17:1), 1999, pp 85-97.

Baille, L., Benyon, D., Macaulay, C., and Pederson, M. G. "Investigating Design Issues in Household Environments," *Cognition, Technology & Work* (5:1), 2003, pp. 33—43.

Boneva, B., Kraut, R., and Frohlich, D. "Using E-Mail for Personal Relationships: The Difference Gender Makes," *American Behavioral Scientist* (45:3), November 2001, pp. 530-549.

Brants, K., and Frissen, V. "Inclusion and Exclusion in the Information Society," Final Deliverable for the European Media and Technology in Everyday Life Network, 2000-2003, 2003 (available online through Research Results at www.emtel2.org).

Cronberg, T., and Sangregorio, I-L. "More of the Same: The Impact of IT on Domestic Life in Japan," *Development Dialogue* (2), 1981, pp. 68-78.

Faulkner, W. "The Technology Question in Feminism: A View from Feminist Technology Studies," *Women's Studies International Forum* (24:1), June 2000, pp. 79-95.

German, L. "Women's Liberation Today," *International Socialism Journal* (101), December 2003, pp. 3-43.

Green, E. "Technology, Leisure and Everyday Practices," in A. Green and A. Adam (eds.), *Virtual Gender: Technology, Consumption and Identity Matters*, London: Routledge, 2001, pp. 173-189.

Green, E., and Adam, A. "On-Line Leisure: Gender and ICTs in the Home," *Information, Communication and Society* (1:3), 1998, pp. 291-312.

Grint, K., and Gill, R. *The Gender-Technology Relation: Contemporary Theory and Research*, London: Taylor and Francis, 1995.

Habib, L., and Cornford, T. "Computers in the Home: Domestication and Gender," *Information Technology & People* (15:2), 2002, pp. 159-174.

Haddon, L. "Explaining ICT Consumption: The Case of the Home Computer," in R. Silverstone and E. Hirsch (eds.), *Consuming Technologies: Media and Information in Domestic Spaces*, London: Routledge, 1992, pp. 82-96.

Harman, C. "From Common Sense to Good Sense," *Socialist Review* (292), January 2005, p. 17.

Howcroft, D., and Trauth, E. "The Choice of Critical Information Systems Research," in B. Kaplan, D. P. Truex, D. Wastell, A. T. Wood-Harper, and J. I. DeGross (eds.), *Information Systems Research: Relevant Theory and Informed Practice*, Boston: Kluwer Academic Publishers, 2004, pp. 195-211.

Huws, U. *The Making of a Cybertariat: Virtual Work in a Real World*, London: The Merlin Press, 2003.

Hynes, D. "Digital Multimedia Consumption/Use in the Household Setting," paper presented at International Association for Media and Communications Research, Barcelona, Spain, July 21-26, 2002.

Kan, M. Y. "Gender Asymmetry in the Division of Domestic Labor," unpublished manuscript, Department of Sociology, University of Oxford, 2001 (available online at http://www.iser.essex.ac.uk/bhps/2001/docs/pdf/papers/kan.pdf).

Kay, T. "Women's Work and Women's Worth: The Leisure Implications of Women's Changing Employment Patterns," *Leisure Studies* (15), 1996, pp. 49-64.

Kvasny, L. "The Existential Problem of Evil and IT in the Hotel Civilization," keynote speech presented to the Second International CRIS Workshop: Critical Reflections on Critical Research on Information Systems, July 14, 2004 (available online at www.isi.salford.ac.uk/cris).

Kvasny, L., and Keil, M. "The Challenges of Redressing the Digital Divide: A Tale of Two US Cities," *Information Systems Journal* (16), 2006, pp. 23-53.

Mandelson, P. "Foreword" to *Competitive Advantage in the Digital Economy*, Department of Trade and Industry, London, 2001 (available online at http://www.dti.gov.uk/comp/competitive/pdfs/ec_pdf1.pdf).

Maynard, E. M., and Pearsall, S. J. "What About Male Mature Students? A Comparison of the Experiences of Men and Women Students," *Journal of Access Studies* (9:2), 1994, pp. 229-240.

MINTEL. *Family leisure Trends—UK*, MINTEL International Group, Ltd., March 2000.

Moore, K. *Versions of the Future in Relation to Mobile Communication Technologies*, unpublished Ph.D. thesis, University of Surrey, United Kingdom, September 2003.

Morley, D. *Home Territories Media Mobility and Identity*, London: Routledge, 2000.

Patel, D., and Pearson, I. D. "Hype and Reality in the Future Home," *BT Technology Journal* (20:2), 2002, pp. 106-115.

Peters, P., and Raaijmakers, S. "Time Crunch and the Perception of Control Over Time from a Gendered Perspective: The Dutch Case," *Society and Leisure* (21:2), Autumn 1999, pp. 417-433.

Phillips, P., Friday, A., and Cheverst, K. "Understanding Smart Environments: A Brief Classification," paper presented at the First Equator IRC Workshop on Ubiquitous Computing in Domestic Environments, University of Nottingham September 13-14, 2001 (available online at http://www.equator.ac.uk).

Richardson, H., and French, S. "Exercising Choices: The Gender Divide and Government Policy Making in the 'Global Knowledge Economy,'" in *The Transformation of Organizaitons in the Information Age: Social and Ethical Implicatoins* (6th International ETHICOMP Conference), J. A. A. A. Lopes, D. I. Alvarez, S. Rogerson and T. Ward Bynum (eds.), Lisbon, November 2002.

Rout, P. A. "Digital Homes—For Richer For Poorer, Who Are They For?," *BT Technology Journal* (20:2), April 2002, pp. 96-105.

Silva, E. B. "The Politics of Consumption at Home: Practices and Dispositions in the Uses of Technologies," Pavis Papers in Social and Cultural Research, The Open University, Milton Keynes, UK, 2000.

Silverstone, R. "Media and Technology in the Everyday Life of European Societies," Final Deliverable to the European Media and Technology in Everyday Life Network, 2000-2003, 2003 (available online at Research Results on www.emtel2.org).

Silverstone, R., and Hirsch, E. *Consuming Technologies: Media and Information in Domestic Spaces*, London: Routledge, 1992.

Steward, J., and Williams, R. "The Wrong Trousers? Beyond the Design Fallacy: Social Learning and the User," in *Handbook of Critical Information Systems Research Theory and Application*, D. Howcroft and E. Trauth (eds.), Cheltenham, MA: Edward Elgar, 2005.

Tonkiss, F. "Using Focus Groups," in C. Seale (ed.), *Researching Society and Culture*, London: Sage Publications, 2004.

Venkatesh, A. "Computers and Other Interactive Technologies for the Home," *Communications of the ACM* (39:12), 1996, pp. 47-54.

Wajcman, J. *Feminism Confronts Technology*, Cambridge, UK: Polity Press, 1991.

Wajcman, J. "Reflections on Gender and Technology Studies: In What State is the Art?," *Social Studies of Science* (30:3), 2000, pp. 447-464.

Ward, K. "An Ethnographic Study of Internet Consumption in Ireland: Between Domesticity and Public Participation," Key Deliverable to the European Media and Technology in Everyday Life Network, 2000-2003, 2003 (available online at   Research Results on www.emtel2.org).

Wharton, A. S. *The Sociology of Gender*, Oxford, UK: Blackwell. 2005.

Wilson, M., and Greenhill, A. "A Critical Deconstruction of Promises Made for Women on Behalf of Teleworking," *Critical Reflections on Critical Research in Information Systems* (2nd International CRIS Workshop), A. Adam, A. Basden, H. Richardson, and B. Robinson (eds.), University of Salford, UK, July 14, 2004.

About the Author

Helen Richardson is a senior lecturer in Information Systems and joined the University of Salford in 1998 after a varied career including working in the field of Social Care and running a Research and Training Unit promoting Positive Action for Women at Work. She is engaged in critical research in IS including issues of gender in the ICT labor market. Helen can be reached at H.Richardson@salford.ac.uk

13 WOMEN AND ICT TRAINING: Inclusion or Segregation in the New Economy?

Hazel Gillard
Nathalie Mitev
London School of Economics
London, U.K.

Abstract   *With the digital revolution narrated as the means for social cohesion in the globally competitive national economy, policy and corporate moves are afoot to increase the inclusion of women into the ICT arena, particularly those who have traditionally remained on the fringes of societal inclusion such as lone women parents. By equipping them with ICT skills, such as network engineering, and utilizing their "soft" relational expertise, greater employability and opportunity is seen as the route toward inclusion. Yet a tension emerges between policy and practice, where such women are finding it hard to gain work, for the ICT industry, renown for its long hours culture, is slow to implement government recommendations for greater work flexibility and their soft skills remain unrecognized. This paper positions this tension within a wider labor market background that focuses on part-time work, for a general lack of full-time flexibility means women with care responsibilities have a limited range of employment choice. Part-time employment is frequently reflective of dead-end jobs and a catalog of inequalities, where occupational segregation and discrimination point to the feminization of low-level ICT skills. This gendered relation to the labor market is hidden by the narrative of inclusion through ICT skills acquisition. Furthermore, the relational association reduces women and men to normative gendered identities and roles which will do little to challenge existing stereotypes of technical expertise. The paper concludes that rather than inclusion, the possible result is further gendered inequalities and exclusion.*

1 INTRODUCTION

It is often argued that we now live in a new world brought together by new technologies, generating a "new economy" with a global reach (Castells 1996; Hanseth

Please use the following format when citing this chapter:

Gillard, H., and Mitev, N., 2006, in IFIP International Federation for Information Processing, Volume 208, Social Inclusion: Societal and Organizational Implications for Information Systems, eds. Trauth, E., Howcroft, D., Butler, T., Fitzgerald, B., DeGross, J., (Boston: Springer), pp. 185-202.

and Braa 2000). In such an economy, ICT infusion, can impose corporate values and aspirations (Kallinikos 2001). Increasingly permeating our everyday existence and our social interaction, this ICT infusion has become "an expression of our interests, an implementation of our values, an extension of ourselves, a form of our lives" (Dahlbom 1996, p. 14). This growth in global ICTs is accompanied by a belief in a series of interconnected socio-economic improvements for the socially excluded and the British nation. By enhancing employability through ICT skills acquisition, greater gender equity and inclusion will boost the nation's global economic competitiveness.

The growth of new technologies is supported by deregulation frameworks that liberalize the labor environment to ensure continued expansion across industrial sectors and enable cross-border migration. This deregulation market climate is woven in a context of ICT expansion and a privileging of knowledge work, where a shift in the West from factory work to white-collar service industries and office technology is said to herald the new economy. This background of ICT productivity plays a critical role in shaping demand for specific expertise, with citizens required to be cognizant of ICT skills, and this imperative generates issues around training and gender. A drive to update and reskill the British population is in full swing, with ICT proficiency seen to open up employment prospects, particularly for those deemed to be outside of mainstream society, and women form a large percentage of these socially excluded groups (Osborn et al. 2000; Rees 2002). "A vision of a modern, fairer and more prosperous Britain...means harnessing the skills and potential of every member of society" (Tony Blair, "Foreword" to DTI 2004). Regarded as the way to connect excluded groups to the new "information society," this harnessing requires that the nation's skills base keeps pace with ICT use in employment, and that strategic partnerships with relevant business, pedagogic and government bodies are built (DTI 2001).

This paper first briefly considers the ICT policy narrative on social exclusion and women's inclusion in Britain in the light of ICT training as a vehicle for social cohesion. We then examine a business-led ICT vendor-specific training scheme in place in many UK educational establishments, and present the narratives of women students enrolled in this training scheme.

2 METHODOLOGY

Data was gathered through in-depth interviews and participant observation (e.g., through attending instructor training modules) and from government and business documentation and conferences. In total, 48 people were asked to talk about their experiences and identify what they regarded as the most critical issues influencing the effectiveness of the ICT training course. The interviewees included three female representatives of the business organization and its public/private training program; four female and two male pedagogic managers or heads of department; four female and three male tutors; two female and one male trainee tutors; and twenty female and nine male students, of which seven were lone women parents. A narrative methodology was chosen to provide rich accounts within their localized settings, and to give expression to the hidden stories behind the statistics (Czarniawska 1998; Riessman 1993; Trauth 2002).

During field work over a period of 9 months between 2002 and 2004, a cross-section of four educational sites was visited in South East England and Scotland: a higher education university, a further education institution, a women's technical college, and a women's technical and education center. These latter two educational institutions provide a second chance and a more flexible route toward education and employment for many who have been caught in the downward spiral of absenteeism from schooling, or have been labeled as "failures," or experienced low or semi-skilled work or unemployment. All of these educational establishments run the same standardized vendor-specific ICT training program in computer network engineering, although the style of delivery and supplementary content varied considerably. Our objective is to contrast the broader ICT policy and pedagogy narratives with the actual experiences of students and staff engaged with this training program, and to connect rhetoric with reality. The exclusion and inclusion policies within contemporary market dynamics claim to privilege ICT skills and gendered expertise, but what are women's actual experiences?

3 ICT POLICY NARRATIVE: PRODUCTIVITY FOR THE NEW ECONOMY

The infusion of ICT and the transformation of occupations have given rise to a perceived skills crisis on a global scale. A lack of key ICT professionals, such as network engineers, computer analysts, and programmers generates an anticipated 32 percent shortfall between demand and supply (Millar and Jagger 2001). An emphasis is that the workforce should not only be ICT literate, but also cognizant of relational expertise that is highly valued in the new economy's customer-oriented business environments, such as working in teams and communicative abilities. This skills shortage is regarded as a serious threat to the commercial exploitation of ICT, inhibitory of economic competitiveness, and reflective of an inability to adjust to change (DTI 1998; 2003a).

The government's solution is to turn round what it perceives as two key contributory factors to this skills shortage: a legacy of low skill levels, and the low participation of women in the labor market, particularly in the ICT sector (DfEE 1998; Greenfield et al. 2002). Deregulation of the labor market and the increased participation of women are key microeconomic strategies of the British government (DTI 2000, 2001, 2003a). Such strategies are seen to help kick-start the economy by facilitating greater work flexibility, and addressing the skills shortage and the high levels of social exclusion. To address the low skill levels, a key site for change is the restructuring of further education and training. The government's goal is that education becomes a life-long learning process; that vocationally oriented training programs and qualifications are standardized and consolidated, specifically those related to ICT; and that e-learning becomes more mainstream (DfEE 1998; DfES 2003). This new pedagogic culture promises "skills of the future" with enhanced job prospects, better pay and promotion, and flexible work arrangements. The British government, together with major ICT companies, is ensuring mechanisms are in place to train and retrain the workforce, specifically those who have traditionally stood outside employment like lone women parents. Reskilling the workforce and the socially excluded through vocational training has become the focus of both government and European policy and business attention, since there is an imperative to counterbalance a failure of supply to meet demand (DTI 1998; COM 2001, 2002). In the late 1990s, a doubling of ICT professions in Europe led to 10.26 million posts (Webster 2003b), generating a significant skills shortage that is predicted to rise by over 1.7 million in Europe alone (Rübsamen-Waigmann et al. 2002; Valenduc 2003). This shortage means "fishing from a wider pool," and finding new ways of working, combining both managerial, technical expertise, and relational expertise (Rübsamen-Waigmann et al. 2002, p. 5).

Britain has high levels of social exclusion, compared with the rest of Europe, with a poor inclusion record and lack of interdepartmental cohesion (Kennedy 1997; SEU 2004). The Social Exclusion Unit (SEU) was set up in 1997 to address this and coordinate policy formulation. The term *social exclusion* implies standing outside of mainstream society, and is indicative of a rupture in the social bond between sets of people and society (DFID 2002). It reflects an attempt to broaden analysis from a one-dimensional view of poverty to include high levels of low skills, lone parent families, unemployment, poor housing, high crime rates, poor health and family breakdown that are seen to create deep-rooted, long-term social and economic problems (Durieux 2003; SEU 2004). Caught in these cycles of exclusion, people who have low educational achievement and a history of low labor market inclusion are positioned outside mainstream society.

Internet technology is seen as the way to combat such exclusion, with the narrative of a digital divide, or a "two speed eEurope" (CEC 2000), conveying an analysis of a division between those who have access to ICTs and those who don't. The digital divide is a dualism first coined by the Clinton administration in 1995 (Lu and Wang 2003; Strover 2003). Those who lack access are perceived to be at risk of exclusion from the influx of new technological developments, and risk exclusion from the new economy (Castells 2001; Norris 2001). Access to the digital economy is today regarded as vital for better employment prospects and improved educational access, since the Net is seen as having the ability to "put the world at your fingertips" (Castells 1996).

With women perceived as being in danger of digital exclusion, they are being targeted for skills enhancement and labor market inclusion (Valenduc 2003; Webster 2003a). While the ICT sector is expanding in Britain, the level of women represented in it is decreasing, both in industry and academic disciplines (Panteli et al. 1999; Panteli, Stack, and Ramsey 2001; Robertson et al. 2001). This low participation by women is widely acknowledged in government circles to threaten Britain's productivity and global competitiveness (Rees 2002; Roberts 2001). Women are regarded as "the single biggest, most undervalued and underused human resource" (Greenfield et al. 2002, p. 36), and not to utilize them is to rob society of their diverse talents of communication, sharing, cooperation, forgiveness, and less ego-centered, pragmatic engagements with the world: the relational, soft skills in demand in today's customer oriented management (DTI 2003b; Webster 2003a). Women's inclusion is seen to offer them viable and marketable skills, thereby gaining economic independence and a viable career development. Not only will it improve their own personal circumstances, but it will also have beneficial impacts on their families (Rochlin and Boguslaw 2001).

The wastage of women's skills as a result of the "leaky pipeline" and institutional discrimination that impedes women's careers is seen as a matter of urgency, since it holds constant across national and disciplinary boundaries (Osborn et al. 2000; Rees 2002; Rübsamen-Waigmann et al. 2002). In encouraging more women to enter the workforce, not only will they be able to tackle these legacies of wastage, but also diversify and improve the nation's skills base, foster excellence and innovation through the creation of new products, and strengthen market competitiveness (DTI 2003b; Rübsamen-Waigmann et al. 2002).

4 ICT TRAINING FOR BUSINESS

According to various British government bodies, the profusion of ICT means that new skills should be part of pedagogic curricula (DfES 2001; DTI 2002). This concern is linked to the narrative of demand for ICT skills that is outstripping an ability of education to produce them (DTI 1998, 2001, 2004b; DfEE 1999; DfES 2003; Millar and Jagger 2001). Therefore, an urgent need is radically overhaul the system to address the nation's low skill levels, with a reform of ICT teaching at NVQ (national vocational qualification) level 3 (DfES 2003; Fryer 1997). This is the level at which the network engineering module is pitched, and represents a relatively low-level ICT occupation. With identification and consolidation of key ICT skills regarded as critical (Dearing 1996; DfEE 1998; Kennedy 1997), the vendor-specific training program meets this requirement by providing a universal and standardized e-learning platform.

E-learning vendor programs are attractive because they offer multiple access points to education and training in ICT, and provide recognized qualifications. Both are argued to be paramount in encouraging career migration and transition, particularly for women with lower skills who may be facing redundancy, or hoping to return to the job market after a break (Fryer 1997; Greenfield et al. 2002). Understanding what the ICT industry needs is vital, with better career information and wider dissemination of the idea that most jobs today involve both ICT skills and face-to face customer interaction (DTI 2001; Millar and Jagger 2001).

An array of European directives on gender affirmative action policies and strategies, which the British government and many large ICT businesses endorse, constitute part of a drive toward digital citizenship and the feminizations of ICT (Osborn et al. 2000; Rees 2002). To support notions of *difference* and *equity*, changes in ICT stereotypes image and corporate culture are advocated to ease the strain of long, anti-social working hours and facilitate women's inclusion, with improved flexible work arrangements to enable a healthier balance between work and private responsibilities (Work and Parents Taskforce 2001). This change is designed to challenge assumptions about who engages with ICT work and the established masculine techno-culture which is "stuck in a time warp," as expressed by a business representative. The ICT company we studied makes use of marketing imagery by showing women in action-oriented roles and proactively attempts to recruit them into its training program. In the words of one ICT key business representative, we need to "educate people on how to be educated." The myth of ICT jobs as lacking human interaction, variety, or personal satisfaction this company regards as outdated, for the reality is that while programming or technical skills are required, a broader range around communication, teamwork and business awareness are key components. With this framework in mind, the paper now turns to the narratives of women on the network engineer training program, and highlights their actual experiences of this inclusion vehicle.

5   NARRATIVES

While the above policy and corporate strategies of inclusion appear to address the assumptions surrounding women's ICT exclusion, there seems to be mismatch between the perceived skills crisis and the reality of the ICT labor market, as narrated by a community education manager:

> *We weren't confident, we're still not confident, that what we're providing from the daytime group is actually...in a position to avail themselves of that shortage...data we were given of...the huge job shortage in this area, 80,000 vacancies...okay, that changed, partly because of the downturn in the economy...which did hit IT obviously...I think the shortage is certainly a lot less severe than it was.*

This downturn in the ICT economy is reflected in the difficulty many students experience when seeking employment, as one male university student voiced:

> *A lot of the students are...actually worried [because] they don't have the experience, and most of them [employers] actually want 1 year experience, [or] 2 years experience....There isn't any work...the companies who are looking for people actually need x amount of years in experience which...none of us I think [have].*

Many students were not finding work after completion of the training program, as one woman community education manager expressed:

> *It's proving, for us, a very tough industry to break into, the technical, to develop the relationship with the employers...I suspect women going out into that situation are potentially going to find it tougher than the young men going out into that situation, [because] they're likely to go into departments where...the culture of the departments are very entrenched male cultures.*

The lack of work experience and "entrenched male cultures" were particularly worrying for female students and staff in general, particularly since they were finding that the qualification was not recognized by ICT employers, as another community education manager commented:

> *The labor market doesn't necessarily agree with the qualification, not necessarily the qualifications we deliver but the qualifications in general...not particularly bothered about NVQs.*

This conundrum was articulated by another community education manager as reflecting the risk involved in letting a newly qualified yet inexperienced person work in a highly strategic networked environment:

> *The reality of the situation is most employers will not let the newly qualified person anywhere near their network system...employers are worried about [the] risk...to systems cock ups [errors]...[there is a] general fear of failure.... Not surprisingly...it's very difficult to find appropriate work experience for somebody doing a qualification...nobody will let them near a network...[it's] very difficult to get the experience, very difficult to get your foot in the door, and without that it's very, very difficult to get a job...it is a real catch 22.... This is indicative of the low risk attitude that we are finding, that the private sector is efficient and risk-taking...I find [that] laughable...they're immensely conservative...and in a way you can appreciate why...[because] if you've got somebody with 10 years experience and somebody who has just come out of college....On the one level, you can understand them playing it safe...on the other level, perhaps they ought to be looking at potential rather than actual.... The two things are very, very different.*

For women, the quest to find work was problematic given the industry's long working, anti-social hours, as narrated by a lone woman parent who simultaneously worked in the ICT industry and attended the program at university during her free time:

> *You cannot do IT to be fair if you have got children...you have to be 7 o'clock in the morning to turn up and make sure the backup is run and do the monthly backups. You have to run your child and drop her off at the child-minders... you just can't do that...if your network does go down and somebody needs to come out 10 o'clock at night...they're going to need you to be there and...if you were a single mother with a child, it would be virtually no way you could do that because where, where would you leave your child at 10 o'clock at night.*

And if a student is a low-skilled, black, lone parent, employability is even more problematic, as a community education manager narrated:

> *Most employers would [employ]...graduates...in preference to a black, lone parent.*

This racial, low-skilled, and care responsibility discrimination was not challenged in some pedagogic institutions, particularly with regard to gendered abilities, as the narrative of a male university head of department reveals:

> *The ladies of the class do have slightly different problems from the males because of their backgrounds and their experiences, and I do have this thing that, yes, females do think differently from males...I don't think I'm sexist in anyway but...men are more lateral thinking than women...with the sort of*

technical engineering type subjects...you can't just sort of look at the problem there [indicates a small area with hands], you've got to look that way as well [widens hands], what's going on around there....Think about what the engineers are doing, they don't...just look around there, they're looking over that hedge and over the next one and the third one as well. They are thinking ahead and programming, that's their way of thinking...you've got to put these things together and make them work...some women...they're not very confident...they're just not looking here [in front of his nose]...and they can't look sideways either...a woman...doesn't seem to be able to do that.

The employability conundrum, combined with overt gendered stereotyping, is further reinforced by the lack of part-time work. An additional barrier for lone parents involved finding extra time to keep pace with constant changes in network information, as a woman parent and student narrated:

I really want to work part-time locally, but the industry is not here to do part-time work. Part-time work is like gold dust....If I had full-time work, I would have to employ someone to clean and iron....The problem with IT jobs is that they require continuous retraining. With a family how do you fit this in? The skills become obsolete. You go for a job and you're disadvantaged. I've been doing this for 20 years and technology is changing so fast. There used to be a plateau of skill levels but now there is no plateau any more....It adds pressure to you because of the family, I need to shop and cook and study.

Many socially excluded women with care responsibilities are disadvantaged when competing with male colleagues, as a lone woman parent and part-time university student, who had some experience of work interviews, remarked:

I'm also realistic to know that when it comes to interviews I'm sure that...if there is a man going with the same amount of experiences as me...they will take a man, so I'm realistic as well to know that it's not as easy to get a job in IT as a woman...as soon as you go into really technical...and network administration [work], I do think it's harder for you to get into those types of jobs...I'm sure, if you have a child I don't think, I don't think they would employ you, they won't say it, but I think that is the case.

This reveals many barriers: a shortage of employment, lack of network engineering experience, masculine techno-cultures, lack of qualification acknowledgment, fear of network malfunction, care conflicts, gendered and racial stereotyping, limited flexible work availability, the need to keep pace with technological advancements, and the industry's preference to recruit single men. Many students, particularly those with care commitments, realized that the ICT environment was not a particularly attractive arena, as a married student with two small children who had previously worked in banking narrated:

They [banking] were open to different ways of working, but I don't feel that has reached the male dominated computer world yet...it is inflexible in its

*working patterns.....At the end of the day, my family comes first. I don't feel
I'm available 24/7.*

The anti-social hours and the barriers reflect the ICT industry's recalcitrance in changing
its competitive "new frontier" culture, and this is in evidence in terms of the onus on
relational skills.   These skills are not yet valued, as a male community education
manager articulated:

*It's an extremely macho industry, the hours...sort of new frontier culture...it's
so unattractive, the role models are still...there's not really the focus on people
skills that actually are increasingly important within the sector itself, but
perhaps aren't being seen and recognized as being particularly important...it
is actually getting worse despite all these initiatives from employers.*

These question the call for greater diversification of the workforce, and reinforce
the argument that ICT skills acquisition alone is insufficient in addressing inclusion.
Despite the policies and initiatives, the needs of business and students' expectations
were mismatched, presenting a fundamental problem for pedagogy. The general lack
of students' awareness, particularly women's, of what the ICT industry entailed was
expressed by a head of business development in a community education college:

*There's an incongruency of women and the hard reality...[there is a] lack of
awareness of the IT world...the reality of the networking environment...there
is a mismatch of expectation...women have no concept of what the industry is
like...[they] think that they can do the job, but the reality is when it comes to
what does that mean to their lives, they often aren't able to fit that in with their
lives. ...Much of the work is shift based, call-center, 24 hour cover... [there are
problems in] bringing women in raw to IT, [they have] no skills, no IT skills,
not much work experience in the industry.*

This mismatch was summarized by a single woman student, aware of some of her
colleagues' care responsibilities:

*[This is] the whole contradiction...I feel the majority of their funding is based
on maybe women getting back, single mothers getting back into work...it's
going to be shifts...there you have the wonderful contradiction...I mean I
appreciate what the man [a manager] said because part of it is true...
networking is a 24/7 thing...it's not a 9 to 5 and "oh little Johnny's got a cold
today." Tough!*

Students are unprepared for the realities of the industry, and unsurprisingly frustration
and annoyance emerged, as one single woman strongly articulated:

*All these so called incentives—we want more women in engineering; we want
more women in IT; we want more women in this...it's lip service...the bottom
line is [that] if you happen to be a woman, that's what you want to do, you'll
do it....This is what the government is always whittering [talking] on about,*

mothers and children and education, and get them off the dole [welfare benefit].

ICT inclusion programs, therefore, run the risk of reinforcing low-self esteem, disenfranchisement, and exclusion, as one lone woman parent student remarked:

The course is geared to attract single mums but...they're obviously targeting women who haven't got a clue until they get halfway through the course, and they realize "hold on a minute"...if they start investigating on jobs and issues and what's realistically out there...they'd given you false information because they wanted bums on seats...it's money...a computer conveyor belt...don't throw me in at the deep end [to] drown basically...I need a job that isn't going to take up much time as I don't have the support...they knew my situation, this is what's so frustrating, they knew it was difficult for me...I was naïve...it's frustrating when you know you can achieve something...there's no support... they've made me feel [extremely undermined], and that's just killed me...these women like me who are thinking of getting out of the rat race...they're demotivating me...they're setting us up to fail...at the end of the day, it's down to us.

These themes appear in all our geographical sites, rural and urban, across educational institutions, across ethnicity, age, parenthood, and experience. For women, especially as lone parents, these commonalities include negative notions of self-confidence, the poor prospects of working in the ICT industry, their pressing childcare responsibilities, and consequently their sense of identity and range of possibilities, which do not necessarily fit with the policy and corporate narratives of inclusion.

6   DISCUSSION: A POLITICAL ECONOMY OF WOMEN AND THE LABOR MARKET

To understand how this mismatch between policy and practices emerges, an overview of women's relation to the labor market helps. Historically, there has been a legacy of gendered labor inequalities, in part because women continue to remain the primary care providers (Walby and Olsen 2002; Wallace 2002). For many, particularly those married, access to full-time work has been restricted by the view that they are not primary workers (Walby 1997; Walby and Olsen 2002). This legacy is displayed in women's disproportionate representation in part-time employment, and in their clustering in a limited range of low-level ICT occupations. This reflects a political economy of women's labor characterized by inequalities and rigidities that manifest a contradictory relation to productivity.

In 2000, five times as many women (44 percent) as men (9 percent) were economically active in part-time employment in Britain (Cousins and Tang 2002; DfES 2003; Walby and Olsen 2002); a statistic which held for 2004 (National Statistics 2004). This heavy representation of women in part-time work is due to a lack of flexibility in full-time employment, and the acute shortage in affordable and suitable care arrangements (Walby 1990, 1997; Webster and Valenduc 2003). With Britain having the lowest childcare provision compared to other European nations, this presents a major obstacle to their inclusion (Cousins and Tang 2002; Kennedy 1997). Women's lower levels of education and training means part-time work may be their only option (Rees 1992; Walby and Olsen 2002; Wallace 2002). Such work is generally low or semi-skilled, with less status than full-time employment, and poorly unionized (DTI 2002; Rubery et al. 1999).

A pay differential of 40 percent in 2002, rising to 43 percent in 2005 is common in part-time employment (Bulman 2002; Hibbett and Meager 2003). This also extends to women in full-time work, on average, being paid 18 or 19 percent less than their male counterparts (DfES 2003; Walby 1997). Part-time work tends to miss out on in-house training and has limited promotion opportunities, with many women's skill levels not increasing in comparison to those in full-time posts (DTI 2002; Walby and Olsen 2002). These pay differentials are attributable to women's lack of labor market experience, a result of interrupted employment, largely due to care responsibilities (Rees 1992; Walby and Olsen 2002). Unless women are protected by maternity leave, many experience downward mobility when they reenter the labor market, where their skills are under-utilized and the number of children having a detrimental effect on their earnings (Rees 1992; Rubery et al. 1999; Walby and Olsen 2002).

Flexible work, for many women, is characterized by low skills, inequalities of pay, weaker conditions of service, fewer training and promotion opportunities, lower status, little labor protection, and greater instability (Cousins and Tang 2002; Greenfield et al. 2002). These have an adverse influence on productivity by poorly utilizing their skills and restricting their labor market mobility (Walby and Olsen 2002). Additionally, the ICT industry is not renown for regular part-time employment. It is not viewed as suited to part-time, flexible employment, with only 18 percent of workers not on full-time conditions of service in 2000, of which 15.7 percent were women and 2.3 percent men (Millar and Jagger 2001). The industry has been slow to adopt work flexibility, with line managers resistant to change and unable to see the business case (DTI 2002; Walby and Olsen 2002). Concerned with the cost of additional recruitment, difficulties in managing a remote team, and the complexity in juggling projects, resources and changing customer requirements tend to govern working conditions and reduce choice in flexible working arrangements (DTI 2002; Vendramin 2003). With call availability in network engineering often over a 24-hour period 7 days a week, regular part-time work is viewed as inadequate.

Part-time contracts are most prolific in call centers, characterized by poor or absent unionization, staffed by low skilled women, under adverse conditions and poor remuneration (Belt et al. 2000; Wilson and Greenhill 2004). Finding part-time network engineer work is like finding gold dust. Breaks in employment mean that an employee will have to catch up on ICT knowledge and practices (Millar and Jagger 2001; Walby and Olsen 2002). This pressure is further amplified by a perception that either you have a dedicated, successful career or you have a balanced life (DTI 2002; Kodz et al. 2002). Being seen as less committed, an employee will be disadvantaged in the light of company practice to promote people abreast with ICT trends, rather than face the expense of updating skills.

In addition, the ICT sector displays a gendered segregation, which curtails the scope and potential for employability for women with care responsibilities (Rubery et al. 1999;

Walby 1990, 1997; Webster 2003b). Women run the risk of being excluded in sites of increasing technical ghettoization (Wajcman 1991; Wilson and Howcroft 2000). This pattern of exclusion points to the feminizations of low-level ICT skills, where women are excluded from higher level positions (Rees 1992). Women still push the buttons but rarely engage with the more status oriented design or configuration of new technologies (Cockburn 1983, 1985; Wajcman 1991; Rees 1992).

This snapshot of low-skilled women in relation to the labor market, and the lack of suitable and regular part-time employment in the ICT sector, points to a contradiction that underpins the strategies to include socially excluded women, and at its heart lies the narrow focus on ICT employability. That women's employment is cataloged by inequalities is not fully accounted for by strategies of inclusion that pander to superficial narratives on legacies of low skill levels and the low participation of women. Yet, while these inequalities may jeopardize productivity, there appears to be an interdependence between the nation's competitive edge and women's cheaper, more flexible forms of labor (Cockburn 1985; Wajcman 1991; Walby 1990). By unraveling yet another labor market rigidity —discrimination (Rees 1992; Walby 1990, 1997; Webster 2003b)—we may begin to understand the recalcitrant inequity characteristics of many women's engagement with the labor market. This rigidity is brought to the fore by the association of women and relational expertise, and points to the symbolic and essentialist reinforcement of exclusionary mechanisms.

The ICT industry, renown for its youthful, masculine techno-culture, is a hard and unfriendly environment for women to enter or succeed in (Bowker and Star 2000; Faulkner 2000; Moreau 2003), despite equity and diversity legislation. While some women do manage to mold a career (Adam 1997; Henwood 2000), the ICT arena generally presents an unattractive and competitive new frontier philosophy that is not only recalcitrant to new initiatives, but also to recognizing relational skills. Enhanced employability for women through their perceived relational strengths does not take place for these skills tend not to be recognized, or rewarded (Rees 1992; Webster 2003a). Rather, what emerges during the feminizations of a particular occupation is the lowering of skills status, or deskilling (Rees 1992).

7   CONCLUSION

This paper sought to present an account of ICT inclusion policies with particular regard to network engineer training, and to match the rhetoric with the reality for socially excluded people, particularly women and lone parents. Our findings show that inclusion is not as straightforward as equipping the socially excluded with the required skills to open doors to their employability, for, in the case of women, the ICT industry remains recalcitrant in recognizing their value, preferring to recruit men (Millar and Jagger 2001; Rees 1992; Webster 2003b). This practice will not be challenged by the association of women and relational skills, since their value is seen to reside not in their technical expertise, but in symbolic personal and behavioral characteristics (Payne 1999). This symbolic association totters dangerously close to essentialism by reducing women to their "feminine" qualities (Faulkner 2000, 2004; Rommes and Faulkner 2003), and is reflected in strategies that attempt to feminize ICT by revamping ICT's masculine image through stereotyped notions of what women and young girls are perceived to be interested in. Yet the reality is that the industry is a male preserve, and any attempt to portray it as otherwise risks further disenfranchisement for those who do not fit or accept the normative and gendered practices. Equality of opportunity cannot be women's reality within this model of inclusion, for by homogeneously presenting them as relational, their differences are sidelined and invalidated.

By so shaping women's inclusion through recognition of their soft relational skills, normative gendered identities and roles are affirmed and differences are silenced (Bowker and Star 2000; Webster 2003b). This narrative of inclusion gives concreteness to women's and men's immutable natural abilities, denies other strengths, the gender crossing of skills, and positions women in low skilled, low status work and outside of technical expertise. In affirming essentialist skills to particular genders, historical and socio-political legacies of value are perpetuated and reinforced, and while society may then appear ordered and known, individuals struggle to find their place or be heard. Difference is silenced by this Western canon of purity (de Beauvoir 1972).

If marginality, or exclusion, is about not fitting into practices and beliefs perceived as the norm, and about crossing the borderlands of these recalcitrant narratives (Bowker and Star 2000), then how may socially excluded groups achieve inclusion if these borderlands of difference and ambiguity are silenced? The narratives of diversity and equity, while seeking to validate difference, do the opposite by imposing essentialist, socially constructed characteristics, in this case, of gender. By materially reinforcing gendered symbolic values in economic and technical deterministic inclusion, normative roles and identities seamlessly disappear into black-boxed infrastructures and discriminatory practices of taken-for-granted habit (Bowker and Star 2000). The mono-causal government analysis of exclusion, where the key to a more prosperous and healthier life lies in employability through ICT skills acquisition, belies the complexity of why people continue to remain on the fringes of society. For some, it is a choice; for others, the choice is constituted by discrimination and a catalog of inequalities and barriers that the narratives reflect and policy does not.

Contrary to the narratives of inclusion, the labor market dynamics present fundamental tensions for people classified as socially excluded, and its deregulation may serve to jeopardize rights hard won. In formulating economic citizenship into educational arenas through the narratives of equality and diversity, socially excluded citizens are encouraged to cultivate an ethos of individualization, responsibility, and obligation, one that requires full ownership and accountability for the management of their personal socio-economic circumstances (Bauman 2000; Beck and Beck-Gernsheim 1995; Lister 1997). This ethos may not so easily be fostered for those on the fringes of society, for the reality of inclusion in terms of suitable and well-paid ICT employment continues to elude them. In assuming equality if skills acquisition is offered, the policy narrative of inclusion airbrushes the labor market relation that many women, particularly those with care responsibilities, experience, airbrushes their different needs and aspirations and thereby risks reinforcing their exclusion.

References

Adam, A. "What Should We Do with Cyberfeminism?," in R. Lander and A. Adam (eds.), *Women in Computing*, Exeter, UK: Intellect Books, 1997, pp. 17-27.

Bauman, Z. *Liquid Modernity*, Cambridge, UK: Polity Press, 2000.

Beck, U., and Beck-Gernsheim, E. *The Normal Chaos of Love*, Cambridge, UK: Polity Press, 1995.

Belt, V., Richardson, R., and Webster, J. "Women's Work in the Information Economy," *Information, Communication & Society* (3:3), 2000, pp. 366-385.

Bowker, G., and Star, S. L. *Sorting Things Out*, Cambridge, MA: The MIT Press, 2000.

Bulman, J. "Patterns of Pay: Results of the 2002 New Earnings Survey," *Labor Market Trends* (110:12), 2002, pp. 634-655.

Castells, M. *The Internet Galaxy: Reflections on the Internet, Business and Society*, Oxford, UK: Oxford University Press, 2001.

Castells, M. *The Rise of the Network Society*, Oxford, UK: Blackwell Publishers, 1996.

CEC. "Building an Inclusive Europe," Communication from the European Commission, Brussels, 2000.

Cockburn, C. *Brothers: Male Dominance and Technological Change*, London: Pluto Press, 1983.

Cockburn, C. *Machinery of Dominance: Women, Men and Technical Know-How*, London: Pluto Press, 1985.

Cousins, C., and Tang, N. "The United Kingdom" in C. Wallace (ed.), *Households, Work and Flexibility: Critical Review of Literature*, Vienna: HWF Series of Project Research Reports, HWF Research Consortium, 2002.

COM. "The eLearning Action Plan: Designing Tomorrow's Education," Commission of the European Communities, Brussels, 2001.

COM. "eEurope 2005: An Information Society for All," Commission of the European Communities, Brussels, 2002.

Czarniawska, B. *A Narrative Approach to Organization Studies*, Thousand Oaks, CA: Sage Publications, 1998.

Dahlbom, B. "The New Informatics," *Scandinavian Journal of Information Systems* (8:2), 1996, pp. 29-47.

de Beauvoir, S. *The Second Sex*, Harmondsworth, UK: Penguin Books, 1972.

Dearing, R. "Review of Qualifications for 16-19 Year Olds," The Robert Dearing Report, London: Skills Council Academic Authority, 1996.

DfEE. "The Learning Age: A Renaissance of a New Britain," Green Paper, Department for Employment and Education, Nottingham: DfEE Publications, February 1998.

DfEE. "Skills for the Information Age," The Stevens Report, Department for Employment and Education, Nottingham: DfEE Publications, 1999.

DfES. "Skills for Life—The National Strategy for Improving Adult Literacy and Numeracy," Department for Education and Skills (Department of Employment and Education), London, 2001.

DfES. "21st Century Skills: Realising Our Potential," Department for Education and Skills (Department of Employment and Education), London, 2003.

DFID. "Social Exclusion in Pro-Poor Infrastructure Provision," Department for International Development, London, 2002.

DTI. "Excellence and Opportunity—A Science and Innovation Policy for the 21st Century," Department for Trade and Industry, London, 2000.

DTI. "Fairness for All: A New Commission for Equality and Human Rights," White Paper, Department of Trade and Industry, in association with the Department for Constitutional Affairs, Department for Education and Skills, Department for Work and Pensions, and the Home Office, London, 2004 (available online at http://www.womenandequalityunit.gov.uk/).

DTI. "Maximising Returns to Science, Engineering and Technology Careers," A report for the Office of Science and Technology and the Department of Trade and Industry, prepared by People Science and Policy Ltd. and the Institute for Employment Research, University of Warwick, 2002.

DTI. "Opportunity for All in a World of Change," White Paper, Department for Trade and Industry, London, 2001.

DTI. "Our Competitive Future: Building the Knowledge Driven Economy," Department for Trade and Industry, London, 1998.

DTI. "A Strategy for Women in Science, Engineering and Technology," Department for Trade and Industry., London, 2003a (available online http://extra.shu.ac.uk/nrc/section_2/publications/reports/R1428_Strategy_for_Women_in_SET.pdf).

DTI. "Women in IT Conference: Engaging & Retaining for Success," Department of Trade and Industry and the Department of Education and Skills, London, January 22, 2003b.

DTI 2004

Durieux, D. "ICT and Social Inclusion in the Everyday Life of Less Abled People," Key Deliverable, European Media and Technology in Everyday Life Network, 2003.

Faulkner, W. "Strategies of Inclusion: Gender in the Information Society," Symposium on Gender and Information and Communication Technologies: Strategies of Inclusion, Brussels, January 2004.

Faulkner, W. "The Technology Question in Feminism: A View from Feminist Technology Studies," Strategies of Inclusion: Gender and the Information Society, Brussels, 2000 (available online at http://www.rcss.ed.ac.uk/sigis/).

Fryer, R. H. "Learning for the Twenty-First Century," The Fryer Report, White Paper, First Report of the National Advisory Group for Continuing Education and Lifelong Learning, London, 1997.

Greenfield, S., Peters, J., Lane, N., Rees, T., and Samuels, G. "SET Fair: A Report on Women in Science, Engineering and Technology," The Greenfield Review, commissioned for the Department of Trade and Industry, London, November 2002.

Hanseth, O., and Braa, K. "Globalisation and 'Risk Society,'" in C. U. Ciborra and Associates (eds.), *From Control to Drift: The Dynamics of Corporate Information Infrastructures*, Oxford, UK: Oxford University Press, 2000.

Henwood, F. "From the Woman Question in Technology to the Technology Question in Feminism: Rethinking Gender Inequality in IT Education," *The European Journal of Women's Studies* (7), 2000, pp. 209-227.

Hibbett, A., and Meager, N. "Key Indicators of Women's Position in Britain," *Labor Market Trends* (111:10), 2003, pp. 503-511.

Kallinikos, J. "Recalcitrant Technology: Cross-Contextual Systems and Context-Embedded Action," Working Paper 103, London School of Economics and Political Science, 2001.

Kennedy, H. "Learning Works: Widening Participation in Further Education," The Further Education Funding Council, London, 1997.

Kodz, J., Harper, H., and Dench, S. "Work-Life Balance: Beyond the Rhetoric," IES Report 384, Institute for Employment Studies, March 2002 (available through http://www.employment-studies.co.uk/pubs/)

Lister, R. "Citizenship: Towards a Feminist Synthesis," *Feminist Review* (57), 1997, pp. 28-48.

Lu, A-X., and Wang, H. "The Problems and Prospects of Teaching in the Digital Age," panel presentation to the Informing Science and Information Technology Education Joint Conference, Pori, Finland, June 24-27, 2003.

Millar, J., and Jagger, N. "Women in ITEC Courses and Careers," A report for the Department of Trade and Industry, Department for Education and Skills, and Women and Equality Unit, Suffolk, UK: DfES Publications, 2001.

Moreau, M-P. "Work Organization and Working Conditions" in P. Vendramin, G. Valenduc, C. Guffins, J. Webster, I. Wagner, A. Birbaumer and M. Tolar (eds.), *Conceptual Framework and State of the Art: Widening Women's Work in Information and Communication Technology*, Namur, Belgium: Foundation Travail-Université, 2003 (available online at http://www.ftu-namur.org/www-ict).

National Statistics. "Labor Market Statistics," Office for National Statistics, London., June 2004. (http://www.statistics.gov.uk).

Norris, P. *Digital Divide: Civic Engagement, Information Poverty, and the Internet Worldwide*, Cambridge, UK: Cambridge University Press, 2001.

Osborn, M., Rees, T., Bosch, M., Ebeling, H., Hermann, C., Hilden, J., McLaren, A., Palomba, R., Peltonen, L., Vela, C., Weis, D., Wold, A., Mason, J., and Wenneras, C. "Science Policies in the European Union: Promoting Excellence through Mainstreaming Gender Equality," A report from the ETAN Network on Women and Science, Office for the Official Publications of the European Communities, Luxembourg, 2000.

Panteli, N., Stack, J., Atkinson, M., and Ramsey, H. "The Status of Women in the UK IT Industry: An Empirical Study," *European Journal of Information Systems* (8), 1999, pp. 170-182.

Panteli, N., Stack, J., and Ramsey, H. "Gendered Patterns in Computing Work in the Late 1990s," *New Technology, Work and Employment* (16:1), 2001, pp. 3-17.

Payne, J. "All Things to All People: Changing Perceptions of 'Skill' Among Britain's Policy Makers Since the 1950s and Their Implications," SKOPE Research Paper No. 1, Warwick University, 1999.

Rees, T. "The Helsinki Group on Women and Science: National Policies on Women and Science in Europe," Office for Official Publications for the European Communities:, Luxembourg, 2002.

Rees, T. *Women and the Labor Market* London: Routledge, 1992.

Riessman, C. K. *Narrative Analysis*, London: Sage Publications, 1993.

Roberts, G. "SET for Success: The Supply of People with Science, Technology, Engineering and Mathematical Skills," The Report of Sir Gareth Roberts' Review, London, 2001.

Robertson, M., Newell, S., Swan, J., Mathiassen, L., and Bjerknes, G. "The Issue of Gender Within Computing: Reflections from the UK and Scandinavia," *Information Systems Journal* (11), 2001, pp. 111-126.

Rochlin, S., and Boguslaw, J. "Business and Community Development: Aligning Corporate Performance with Community Economic Development to Achieve Win-Win Impacts," The Center for Corporate Citizenship at Boston College, 2001.

Rommes, E., and Faulkner, W. "Conclusion," in E. Rommes, I. van Slooten, E. van Oost, and N. Oudshoorn (eds.), *Designing Inclusion: The Development of ICT Products to Include Women in the Information Society*, Strategies of Inclusion: Gender and the Information Society, 2003 (available online at http://www.sigis-ist.org/).

Rubery, J., Smith, M., and Fagan, C. *Women's Employment in Europe: Trends and Prospects*, London: Routledge, 1999.

Rübsamen-Waigmann, H., Sohlberg, R., Rees, T., Berry, O., Bismuth, P., D'Antona, R., De Brabander, E., Haemers, G., Holmes, J., Jepson, M. K., Leclaire, J., Mann, E., Neumann, J., Needham, R., Christian, N., Vela, C., and Winslow, D. "Women in Industrial Research: A Wake Up Call for European Industry," A report for the European Commission from the High Level Expert Group on Women in Industrial Research for Strategic Analysis of Specific Science and Technology Policy Issues (STRATA), European Commission Directorate-General for Research, Luxembourg, 2002.

SEU. "Preventing Social Exclusion," A report by the Social Exclusion Unit, London, 2004 (available online at http://www.socialexclusionunit.gov.uk/).

Strover, S. "Remapping the Digital Divide," *The Information Society* (19), 2003, pp. 275-277.

Trauth, E. "Odd Girl Out: An Individual Difference Perspective on Women in the IT Profession," *Information Technology and People* (15:2), 2002, pp. 98-117.

Valenduc, G. "Mapping ICT Profession" in P. Vendramin, G. Valenduc, C. Guffins, J. Webster, I. Wagner, A. Birbaumer, and M. Tolar (eds.), *Widening Women's Work in Information and Communication Technology: Conceptual Framework and State of the Art*, Namur, Belgium: Foundation Travail-Université, 2003 (avaialble online at http://www.ftu-namur.org/www-ict).

Vendramin, P. "Describing the Various Dimensions of the Gender Gap in ICT Professions" in P. Vendramin, G. Valenduc, C. Guffins, J. Webster, I. Wagner, A. Birbaumer, and M. Tolar (eds.), *Widening Women's Work in Information and Communication Technology: Conceptual Framework and State of the Art*, Namur, Belgium: Foundation Travail-Université, 2003 (avaialble online at http://www.ftu-namur.org/www-ict).

Wajcman, J. *Feminism Confronts Technology*, Cambridge, UK: Polity Press, 1991.

Walby, S. *Gender Transformations*, London: Routledge, 1990.

Walby, S. *Theorizing Patriarchy*, Oxford, UK: Blackwell Publishers, 1990.

Walby, S., and Olsen, W. "The Impact of Women's Position in the Labor Market on Pay and Implications for UK Productivity," Report to Women & Equality Unit, London: DTI Publications, November 2002.

Wallace, C. "Overview" in C. Wallace (ed.), *Households, Work and Flexibility: Critical Review of Literature*, Vienna: HWF Series of Project Research Reports, HWF Research Consortium, 2002.

Webster, J. "Gender Issues in European Socio-Economic Research on the Information Society," in P. Vendramin, G. Valenduc, C. Guffins, J. Webster, I. Wagner, A. Birbaumer, and M. Tolar (eds.), *Widening Women's Work in Information and Communication Technology: Conceptual Framework and State of the Art*, Namur, Belgium: Foundation Travail-Université, 2003a (avaialble online at http://www.ftu-namur.org/www-ict).

Webster, J. "Working in the New Economy—The View from the Employee," UK Work Organization Network, London, 2003b..

Webster, J., and Valenduc, G. "Mapping Gender Gaps in Employment and Occupations" in P. Vendramin, G. Valenduc, C. Guffins, J. Webster, I. Wagner, A. Birbaumer, and M. Tolar (eds.), *Widening Women's Work in Information and Communication Technology: Conceptual Framework and State of the Art*, Namur, Belgium: Foundation Travail-Université, 2003 (avaialble online at http://www.ftu-namur.org/www-ict).

Wilson, M., and Greenhill, A. "Gender and Teleworking Identities: Reconstructing the Research Agenda," in *Proceedings of the 12th European Conference on Information Systems*, Turku, Finland, June 2004.

Wilson, M., and Howcroft, D. "The Role of Gender in User Resistance and Informatin Systems Failure," in R. Baskerville, J. Stage, and J. I. DeGross (eds.), *Organizational and Social Perspectives on Information Technology*, Boston: Kluwer Academic Publishers, 2000, pp. 453-471.

Work and Parents Taskforce. "About Time: Flexible Working," London, 2001 (available online at http://www.workandparentstaskforce.gov.uk).

About the Authors

Hazel Gillard is currently finalizing her Ph.D. at the London School of Economics, Department of Information Systems. Her research interests lie in government and corporate valorization of ICT productivity to tackle socio-economic and gendered exclusion; in the philosophy of technology; and in pedagogy as a vehicle for social and personal change. With a diverse background in social anthropology and computer science, she has taught extensively in a variety of public sector educational institutions, traveled widely and is also a shiatsu practitioner. Hazel can be contacted at h.gillard@lse.ac.uk.

Nathalie Mitev is a senior lecturer at the London School of Economics and has held previous lecturing positions at Salford University and City University in the UK. She has French postgraduate degrees, an MBA, and a Ph.D. Her research career initially concentrated on information retrieval and human-computer interaction and then moved to the organizational and social aspects of IS. She has published on IS implementation issues in small businesses, and the health, tourism, travel, and construction industries. Her theoretical interests are the social construction of technology and she has applied actor-network theory to analyzing IS failures. She is particularly interested in how social constructionist approaches contribute to critical IS research. Nathalie has published in major IS journals and conferences, including *European Journal for Information Systems, Journal of Information Technology, Information Technology and People*, the European Conference on Information Systems and the International Conference on Information Systems. She has been track chair for various conferences such as IRMA, ICIS, and Decision Sciences Institute. She is a visiting professor at Aarhus University School of Business in Denmark. Nathalie can be reached at n.n.mitev@lse.ac.uk.

14 SOCIAL INCLUSION AND THE SHIFTING ROLE OF TECHNOLOGY: Is Age the New Gender in Mobile Access?

Carl Adams
Tineke Fitch
University of Portsmouth
Portsmouth, U.K.

Abstract   *Information and communication technologies (ICT) are at the heart of government social inclusion policy. However, the "digital divide" remains and social inclusion and technology are closely linked: Not having access to technology is often seen both as part of the inclusion/exclusion problem and part of the solution by enabling access to information resources through different channels. Yet, we argue that by using technology to address an inclusion/exclusion problem, it will also result in moving the problem from one area to another. The arguments in this paper have been informed by two empirical studies around a ubiquitous technology, the mobile phone. One study is primarily based on the 18 to 25 year old age groups; the other mostly on retired people. The studies show clear differences between age groups and gender in adoption and use of the mobile telephone.*

Social inclusion is multifaceted; it is not an either/or measure and many attributes are subjective and depend on context. Social inclusion for mobile access is also closely linked to deeply embedded structures within society, such as those traditionally associated with gender. Technology may be changing these structures; indeed, age may be the new gender. The family or social unit may also be a useful entity to consider in the exclusion debate. Technology is being used to address social exclusion; however, we suggest that while some leveling may result, there may also be different social exclusion fronts emerging.

1   INCLUSION AND TECHNOLOGY

This paper examines social inclusion and exclusion and the role of technology through a ubiquitous technology: the mobile phone. The aim of the paper is to see how

Please use the following format when citing this chapter:

Adams, C., and Fitch, T., 2006, in IFIP International Federation for Information Processing, Volume 208, Social Inclusion: Societal and Organizational Implications for Information Systems, eds. Trauth, E., Howcroft, D., Butler, T., Fitzgerald, B., DeGross, J., (Boston: Springer), pp. 203-215.

technology impacts inclusion activity in technology dominated societies. The paper draws upon some government practice and thinking in addressing exclusion within the digital divide. Two empirical studies on mobile phone use and adoption are used and related to current thinking about social exclusion. There are many definitions of the terms *social inclusion* and *exclusion* (Britton and Casebourne n.d.) and the terms are used differently in different contexts, although the Scottish government's definition brings out most of the common attributes:

> Social inclusion is about reducing inequalities between the least advantaged groups and communities and the rest of society by closing the opportunity gap and ensuring that support reaches those who need it most.[1]

Social inclusion is about reducing the inequalities between differently advantaged groups, particularly when providing support and services. Social inclusion and exclusion have been very topical areas of concern in the United States, particularly during the Clinton years, as well as in the Europen Union and many other countries in recent years (Warschauer 2002). This has resulted in government policies aimed at reducing inequalities between the least advantaged groups and the rest of society. Much of this policy has been focused on closing the opportunity gap by giving fair access to resources and usually follows altruistic motives and rhetoric.

> The idea of "social inclusion" is now the central legitimating concept of social policy in Europe and elsewhere. There is a general agreement that inclusion is a good thing, and that exclusion is a bad thing, both because it is unfair, and because it damages social cohesion. There is also very little clarity about what inclusion or exclusion actually mean, and indeed to some extent the unifying function of these terms depends on that lack of clarity (Levitas 2003, p. 1).

Information and communication technologies (ICTs) are at the heart of government social inclusion policy, which is unsurprising, as increasing use of technology has created a "digital divide." For instance, one of the flagship inclusion projects for the UK government is "Inclusion through Innovation," which focuses on how ICT can be used to generate equality of opportunity for disadvantaged groups in society.

> The Social Exclusion Unit project, "Inclusion through Innovation," is focused on identifying the specific needs of the most disadvantaged groups and exploring how Information and Communication Technologies (ICT) can help to address these needs, both through improved service delivery and through empowerment of service users.[2]

---

[1]This definition of social inclusion is taken from Scottish Executive People & Society (http://www.scotland.gov.uk/Topics/People/Social-Inclusion).

[2]From the Social Exclusion Unit "Inclusion through Innovation" Project website (http://www.socialexclusionunit.gov.uk/).

In this project, like many other government based projects, *technology* is seen as one of the main answers to address inequalities of opportunity. This is particularly so with the so-called digital divide, between those who can and cannot make use of ICT in its full glory. This view is supported with fairly compelling evidence.

> The Social Exclusion Unit has reviewed a large amount of evidence which appears to support the view that ICT can potentially help improve outcomes for people across a number of key areas including:
> *   Addressing educational underachievement:
> *   Addressing worklessness
> *   Addressing social isolation[3]

Social inclusion is key to government social policy and ICT is used as an indicator of the level of exclusion and a facilitator to improve access to services. For instance, one area that is at the forefront of such ICT based social inclusion policy is healthcare provision. Healthcare illustrates many of the challenges of providing inclusion discussed earlier, but also highlights other aspects, notably that there is an inherent funding versus provision dilemma and that it is usually very political. As Fitch and Adams (2006, p. 6) note,

> Healthcare is a highly politicized arena....The larger political dimension brings in other challenges. When there is a change of governing political party then there is a political need for the new party to deliver on electoral promises before the next round of elections. This equally applies to changes in political or executive healthcare posts, with new incumbents wishing a "return" on their investment, with improvements within tight timeframes.

In the UK, technology is seen as one of the main tools to achieve equity of health-care provision as well as to keep down the healthcare provision costs. For instance, in "Delivering the NHS Plan" (DoH 2002) and the influential Wanless report (Wanless 2002), investment in information technology is identified as a fundamental route to providing and improving service provision and keeping costs down. After the Wanless report, a new IT director for the National Health Service, with a £12 billion budget, was appointed in September 2002 to implement the NHS information strategy and achieve the "effective use of IT" promoted in the report. As noted in the Wanless report,

> Without a major advance in the effective use of ICT...the health service will find it increasingly difficult to deliver the efficient, high quality service which the public will demand. This is a major priority which will have a crucial impact on the health service over future years (Wanless 2002, p. 5).

These political and funding dimensions to healthcare systems in the UK have also been noted by the European Observatory on Health Care Systems.

---

[3]From Age Concern's comments on the Social Exclusion Unit (http://www.ageconcern.org.uk/ageconcern/).

Health policy is currently **the** most high profile item on the political agenda. Debate and public policy is focusing on both the finance and provision of healthcare (EOHCS 2002, p. 113)

So technology plays a key role in many government social policy as well as political programs. Technology is seen as one of the keys to achieving inclusion as well as reducing the costs of such service provisions and gaining and keeping the political favor of the electorate.

However, technology by itself cannot address the exclusion problem, a theme that Mark Warschauer demonstrates through case study vignettes.

Each of the programs described in the preceding vignettes was motivated by a sincere attempt to improve people's lives through ICT. But each program ran into unexpected difficulties that hindered the results. Of course any ICT project is complicated, and none can be expected to run smoothly. But the problems with these projects were neither isolated, nor random. Rather, these same types of problems occur again and again in technology projects around the world, which too often focus on providing hardware and software and pay insufficient attention to the human and social systems that must also change for technology to make a difference (Warschauer 2002, p. 7).

Access to ICT is embedded in a complex array of factors encompassing physical, digital, human, and social resources and relationships. Content and language, literacy and education, and community and institutional structures must all be taken into account if meaningful access to new technologies is to be provided (Warshauer 2002, p. 7).

Social exclusion issues are politically charged and intrinsically linked to technology, with investment in technology often being used as a means to increase inclusive provision of services. But achieving inclusion through technology is likely to involve more than just providing the hardware and software; an understanding is also needed of the wider human aspects and social environment (Warschauer 2003).

The next section will examine two research studies into the use and adoption of one of the most ubiquitous technologies used in the Western world, the mobile phone. The studies cover two different age groups, young adults and retired people, and comparisons are made between the use patterns of both groups.

2   RESEARCH STUDIES: MOBILE TECHNOLOGIES

Several business and social commentators argue that the future is mobile (e.g., Economist 2002; Thomas 2003) with many information services, business practices and social activities being based around increasingly sophisticated mobile devices. This view was extolled by British Telecom's marketing in the late 1990s, proclaiming that geography is history, and reinforced with more recent, similar marketing by telecommunications and computer companies with the clear expectation that technology-enabled mobile working and living is becoming a significant aspect of society. People have the ability to work, communicate and socialize independently of geographical location. Mobile phone technologies play an integral part in this technology-enabled mobile world, providing people with the ability to communicate and access information seemingly wherever they are. In addition, mobile phones are truly pervasive, with adoption levels of 70 percent in many countries and even over 100 percent for some user groups (i.e., some groups have more than one mobile phone). However, according to Warschauer's (2002) perspective, just "having" a mobile phone does not necessarily guarantee the mobile phone owner the full potential of communication and information access. Indeed, the pervasiveness of mobile phones provides a good base to examine the wider human aspects and social environment identified by Warschauer.

Two empirical works are used to examine very different groups of mobile phone users. One of the studies, focusing on young adults' use of mobile phones, has been running for 5 years and a fuller description of this study can be found in Adams et al (2003) and Adams and Millard (2003). The other study, focusing on retired users of mobile phones, had a preliminary report in Jeffcote et al (2003) and the full report is awaiting publication. Individually, each of these studies raised some interesting aspects of mobile phone use in each of the user groups. However, combining and comparing the studies brings out some pronounced inclusion and exclusion attributes of using mobile technologies and the services to which they give access. Both studies investigated how people used their mobile phones, how attached people are to them, and a range of related issues around the use of mobile phones.

The young adults study was based on a questionnaire survey given to university students, and included responses for one of the years from three different universities in different countries. The other years were limited to one university in the UK. The number of responses now exceeds 1,200. Focus groups of students have also been used to confirm the questionnaire responses and to get a deeper understanding of the issues surrounding mobile phone use for the young adult student group.

The other study was aimed at addressing a lack of research into mobile use by older age groups at the time. The study revolved around a qualitative survey of a sample from the general public conducted through the Mass-Observation Archive (MOA) at the University of Sussex in the UK. The survey (called a "directive" within the MOA), was sent out to a self-selecting panel of people across the UK. The panel is biased toward the older population with the average age of panel members being over 60 years old. The panel also contains gender biases with approximately two-thirds of the panel members being female. However, the panel does represent people from a wide selection of socio-economic backgrounds and is likely to provide a good window into every day contemporary life (Sheridan 1996). For the purpose of the study, it provided a rare window into mobile phone use and issues for the older community. The study consisted of a directive (survey) on mobile phone use in 2002 and a comparison with a previous directive in 1996 on (landline) phone use. The 2002 directive contained open-ended questions, or themes, that panel members could write about. The MOA administers the distribution, collection, and coding of the directives and associated responses. The confidentiality of each respondent is ensured by a coding system that enables researchers to identify the gender, occupation, town (or approximate location), and age of respondents, without actually giving information that could identify a respondent. The average age of respondents for the 2002 directive was 64, with over 60 percent of respondents being retired. The number of panel members that responded was 193 (140 female, 53 male), and represented 56 percent of the panel population. The responses provided a rich set of data, ranging from a few paragraphs to several pages of unstructured prose. Mobile phone ownership among the panel members was over 60 percent, which compared with an ICM poll in 2002, giving mobile phone ownership of the 60+ age group of about 50 percent.

Comparing the two different studies has its own challenges, given that they involved different methods and different types of responses. This will be discussed later in the paper. The comparisons below cover some of the main issues brought out by either one group or by both groups of responses.

2.1 Attachment to Mobile Phones

The study of young adults asked explicit questions about how attached people were to their mobile phones, whereas the questions to the retired age group were more open ended. However, attachment to mobile phones was one of the most often identified themes for the older age group responses.

The young adults as a group had more attachment to their mobile phones than the older age group. Indeed, the young adult responses indicate a very close attachment, with respondents taking their phones just about everywhere, the majority of them willing to return home even when running late to collect their phone if they had inadvertently left home without it.

Interestingly, the responses from the older age groups indicated some also had a very close attachment to their mobile phones, although the responses were split roughly in half between those that did and those that did not. The attachment to mobile phones for the older generation seemed to be based around a need to be in contact with a specific group (such as close family), whereas the attachment for the younger age group seemed to be more complex.

2.2 Gender and Generation Issues

Some responses brought out gender differences; for instance, both studies investigated reasons for having a mobile phone. For the young adults being able to be contacted and to be able to contact other people were the two highest ranked. However, the locus of control (i.e., being able to be *contacted* and being able to *contact*) seems to have been different for many people, since they placed one attribute higher than the other. For some people, it is more important to have the ability to be contacted than to be able to contact other people; for others it is the other way round. There was a slight gender bias here with males rating more highly the ability to *contact* than be *contacted,* while it was the other way round for females. Interestingly, this gender difference was more pronounced in different groups of young adults at different universities, possibly indicating a wider set of influences at play.

For the older age group of respondents, there were some gender differences but these were more complex and were muddled with aspects of partner and offspring influences. There were *paternal* and *reverse parental* elements in the responses, where one of the partners (usually the male) "viewed" a need for the other partner to be either contactable or have the ability to contact. The responses seemed to imply something similar originating from the children of the respondents, for instance where the respondents retell a story of their son/daughter buying them a mobile so that they can call or be called by the son/daughter. The generation issue of purchasing and exerting influences on use (i.e., *by* the offspring *for* the parents) seemed to be very similar to the power issues in engendered technologies. There were several examples of the respondents' children not only influencing the purchase of the mobile phone (i.e., buying, giving, choosing) but also influencing how and when it is used (i.e., training, showing how to use, being the main initiator of calls or texts). Also, having the ability *not* to be contacted was a very strong issue for many of the older age group respondents, both male and female.

2.3 Mobile Phones, Safety, and Wider Use

For the young adult respondents, a substantial proportion indicated that the mobile phone makes them feel safe, such as when driving a car or to a lesser extent when walking. The questionnaire also asked for areas of concern regarding using mobile phones. "Theft of mobile phones" had a high response; however, "loss of personal information" had a slightly higher response. The loss of the phone itself seemed to be less important than the loss of the phone's personalized functions, such as personal data.

These results seem to imply that the mobile phone is more than a communication device: the mobile phone is fulfilling support functions contributing to perception of being safe, keeping and providing personal information, as well as providing a contacting and contactable function. The respondents seem to have a very close attachment and relationship with their mobile phones. The relationship seems to be complex (Adams and Millard 2003, p. 5).

Correspondingly for the older age group of respondents, safety also played an important role, although it was usually as a just-in-case rather than a continual feel safe function. For instance, older respondents would typically retell a tale of how they bought (or were bought) a mobile phone after an event such as breaking down in a car, but also they would as likely describe keeping the mobile in the car and not even have it switched on. The concern of any loss, if the respondents raised it, was mostly just focusing on the loss of the phone and not of any data.

This seems to highlight some very clear differences in use emerging from the two studies: the younger age group seem to be using the mobile phone for a variety of functions, much of which revolves around socializing and a range of access to information and services via their mobiles; the older age group seem to be using the mobile phone "just as a phone" and not utilizing the extra functionality and access to services via their mobiles. It was clear that the population of older respondents were very diverse in their attitudes and the ways they used the technology. There were stark contrasts from attitudes of "hating" the devices to "can't live without" (although these were fewer), or from constant, everyday use to being locked away for most of the time. There were also some gender and age differences in how people perceived and used the mobile phones (e.g., duration and type of calls, how they viewed other people using mobile phones).

3   REVISITING INCLUSION AND EXCLUSION AND MOBILE USE

The studies bring out some differences of use and access to mobile phones for the two groups. For the older age group, relatively few respondents were using SMS and the more sophisticated functions of mobile phones, even when they had had a mobile for several years. Indeed, many kept their mobile phones switched off and preferred using landline phones for most calls. Attitudes toward mobile phones varied considerably, ranging from people hating the mobile phones to people saying they couldn't live without them. For many people there was a grudging acceptance and tolerance of mobile phones, with many identifying benefits such as security or emergency use. In contrast, the younger age group were far more embracing of functions and attitudes toward the use of the mobile phones. Some quite sophisticated use was identified where the mobile was an integral part in the socializing, studying, working, and general living. There also seemed to be some parent-child role reversal as the sons and daughters were buying phones for their parents, which is different from the younger age groups, where the parents buy phones for their children. The same seems to be true with using the more sophisticated functionality of the mobile devices: where in the past it may have been the parents showing their children how to use something, with mobiles it is often the children showing the parents.

The comparisons of mobile phone use for the young adults and the older generation seems to confirm Warschauer's (2002) view that achieving inclusion through technology is likely to involve more than just providing the hardware and software. An understanding is also needed of other factors such as the wider human aspects and the social environment. Below are some of the factors that seem relevant from comparing the two different age groups' use of mobile phones.

3.1 Inclusion–Exclusion Is Relative

One could take the meaning of *relative* to be both meaning "family/social relations" and "'relative to context." For the older age group, accessing and using the mobile technology was influenced, or even directed, by other family members, notably children. The family or social unit, where it exists, may therefore be a useful entity to consider in the inclusion–exclusion debate.

The relative to context meaning is drawn from the very different use patterns, needs, and context for the different groups. For the young adult age group, the mobile was fulfilling many needs (e.g., communication, security, socializing, playing, information), whereas the older group had a different, more limited set of needs. The younger group were using the mobile technology to explore, define, and refine their needs. The older age groups already had well defined needs, and were mostly fulfilling those with their existing activities. There are clear parallels for technology access on national and international scales; for instance, access to technology within the majority of the technologically developed West is likely to be considerably different from access in other parts of the world, since they would have different needs and different contexts with which to contend. Inclusions and exclusions have to be considered within the context of the environment, whether it is on a national scale, in the work environment, or even in the home environment.

3.2 Inclusion–Exclusion of Access is Subjective

Although both studies indicated people with both high and low levels of access to the technology, the access was fairly granular. The younger age group had higher levels of access and a wider, more sophisticated level of use. There was also quite a range in use patterns. The range and granularity of use was considerable in the older age group as well. Deciding whether and who had inclusive or exclusive access was not clear-cut. Further, as Levitas (2003) identified, there is little clarity about what inclusion or exclusion actually mean. One could argue that exclusion and inclusion are subjective terms and could be considered on a sliding scale rather than on a fixed metric; that is, people toward the "inclusive" end of the scale have greater access to resources than those toward the "exclusive" end.

3.3 Technologies Moves the Inclusion–Exclusion Barriers

There seems to be a pattern of changing access needs, barriers, and practices emerging from the different levels of use for the respondents in both studies. For instance, at a basic level, barriers to inclusive use could relate to having access to a mobile phone and some basic training on how to use it. For less basic use, barriers to inclusion could be having the right type of phone with access to the Internet or signal coverage in all the areas the users want. For more sophisticated and enabling use, barriers to inclusion could include access to even more sophisticated information or location-aware services and infrastructure. Cost issues also seem interlinked here. As the technology evolves, the initially expensive sophisticated technology used by the "first to market users" invariably evolves to be the basic technology used by other groups. This was demonstrated in the older age groups respondents, a significant proportion of which had hand-me-down phones from their children or other relatives.

The needs and the barriers for exclusion move as the technology evolves. Technology changes things. This concept is not new. For instance, Hebert (1998, p. 69), studying healthcare provision in five community hospitals, noted

> results suggest that, for specific tasks, IT increased efficiency and productivity—a single employee was able to complete more tasks. However, this produced other consequences not predicted. Participants noted this change did not "free up time" to spend with patients, but meant there were potentially more opportunities to provide services and more tasks to complete.

So in Hebert's study, technology that was meant to increase quality of service to patients often resulted in less frequent and shorter contact between staff and patients, as staff time was increasingly taken up with computer-oriented tasks. Issues and barriers to providing equity of patient service moved from "things healthcare staff did with *patients*" to "things healthcare staff did with *technology*."

When considering inclusion issues, then, some understanding is needed of the intricate and evolving role of technology. Technology will help define and move the barriers to inclusion as it evolves.

4   TECHNOLOGY CHANGES STRUCTURES: IS AGE THE NEW GENDER?

The idea that technology defines and moves barriers has further meaning when we consider the earlier age/gender observation and discussion. There is a link between gender and technology use. For instance, in the use of Internet technologies, differences have been noted, some arguably related to traditional gender roles and barriers (e.g., Turkle 1995; Wallace 1999). In addition, women communicate differently and can be more self-deprecating and less confident than men (Tannen 1990).

However, the gender literature raises several more fundamental inclusion issues relating to access to technology, work, wealth, and standing (e.g., Rantalaiho and Heiskanen 1997a, 1997b; Wajcman 1991). Work and corresponding societal structures and practices are geared to favor men over women. Technology plays a part in facilitating and perpetuating gender work and social role differences by providing both channels and barriers to access.

Males may be more involved in "higher" activities of designing and making technology while females may be more involved in "lower" activities of using the technologies. Generally there is a bias toward exerting influences on working and social practice *by* males *for* females. This is likely to be engrained in the deeply rooted structures. As Rantalaiho and Heiskanen (1997b, p. 191) note,

> Quite often "gendered" means the common hierarchical difference between men and women, between the masculine and the feminine, with men and masculinity in the dominant position. The difference is quite strong in the working life all over the world, and also where gender equality is an acknowledged ideology.

They also note, however, that the differences can be subtle and unintentional.

> Gendered hierarchies are not always visible or audible at the workplace level. It is rather rare in the present Western part of the globe that a researcher can point to open and conscious discrimination of women. Instead, the prevailing construction of women's hierarchically lower positions is a delicate practice in which women and men mostly do not intentionally indulge. Gender is constructed at the workplace in the daily work process and it is involved in solutions about how to organize the work. Some jobs and tasks almost unnoticeably become defined as feminine and others as masculine (p. 191).

The earlier discussion shows a younger generation embracing, adopting, and engrossing themselves in the technology *and* using this "expertise" to direct and inform the older generation (of both sexes) in the use of such technologies. There seems to be embedded *hierarchical difference* between the young and the old, not only in use but in design (i.e., with mobile technology designed by and for the young and not the old). In using the more sophisticated mobile technology, there seem to be well-defined hierarchical structures emerging, with many activities becoming firmly the realm of the young.

Perhaps we are seeing some changes in the deeply embedded gender role structures here, with the younger generation taking on what used to be the confident, masculine roles and older generation taking on the less confident, feminine roles. With a continually changing and evolving technology, such as mobiles, the older less confident may become more excluded from the facilities the technology offers.

5 CONCLUSION AND AREAS FOR FURTHER RESEARCH

The paper has argued that ICTs are at the heart of government social inclusion policy but that social exclusion and technology are inextricably linked. Technology, and access to it, is often seen as part of the exclusion problem, as well as part of the solution to enable access to information resources.

Two empirical studies, one looking at the use of mobile technologies by a 18 to 25 year old age group and the other of mostly retired users, have been used to examine inclusion and exclusion issues. There are limitations with this research. The studies were different, involving different methods and different types of responses. In addition, the focus of each study was not on inclusion or exclusion, and it was only once both studies were completed and the results combined that inclusion and exclusion emerged as issues. Combining the results and responses of both studies has proved challenging. There have been some subjective decisions over which data to use and how to combine elements in one data set with a different data set. Clearly further research is needed to examine the age and ICT dimension of inclusion. Such research needs to follow a consistent focus and methodological approach. The target sample would need to be more fully representative of the population, such as involving different economic groups and more delineated groups, possibly involving younger age groups. The study will need a ubiquitous technology, such as a mobile phone, to provide a common focus for investigation.

Limitations aside, several themes derive from examining these two sets of respondents. Using technology shifts the inclusion and exclusion problem landscape. Social inclusion is multifaceted and not a simple either/or situation, and should be considered rather as a subjective sliding scale dependent on context rather than an absolute. The family or social unit where it exists may also be a useful entity to consider in the exclusion debate. The studies show some clear differences between age groups and gender. The paper has shown that technology impacts inclusion activity in technology dominated societies, although further research is needed. The paper argues that we may be seeing some structural changes in society along the structural lines traditionally associated with gender. As the paper argues, age may be the new gender.

References

Adams, C., Avison, D., and Millard, P. "Personal Trust Space in Mobile Commerce," paper presented at the Sixth International Conference on Electronic Commerce Research (ICECR-6), INFORMAT, Dallas, TX, October 23-26, 2003.

Adams, C., and Fitch, C. "Mobile Support for Community Healthcare: A Janus View," in E. Lawrence, B. Pernici, and J. Krogstie (eds.), *Mobile Information Systems*, New York: Springer 2004, pp. 341-349.

Adams, C., and Millard, P. "Personal Trust Space and Devices: 'Geography Will *Not Be* History' in the M-Commerce Future," paper presented at the Hawaii International Conference on Business (HICB), Honolulu, HI, June 18-21, 2003.

Britton, L., and Casebourne, J. "Defining Social Inclusion," Working Brief 136, Centre for Economic and Social Inclusion, n.d. (available online at http://www.cesi.org.uk/docPool/defsocinc.pdf).

DoH.   "Delivering the Plan," Department of Health, 2002 (available online at http://www.doh.gov.uk/).

Economist. "Computing's New Shape," *The Economist*, November 23, 2002, pp. 9-10, 85-87.

EOHCS. "Healthcare Systems in Eight Countries: Trends and Challenges," European Observatory on Health Care Systems, London School of Economics, 2002.

Fitch, C. J., and Adams, C. "Mobile Supported Patient Care: The Dichotomy of National and Local Needs," in I. Kushchu (ed.), *Mobile Government: An Emerging Direction for e-Government*, Hershey, PA: Idea Group Publishing 2006 (forthcoming).

Hebert, M. A. "Impact of IT on Health Care Professional: Changes in Work and the Productivity Paradox," *Health Services Management Research* (11), 1998, pp. 69-79.

ICM. "Retail Week Survey," January 2002 (available online at http://www.sussex.ac.uk/library//massobs/archive_publications.html).

Jeffcote, R., Adams, C., and Su, Q. "Mobile Telephones: Just Another Gendered Technology?," paper presented at the IFIP8.2 OASIS Working Conference and SIG at the International Conference on Information Systems, Seattle, WA, December 14, 2003.

Levitas, R. "The Idea of Social Inclusion," paper presented at the Social Inclusion Research Conference, The Canadian Council on Social Development and Human Resources Development, Ottawa, March 27-28, 2003 (available online at http://www.ccsd.ca/events/inclusion/papers/rlevitas.htm).

Rantalaiho, L., and Heiskanen, T. (eds). *Gender Practices in Working Life*, London: Macmillan Press, 1997a.

Rantalaiho, L., and Heiskanen, T. "Persistence and Change of Gendered Practices," in L. Rantalaiho and T. Heiskanen (eds.), *Gender Practices in Working Life*, London: Macmillan Press, 1997b., pp 191-196.

Sheridan, D. "Damned Anecdotes and Confabulations: Mass-Observation as a Life History," Mass-Observation Archive Occasional Paper No. 7,University of Sussex Library, UK, 1996 (available at http://www.sussex.ac.uk/library//massobs/archive_publications.html).

Tannen, D. *You Just Don't Understand. Men and Women in Conversation*, New York: William Morrow Publications, 1990.

Thomas, D. "M-commerce: A False Start?," *Computer Weekly*, January 16, 2003, p. 18.

Turkle, S. *Life on the Screen: Identity in the Age of the Internet*, New York: Simon and Schuster, 1995.

Wajcman, J. *Feminism Confronts Technology*, Cambridge, UK: Polity Press, 1991.

Wallace, P. *The Psychology of the Internet*, Cambridge, UK: Cambridge University Press, 1999.

Wanless, D. "Securing Our Future Health: Taking a Long-Term View—The Wanless Report," HM Treasury, 2002 (available online at http://www.hm-treasury.gov.uk/Consultations_and_Legislation/wanless/consult_wanless_final.cfm?).

Warschauer, M. *Technology and Social Inclusion: Rethinking the Digital Divide*, Cambridge, MA: MIT Press, 2003.

Warschauer, M. "Reconceptualizing the Digital Divide," *First Monday* (7:7), July 2002 (available online at http://www.firstmonday.org/issues/issue7_7/warschauer/).

About the Authors

Carl Adams is a principle lecturer at the University of Portsmouth. He has a Ph.D. in Information Systems development and an M.Sc. in Management Science, both from Southampton University, UK. His research interests are in Information Systems, mobile technologies and the impact of technology on society. He can be reached at carl.adams@port.ac.uk.

Tineke Fitch is a senior lecturer at the University of Portsmouth, with a Ph.D. in health informatics and telemedicine and an M.Sc. in Information Systems plus qualifications in business and human resource management. Prior to joining the University of Portsmouth, she held management positions in industry and the UK National Health Service. She is a senior member of the Centre for Healthcare Modelling and Informatics at the University's School of Computing and her research includes the use of telemedicine in elderly care and social aspects of e-health applications. She can be reached at tineke.fitch@port.ac.uk.

15   WEB ACCESSIBILITY: A Digital Divide for Disabled People?

Alison Adam
David Kreps
University of Salford
Salford, U.K.

Abstract   *The focus of this paper is Web accessibility for disabled people. Much of the Web remains inaccessible or difficult to access by people across a spectrum of disabilities and this may have serious implications for the potential use of the Web for increasing social inclusion. The topic of disabled Web access is introduced through a consideration of four discourses: digital divide, social construction of disability, legal, and Web accessibility. The lack of dialogue between these permits a passive liberal approach toward disability discrimination to prevail and this political position has become inscribed in widely used automatic software tools resulting in a reinforcement of the view that Web site accessibility approval may, in many cases, be deemed an empty shell.*

1   INTRODUCTION

After more than a decade of development of the World Wide Web, despite the consolidation of Web accessibility standards, and despite the enactment of strong disability discrimination legislation in many Western countries, much of the Web remains inaccessible to disabled people. A recent UK study of accessibility of public Web sites put a figure of less than 20 percent on Web sites that meet even the most basic accessibility standards across a spectrum of disabilities including hearing, motor, and sight impairment (DRC 2004). Given the growing use of the Internet and WWW for information, education, social contact, and, increasingly, the provision of goods and services, a digital divide between disabled people and those whom society does not categorize as disabled, threatens to open up and grow. If much of the Web remains inaccessible to disabled people, this may severely limit the potential of the Web to act as a platform on which to build social inclusion. Our research question is, therefore: How can an understanding of the major discourses surrounding access to digital technologies by people with disabilities contribute to an understanding of why Web accessibility remains as a persistent problem?

Please use the following format when citing this chapter:

Adam, A., and Kreps, D., 2006, in IFIP International Federation for Information Processing, Volume 208, Social Inclusion: Societal and Organizational Implications for Information Systems, eds. Trauth, E., Howcroft, D., Butler, T., Fitzgerald, B., DeGross, J., (Boston: Springer), pp. 217-228.

We argue that the complexities of Web accessibility are best understood and analyzed against a set of relevant discourses and that part of the reason for the obduracy of Web inaccessibility lies in crucial gaps in their engagement with each other. In the following sections we characterize the relevant discourses in terms of the digital divide discourse, the social construction of disability discourse focusing, for the present purposes, on World Wide Web access by the disabled, the legal discourse where we briefly describe the burdens that disability discrimination demands put on those who design Web sites and the Web accessibility discourse, including a brief history of the development of Web accessibility guidelines. There is a raft of such guidelines, the majority of which cannot be adequately checked by automatic software. We describe, briefly, three of the guidelines which are inadequately addressed by automatic checkers. Having described these discourses, the next section continues by making the argument that their lack of appropriate engagement, in certain places, leaves in place a traditional, often passive, liberal approach toward inclusion of the disabled in Web accessibility terms. Indeed, we make the stronger claim that such a political position can be seen as inscribed in automatic accessibility checking software, resulting in the accessibility stamp of approval which they confer being appropriately deemed an "empty shell" (i.e., the gap between espoused policy and actual practice resulting in an equality policy that is meaningless; Hoque and Noon 2004).

Our research methodology for arriving at a set of credible discourses was drawn from our personal histories as researchers in this and related areas. The first author has researched gender issues in IS and computer ethics with a knowledge of digital divide literature and social shaping of technology and was struck by the parallels between rhetoric on women's and disabled people's access to digital technology. The second author is an active Web developer with specialist technical knowledge of Web accessibility, whose own research into cyborgism had led him into the disability studies field, with a particular interest in disabled access to ICTs. It then became an exercise in piecing together our respective expertise and searching for literature where we felt there were gaps. Finally, we fashioned what we hope is a convincing model of the relevant discourses.

2   DIGITAL DIVIDE DISCOURSE

Although the concept of the digital divide or the postulated divide between the "information haves" and the "information have-nots" is relatively recent (probably first coined explicitly in 1995; Servon 2002, p. 24), it has rapidly become the peg on which to hang policy concerns (Selwyn 2004; U.S. Department of Commerce 2000). A wider spectrum of writing, much of it academic, that postulates inequalities between those who have access to digital networked technologies and those who do not, has also developed (e.g., Loader 1998; Marshall et al. 2003; Norris 2001; Servon 2002). Following Selwyn (2004), we urge caution in embracing the term *digital divide* uncritically as there are conceptual limitations to the dichotomous conception of such a divide with its tendency to equate access with simplistic views of availability of technology. Accepting this caveat, the literature (i.e., policy and academic wings) offers a natural starting place to look for analyses of questions of disabled access to the Internet. However, the problem is not what the digital divide discourse says about disabled access, but what it does not say. Digital divide literature is surprisingly reticent about disability, with several of the major works in the field offering no discussion of disability (Loader 1998; Marshall et al. 2003; Norris 2001; Servon 2002) or only a passing mention of the form "gender, race, disability, etc."

Arguably, the focus of the digital divide has traditionally been the divide between rich and poor, between developed and developing countries. Yet gender, as an analytical device, has quickly become part of the repertoire of the digital divide (Cooper and Weaver 2003). It is also notable that otherwise sophisticated analyses include references to demographics such as age without considering disability as well (Selwyn 2004). Importantly, the relative absence, or at least late arrival, of disability in the academic wing of the digital divide is replicated in the policy wing. Disability was first considered only in the fourth of the U.S. Government's "Falling through the Net" reports of the mid to late 1990s (U.S. Department of Commerce 2000). What are the effects of leaving disability out in the cold?

As Selwyn (2004) argues, the explosion of interest in the digital divide is a central plank in the wider theme of social inclusion and exclusion in policy terms. Indeed, the shift toward a "socially inclusive" policy agenda in countries such as the United Kingdom, United States, and France is intimately entwined with notions of a digital divide. Selwyn (2002, p. 2) notes, "the convergence of these 'information society' and 'inclusive society' discourses into an ongoing debate over the potential of ICTs to either exacerbate or alleviate social exclusion." In the UK, "New Labour" has seized upon information and communications technologies (ICT) as the defining feature of modern citizenship. Nevertheless, within the digital divide discourse from the policy wing, critical discussion of how governments use technology to achieve social inclusion is somewhat thin. The prevailing view, at least within UK government policy, is of a clear divide between "connected" and "unconnected" citizens with the twin specter of the digital divide reinforcing existing social divides and creating a new digital version at the same time. As Selwyn (2002, p. 16) suggests, this follows the traditional "technologification" of areas such as education and health; social exclusion is next in line for the technical fix.

3   SOCIAL CONSTRUCTION OF DISABILITY DISCOURSE AND WEB ACCESS

Disability, itself, is clearly a contested term. As attitudes and understanding undergo changes toward more tolerance, so does acceptable terminology. Witness how the term *crippled* would now be universally regarded as offensive and that the term *handicapped* has more recently dropped from favor. It may be that *disability* as a term might have a limited span as it too conjures up a negative image of being measured against some norm of ability. The term *differently abled* is sometimes used and may be seen as preferable to disabled. Yet differently abled also implies being different to some norm of ability, so this term is not unproblematic. This signals the impossibility of ever achieving a neutral term—all carry the weight of political baggage. Understandably, individuals may resist being lumped together as a group and individual differences in circumstances make a huge difference to one's experience (see Trauth et al. 2004). Nevertheless, a key political strategy to press for change involves identifying oneself as a member of a group of people who have similar issues and concerns. Hence the identity politics of disability remain important.

Such views are borne out by the tensions between the charity and medical models of disability which have hitherto prevailed (Fulcher 1989) and the newer models which challenge them. The medical model of disability emphasizes impairment as loss where the deficit is seen as belonging to the individual and where the presumed status and neutrality of professional medical judgement takes disability out of the political arena, emphasizing its supposed nature in terms of personal issues for medical judgement. The charity model sits alongside such a view in assuming that disabled individuals are to be the objects of pity and are requiring of charity rather than necessarily having a set of rights within the welfare state and within government policy (Goggin and Newell 2000). However a more radical approach is represented by the social, social barriers, or social construction of disability model, which emphasizes that locating disability in the individual as opposed to society is a political decision.

Available and appropriate technology, and how it is used, is an integral part of the social model of disability. Disability can be created by designing technology in such a way that some people cannot use it—a crucial point to which we return when considering Web site accessibility. As Goggin and Newell (2000, p. 128) note, "Disability can thus be viewed as a constructed socio-political space, which is determined by dominant norms, the values found in technological systems, and their social context." They argue that research has focused on analysis of particular types of impairment with the development of technical solutions specifically to address these, thus reflecting the dominant medical paradigm of disability (p. 132).

Counter to the social model, one might argue that a poor technological design could beget a short term impairment rather than a long term disability and that a *handicap* refers to the relationship between a person and their environment (Cook and Hussey 2001). However, if a technology persists in being unusable for years where it could readily be made usable, the distinction between short-term handicap and long-term impairment becomes blurred.

Understanding disability against the social model makes feasible a more focused challenge to the prevailing norms and power relations in society. In other words, the onus is on the wider society to make the Internet and Web accessible, rather than the onus being on the individual disabled person to acquire specific technical aids and/or to struggle with poorly designed and often inaccessible Web sites. The social or social construction model moves away from the idea of disability as individual deficit, locating it instead in terms of barriers in the social environment. "It is not bodily impairment as such, but rather social discrimination and biases that in fact produce 'disability.'" (Guo et al. 2005, p. 51). Hence, one might argue that a poorly designed Web site could be regarded as creating disability.

4   LEGAL DISCOURSE

In several Western countries, including the United States, the United Kingdom, Australia, and countries in the European Union, legislation has been enacted to ensure that individuals are not discriminated against on the grounds of disability, gender, race, and, more recently (at least in the UK), age. In each of these regions where legislation is in force, to prevent discrimination against the disabled, this legislation is widely interpreted as mandating the use of accessibility techniques on the Web. Section 508 of the U.S. Rehabilitation Act (1973; updated in 1998) uniquely spells out specific requirements of federal Web sites to ensure their accessibility to disabled users, although this falls short of the benchmark accepted elsewhere and applies only to federal, and not private sector, Web sites.

In the UK, the Disability Discrimination Act (1995) came into force in phases over a period of almost 10 years. It is now unlawful to discriminate against disabled people by refusing them service, providing service on worse terms, or providing a lower standard of service. It also requires service providers to make reasonable adjustments to the way they provide their goods, facilities and services to make them accessible. The owner of any public facing Web site, public or private sector, is a "service provider" under the terms of the Act, and must therefore comply with the law (DRC 2002).

In Europe, the eEurope Actions Plan 2002 and 2005, followed by EU Council and EU Parliament resolutions (EU Parliament 2002), mandate accessibility standards for all public Web sites. European national legislation on disability discrimination as it relates to the provision of services, has also been interpreted as including services delivered electronically.

The chairman of the UK Disability Rights Commission, Bert Massie, however, states that, "the industry should be prepared for disabled people to use the law to make the Web a less hostile place" (DRC 2004). These are strong words; they explicitly urge disabled people to look to the law if their needs are not met.

5 WEB ACCESSIBILITY DISCOURSE

In this section we briefly consider how technical development of the Web, and attempts to regulate it, have contributed to the development of the Web accessibility discourse. We hope to clarify, briefly, three of the specific ways in which Web sites may be inaccessible to disabled people and to explain why automatic software checkers will not necessarily flag such problems.

Central to the Web accessibility movement is the World Wide Web Consortium (W3C), the body established by Berners-Lee in 1994 to try to marshal the phenomenal growth of the Web his mark-up language, HTML, has spawned. The exponential growth of the Web encouraged unregulated, complex, and cumbersome plug-ins and unwieldy new versions of HTML. In response to this, the W3C began creating a new foundational language for the future of the Web: extensible mark-up language (XML).[1]

XML is at the heart of Berners-Lee's concept of the Semantic Web, and his wish, through the universal application of rigorously quality processed international standards for code languages, to see machines talking to one another on our behalf. Parallel with these developments, the W3C undertook an exercise entitled the Web Accessibility Initiative (WAI), which in 1999 published its Web Content Accessibility Guidelines (WCAG). As part of the initiative, new elements and attributes were introduced into the code to help make it more accessible to disabled people.

The WCAG provide a set of guidelines for creating Web pages that are accessible to all, regardless of sensory, physical, or cognitive ability. To provide Web developers with a graded approach to the implementation of accessibility, three levels have been

---

[1] HTML and XHTML Frequently Asked Questions from the W3C site, http://www.w3.org/MarkUp/2004/xhtml-faq.

defined—Level A, Level AA, and Level AAA—which cover items on Web pages that *must*, *should* and *may*, respectively, be made accessible in order for individuals with disabilities to access content. Most governmental directives specify Level AA as the minimum requirement, although the U.S. Section 508 falls somewhat short of this. The EU Council and Parliamentary resolutions specify the W3C's Web accessibility standards, mandating compliance, Europe-wide, with WCAG Level AA (Council of Europe 2003).

The development of accessibility standards is part of the wider story of the development of the Web, a classic tale of free market profit making versus nonprofit making, nonproprietary regulation. In European terms, the pendulum has swung markedly toward regulation and standardization. Given the active approach that disability discrimination legislation requires, this would seem to be a very positive move toward achieving accessibility. The free market will not emphasize accessibility unless it is compelled to do so (although it may well be compelled if the exhortations of the DRC to the disabled community to test the legislation are anything to go by) or unless it sees compliance as profitable.

Either way, we cannot expect a World Wide Web modeled on the liberal values of the free market to produce an equitable and accessible space of its own accord. Accessibility and end to discrimination are not emergent properties of private profit-making environments, quite the opposite (Winner 1997). Unfortunately positive moves toward standardization, with the potential for achievable accessibility standards are undermined both by the quantity of old style HTML sites still in existence, which are full of inconsistencies, and on a reliance on automatic checkers, which cannot possibly provide the necessary accessibility checks, as we now describe.

Automated approaches to checking Web pages against these guidelines have proliferated. Space permits a consideration of only three of the most common of these accessibility problems but a comprehensive list of the many accessibility traps may be found in Kreps and Adam (2006). Accessibility checking programs include A-Prompt (one of the better ones), Bobby (once the most popular one, now renamed WebExact), LIFT, and many others. The W3C maintain a list of such tools on their Web site,[2] but are careful not to endorse any of them, and they do not provide their own software tool to check Web pages against their accessibility guidelines. The situation remains that the guidelines simply cannot be properly tested in an automated manner, and for many of them, only a human check is possible.

In the remainder of this section, we describe three typical problems where an automatic checker would pass a Web site as accessible while it remains inaccessible to many users. These examples relate (mainly) to visually impaired people. The findings of a major study (DRC 2004) showed visually impaired users having the most problems with accessibility. However, the report found that users with hearing and motor impairments also have many difficulties with Web accessibility. This acknowledges that there is a wide spectrum of accessibility issues which affect users differently. However, for reasons of space, we describe a group of visual accessibility issues here.

Ritchie and Blanck (2003, p. 19), in their survey of centers for independent living (CILs) service delivery via Web sites, highlight the absence of a text equivalent

---

[2]Evaluation, Repair, and Transformation Tools for Web Content Accessibility, http://www.w3.org/WAI/ER/existingtools.html.

description of graphic images (ALT or alternative text errors), as the main error that caused the Web sites surveyed in their research to fail the Bobby software. ALT tags on images either being nonexistent or unhelpful is one of the key problems experienced by blind users in the UK's Disability Rights Commission survey of Web accessibility which involved a user panel of disabled people and which found less than 20 percent of public Web sites meeting the most basic accessibility level (DRC 2004, p. 29).

The provision of a text equivalent for every non-text element is one of the most basic W3C Web accessibility guidelines (WCAG 1.1). However it is eminently feasible for a Web site to pass automated software tools on this count and yet be providing a text description that is inadequate at best and meaningless at worst.

Visually impaired people use speech synthesis software that reads out the text on Web pages. Indeed, screen readers and voice browsers are perhaps the most commonly known assistive technologies used by disabled people to surf the Web. The IMG element of HTML is used to place an image on a Web page. The ALT attribute of this element was introduced in HTML 2, so that Web authors could provide a text equivalent for images. The UK's RNIB (Royal National Institute for the Blind) recommends using five words as the usual number required to produce a meaningful tag (e.g., ALT = "dog leaps for a stick"). Speech synthesis software then reads the ALT text back to the user. Unfortunately, automatic checkers will accept, for example, ALT = image.jpg in the code, as a valid ALT attribute. They cannot check whether the text supplied is actually meaningful.

Speech synthesis software enables visually impaired users to "skim" pages, in a similar way that sighted users "scan" pages. Such software reads out only the headings and subheadings, until a keypress stops the skimming process and the software reads out the paragraphs beneath the subheading selected. The HTML elements <H1> to <H5> create headings and subheadings, and <p> denotes a paragraph. Automated software checkers can only detect the absence of <H1> – <H5> in code, and recommend a human check; they cannot detect when a heading or subheading has been placed in a <p>.

Forms on Web pages enable interaction for a wide range of purposes, from simple feedback to complex transactions. Speech synthesis software reading out the text beside form fields, so that visually impaired users know where to input their details, relies upon specific elements in the HTML code to ensure that the right labels are clearly associated with their corresponding input fields. A poorly coded form, while clear to sighted users, might easily lead a visually impaired user to type the expiry date of their card into the security id input field, their post code into the county field, and so on. An automated software checker can only check for the absence of the <label> element and the <for> attribute in HTML forms. Human comprehension is required to correctly associate labels with their form controls, making the forms usable.

6 THE NEGATIVE EFFECTS OF AUTOMATED APPROACHES

The problem is not only that automated approaches to checking Web pages for accessibility are insufficient and unable to substitute for a human check. The existence and proliferation of such software has, in certain respects, actually hampered the global project of making the Web more accessible so it may be worse than an empty shell.

Hoque and Noon (2004) coined this term to describe the effects of equality and diversity policies in the workplace, but the concept may be extended to apply to the inequalities relating to Web accessibility. They claim that, in many instances, equality policies are passive instruments which make little difference to the material experiences of workers subject to unequal conditions and practices. This is because the equality policies do not carry with them a recognition of the reasons inequalities occur and have no means of changing the inequality. The organization that has developed the policy believes it has done its job and has to do nothing more to achieve equality in the workplace. The equality and diversity policy is, therefore, an empty shell. Similarly, a "badge of accessibility," such as the approval of an automatic checker, may engender the view that nothing more needs be done to make a Web site accessible. The approval of the Web site is then an empty shell.

The Level A, Level AA, and Level AAA of the Web Accessibility Initiative has been used by a very popular tool called Bobby. Bobby was, and its replacement WebExact is, a very useful tool, insofar as it can quickly and effectively show how *inaccessible* a Web page is, but it is all too often misunderstood. Many organizations—including disability organizations—falsely believe that simply passing such tests will satisfy their Web accessibility obligations. For them, the measure of accessibility is whether or not their pages can attain the "Bobby Approved" icon. Therefore, the Bobby icon appeared to represent an achievable standard and a tangible, cost effective reward for efforts made toward Web accessibility. But it is really quite patronizing for disabled visitors to Web sites to be told that because it is a Bobby Approved page it is accessible to all. As we have seen above, where the alternative text on an image says "photo1.jpg, 5100bytes," the page would have successfully attain the Bobby Approved icon.

Interestingly, this tool has been subject to so much criticism on this count that it has finally, in 2005, been consigned to history, replaced by a tool that makes fewer claims.[3] The Bobby-approved icon, however, like the "tag soup" of old style HTML it often accompanies, will be adorning Web pages for a good while to come.

It has been a commonplace experience among Web developers tendering for work in the public sector in Europe, where the WAI Level AA benchmark is mandated for all Web sites, to find the specifications in the "invitation to tender" actually listing Bobby Approved as the required benchmark of accessibility. So, a tool that cannot possibly do the job of all the checks required is actually listed as the benchmark. If the authors of such tender documents are confused about what is required, then it is no wonder that, as the UK Disability Rights Commission reveal in their report, "The Web: Access and Inclusion for Disabled People—A Formal Investigation" (DRC 2004), 81 percent of the 1,000 Web sites included in the investigation failed "to satisfy the most basic Web Accessibility Initiative category"—Level A.

Hence the Bobby icon, despite the best intentions of its designers who, in any case recommended that Web developers use Bobby only as a first step to ensure accessible Web page design, may be unintentionally promoting social exclusion.

---

[3]WebExact, http://Webxact.watchfire.com/.

7   DISSECTING THE DISCOURSES: IMPLICATIONS OF LIBERALISM AND TECHNOLOGICAL DETERMINISM

Critics of liberalism (Adam 2005) note the problems of liberal discourse where there may be a general will toward a more equal and fairer society but where the deeper social and cultural structures of society, which are implicated in causing the inequality in the first place, are left unexplored. Sometimes a liberal agenda prevails because asking more searching questions raises the specter of substantial discrimination and oppression. This in turn, raises the question of who is doing the discriminating and oppressing and what advantages they are levering against other groups. The language of *inequality* and *underrepresentation* sounds more neutral and presents less of a challenge to the *status quo* than *oppression* and *discrimination*.

The liberal approach is manifest in, at least, the policy wing of the digital divide discourse where it is assumed that access to technology brings social inclusion without posing deeper questions of how this may come about and also without understanding the different types of exclusion—in other words, that there may be several digital divides. Not surprisingly, commentators (Adam 2005) have noted the alliance between liberalism and technological determinism. A liberal approach is one that accepts the objectivity of the world and the inevitability and desirability of technological development to the extent where technological access has historically been seen as the key to equality in contemporary policy discourse (Selwyn 2004). Such arguments are reproduced in the technologification to cure social ills rhetoric described by Selwyn (2002). Additionally, the paucity of discussion on disability within the (policy *and* academic) digital divide literature further entrenches the liberal position. This is partly because there simply has not been enough discussion and awareness, where it may be assumed that disabled access will "come out in the wash" when social inclusion is dealt with as a blanket phenomenon.

The approach of policy-oriented digital divide literature tends to be uncritical of technology and has paid insufficient attention to the details of disability. This contrasts with the view that sees disability as socially constructed even to the extent that technology may be seen as designed, albeit unintentionally, to create disability. This signals a major disjunction between these two discourses.

However, the legal discourse encapsulated, for instance, in the UK Disability Discrimination Act and surrounding discussion, does not sit comfortably with current technologification policy. In putting the onus on the service provider to make Web sites accessible, rather than on the disabled person to find a way of accessing what might be somewhat inaccessible sites, the law recognizes that the barrier lies not with the disability but with the technology and, by extension, those who create and design the technology. Additionally, the law recognizes that disabled people have rights. These two aspects are central planks of the social construction model. Therefore, we contend that UK law, at least implicitly, contains some elements of the social construction model.

The Web accessibility movement has largely concentrated on the technical aspects of the problem. Understandably, there are huge and sophisticated technical problems to be solved before Web accessibility can be achieved and much has already been accomplished by WAI and others. However Web accessibility discourse has, to date, overlapped fairly minimally with the digital divide, social construction, and legislative discourses, meaning that, so far, it has not been in the best position to take advantage of the more radical arguments of the social construction and legal discourses on barriers and rights, which could be used, very positively, to fuel its campaign.

Without a united voice, from the complete spectrum of relevant discourses from digital divide, through social construction and legal, on to Web accessibility, pressing for active rights of disabled people against constructed barriers to Web accessibility, a relatively passive liberal approach toward disabled access may yet prevail.

8   THE PROBLEM WITH ACCESSIBILITY SOFTWARE: INSCRIBING A LIBERAL VIEW OR CREATING DISABILITY

Finally, we argue that by relying on automated Web site accessibility software we are, in an important sense, designing into information systems the problematic liberal view of equality that we identify above, which results from the lack of engagement between the relevant discourses. Many such "accessibility approved" stamps of respectability found on the Web then fall into the category of empty shells. So the problems we highlight above are exacerbated by automatic software. This may be regarded as a form of inscription. As Akrich (1992) argues, particular political positions can be designed into or inscribed into technology. One legendary story of inscription in the design of technology is Winner's (1999) account of the road network on Long Island designed with low bridges so that buses could not pass underneath. Apparently this was a deliberate intention of the designer, to exclude poor and black people, who were more likely to be bus rather than car users, from parks. (Although the near mythical status of this story has since been fatally wounded by Steve Woolgar, who famously produced the appropriate Long Island bus timetable at a conference in 1999!)

In the present case, we are arguing that a liberal view of equality and access has been inscribed in the design of accessibility testing software. This is partly because disabled people have not been involved in the testing of Web sites and partly because the passive view of access prevails, where we need not think too much about what access means, rather we accept what the tool gives us. Also, following the social construction of disability discourse, we must consider that the proliferation of all of these inaccessible Web sites is creating disability. Hence, not just liberal politics, but even disability itself, can be regarded as inscribed in the design of this technology.

9   CONCLUSION

In this paper we have attempted to understand the exceedingly complex, somewhat troubled, and multifaceted picture of disabled access to the Web through a set of relevant discourses. We note the tension between the active approach demanded by disability discrimination legislation, supported by the social construction model and disabled rights discourse and the passive, liberal approach that is often taken toward inclusivity. The policy wing of the digital divide discourse has failed to dispel the latter in its lack of interest in disability and its enthusiasm for technologification. The Web accessibility movement, with its necessary concentration on technical aspects and standardization sees Web accessibility largely in technical terms and therefore is not availing itself of the more radical arguments of the social construction and legal movements which could be used to positive effect in its campaigns.

The liberal approach to disabled access, which tends to prevail in the teeth of the disjunctions in the relevant discourses, can be regarded as inscribed in software tools. This is reinforced by the inability of software to check for meaning so that humans are always required. Taking the popular Bobby icon as an example, we argue that having a badge of respectability can be counterproductive. If we want to get beyond passive and ineffective approaches to accessibility, given in any case that the legislation demands it, and pressure groups such as the UK Disability Rights Commission will actively press for testing the legislation, we should heed the calls of these groups. This must be coupled with a clear need for human intervention rather than automatic checking, to involve disabled people much more directly in the design and testing of Web sites. Only in this way can we expect to see genuine steps taken toward making the World Wide Web socially inclusive for disabled people.

References

Adam, A. *Gender, Ethics and Information Technology*, Basingstoke: Palgrave Macmillan, 2005.

Akrich, M. "The De-scription of Technical Objects," in W. E. Bijker and J. Law (eds.), *Shaping Technology/ Building Society: Studies in Sociotechnical Change*, Cambridge, MA: MIT Press, 1992, pp. 205-224.

Cook, A. M., and Hussey, S. *Assistive Technologies: Principles and Practices*, St Louis, MO: Mosby, 2001.

Cooper, J., and Weaver, K. D. *Gender and Computers: Understanding the Digital Divide*, Mahwah, NJ: Lawrence Erlbaum Associates, 2003

Council of Europe. "Council Resolution on the Implementation of the eEurope 200-5 Action Plan," Brussels, January 2003 (http://www.eu.int/information_society/eeurope/2005/doc/all_about/resolution. doc).

DRC. "Disability Discrimination Act: Code of Practice," Disability Rights Commission, UK Parliament 2008_223, 2002 (http://www.drc-gb.org/thelaw/practice.asp).

DRC. "The Web: Access and Inclusion for Disabled People," Disability Rights Commission, London, 2004 (http://www.drc-gb.org/library/webaccessibility.asp).

EU Parliament. "European Parliament Resolution on the Commission Communication eEurope 2002: Accessibility of Public Web Sites and their Content," (COM(2001) 529–C5-0074/2002 –2002/2032(COS)), European Union, 2002 (http://europa.eu.int/information_society/policy/accessibility/).

Fulcher, G. *Disabling Policies?*, London: Falmer Press, 1989.

Goggin, G., and Newell, C. "An End to Disabling Policies? Toward Enlightened Universal Service," *The Information Society* (16), 2000, pp. 127-133.

Guo, B., Bricout, J. C., and Huang, J. "A Common Open Space or a Digital Divide? A Social Model Perspective on the Online Disability Community in China," *Disability & Society* (20:1), 2005, pp. 49-66.

Hoque, K., and Noon, M. "Equal Opportunities Policy and Practice in Britain: Evaluating the 'Empty Shell' Hypothesis," *Work, Employment and Society* (18:3), 2004, pp. 481-506.

Kreps, D., and Adam, A. "Failing the Disabled Community? The Continuing Problem of Web Accessibility," in P. Zaphiris and S. Kurniawan (eds.), *Human Computer Interaction Research in Web Design and Evaluation*, Hershey, PA: Ideas Group, 2006 (forthcoming).

Loader, B. D. (ed.). *Cyberspace Divide: Equality, Agency and Policy in the Information Society*, London: Routledge, 1998.

Marshall, S., Taylor, W., and You, X. (eds.). *Closing the Digital Divide: Transforming Regional Economies and Communities with Information Technology*, Westport, CT: Praeger, 2003.

Norris, P. *Digital Divide: Civic Engagement, Information Poverty, and the Internet Worldwide*, Cambridge, UK: Cambridge University Press, 2001.

Ritchie, H., and Blanck, P. "The Promise of the Internet for Disability: A Study of On-Line Services and Web Site Accessibility at Centers for Independent Living," *Behavioral Sciences and the Law* (21), 2003, pp. 5-26.

Selwyn, N. "'E-stablishing' an Inclusive Society? Technology, Social Exclusion and UK Government Policy Making," *Journal of Social Policy* (31:1), 2002, pp. 1-20.

Selwyn, N. "Reconsidering Political and Popular Understandings of the Digital Divide," *New Media & Society* (6:3), 2004, pp. 341-362.

Servon, L. J. *Bridging the Digital Divide: Technology, Community and Public Policy*, Malden, MA: Blackwell, 2002.

Trauth, E. M., Quesenberry, J. L., and Morgan, A. J. "Understanding the Under Representation of Women in IT: Toward a Theory of Individual Differences," in M. Tanniru and S. Weisband (eds.), *Proceedings of ACM SIGMIS '04*, New York: ACM Press, 2004, pp. 114-119..

U.S. Department of Commerce. "Falling Through the Net: Toward Digital Inclusion," Washington, DC: National Telecommunications and Information Administration, 2000 (available online at http://www.ntia.doc.gov/ntiahome/fttn00/contents00.html).

Winner, L. "Cyberlibertarian Myths and the Prospect for Community," *ACM Computers and Society* (27:3), 1997, pp. 14-19.

Winner, L. "Do Artefacts Have Politics?," in D. MacKenzie and J. Wajcman (eds.), *The Social Shaping of Technology*, Buckingham, UK: Open University Press, 1999, pp. 28-40.

About the Authors

Alison Adam is a professor of Information Systems and is currently Head of the Information Systems Institute at the University of Salford. Her research interests lie in critical information systems, gender and information systems, and computer ethics. Her recent book, *Gender, Ethics and Information Technology*, brings together these themes. Alison may be contacted at a.e.adam@salford.ac.uk.

David Kreps holds a BA(Hons) in Theatre and Arts Management, an MA in Cultural Studies, and a Ph.D. in the Sociology of Technology. David spent several years as a local government officer, running arts centres, and has been chairman of Kaos Theatre UK since 1997. He has been making Web sites since 1995, and is director of fourquarters IS Ltd. (http://www.fourquarters.biz). After several years lecturing part-time, David joined the Information Systems Institute at the University of Salford in January 2004. He has since worked on the creation of the eGovernment Master's program delivered from September 2004, and lectures in Information Society and World Wide Web development. David can be contacted at d.g.kreps@salford.ac.uk.

Part 5

Ethical Issues

16 RESPONSIBLE MANAGEMENT OF DIGITAL DIVIDES: An Oxymoronic Endeavor?

Bernd Carsten Stahl
De Montfort University
Leicester, U.K.

Abstract   *This paper critiques the notion of responsible management of information systems by pointing out the intrinsic contradiction inherent in the idea of managing morality and ethics in information systems. The paper, being part of the tradition of critical research in IS, uses the example of managing digital divides to argue that a traditional view of management (here called heroic management) leads to conceptual problems. It will develop two basic arguments that undermine the possibility of responsible heroic management of digital divides: (1) Normative issues related to digital divides cannot be managed because management is part of the construction of the problem and therefore lacks the detached and objective viewpoint required for rational management. (2) The very concept of responsibility, if taken seriously and applied responsibly (here called reflective responsibility) requires a participative approach that contradicts the traditional top-down approach of heroic management. The paper will conclude with a discussion of what form management of IS needs to take if it wants to be responsible.*

Keywords   Digital divides, responsibility, heroic management, critical research in information systems, ethics, morality, law

1   INTRODUCTION

Digital divides are one of the central problems created by information and communication technology. There is a range of literature on digital divides but there is no agreement on what constitutes them, why they are problematic, and how they should be addressed. I will briefly outline some of the problems of digital divides and argue that they are first and foremost ethical issues. If digital divides are ethically problematic, then conventional wisdom in information systems would suggest that they need

Please use the following format when citing this chapter:

Stahl, B.C., 2006, in IFIP International Federation for Information Processing, Volume 208, Social Inclusion: Societal and Organizational Implications for Information Systems, eds. Trauth, E., Howcroft, D., Butler, T., Fitzgerald, B., DeGross, J., (Boston: Springer), pp. 231-243.

to be managed right in order to solve the problem. The main argument of this paper is that such a conventional understanding of IS as something that can be managed in a rational traditional top-down manner (here called heroic management) is flawed. This becomes particularly obvious in the case of ethically charged issues such as digital divides. Using a critical approach, I will argue that the idea of heroically managing ethical issues in IS is intrinsically flawed and self-contradictory because (1) management produces some of the problems it sets out to solve and (2) the nature of responsible management precludes an heroic approach.

In order to develop this argument, I will first discuss the concept of digital divides and why they are problematic. In a second step, I will question the concept of management and develop my critique of heroic management based on the idea of responsibility. In the conclusion, I will discuss the consequences this will have for managing ethical issues.

2   MANAGING DIGITAL DIVIDES

Digital divides are multifaceted issues. They are often discussed in terms of politics and power (Norris 2001). However, the reason why we seem to believe that political solutions must be found is that digital divides are closely linked to social divides and create social injustices (UNDP 1998). There is an enormous amount of inequality in the world (Castells 1997; Schiller 1999) and there seems to be an implicit agreement among many scholars with an interest in divides that this constitutes a moral problem. In this paper I take the view that this perception of moral relevance is at the bottom of attention to digital divides. This does not rule out other approaches but it will provide the necessary link to the concept of responsibility developed later. The section will give a brief introduction to the concept of digital divides and then discuss how a traditional view of management can be applied to digital divides.

2.1 Digital Divides

The idea of the digital divides needs to be seen in the context of social justice and is related to a number of phenomena. For this reason I use the plural rather than the possibly more widely used singular of digital divide (see Rookby 2006). Like most concepts, *digital divides* is hard to define and can be ambiguous (Walsham 2003). The essence of the term is that it reflects a concern that the use of ICT can have an influence on divides and the resulting chances to live a fulfilled and autonomous life. Digital divides are often described in the context of economic development. They can refer to differences between as well as within countries (Kvasny 2002; Kvasny and Keil 2002).

The concept of a digital divide has been discussed since approximately the mid 1990s. In a narrow sense, it refers to "significant demographic gaps in computer and Internet access and usage" (Hacker and Mason 2003, p. 99). During the last decade there has been a large amount of research that tried to establish the reality and relevance of the digital divide. In the United States, for example, the National Telecommunications and Information Administration has collected a large amount of data for a variety of reports, some of which share the title "Falling Through the Net" (see www.ntia.doc. gov). Such a collection of statistics has been criticized as being one-dimensional and ideologically motivated (Hacker and Mason 2003). The approach also structures the possible problem by positing that different levels of access are a problem and by concentrating on the lack of access. This by necessity neglects some aspects such as the possible formation of digital elites (see McSorley 2003). It has furthermore been remarked that there are considerable methodological problems when measuring digital divides. Some authors doubt whether the concentration on the digital divide that we find in some streams of research is actually helpful or whether we should not look at more fundamental issues such as the structure and design of the Internet (Couldry 2003).

One can thus state that there is no clear definition of digital divides. It is unclear how they can be described and why they constitute a problem. Digital divides and social divides are, therefore, often closely related and can be seen as expressions of the same problem (Moss 2002; Parayil 2005).

2.2 Digital Divides in Organizations

The literature on digital divides concentrates on divides between countries or socio-economic groups within countries. It rarely touches on issues within organizations. Where it does, it concentrates on digital divides between organizations (Dewan and Riggins 2005). However, there seems to be no profound reason why individual digital divides within organizations are underrepresented. If digital divides are problematic because they affect power, abilities to participate and flourish, then it is easy to see that they apply to organizations as well. There are companies where parts of the workforce have access to ICT and others do not, which corresponds to power differentials. There is some overlap with hourly paid and salaried workers and thus with a more traditional distinction between knowledge and manual workers and socioeconomic classes. However, ICT is moving into more and more areas of work, including those that used to be manual. But even then, there is a difference between those who can and are allowed to use the technology and those who can but may not. Issues of inclusion and well-being that form the moral basis of discussions of digital divides are thus pertinent within organizations as well as within nation states.

These considerations do not seem to be developed in the literature. They also go beyond the confines of this paper. It would be interesting to consider how the literature on digital divides and the literature on organizational use of ICTs might be linked. One relevant aspect would be the question of participation, which is often discussed in conjunction with e-democracy. If such thoughts were extended to commercial organizations, they might have revolutionary implications regarding the distribution of power and resources. At the moment, however, there seems to be nothing more than recommendations for researchers to "examine the extent and impact of the digital divide on the individual worker, the workplace and employers." (Dewan and Riggins 2005, p. 314).

2.3 Problems and Management of Digital Divides

Digital divides produce a number of problems that I cannot discuss in depth here. They concentrate our attention on technology, where social issues should be considered. They can appear to reveal problems of justice where differences in access are chosen voluntarily. They can even be expressions of Western cultural imperialism that promotes a particular view of the problem and thereby of the possible solution. Despite these problems, it seems reasonable to assume that digital divides are relevant ethical problems that may react to moral intervention (see Kvasny and Truex 2000).

If digital divides are ethically problematic, then one needs to ask how they can be addressed. The traditional answer to this would be to have them managed in a responsible way, so that the problems are overcome. The majority of digital divide issues discussed above relate to the national or international level. "Managers" in charge of such issues will therefore often be politicians, national or international bureaucrats, or representatives of multinational organizations. However, digital divides issues can just as well appear on the organizational level. The responsible manager would then be a normal company manager. A responsible approach to managing ethical issues in the traditional view would be to determine the problem, find a solution, and then implement it. The main argument in this paper is that such a traditional approach is self-defeating because there are intrinsic and conceptual contradictions between the ideas of management and responsibility.

3   RESPONSIBLE MANAGEMENT OF DIGITAL DIVIDES

In this section I will briefly discuss the critical approach used in the current paper. I will then introduce the term *heroic management* as a description of the traditional view of management. This will lead to a discussion why heroic management is a problematic approach to ethical issues in ICT.

3.1 The Critical Approach to Management

This paper follows the critical research paradigm. This means, first of all, that it follows a *critical intention* not only to describe reality, but to change it, which is typical of critical research (Alvesson and Deetz 2000; Cecez-Kecmanovic 2001; Ngwenyama and Lee 1997). The main way in which the critical intention is usually realized is by promoting emancipation (Alvesson and Willmott 1992; Hirschheim and Klein 1994 Klein and Myers 1999; McAulay et al. 2002; Ngwenyama and Lee 1997; Varey et al. 2002). A fundamental problem is how research can emancipate. In this case the answer is that the exposure of a conceptual contradiction in the idea of managing digital divides will open up discursive closures. By demonstrating that a traditional approach to digital divides is incapable of addressing the problem, individuals will be freed from reliance on the problematic approach. This refers to people facing digital divide issues but also managers who may be in a situation where they are ascribed responsibility which they cannot discharge. The importance of language is a central feature of critical research, despite the lack of a recognized methodology (see McGrath 2005). This paper will follow that tradition by attempting to promote emancipation by exposing conceptual contradictions.

3.2 Heroic Management

Etymologically, the verb "to manage" (originally probably derived from the Latin *manus*, the hand) comes from the Italian *maneggiare* to handle, to be able to use skillfully, and originally referred to the handling of horses. Today it means "to conduct, carry on, supervise, or control."[1] While *management* thus has a wide meaning compatible with different styles of solving problems, it often aims to convey a more specific meaning, which might be termed *heroic management* (Gosling and Minzberg 2003). My use of this term has been inspired by the idea of *postheoric management* (Baecker 1994) and the recognition that actual management practices still have a long way to go before they become "post" heroic.

Heroic management stands for the type of management typically taught in many business schools and propagated by management magazines. It depicts the manager as the individual who is personally responsible for success or failure of organizational activities. This orthodox or business school view of management is supported by a relatively standardized and coherent body of knowledge comparable to that of other academic disciplines such as law or medicine (Knights and Willmott 1999). Management takes place in most levels of organizations but the main interest lies in top level management where the strategy of companies is decided (Bourlakis and Bourlakis 2003). Indeed, conventional management wisdom suggests that every organization must have a strategy and that it will be lost in the turbulent environment if it does not have one (Knights and Morgan 1991). Managers are in charge of creating the strategy and aligning organizational efforts with it. A considerable amount of effort is therefore spent describing the qualities and characteristics of the manager. The manager is a role model for employees (and for students of management). He (and he is rarely a she) is "seen as someone who represents what society believes in and whose behavior is regarded to be, in principle, morally correct" (Introna 1997 p. 23). Examples of the managerial virtues are rationality (Newell et al. 2001), motivation, effectiveness, and efficiency. But there are also less tangible virtues. The manager is reliable and keeps his calm in the storm. He is a leader but also reassuring and helpful. The fact that few, if any, individuals actually combine all of these characteristics does not diminish their importance as an ideal type. It is justified to call this understanding of management heroic management because the individual manager is depicted as a hero, the savior of the organization. And just like the term heroic has the connotation of good and desirable, the same is true for the term management (Lawler 2004).

Despite the fact that it is probably the predominant view of management, heroic management also runs into problems. One academic approach that is interested in the downsides and weaknesses of heroic management is critical management studies (Alvesson and Deetz 2000). The problems of heroic management can be divided in practical, theoretical, and ethical ones.

The main practical problem is that heroic management often does not work. The heroic approach to project management, for example, does not seem to affect the outcome of projects (Couillard 1996). Managers are caught up in webs of relationships which make it hard for them to establish their heroic leadership, and even if they do,

---

[1]Oxford English Dictionary, 2004, "Management" (online at http://athens.oed.com/).

there are conflicts with other managers holding similar positions as well as internal conflicts regarding other roles managers may play (Knights and Willmott 1999).

Theoretical problems concern the fundamental reasons why heroic management tends to fail. These include the fact that the very idea of heroic management is a socially constructed category which may be more or less suited to a specific situation, depending on the composition of the group to which management is applied. This means that the acceptability of heroic management is not in the hands of the manager, diminishing his control of success or failure. Another theoretical argument against the concept of heroic management is that it overlooks the fundamental determinants of humans who act as managers. Managers are not the abstract rational *homines economici* described in parts of the management literature; they are being-in-the-world in a Heideggerian sense (Heidegger 1992; see also Ciborra 2002; Introna 1997). They are incapable of leaving their bodily situatedness, the fact that they are always caught up in situations (Lawler 2004) as well as the ideologies and discursive webs surrounding them (Levy et al. 2003). The myth of rationality, on which heroic management is built, is thus exposed as untenable. Rational decisions in a decision-theoretic model are the rare exception for managers who have to make do in bounded rationality, and for whom emotions are often more important than objective information (Fineman 2001). Managers have to make sense of an uncertain and changing world (Hughes et al. 2002; Thomas 1999).

The myth of rationality, which I assume to be at the base of heroic management and its failure, deserves more attention than I can give it here. It goes back to Max Weber's distinction of different types of rationality, and most importantly to his idea of purposive rationality (*Zweckrationalität*). This type of limited rationality is typical for the organization of capitalist economies and thus a central issue of critical research (see Habermas 1984; Stahl 2005). It is closely related to the myth of control, namely that managers can and want to control social action according to their ends. I contend, without being able to argue the point in detail, that the basis of the problems is a limited understanding of rationality, which, if transcended, would overcome the myth of control as well as heroic management.

Another point of critique of the heroic ideal comes from feminist scholars. Adam (2001) shows that the concept of the lone savior/hero is not confined to management but finds its equivalent in engineering as well. She argues that this is problematic because it is a gendered description which gives preference to behaviors that are traditionally associated with men. It thereby gives rise to ethical approaches which emphasize the confrontational nature of ethics and therefore can be blind to more efficient conciliatory solutions. The metaphor of the hero is thus not only misleading but also ethically problematic. This line of argument can lead us to the question of the link between responsibility and heroic management.

3.3 Heroic and Responsible Management?

We have now seen that heroic management is *per se* problematic. Apart from the arguments outline above, there are other issues that the critical management literature so far has not picked up on. The one aspect that I want to develop in this paper is the difficulty of combining heroic and responsible management. Initially, *responsible management* here stands for the use of management to address and solve ethical and moral issues. These are issues that have to do with good and bad, right and wrong, and with the question how we justify such distinctions (for a detailed account of responsible management in IS, see Stahl 2004). Responsible management is thus the desirable approach to issues such as digital divides. Digital divides seem to be a topic where there is a strong initial perception that something is wrong and should be changed. It is not always obvious, however, what exactly is wrong and how it should be changed or by whom. Managing digital divides responsibly would mean identifying the problems, finding solutions, and resolving the issues. While this is generally difficult, I think that there are two reasons why it is fundamentally impossible to use the traditional heroic way of managing for such issues of responsibility: the problem of self-awareness and the problem of conceptual consistency.

3.3.1 Problem I: Detached Rationality and Objective Reality—The Problem of Self-Awareness

Responsibility ascriptions are complex social processes that can raise problems for a variety of reasons, which this paper will not be able to cover. There are, however, structural problems of responsible heroic management that cannot be overcome in the traditional top-down objectivist mindset. The attempt to manage digital divides clearly shows this. There are moral issues of distribution and equality of access. There are ethical issues of finding supporting arguments for the solution to moral issues. But there is also the problem that it is not completely clear what the problem is. The issues related to digital divides are not objectively given. Rather, they are based on individual and social experiences and develop over time. They are culturally variable and depend on a number of immeasurable factors. A heroic top-down approach will be unable to identify all of these, not because of a lack of effort, but because they have no objective context-independent reality that would allow describing them in an algorithmic way.

An important aspect of this problem is that management is not a detached entity with a privileged observer position with regard to digital divides but an involved agent that constitutes part of the problem. Managerial or political decisions set the framework for questions of access. National or local questions of divide are directly linked to the institutional environment and also to local management styles. The same can be said for divides within organizations, which will depend to a large extent on managerial decisions. Furthermore, political or management decisions regarding digital divides are necessarily based on preconceived moral ideals and (often implicit) ethical convictions. These will rarely be identical to those of the citizens or employees who are affected. Political leadership and management thus introduce and privilege a certain morality, which in itself will usually constitute an ethical problem.

I should clarify that these problems are not caused by bad leaders or bad management practices. Rather, they are intrinsic in heroic management that takes an objective reality for granted and believes that problems can be addressed from a detached and rational point of view. A resulting fundamental problem is that legitimate concerns of citizens or employees based on their moral or ethical views cannot be accommodated in such an objectivist world view. That means that where concerns are raised, these will typically be considered resistance to change, which leadership must overcome. Since the affected citizens or employees see their objections as justified, management will have to make use of formal powers to overcome the perceived resistance. This will not solve the underlying problem but instead create another moral issue.

3.3.2   Problem II: Responsible Use of Responsibility—
The Problem of Conceptual Consistency

The second problem of the attempt to manage responsibly within the mindset of heroic management refers to the concept of responsibility itself. There are three fundamental characteristics of responsibility: openness, affinity to action, and teleology. I have elsewhere developed in more depth the concept of *reflective responsibility* (Stahl 2004). The basic idea of reflective responsibility is that a normative idea like responsibility should be applicable to itself without contradiction. That means that the use of the concept of responsibility should be a responsible action. Or, to break this down to the main characteristics, an ascription of responsibility should be open, lead to action, and support the intended *telos*, the aim of responsibility. Reflective use of responsibility should thus determine whether an ascription is indeed viable and whether it can achieve its aims.

Considering this question will require attention to detail in every single case, which is impossible to do in an academic paper. There are, however, a number of issues that can be discussed in general terms. These can be divided according to the main dimensions involved: subject, object, and authority. The subject is the entity that is responsible. In heroic management, this will be a manager. The higher up in the hierarchy, the more responsibility one will expect. This exclusive focus on individual responsibility is problematic, however, because in complex modern organizations, it is usually not trivial to draw a direct line between individuals and certain actions or decisions. This problem is exacerbated when we look at political settings, which dominate digital divides issues. Many decisions are taken by collectives or emerge from the history of the organization without being attributable to a single person. Moreover, individuals do not meet all of the conditions that need to be fulfilled in order for responsibility to be acceptable: freedom, knowledge, and power (Fischer 1999; Goldman 1999). Individuals higher up in the hierarchy will often have more freedom and power, but they lack the local knowledge of pertinent problems. Those individuals who have the local knowledge typically have no power to change things. With regard to digital divides this means that it is not clear who should be held responsible.

The subject is responsible for the object of responsibility. A traditional approach would define the objects at the outset. For digital divides, this might include measures of access for different groups or the availability of technology or education. Even where they were not contentious, such objects would be problematic. The main problem here is what we call *side effects*. Side effects are those consequences of actions that are caused but not intended. The provision of technology or access can lead to unwanted consequences. Where equality of access should create equality of use and opportunities, it is possible that those who are better educated anyway will profit most. Equaling the digital divide may mean that resources have to be expropriated and redistributed, thus creating new problems of justice. Technology, once provided can be misused, for example for hate speech, promotion of terrorism, or child pornography.

The main problem of the object of ascription is that a top-down objectivist approach is likely to miss a considerable number of the most relevant issues, including most moral questions. Again, this is not the case because managers do a bad job, but because moral problems are context-dependent and emerge from continuous interaction. They are thus not completely identifiable from an external observer's position, a position assumed by heroic management.

The main problem with heroic management in this context is that it privileges a particular viewpoint, namely, that of management in the process of establishing and sanctioning responsibility. Most ethical theories are based on the idea that ethical evaluations must be impartial. A heroic and detached approach to responsibility can, by definition, not be impartial because, even when considering other stakeholders' views, it determines outcomes on the basis of management's view of the world.

A traditional approach to responsible management of digital divides thus falls short of the requirements of responsibility with regard to the major dimensions: subject and object. If it cannot identify the right subject, it will miss some of the relevant objects and it will not be based on an acceptable set of norms and thus not produce viable sanctions. To reiterate the point: This is not because managers are bad people or because management does not do its job well. The problems I have discussed are structural and conceptual. They are based on the intrinsic contradiction between a traditional and heroic approach to management and the requirements of responsibility.

4 REFLECTIVE AND RESPONSIBLE MANAGEMENT: THE SOLUTION?

So far the paper has argued that there are substantial conceptual problems related to the attempt to responsibly manage the normative problems raised by digital divides. To return to the question in the title of this paper, responsible management of information systems indeed seems to be an oxymoron, at least in so far as management is understood in the traditional top-down scientifically rational way, which I have termed heroic management. What conclusions can we draw from this? The simplest one would be to stop speaking of responsibility and management. However, responsibility is a concept closely linked to management and managers tend to be proud of the fact that they are responsible people. It also allows highlighting ethical issues such as digital divides. The next solution is thus to simply ignore the issues raised in this paper. Heroic management that concentrates on political or organizational imperatives and neglects the wider context can still be promoted. It will have blind spots and not be sensitive to the moral and ethical issues discussed in this paper, but it can be used to further specific ends. Anecdotal evidence suggests that this is the solution frequently chosen. Such an approach has two major disadvantages: an ethical and an organizational one. The ethical disadvantage is that responsibility understood in a top-down strategic manner will fail to pick up on many moral problems raised by digital divides. Furthermore, it does not have the ethical breadth to deal with those it does pick up. It will thus ignore relevant and legitimate concerns or will try to suppress them as unjustified resistance to change.

The political and organizational problem of the approach is its insensitivity to moral and ethical questions, which can lead to problems of implementation. When solutions to problems of digital divides are sought by implementing decisions agreed upon by individual leaders, it is likely that this will lead to resistance because legitimate concerns have been overlooked. The heroic approach can, therefore, backfire.

The alternative to this unsatisfactory approach would be to understand the concept of management in a different way, in a way that is compatible with the concept of responsibility. This is where we come back to the idea of reflective responsibility introduced earlier. Reflective responsibility is the attempt to realize the ascription of responsibility in such a way as to render it a responsible activity. This means that responsibility is ascribed in such a way that it will be open (in terms of process and outcome), that it will have manifest results, and that it furthers the original intention of the ascription. It goes far beyond the confines of this paper to describe the details of reflective responsibility (for an in-depth discussion, see Stahl 2004). Suffice it to say that reflective responsibility will require participative processes that define all steps and dimensions of responsibility in an interdependent way. That means that an instance of responsibility needs to be defined in terms of subject, object, and norms or sanctions. The subjects need to be chosen so that they can affect the outcomes, adhere to the norms, and react to the sanctions. In terms of digital divides, this will mean that there is no one single ascription of responsibility but rather a web of interlinking responsibilities that will refer to one another. Subjects will most likely include political leaders or individual managers but they will not be confined to these. It is possible for individual citizens to become subjects of responsibility or collectives or whole organizations. This reconceptualization of responsibility subjects may open avenues for paying closer attention to gender issues, for example by underlining the importance of hero helpers or sybils (Adam 2001) as counter-metaphors to the lone hero.

The objects will include the traditional (equality of access, provision of technology, provision of education) but they will go beyond these, covering questions of respect, minority issues, unintended side-effects, and whatever else the affected parties find worthy of ascribing responsibility. The relationship between subject and object will be defined on the basis of acceptable norms, which can be economic ones (profit maximization), but which can also be explicitly ethical (autonomy, freedom, justice) or of a different nature (tradition, local culture).

It should be clear that such a web of responsibility requires a fundamentally different type of interaction between leaders and other stakeholders from the one implied in heroic management. In practice, the process of responsibility ascription will look more like Habermasian discourse (Habermas 1981) or a stakeholder debate in the sense of stakeholder management (Donaldson and Preston 1995). It also embodies the ideal of democracy with autonomous and independent citizens. The main advantage of this reflective approach to responsible management of normative issues of IS is that it allows the identification and consideration of the wide range of moral and ethical issues that are potentially raised by digital divides. It faces neither of the two main problems of heroic management discussed in this paper. Since it is not a one-sided, top-down and power-based responsibility, leadership does not have the most important place. Leaders are, of course, legitimate stakeholders in the process of ascription and they can argue for their desired objectives. However, they need to take into consideration the viewpoints of other stakeholders. This allows a definition of the problems (objects of responsibility) that overcomes the partial interests of management. The ascription is, therefore, not fraught with the problem of self-awareness. By considering questions of realizabiltiy and desirable outcomes, the process of ascription also addresses the second main objection raised above. The simultaneous definition of subject, object, and authority allows the development of viable ascriptions. Finally, the web of responsibility created in this way needs to remain open to revision and thus is not a static construct. It can react to changes by adding or modifying ascriptions.

The critical reader can raise a number of objections to the model of reflective responsibility. The main ones are that it is a hugely complex undertaking, particularly when applied to large processes, and that it does not offer a guarantee of success. These points of critique are valid but can be countered from the point of view of reflective responsibility. It is an intrinsic characteristic of reflective responsibility that it is modest in its goals; that it aims to further the moral objectives of the community of discourse without claiming that it will achieve perfection. The counterargument would thus be that the reflective approach at least offers the possibility of overcoming the short-comings of heroic responsibility and that such an attempt should be worth the cost, first because it can help overcome organizational problems, and second because it is a morally acceptable way to deal with the other. There are, of course, other counter-arguments, which aim at the heart of participatory approaches, which I cannot discuss here (see Kvasny and Truex 2000; Wilson 1997).

There is, however, another reason why it is difficult to accept this approach. The role of the leader in this setting changes drastically. He is no longer the lone and rational hero who brings salvation to the organization. Instead, he becomes an involved member of a community and, at best, a facilitator of discourses. This goes counter to the self-description of many leaders as well as our social perception of them. It requires a wider discourse aimed at redefining management and leadership. Without such a discourse and a change of our understanding of the role of managers, the heroic approach to managing responsibly is likely to prevail despite its oxymoronic nature, which will render it impossible to address the moral and ethical issues of digital divides.

References

Adam, A. "Heroes or Sibyls? Gender and Engineering Ethics," *IEEE Technology and Society Magazine* (20:3), 2001, pp. 39-46.

Alvesson, M., and Deetz, S. *Doing Critical Management Research*, London: Sage Publications, 2000.

Alvesson, M., and Willmott, H. "On the Idea of Emancipation in Management and Organization Studies," *Academy of Management Review* (17:3), 1992, pp. 432-464.

Baecker, D. *Postheroisches Management. Ein Vademecum.* Berlin: Merve, 1994.

Bourlakis, C. A., and Bourlakis, M. A. "Logistics, Information Technology and Retail Internationalization: The Formation of International Strategic Retail Networks," in L. A. Joia (ed.), *IT-Based Management: Challenges and Solutions*, Hershey, PA: Idea Group Publishing, 2003, pp. 257-276.

Castells, M. *The Information Age: Economy, Society, and Culture. Volume II: The Power of Identity*, Oxford, UK: Blackwell, 1997.

Cecez-Kecmanovic, D. "Doing Critical IS Research: The Question of Methodology," in E. Trauth (ed.), *Qualitative Research in IS: Issues and Trends*, Hershey, PA: Idea Group Publishing, 2001, pp. 141-162.

Ciborra, C. *The Labyriths of Information-Challenging the Wisdom of Systems*, Oxford, UK: Oxford University Press, 2002.

Couillard, J. "The Role of Project Risk in Determining Project Management Approach," *Project Management Journal* (26:4), 1995, pp. 3-15.

Couldry, N. "Digital Divide or Discursive Design? On the Emerging Ethics of Information Space," *Ethics and Information Technology* (5:2), 2003, pp. 89-97.

Dewan, S., and Riggins, F J. "The Digital Divide: Current and Future Research Directions," *Journal of the Association for Information Systems* (6:12), 2005, pp. 298-337.

Donaldson, T., and Preston, L. E. "The Stakeholder Theory of the Corporation: Concepts, Evidence, and Implications," *Academy of Management Review* (20:1), 1995, pp. 65-91.

Fineman, S. "Fashioning the Environment," *Organization* (8:1), 2001, pp. 17-31.

Fischer, J. M. "Recent Work on Moral Responsibility," *Ethics* (110:1), 1999, pp. 93-139.

Goldman, A. I. "Why Citizens Should Vote: A Causal Responsibility Approach," in E. F. Paul, F. D. Miller, and J. Paul (eds.), *Responsibility*, Cambridge, UK; Cambridge University Press, 2003, pp. 201-217.

Gosling, J., and Mintzberg, H. "The Five Minds of a Manager," *Harvard Business Review* (81:11), 2003, pp. 54-63.

Habermas, J. *Theorie des kommunikativen Handelns*-Band I+II. Frankfurt: Suhrkamp Verlag, 1981.

Hacker, K. L., and Mason, S. M. "Ethical Gaps in Studies of the Digital Divide," *Ethics and Information Technology* (5:2), 2003, pp. 99 -115.

Heidegger, M. *Sein und Zeit* (17th ed.), Tübingen, Germany: Max Niemeyer Verlag, 1993.

Hirschheim, R., and Klein, H. K. "Realizing Emancipatory Principles in Information Systems Development: The Case for ETHICS," *MIS Quarterly* (18:1), 1994, pp. 83-109.

Hughes, J. A., Rouncefield, M., and Tolmie, P. "The Day-to-Day Work of Standardization: A Sceptical Note on the Reliance on IT in a Retail Bank," in S. Woolgar (ed.), *Virtual Society? Technology, Cyberbole, Reality*, Oxford: Oxford University Press, 2002, pp. 247-263.

Introna, L. *Management, Information and Power: A Narrative of the Involved Manager*. London: MacMillan, 1997.

Klein, H. K., and Myers, M. D. "A Set of Principles for Conducting and Evaluating Interpretive Field Studies in Information Systems," *MIS Quarterly* (23:1), 1999, pp. 67-94.

Knights, D., and Morgan, G "Corporate Strategy, Organizations, and Subjectivity: A Critique," *Organization Studies* (12:2), 1991, pp. 251-273.

Knights, D., and Willmott, H. *Management Lives: Power and Identity in Organizations*, London: Sage Publications, 1999.

Kvasny, L. "A Conceptual Framework For Examining Digital Inequality," in R. Ramsower and J. Windsor (eds.), *Proceedings of the Eighth Americas Conference on Information Systems*, Dallas, TX, 2002, pp. 1798-1805.

Kvasny, L., and Keil, M "The Challenges of Redressing the Digital Divide: A Tale of Two Cities," in L. Applegate, R. D. Galliers, and J. I. DeGross (eds.), *Proceedings of the 23rd International Conference on Information Systems*, Barcelona, Spain, 2002, pp. 817-828.

Kvasny, L., and Truex, D. "Information Technology and the Cultural Reproduction of Social Order: A Research Program," in R. Baskerville, J. Stage, and J. I. DeGross (eds.), *Organizational and Social Perspectives on Information Technology*, Boston: Kluwer Academic Publishers, 2000, pp. 277-294.

Lawler, J. "Meaning and Being: Existentialist Concepts in Leadership," *International Journal of Management Concepts and Philosophy* (1:1), 2004, pp. 61-72.

Levy, D. L., Alvesson, M., and Willmott, H. "Critical Approaches to Strategic Management," in M. Alvesson and H. Willmott (eds.), *Studying Management Critically*, London: Sage Publications, 2003, pp. 92-110.

McAulay, L., Doherty, N., and Keval, N. "The Stakeholder Dimension in Information Systems Evaluation," *Journal of Information Technology* (17), 2002, pp. 241-255.

McGrath, K. "Doing Critical Research in Information Systems: A Case of Theory and Practice Not Informing Each Other," *Information Systems Journal* (15), 2005, pp. 85-101.

McSorley, K. The Secular Salvation Story of the Digital Divide," *Ethics and Information Technology* (5:2), 2003, pp. 75-87.

Moss, J. "Power and the Digital Divide," In: *Ethics and Information Technology* (4:2), 2002, pp. 159-165.

Newell, S., Swan, J., and Kautz, K. "The Role of Funding Bodies in the Creation and Diffusion of Management Fads and Fashions," *Organization* (8:1), 2001, pp. 97-120.

Ngwenyama, O. K., and Lee, A. S. "Communication Richness in Electronic Mail: Critical Social Theory and the Contextuality of Meaning," *MIS Quarterly* (21:2), 1997, pp. 145-167.

Norris, P. *Digital Divide—Civic Engagement, Information Poverty, and the Internet Worldwide*, Cambridge, UK: Cambridge University Press, 2001.

Parayil, G. "The Digital Divide and Increasing Returns: Contradictions of Informational Capitalism," *The Information Society* (21:1), 2005, pp. 41-51.

Rookby, E. (ed.). *Information Technology and Social Justice*, Hershey, PA: Idea Group Publishing, 2006.

Schiller, D. *Digital Capitalism: Networking the Global Market System*, Cambridge, MA: MIT Press, 1999.

Stahl, B. C. "The Obituary as Bricolage: The Mann Gulch Disaster and the Problem of Heroic Rationality," *European Journal of Information Systems* (14), 2005, pp. 487-491.

Stahl, B. C. *Responsible Management of Information Systems*, Hershey, PA: Idea Group Publishing, 2004.

Thomas, R. J. "What Machines Can't Do: Politics and Technology in the Industrial Enterprise," in D. MacKenzie and J. Wajcman (eds.), *The Social Shaping of Technology* (2nd ed.), Maidenhead, UK: Open University Press, 1999, pp. 199-221.

UNDP. *Human Development Report 1998*, United Nations Development Programme, New York: Oxford University Press, 1998.

Varey, R. J., Wood-Harper, T., and Wood, B. "A Theoretical Review of Management and Information Systems Using a Critical Communications Theory," *Journal of Information Technology* (17), 2002, pp. 229-239.

Walsham, G. "Development, Global Futures and IS Research: A Polemic," paper presented at IS Perspectives and Challenges in the Context of Globalization, IFIP Working Groups 8.2 and 9.4 Joint Conference, Athens Greece, June 15-17, 2003.

Wilson, F. A. "The Truth is Out There: The Search for Emancipatory Principles in Information Systems Design," *Information Technology and People* (10:3), 1997, pp. 187-204.

About the Author

Bernd Carsten Stahl is a senior lecturer in the Faculty of Computing Sciences and Engineering and a research associate at the Centre for Computing and Social Responsibility of De Montfort University, Leicester, UK. His interests cover philosophical issues arising from the intersections of business, technology, and information. This includes the ethics of computing and critical approaches to information systems. He is the editor-in-chief of *International Journal of Technology and Human Interaction*. He can be reached at bstahl@dmu.ac.uk.

17 PRIVACY, SECURITY, AND TRANSPARENCY: ICT-Related Ethical Perspectives and Contrasts in Contemporary Firms

Antonino Vaccaro
Carnegie Mellon University
Pittsburgh, PA U.S.A.
and Instituto Superior Técnico
Lisbon, Portugal

Abstract   *This paper analyzes the ethical perspectives associated with the introduction and use of information and communication technologies in contemporary firms. It presents a three-dimensional ethical model that introduces the transparency concern, and its related impact on the digital divide question, as the new ethical perspective of contemporary business organizations.*

Keywords   Business ethics, information ethics, information and communication technologies

1   INTRODUCTION

The impressive development of information and communication technologies (ICT) in recent decades has supported a widespread diffusion of these tools in the social and economic life of developed countries around the world. The pervasive adoption of virtual applications has significantly changed cultural, social, and economic equilibria through a radical modification of social relationships in private, public, and professional dimensions. The aim of the current work is to point out and analyze the ethical perspectives of ICT adoption and use at the firm level in contemporary business organizations. This will be accomplished by reviewing the current literature about the subject by focusing upon varied research fields such as business ethics (e.g., Crane and Matten 2004), information ethics (e.g., Floridi and Sanders 2002), media ethics (e.g., Bettetini and   Fumagalli 2002), ethics and technology (Tavani 2004), and computer ethics

Please use the following format when citing this chapter:

Vaccaro, A., 2006, in IFIP International Federation for Information Processing, Volume 208, Social Inclusion: Societal and Organizational Implications for Information Systems, eds. Trauth, E., Howcroft, D., Butler, T., Fitzgerald, B., DeGross, J., (Boston: Springer), pp. 245-258.

(Johnson 2001), among others.[1] In this sense, we acknowledge that the state of the art lacks an integrated review of the different perspectives concerning this theme offered by the research of social sciences.

This paper contributes to the literature in several ways. First, it introduces and defines the various forms of transparency as a new, important ethical perspective for contemporary business organizations. To the best of our knowledge, it is the first work that approaches this theme in the context of management of information systems and business ethics disciplines. Moreover, as we will see, internal transparency represents an important ethical concern inside the digital divide discourse. Second, this paper provides an integrated vision of the various ICT-related ethical problems that affect contemporary companies presenting an integrative model based on the review of the literature of a wide group of research fields. Third, useful considerations and implications for practitioners and scholars are provided.

The remainder of the paper is organized as follows. First, some preliminary definitions and considerations to focus our conceptual path are provided. The Rawlsian "veil of ignorance" is introduced, followed by three parts analyzing, respectively, privacy, security, and transparency concerns. The final section provides a brief discussion and a series of related considerations and policy implications.

2   SOME INTERESTING DEFINITIONS AND PRELIMINARY CONSIDERATIONS

In recent decades, various authors have emphasized and described the uniqueness of the features and capabilities of ICT (e.g., Moor 1985; Tavani 2004). As a consequence, there has been an over-evaluation of ICT-related ethical problems. Argandoña (2003, p. 7) argued that the ethical neutrality of ICT can be legitimately questioned because "any technology that can be used immorally must be developed with caution." Indeed, he points to the example of a category of ICT tools (i.e., monitoring technologies) that are "more likely to be used for illicit purposes" (p. 7). Following Argandoña's perspective, we analyze a broad definition of ICT in order to determine whether the core categories of uses associated with new virtual technologies can be related to ethical or nonethical purposes.

Information technology (IT) or information and communication technology (ICT) is the technology required for information processing. In particular the

---

[1] We did not set out to study (1) uses of ICT already recognized as illegal, such as development and diffusion of computer viruses, computer piracy, unauthorized information access, computer fraud, or corporate sabotage, (2) the ethical impact of ICT adoption for social purposes by private or institutional actors, or (3) the different conceptions of ethical uses of ICT in the population of users.

use of electronic computers and computer software to convert, store, protect, process, transmit, and retrieve information from anywhere, anytime.[2]

If we consider **human writing**, we can verify that its definition and its ultimate objectives are similar to those of ICT because human writing is simply an old, "traditional" form of ICT. To support our observation we will **adapt** the definition of ICT to human writing.

Human writing is the technology required for information processing. In particular, the use of characters, paper, and ink to convert, store, process, transmit, and retrieve information anywhere, anytime.

Whatever the ethical position of the reader, surely human writing is believed to be ethical. As we have recognized, ICTs represent a wider form of information transmission just as human writing was several millennia ago in relation to previous methods of communication. This consideration assures us that *a priori* the main uses associated with ICT are similar to traditional writing. Consequently, assuming the ethical neutrality of ICT, our investigation will focus on the uses of these technologies in the specific context of our interest, business organizations.

3 IDENTIFYING THE ETHICAL QUESTIONS

Our approach to identifying the ethical questions posed in this work is based on the Rawlsian theory of justice as fairness (Rawls 1971). We have chosen this philosophical theory for various reasons. First, Rawls' ethical model has changed contemporary ethical philosophy (Abbá 1995), supporting a new and effective way to approach the pluralism of contemporary society. Second, the theory of justice as fairness has been applied in diverse practical ethical questions related to egalitarian issues such as feminism cases (e.g., Moller Okin 1989), the defense of homosexual rights (e.g., Dobbs 2004), and specific ICT-related ethical debates such as privacy and employee surveillance (e.g., Introna 2001). Third, as we will see in the following passages, the Rawlsian approach to identifying ethical questions allows a wide applicability and generalization of the insights introduced in the model.

Rawls proposes a public morality developed through a social contract in which all actors are in an "original position." The idea is "to nullify the effects of specific contingencies which put men and women at odds and tempt them to exploit social and natural circumstances to their own advantage" (Rawls 1971, p. 136). Under the veil of ignorance, the condition in which no one knows in which social position they will live, everyone would agree to some basic rules of society. Moreover, Rawls assumes that agents involved in the development of public morality are rational and their objective

---

[2]The definition is from the wikipedia encyclopedia, The choice of this reference for our definition is not fortuitous. We analyzed more than 50 definitions in the MIS literature, in dictionaries, etc. It is consistent and comprehensive of all references analyzed.

is social cooperation between equals with the intention of reciprocal advantage.[3] Therefore, our basis for identifying and proposing the ethical considerations will be the question: **Under the veil of ignorance, will a rational actor agree with the development of this kind of use of ICT tools in firms' activities?**

In relation to the introduction of ICT into our society, the main ethical problems recognized in the various literatures relate to a wide set of concerns, such as privacy (e.g.,Introna 1996; Ottensmeyer and Heroux 1991), intellectual property (e.g., Winter et al. 2004), workplace conditions (e.g., Brown and Duguid 2000; Castells 1996; Perrolle 1998), security of individuals (e.g., Fung and Lee 1999), and the digital divide (Tavani 2004). We recognize within this heterogeneous and wide range that the problems affecting firms' activities can be described along two main dimensions: the first is privacy, the second security and safety of individuals. In this work we propose another dimension that, to the best of our knowledge, has not been approached in detail in the literature: **firms' transparency**. As firms' activities are both internal and external, we will consider for each of the introduced dimensions two levels of ethical investigation and analysis, which we will define respectively as internal and external levels. We therefore propose a three-dimensional (privacy, security, and transparency) and two-level (internal and external) model, useful for both scholars and practitioners to frame the main ethical problems arising from the adoption and use of ICT for firms' activities[4] (see Figure 1). The model presents an ethical question for each couple dimension/level. The assumption that actors involved in the ethical discourse have heterogeneous ethical beliefs suggests proposing appropriate ethical questions, rather than propositions, in order to allow a wide usability and generalization of the offered insights.[5] Each of these questions should be taken as representative of inquiries into a wider series of specific ethical issues that affect the management of information systems in the selected dimension and level of analysis.

4   THE FIRST DIMENSION: MULTIPLE, VARIEGATED FACES OF THE PRIVACY

In the last decade, problems related to the respect of personal privacy have widely interested intellectuals, practitioners in every managerial field, and institutions at every level. As Tavani (2004, p. 42) pointed out, "of all the ethical issues associated with the use of cybertechnology, perhaps none has received more media attention than the concern about the loss of personal privacy in the Internet era."

---

[3]These are perfectly reasonable assumptions with which to approach our ethical problems at the firm level: social cooperation in order to allow reciprocal advantage and rationality of agents are necessary starting points for every business organization.

[4]The model does not cover intellectual property concerns because we did not find in the literature indications regarding the impact of these issues at the firm level. Moreover, we expect that intellectual property problems are or should be adequately regulated by the national norms under which each company operates.

[5]Other referred works in the business ethics field (e.g., Nash 2003) have adopted this editorial and methodological strategy.

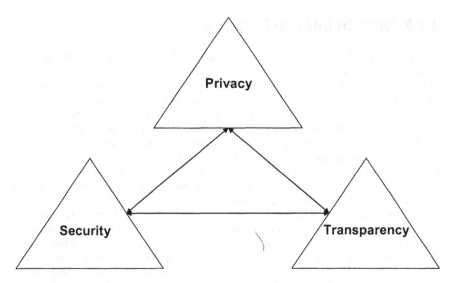

Figure 1. The Three Dimensions of the Model

It is a shared belief that ICT have created a surveillance society in which the issue of individual privacy is no longer space and time bound (Barlow 1991; Introna 1996, 2002; Lyon 1994) and affects each individual at different levels. There is in fact irrefutable evidence that the computer as a work tool enables new forms of surveillance (Ottensmeyer and Heroux 1991) and that the advent of electronic commerce brings with it a host of ethical issues surrounding customer privacy (Sarathy and Robertson 2003). We will refer to privacy as the concept of a person's right to control information about him/herself and the situations over which such a right may be legitimately extended[6] (Cranford 1998).

Analysis of the literature confirms that two actors have been mainly affected by the introduction and diffusion of ICT tools inside firms' organizations: **employees and customers**. For example, Spinello (2004) provided a series of case studies showing that the possibilities arising from the use of ICT caused serious privacy issues in relationships with both customers and employees. Thus, privacy concerns affect ICT use in contemporary companies at two different levels: the **external**, in the relationships with customers, and **internal**, in management's interaction with employees.

---

[6]This definition is consistent with others in the literature such Mason (1986), Shaw, (2003), and the Oxford and Webster Dictionary. While the term privacy was first used in English in about 1450, its importance was recognized for the first time in an official document of the 19th century. In a ruling dated 1888, an American judge, Thomas Cooley, defined privacy as the right "to be let alone." Two years later, Warren and Brandeis (1890) recognized "recent inventions and business methods," like "instantaneous photographs and newspaper enterprise," as causes of new forms of privacy violation.

4.1 Privacy in Internal Relationships

In the internal dimension, the privacy of the workforce is mainly violated due to the ability to monitor the activities of employees continuously and without limits. Managers can in fact observe in real time what exactly an employee is doing through the use of a multitude of basic and inexpensive computer-based monitoring products that allow them to track Web use, observe downloaded files, discover how much time employees spend on various Web sites, etc. (Hartman 2001). Marx (1999) suggests that ICTs have enabled contemporary companies to develop an organizational behavior similar to that of the **ideal prison** proposed by the philosopher Jeremy Bentham in 1791: a building of polygonal structure with a central tower that offers a full view of rows of glass walled cells, where the mirrors around the tower made it possible for the guards to look into each cell while staying invisible to prisoners.

The development and use of electronic tools in contemporary firms has supported a change in the principal–agent relationship. It seems evident that ICTs have increased the principal's control over the activities of the agent. In this new situation the flow of information favors the principal, who has gained multiple ways to control the agent.[7]

On the other hand, in every work relationship there is a reasonable limit to the control exercised by the principal beyond whom the agent can invoke a natural respect for his/her physical privacy. Many workers in fact resent such monitoring (Marx 1992), feeling violated and powerless (Marx and Sherizen 1986).

A balance between employers' interest in managing the workplace and employees' privacy interests should be reached in every business organization (Hartman 2001). Every person under the veil of ignorance would agree on the need to set a limit on the control of his/her work activities exercised by the principal. Thus, our first question is: **Under the veil of ignorance, what could be the ethical limit related to the use of ICTs in order to control employees' activities during working hours?**

4.2 Privacy in the External Relationships

More rapidly available and more accurate information does not affect only the principal–agent relationship within firms but also has raised new questions related to the information privacy[8] of all actors external to the firm's organization and customers in particular.[9] Indeed, contemporary firms have the opportunity to collect and analyze

---

[7]A reduction of asymmetric information in the principal-agent relationship does not *per se* offer particular new ethical questions. While economic theory has resolved the principal–agent relationship through adequate incentive mechanisms, a reduction of the asymmetry *per se* should reduce the possibility of morally hazardous behaviors.

[8]Information privacy is the right to determine how, when, and to what extent private data about us is released to others (Simms 1994).

[9] The problem of information privacy has a limited impact at the internal level and in particular in the employee-employer relationship. The introduction of ICTs has in fact only improved the effectiveness of the acquisition and storage of information that was already available in the past. A different scenario is instead offered by the use of ICT in external relationships due to the multiple different possibilities to acquire new and more detailed items of information.

customers' personal data, with an accuracy and precision that necessitate serious reflection on the limits of these practices. For example, everyone who connects to a company Web site can easily be identified through the IP number of the PC or through Internet cookies; the private and personal information that we submit to be admitted to fidelity firms' programs can be processed for different uses from those officially declared, etc. The lack of a unique international regulation enhances this problem, because customers can not know the national laws of Web site they would visit. Moreover, as Smith and Hasnas (1999) have demonstrated, in addition to the various points of view of institutional and governmental actors, different business ethics theories can support contrasting solutions regarding the use of personal data. Under the veil of ignorance everyone would agree on the need to define a limit regarding the use of his/her personal information by a company or other kinds of institutions. Thus, our second question is: **Under the veil of ignorance, what could be the ethical limit related to the use of ICTs in order to collect and exploit customers' personal (private) data?**

5 THE SECOND DIMENSION: SAFETY AND SECURITY OF INDIVIDUALS

The introduction and diffusion of ICTs have raised ethical questions related to safety and security of individuals both inside and outside the firm. At the internal level, firms' working styles have been transformed by the advent of personal computers and electronic networks with a consequent request of attention to the respect for working conditions. At the external level, firms have started to replace the traditional market, understood as a physical place to interact economically, with virtual markets, in which all kinds of relationships are mediated through ICT. The loss of physical, personal contact has consequently enhanced the ethical perspectives and problems related to the security of individuals engaged in ICT-enabled business activities.

5.1 Security of Individuals Within the Firm: Acceptable Work Conditions

Employees' security has represented an ethical concern of business organizations since their constitution. Although the image of exhausted factory workers is far from our perception of contemporary firms, there is still a need to confirm if work environments respect human dignity. The shift, in many sectors of human engagement from physical to mental processes does not *a priori* guarantee better conditions for the workforce. The automation of administrative procedures can lead to stressful conditions for office employees that have to face a continuous, interminable flow of activities (Perrolle 1998, p. 104). The **old** requirement for acceptable work conditions reappears in the important themes of contemporary management practice and theory and, in particular, as pointed by Brown and Duguid (2000), in the context of the wide reengineering processes caused by the introduction of new virtual technologies inside business organizations. Under the veil of ignorance, everyone would in fact agree on the need to define rules and guidelines regarding the requirements necessary to guarantee decent work environments. Who would risk being allocated to an uncomfortable, unpleasant work position? Thus, our third question is: **Under the veil of ignorance, what could be the requirements related to the use of ICTs that guarantee decent working environments for every employee?**

5.2 Security of Individuals Outside the Boundaries of the Firm

The open, interconnected, and unregulated global nature of the Internet has heightened concerns about the security of economic activities enabled by ICT (Fung and Lee 1999). The market, in the sense of a physical place to meet people and to develop economic exchanges, has been in fact replaced in many situations by virtual e-commerce. This change has led to the loss of many control mechanisms that had matured in traditional markets. The extent of new virtual markets, the lack of personal contact, and the lack of a single international legal system have enhanced the importance of security in Internet-based economic transactions.

Firms have replaced traditional markets in two ways. The first is by creating a virtual shop in which a customer can find and buy goods electronically in a transaction that involves only the customer and the company. The second is the creation of a "marketplace" in which buyers and sellers can virtually meet their counterparts and carry out economic transactions. In the first situation, the current technology provides all the conditions necessary to guarantee customers' security. An honest company in fact has all the technological tools to provide detailed information on the goods sold and the conditions of the purchase. The real security of a virtual transaction itself can be guaranteed with adequate encryption, digital signatures, and third party authentication; such methods have been addressed in detail in the trade and computer science literature ((Bhimani 1996; Varadharajan et al. 1997) and adequately implemented in the real market through the collaboration of financial and ICT leaders (Shapiro and Varian 2000).

At the same time, the diffusion of marketplaces suggests ethical questions related to the rules of exchange governing transactions between external actors. As a single firm has the opportunity to create a virtual place in which it can conduct economic activities, all the rules in this area are created and controlled by the firm itself. In other words, the transactions of different actors extraneous to the company are regulated through the marketplace by a firm that imposes certain rules rather than others. In this context the firm acts as a mediator but has a limited set of data on the actors of the transaction and the object of the transaction. The marketplace is consequently a virtual area in which there is a situation of asymmetric information between the actors involved in the transaction and in which the rules are written by a company. The fourth question that we propose is, therefore: **Under the veil of ignorance, what are the rules governing transactions that should be imposed by firms in order to guarantee customers' security in the e-marketplace?**

6 A NEW DIMENSION: CORPORATE TRANSPARENCY

The importance of transparency and its impact on market efficiency has been widely analyzed in the micro-finance and economics fields (e.g., Bias 1993; Fleming and Remolona 1999; Ho and Hans 1983) but it has not been closely examined at the firm level. In the following passages we will distinguish between external and internal transparency. The former is defined as the degree of completeness of information, regarding its own business activities, provided by each company to the market. The latter is defined as the degree of virtual connectivity (i.e., availability to access through ICT tools) of the workforce to the external environment.

6.1 External Transparency as the New Ethical Imperative

The advent and spread of Internet technology has reduced the distance between firms and a part of developed society. Indeed, firms have the option to disseminate a well controlled set of information through their Web sites. The consequent ethical question is related to the degree of transparency companies should adopt in their new virtual relationships with society. In an ideal society, under the veil of ignorance, everyone would be able to obtain detailed information about the firm's activities, under the guarantee of not using it for commercial or personal benefit, anyone should be able to obtain all information regarding the firm's activities. In real life we can find an already existing similar condition: an increasing number of restaurants have created transparent kitchens that can be checked by customers. While it is not easy to copy the art of chefs through a brief view, these restaurants have decided to increase their customers' knowledge of their internal operations. Moreover, protests organized by consumer associations against multinational companies whose activities are deemed unethical clearly express the real and growing interest in the way business activities are conducted.

Companies around the world have already opened up their information systems to important suppliers and customers to improve their operational effectiveness, reducing costs and lead times. On the other hand, it could be argued that extensive and detailed information on internal activities could be used by competitors to threaten a firm's market position.

While a firm has the right to preserve its business position, it is possible to argue that the degree of transparency of firms' activities could be increased to comply with the request of more detailed information expressed, around the world, by customers . Thus our fifth ethical question will be: **Under the veil of ignorance, what could be the expected level of a firm's transparency through ICT in its relationships with the external environment?**

6.2 Internal Transparency: A Social Inclusion Perspective

Today, employees' ability to access the external environment during working hours is greater than it was two decades ago: the Internet provides a wide range of opportunities such as the browsing of Web sites, e-mail, and chat programs (e.g., Windows Messenger). As pointed out in the literature (e.g., Capurro 2000), while in the past the exchange of important information was based on vertical dimensions (top–down relationships along the social or organization structure), the introduction of ICT has supported multidirectional (i.e., both horizontal and vertical) interactive communications. In the firm context, this means that each employee can obtain all kinds of information from a wider range of actors and sources both inside and outside the company's boundaries.

On the other hand, the frequent attempts by employees around the world to use firms' PCs for personal use or for illicit purposes, such as downloading pornography, have resulted in the spread of various forms of limitations on employees' use of ICT tools in their contact with the external environment. While the promise of Internet technology was the creation of a single, global, open network, reducing the multiple externalities of information transactions, a common practice of companies, is in direct opposition to this trend because it limits employees' access and external connections. Indeed, Castells (1996) has proposed a classification of employees based on their level of interconnection with other individuals through ICT tools, in particular the networkers, who are able to establish relationships without constraint, the networked, those individuals that are connected to the Net but are constrained in their communications, and finally the switched-off, who are not linked to the Net.

Assuming that it is reasonable to prevent the use of a company's information systems for personal purposes unrelated to the firm's business activities during working hours, there is neither a managerial nor an ethical basis for limiting employees' interactions with the external environment. The Internet connections available inside the firm can be, in many cases, the sole opportunity for employees to have access to the Web. Contemporary firms consequently have the **opportunity to reduce the digital divide exclusion** allowing their workforce to use the Internet connection in specific and controlled circumstances. For example, the Banca d'Italia, the Italian central bank, allows employees to use, during lunch break and outside working hours, special PC locations for Web navigation and personal e-mail (Vaccaro and Madsen 2006). Moreover, other solutions can be found in relation to specific organizational and business circumstances. Indeed, with adequate and well-defined controls, there are neither ethical nor technological reasons to forbid employees to use firms' Internet connections for personal reasons outside working hours.

Under the veil of ignorance, everyone would agree on the need to develop norms and guidelines governing the transparency of companies' information systems for employees in their relationship with the external environment in order to guarantee the social inclusion of workforces.

Thus, our last question is: **Under the veil of ignorance, what could be the ethical limit to the reduction of ICT transparency (possibility of information exchange) between workers and the external environment in order to allow the social inclusion of the workforce?**

7   DISCUSSION AND CONCLUSION

The path we have followed has revealed the presence of a wide variety of ethical needs and demands related to the use of ICTs in contemporary business organizations.

Some of these themes are well-known, old problems, such as those related to acceptable working conditions, which have been transposed to the technological world. Others, such as privacy concerns, are old ethical issues that have been enhanced in degree and complexity by the potential of ICTs. Finally, there are other ethical issues, like transparency, that are related both to the increased ethical attention of contemporary society to business activities and to the social modification caused by the diffusion of ICTs. In this new scenario, the transparency dimension is very important because it refers both to the customer's increasing need to be more conscious of firms' business practices and to the digital social inclusion of employees. In particular, this last concern represents a *condicio sine qua non*, a preliminary necessary step, that business organizations should adequately understand and resolve in the development of their strategy and practices.

It is undeniable that the different ethical dimensions analyzed above can be shown to be, in various organizational circumstances and in relation to different individual ethical beliefs, in a trade-off situation. Security and privacy, for example, can be conflicting requirements in the management of external relationships. How in fact is it possible to guarantee security and privacy at the same time in a marketplace? What is the ethical limit that distinguishes right from wrong in the acquisition and use of personal data in order to protect the security of individuals?

Analogously, a manager may see conflicts between the requirements for transparency and for security. What is the level of transparency beyond which there is a real risk of endangering employees' safety? Or, what is the level of transparency beyond which the firm's existence itself can be endangered by competitors accidentally becoming able to spy and to copy? Conversely, it is possible to find organizational and environmental conditions in which some problems, which belong to two of the different dimensions introduced, are compatible or synergic. Moreover, the introduction of different religious, cultural, and ethical points of view can only complicate our discourse, leading to the analysis of highly specific and particular problems from which it is difficult or impossible to extrapolate useful insights for scholars and managers.

A final concern is related to the vision of ethical problems not only as **static** but also as **dynamic social processes**. From the point of view of the firm, ethical beliefs are in fact highly dynamic processes related to internal and environmental variables. First, as MacIntyre (1998) has pointed out, ethical demands and needs are generally modified in the same community along the temporal dimension. While the temporal horizon proposed by MacIntyre is considerably longer than the average firm's existence, globalization processes and telecommunications have accelerated social change and consequently contemporary firms have to take account of such individual and collective modifications. Second, entry into new markets, in both geographical and sectoral or technological terms, can bring firms to face with new ethical issues. Third, modification of a market segment in the same geographical area and employees' intergenerational shifts can modify stakeholders' ethical requirements.

Thus, there appears to be no way to approach and resolve these problems, due to the complexity, interdependence, and dynamism of the individual, collective, and social variables involved in such processes.

We argue that there is not in fact a single, well-defined recipe for approaching such problems but also that it is possible to define an organizational strategy to face them. The way we propose is based both on clear transparency concerning firms' policies on the use of ICTs and the development of a **participatory system** in which all actors involved in firms' activities are not only well informed but also able to **interact with the firm itself** in relation to ICT ethical problems. In other words, we propose that problems related to the use of ICT within business corporations can be resolved through appropriate exploitation of the opportunities offered by the electronic and virtual technologies themselves. For example, the creation of an internal committee could enable communication between top management and the whole workforce; the creation of a special page on the firm's Web site could enable the development of open dialogue with customers, suppliers, and society in general.

In a deliberately provocative way, we are proposing to use the potentialities of ICT to develop a **dynamic approach** to the multiple, varied, and contrasting ethical expectations of society.

This strategy can present various problems due to the lack of guidelines on how each ethical requirement should be weighted in the process of developing the company's ethical position. For example, should the employees' or the customers' expectations be considered more important in the definition of the firm's ICT policies? Or, in the event of opposing points of view between employees and employers, who should be considered the more important? The answers to such questions are based on the unique features that characterize each firm, on its history, strategic objectives, environmental and cultural variables, and are beyond the scope of this work.

On the other hand, only the combination of an **open participatory system** and of **clear transparent policies** can guarantee that firms take into account not only the different ethical expectations of individuals and groups but also the continuous modifications within society and along the temporal dimension. Thus, instead of approaching ethical problems through the development of a rigid set of norms, contemporary firms have the possibility to explore the various dynamic ethical trajectories of their stakeholders and to modify their position accordingly.

The first step of this long and difficult process requires the real digital inclusion of all stakeholders. In relation to this concern, contemporary business organizations can and should provide a real contribution to the society, looking first at their internal organizations and guaranteeing to all employees the possibility to exploit the great opportunities offered by new virtual technologies, with the hope that ICT will became a tool of integration and not another cause of social inequality.

Acknowledgments

The author is grateful to João César das Neves for the generous support he provided during the development of the paper.

References

Abbà, A. *Quale Impostazione per La Filosofia Morale?*, Rome: LAS, 1996.
Argandoña, A. "The New Economy: Ethical Issues," *Journal of Business Ethics* (44), 2003, pp. 3-22.
Barlow, J. P. " Electronic Frontier: Private Life in Cyberspace," *Communications of the ACM* (34:8), 1991, pp. 23-25.
Bettetini, G. , and Fumagalli, A. *Quel Che Resta Dei Media*, Rome: Franco Angeli, 2002.

Bias, B. "Price Formation and Equilibrium Liquidity in Fragmented and Centralized Markets," *Journal of Finance* (48:1), 1993, pp. 157-185.

Bhimani, A. "Securing the Commercial Internet," *Communications of the ACM* (39:6), 1996, pp. 29-35.

Brown, J. S., and Duguid, P. *The Social Life of Information*, Boston: Harvard Business School Press, 2000.

Capurro, R. "Hermeneutics and the Phenomenon of Information," in C. Mitcham (ed.), *Metaphysics, Epistemology, and Technology. Research in Philosophy and Technology* (Volume 19), Amsterdam: Elsevier, 2000, pp. 79-85.

Cooley, T. *A Treatise on the Law of Torts* (2nd ed.), Chicago: Callaghan, 1888.

Castells, M. *The Rise of the Network Society*, Oxford, England: Blackwell Publishers, 1986.

Crane, A. , and Matten, D. *Business Ethics*, Oxford, England: Oxford University Press, 2004.

Cranford, M. "Drug Testing and the Right to Privacy: Arguing the Ethics of Workplace Drug Testing," *Journal of Business Ethics* (17:16), 1998, pp. 1805-1815.

Dobbs, R. R. "Application of a Justice as Fairness Perspective to Laws Banning Same Sex Marriage," *Californian Journal of Health Promotion* (2), 2004, pp. 15-23.

Fleming, M., and Remolona, E. "Price Formation and Liquidity in the U.S. Treasury Market: The Response of Public Information," *Journal of Finance* (54:5), 1999, pp. 1901-1915.

Floridi, L.., and Sanders, J. W. "Mapping the Foundationalist Debate in Computer Ethics," *Ethics in Information Technology* (4), 2002, pp. 1-9.

Fung, R. K., and Lee, M. K. "EC-Trust (Trust in Electronic Commerce): Exploring the Antencedent Factors," in W. D. Haseman and D. L. Nazareth (edsl), *Proceedings of the Fifth Americas Conference of Information Systems*, Milwaukee, WI, August 13-15, 1999, pp. 517-519.

Hartman, L. Technology and Ethics: Privacy in the Workplace," *Business and Society Review* (106:1), 2001, pp. 1-27.

Ho, T., and Hans, S. "The Dynamics of Dealer Markets under Competition," *Journal of Finance* (38:4), 1983, pp. 1053-1074.

Introna, L. D. "The (Im)possibility of Ethics in the Information Age," *Information and Organization* (12:2), 2002, pp. 71-84.

Introna, L. D. "Privacy and the Computer: Why We Need Privacy in the Information Society," paper presented at ETHICOMP96, Pontificial University of Salamanca, Madrid, Spain, November 6-8, 1996.

Introna, L. D. "Workplace Surveillance, Privacy, and Distributive Justice," in R. A, Spinello and H. T. Tavani (eds.), *Readings in Cyberethics*, Sudbury, MA: Joines and Bartlett Publishers, 2001, pp. 418-429.

Johnson D. G. *Computer Ethics* (3rd ed.), Upper Saddle River, NJ: Prentice Hall, 2001.

Lyon, D. The Electronic Eye, London: Polity Press, 1994.

Macintyre, A. *A Short History of Ethics*, Notre Dame, IN: University of Notre Dame Press, 1998.

Marx, G. T. "Let's Eavesdrop on Managers," *Computerworld* (26:16), 1992, p. 29.

Marx, G. T. "Measuring Everything that Moves: The New Surveillance at Work," in I. Simpson and R. Simpson (eds.), *The Workplace and Deviance*, Greenwich, CT: JAI, 1999.

Marx, G. T. , and Sherizen, S. "Monitoring on the Job: How to Protect Privacy as Well as Property," *Technology Review* (89), November-December 1986, pp. 63-72.

Mason, R. O. "Four Ethical Issues of the Information Age," *MIS Quarterly* (10:1), 1986, pp. 5-12.

Moor, J. H. "What Is Computer Ethics?," *Metaphilosophy* (16:4), 1985, pp. 266-275.

Moller Okin, S. *Justice, Gender and the Family*, New York: Basic Books Inc., 1989.

Nash, L. "Ethics Without Sermon," in *Harvard Business Review on Corporate Ethics*, Boston: Harvard Business School Press, 2003.

Ottensmeyer, E. J. , and Heroux, M. A. "Ethics, Public Policy and Managing Advanced Technologies: The Case of Electronic Surveillance," *Journal of Business Ethics* (10), 1991, pp. 519-526.

Perrolle, J. *Computers and Social Change: Information, Property, and Power* (Web Edition), Belmont, CA: Wadsworth Publishing Company, 1998.

Rawls, J. *A Theory of Justice*, Boston: Belknap Press, 1971.

Sarathy, R., and Robertson, C. J. "Strategic and Ethical Considerations in Managing Digital Privacy," *Journal of Business Ethics* (46:1), 2003, pp. 111-126.

Shapiro C. , and Varian, H. R. *Information Rules: A Strategic Guide to the Network Economy*, Boston: Harvard Business School Press, 2000.

Shaw, I. F. "Ethics in Qualitative Research and Evaluation," *Journal of Social Work* (3:1), 2003, pp. 9-29.

Simms, M. "Defining Privacy in Employee Health Screening Cases: Ethical Ramifications Concerning the Employee/Employer Relationship," *Journal of Business Ethics* (13:1), 1994, pp. 315-325.

Smith, H. J., and Hasnas, J. "Ethics and Information Systems: the Corporate Domain," *MIS Quarterly* (23:1), 1999, pp. 109-127.

Spinello, R. *Case Studies in Information Technology Ethics* (2nd ed.), Upper Saddle River, NJ: Prentice-Hall, 2004.

Tavani, H. T. *Ethics and Technology, Ethical Issues in an Age of Information and Communication Technology*, New York: John Wiley & Sons, Inc., 2004.

Vaccaro, A., and Madsen, P. "Firm Information Transparency: Ethical Questions in the Information Age," Working Paper, Carnegie Mellon University, 2006.

Varadharajan, V., Pieprzyk, J., and Mu, Y. "Information Security and Privacy," in *Proceedings of the Second Australian Conference*, Sydney, Australia, July 7-9, 1997.

Warren, S., and Brandeis, L. "The Right to Privacy," *Harvard Law Review* (4:5), 1890, pp. 193-196.

Winter, S. J. , Stylianou A. C., and Giacalone R. A. "Individual Differences in the Acceptability of Unethical Information Technology Practices: The Case of Machiavellianism and Ethical Ideology," *Journal of Business Ethics* (54:3), 2004, pp. 275-296.

About the Author

Antonino Vaccaro is currently a visiting research scholar at Carnegie Mellon University and an assistant researcher at the IN+ Center for Innovation, Technology, and Policy Research of Lisbon. He is also collaborating with the Catholic University of Lisbon for the creation of the first Portuguese center of business ethics and social responsibility. Antonino can be reached at vaccaro@andrew.cmu.edu.

Part 6

Technology and its Consequences

18 DEVELOPING OPEN SOURCE SOFTWARE: A Community-Based Analysis of Research

Joseph Feller
Patrick Finnegan
David Kelly
Maurice MacNamara
*University College
Cork, Ireland*

Abstract   *Open source software (OSS) creates the potential for the inclusion of large
and diverse communities in every aspect of the software development and
consumption life cycle. However, despite 6 years of effort by an ever growing
research community, we still don't know exactly what we do and don't know
about OSS, nor do we have a clear idea about the basis for our knowledge.
This paper presents an analysis of 155 research artefacts in the area of open
source software. The purpose of the study is to identify the kinds of open
source project communities that have been researched, the kinds of research
questions that have been asked, and the methodologies used by researchers.
Emerging from the study is a clearer understanding of what we do and don't
know about open source software, and recommendations for future research
efforts*

1   INTRODUCTION

The licensing and distribution terms of OSS create the potential for the inclusion
of large and diverse communities in every aspect of the software development and
consumption life cycle. This social inclusion takes many forms. For example,

*   A third-party is potentially able to deliver services in level-field competition with
    the creator of the software, leveraging the open nature of the source code; this
    lowers barriers to entry for smaller service providers and provides autonomy to

Please use the following format when citing this chapter:

Feller, J., Finnegan, P., Kelly, D., and MacNamara, M., 2006, in IFIP International
Federation for Information Processing, Volume 208, Social Inclusion: Societal and
Organizational Implications for Information Systems, eds. Trauth, E., Howcroft, D.,
Butler, T., Fitzgerald, B., DeGross, J., (Boston: Springer), pp. 261-278.

software users who are no longer locked-in to a single vendor (Woods and Guliani 2005).

• User and developer communities can potentially share or assume the burden of innovation, a process traditionally located privately within the firm (Von Hippel 2005).

• Low acquisition costs, user-empowering freedoms, and the removal of information asymmetry potentially serve as powerful tools in combating the digital divide and in creating autonomy and local knowledge resources in the developing world (see, for example, Feller et al. 2003; James 2003; Steinmueller 2001; Yee 1999).

• OSS is seen as a mechanism by which public bodies can improve the transparency of, and provide wider access to, government services (see, for example, the archive of policy documents and case studies in the Center of Open Source and Government at http://www.egovos.org/).

Given these potential implications, it is unsurprising that, since the coining of the term in 1998, OSS has enjoyed a wide-spread surge in interest among users, developers, for-profit and nonprofit organizations, governments, and—last but certainly not least—researchers. However, with 6 years of research behind us, we still don't know exactly what we do and don't know about the phenomenon, nor do we have a clear idea about the basis for our knowledge. This paper presents an analysis of 155 research artefacts, mostly peer-reviewed, published between 1998 and 2004. The analysis focuses on three questions.

1. What types of OSS projects have been the subject of research?
2. What areas or topics have been the subject of research?
3. What methodologies have been used?

The rationale behind asking these questions is fundamental. OSS is surrounded by hype and hope—that it will revolutionize software development, the software industry, and, potentially, the information society. To separate hype from reality, and to help realize the potential benefits of OSS, the academic community needs to take stock of the research to date and clearly articulate the work that remains to be done.

2 THEORETICAL FOUNDATION AND RESEARCH METHOD

It has been argued that the structured identification of required future research directions is important, particularly in an emerging research area (Culnan 1987). The examination of previous work enables both the determination of progress made (Farhoomand 1987), and also the identification of work required in the future to further develop a field of study (Alavi and Carlson 1992). Such an approach has been used at both a disciplinary level—for example, within Information Systems (Alavi and Carlson 1992; Chen and Hirschheim 2004; Claver et al. 2000; Farhoomand and Drury 1999; Orlikowski and Baroudi 1991), Software Engineering (Glass et al. 2002), and Computer Science (Ramesh et al. 2004)—and at a thematic or subfield level (e.g., Romano and Fjermestad 2002). Such works have surveyed the existing literature to investigate the paradigmatic approaches to research (e.g., Chen and Hirschheim 2004; Orlikowski and Baroudi 1991), the research methods or strategies used (e.g., Chen and Hirschheim 2004; Claver et al. 2000; Farhoomand 1987; Orlikowski and Baroudi 1991), and topics investigated (e.g., Farhoomand 1987; Glass et al. 2002; Ramesh et al. 2004; Romano and Fjermestad 2002).

Previous efforts at assessing the state of knowledge within an field have limited their sample to a specific number of outlets in order to investigate the methods being used (e.g., Chen and Hirschheim 2004; Farhoomand and Drury 1999) or the paradigmatic focus into which the research falls (e.g., Chen and Hirschheim 2004; Orlikowski and Baroudi 1991). In order to take into account the multidisciplinary nature of research in the area of OSS, the literature search was not confined to specific publications within any one discipline. Rather, a strategy of exploring a range of outlets was employed, following similar efforts by Romano and Fjermestad (2002).

Candidate papers were discovered through keyword searches of citation indices (e.g., EBSCO, Science-Direct, IEEE, ACM Portal), by using existing bibliographies of OSS research, and through recursion using the references cited within papers. In addition to a range of journals from various disciplines (see Table 1), a variety of international conferences and three books (DiBona et al. 1999; Koch 2004; Raymond 1999) were also reviewed. In total, 155 research artefacts published since 1998 were reviewed. Of these, 99 were journal papers, 37 were conference papers, and the remaining 21 consisted of various books, reviews and commentaries.

A number of limitations are evident in the approach used for identifying artefacts. In employing a strategy of exploring as many outlets as possible, the research sources used were not limited to ranked journals, as was the case in similar research evaluation efforts (e.g., Farhoomand and Drury 1999). Additionally, research on OSS in specific application spaces exists in specialized publications that were not included, thus the identification of all relevant literature can not be guaranteed. Finally, by not including publications prior to 1998, there is an implication that there was no literature in the area of OSS produced prior to that date. Such a view would be inaccurate, however, as the majority of publications prior to this year were both descriptive and published in non-peer-reviewed outlets, thus they were not included in the study.

Classification systems provide a means to communicate the contents of a field of study, and thereby enable the generalization and communication of findings (Vessey et al. 2002, 2005). For this study, each artefact was first analyzed to determine the type(s) of development community the research artefact investigated. Following the characterization by primary OSS community, each artefact was further categorized by (1) research focus and (2) research method. Within research focus, artefacts were categorized as software engineering issues, economic and business model issues, socio-cultural and organizational issues, and software application space. Table 2 illustrates some sample topics associated with each focus area. Table 3 illustrates the methodological labels.

Table 1. List of Journals Covered

ACM Transactions on Software Engineering and Methodology	IEEE Review
Briefings in Bioinformatics	IEEE Software
Business Horizons	IEEE Transactions on Consumer Electronics
Communications of the ACM	IEEE Transactions on Software Engineering
Computer	Information Systems Journal
CPA Journal	International Review of Industrial Property and Copyright Law
Electronic Markets	Journal of Law, Economics and Organization
European Journal of Information Systems	Organization Science
First Monday	Research Policy
IEE Proceedings–Software	Information, Technology, and People
IEE Proceedings–Software Engineering	Sloan Management Review
IEE Proceedings–Software Engineering,	The Information Society
IEEE Computer	Transactions in GIS

Table 2. Research Focus Areas with Sample Topics

Focus Area	Sample Topics
Software Engineering Issues	• Version Control • Software Architecture • Development Methodology
Economic and Business Model Issues	• Revenue Models • Resource Allocation • Market Drivers
Socio-Cultural and Organizational Issues	• Conflict Resolution • Motivation • Legal Issues
Software Application Spaces	• Specific Vertical Sector (Automotive, Health, etc.) • Specific Horizontal Sector (Financials, Human Resources, etc.) • Software Acquisition and Management

Table 3. Research Methdology Labels with Definitions

Label	Definition
Anecdotal/Descriptive	Little or no formal data-gathering methodology.
Secondary	(Re-)Analysis of previous research.
Case Study	Formal, high-depth data gathering focused on a single research site.
Cross-Case	Formal, medium-depth data gathering focused on 2-3 research sites with comparative analysis.
Field Study	Formal, low-depth data gathering across a wide number of research sites with comparative analysis.
Survey	High-volume structured questionnaire.
Experiment	Laboratory or field-experiment.

Table 4. Analysis of Artefacts per Publication Outlet

Year	Journals	Conferences
1998	3	0
1999	12	0
2000	6	7
2001	17	5
2002	17	8
2003	20	12
2004	24	5
Total	99	37

3   FINDINGS

OSS research has been increasing steadily in recent years. Analysis of the outlets used in the publication of such research (see Table 4) shows that journals (particularly special issues) have been the predominant means for the communication of findings.

3.1 Communities of OSS Development

Our analysis began by classifying the unit (community) within which the software was developed. The objective of this exercise was to provide a means of describing the groups involved as a set of organizational forms (see Doty and Glick 1994). In doing so, four community types were identified: *ad hoc* communities, standardized communities, organized communities, and commercial organizations. The key differentiating characteristics of these community types are summarized in Table 5.

Table 5. Characteristics of OSS Community Types

	Ad Hoc Communities	**Standardized Communities**	**Organized Communities**	**Commercial Organizations**
General Structure	Small, informal communities of practice collaborating "in the wild" on OSS projects of limited size (as measured by number of users and developers)	More mature (older, more stable) communities of practice with more formalized software development and management standards in place to address larger project sizes.	Very mature communities of practice which go beyond the creation of standardized practices to the formal (legal) establishment of an organizational entity.	Communities of practice embedded in formal (legal) profit-seeking firms.
Environment	Internet-based collaboration tools, generally hosted by a third-party (e.g., the SourceForge repository).	Self- or third-party hosted Internet-based collaboration tools. Generally used in conjunction with a self-hosted or sponsored identity-building environment (e.g., a group (rather than project) Web page).	Self-hosted Internet-based collaboration tools. Mature identity building environment. Possible physical collocation of some project members.	Self-hosted Internet-based collaboration tools and mature identity building environment. Physical collocation of some project members. Explicit integration with corporate development, communication and management structures.
Goals	Driven by individual goals, e.g., to meet personal computing requirements, to collaborate with others, to share output with the community, to gain personal reputation, to learn, etc.	Goals from *ad hoc* communities plus group-focused goals like quality assurance, project management, standardization, all towards the overall goal of building a public good.	Goals from standardized communities plus the need to provide legal protection for contributors and engage in organization-to-organization relationships with other organizations, firms, governments, etc. Desire to give project a "life of its own" independent of individual members.	Many of the goals from organized communities plus the desire to effectively utilize OSS dynamics, and to interact with wider communities, in order to generate share-holder value.

	Ad Hoc Communities	Standardized Communities	Organized Communities	Commercial Organizations
Methods	Individual-based methods with little formal documentation or standardization.	Standardization and documentation of key development methods and processes.	Standardization and documentation of key development methods and processes, formal project and organizational management.	Standardization and documentation of key development methods and processes, formal project and organizational management.
User Community	Users are generally other developers, early-adopters and power users.	Users are generally other developers, early-adopters and power users.	Users are both other developers, early-adopters and power users as well as main stream end users.	Users are both other developers, early-adopters and power users as well as main stream end users. Users are treated as customers.
Licensing	Generic licensing	Generic licensing, possibly project specific licensing.	Project specific licensing.	Corporate licensing.

3.1.1   General Structure

The use of general formal structure in the development of classifications based on organizational characteristics on the basis of formalization, specialization, and levels has been proposed by McKelvey (1978). Here, general structure refers to the organizational size, formality of structures, and legal standing held by each software production community. Gacek and Arief (2004) found that size alone is not a distinctive measure of an OSS project, with the code base and community varying between projects. It is with this in mind that the formalization of software development practices and management standards, and the establishment of a formal (legal) organizational entity are included as additional differentiating factors within the general structure dimension.

In the case of *ad hoc* communities, the size of project groups (as measured by the number of developers and users) is small with little formal structure. Illustrative of the size of such projects are the results of the Orbiten Free Software Survey, which found that 75 percent of projects had only one author participating (Ghosh and Prakash 2000). Capiluppi et al. (2003), following an analysis of the FreshMeat portal (http://freshmeat.net), reported that 57 percent of projects have one or two developers, and 80 percent have less than 11 subscribers (a proxy of users of the project's application).

The addition of formalized software development and management standards separates *ad hoc* OSS communities from standardized communities within the dimension of general structure. As projects mature, increased numbers of users, a growing code base, and a need to facilitate larger scale, distributed development requires the implementation of project management tools and techniques.

The key differentiating factor between standardized communities and organized communities is the move beyond formal standardized practices, and to becoming a formal legal organizational entity. The establishment of such noncommercial organizations enables the formalization of the projects' administrative functions in a board of directors, while allowing its further development and advancement to remain with willing individual developers. Well known examples of projects within the organized community classification are Apache and Mozilla.

The final community classification identified is that of a commercial organization. The general structure of communities within this grouping is that of a community of practice, which is a formal (legal) profit-seeking firm. Projects falling within this classification can be categorized as those emerging from organizations with either "pure-play" open source business models, or with a hybrid (i.e., a mix of both proprietary and open source) business model. Examples of projects classified under the commercial organization heading are OSS projects emerging from Red Hat, Sun, IBM, and Sony.

3.1.2 Environment

The development environment refers to both where development occurs and the tools utilized to facilitate communication and collaboration in the development process. *Ad hoc* communities use primarily Internet-based collaboration tools, which are generally hosted by a third-party, for example the SourceForge (http://sourceforge.net) repository. Such projects are generally of a size that does not warrant the maintenance of an independent Web presence (Feller and Fitzgerald 2002). The use of such Internet-based collaboration tools enables geographically dispersed project members to communicate and share source code (Moon and Sproull 2000). Development within a standardized community generally takes place using either a self- or third-party hosted Internet-based collaboration environment. Often, in conjunction with this, a self-hosted or sponsored identity-building Web page is also maintained. While development within standardized communities is generally distributed, within an organized community there is also the possibility of physical collocation of project members (e.g., Lussier 2004). In addition, identity building is again supported by group (versus project) Web pages, for example, the Mozilla Organization (www.mozilla.org) and the Apache Software Foundation (www.apache.org). Within commercial organizations, development can also rely on higher levels of physical collocation of project members and involves explicit integration with corporate development, communication, and management structures. As with organized communities, commercial organizations are more likely to use self-hosted Internet-based collaboration tools in order to facilitate development with geographically dispersed members.

3.1.3 Goals

The motivation of the participants involved in OSS production has been the subject of a wide range of research (see, for example, Hars and Ou 2001; Hertel et al. 2003; von Hippel and von Krogh 2003). At the level of the *ad hoc* community, participants are driven primarily by individual goals. Such individual goals can be to meet personal computing requirements or fill a void in functionality (Nakakoji et al. 2002), or to learn new programming languages (Feller and Fitzgerald 2002; Ye et al. 2002). Other individual goals that have been identified are to share output with a community (Berquist and Ljunberg 2001; Feller and Fitzgerald 2002) or to enhance reputation with peers (Berquist and Ljunberg 2001; Gacek and Arief 2004). Within the standardized community, while the individual goals are still present, more group focused goals aimed at project development also emerge. These include quality assurance, project management, and standardization, all of which contribute to the good of the overall project or community. Within the organized community space, again the goals of the previous two communities are subsumed. There is also the objective of both providing a level of legal protection to contributors, and enabling the interaction between the community and other established legal entities, such as nonprofit organizations, companies, or governments. The establishment of a formal (legal) entity also allows the project to be given a life of its own, independent of individual contributors. The final community classification, commercial organizations, subsumes many of the goals of the previous community types. Such organizations also have the objective of leveraging the knowledge and competencies of the wider OSS development community in order to generate shareholder value (Brown and Booch 2002).

3.1.4 Methods

Development method used gives another dimension by which to classify communities. In the area of *ad hoc* communities, individual-based methods with little formal documentation or standardization are used. Given the low numbers of contributors and users of such projects, as discussed in the "General Structure" section above, the need for more formalized development methods and processes in such projects is relatively low. Higher levels of development method and process standardization and documentation can be found within projects classified as belonging to a standardized community. Such formalization is required to deal with growing project code and contributor community sizes and to enable wider distributed development. As with the standardized community, projects classified as belonging to an organized community rely on the standardization and documentation of methods and processes in order to facilitate larger scale distributed development. An example of such a formalized approach to development is evident within the PyPy project where agile development methods are combined with the frequent use of Sprints, involving the collocation of project members for a short time, to complement distributed development (During 2005). In addition to formalization, the establishment of a formal organizational structure also includes more structured approaches to project and organizational management (for example, Mockus et al. 2002). The level of formalization within commercial organizations reflects that identified in organized communities. However, hybrid development approaches consisting of aspects of traditional and Open Source development approaches (Mockus et al. 2000, 2002) may also be present as organizations attempt to take advantage of the strengths of OSS development methods (see, for example, Dinkelacker et al. 2002).

3.1.5 User Community

Research on OSS user profiles is lacking (Feller and Fitzgerald 2002). It has been argued that OSS diffusion has occurred primarily in areas where the end-user is technically sophisticated, many of whom are developers and wish to modify the source code themselves (Lerner and Tirole 2000; West and Dedrick 2001). Within the community classification, users of projects within the *ad hoc* and standardized community spaces are generally other developers, early-adopters, and "power-users" that possess the technical skills to use, adapt, and maintain such software. Within the organized community space, there is again an overlap between these types of users, and more mainstream end-users. An example of such a situation is the ongoing development of the Mozilla range of software products which are aimed at the personal end-user or desktop market segment. Within the commercial organization community, the user group is similar to that of the organized community. Users within this area are, however, treated as customers with the possible inclusion of value-added services such as technical support, training, documentation, or consultancy.

3.1.6 Licensing

The choice of license within OSS is used to impose a variety of restrictions on users (Lerner and Tirole 2005). Such licenses often specify the conditions under which the software may be used, modified, or distributed and the restrictions in place on copyright and the software's open source status.[1] The legal implications resulting from the use of different licensing structures can vary widely (Ruffin and Ebert 2004). This results in the choice of licence imposed impacting a range of stakeholders, including the community of programmers working on the project, the end users, other open source projects that will later compete with or complement the project, and commercial vendors or support providers (Lerner and Tirole 2005). Given both the range of licenses available and their differing uses (Lerner and Tirole 2005; Wu and Lin 2001), license alone does not provide a useful means to classify OSS community types. This is because the level of restriction placed on projects through their license can vary depending on the environment in which the software is to operate, the intended user audience, and the maturity of the project (Lerner and Tirole 2005). The type of licensing structure imposed does, however, provide an additional dimension upon which a broader classification can be based.

Within *ad hoc* communities generally, generic licensing will be used, perhaps because of the range of generic licensing available and the fact that project initiators within this space may not want to develop specific licensing. Examples of such generic licensing options are GNU's GPL and LGPL, as well as public domain licensing options. Within the standardized community space, licensing options can include either generic licences or licences developed specifically for the project. Organized community OSS projects are more likely to implement project-specific licences, with

---

[1]Adapted from the Open Source Initiative, Open Source Definition, Version 1.9 (http://www.opensource.org/docs/definition.php).

examples being the Apache Software License and the Mozilla Public Licenses. Commercial organization communities are more likely to use corporate licensing structures specific to their project, often with the objective of retaining a level of control over the software's development and subsequent use. Examples of such corporate licensing structures include the Apple Public Source License, the IBM Public License, the Zope Public license, as well as a range of non-OSI (Open Source Initiative) approved proprietary licensing structures.

3.2 Characterization of Research on OSS Communities

As shown in Figure 1, nearly two-thirds of the research artefacts analyzed drew data from the standardized and organized community types. It would appear that this is at least partially because the "headliner" OSS projects, such as Apache, Mozilla, Perl, and Linux fall into these categories and have each been quite extensively researched. Within the remaining one-third of artefacts, there was a 2:1 ratio of commercial organizations to *ad hoc* communities. Again, this is partially because of high profile commercial organizations like Sun and IBM, and also due to the fact that commercial organization focused research covered a wider range of topics than the *ad hoc* community focused research.

In looking at the OSS production communities which have been studied (Figure 2), it is interesting to note that there has been little change in the numbers of artefacts focusing on commercial organizations since 2001. It is instead the *ad hoc* and organized community classifications that have shown consistent growth in recent years. There are a number of possible explanations for such findings. The growing awareness of and interest in the "headliner" open source projects within both the research and business communities has led to increasing levels of research being conducted. The second possible explanation is that research in the area of OSS in general (i.e., not specifically relating to individual projects or community types) has been increasing. As the community classification scheme used assigns multiple classifications to such general research, it is possible that the trends presented have been influenced.

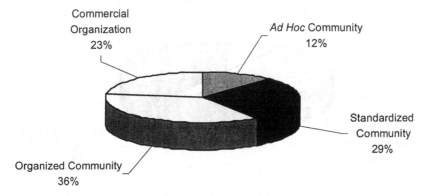

Figure 1. Overall Percentage of Artefacts Classified by Community

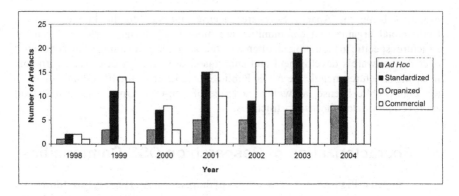

Figure 2. Yearly Analysis of Communities Researched

As shown in Figure 3, half of the research artefacts focused on socio-cultural and organizational issues, and nearly one-third focused on software engineering issues. This is a provocative finding given the strong software engineering/information systems nature of the conferences and journals in which the artefacts were published/presented. While more extensive analysis is needed, it would appear that the research community finds the collaborative "human" aspect of OSS to be more "research-worthy" than the technical aspects. Figure 3 also shows that a roughly equal number of artefacts focused on economic and business model issues and software application spaces (approximately 10 percent each). These artefacts within the area of software application spaces tend to be more recent, as illustrated in Table 6, and are arguably evidence of a shift in focus from OSS production to OSS consumption and exploitation.

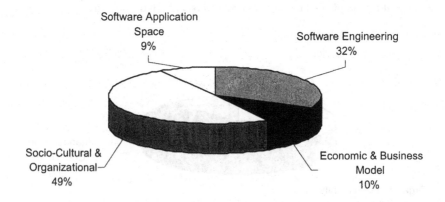

Figure 3. Overall Percentage of Artefacts Classified by Research Area

Table 6. Yearly Analysis of Research Areas

Year	Software Engineering	Economic & Business	Socio-Cultural & Organizational	Application Space	n
1998	0%	33%	67%	0%	3
1999	9%	26%	56%	9%	23
2000	43%	0%	50%	7%	14
2001	20%	20%	48%	12%	25
2002	41%	4%	42%	13%	24
2003	34%	13%	25%	28%	32
2004	33%	12%	40%	15%	33

Table 7 presents a more detailed view of the data, highlighting intersections between the OSS community types and the areas of research. Within the *ad hoc* communities space, there is no research focused on economic and business model issues and software application spaces; rather, the research is divided between socio-cultural and organizational issues and software engineering issues, in roughly the same proportions as the overall collection. Within the standardized and organized communities categories, we again see the same dominance of socio-cultural and organizational issues and software engineering issues, with a gradual increase in the other research areas. This is not particularly surprising, as much of the research on economic and business model issues and software application spaces requires projects and products to be of a much higher level of complexity than can be found in *ad hoc* communities. Finally, the commercial organizations space breaks free from the overall distribution pattern discussed previously, with all four research areas represented in a more-or-less even way. Unsurprisingly, research on economic and business model issues dominates this space.

Figure 4 provides an overview of the research methods used to study OSS development communities. Most significant here is the identification that the dominant form of research present within the area is informal work, with 42 percent of research to date conducted using anecdotal or descriptive methods. While there has been some fluctua-

Table 7. Count by Community/Focus Intersection

	Ad Hoc Community	Standardized Community	Organized Community	Commercial Organization	Subtotals
Software Engineering	13	28	31	14	86
Economic & Business Model	0	2	7	18	27
Socio-Cultural & Organizational	19	43	53	18	133
Software Application Space	0	4	7	12	23
Subtotals	32	77	98	62	**269**

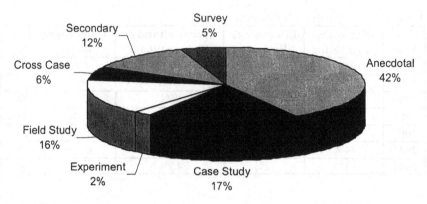

Figure 4. Overall Percentage of Artefacts Classified by Research Method

tion in the amount of informal work conducted between 1998 and 2004, it forms the basis for much of the OSS body of knowledge. Such findings are perhaps illustrative of the relative immaturity of the field.

Within the research on *ad hoc* communities, the sampling approach dominates; anecdotal data and broad, shallow field studies are the most common, with only a few deeper single case studies. As we move into the standardized communities, there is an increase in case study based research, particularly in the area of software engineering issues. To a certain extent, this can be explained in terms of accessibility: case study research requires a clearly bounded subject, and this is more readily accomplished with standardized communities than with *ad hoc* communities. Also, by definition, standardized communities display more concrete "researchable" software engineering practices. The trend toward increasing depth of research continues with the work focused on organized communities, where we see very strong single and cross-case analysis. There is also a marked increase in the gathering and analysis of quantitative data. Again, this may be due to accessibility: the stability of organized communities provides more opportunity for this type of research. Interestingly, and importantly from the point of view of the gap-analysis, within the commercial organizations space, we see a certain swing back toward anecdotal data collection and analysis.

The low number of in-depth, empirical research artefacts in the areas of both economic and business model issues and software application spaces stand out as noteworthy findings when the intersection of topic and methodology is reviewed (Table 8). When viewed within the context of increasing levels of commercial interest in OSS, the dearth of established research in these areas is particularly significant.

4   CONCLUSION

Based on our analysis, we argue that the OSS research literature requires greater discipline and rigor—deeper research, more quantitative data, and more robust cross case-analysis. There is also a need for greater understanding of the similarities and differences between community types (cross-community analysis) and for more inter-

Table 8. Research Topic/Research Methodology Intersection

	Software Engineering	Economic & Business Model	Socio-Cultural & Organizational	Software Application Space
Anecdotal	11	14	26	16
Case Study	14	2	11	4
Experiment	1	0	1	2
Field Study	9	4	7	0
Cross Case	4	1	5	0
Secondary	3	0	10	1
Survey	2	0	6	0

disciplinary research (cross-topic analysis). Building on these deeper descriptions, the research community could then address the more fundamental gap in our knowledge, namely the relative lack of robust models and theories.

It is evident that commercial organizations are underrepresented in the research, not just in terms of quantity, but more importantly in terms of depth of research. In addition, our understanding of economic and business models and software application spaces is also quite limited. These are critical gaps in the body of OSS knowledge in the context of social inclusion, as commercial and community OSS groups need to understand each other to realize the social inclusion potential of OSS highlighted in the introduction to this paper. Thus, we argue that future OSS research must address the convergence—and potential conflict—of the goals of the different communities that constitute the open source environment: individual and organizational users, software developers "in the wild," in nonprofit organizations, and in commercial firms, and policy makers seeking to make sense of the role of software in the wider information society.

Acknowledgments

This paper is based on research funded by the European Commission via IST Project 004337, CALIBRE (http://www.calibre.ie).

References

Alvai, M., and Carlson, P. "A Review of MIS Research and Disciplinary Development," *Journal of Management Information Systems* (3:4), 1992, pp. 45-62.

Bergquist, M., and Ljunberg, J. "The Power of Gifts: Organizing Social Relationships in Open Source Communities," *Information Systems Journal* (11:4), 2001, pp. 305-320.

Brown, W. A., and Booch, G. "Reusing Open-Source Software and Practices: The Impact of Open-Source on Commercial Vendors," in C. Gacek (ed.), *Software Reuse: Methods, Techniques, and Tools*, New York: Springer-Verlag, 2002, pp. 123-136.

Capiluppi, A., Lago, P., and Morisio, M. "Characteristics of Open Source Projects," in *Proceedings of the 7th European Conference on Software Maintenance and Reengineering*, Los Alamitos, CA: IEEE Computer Society Press, 2003, pp. 317-327.

Chen, W., and Hirschheim, R. "A Paradigmatic and Methodological Examination of Information Systems Research from 1991 to 2001m" *Information Systems Journal* (14:3), 2004, pp. 197-235.

Claver, E., Gonzales, R., and Llopis, J. "An Analysis of Research in Information Systems," *Information and Management* (37:4), 2000, pp. 181-195.

Culnan, M. J. "Mapping the Intellectual Structure of MIS, 1980-1985: A Co-Citation Analysis," *MIS Quarterly* (11:3), 1987, pp. 340-353.

DiBona, C., Ockman, S., and Stone, M. *Open Sources: Voices from the Open Source Revolution*, Cambridge, MA: O'Reilly and Associates, 1999.

Dinkelacker, J., Garg, P. K., Miller, R., and Nelson, D. "Progressive Open Source," in *Proceedings of the 24th International Conference on Software Engineering*, Orlando, FL, May 19-25, 2002, pp. 177-186.

Doty, D. H., and Glick, W. H. "Typologies as a Unique Form of Theory Building: Toward Improved Understanding and Modeling," *Academy of Management Review* (19:2), 1994, pp. 230-251.

During, B "Agile Methods in the PyPy Project," paper presented at the Second International Calibre Conference Limerick, Ireland, September 9, 2005.

Farhoomand, A .F. "Scientific Progress of Management Information Systems," *DataBase* (18:4), 1987, pp. 48-56.

Farhoomand, A. F., and Drury, D. H. "A Historiographical Examination of Information Systems," *Communications of the Association for Information Systems* (1:19), 1999.

Feller, J., and Fitzgerald, B. *Understanding Open Source Software Development*, Harlow, UK: Pearson Education Ltd., 2002.

Feller, J., Fitzgerald, B., Ljungberg, J., and Berquist, M. "Open Source and Free Software: Organizational and Societal Implications," in M. Korpela, R. Montealegre, and A. Poulymenakou (eds.), *Organizational Information Systems in the Context of Globalization*, Boston: Kluwer Academic Publishers, 2003, pp. 461-464.

Gacek, C., and Arief, B. "The Many Meanings of Open Source," *IEEE Software* (21:1), 2004, pp. 34-40.

Ghosh, R. A., and Prakash, V. V. "The Orbiten Free Software Survey," *First Monday* (5:7), 2000.

Glass, R. L., Vessey, I., and Ramesh, V. "Research in Software Engineering: An Analysis of the Literature," *Information and Software Technology* (44:8), 2002, pp. 491-506

Hars, A., and Ou, S. "Working for Free? Motivations of Participating in Open Source Projects," in *Proceedings of the the 34th Hawaii International Conference on System Sciences* (Volume 7), Los Alamitos, CA: IEEE Computer Society Press, 2001, p. 7014.

Hertel, G., Niedner, S., and Herrman, S. "Motivation of Software Developers in Open Source Projects: An Internet-Based Survey of Contributors to the Linux Kernel," *Research Policy* (32:7), 2003, pp. 1159-1177.

James, J. *Bridging the Global Digital Divide*, Cheltenham, UK: Edward Elgar Publishing Ltd.., 2003.

Koch, S. *Free/Open Source Software Development*, Hershey, PA: Idea Group Publishing, 2004.

Lerner, J., and Tirole, J. "The Simple Economics of Open Source," Working Paper 7600, National Bureau of Economic Research, Cambridge, MA, 2000.

Lerner, J., and Tirole, J. "The Scope of Open Source Licensing," *The Journal of Law, Economics, and Organization* (21:1), 2005, pp. 20-56.

Lussier, S. "New Tricks: How Open Source Changed the Way My Team Works," *IEEE Software* 21:1), 2004, pp. 68-72.

McKelvey, B. "Organizational Systematics: Taxonomic Lessons from Biology," *Management Science* (24:13), 1978, pp. 1428-1440.

Mockus, A., Fielding, R., and Herbsleb, J. D. "A Case Study of Open Source Software Development: The Apache Server," in *Proceedings of the 22nd International Conference on Software Engineering*, New York: ACM Press, 2000, pp. 263-272.

Mockus, A., Fielding, R., and Herbsleb. J. D. "Two Case Studies of Open Source Software Development: Apache and Mozilla," *ACM Transactions on Software Engineering and Methodology* (11:3), 2002, pp. 309-346.

Moon, J. Y., and Sproull, L. "Essence of Distributed Work: The Case of the Linux Kernal," *First Monday* (5:11), 2000.

Nakakoji, K., Yamamoto, Y,, Nishinaka, Y,, Kishida, K., and Ye, Y. "Evolution Patterns of Open-Source Software Systems and Communities," in *Proceedings of the International Workshop on Principles of Software Evolution*, New York: ACM Press, 2002, pp. 76-85.

Orlikowski, W., and Baroudi, J. J. "Studying Information Technology in Organizations: Research Approaches and Assumptions," *Information Systems Research* (2:1), 1991, pp. 1-28.

Ramesh, V., Glass, R. L., and Vessey, I. "Research in Computer Science: An Empirical Study," *Journal of Systems and Software* (70:1-2), 2004, pp. 165-176.

Raymond, S. E. *The Cathedral and the Bazaar*, Sebastapol, CA: O'Reilly and Associates, 1999.

Romano, N. C., and Fjermestad, J. "Electronic Commerce Customer Relationship Management: An Assessment of Research," *International Journal of Electronic Commerce* (6:2), 2002 pp. 61-113.

Ruffin, M., and Ebert, C. "Using Open Source Software in Product Development: A Primer," *IEEE Software* (21:1), 2004, pp. 82-87.

Steinmueller, W. E. "ICTs and the Possibilities for Leapfrogging by Developing Countries," *International Labor Review* (140:2), 2001, pp. 193-210.

Vessey, I., Ramesh, V., and Glass, R. L. "Research in Information Systems: An Empirical Study of Diversity in the Discipline and its Journals," *Journal of Management Information Systems* (19:2), 2002, pp. 129-174.

Vessey, I., Ramesh, V., and Glass, R. L. "A Unified Classification System for Research in the Computing Disciplines," *Information and Software Technology* (47:4), 2005, pp. 245-255.

Von Hippel, E. *Democratizing Innovation*, Cambridge, MA: MIT Press, 2005.

Von Hippel, E., and von Krogh, G. "Open Source Software and the 'Private-Collective' Innovation Model: Issues for Organization Science," *Organization Science* (14:2), 2003, pp. 209-223.

West, J., and Dedrick, J. "Proprietary vs. Open Standards in the Network Era: An Examination of the Linux Phenomenon," in *Proceedings of the 34th Hawaii International Conference on System Sciences* (Volume 5), Los Alamitos, CA: IEEE Computer Society Press, 2001, p. 5011.

Woods, D., and Guliani, G. *Open Source for the Enterprise*, Sebastapol, CA: O'Reilly Associates, 2005.

Wu, M., and Lin, Y. "Open Source Software Development: An Overview," *IEEE Computer* (34:6), 2001, pp. 33-38.

Ye, Y., Kishida, K., Nakakoji, K., and Yamamoto, Y. "Creating and Maintaining Sustainable Open Source Software Communities," in *Proceedings of International Symposium on Future*

Software Technology, Software Engineers Association, Wuhan, China, October 23-26, 2002 (CD-ROM).

Yee, D. "Development, Ethical Trading and Free Software," *First Monday* (4:12), 1999.

About the Authors

Joseph Feller is a senior lecturer in Business Information Systems, University College Cork, Ireland. His work on open source software includes coauthorship of two books (*Perspectives on Free and Open Source Software*, The MIT Press, 2005, and *Understanding Open Source Software Development*, Addison-Wesley, 2002) as well as international conference and journal papers. He coauthored "A Framework Analysis of the Open Source Software Development Paradigm," which was awarded Best Paper on Conference Theme at the 21st International Conference on Information Systems (ICIS 2000). Joseph was the lead organizer of the IEE/ACM workshop series on Open Source Software Engineering from 2001 through 2005, and has been a speaker and panelist on the topic at academic conferences, industry workshops, and European Commission briefings and roundtables. Joseph is a member of the EU FP6 Coordination action project CALIBRE (www.calibre.ie), co-leading the dissemination and awareness work package and conducting research on open source software business models. He can be reached at jfeller@afis.ucc.ie.

Patrick Finnegan holds a Ph.D. in Information Systems from the University of Warwick, and is currently a senior lecturer in Management Information Systems at University College Cork. His research interests include electronic business and IS strategy. He has published his research in a number of international journals and conferences including *The International Journal of Electronic Commerce, Information Technology & People, DataBase, Electronic Markets, The Information Systems Journal*, the European Conference on Information Systems, the International Conference on Information Systems, and the Americas Conference on Information Systems. Patrick can be reached at pfinnegan@afis.ucc.ie.

David Kelly is currently pursuing a Ph.D. in Information Systems at University College Cork. His research interests include innovation adoption, ambient intelligence, standards, and open-source software. David can be reached at d.kelly@ucc.ie.

Maurice MacNamara is currently pursuing a Ph.D. in Information Systems at University College Cork. His research focuses on the collaborative development of software systems for knowledge sharing. Maurice can be reached at mmacnamara@bismail.ucc.ie.

19 UNDERSTANDING MEANING AND BRIDGING DIVIDES: The Use of an African Metaphor for the South African Open Source Center

Elaine Byrne
University of Pretoria
Tshwane, South Africa

Bob Jolliffe
University of South Africa
Tshwane, South Africa

Nhlanhla Mabaso
Meraka Institute
Center for Scientific and Industrial Research
Tshwane, South Africa

Abstract   *This paper describes a conscious attempt to use metaphor to both promote and reinterpret ideas and values from the global free and open source software movement in the context of South Africa. A case study is given of an initiative launched by the South African Council for Industrial and Scientific Research to stimulate awareness and promote the use of free and open source software in South Africa and the region. The new Open Source Center made use of an African language metaphor to relate the concept of shared intellectual property in software to traditional communal land management. Whereas Western metaphors are commonly used in the field of organizational studies and Information Systems to facilitate meaning, the deliberate use of an African language metaphor to describe software systems is less common (even in Africa). This paper provides a background as to why such a metaphor was chosen as well as some reflection on its effectiveness.*

Keywords   Metaphors, open source software, free software, South Africa

Please use the following format when citing this chapter:

Byrne, E., Jolliffe, B., and Mabaso, N., 2006, in IFIP International Federation for Information Processing, Volume 208, Social Inclusion: Societal and Organizational Implications for Information Systems, eds. Trauth, E., Howcroft, D., Butler, T., Fitzgerald, B., DeGross, J., (Boston: Springer), pp. 279-293.

1   INTRODUCTION

Most of us who are connected in some or other way to the field of Information Systems share a roughly common understanding of what software is. Many of us will recall early courses in computer literacy where terms like hardware and software were introduced. At the risk of some inaccuracy, we might say that software refers to the programs which execute on programmable computers, or hardware. Though the terminology is far from intuitive, particularly to the large majority of people who would not be classified as "computer literate," we feel that, given access to a computer and its programs, the term software can be reasonably easily explained and understood.

There has been considerable interest in recent years in a "species" of software which is variously referred to as open source software, free software, free/open source software (FOSS) and even free/libre/open source software (FLOSS). The choice of terminology is somewhat contested, reflecting, as we shall see below, different political or philosophical strands within the communities of practitioners, users, and developers who create and sustain the software. Without wishing to pass judgment on any of these positions we will proceed in this discussion using the term FLOSS. It has been the experience of the authors that a significant majority of people (even those who understand what software is) find the concept of FLOSS counterintuitive, confusing, and, at least at first pass, unconvincing. This situation is not improved by the lack of clear consensus on terminology and approach within the FLOSS "movement."

These difficulties would not be worthy of much discussion, except that it is widely believed that this "stuff" has some merit and that it may even have an important role to play in the development of a more open, equitable, affordable, and empowering vision of an information society. In 2002 in South Africa, the National Advisory Council on Innovation (NACI)[1] produced a report entitled "Open Software and Open Standards—A Critical Issue for Addressing the Digital Divide," in which this view was clearly articulated. The decision to set up a center in 2003 to promote and support the adoption and development of FLOSS within South Africa and the region was an outcome of the NACI report. Two of the authors of this paper were involved in the initial setup phase of the project. One of the authors continues to be the manager of this center.

Our early experience of FLOSS advocacy indicated that explaining FLOSS to key decision makers, who had been thoroughly immersed in a dominant narrative of software as exclusively private intellectual property, was a nontrivial task. What was needed was a metaphor.

This paper illustrates how metaphors can be used in organizational change and how the use of a particular metaphor (*meraka*[2]) was used strategically to effect such a change in the Open Source Center (OSC) at the Center for Scientific and Industrial Research (CSIR) in South Africa. The use of a common concept from everyday life helped over-

---

[1]The National Advisory Council on Innovation (http://www.naci.org.za/) is a body set up by a South African Act of Parliament to advise the then Minister of Arts Culture Science and Technology, as well as the Cabinet as a whole, on science and technology issues.

[2]*Meraka* is a term used in Lesotho, South Africa, and Botswana to describe common grazing land. People may engage in private or communal productive activity on this land, but the land itself is kept for the common good. Its use in Botswana has been described by Arntzen (1989).

come some of the difficulties with explaining and understanding the concept of FLOSS beyond the software community. This particular metaphor supported the desire by the management for an African image for the Center, while at the same time bringing to the forefront some of the resistance and difficulties in pursuing this image.

To place the case study and its use of the metaphor *meraka* in context, we first describe briefly the common usage of metaphors in organizational change and Information Systems development literature. In section 3 we describe the current debate between the concepts of *free* and *open source* software. Section 4 introduces the case study of the OSC in the Meraka Institute, and section 5 presents a discussion of the case study in light of the previous debates presented in section 2 and 3. In the last section, we conclude with the more general contributions that this paper makes.

2   IS AND METAPHOR USE

Metaphors are used in everyday life to facilitate meaning. For example, we commonly hear phrases such as "eating your words," "winning an argument," or "having a heart of stone." A metaphor is defined as "use of a word or phrase to indicate something different from (though related in some way to) the literal meaning" (*Oxford Advanced Learner's Dictionary* 1989). Metaphors can be seen as a symbol, a figure of speech, a simile, an image or an allegory. They help make sense of situations, help in understanding new concepts or existing situations. Metaphors help put meaning into experiences and are useful in balancing apparent paradoxes or contradictions (Ott 1989; pp. 29-30 quoted in Kendall and Kendall 1993, p. 150). In the case of FLOSS, we were looking for a metaphor to lend possible meanings to a complex concept in easy to understand terms. In this way it would serve many functions, in fact address Weaver's (1967, quoted in Kendall and Kendall 1993, p. 150) four main functions of metaphors: supplying concreteness or actualization of an abstract idea, clarifying the unknown, expressing the subjective, and assisting thought. *Meraka* was the metaphor chosen.

The potential for metaphors within organizations and IS have long been recognized. The use of metaphors to maintain or change the organizational culture is a common theme in organizational literature. It is also a way of knowing the principle ways in which people endow experience with meaning. Although in relation to narratives Ramiller notes (2001, p. 290) that

> a story never really "tells itself." In finding meaning in a narrative the listener also draws on personal experience, cultural convention, and knowledge of the social context to which the narrative refers—plus a learned facility with the task of interpreting stories.

Metaphors can be used in a similar way.

2.1 Organizational Studies and Metaphors

Krefting and Frost (1995) argue that in addition to capturing the complexity of an organization in the members' own terms "metaphors may also serve in grasping an existing culture, framing a new culture, or generating change where current organizational culture is perceived to be less than optimal" (p. 158). They investigate how culture in organizational settings can be managed through the therapeutic use of metaphors using two constructs: the degree of heterogeneity (homogeneity) and location of blockages (conscious-unconscious). Krefting and Frost endorse the use of metaphors in situations of organizational change: "Metaphors may serve as models or paradigms that can help focus attention on what currently exists, frame other possibilities where change is perceived as desirable, and initiate action towards such change" (p. 168).

Walsham (1993, p. 37) comments on how little work has been done on subcultures and metaphors within organizations. One exception to this is the work by Young (1989), in which the author shows how the symbol of the rose within an organization was viewed as having a fixed meaning by management, but in fact hid the different feelings and loyalties of two main groups of shop floor workers in a textile company. Thus the same symbol or metaphor can have very different meanings within an organization. Young concludes that, "It is this tension between fragmentation and unity which I argue is the organizational culture, while the symbols, artefacts, myths, etc., informing organizational events are the explicit manifestation of it" (pp. 203-204).

Walsham uses metaphors in an interesting way to understand the process of change within an organization. Using the metaphors of power and culture, the political metaphor encourages us to see organizations as loose networks of people with divergent interests who gather together for the sake of expediency (Morgan 1986). Power is viewed as a medium through which conflicts are resolved. Foucault saw the panoptican as a metaphor for modern society. Walsham concludes his discussion of metaphors:

> Metaphors can also assist with the linking of academic practices with that of practitioners. Ramiller (2001) in his account of the Airline Magazine Syndrome shows how we can link academic literature with practical problems through the use of narratives. This is equally applicable to the use of metaphors. In this way, though challenging, metaphors can assist in some instances with combining the rationality of the academic world with the rationality of practitioners (Walsham 1993, p. 39).

In summary, within the organizational and management literature, metaphors have been used to understand or manage organizational culture; are the manifestation of the tensions between unity and fragmentation within an organization; assist with understanding the process of change; and provide a link between academic practices and the practices of practitioners.

2.2 Information Systems and Metaphors

Although there is no common or standard approach in the use of metaphors in systems analysis and design, metaphors have been used frequently in information systems literature (Hirschheim and Newman 1991; Walsham 1993). Walsham notes that the use of metaphors in information systems literature is mainly implicit, with the exception of Hirschheim and Klein (1989), who look at metaphors in terms of the alternative view of role of systems analyst, and Madsen (1989), who believes that we can consciously use metaphors.

As information systems are social constructs, it is not surprising that there are a number of reasons why they are used in this field. Walsham (1993) and Hirschheim and Newman (1991) outline some of the reasons. Metaphors

- help liven up speech and writing;
- are an unexpected and creative device for evolving new images of known situations;
- build on the belief that our reality is defined through metaphors—metaphors are pervasive in everyday life (Lakoff and Johnson, 1980);
- are a way of thinking and seeing ("a way of thinking and a way of seeing that pervade how we understand our world generally," Morgan 1986, p. 12);
- are the ways we think and act (Boland 1987);
- provide fresh insight into existing situations with the use of new metaphors (Mangham and Overington 1987);
- can assist in tapping unconscious material in human minds (Krefting and Frost) 1995); and
- can facilitate change while maintaining stability (Pondy 1983).

Based on these reasons a number of common metaphors, such as war, journeys, and orchestra, are used in the field of information systems. A more comprehensive list of the metaphors used is given in Table 1.

The use of metaphors as indicated in Table 1 illustrate the various positive roles metaphors can play in IS development. However, from an information engineering perspective, Beath and Orlikowski (1994) show how the use of metaphors in IS development can, on one level, hide the underlying philosophy and motivation in user-involvement in IS development processes, but at another level reveal the true conscious or unconscious meaning behind the IS design techniques. The use of the metaphor *player* (either in an acting or sports context) fits in with the image of the developer of the IS being largely in control of the overall schema and the users participating in this plan. "Players participate on others' terms, in that the rules of the game or the script of the play are devised by and commanded by others (for example, game officials, umpires, coaches, playwrights, directors, and producers)" (Beath and Orlikowski 1994, p. 361). In the text they explored, Beath and Orlikowski discovered that "users seem to have little direct control over the nature and frequency of their contribution, the content and context of interaction, and the timing of events" (p. 361). They also came across the use of the missionary metaphor for systems analysts:

With this metaphor, the text implies that information technology is a religion, that analysts are priests, and that systems development methodologies are scriptures that will lead the heathens (the users) to their salvation. Users are unsophisticated "villagers," and their views are "folklore," hence, discountable. The analyst's job is to offer the users "a promise" of a better life....In this claim the metaphor is quite accurate—although, one suspects, not in the way implied in the text—for missionaries' modus operandi is to convert the natives to their view of the world, rather than to try and accommodate the natives' views. In the referenced religious tradition, there is little modification of the faith by the converted (Beath and Orlikowski 1994, p. 361).

Table 1. A Summary of the Use of Metaphors in Information Systems Literature

Metaphor	Use of Metaphor	Source
War, organism, city-state (society), and team sports	Metaphors are useful in enacting corporate strategy and linking strategic planning with IT planning.	Mason (1991)
Construction of the palace of Versailles	A metaphor for IS design.	Allen and Lientz (1978)
No common metaphors suggested nor are metaphors investigated which already are resident in systems development methodologies	Introducing metaphors in IS design rather than discovering the metaphors which the users rely on in their dialogue.	Madsen (1989)
Six main metaphors are used: journey, war, game, organism, society and machine and; three metaphors emerged from the language of IS users: family, zoo and jungle	Analysts who are aware of the existence of metaphors will see systems development process in a very different light. Kendall and Kendall (1993) take examples from various IS design approaches that fit the different metaphors best—for example SDLC as a game; structured methodologies and CASE tools as a machine; prototyping as a journey; project champion as the jungle; ETHICS as a family; SSM as a zoo; multiview as a society, and; IS development deteriorating into war.	Kendall and Kendall (1993)
Game, garden, orchestra, journey and machine	Metaphors as a means of examining phenomena from different angles.	Gallupe (2000)
No particular metaphor used	A metaphor is essentially a way of understanding and experiencing one kind of thing in terms of another. IS development has been too narrowly conceived and the use of symbolism will assist with moving out of this very narrow focus.	Hirschheim and Newman (1991)

A similar example is given using the "The Tower of Babel," which serves to reinforce the dichotomy between users and analysts. Beath and Orlikowski's examples illustrate that metaphors can be used to mislead and/or direct an organization in certain ways. In their analysis of a text on the participatory nature of IS design, Beath and Orlikowski discovered that "users seem to have little direct control over the nature and frequency of their contribution, the content and context of interaction, and the timing of events" (p. 361). The use of a particular metaphor excludes other meanings. Metaphors are also culturally and context specific. Boland (1987) identifies five metaphors which he feels guide systems development, but which are really dangerous fantasies "and not suited for guiding serious thought" as "they reify the human actor in ISD, and inevitably lead to dysfunctional consequences" (p. 367). The examples he gives are: Information as structured data, as an object or entity; organization is information; information is power; information is intelligence; and information is perfectible. Additionally, even though Kendall and Kendall (1993) endorse the use of metaphors by systems analysts, they conclude that in relation to practice, systems developers should be aware that users are enacting metaphors and this may guide the developer in choosing a methodology.

One of the other contemporary debates that the choice of the metaphor *meraka* is inextricably linked with is that of the open and free source debate. We briefly discuss this debate in the next section before describing the South African case study.

3 THE OPEN SOURCE AND FREE SOFTWARE DEBATE

Early writings on the FLOSS community frequently characterized (or caricatured) it as a hegemonic grouping with a common hacker culture (Raymond 1999). It is interesting, from the perspective of this paper, that Eric Raymond's important trilogy of papers made heavy use of metaphor to support his arguments: "The Cathedral and the Bazaar" (in which the proprietary software development model was contrasted to the bazaar-like approach of FLOSS development) (Raymond 1998b), "The Magic Cauldron" (which makes reference to the mythical Welsh Ceridwen's magic cauldron as an inexhaustible supply of creative plenty) (Raymond 2000), and "Homesteading the Noosphere" (likening the first appropriation of FLOSS projects to the frontier type practice of homesteading previously "unowned" land) (Raymond 1998b). This last image is actually quite a disturbing one in the context of FLOSS adoption in countries that were formerly colonies, where the historical colonial practice of homesteading has a far from positive connotation and the notion of "unowned" land simply reflected a disregard for all forms of land ownership which did not take the form of title deeds registered in a colonial deeds office. Nevertheless, Raymond's early writings played a vital part in starting off the process of understanding what was happening with this new FLOSS phenomenon. It was clear, whether one accepted Raymond's characterization or not, that by the end of the 1990s, FLOSS had established itself as being important, being of some value, and being potentially disruptive to the established models of creating software and doing business.

One of the more interesting fault lines in the global FLOSS "movement" is that between free software and open source software. It is possible to make too much of this divide as it can be argued that the difference is really a rather subtle one that has very little practical impact on the users of FLOSS. In most cases, the two alternative terminologies describe a broad intersection of essentially the same software.

> "Free software" and "Open Source" describe the same category of software, more or less, but say different things about the software, and about values. The GNU Project continues to use the term "free software," to express the idea that freedom, not just technology, is important (Stallman 1999).

The Free Software Foundation was founded by Richard Stallman and was built around the GNU GPL (general public licence). A large number of important software projects have been licenced under the GPL, including the gcc compiler (a necessary tool for compiling much of the FLOSS software in existence today), the linux operating system kernel, and the Gnome and KDE desktop management software. For Stallman, the notion of free software (that is free as in speech, not free as in beer) is a conscious attempt to politicize and create a movement.

Eric Raymond and Bruce Perens were founding members of the Open Source Initiative (OSI) in 1998, which popularized the term open source software (OSS). For the OSI, Stallman's notion of free software was obstructing the broader potential of FLOSS. The word *free* was ambiguous and would be viewed with suspicion by the corporate world. Raymond's "Cathedral and the Bazaar" trilogy made the case that OSS was technically a better way to produce software than the traditional "cathedral" style of proprietary software production. So whereas Stallman argues passionately that the collaboration and sharing that is an essential aspect of free software is a desirable goal in its own right, the OSI introduced a more instrumental justification: the collaborative and shared model of software development was to be encouraged primarily because it resulted in better software.

Reflecting back, in 2006, it is clear that FLOSS has continued to thrive and grow, attracting new groups of interest, not least of which have been large corporations such as IBM, Oracle, and HP and governments of developed and developing countries such as Brazil, India and South Africa. A consequence of this expansion has been the need to reflect upon the validity, legitimacy, and continued usefulness of the theories of early Raymondism.[3] In a recent special issue of First Monday, Lin (2005) outlines the need for such a sociological reflection:

> However, I argue that such a view, partially valid in explaining the FLOSS development, not only ignores the diversity of population and their different articulations, interpretation on and performances towards developing FLOSS, but also neglects the different environments and contexts where FLOSS is deployed, developed and implemented.

The phenomenon of FLOSS has also captured the attention of those working outside the field of computer software. There have been a number of efforts to conceive of FLOSS as part of a broader digital commons (see, for example, Boyle 1997). Boyle uses the concept of a commons as a metaphor to (1) highlight the case for different ownership models of so-called intellectual property and (2) to evoke a comparison with the period of Enclosures which characterized a rapidly industrializing Britain in the 17th, 18th, and 19th centuries (Thompson 1963). Comparing the rapid expansion of the scope of copyright, patent, and trademark protection which marked the end of the 20th century

---

[3]Raymondism is a term coined by Nikolai Bezrokov (see http://www.softpanorama.com) in which he describes the thinking behind "The Cathedral and the Bazaar" as an anarchic right-wing libertarianism or vulgar marxism. Raymond's reaction to being termed a marxist (vulgar or otherwise!) gave rise to a particularly vitriolic exchange between the two in the annals of First Monday.

with this earlier period of enclosure is a theme which has also been picked by others including, for example, May (2000).

The idea of a commons is clearly a powerful metaphor for at least some aspects of FLOSS. In the Southern African context, there is no need to refer to a leafy image of "olde England" as all of the major indigenous languages have a rich vocabulary for describing various forms of commons land usage and management, many of which are still in common usage. After considering a number of options[4] the seSotho word, *meraka*, was adopted as the symbolic name for the new FLOSS center.

4   SOUTH AFRICAN CASE STUDY: OPEN SOURCE CENTER

4.1 Research Approach

The case study of the CSIR's OSC was chosen for two reasons. First, two of the authors, as mentioned in the introduction, were closely linked with the center's formation in 2002 and its continued operation since. One of the authors is the manager of the center and the other was initially part of the setup team. Second, the remaining author has been investigating the use of metaphors as part of IS research strategies and all metaphors commonly found in the literature were Western. The conversation on how the use of an African metaphor was used in the naming of the OSC started after the manager of the OSC presented a guest lecture on open source software to postgraduate IS students.

The backgrounds of two of the authors—their lived experiences—were the main sources of primary data for the case study. A number of discussions were held between the three authors during which the history of the OSC was debated and traced. Often this necessitated the search for documentation of this history and further discussions so that agreement could be reached on the sequencing of events. Secondary data was obtained through the interrogation of documents and reports published by the OSC against this experience and background. Therefore, along with other interpretive researchers in the IS field (Lee 1994; Myers 1994; Walsham 1993), the position that our knowledge of reality is a social construction by human actions was adopted. In order to understand the origin of the metaphor used by the OSC, an attempt was made to understand the meanings assigned to the metaphor and the context in which it was chosen.

A variety of stakeholders' opinions on their interpretation of the metaphor *meraka* was not sought, as the purpose of the case study and the data collected was to document the rationale behind the use of the metaphor. This was part of the authors' reflective

---

[4]For example, the Zulu word *idlelo* has approximately the same meaning as *meraka*. *Idlelo* was used as the title of the First Conference on the African Digital Commons held at the University of the Western Cape in January 2003. The *Idlelo* mailing list is still one of the most active lists dedicated to discussion of FLOSS issues on the African continent. The second *Idlelo* conference took place in Nairobi, Kenya, in February 2006.

process on the establishment of the organization. Other interpretations of the metaphor, which may contradict or even encapsulate the meaning of the metaphor as described here, would be an interesting topic for further research.

4.2 The OSC Case Study

The OSC was formally launched in October 2003 by the CSIR and the Department of Science and Technology in the city of Tshwane, South Africa. The overarching objective in establishing the center was to stimulate the awareness, understanding, and optimization of FLOSS benefits in Southern Africa, while contributing to similar efforts on the continent and the rest of the world. Part of the strategy for creating awareness and facilitating understanding of FLOSS is through developing and sustaining networks—consisting of members from government, industry, civil society, education, academia, and the open source community. The OSC works through three key areas: OpenSpeak, OpenMentor, and OpenProject.

- OpenSpeak focuses on developing partnerships, creating awareness, and providing information on FLOSS resources.

- OpenMentor aims to address the skills challenge by facilitating access to and development of learning and training materials for FLOSS.

- OpenProject intends to stimulate local adoption, adaptation, development, and testing of FLOSS.

The search for the name for the OSC was based on a number of factors or influences:

- the difficulty in explaining FLOSS
- the OSC had to appeal to a broad African audience, including policy makers, members of the government and the general public
- awareness that the common property relations implicit in FLOSS licences resonated with the familiar concepts of communal land and water rights on the African continent

After a brainstorming session and a number of wide-ranging discussions with a broad audience, the OSC adopted the name *Meraka* because it captures the notion of collective property rights, development, and collaboration within Southern Africa that is consistent with the FLOSS philosophy.

FLOSS is very much like a digital *meraka*. Unlike most proprietary software, open source software is available at little or no cost. The inner workings of FLOSS are also available to all who want to see it and use it. Unlike proprietary software, the source code for an open source software application is not a closely guarded secret of any individual or organization. The open and free availability of the source code allows and encourages a model of development, testing and modification based on public collaboration.

5 DISCUSSION

Within a year of the OSC being established at the CSIR, the ICT related units of the organization underwent a substantial restructuring. The fledgling African Advanced Institute for Information and Communication Technologies (AAIICT) initiative was revived under the name of the Meraka Institute and the OSC was incorporated within this institute.

Whereas the use of the metaphor *meraka* had supported the aims of the OSC in a number of ways, the metaphor now contributed to the broader South African transformation drive by getting people to see themselves as *bamerakeng*[5] and not just members of yet another entity with an English name. One example of the effectiveness of this is the recent signing of an agreement with the United Nations Development Programme (UNDP). The agreement develops the strategy on how to boost the open source capacity for the region through a knowledge networking project. By selecting an indigenous institution such as the Meraka Institute to be the implementing agency, the UNDP hopes to encourage South-South cooperation[6] and extend the benefits of the project to the rest of the continent.

Simultaneously the metaphor allowed the organization to affirm its position with regard to the digital commons. Beyond the South African situation, the use of indigenous metaphors has also found acceptance within the African continent, where the concept of communal land and ownership still plays an important part in peoples' lives. The *idlelo* mailing list, for instance, has continued to grow. The Kenyans even introduced the concept of *Kiwanja*, which is the kiSwahili translation of *Idlelo* and *Meraka*. Various contributors to the *idlelo* mailing list have also used a range of metaphors in their projects and reports. These include the various African names for gnu/linux distributions like Mambo, Impi, and Ubuntu. The Asiasource report (Noronha 2005) uses many metaphors. In this way, the term has opened up a wider discussion on how our countries are connected through a common culture, and how we can collaborate in the open source arena—opened up the discussion in the region.

Meraka has enabled people to draw a meaningful line between lessons from the agricultural age and challenges of the knowledge age. In a country where both realities still exist, this is important. This was well illustrated during a live radio broadcast by Jozi FM that was done in support of the Software Freedom Day activities in Soweto. The timing of the event coincided with a program focusing on traditional music. Some of the folk songs and poetry that were aired during this program resonated with the FLOSS celebration that was taking place. The intermittent interviews that took place with various "geeks" reaffirmed this connection. During one of the interviews, the idea of extending the Translate[7] project into local slang known as *tsotsitaal* was investigated. The host of the show summed it up at the end by pointing out that the program was more successful because it combined popular traditional folklore with leading edge technology phenomena like free software.

---

[5]Directly translated as "the people of *meraka*."

[6]"South-South" is a term commonly used to denote relations between developing countries (which are mostly, but not always, in the South), as distinct to partnerships between developing and so-called developed countries.

[7]Translate.org.za aims to make free software available in local languages.

In summary, the use of the metaphor *meraka* has enabled the articulation of thinking behind the concept of free software without being caught up in the free/open source debate. It has also allowed for a demonstration of the broadness and depth of the thinking behind some of the related initiatives. Consequently it has become relatively easy to extend the concept beyond software to other important aspects of the digital commons.

However, there has also been some resistance. As Young (1989) showed in his analysis of the meanings of the rose in an organization, the metaphor *meraka* may not be viewed in the same way by all members in the CSIR. Although people readily warm up to the name when they understand what it means, there were problems with the initial association of common grazing land with a cattle post. However, this is soon resolved when people get to see the name in the context of the organization. Additionally there was also some concern over the "Africanness" of the name of the organization. For example, the term *marakas* meaning chaos or a shambles in Afrikaans is the name given to the organization in the corridors by some members of the organization.

In general, though, there have been positive benefits from the use of the metaphor. Along with those listed above, we conclude with one example where the metaphor assisted in lobbying the much needed political support and "buy-in" from the government. At the launch of the Meraka Institute, the Minister of Communications explained the name by articulating the vision of a free, shared digital commons:

> I am proud to formally announce that this institute will be known as the Meraka Institute. The name is a Sesotho word which has different interpretations, but in this instance relates to a common space that is shared by a community for creative and productive activity (Minister of Communication 2005).

6   CONCLUSION

This paper shows how using an indigenous metaphor played an important role in the transformation process of a FLOSS organization in South Africa. In line with the traditional use of metaphors, the use of the term *meraka* helped align the organization with the broader transformational issues taking place in South Africa.

Additionally, most of the literature on metaphors relies on Western concepts and philosophy. This paper shows the potential role that indigenous metaphors can play. The use of a Southern African concept of communal land and the metaphor *meraka* shows how metaphors can make it easier to understand in that context and help bridge the divide between everyday life and the more technical aspects of life. The metaphor also has wider implications; it illustrates how in this case it assists with overcoming some of the global issues around free and open software, which is fundamentally rooted in a Western conception of property that is ill-suited for FLOSS.

An important characteristic of the debate between Stallmanism and Raymondism is that, despite appeals in both cases to universal values, there is something peculiarly American about it all. In the "land of the free," the terms *free* and *freedom* appeal to a strong vein of identity within that nation's psyche. Referring back to Lin's suggestion of the need for sociological reflection, debates about whether one form of licence is more free than another do not resonate in the same way with a South African society, which has its own very powerful tradition of interpretation of, and struggle for, freedom. We are left with a sense that, whereas the social values emphasized by Stallman (and de-emphasized by the open source approach) are a significant factor in the potential attractiveness of FLOSS as a tool for development and growth in South Africa, there is a need to reimagine, to reinterpret, and perhaps to "re-vocabularize" these powerful ideas to better integrate them with both our tradition and our projected development trajectory. We find ourselves almost entirely in agreement with Stallman, and even grudgingly respectful of Raymond—we simply believe that we can, and should, find better words which better express the meaning and potential of FLOSS according to our own image.

References

Allen, J., and Lientz, B. P. *Systems in Action*, Santa Monica, CA: Goodyear Publishing Company, Inc., 1978.

Arntzen, J. W. *Environmental Pressure and Adaptation in Rural Botswana*, unpublished PhD Thesis, Vrije Universiteit te Amsterdam, 1989.

Beath, C. M., and Orlikowski, W. J. "The Contradictory Structure of Systems Development Methodologies: Deconstructing the IS-User Relationship in Information Engineering," *Information Systems Research* (5:4), 1994, pp. 350-377.

Boland, R. "The In-Formation of Information Systems," in R. Boland and R. A. Hirschheim (eds.), *Critical Issues in Information Systems Research*, Chichester, UK: John Wiley & Sons, Inc., 1987, pp. 363-379.

Boyle, J. "A Politics of Intellectual Property: Environmentalism for the Net?," *Duke Law Journal* (47), 1997, pp. 1, 87-116.

Gallupe, R. B. "Images of Information Systems in the early 21st Century," *Communications of the AIS* (3:3), 2000.

Hirschheim, R. and Klein, H. "Four Paradigms of Information Systems Development," *Communications of the ACM* (32:10), 1991, pp. 1199-1216.

Hirschheim, R., and Newman, M. "Symbolism and Information Systems Development: Myth, Metaphor and Magic," *Information Systems Research* (2:1), 1989, pp. 29-62.

Kendall, J. E., and Kendall, K .E. "Metaphors and Methodologies: Living Beyond the Systems Machine," *MIS Quarterly* (17:2) June 1993, 149-171.

Krefting, L. A., and Frost, P. J. "Untangling Webs, Surfing Waves, and Wildcatting: A Multiple-Metaphor Perspective on Managing Organizational Culture," in P. J. Frost, L. F. Moore, M. L. Louis, C. C. Lundberg, and J. Martin (eds.), *Organizational Culture*, Thousand Oaks, CA: Sage Publications, 1995.

Lakoff, G., and Johnson, M. *Metaphors We Live By*, Chicago: University of Chicago Press, 1980.

Lee, A. S. "Electronic Mail as a Medium for Rich Communication: An Empirical Investigation Using Hermeneutic Interpretation," *MIS Quarterly* (18:2), June 1994, pp. 143-157.

Lin, Y. "The Future of Sociology of FLOSS," *First Monday*, Special Issue #2: Open Source, October 3 2005 (available online at http://firstmonday.org/issues/special10_10/).

Madsen, K. H. "Breakthrough by Breakdown: Metaphors and Structured Domains," in H. K. Klein and K. Kumar (eds.), *Systems Development for Human Progress*, New York: North Holland, 1989, pp. 41-53.

Mangham, I. L., and Overington, M. A. *Organizations as Theatre: A Social Psychology of Dramatic Appearances*, Chichester, UK: John Wiley & Sons, 1987.

Mason, R. M. "Metaphors and Strategic Information Systems Planning," in J. Nunamaker, Jr. and R. H. Sprague, Jr. (eds.). *Proceedings of the Twenty-Fourth Annual Hawaii International Conference on Systems Sciences* (Volume 4), New York: Plenum Publishing, 1991, pp. 231-240.

May, C. *A Global Political Economy of Intellectual Property Rights*, London: Routledge, 2000.

Minister of Communications. Keynote address by the Minister of Communications at the launch of the Meraka Institute, May 17, 2005 (online at http://www.meraka.org.za/).

Morgan, G. *Images of Organizations*, Beverly Hills, CA: Sage Publications, 1986.

Myers, M. D. "A Disaster for Everyone to See: An Interpretive Analysis of a Failed IS Project.," *Accounting, Management and Information Technologies* (4:4), 1994, pp. 185-201.

NACI (National Advisory Council on Innovation). "Open Software and Open Standards—A Critical Issue for Addressing the Digital Divide," 2002 (online at http://www.naci.org/).

Noronha, F. "Opting for a Week on the Wrong Side of the Digital Divide," *Tactical Technology Collective*, 2005 (online at http://www.africasource.org/).

Ott, J. S. *Organizational Culture Perspectives*, Chicago: Dorsey Press, 1989.

Oxford Advanced Learner's Dictionary (4th ed.), Oxford, UK: Oxford University Press, 1989.

Pondy, L. R. "The Role of Metaphors and Myths in Organization and the Facilitation of Change," in L. R. Pondy, P. J. Frost, and T. D. Dandridge (eds.), *Organizational Symbolism*, Greenwich, CT: JAI Press, 1983, pp. 157-166.

Ramiller, N. C. "Airline Magazine Syndrome: Reading a Myth of Mismanagement," *Information Technology and People* (14:3), 2001, pp. 287-303.

Raymond, E. S. "A Brief History of Hackerdom," in C. Di Bona, S. Ockman, and M. Stone (eds.), *Open Sources: Voices from the Open Source Revolution*, Sebastopol, CA: O' Reilly and Associates, 1999.

Raymond, E. S. "The Cathedral and the Bazaar," *First Monday* (3:3), March 1998a (available online at http://www.firstmonday.org/issues/issue3_3/raymond/index.html).

Raymond, E. S. "Homesteading the Noosphere," *First Monday* (3:10), October 1998b (available online at http://www.firstmonday.org/issues/issue3_10/raymond/index.html).

Raymond, E.S. "The Magic Cauldron," Version 3.0, 2000 (available online at http://www.catb.org/~esr/writings/cathedral-bazaar/magic-cauldron/).

Stallman, R. "The GNU Operating System and the Free Software Movement," in C. DiBona, S. Ockman, and M. Stone (eds.), *Open Sources: Voices from the Open Source Revolution*, Sebastopol, CA: O'Reilly and Associates, 1999.

Thompson, E. P. *The Making of the English Working Class*, New York: Penguin Books, 1963.

Walsham, G. *Interpreting Information Systems in Organizations*, Chichester: Wiley and Sons, 1993.

Weaver, R. M. *A Rhetoric and Handbook*, New York: Holt Reinhart and Winston, 1967.

Young, E. "On the Naming of the Rose: Interests and Multiple Meanings as Elements of Organizational Culture," *Organization Studies* (10:2), 1989, pp. 187-206.

About the Authors

Elaine Byrne is a senior lecturer at the Department of Informatics, University of Pretoria. She recently obtained her doctorate from the University of the Western Cape, Cape Town, South Africa, in Public Health on the design and development of community based health information systems. Her general research interest areas are information systems and social development, qualitative research methodology, and health information systems. Elaine may be contacted at elainebyrne@up.ac.za.

Bob Jolliffe is a senior lecturer in Computer Science at the University of South Africa, where he completed his M.Sc. in 2002. He is actively involved in the Free/Open Source

Software movement in South Africa. His current research is directed toward the effects of the patent system on innovation in computer software in developing countries. Bob may be contacted at jollirm@unisa.ac.za.

Nhlanhla Mabaso has worked in a range of ICT areas. After completing his B.Sc. (Computer Science and Applied Maths) at the University of the Witwatersrand, he worked as a software engineer for an airline. He later took on other responsibilities as a systems analyst for an Internet service provider working on a range of areas including systems administration, Internet hotline, online databases as well as strategic consulting. By the time he completed his Master's in Business Administration studies, he had moved into the area of management within the private and later he public sector where he was Chief Information Officer. He is currently involved in the Meraka Institute's Open Source Centre initiative hosted at the CSIR. All this work has necessitated the establishment of a wide range of local and international partnerships, with partners from within Africa, Brazil, China, Finland, the European Union, and India. He is currently the coordinator of the Free Software and Open Source Foundation for Africa (FOSSFA). Nhlanhla may be contacted at nmabaso@csir.co.za.

20 WEBLOGGING: Implementing Communities of Practice

Leiser Silva
Elham Mousavidin
Lakshmi Goel
University of Houston
Houston, TX U.S.A.

Abstract   *This paper centers on the emergent phenomenon of weblogging. Even though the total number of weblogs is increasing at an exponential rate, little formal study has been done on this phenomenon. This paper provides two main contributions. First, it describes the phenomenon of weblogging and conceptualizes it, discussing significant attributes of weblogs that set it apart from traditional communication means. Second, it establishes a framework grounded in the theory of communities of practice that provides a lens to study the potential role of weblogging in organizational communication. The research approach is qualitative and analysis is done by interpreting the content of a weblog through a hermeneutic approach. Weblogging can be seen to foster social inclusion based on its characteristics and nature. Our study shows that by its features of interaction and informality, weblogging cultivates social inclusion, particularly that of employees working in a corporation. The paper concludes by reflecting on the potential of weblogging for enabling informal means of communication in organizations.*

1   INTRODUCTION

A weblog (or blog) is a self-publishing website that is updated on a regular basis. The word *blog* has been defined by the Merriam-Webster dictionary as "a web site that contains an online personal journal with reflections, comments and often hyperlinks" and has been identified as the most looked-up word in the year 2004.[1] Contents of a

---

[1]BBC News, "'Blog'" Picked as Word of the Year," December 1, 2004; see http://news.bbc.co.uk/2/hi/technology/4059291.stm.

Please use the following format when citing this chapter:

Silva, L., Mousavidin, E., and Goel, L., 2006, in IFIP International Federation for Information Processing, Volume 208, Social Inclusion: Societal and Organizational Implications for Information Systems, eds. Trauth, E., Howcroft, D., Butler, T., Fitzgerald, B., DeGross, J., (Boston: Springer), pp. 295-316.

weblog are written mostly in a casual manner and are archived reverse chronologically. The number of blogs continues to grow. Approximately 25.8 million blogs were being tracked by Technorati, a real-time search engine that maintains updated information on blogs, in January 2006.[2] As blogs become an increasingly familiar sight on cyberspace and tools further improve, the prevalent exponential trend in growth is expected to continue (Schiano et al. 2004).

Organizations are increasingly adopting weblogs due to their dynamic and informal nature. Corporations such as Microsoft, Sun Microsystems, Google, and Yahoo, amongst many others, have recognized the potential of using weblogs, and maintain their own weblogs (Rosencrance 2004; Taulli 2006). These weblogs provide real-time information and enable all visitors to give feedback. Weblogs are a two-way channel of communication between customers and firms. They also enable informal communication among employees within an organization. In a sense, weblogs can be seen to give organizational voice to employees. Through weblogs, employees that would not usually "speak up" or participate—due to reasons that are based on personality, gender, or geographic location (Bowen and Blackmon 2003)—have a channel to express their opinion. By analyzing the phenomenon of weblogging, this paper identifies the characteristics of weblogs which make this happen. We argue that weblogs facilitate social inclusion of voices that may not have been heard in the absence of this form of communication.

The social dynamism of weblogs is manifested through different applications ranging from personal diaries to political forums. For example, in the 2004 U.S. Presidential election, weblogs were extensively used by political parties. Presidential candidate John Kerry had his own official weblog[3] to communicate with supporters, obtain their feedback, and provide information about the campaign. At the same time, CNN had its own official weblog[4] to provide up-to-date information about the ongoing election process. The social impact of weblogs was evident early in the night of the election in the strong belief that John Kerry was winning. This belief stemmed from the exit poll results that were published on weblogs even though the mainstream broadcasting media did not announce them.

Thus, given the relevance of weblogs, manifested in their exponential growth and their impact in mass media as well as in corporations, we decided to conduct an interpretive study (Walsham 1995) to examine their main attributes. Accordingly, the objective of this paper is to conceptualize weblogs; that is, to establish their properties and attributes as well as to propose a theoretical lens that would help researchers and practitioners make sense of this phenomenon.

The organization of the paper is as follows. We begin by defining weblogs; we do so by identifying the attributes that distinguish them from other Internet based communication technologies. We then discuss our theoretical lens, communities of practice (Brown and Duguid 1991, 1998; Lave 1991; Lave and Wenger 1991; Wenger 1998, 2000;Wenger et al. 2002; Wenger and Snyder 2000). In the subsequent section, we

---

[2]See http://www.technorati.com.
[3]The page, located at http://blog.johnkerry.com/blog/archives/week_2004_10_31.html, while still a valid site, is currently inactive.
[4]Located at http://www.cnn.com/2004/ALLPOLITICS/blog/10/13/one.blog/index.html.

apply this lens to conduct a hermeneutic interpretation (Sanders 1982) of a corporate blog. This interpretation allows us to propose a model for understanding the life cycle of a corporate weblog. We conclude by reflecting on the potential impact of weblogging on organizational communication.

2 WEBLOGGING

2.1 Attributes of Weblogs

Early versions of what is known as a weblog today (i.e., traditional websites) are in the form of static or noninteractive web pages. Weblogs usually have a central theme and attract regular visitors who interact and form interlinked micro-communities (Herring et al. 2005; Kumar et al. 2003). This interaction is the basis for the dynamic nature of weblogs. Some popular weblogs, for example Glenn Reynolds' site,[5] are visited by as many as 100,000 readers each day.[6] The content of weblogs is mainly text. However, weblogs can support photos and other multimedia content as well. The posts center around the main theme of the weblog,[7] with links to other weblogs or websites on the Internet. Most weblogs allow readers to leave their comments on existing posts (Blood 2002). Hence weblogging lends itself appropriately for task-related collaboration as well as informal communication. It can also be a channel for distributing information in organizations (e.g., notification of organizational decisions), two-way stakeholder communication (interaction with customers or vendors), team-building (exchange of ideas, brainstorming), informal dialogs, and problem solving. Most weblogs today feed into RSS-aware programs called aggregators. RSS (really simple syndication) is a format that syndicates information items from other websites, weblogs, wikis, or even changelogs of concurrent versions system (CVS) check-ins. An organization can use an aggregator by checking RSS feeds of news websites, new additions on supplier websites, technical updates, etc.

2.2 Strengths

Weblogs are created and read by individuals who share similar interests and who want to interact and communicate with like-minded people. In contrast with traditional communication systems that are usually formal and top-down driven, weblogs offer an informal and dynamic means to share information. They offer a platform for meeting and sharing ideas at one's convenience and hence enable communication between people that might not have been possible face-to-face. This engenders inclusion of indi-

---

[5]http://www.instapundit.com/

[6]"Blogging is Booming," R. E. Bruner (http://www.imediaconnection.com/content/3162.asp).

[7]Weblogs can have different themes. There are community weblogs (such as Metafilter), corporate weblogs (Yahoo) and weblogs that concentrate on philosophical discussions (www.plastic.com).

viduals and encourages participation. With the tools available today, weblogs require minimal technical skills to setup, use, and maintain. In addition, weblogs can support multiple users in terms of accessibility for reading as well as making contributions. Weblogs, known as mBlogs, can also be accessed through mobile devices. Intranet webogs can be accessed organization-wide. A fast search feature enables archived information to be retrieved quickly. The ease of use and ubiquitous access allows inclusion of people with limited technical knowledge.

Dynamism and interaction exhibited by weblogs come from allowing users to post new topics as well as comment or reply to previous posts. Being highly interactive, weblogs are "hit" at a higher rate than static or conventional websites. Since search engines work on factors such as content relevance, number of incoming links from other sites, and rate of updating, use of weblogs increases the presence of an organization in cyberspace. Weblogs enable businesses to publish and disseminate information faster than e-newsletters or other conventional forms of electronic communication. Weblogs also have the potential to help organizations reduce costs related to storing digital information. Even though storage cost is decreasing steadily, it still remains a problem. E-mailing or sending out e-newsletters to individual employees may cause clutter in their mailboxes and decrease available storage space. Bad housekeeping habits of employees in keeping their mailboxes "clean" can further aggravate storage problems. Maintaining a central weblog to provide the same information prevents these conceivable problems by organizing the information in one location for easier reference.

2.3 Challenges

Despite its potential, blogging, as a new technology, is not devoid of challenges. One of those is the high abandonment rate. Due to the ease and fairly low requirements for installing them, many users set up their own blogs. However, not all blogs are read consistently and have an ardent membership. Most of them simply are not visited at all. In the terminology of bloggers these blogs are "unpopular." The popularity differentiates a successful weblog from one that is doomed to failure. This results in unnecessary clutter of inactive blogs. Furthermore, since weblogs enable informal communication, employees may easily misuse them. Weblogs may result in a waste of company resources as employees use them for entertainment and leisure.

Another important concern is that weblogs, being a source of documented information, can cause legal problems because of breaches of privacy and confidentiality. This is a risk particularly for employees who own personal weblogs that identify them with the companies for which they work. Accidental references may lead to action against the company for libel or defamation, leakage of sensitive information, data protection, and confidentiality issues (Twist 2005). Hence, most companies are concerned about the content of the personal weblogs that their employees maintain. This concern at times has led to several employees being fired or banned from publishing on their weblogs. For example, in November 2004, Delta Air Lines fired one of its flight attendants because she had pictures of herself posing in her work uniform posted on her weblog (Twist 2004). This tension between the rights of individuals to express themselves and the confidentiality required by corporations for which they work has been the center of attention of other academics. For instance, Suitt et al. (2003) tell the fictional story of an individual whose messages in her blog affected the reputation of the company that employed her, and eventually hit the company's revenue.

The marked interest of companies in the content of their employees' weblogs seems clearer in the field of journalism. For example, Boese (2004) wrote about two journalists, Josh Kucera from *Time* Magazine and Kevin Sites from CNN, whose weblogs were banned by their employers. Both journalists wrote about the Iraq war on their weblogs. According to Boese, the writings of these journalists were found to be more immediate and compelling than what appeared in *Time* and on CNN. Therefore, *Time* and CNN prohibited these journalists from publishing on the web to protect the companies' images. In another instance, Palser (2003) wrote about the story of three journalists' weblogs that were stopped prematurely because the employers of these journalists believed that those weblogs were a conflict of interest. As seen in several cases, the lack of explicit rules has created some problems for employers and their blogging employees. Legal expert Nick Locket from hi-tech DL Legal says, "Blogs can be good for companies, but what is clear is that the rules on blogs are hazy and inconsistent, and bloggers should be alert about what they are doing" (Twist 2005, p. 1).

All these features suggest the potential and limitations of weblogging for enabling communications in firms. This is relevant given the challenges faced by organizations in managing communications and information exchange (Alavi and Leidner 2001; Cole 1998; Davenport and Prusak 1997; Nonaka and Takeuchi 1995). In order to highlight the attributes of weblogging, we compare it with other means of electronic communication. A summary of this comparison is presented in Table 1.

3 THEORETICAL BACKGROUND

In this section we introduce our theoretical lens: communities of practice (Brown and Duguid 1991, 1998). Communities of practice posits a social theory of learning (Lave 1991; Lave and Wenger 1991; Wenger 1998, 2000; Wenger et al. 2002). From this perspective, learning is conceived as the generation and transmission of tacit knowledge through the sharing of experiences mainly through narratives and informal communications (Boland and Tenkasi 1991; Lave 1991; Lave and Wenger 1991; Wenger 1998, 2000). Since organizations apply weblogs to communicate in an informal and interactive manner with their employees and customers, often with the purpose of managing knowledge (Jantsch 2004, Manjoo 2002),[8] we argue that communities of practice is an appropriate lens for looking into the weblogging phenomenon. Accordingly, below we discuss in detail the different concepts of the theory of communities of practice and how they are related to our study.

---

[8]Given the scope of this paper, its purpose is not to contribute to the theory of communities of practice (although interesting) but to use it as a lens to make sense of corporate weblogs.

Table 1. Weblogging and Conventional Electronic Media

Medium	Editability	Dynamism	Archiving	Asynchronicity	Informality	Cost	Cultural Impact	Reciprocity	Reach	Ease of Use
Newsgroups	L	M	M	H	M	L	L	M	M	M
Bulletin Boards	M	M	M	H	M	M	L	M	M	M
E-mail, E-Newsletters	N	N	L	H	M	L	L	M	L	H
Instant Messaging	N	N	L	H	H	L	L	M	L	M
Groups	N	H	H	H	M	L	M	H	M	M
Open Source Systems (Wiki)	H	H	H	H	M	L	L	H	H	M
Video Conferencing	N	H	N	L	M	M	L	M	L	L
Websites	H	M	L	N	L	L	L	N	H	H
Weblogging	H	H	H	H	H	L	H	H	H	H

Notes: 1.   L = Low; M = Medium; H = High; N = None

        2.   The attributes were identified after careful examination of several weblogs, including those of Google, CNN, Microsoft, and conventional electronic media (i.e., e-mail, video conferencing, and databases) (Karahanna and Limayem 2000; Ngwenyama and Lee 1997; Yates and Orlikowski 1992).

               Editability: Ability to change previously posted information

               Dynamism: Rate of change/updating

               Archiving: Ability to maintain records and provide search features

               Asynchronicity: Ability to respond at one's convenience

               Informality: Ability to express information in an informal manner

               Cost: Cost of implementation, use, and maintenance

               Cultural Impact: Ability to support and foster a social function

               Reciprocity: Ability to support two-way communication

               Reach: Number of (unspecified) recipients

               Ease of Use: Effort of implementation, use, and maintenance

3.1 Communities of Practice

A community of practice has been defined by Brown and Duguid (1998, p. 96) as

A group across which know-how and sensemaking are shared—the group which needs to work together for its dispositional know-how to be put into practice....In the course of their ongoing practice, the members of such a group will develop into a de facto community. (Often, the community, like the knowledge, is implicit).

This theory assumes that such communities of practice can span across an organization, or between organizations, and are extremely flexible. Their formation is driven by a common interest to share and exchange information. They are like a "spiral of knowledge" in which individuals' knowledge transforms and builds upon others knowledge to form social and organizational level knowledge (Nonaka 1994). Nonaka's "knowledge creation spiral" concept centers on how knowledge through practice and communities play a symbiotic role. Communities of practice embody this symbiosis to form a unit that generates collective knowledge. Wenger (1998, 2000) emphasizes the informal and pervasive nature of communities of practice and highlights the aspect of learning as a practice of engaging and participating with other community members. Next, we discuss different attributes of communities of practice and how they are related to weblogging.

3.2 Weblogging and Communities of Practice

In conceptualizing communities of practice, Brown and Duguid (1991) identified the key attributes that define a community of practice. These are a collective cooperative venture, synergistic potential, informal support, reach and reciprocity, and interactivity, participation and learning. Using these attributes as a lens, we reflect on how blogs can support the formation of communities of practice. Table 2 contains a summary of this discussion.

A collective, cooperative venture: Communities of practice start with a group of people who have the ability and desire to share common interests. In this sense, media such as e-mail, video conferencing and instant messaging that are either one-to-one or one-to-many (usually a limited number) may not necessarily be the most appropriate media for sharing "group" interests dynamically and in an interactive way. Weblogging, since its inception, has been used for exactly the purpose of communication between like-minded individuals and is strongly a many-to-many medium, fitting the requirement of a collective, cooperative venture. Weblogs are being used by people who share common interests such as literature, nature, adventure sports, particular technologies, and research.

Synergistic potential: Communities of practice are synergistic in nature as they foster communication and sharing of knowledge and ideas in a conversational form. We may consider this way of facilitating communication as continuous. Newsgroups, bulletin boards, e-mail, and open source systems,[9] on the other hand, are discrete in the sense that they do not allow a dialogical way of communication, and hence do not facilitate dynamic conversational exchange. Weblogging provides a technological platform for enabling synergistic interchange as it allows dynamic and interactive sharing of knowledge. This is achieved because the information on a weblog is available to many people at the same time and also because anyone can contribute to what is already pub-

---

[9]Weblogs employing technologies such as XML and PHP may also be considered open source systems. However, for the purpose of this paper, we choose to differentiate between such weblogs and more traditional open source systems such as wikis. We make this differentiation based on the purpose of traditional open source systems such as Linux and Wikipedia, which is to achieve a final goal and thus allows members to edit or "correct" previous posts. In weblogs, the goal is usually to express individuals' opinion and is not under the censorship of subsequent posters.

Table 2. Communities of Practice Versus Weblogging

Community of Practice / Weblog	Collective, Cooperative Venture	Synergistic Potential	Informal Support	Reach and Reciprocity	Interactivity, Participation, Learning
Editability			Y		Y
Dynamism	Y	Y		Y	Y
Archiving					Y
Asynchronocity				Y	Y
Informality	Y	Y	Y		Y
Cost	Y		Y	Y	Y
Cultural Impact	Y	Y	Y		Y
Reciprocity	Y	Y		Y	Y
Reach	Y		Y	Y	
Ease of Use	Y	Y	Y	Y	Y

lished. For example, companies such as Microsoft use weblogging for exchange of ideas among developers. It conducts activities such as brainstorming for developing new products, troubleshooting, and customer relations. Weblogs can hence be used to accumulate ideas and knowledge and generate some synergistic output, whether it is in the form of an idea, a solution, or a product.

Informality: One of the key attributes of a community of practice is that its members interact casually. The level of interaction grows in an atmosphere of informality. Formality, demanded by most electronic communication media used today (such as bulletin boards and e-newsletters), thwarts this attempt at creating an informal atmosphere. Most of these groups are moderated and have a formal tone in their communications. The implicit informal nature of weblogging can greatly support communities of practice. For example, in the field of education, weblogs are being used to facilitate informal communication between students and professors (Stiler and Philleo 2003). Schools such as Harvard University[10] and University of California, Berkeley [11] provide weblogs to their students. Low cost, its informal tone and accessibility (blogs can be accessed through a browser) make blogs appealing to students.

Reach and Reciprocity: Members of a community of practice are accessible to other members and they engage in dialogical actions. We argue that weblogs allow for reach and reciprocity to a higher degree than other Internet communication technologies. Traditional websites, while having a global reach, do not have reciprocity. Media such as e-mail have high reciprocity but negligible reach. In contrast, weblogs, by virtue of their public and interactive attributes, not only have global reach but also facilitate

---

[10] http://blogs.law.harvard.edu/
[11] http://blog.berkeley.edu/index.jsp

multidirectional information exchange. Companies such as Yahoo and Microsoft use weblogs to reach their customers and engage in a dynamic exchange of information.

Interactivity, Participation, Learning: Communities of practice learn and grow as the level of interaction and participation of their members increases (Wenger 1998, 2000). In comparison with weblogs, media such as instant messaging, newsgroups, video conferencing and traditional websites have lower learning functions associated with their usage. In contrast, weblogging—by virtue of its archival and interactive features—is extensively used by journalists (Matheson 2004), lawyers, politicians, teachers (Stiler and Philleo 2003), and developers to retrieve and share collective knowledge. Thus, the weblogs' capacities to store information and provide multidirectional communication enable the reciprocity property of communities of practice.

4 RESEARCH APPROACH

To achieve our research objective we conducted an interpretive study (Walsham 1995) in which the unit of analysis is a corporate weblog. Because of its emphasis on meanings, we considered that an interpretive approach was the most suitable for conducting this research given the nature of our data (i.e., the content of a weblog). In this section we explain the rationale for the selection of the blog and how we interpreted the data.

4.1 Selecting the Corporation

To select the weblog we did an Internet search and looked for weblogs that were implemented by major organizations. In addition, we scanned business articles that talked about corporate weblogging (Bentley 2003; Gartenberg 2003; Jantsch 2004; Leonard 2003; Macdonald 2004; Malik 2003; Manjoo 2002; Miller 2003; Verton 2003; Weidlich 2003). Some weblogs that were mentioned frequently in the media and were found as top search results on the Internet are

- Google, http://googleblog.blogspot.com/
- Yahoo, http://www.ysearchblog.com/
- Sun Microsystems, http://blogs.sun.com/roller/main.do
- Jupiter Research, http://weblogs.jupiterresearch.com/toplevel/
- Macromedia, http://weblogs.macromedia.com/mxna/reports/categoryFeedReport/
- GM, http://gmblogs.com/
- Microsoft, http://blogs.msdn.com/

The content of these weblogs was scanned. Statistics such as their duration, central theme, and readership were observed. Microsoft was chosen because it was one of the early adopters of weblogs as a communication technology and has implemented them for a variety of applications including technical discussions, personal opinions, brainstorming, and customer support (Evers 2004; Miller 2003).

4.2 Selecting the Blog

In addition to online help, documentation, and technical support, Microsoft hosts what they call "Microsoft Technical Communities." These Communities facilitate communication exchanges through different tools such as webcasts, online chats, user groups, and weblogs. Microsoft maintains a community[12] of weblogs, which covers 129 categories such as Microsoft products, technologies, research, and applications. There are around 700 different weblogs owned by Microsoft employees. With the purpose of selecting our unit of analysis (i.e., the corporate blog), we scanned and examined the content of those blogs. A weblog called "Office Development, Security, Randomness"[13] was chosen because, using our criteria, it was representative of a corporate weblog. Like other weblogs of Microsoft communities, this weblog is authored by a developer. Topics posted by the author center around issues concerning technical aspects of his work at Microsoft, as well as personal anecdotes. Primarily, posts on the weblog include things that the author finds interesting in his line of work, and things that he thinks his readers would find useful. Hence, the readership primarily consists of people who are knowledgeable about IT product development and security. The title of the weblog, "Office Development, Security, Randomness...(But mostly randomness)," implies that the author sees the weblog as an informal means of communicating with like-minded individuals. The weblog requires a login to make posts, hence there is a control on who can post. Personal weblogs in organizations are usually required to have a disclaimer on the responsibility of posts. This weblog explicitly states that neither the primary author nor Microsoft is responsible for anything on the weblog. The posts are archived reverse chronologically and can be searched according to the post categories. The statistics of the weblog are

* Name of the weblog: Office Development, Security, Randomness...
* Number of Posts: 181
* Number of Comments: 2053
* Start date: July 2003

4.3 Interpretation

We began by reading all posts[14] and interpreting them against the backdrop of our theoretical lens. Next, we synthesized our initial interpretations in themes (Sanders 1982). This was done through a hermeneutic circle that took us back and forth from the text to theory (Klein and Myers 1999; Taylor 1971). In so doing, we classified the text into categories that corresponded to the components of the concepts of our theoretical framework. Although we found that most themes were related to those concepts, we

---

[12]http://www.microsoft.com/communities/blogs/PortalHome.mspx

[13]http://blogs.msdn.com/ptorr

[14]Our data were the threads posted in the weblog. We downloaded the content from July 2003 through September 2005 and converted it into text files.

also found recurring emergent themes such as commitment to post on behalf of the author, and the lack of explicit rules of language that lead the author to impose norms. Given the large volume of data, it is not possible to present all the quotes collected. Some representative quotes are mentioned in the next section to elucidate each theme. A summary of the themes and their relation to the data and theory are summarized in the Appendix.

5 RESULTS

We structured the themes according to what we interpreted to be the life cycle of a blog. In order to provide structure, we studied the temporal occurrence of the themes. In doing so, we found a certain sequence and identified three stages clearly demarcated in the weblog. This sequence allows us to present the themes in a coherent and systematized manner.

The first stage—the birth of a blog—represents the beginning of a new weblog. Here the author tries to establish the tone and make clear the subject matter of the blog. Certain implicit and explicit rules are set by the author at this stage. The characteristics attained by the blog at this stage are retained through the life of the blog. The second stage occurs when the weblog matures and facilitates learning and knowledge as the result of the members exchanging communications and engaging actively in discussions. At this stage, the author and the readers relate to each other on an individual level. The third stage of the blog—its death—occurs when the author loses his commitment to post regularly. We argue that this could occur due to various reasons including decline in readership of the blog or increase in work load of the author, causing him to lose motivation to expend time on the weblog. In turn, loss of motivation of the author leads to further decline in readership. This circle, we believe, leads to the death of the blog over time. Figure 1 depicts this cycle.[15]

In the rest of this section, we explain in detail the different themes associated with each stage of the lifecycle and relate them to what we considered were the most representative quotations in our data. Figure 1 summarizes this discussion.

5.1 The Birth of a Blog: Setting of Rules, Subject Matter, and Tone (Informality)

A salient attribute of a blog is its informal tone. Thus, unlike technical forums in which there are clear rules and moderators, bloggers, as suggested above, struggle in finding rules that define boundaries of what is allowed and what is not. It is clear that one of the concerns of the owner of the blog is what he is allowed to share with his readers as seen in the following quote:

---

[15]The diagram merely provides a simplified picture, and we are aware that several factors could be brought into consideration in these dynamics. However, our objective is to illustrate our findings and represent our interpretation of the phenomenon.

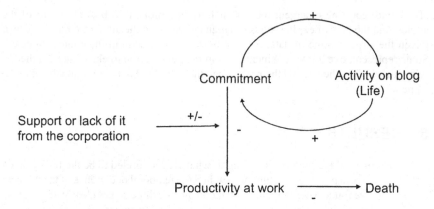

Figure 1. Life Cycle of a Corporate Blog

> *There's lots of stuff I'd like to write about, but it's not very clear if they're "permitted" topics.*

Indeed, this can be an inhibitor for posting on the blog. Another rule that we grasp from our interpretation is the need for the messages to be "legitimate."

> *Thanks to the people who leave legitimate comments on the blog.*

By legitimate, we interpret that the owner of the blog means that the messages have to be faithful to the main theme, which is of a technical nature. However, as we will see below, this does not mean that the participants do not discuss other topics in which they are interested. We found that the language of the blog is casual. This is not explicit anywhere but it is implicitly a common theme in the whole blog. This can be appreciated in the following quote:

> *Today I needed to write a fairly simple piece of code to manipulate some Excel documents, and I chose to do it in VBA. That might sound like heresy for someone who used to work on Visual Studio Tools for Office, but since I switched teams I feel no obligation to use that stuff any more ;-)*

The tone is not only friendly but also reveals interiorities of the work at Microsoft. This warmth and casual language invites people to contribute and also portrays a friendly face of the work at Microsoft. Technical knowledge is also presented in an informal and humorous manner, as illustrated in the following quote:

> *But here I present three easy ways you can disable WSH [Windows Script Host] if you so wish (ha ha, pun intended :-)).*

This relates to the attribute according to which communities of practice share information in a casual manner. We may argue here that a blog that maintains a formal and cold tone would not get too many visits. The same argument can be made about inflammatory remarks, which are not only illegitimate but also unfriendly. The owner of the blog tries to prevent flaming as it would undermine the popularity of the blog and probably deter legitimate participants:

Yes, please don't have a flame war on my blog 😊 *I will delete any flames...*

5.2 The Life of a Blog: Personal Touch—Creation of Knowledge Occurs through Dialogue (Interactivity, Participation, Learning; Collective Cooperative Venture)

We observed how participants of the blog engaged in searching for solutions. Participants' interaction and replies to posts, which were on first-name basis, facilitated arriving at technical solutions.

The other day, Karl Levinson added a comment to my previous entry about the Outlook OM. He raises some interesting points, so I thought I'd reply here...The comments from my last post are still coming in thick and fast... Thanks for being part of the solution! :-)

In the above quote we observe that the messages posted correspond to the sequence in which the topic is being discussed. It shows that the owner of the blog pays attention and reads the messages. We argue that it is essential for the blogger to demonstrate commitment to his readers. This commitment is accompanied not only by the quality of the content, but also by honesty.

*First things first: **I was wrong about uninstalling plug-ins**. Thanks to several helpful posters, you can actually do this via ...*

We can only assume that the readers and participants of the blog sympathize with the openness and honesty of a Microsoft programmer acknowledging that he has been wrong. In addition, the dialogical and personal touch of the blog is observed since the owner of the blog takes personal care of the participants in offering technical solutions.

Based on some of Nicole's feedback, I decided to write a basic app that checked your .NET security settings for you...

We found that the personal touch of the owner of the blog was key for the members to participate in posting messages. This is reflected, for example, in the fact that the blog, in addition to the main technical theme, also allows people to comment on other areas of interest of the owner of the blog, such as coffee.

As I blogged earlier (I think!) I have a rather nice espresso machine at home. You can pick one up for yourself at Whole Latte Love (that pun makes my dear *friend wince :-)) but it's a bit big (and expensive) to have one at work as well, so I took advantage of this really cool offer from illy to get a Francis Francis! X5 machine for only $175. (The catch: you have to buy a year's worth of coffee to go with it).*

Although, clearly this is not the thread that gets the majority of comments, it is, in our view a fundamental component in which the owner of the blog portrays himself as an individual, not as an official, impersonal, or even cold Microsoft employee. We argue that an impersonal blog would not become popular.

5.3 Death of a Blog: End of its Life Cycle

We argue that the dialogical nature of the communication and the personal touch and commitment of the blogger are essential for boosting participation in the blog. These are what make the blog popular. We found that there is a virtuous circle between popularity and commitment that gives life to the blog (see Figure 1). It is the popularity of the blog that makes the owner continue posting. This is illustrated in the following quote:

It would be nice to know how many people (if any) actually read this. Kind of gives one an incentive to write.

Clearly, maintaining this blog is an advantage for Microsoft for improving its image and collecting information from its customers regarding their technical problems. The downside is probably that keeping up with the popularity and expectations of this weblog requires a serious commitment in terms of time and effort on behalf of the employee. This would eventually impact the weblogger's productivity. Moreover, if the weblogger's superiors do not consider his blogging activity as a part of his job duties, the blogger might get into trouble. This in turn might result in less frequent posts. Therefore, we conjecture that one of the reasons a blog may "die" is when the owner cannot keep the level of commitment that makes a weblog popular. In other words, blogs can become victims of their own success. Though there may be other reasons that a blog might die, we argue that the ability and the motivation of the author are key for its life. The ability of the author relates to factors such as support from his organization, time available to him, and his subject knowledge on the topic of the weblog. Since these factors cannot be observed in the data (as they relate to the death of the blog), we formulate this assertion as a conjecture that would require empiric confirmation.

From the data, we observe that the motivation to post comes from the readership and feedback from the readers. When the owner does not post, readers (including other bloggers) stop visiting and posting and that is the beginning of the end. The owner of this blog, conscious of this issue, posted the following message:

Just a quick message to anyone who happens to be reading this that I'm still around.

6   IMPLICATIONS

Several implications stem from the analysis of our data. Some are theoretical, such as our proposed life cycle of a corporate blog and the themes that emerged from our interpretation. These could be subject to confirmatory studies. Moreover, it would be interesting to establish whether other types of blogs exhibit similar properties. We also found that blogs, by means of their informality and interaction, can support communities of practice. In this sense we consider that such a lens is an appropriate theoretical framework for examining blogs. As seen in our analysis, blogging is more than a mere technical phenomenon. It encompasses social and psychological aspects such as group norms and the personality of the blogger. Implicitly setting group norms and rules is vital for the community to be coherent. In terms of the personality of the blogger, we found that an openness to share some aspects of his/her work and personal life are important, as are writing and communication skills. Accordingly, blogs can facilitate social inclusion, as individuals with those particular personality traits can express their thoughts and discuss ideas with other people. Blogs are different from other similar media, such as forums and wikis, in the fact that the blogs are mostly owned by individuals. Since they eliminate social structures, such as membership, and technical barriers due to their technological attributes, such as ease of use and interactiveness (Herring et al 2005), weblogs are suitable for social inclusion on the Internet.

In terms of implications for practice, we found that a corporation interested in deploying blogs as a media of communication with their customers may gain valuable benefits. Concretely, we identify two. One is the opening of their organization and the displaying of a "human side" to their organization. This was clear in our data, particularly when the Microsoft blogger openly shared with his readers interiorities of his work and personal tastes. The other benefit we see is that organizations may gain knowledge of the perception and performance of their products. Accordingly, Microsoft would learn about the problems of their products as well as the meaning that these problems have for their customers. Furthermore, they can offer much more personalized support through blogs. Another practical implication is that managers considering supporting blogs to communicate with customers should bear in mind that employees are going to commit valuable and considerable resources to the maintenance of the blog. Therefore, encouraging the employees to blog and allowing them to spend time as part of their job function is important. As implied by the life cycle proposed in this research, the support from the corporation plays a vital role in popularity or death of a blog. These practical implications are additions to the already known considerations about privacy and confidentiality that are problematic in most new technologies.

7   LIMITATIONS AND FUTURE RESEARCH

In conceptualizing the phenomenon of blogging, we have employed a framework grounded in the theory of communities of practice. We analyzed a blog using our theoretical lens and have proposed a model that represents the life cycle of a corporate blog. Given the scope of this research, we have only succeeded in providing a holistic view of the phenomenon. However, each theme that we found can be researched in more depth. For example, elements of the proposed model can be investigated in further studies. Likewise, the social and psychological aspects of the phenomenon can be full-fledged topics for future research. Literature from the fields of social psychology, psychology, and organizational culture can be drawn upon and used as different lenses to study the same phenomenon. Another interesting line of enquiry could focus on identifying the different reasons for why organizational members decide to blog (i.e., corporate objectives, self promotion) and, once identified, studying how those reasons determine the way blogs evolve further. Thus, scholars can refer to this paper as a broad view on corporate blogging to identify potential topics with a narrower scope.

8 CONCLUSION

Internet-based practices such as blogging continue to evolve and open new possibilities for individuals and organizations. We found that the dynamism and informal attributes of blogs make them an attractive means of communication. This paper constitutes an effort to make sense of an emergent phenomenon such as blogging, whose attributes and fast growth raise a degree of perplexity to which information systems researchers cannot remain indifferent. This paper does not wish to prove that weblogs are conclusively the most effective way to enable informal communication. Sampling and statistical techniques would be needed in order to investigate that research question. Instead, we attempt to find the emergent themes in weblogs. The goal of this paper was not to develop a generalizable theory but, as Walsham (1995) and Lee and Baskerville (2003) posit, to find second order concepts as generalizations of our findings. In this paper we have articulated a set of attributes that, we argue, give blogs their unique dynamism. Moreover, we have proposed a model that depicts the possible life cycle for corporate blogs. All in all, as bloggers continue to innovate their practices and organizations adopt these practices, researchers of information systems have an exciting challenge ahead.

References

Alavi, M., and Leidner, D. E. "*Review*: Knowledge Management and Knowledge Management Systems: Conceptual Foundations and Research Issues," *MIS Quarterly* (25:1) 2001, pp. 107-136.

Bentley, R. "Blogging Touted as a New Business Tool," *Computer Weekly.com* (8), September 22, 2003 (available online at http://www.computerweekly.com/Articles/2003/09/22/197397/ Bloggingtoutedasanewbusinesstool.htm).

Blood, R. "We've Got Blog: How Weblogs are Changing Our Culture," Cambridge, MA, Perseus Publishing, 2002.

Boese, C. "The Spirit of Paulo Freire in Blogland: Struggling for a Knowledge Log Revolution," *Into the Blogosphere*, 2004 (http://blog.lib.umn.edu/blogosphere/ the_spirit_of_paulo_freire.html).

Boland, R. J., and Tenkasi, R. V. "Perspective Making and Perspective-Taking in Communities of Knowing," *Organization Science* (6:4), 1995, pp. 350-372.

Bowen, F., and Blackmon, K. "Spirals of Silence: The Dynamic Effects of Diversity on Organizational Voice," *Journal of Management Studies* (40:6), 2003, pp. 1393-1417.

Brown, J. S., and Duguid, P. "Organizational Knowledge," *California Management Review* (40:3), 1998, pp. 90-111.

Brown, J. S., and Duguid, P. "Organizational Learning and Communities-of-Practice: Toward a Unified View of Working, Learning, and Innovation," *Organization Science* (2:1), 1991, pp. 40-57.

Cole, R. E. "Introduction," *California Management Review* (45:3), 1998, pp. 15-21.

Davenport, T. H., and Prusak, L. *Working Knowledge: How Organizations Manage What They Know*, Boston, MA: Harvard Business School Press , 1997.

Evers, J. "Microsoft's Channel 9 Gets Social with Developers," *ComputerWorld*, April 6, 2004 (available online at http://www.computerworld.com/developmenttopics/development/story/ 0,10801,91979,00.html).

Gartenberg, M. "Blogging for Fun and Profit," *ComputerWorld*, March 3, 2003 (available online at http://www.computerworld.com/developmenttopics/development/webdev/story/ 0,10801,78895,00.html).

Herring, S. C., Scheidt, L. A., Wright, E., and Bonus, S. "Weblogs as a Bridging Genre" *Information Technology and People* (18:2), 2005, pp. 142-171.

Jantsch, J. "Blogging for Business—Great Reasons for Every Business to Start a Weblog," *Webpronews.com*, March 24, 2004 (available online at http://www.webpronews.com/ ebusiness/smallbusiness/wpn-2-20040324BloggingForBusinessGreatReasonsFor EveryBusinessToStartAWeblog.html).

Karahanna, E., and Limayem, M. "E-Mail and V-Mail Usage: Generalizing Across Technologies," *Journal of Organizational Computing and Electronic Commerce* (10:1), 2000, pp. 49-66.

Kumar, R., Novak, P., Raghavan, S., and Tomkins, A. "On the Bursty Evolution of Blogspace," in *Proceedings of the Twelfth International World Wide Web Conference*, Budapest, Hungary, 2003, pp. 568-576.

Klein, H. K., and Myers, M. D. "A Set of Principles for Conducting and Evaluating Interpretive Field Studies in Information Systems," *MIS Quarterly* (23:1), 1999, pp. 67-94.

Lave, J. "Situating Learning in Communities of Practice," in L. B. Resnick, J. M. Levine, and S. D. Teasley (eds.), *Perspectives on Socially Shared Cognition*, Washington, DC: American Psychological Association, 1991.

Lave, J., and Wenger, E. *Situated Learning: Legitimate Peripheral Participation*, Cambridge, UK: Cambridge University Press, 1991.

Lee, A. S., and Baskerville, R. L. "Generalizing Generalizability in Information Systems Research," *Information Systems Research* (14:3), 2003, pp. 221-243.

Leonard, B. "Blogs Begin to Make Mark on Corporate Communications," *HR Magazine* (48:9), 2003, p. 30.

Lucas, J. W., Younts, C. W., Lovaglia, M. J., and Markovsky, B. "Line of Power in Exchange Networks," *Social Forces* (80:1), 2001, pp. 185-214.

Macdonald, N. "The Future of Weblogging," *The Register*, April 18, 2004 (available online at http://www.theregister.co.uk/2004/04/18/blogging_future/).

Malik, O. "Blogging for Dollars," *Business 2.0* (4:10), 2003, p. 40.

Manjoo, F. "Flash: Blogging Goes Corporte," *Wired Magazine*, May 9, 2002 (available online at http://www.wired.com/news/culture/0,1284,52380,00.html).

Matheson, D. "Weblogs and the Epistemology of the News: Some Trends in Online Journalism," *New Media & Society* (6:4), 2004, pp. 443-468.

Miller, R. "Blogging for Business," *EContent* (26:10), 2003, pp. 30-34.

Ngwenyama, O. K., and Lee, A. S. "Communication Richness in Electronic Mail: Critical Social theory and Contextuality of Meaning," *MIS Quarterly* (21:2), 1997, pp. 145-167.

Nonaka, I. "A Dynamic Theory of Organizational Knowledge Creation," *Organization Science* (5:1), 1994, pp. 14-37.

Nonaka, I., and Takeuchi, H. *The Knowledge- Creating Company: How Japanese Companies Create the Dynamics of Innovation*, New York: Oxford University Press, 1995.

Palser, B. "Free to Blog?," *American Journalism Review* (25:5), 2003, pp. 62-63.

Rosencrance, L. "Blogs Bubble Into Business," *ComputerWorld*, January 26, 2004 (available online at http://www.computerworld.com/softwaretopics/software/story/0,10801,89283,00.html).

Sanders, P. "Phenomenology: A New Way of Viewing Organizational Research," *Academy of Management Review* (7:3), 1982, pp. 353-360.

Schiano, D. J., Nardi, B. A., Gumbrecht, M., and Swartz, L. "Blogging by the Rest of Us," in *Proceedings of the Conference on Human Factors in Computing Systems* New York: ACM Press, 2004, pp. 1143-1146.

Short, J., Williams, E., and Christie, B. *The Social Psychology of Telecommunications*, London: John Wiley & Sons, 1976.

Stiler, G. M., and Philleo, T. "Blogging and Blogspots: An Alternative Format for Encouraging Reflective Practice Among Preservice Teachers," *Education* (123:4), 2003, pp 789-797.

Suitt, H., Weinberger, D., Samuelson, P., Ozzie, R., and Motameni, E. "A Blogger in Their Midst," *Harvard Business Review* (81:9), 2003, pp. 30-40.

Taulli, T. "Tapping into the Blogosphere," *Forbes*, January 25, 2006 (available online at http://www.forbes.com/2006/01/24/google-apple-microsoft-cx_tt_0125straightup.html?partner=tentech_newsletter).

Taylor, C. "Interpretation and the Sciences of Man," *Review of Metaphysics* (25:71), 1971, pp. 3-51.

Twist, J. "US Blogger Fired by Her Airline," *BBCNews*, November 3, 2004 (available online at http://news.bbc.co.uk/1/hi/technology/3974081.stm).

Twist, J. "Looming Pitfalls of Work Blogs," *BBCNews*, January 3, 2005 (available online at http://news.bbc.co.uk/2/hi/technology/4115073.stm).

Verton, D. "Blogs Play a Role in Homeland Security," *ComputerWorld*, May 12, 2003 (available online at http://www.computerworld.com/developmenttopics/websitemgmt/story/0,10801,81115,00.html).

Walsham, G. "Interpretive Case Studies in IS Research: Nature and Method," *European Journal of Information Systems* (4), 1995, pp. 74-81.

Weidlich, T. "Executive Life: The Corporate Blog Is Catching On," *The New York Times*, June 22, 2003 (available online at http://www.nytimes.com/).

Wenger, E. *Communities of Practice: Learning, Meaning, and Identity*, Cambridge, UK: Cambridge University Press, 1998.

Wenger, E. "Communities of Practice and Social Learning Systems," *Organization* (7:2), 2000, pp. 225-247.

Wenger, E., McDermott, R., and Snyder, W. *Cultivating Communities of Practice: A Guide to Managing Knowledge*, Boston: Harvard Business School Press, 2002.

Wenger, E., and Snyder, W. "Communities of Practice: The Organizational Frontier," *Harvard Business Review* (78:1), 2000, pp. 139-146.

Yates, J., and Orlikowski, W. J. "Genres of Organizational Communication: An Approach to Studying Communication and Media," *Academy of Management Review* (17:2), 1992, pp 299-326.

About the Authors

Leiser Silva is an Assistant Professor in the Decision and Information Sciences Department at the C. T. Bauer College of Business, University of Houston. He holds a Ph.D. in information systems from the London School of Economics and Political Science. His current research examines issues of power and politics in the adoption and implementation of information systems. In addition, he is looking at managerial aspects of information systems, specifically contextual and institutional factors as well as knowledge management systems. His work has been published or is forthcoming in journals such as *MIS Quarterly, The Information Systems Journal, Journal of the Association for Information Systems, Communications of the Association for Information Systems, European Journal of Information Systems, Information Society, Journal of Information Technology for Development,* and *Information Technology and People.* He has served as an Associate Editor for *MIS Quarterly.* Leiser can be reached at lsilva@uh.edu.

Elham Mousavidin is a Doctoral student in the Decision and Information Sciences Department at the C. T. Bauer College of Business, University of Houston. She received her MBA from C. T. Bauer College of Business in December 2002. Her current research interest lies in the area of Web-based communications and Web-enabled communities. She has been involved in research on Weblogs and their potential applications in organizations and is working on more papers on this topic with her coauthors. Elham can be reached at: emousavi@mail.uh.edu.

Lakshmi Goel is a Doctoral student in the Decision and Information Sciences Department at the C. T. Bauer College of Business, University of Houston. She holds a Master's in Computer Science from the University of Houston, and a Master's in Computer Applications from the University of Pune, India. Her current research looks at organizational learning and knowledge management through information systems. She is interested in strategic, socio-psychological, sociological, and managerial facets of information systems. Lakshmi can be reached at lgoel@uh.edu.

Appendix: Content Analysis

Quote	Interpretation	How the Interpretation Relates to Cop
1. "So here it goes (Jeff, I **promise** this will be a short entry! Honest! Ha ha ha)" 2. "But here I present three easy ways you can disable WSH if you so wish (ha ha, pun intended :-)):" 3. "Today I needed to write a fairly simple piece of code to manipulate some Excel documents, and I chose to do it in VBA. That might sound like heresy for someone who used to work on Visual Studio Tools for Office, but since I switched teams I feel no obligation to use that stuff any more ;-)" 4. "Btw, didn't your mother teach you to always save to disk instead of running files from the online location! tut tut! (posted by a reader)" 5. "People need to be trained about security issues before they can effectively design, write, test, or document a software product. I am sure that some readers might chuckle to themselves here and make a snide remark about how 'Everybody should know about buffer over-runs (BOs) by now!' but there are two things I want to say about that" 6. "Here's a quick story about one such rule that we fixed before the CLR shipped. I'm warning you -- it's obscure and boring and you'll never get the 5 minutes of your life back if you keep reading, but someone wanted me to post about such things so here goes"	Communication is not formal even though the content is.	Informal support
1. "Thanks for being part of the solution! :-)" 2. "This post wouldn't have been possible without all of the great work people at Microsoft are doing around thread modeling" 3. "Thanks to several helpful posters, you can actually do this via Tools -> Options -> Downloads -> Plugins and clicking on the little blue arrows" 4. "(Thanks to Mike and Robert and the other folk who gave this a once-over before posting; any errors are still mine though ;-))"	Readers help at arriving at a solution. The knowledge presented in the post is a cumulative result from various sources.	Synergistic potential

Quote	Interpretation	How the Interpretation Relates to Cop
5. "As a lover of open source and a lover of Firefox, I'd like to say thanks for your helpful suggestions. I hope Firefox will take them on board"		
1. "It would be nice to know how many people (if any) actually read this. Kind of gives one an incentive to write." 2. "I thought everyone had stopped reading but for better or worse I checked and there were a few hundred fresh … comments on my Firefox post" 3. "Only have discovered your blog recently, but I'm turning into an avid reader!"	Author aims at a wide (global) audience for what he has to say. Readers reciprocate.	Reach and Reciprocity
1. "The other day, Karl Levinson added a comment to my previous entry about the Outlook OM. He raises some interesting points, so I thought I'd reply here" 2. "First things first: **I was wrong about uninstalling plug-ins**. Thanks to several helpful posters, you can actually do this via …" 3. "Based on some of Nicole's feedback, I decided to write a basic app that checked your .NET security settings for you…" 4. "As I blogged earlier (I think!) I have a rather nice espresso machine at home. You can pick one up for yourself at Whole Latte Love (that pun makes my dear friend wince) but it's a bit big (and expensive) to have one at work as well, so I took advantage of this really cool offer from illy to get a Francis Francis! X5 machine for only $175. (The catch: you have to buy a year's worth of coffee to go with it). 5. "The other day Eric Wilson asked how to ensure his code never ran with FullTrust. I replied that the "best" way was to refuse permissions you didn't want, and then Nicole Calinoiu replied that maybe requesting optional permissions was better." 6. "Just wanted to let you know that your presentation on VSTO and VSTO2 were awesome... the level of content, detail, and	Interaction by the author with readers at a first name basis. The author receives feedback about posts and rectifies errors he had made. Author adds a personal touch by giving anecdotes from his life.	Personal touch, Interactivity, Participation, Learning; Collective cooperative venture

Quote	Interpretation	How the Interpretation Relates to Cop
reasoning was very much appreciated. Looking forward to your security talk on Office!"		
7. "But, I thought to myself, one way to share some of my experience with all you great folks would be to have a series of 'Dear Diary' entries where (in the grandest tradition of trashy magazines) I will publish letters from "readers" who have sent me their security questions, and provide my answers or advice. Some of these questions will come from real engagements I have had at Microsoft, some will come from questions I've had from external customers in the past, and (maybe) some will come from questions that **you** send in. Then I won't have to fake it any more! :-) Anyway, we'll see how it goes... I'd love to hear your feedback."		
1. "Just a quick message to anyone who happens to be reading this that I'm still around"	Author feels obligated to post regularly	Commitment
2. "A couple of people have asked me about this... I just need to clean up a few things in my 'copious spare time' and then I'll post it to GotDotNet -- I promise!"	Author feels obligated to reply to readers requests	
3. "Sorry for the delay :-("	Author feels obligated to let his readers know about his	
4. "I'll be off-line for a few days, so no comments will get moderated until I return."	absence	
1. "There's lots of stuff I'd like to write about, but it's not very clear if they're "permitted" topics."	Implicit rules and norms set by the author.	Lack of explicit rules
2. "Yes, please don't have a flame war on my blog 🙂 I will delete any flames..."		
3. "Thanks to the people who leave *legitimate* comments on the blog"		
4. "Thanks to everyone who didn't just swear at me (and if I didn't approve your comment, it was because it had too much profanity in it)"		

21 TAKING PEOPLE OUT OF THE NETWORK: A Deconstruction of "Your Next IT Strategy"

Elizabeth Davidson
University of Hawaii, Manoa
Honolulu, HI U.S.A.

Mike Chiasson
Lancaster University
Bailrigg, Lancaster, UK

Sachin Ruikar
University of Hawaii, Manoa
Honolulu, HI U.S.A.

Abstract   *Web services are frequently discussed as "the next big thing" in information technology architecture. The picture painted by pundits, practitioners, IT vendors, and academics is appealing technically: Web service applications "exposed" to one another through standard protocols, navigating through an open infrastructure to search out counterparts over the Internet, with "seamless" integration across business processes and enterprises, without human intervention. However, the vision of a computing architecture that takes "people out of the network" has troubling social implications. In this paper, we utilize deconstruction as an analytic approach to examine a paper that promotes Web services, entitled "Your Next IT Strategy" (Hagel and Brown 2001). Our analytic purpose is to generate interpretations of the text that surface assumptions about how this IT innovation may influence the social organization of IT-related work. Our interpretation suggests that the Web services architecture could contribute to reproduction and consolidation of control among already powerful socio-economic actors, while restructuring and automating the work of IT professionals and other knowledge workers. We conclude with a discussion of deconstruction as a research approach to investigate issues of social inclusion and IT innovation.*

Please use the following format when citing this chapter:

Davidson, E., Chiasson, M., and Ruikar, S., 2006, in IFIP International Federation for Information Processing, Volume 208, Social Inclusion: Societal and Organizational Implications for Information Systems, eds. Trauth, E., Howcroft, D., Butler, T., Fitzgerald, B., DeGross, J., (Boston: Springer), pp. 317-332.

1   INTRODUCTION AND MOTIVATION

The term *Web services* has numerous definitions, most referring to business applications that are built using a set of open, standard protocols and that are shared over the Internet among business processes within and across enterprises. Beyond the technical definitions, the phrase has become an *organizing vision* (Swanson and Ramiller 1997) of how IT assets and business functions can be organized and managed. For some, this organizing vision extends beyond the IT function to the reorganization of business enterprises as loosely-coupled value chains (Hagel and Brown 2001).

In technical terms, the World Wide Web Consortium defines Web services as software applications designed to support machine-to-machine interaction over a network (http://www.w3.org/2002/ws/Activity). There are a number of open standards related to the Web services architecture that will make this possible. Extensible mark-up language (XML) provides a meta-language to create a shared and common structure for the exchange of data between applications. SOAP (simple object access protocol) provides a standard approach to transmitting XML-coded data between different systems and a method to invoke remote applications. WSDL (Web services definition language) is a protocol to describe Web services in a standard, machine-readable format. UDDI (universal description, discovery, and integration service) is a mechanism for applications to dynamically find and use Web services programs. These and other Web services standards are being developed by industry consortia and major IT vendors (see Table 1).

Although Web services technology is an important area of research, our interest in this paper is the purported social and organizational implications of Web services. Consider the following description of the Web services vision:

> The Web services vision is grand: a universal set of communications protocols to enable computer systems and business processes to seek each other out over the Internet, lonely hearts style, and have deep, meaningful interactions with no human intervention. ("The Battle for Web Services," C. Koch, *CIO Magazine*, October 1, 2003)

Table 1. Key Standards Setting Organizations for Web Services

World Wide Web Consortium (W3C) (http://www.w3.org/Consortium/) Firms represented on Advisory Board: ILOG, Boeing, HP, Oracle, Sun Microsystems, IBM, MITRE, Nokia, SAP AG
Web Services Interoperability (WS-I) (www.ws-i.org) Board of Directors: SAP, Intel, BEA Systems, Fujitsu, IBM, Sun Microsystems, HP, Microsoft, Oracle, Webmethods
Organization for the Advancement of Structured Information Standards (Oasis) (www.oasis-open.org) Board of Directors: BEA Systems, Fujitsu Software, OASIS, Center for Document Engineering, UC Berkeley, Sun Microsystems, Nokia, General Motors, Microsoft, Oracle, SAP AG, IBM

This quote illustrates a common theme in Web service discussions: the potential to automate human activity by creating and operating autonomous computer applications. Despite considerable attention to the loss of IT work from Western economies to India, China, and other lower-cost labor markets, "off-shoring" accounts for a small percentage of the IT economy (Carmel and Tjia 2005). A much more significant influence on the future of the IT workforce will be the automation of both IT and non-IT work using computer automation. According to one of the chief architects at Microsoft, outsourcing has historically been a prelude to software automation and mechanization, and future IT work, though less plentiful, will be in the automation of business processes and of IT work (Murphy 2003).

Our purpose is to critically examine the visions motivating automation of work through IT innovations, such as the Web services architecture, in order to understand how humans might be "taken out of the network" (Hagel and Brown 2001, p. 107). One only has to look at the struggles between IT vendors, anxious to shape the IT marketplace to their own advantage (Koch 2003), or the hard political battles fought within industries and organizations to define and shape IT standards, to realize that people are still very much part of "the network." However, the ways in which humans influence the design and use of technologies can be transformed by such organizing visions for IT innovations. Examining these visions brings attention to the potential for inclusion or exclusion of different groups involved with and affected by IT.

To investigate these issues, we utilize deconstruction as an analytic method. Deconstruction involves a critical reading of texts to reveal alternative interpretations that surface and challenge dominant elements and interpretations (Martin 1990). In this paper, we present our deconstruction of an article that promotes a vision for Web services, in order to expose underlying tensions concerning the role of human actors in the development and application of this IT innovation in this discourse. What we reveal is an antipathy to human activity that venerates automation over socio-technical design and the promotion of immediate action by those already in power—executive management and large IT vendors and firms.

In the next section, we provide a brief discussion of deconstruction. We then describe the approach to our deconstructive reading and analysis of this management text. We focus our analysis on *différance* and *supplement* strategies that include technical and exclude social elements. To highlight alternative socio-technical possibilities, we draw on the concept of *potentiality* (Feenberg 2002) in reconstructing a passage of the text, highlighting the social and ethical choices that might be made within the IT architecture. We conclude by discussing the implications for practice and the contributions of deconstruction in researching inclusion and exclusion issues in IS texts.

2 A BRIEF INTRODUCTION TO DECONSTRUCTION

Deconstruction is a form of critical reading of a text, often associated with the literary critiques of Jacque Derrida (1973, 1977, 1982), in which hidden and alternative interpretations of the text's meaning are surfaced. Deconstruction assumes that speech and writing are as much *performative* (i.e., promises and acts) as *declarative* (i.e., factual descriptions) (Royle 2003). There is often an unstated and unstable relationship between the two, which allows multiple interpretations and critique (Royle 2003).

Acknowledging the difficulty in identifying the key tenets of deconstruction (i.e., centering), we suggest one important purpose is to expose dominating interpretations of texts (Royle 2003). Domination is achieved by our inclination to privilege language as natural and factual (i.e., *logocentricism*) and is challenged by disturbing the normal and exploring the excluded possibilities in texts (de-centering) (Royle 2003). In doing so, deconstruction pursues an emancipatory project to uncover excluded possibilities in the text (Norris 2000). A deconstructive reading does not aim to produce a simple, unified, or "true" interpretation but instead reveals the excluded possibilities hidden by the text's dominant interpretation. It thus reveals "power operating in structures of thinking and behavior that previously seemed devoid of power relations" (White 1986, p. 421, quoted in Martin 1990, p. 340).

One approach to a deconstructive reading is to explore *différance*. This term incorporates the idea of "differing," or contrast, and "deferring," or giving way to. *Différance* is represented as dichotomies, which on the surface appear to be natural but in fact privilege one element over the other. For example, in American culture, being *young* is valued over being *old*, as is evident in cultural texts such as movies, television programs, music, and advertisement. The old *differs* from the young and also *defers* to the young in these texts. Related to *différance* is *supplement* (Beath and Orlikowski 1994; Royle 2003), where the privileged element of the dichotomy shares common roots with and depends on the deferred element (*supplement*): the *old* were once *young*; the *old* create and sustain the *young*; thus, *old* is a supplement to *young* in this context.

Deconstruction cannot be reduced to technique and instead requires close reading of the text in context (Kilduff 1993, p. 16); however, a variety of techniques to assist with deconstruction have been identified. Occurrences of both *différance* and *supplement* can be exposed through a deconstructive reading of the text, in which the reader explores words, their position, and their possible meanings. Other techniques include examining the margins of a text such as footnotes or parenthetical expressions, dichotomies, metaphors, double entrendre, tautologies, and silences (unacknowledged ideas or concepts) to expose subordinated elements (Beath and Orlikowski 1994; Martin 1990).

In management studies, deconstruction has been used as an analytic approach to examine gender conflicts in organizational life (Martin 1990), the positivist agenda in organizational theory (Kuduff 1993), and limitations of information systems methodologies (Beath and Orlikowski 1994; Watson and Wood-Harper 1996). Texts drawn from management literatures are analyzed to surface inconsistencies in the text, which may reflect conflicts in the social world to which the text refers. Although seldom used in managerial research thus far, such works can be influential if they achieve what Golden-Biddle and Locke (1993) refer to as criticality by bringing the reader to a deeper perspective on the phenomena examined. Beath and Orlikowski's (1994) deconstruction of a systems development methodology highlighted contradictory attitudes about the users' participation in systems development. This paper has been widely cited in IS research, suggesting its themes resonated with researchers studying user participation.

In this paper, we use deconstruction to examine a text that promotes an IT innovation (Web services) to explore themes of exclusion and inclusion of people. Our goal is not to provide answers about the future (unlike the text we deconstruct) but to raise questions about the social consequences of the dominant organizing vision in this text and the *potentiality* of alternative social outcomes (Feenburg 2002) that might be realized through this innovation. In doing so, we question the dichotomy of social and technical by considering the social nature of technical architectures (Bloomfield 1992; Watson and Wood-Harper 1996).

3   RESEARCH APPROACH AND METHODS

We selected the article, "Your Next IT Strategy," by John Hagel and John Seely Brown, for this deconstruction exercise because we found it to be a compelling example of management discourse on Web services, a highly touted IT innovation. The article presents a high-level vision, written by well-known and respected technology strategists, of how the Web services technical architecture will be applied in business practices. This vision is directed to executives, who are the target audience for *Harvard Business Review*. Although the article apparently is well known,[1] we chose this article based not on its influence among executives but because of the article's assertion that "taking people out of the network" (p. 109) is a key element of the "next IT strategy." This suggested that the text would provide an interesting source for themes of social inclusion and exclusion related to Web services.

To go about the deconstruction, we followed the process outlined by Beath and Orlikowski (1994), beginning with each author doing several close readings of the text to identify themes of interest. We focused on *différance*, that is, dichotomous relationships that underlie the text's discursive structure, and *supplement*, the ways in which the subordinate element in a dichotomous relationship supplements or makes possible the privileged element. We shared our interpretations to refine our analytic focus on emerging themes of inclusion and exclusion. Table 2 summarizes themes we addressed and provides examples.

In the next iteration, we again examined the text line-for-line, reassessing each statement's relevance to these themes. We utilized other analytic techniques, such as scrutinizing metaphors and identifying non sequiturs to examine how *différance* and *supplement* are represented. Table 3 summarizes the techniques that we employed and provides brief examples. The results of this analytic process are described in the following section.

---

[1]A search of Google's scholarly database (scholar.google.com) identified more than 90 citations to this paper in academic publications and a Web of Science search identified 16 citations (as of January 2006). A narrow search of Google's full database (using the paper's exact title and last name of authors) revealed over 9,500 mentions of the paper in other business publications, blogs, websites, and so on.

Table 2. Themes of *Différance* and *Supplement* in the Deconstruction Analysis

Différance	Supplement
CHANGE: "a steady stream of new, Internet-based services will come on-line...all your old assumptions about IT management will be overturned" (p. 106)	**STATUS QUO**: "In supplying these functions, traditional companies have an important advantage" (p. 113)
NEW: "The New Architecture" (p. 106)	**OLD**: "Build on your existing systems" (p. 110)
OPEN: "openness and modularity" (p. 106)	**CLOSED**: "existing application is left intact but is 'exposed'" (p. 110)
OUTSOURCE: "shifting responsibility for maintaining systems to outside providers" (p. 108)	**INSOURCE**: "The distinction between users and suppliers of Web services will fade" (p. 113)
FREEDOM: "Companies will no longer find themselves stuck with outdated or mediocre applications and hardware" (p. 108)	**CONSTRAINT**: "A robust service grid is vital to accelerating and broadening the potential impact of Web services. Without it, Web services will remain relatively marginal to the enterprise" (p. 106)
AUTOMATION: "applications will be able to talk freely with other applications, without costly reprogramming" (p. 109)	**HUMAN ACTIVITY**: "Traditional distributors spend years learning the shades of meaning used by different buyers and sellers ...it is only then the distributor will have the knowledge and the authority to create a standard rating system" (p. 112)

4   A DECONSTRUCTIVE READING OF "YOUR NEXT IT STRATEGY"

The following sections present our analysis of this text. We organize our own text around the six themes outlined in Table 2. The first section considers each theme in terms of *différance*; the second section illustrates how *supplement* is present in the text.

4.1 Themes of *Différance*

The text of "Your Next IT Strategy" begins with an assertion that Web services are a new IT innovation that, unlike the innovations in the so-called "dot.com boom," will change the way companies manage their IT resources, the types of business opportunities they will pursue, and the way their businesses will be organized. The *différance* of *change* and *status quo* presents a call to action and a warning to the reader that "your

Table 3. Analytic Strategies for Deconstruction

Analytic Strategy	Examples from "Your Next IT Strategy"
Dismantling a dichotomy	"The Web services architecture is completely different" (p. 106) (This new and completely different architecture depends on existing architectures and IT capabilities to be realized.)
Attending to disruptions and contradictions	"Taking the people out of the network, the architecture will enable connections between applications—both within and across enterprises—to be managed automatically" (p. 109) (Humans create and operate the standards, protocols and applications that permit automation.)
Scrutinizing naturalness claims or arguments	"Shared meaning will naturally increase as the use of the Web services architecture expands" (p. 113) ("Meaning" is synonymous with standardized definitions that must be "hashed out" through human effort.)
Examining silences	"big staffs to keep everything up and running" (p. 106) (Workers who create IT capabilities are referred to only as burdens to be shed.)
Focusing on marginalized elements	"Big Changes for your IT Department" (p. 108) (Implications for IT professionals are put in a "sidebar" panel; only the CIO's role is considered.)
Interpreting metaphors for multiple meanings	"restrictive enterprise silos" (p. 106) (ERP and other integrated systems are "silos" that prohibit interaction.)
Analyzing double-entrendres	"In the process, many companies will find themselves turned inside out, with their formally well-guarded core capabilities visible and accessible to all" (p. 113) (Turning inside out is both "desirable" and threatening.)

Adapted from Martin (1990, p. 355, Figure 1) and Beath and Orlikowski (1994, p. 356, Table 2).

old assumptions about IT management will be overturned" (p. 106). At the same time, there are promises that change will "create substantial benefits...without high-risk, big-bang approaches," and offers instead "immediate efficiency gains" (p. 106). The benefits of change are so "compelling" (p. 112) that resistance appears to be futile.

The change to Web services depends on *différance* of the *new* IT architecture and the *old* IT architecture. *Old* IT is referred to as a "mishmash of disparate systems," "data silos," "massively complex," "hodgepodge," "inflexible," and "fiendishly difficult to change," all in one paragraph (p. 106). Even relatively recent systems are characterized as "restrictive enterprise silos." In contrast, the *new* IT (Web services) is "open," "modular," "less risky," "efficient," "easy," and provides the "best tool for the job at hand" (p. 108).

The *new* IT architecture will be realized through *open* rather than *closed* technology, through an array of open standards. An "open standard" is a contradiction in terms, because a standard defines the normal, expected, permissible, and thus is closed to other possibilities. In the case of Web services and other Internet protocols, *open* could mean open to inspection and use by all IT vendors and business organizations, in contrast to the *old*, proprietary IT architectures that were "sealed" from other systems and users (customers, suppliers, competitors, or the merely curious). Despite important and pronounced social and organization change resulting from the technology, the *open* architecture of Web service standards is explained very briefly in the text, then set aside in a colorful diagram ("An Overview of Web Services," p. 107). The section presents a very high-level description composed of acronyms and unexplained terms. The high-level nature of this description leaves the *open* architecture *closed* to the reader, suggesting the reader need only *look over* rather than *look into* the architecture.

The text proclaims that the *openness* of the *new* IT architecture makes possible major *changes* by turning "IT assets," and ultimately the organization, "inside out." Again, the *différance* of *out-sourcing* and *in-sourcing* is dramatic. What are *in-sourced* are "rigid business processes" that lock a company in "unit silos" and "enterprise silos" (p. 106), preventing the company from adjusting to change, and burdening the company with unnecessary investments in humans and computers. *Outsourcing*, on the other hand, reduces the need to invest in internal assets by making it possible to lease the *new* and abandon the *old*.

The leasing of IT processing capability (and ultimately business process capability) is possible through the *new* and *open* market that Web services will provide. The metaphor of the Swiss Army knife (p. 108) is perplexing here. The *in-sourced* IT application, like the Swiss Army knife, "does a lot of things, but it may not do any of them particularly well" (p. 108). In the case of Web services, highly specialized applications will be leased as needed. However, the Swiss Army knife is a handy little tool, much lighter and easier to carry than hammers, corkscrews, scissors, and so on, as campers or soldiers might agree. Equating the burdensome *old*, *closed* IT application with a small, flexible, and handy tool—the quintessential definition of a Web service application—appears as a contradiction that disrupts the text's logic.

The *change* that the *new*, *open*, *out-source-able* IT architecture will bring also gives the company *freedom* from the *constraint* of the *old* architecture. The language here implies a type of interorganizational promiscuity and youth. The firm engages in flexible, changeable "loose couplings" (p. 109) with outside service providers with little risk or commitment and dismisses the *old* as "out of date or mediocre" (p. 108). Instead, the firm can "plug-and-play" with the most up-to-date technology available to remain flexible and competitive (p. 108).

Freedom from the *constraint* of the *old* IT architecture implies that the firm is also free from the *constraints* of *human activity* the *old* IT entailed. In fact, flesh-and-blood humans are largely absent from the text. The *automation* of the *new*, *open*, *outsourced* market of Web services "reduces the need for manual work" and "the need for hiring numerous IT specialists" (p. 108). This is desirable, because human systems are "inefficient, slow, and mistake ridden" (p. 109). *Automation*, in contrast, is efficient, flexible, and simple. Automated applications will "talk freely with other applications" (p. 109) and the company can avoid the pitfalls of human activity, as the Web services architecture takes "people out of the network" (p. 109).

What *human activity* will be involved in the new IT architecture? Individual humans have no articulated role to play in the Web services architecture in the text, except as customers whose needs will be fulfilled. (We suppose the *automation* process will be complete when the customer is also a Web service.) The firm's senior managers appear to be needed to oversee leasing Web service applications from the "best" third-party providers or to direct development of the firm's own Web service applications. These managers will only need to ask questions about the firm's implementation of the Web services architecture (p. 109). However, the people available to provide responses are absent from the text. The only IT professional mentioned is the CIO (p. 108), who will be too occupied as a "strategist," "entrepreneur," "knowledge broker," "relationship manager," and "negotiator" to do any planning, designing, or coding of Web Service applications. (Perhaps the senior managers will have to question the Web services applications directly, assuming that these questions can be rendered meaningful in XML.)

Despite this absence of humans, we do see in the text a continued and heightened role for large IT vendors: the "new singers" of the "chorus of promises" about Web services are the "big providers of computer hardware, software and services" (p. 105). These vendors and large firms like GM are developing the standards and protocols (see Table 1) and leading the call to action that *change* requires: "The early movers like Merrill Lynch, GM, Dell play key roles by providing their business partners with compelling reasons to use Web services" (p. 112). That is, Web services will apparently be imposed on smaller firms by these dominant firms. "Traditional companies have an important advantage" (p. 113), not only because they have the resources to invest in Web services and the market power to compel other firms, but they also have the name recognition and legitimacy to supplement the "trust" promised by the Web services "service grid." Citibank is cited as an example on page 113 of how an established firm used its name recognition to establish dominance in online financial transactions.

4.2 Themes of *Supplement*

Having seen how *différance* excludes *old, closed, in-sourcing, constraint*, and *human activity*, we now consider how *supplement* reintroduces these subordinated elements back into the text, augmenting and sometimes replacing the naturalized and dominating elements.

First, the dramatic *change* in IT infrastructure depends on the power and influence of the major IT vendors and the cadre of large, powerful firms that compel others to switch to Web services, as we note above. That is, it appears that the *changed* world depends on the *status quo*. The *new* IT architecture itself is too immature and will require "years of investment and refinement...before a mature, stable architecture is in place" (p. 109). To transition to this *new* world, the *old* IT applications—inefficient, inflexible, and burdensome as they may be—will be renewed through a process called "node enablement," which "is often as simple as creating an explicit record of the connection specifications of an application...along with the application's name, its Internet location, and procedures for connecting with it" (p. 110). In computer science parlance, Web services become simply a standardized interface "wrapper" around a propriety software module, allowing what has been hopelessly *closed* to become delightfully *open*: "the existing application is left intact but is 'exposed' so that it can be found and accessed by other applications in the Web services architecture" (p. 110).

Despite an urgency to *outsource*, in order to move not only IT applications but business functions to "the edge," firms are advised to move cautiously, learning "what works and what doesn't" and resisting the urge to "engage with too many partners too fast" (p. 111). As a result, the strategies for implementing Web services are incremental, involving "edge" systems that are already connected to outside customers and suppliers (p. 110). Eventually, distinctions between *in-sourcing* and *out-sourcing* disappear, as "the distinctions between users and suppliers of Web services will fade" and "over time, the location of particular capabilities—whether inside or outside the walls of any company—will become less important" (p. 113).

As *change* is built upon the *status quo*, *old* supplements *new*, *closed* become *open*, and *in-sourcing* and *out-sourcing* coexist, we see that the *freedom* promised by the Web services chorus (p. 105) depends on a surrender to the *constraints* of the service grid: "the importance of the service grid will become increasingly apparent...without the security, reliability, and performance auditing that service grid utilities can provide to their customers, few enterprises will be willing to offer, much less subscribe to, such mission-critical services" (p. 113). In the depiction of the Web services architecture (p. 107), the service grid is a governing and autonomous system to which companies submit: it facilitates, orchestrates, determines correct ways of interacting, ensures reliability, monitors performance to ascertain conformance, "assures users of Web services that they will obtain agreed-upon levels of performance and will be compensated for damages if performance falls below these levels" (p. 107), as well as bills and ensures prompt and full payment. It is the legislative, executive, and judicial functions combined, and all, we are to assume, highly automated.

The text is largely silent about where this governing function will reside and who will control it, noting only that third-party vendors (the big IT suppliers) will provide the service grid and thus control the Web services infrastructure, further consolidating their power and that of their close partners. The text is also silent about how these governmental functions will be carried out by automated agents. Will these automated programs have programmed features that allow them to punish other automated programs for noncompliance, or will they reach out from the technical infrastructure to sanction the offending program's human counterpart?

Given these disruptions and unanswered questions in the text, Web services *automation* appears to depend entirely on *humans* to enable the Web services architecture and to imbue it with human-like capabilities of language, meaning, and communication. Table 1 attests to the number of people in primarily large and powerful organizations who are involved in the specification of the Web services architecture. What is not evident in the table is the extensive work required by human actors (IT and business professionals) to translate their human meaning into a language for computers. Just as humans in the "swivel chair network" integrate the "primitive patchwork" of previous automation to create the illusion of a "single, streamlined system" (p. 109), *human activity* will be extensively involved in creating the shared terminology that will enable computers to talk to computers: "Subtleties of meaning have to be hashed out before business can be conducted in all its inevitable complexity" (p. 111) and *automation* can take over.

Surfacing the *human* supplement to *automation*, we see a conundrum: humans communicate with humans (over standards) so that computers can communicate with computers (in day-to-day business processes) so that humans don't have to communicate with humans. We imagine that if "shared meaning will naturally increase as the use of the Web services architecture expands" (p. 112), computers may eventually be taught (by humans) to negotiate their own standards, creating their own language to substitute automated "meaning" (i.e., standard definitions) for human meaning, and by doing so, advance the *différance* of *automation* over *human activity* toward the realms of science fiction.

5   DISCUSSION AND IMPLICATIONS

Through our deconstruction of the text "Your Next IT Strategy," we explored underlying themes of inclusion and exclusion related to an IT innovation (Web services) that many expect will shape IT and non-IT work in the future. These inclusion-exclusion logics suggest an antipathy for human activity, particularly the contributions of IT workers who develop and support IT in organizations, a veneration of automation that ignores the technical limitations of automation, and a conservative agenda that builds on and extends the status quo of powerful actors in the IT sector, masked by the appearance of change and freedom.

Our interpretation of the text is no more correct than other readers' interpretations. Nor do we claim that we have interpreted the authors' explicit or implicit intentions. We also note that our own text, including the following reconstruction of a passage from the article, is itself open to deconstruction. Instead, we suggest that the value of our deconstruction comes from exploring the declarative and performative possibilities that could arise from this text. Through this deliberate "play," as described by Derrida (Royle 2003), excluded possibilities for the development and use of Web services might be surfaced and thus included in the discussion of social practices and ethical choices related to this IT innovation.

Moreover, we suggest, as others do, that deconstruction attempts to finish the unfinished project of modernity (Norris 2000). It does so by exposing the "conditions of possibility" for interpretation (Norris 2000, p. 81). We find this approach consistent with Andrew Feenburg's work on technical potentiality. Feenburg (2002) suggests that there is much confusion about the effects of technologies because writers mix primary (i.e., embodied in technology) and secondary (i.e., revealed in specific contexts) instrumentalization. Primary instrumentalization occurs when technical objects are isolated from their original context, analyzed in terms of their utility, and transformed into a technically universal and useful form. Often, primary instrumentalization serves the interests of managers, who wish to control workers and work practices. Secondary instrumentalization arises during the inevitable social construction of technologies in concrete settings. Through a process of systematization, technical objects are combined and re-embedded in a social context. Systemization is mediated to a large degree by ethical and aesthetic concerns, and thus outcomes are indeterminate, subject to human agency and initiative.

Potentialities are the possible secondary instrumentalizations that could emerge as technologies are implemented in particular settings. A potentiality is a particular set of secondary qualities that are possible in a given situation, but are as yet unrealized within that situation. Feenburg suggests a philosophy of technology based on potentiality that "exposes the obstacles to the release of technology's integrative potential and thus serves as the link between political and technical discourse" (p. 177).

Here, the text of "Your Next IT Strategy" emphasizes the primary qualities of Web services and proposes a set of secondary qualities that will shape every context, regardless of ethical, social, or human influences. The result is an organizing vision that largely excludes consideration of the social contexts in which IT innovations are deployed. Context includes the specific actions of and the social, economic, political, and economic implications for human actors. Such a context-free vision inhibits the reader from examining political choices during secondary instrumentalization and creates obstacles to the realization of democratic practices in socio-technical design.

We suggest that alternative potentialities can be surfaced by de-centering the dominant interpretations of a text through deconstruction. In the previous section, we de-centered the dominant interpretation of the text through our deconstructive reading and analysis, exposing issues of social exclusion and inclusion. We now continue to de-center the text to highlight alternative potentialities for the Web services architecture, using the analytic technique of reconstruction (Martin 1990). This technique involves further play with the text, as words and phrases are altered so as to produce a new text, one that brings to the foreground political assumptions and social tensions. Here, we reconstruct the brief passage from "Your Next IT Strategy" that inspired our deconstruction, to point to potentialities for building Web services infrastructure in socially accountable and ethical ways.

The passage begins with the story of Merrill Lynch (a large, powerful firm) and its struggle with old, closed, and inflexible IT systems. The chief technology officer is quoted as comparing these systems to a Potemkin village in czarist Russia. The metaphor of a Potemkin village refers to Grigori Potemkin, who was believed to have painted the exteriors of impoverished villages to impress Catherine the Great.[2] Thus, a "Potemkin village" is a false front or construct, which hides a damaged and unseemly reality.[3] The story explains that employees of Merrill Lynch (embodied as a "swivel chair network") have been creating the "illusion of a single, streamlined system" from a "primitive patchwork" of internal systems (p. 109). Rather than celebrating the achievements of these human heroes, the Web services architecture is poised to remove them from the network so that true automation can take over, and the false front can become a true front:

> The Web services architecture promises to solve this problem. By taking the people out of the network, the architecture will enable connections between applications—both within and across enterprises—to be managed automatically (p. 109).

---

[2] See Bartelby.com (http://www.bartleby.com/61/0/P0480000.html).
[3] See Wikipedia.org (http://en.wikipedia.org/wiki/Potemkin_village). Ironically, some historians now believe that Potemkin did in fact help improve socio-economic conditions in these villages rather than merely put on an appearance.

This statement reveals the tension between *automation* and *human activity* evident throughout the text. If the humans in the "swivel chair network" compensate for the limitations of the automated system (*supplement*), removing the people from the network will cause the system to collapse. Perhaps it is not people who are to blame for the false front but automation, and thus it is automation that should be removed. In our first reconstructive step, we therefore switch "people" and "automation":

> The Web services architecture promises to solve this problem. By taking *automation* out of the network, the architecture will enable connections between applications—both within and across the enterprises—to be managed by *people*.

Although this phrasing is more human-centered, it suggests a return to yesteryear that is politically (if not objectively) naive. It is difficult to deny the benefits of appropriate automation, despite the inevitable loss of jobs and expertise due to any automation. For example, the automation of the telephone switch eliminated telephone operators from the phone network but allowed for reliable, inexpensive global communications. It would be reactionary and politically difficult to completely dismiss automation and is thus an unrealistic potentiality. However, by focusing exclusively on "taking out" human activity, the text produces an impossible and ethically irresponsible outcome—a weak potentiality. As a second attempt at reconstruction, we suggest that the preference for taking things *out* be reconsidered, and instead, something needs to be put *in* to business processes, that is, automation. Thus we replace "taking out" with "putting in":

> The Web services architecture promises to solve this problem. By *putting automation into* the network, the architecture will enable connections between applications—both within and across the enterprises—to be managed by people.

Now we see the potentiality of automation supplementing human activity, rather than humans supplementing automation, at least for those humans doing the managing. We are still disturbed by the non sequitur of the Web services architecture promising anything to anyone. It is humans who make promises. We have seen that development and maintenance of the Web services architecture depends on humans, particularly the humans in charge of large IT vendors and other firms that will compel use of this IT innovation. Acknowledging that all technologies result from human endeavors, and that the reference to "Web services architecture" masks substantial human effort and agency involved in its construction, maintenance, and implementation, we attribute responsibility for promises and actions related to the IT innovation to the humans who create and utilize the technology:

> The *people who are developing and promoting the Web services architecture* promise to solve this problem. By putting automation into the network, these *people* will enable connections between applications—both within and across the enterprises—to be managed *by people who implement and utilize the architecture.*"

Our reconstruction of this passage of text has removed some of the obstacles to acknowledging human participation and agency in the Web services architecture by recognizing their hidden and subordinate role in the text, and we can begin the discussion of where human responsibility, accountability and benefits might accrue. In doing so, we can explore various potentialities in Web services technology by acknowledging the pragmatic and ethical choices in who develops, who controls, who is accountable for, and who benefits from this IT innovation. Deconstruction and reconstruction could continue ad infinitum, and our text is itself open to these processes. We end here, having put the subordinated and absented "people" back into the network.

6   CONCLUDING REMARKS

Our deconstruction of a well-known management article promoting the Web services architecture highlights an organizing vision in which human activity defers to automation and the technical changes made possible through this IT innovation reinforce and consolidate the status quo of powerful social actors. By promoting an organizing vision focused on primary instrumentalization of technical features and a universal set of secondary qualities, this vision excludes consideration of alternative social and ethical implications of this IT innovation, which might be possible through secondary instrumentalization. Our reconstructions of one segment of the text attempts to reintroduce human agency and accountability into the design and management of this IT innovation and suggests the possibility that people should not be taken out of this socio-technical network but instead be put in charge of and held accountable for it. By doing so, we open the discussion to questions of social, political, and ethical choices in the design, management, and implementation of the innovation. Our critique does not mean that we are in opposition to Web services and automation. However, we recognize that technologies are the product of human creativity, agency, and intention, thus they are open to alternative designs and effects—including those that privilege human activity and choice over automation and that include rather than exclude the human actors who produce, operate, and utilize automated business processes such as IT professionals and technology users.

An implication for practice from our study involves our role as IT educators. Through our own deconstructive readings of management texts on IT innovation, we can bring insights that challenge our students to critique organizing visions for IT innovations on social and ethical grounds as well as on economic and technical grounds. We might also encourage and instruct students on how to do deconstructive readings themselves. If students develop a greater appreciation of alternative scenarios about the future effects of IT innovation, deconstruction achieves a degree of criticality (Golden-Biddle and Locke 1993).

As researchers, deconstruction can help us to think critically about the unspoken texts within the texts of IT innovation. By closely examining the organizing visions for IT innovations that others produce, and that we ourselves develop or to which we contribute, we can explore the tensions inside and outside the text about the social, economic, political, and ethical implications of IT innovations. As scholars, we tend to focus on what has been or is happening with information technology and to limit our future projections to the development of the technical in technical systems. We could also assert a role and assume a responsibility to consider the numerous social possibilities that could emerge from technical systems, not only as they apparently exist today but also as they could exist in the future. The potentialities of IT innovations such as Web services are many. It will be through the purposeful exploration of these possibilities that social practices will evolve. In the hurry-up world of academic publishing, we could use Derrida's advice: slow down and carefully construct and deconstruct our texts, in order to develop an expanded awareness of the topics to which we wish to speak. Only then can we speak intelligently and responsibly about the potentialities of IT and organizational practice.

References

Beath, C. M., and Orlikowski, W. J. "The Contradictory Structure of Systems Development Methodologies: Deconstructing the IS-User Relationship in Information Engineering," *Information Systems Research* (5:4), 1994, pp. 350-377.

Bloomfield, B. "Understanding the Social Practices of Systems Developers," *Journal of Information Systems* (2), 1992, pp. 189-206.

Carmel, E., and Tjia, P. *Offshoring Information Technology*, Cambridge, UK: Cambridge University Press, 2005.

Derrida, J. *Of Grammatology* (translated by Gayatre Spivak), Baltimore, MD: John Hopkins University Press, 1977.

Derrida, J. *The Margins of Philosophy* (translated by Alan Bass), Chicago: University of Chicago Press, 1982.

Derrida, J. *Speech and Phenomenon*, Evanston, IL: Northwestern University Press, 1973.

Feenburg, A. *Transforming Technology: A Critical Theory Revisited*, Oxford, UK: Oxford University Press, 2002.

Golden-Biddle, K., and Locke, K. "Appealing Work: An Investigation of How Ethnographic Texts Convince," *Organization Science* (4:4), 1993, pp. 595-616.

Hagel, J., and Brown, J. S. "Your Next IT Strategy," *Harvard Business Review* (79:9), 2001, pp. 105-113.

Kilduff, M. "Deconstructing *Organizations*," *Academy of Management Review* (18:1), 1993, pp. 13-21.

Koch, C. "The Battle for Web Services," *CIO Magazine*, October 1, 2003 (available online at http://www.cio.com/archive/100103/standards.html).

Martin, J. "Deconstructing Organizational Taboos: The Suppression of Gender Conflict in Organizations," *Organization Science* (1:4), 1990, pp. 339-359.

Murphy, C. "Future View: Software Jobs Will Be Mechanized in the Long Run," *Information Week*, November 17, 2003 (available online at http://www.informationweek.com/showArticle.jhtml?articleID=16100723).

Norris, C. *Deconstruction and the Unfinished Project of Modernity*, New York: Routledge, 2000.

Royle, R. *Jacques Derrida*, London: Routledge, 2003.

Swanson, B., and Ramiller, N. "The Organizing Vision in Information Systems Innovation," *Organization Science* (8:5), 1997, pp. 458-474.

Watson, H., and Wood-Harper, T. "Deconstruction Contexts in Interpreting Methodology," *Journal of Information Technology* (11), 1996, pp. 59-70.

White, S. "Foucault's Challenge to Critical Theory," *American Political Science Review* (80:2), 1986, pp. 419-431.

About the Authors

Elizabeth Davidson is an associate professor and chair of the Information Technology Management Department at the University of Hawaii, Manoa. Her research examines the social implications of information technology development and use in organizational settings. Her theoretic focus is on socio-cognitive processes and the influence of institutional environments on IT-related organizational change. In recent years, Elizabeth has investigated these issues in the health care sector to examine the possible consequences of health care information technologies on organizational structure and professional practice. Elizabeth can be reached by e-mail at Elizabeth.Davidson@hawaii.edu.

Mike W. Chiasson is a senior lecturer at Lancaster University's Management School, in the Department of Management Science. His research examines how context affects IS development and implementation, using a range of social theories (actor network theory, structuration theory, critical social theory, ethnomethodology, and institutional theory). In studying this question, he has examined various development and implementation issues (privacy, user involvement, diffusion, outsourcing, cyber-crime, system development conflict) within medical, legal, engineering, entrepreneurial, and governmental settings. Mike can be reached by e-mail at m.chiasson@lancaster.ac.uk.

Sachin Ruikar is a Ph.D. student in International Business at the University of Hawaii College of Business Administration. His research interests include the globalization of information technology development and other forms of knowledge work and its consequences for system design and architecture. Sachin can be reached by e-mail at ruikar@hawaii.edu.

22 INSTITUTIONS, COMMUNITY, AND PEOPLE: An Evaluation of a Longitudinal Digital Divide Experience

Barbara J. Crump
Massey University
Wellington, New Zealand

Abstract   *A community computing center was established in late 2001 in a city council high-rise apartment block in Wellington, New Zealand's capital city. The center was one of five computing hubs (centers) of the Smart Newtown Project, established with economic and social inclusion objectives, in the lower socio-economic suburb of Newtown. The project aim was to reduce inequalities of access to information and communications technology (ICT). A partnership approach was adopted that included multiple stakeholders: city council employees and councillors, a communications trust, universities, staff of a computer corporation, and some apartment residents. After 4 years of operation, the center was closed and remains so at the time of writing. Using a theoretical framework that includes Warschauer's (2003) model of ICT for social inclusion, the concept of social capital, and Oldenburg's (1991) third place, this paper examines reasons for the center's closure. The main findings reveal that low social capital and the inadequate support of social resources in the form of the community and an institution were key factors in the closure of this initiative. Recommendations are made for implementing future projects.*

Keywords   Community computing, sustainability, ICT, social inclusion, social capital, digital divide

1   INTRODUCTION

In May 2005, the New Zealand government launched its digital strategy with the aim of "creating a digital future for all New Zealanders whether they are at home,

Please use the following format when citing this chapter:

Crump, B.J., 2006, in IFIP International Federation for Information Processing, Volume 208, Social Inclusion: Societal and Organizational Implications for Information Systems, eds. Trauth, E., Howcroft, D., Butler, T., Fitzgerald, B., DeGross, J., (Boston: Springer), pp. 333-346.

school, work or in the community."[1] The strategy aims at positioning New Zealand as a world leader in using information and technology to realize its economic, social, environmental, and cultural goals, to the benefit of all its people. The focus is on spreading the benefits of information and communications technology (ICT)[2] right across the economy and "ensuring all Kiwis [New Zealanders] can participate."[3] The community sector is one of the three "agents of change" identified as necessary for meeting the New Zealand government's goal of raising people's awareness of the potential of ICT. Business and government are the other two agents and these, together with the enablers of content, connection, and confidence will, it is believed, form the foundation for realizing the full benefits of ICT.

Nearly 5 years prior to the launch of the digital strategy a partnership was formed between the Wellington Regional Economic Development Agency (WREDA, an agency representing the Wellington region's local government councils), and Fujitsu New Zealand Ltd., a computer corporation. Employees of these organizations, together with some tenants of a council high-rise apartment block, were interested in addressing economic and social inequalities that they believed could arise from disadvantaged people being excluded from the information society. Many of them were aware of digital divide strategies that had been implemented within low-income, high-unemployment, and ethnically diverse communities, characteristics of groups identified as those more likely than others to be left behind in the information revolution. Some of these initiatives focused on the establishment of community computing centers that offered free Internet access and introductory classes and there was enthusiasm from Fujitsu and some agency employees for establishing such a center at the Newtown Park Flats (NPF). Representatives of the Wellington City Council and WREDA called two consultative meetings at the flats (apartments) outlining the proposal to tenants interested in participating in this project. Although there was a very low attendance of tenants at the two meetings (representing about 5 percent and 2 percent of the total tenant population respectively), those present expressed interest in this community project, ultimately resulting in the establishment of the computing center at NPF. This center was the second to be launched as part of the five-hub project planned for the Smart Newtown Project.

2   THE SMART NEWTOWN PROJECT

The aim for the Smart Newtown Project was to narrow the digital divide and had specific objectives of

*   Improving educational achievement and interest in participation in further education

---

[1]Community Net, Community Centre News, "The Digital Strategy—Creating a Digital Future," http://www.community.net.nz/CommunityCentre/News/National/digital-strategy-announce.htm.

[2]A term that includes technologies such as computers and communications such as satellites, mobile phones, and the Internet to process, transmit, and store data.

[3]"The Digital Strategy: Creating Our Digital Future," 2005, www.digitalstrategy.govt.nz.

- Improving short and long term employment prospects
- Developing ICT skill levels among disadvantaged groups
- Enhancing economic and social benefits for the wider community
- Strengthening intra-family relationships and cooperation
- Extending social networks and greater community interaction
- Improving opportunities for residents' expression of cultural heritage
- Improving flow of information between home and school

Newtown was chosen as the pilot community because of its diverse needs and breadth of ethnic groups—46 percent come from 41 ethnic groups other than Maori or Pakeha (European New Zealanders) and less than 40 percent of households had access to the Internet (2001 census statistics, cited in Smart Newtown Project 2003). The project partnership model included multiple stakeholders beyond the council and computer corporation; there were also representatives from a communications-based charitable trust, three educational institutions (a polytechnic and two universities), and community organizations.

By 2001, five computing hubs were established in the Newtown suburb. These were at the local primary school, the community cultural center, NPF, the public library, and the Pacific Island Cultural Center. Four of the centers offered free computing facilities and Internet access from a public location, and at some of the centers intro-ductory computing lessons were available. Thus the project focus was on "communities of place rather than communities of interest" (Pigg and Crank 2004) Such centers provide a "route to inclusion," attracting and involving new users and facilitating a new mode of participative learning within a supportive and stimulating social context (Liff et al., undated, p. 1).

One of the communities of place in the Smart Newtown Project was the Fujitsu computing room, established at the NPF, one of Wellington City Council's largest housing complexes. After 4 years of operation and participation by tenants of the NPF, the Fujitsu room closed and remains so at the time of writing.

This paper examines the events which led to the closure of the Fujitsu room. The author was one of the researchers involved in two separate, contracted Smart Newtown research projects and the design and method used for the projects are described in the next section.

3   RESEARCH DESIGN

The first research project (pilot study) was an evaluation of the 1-year pilot, implementation phase, contracted by WREDA. This resulted in a report to the City Council and other key stakeholders (McGregor et al. 2002) that provided recommen-dations relating to the economic and social inclusion objectives listed earlier. The second project (post study) was funded by Massey University and extended over 2 years of the post-implementation period. The main goal of this project was to investigate sustainability, governance, and management issues, identified from the first study's report as requiring further research.

A mixed-method design, incorporating both quantitative and qualitative approaches, was adopted for both studies. Data were collected for breadth (user and nonuser surveys) and depth (interviews with key staff, volunteers, and other stakeholders; narratives from users; document analysis). In addition, on-going observation and participation by the three researchers involved in the study added a further dimension to the evaluation. The user survey developed and used in the pilot phase of the project was refined and used again during the post-implementation phase.

The hubs operated on a drop-in basis. It was impossible, therefore, to define a population from which to draw a sample. Potentially the population was the entire Newtown community, although the statistics showed there were participants from outside the immediate Newtown area. The population base for the Fujitsu room was mostly from the NPF. The pilot study resulted in a convenience sample of 118 completed, usable user questionnaires and 159 nonuser survey forms. The nonuser survey was not repeated during the post study phase and the user survey resulted in 111 usable questionnaires. For both studies, a total of 47 interviews were held with volunteers and key stakeholders, and computer users participated in 53 informal narratives and discussions.

4   THEORETICAL FRAMEWORK

Warschauer's (2003) model of ICT access for social inclusion provided the theoretical framework for this study. He acknowledges the complicated nature of ICT projects and believes that ICTs and social inclusion intersect. The four sets of resources that Warschauer believes have an iterative relation with ICT use are physical (computers and telecommunication), digital (relevant content in diverse languages), human (literacy and education), and social (community and institutional support). They contribute to effective usage and, once effectively used, feed into promotion and extension of the resources. Warschauer (p. 77) notes that while community computing centers have "embraced" the need to provide the physical resources, such as hardware and telecommunications, there is often implicit reliance on social capital—the norms, trust, and networks thought to exist within the community where the computing center is established.

Important attributes of social capital relate to the personal relations that people have in their family and community which encompass information, influence, social credentials, and reinforcement (Lin 2001). These supportive, emotional, and personal factors can be shared through bonding social capital and bridging social capital (Putnam 2000). The strong ties of bonding social capital result from dense, inward-looking social networks such as among family members and close friends and provide emotional support.

Bridging social capital is associated with large, loose networks over a wider and more diverse group and is considered important for economic and social development. These "weak ties" (Warschauer 2003) are considered important because they provide access to different people, different information, and different social networks beyond our immediate circle.

Tied up with the notion of community is the idea that these strong and weak ties result in networks, norms, and trust, thus enabling members of a community to act together more effectively to pursue shared objectives. Informal gathering places, close to home, are considered essential to a community because they create a sense of place, promote companionship, nourish relationships, and encourage sociability (Oldenburg 1991). Oldenburg calls such locations "third places," the first being the home and the second being work.

Another aspect of social capital that Hopkins (2002) discusses is the competitive aspect, experienced by those who struggle for power through control of networks and relationships. She examines other theoretical positions and refers to the French social theorist Pierre Bourdieu, who defines social capital as "the aggregate of the actual or potential resources which are linked to the possession of a durable network of more or less institutionalized relationships of mutual acquaintance and recognition" (Bourdieu 1986, p. 248). Access to these resources varies with the individual and, within the field of social relationships, they struggle to maximize their own access at the expense of others. Social capital has, therefore, the potential for the reproduction of social inequality and social exclusion for those who do not have the advantages and opportunities that accrue through membership in certain communities (McClenaghan 2000). Where there is fragmentation among the community in terms of competing groups for scarce resources, lack of trust and poor network connections between and amongst the groups, the stock of social capital is likely to be very low and the benefits of social capital will not be realized.

Warschauer's model of ICT for social inclusion, the notion of social capital as a critical component in shaping access to technology, and the influence of third place, provide a useful theoretical framework to examine the factors that contributed to the closure of the Fujitsu Computing Room. The next section describes the NPF Fujitsu Room.

5   THE FUJITSU ROOM

The NPF house approximately 450 disadvantaged people such as those on low incomes and others who would otherwise struggle to find a safe and secure roof over their heads. A large number of the tenants (40 to 50 percent) are state beneficiaries and a few of the residents are housed at NPF as part of their transition into the community after prison terms. Because the majority of the flats are studios and others have only one bedroom, few families are housed in the complex and there is a high transitory tenancy in the flats. The NPF complex is located within an area that has social problems such as graffiti and vandalism of public areas and instances of ethnic gang fighting. The Fujitsu room had a panic button that was monitored 24 hours a day by the Wellington City Council security unit (Smart Newtown Project 2003).

The Fujitsu room initially appeared to have many of the third place characteristics Oldenburg (1991) found to be attractive in encouraging patronage. The room was in an accessible, ground floor location in one of the six blocks of the high-rise complex, thus providing easy, communal access in a quasi-public space. In the early years, there were frequent regulars and little interference from a host, such as a manager or coordinator. The center appeared to have further attributes of a third place: it became a neutral place away from home and work where people felt comfortable, was socially inclusive in terms of participation, and stimulated connection with others.

5.1 Human, Social and Physical Resources

The human, social, and physical resources, identified as essential for effective use of ICTs (Morino 2000; Warschauer 2003), also appeared to be available. There was an unpaid, volunteer coordinator who was an early and enthusiastic supporter of the project and who accepted management responsibilities associated with the computer room. Institutional and financial support was provided from the housing division of the city council, WREDA, and Fujitsu New Zealand Ltd., the organizations responsible for initiating and implementing the project.

The physical resources of 11 computers, printer, application and anti-virus software, on-going help desk, anti-virus protection, and basic maintenance support were provided by Fujitsu. The user interface was in English only. Opening hours were advertised as 10:00 a.m. to 5:00 p.m. weekdays, Saturdays 10:00 a.m. to 8:00 p.m. and Sundays 1:00 p.m. to 5:00 p.m. Some of the volunteers responsible for managing the room would informally assist people new to computing. After 8 months of operation, a polytechnic provided a free, self-paced training program for anyone interested in learning basic computing skills and applications. The polytechnic paid the room coordinator for the class hours (typically averaging 4 hours per week) during which time he was on hand to problem solve and offer users assistance as required. The coordinator received no other payment for his management duties, which included monitoring Internet access to ensure ethical use, establishing and displaying room-use rules, times of opening, volunteer rosters, and so on.

5.2 Teething Problems

In the first few months of implementation, there were technical and personnel problems. The volunteer coordinator (who had little computing experience) proved unsuited to manage the facility and these troubles dampened residents' enthusiasm. However, a new volunteer coordinator was recruited who was familiar with computers and proved capable of providing the day-to-day computer support and management necessary to run the environment.

5.3 Significant Nonuse

Despite these changes it became apparent, for reasons that were unclear, that there was significant nonuse by tenants. A 17-question survey was used to establish whether the tenants used the computer room or not and to understand the reasons for nonuse (Crump and McIlroy 2003). The total sample was 159 ethnically diverse people (57 percent of the 275 occupied flats). The majority of respondents (69 percent) were aged between 19 and 55 years with 62 percent male, and 38 percent female. Nearly 70 percent stated that they were state beneficiaries.

The results revealed that 73 percent of those surveyed did not use the computer center and the majority (75 percent) did not have a home computer or use one elsewhere. A more positive finding was that 78 percent of respondents were aware of the computer center's existence but 82 percent of them did not know its opening hours. The nonuser participants were asked if they were interested in using the computer center and, if not, what would encourage them to do so. Only 37 percent indicated interest and the other 63 percent were asked what might encourage them. The participants responded to a number of variables that related to access such as the hours of opening of the computer room, through to social variables such as "someone to go with," and cultural factors such as "ethnic groups only." Five variables related to computer training such as "more classes" and 11 variables explored social aspects that included cultural and gender preferences and attitudes toward computers. The variable most nominated was simply "not interested"; the tenants lacked the motivation to use the computer.

5.4 Positive Outcomes

Subsequent to the survey, attendance increased, resulting in positive individual outcomes for the users. While there was a high drop-out rate of those enrolled in the free classes, there were also many who completed the courses. Observation and discussion with the users revealed varied usage of the computers that included study, job hunting, genealogy, games, and Maori culture. Employees of the housing division of the council noted a more positive NPF environment. Graffiti had reduced and there was approximately a 5 percent increase in the NPF occupancy rate because people wanted to live in a complex with a computing facility.

5.5 Change for the Worse

However the environment of the Fujitsu room changed gradually for the worse. First, the numbers of volunteers declined, resulting in erratic opening times for the room and occasions when it was closed for days at a time. Second, the coordinator became disillusioned with his unpaid role and there was increasing acrimony among different users and the coordinator. The coordinator had, on numerous occasions, been promised by staff of the Wellington City Council that he would be paid for his work and "the contract would soon arrive." These promises were never made good yet continued to be promised over an 18 to 20 month period. Eventually, he resigned. Third, the computer room opening times were unpredictable, resulting in scheduled classes not running. Fourth, there were occasions when rival gangs fought in the courtyard onto which the computer room opened, resulting in police intervention. Fifth, usage of the computer room dwindled to a very small core group of male users.

The Fujitsu room was no longer the well-functioning third place with Oldenburg's essential criteria of an unobtrusive host and a safe, relaxed, and neutral place away from home where people felt welcome and regularly gathered.

The final, and catalytic, negative change related to the abuse of download volume. It was noted on several observational visits that private laptops were being brought into the room and connected to the system. Subsequently the city council received a statement for a "blow-out" monthly bill (over $20,000) for the Internet connection cost. This was the catalyst for the room closing and it remains so at the time of writing this paper—just 4 years since its opening.

6 ANALYSIS OF REASONS FOR THE CLOSURE

Reasons for the closure of the Fujitsu center are explored in this section using an analytical framework that includes Warschauer's (2003) model for ICT access and the concept of social capital. As discussed earlier, Warshauer's model specifies the four components of social, human, digital, and physical resources. He considers all four components as essential for effective use of ICT and, if handled well, promoting social inclusion among disadvantaged groups.

6.1 Social Resources

Institutional and community resources are the strands that contribute to the social category. Warschauer believes these are critical to community computing projects and analysis shows that, after a mostly positive initial period, deficiencies in three of these resources contributed to the deteriorating situation at the Fujitsu room, ultimately resulting in its closure.

6.1.1   Institutional

Short, medium, and long term strategic planning is vital for any project's success and must take into account the context within which the project is situated. The NPF project suffered from a lack of a long-term and well-planned strategy, beyond the pilot phase, which factored in sustainability issues of funding and human resources, especially of volunteers. Fujitsu New Zealand Ltd. met its obligations as defined by the memoranda of understanding between it and the city council. However, interviews with city council staff and councillors reveal that they felt there was too much idealism by individuals originally involved in the project and enthusiasm for the project detracted from council addressing longer-term sustainability issues (especially financial sustainability).

Governance and management issues were problems with the NPF project. There was a lack of champions, particularly a central coordinator responsible for the project overview and liaison among stakeholders. Restructuring of WREDA meant that responsibilities for community ICT initiatives were moved to the city council, with the subsequent loss of the initial champion driver. While some council individuals took a personal interest in the project, there was no official policy, unit, or the high-level backing necessary in the council for community computing projects and, in particular, the NPF project. This situation makes it easier to understand why the coordinator was so shabbily treated with regard to the promises of paid employment. There was an erosion of trust that damaged the relations between council members and the coordinator when the paid contract never eventuated. Trust was further eroded when a different coordinator at another Newtown hub signed a contract for paid employment with the council. This established a "norm of reciprocity" (Putnam 2000, p. 19) between council and the other hub coordinator. The council's actions created inequality, deepened mistrust, and damaged the measure of connectedness between council employees and some of the NPF tenants.

6.1.2 Community

During discussions with the project's stakeholders, the over-dependence on volunteers was identified as an on-going problem and several people said they believed there were unrealistic expectations for the flat volunteers. The very low attendance at the two consultative meetings with tenants of NPF should not have been interpreted as significant community involvement and ownership that would result in a continuing pool of volunteers, especially when there was little evidence of strong social capital with existing networks. The over-reliance on voluntary resources and New Zealand's national and local government policies being biased toward projects rather than process or sustainability has been noted by Williamson and Dekkers (2005).

While there was (and still is) no formal measure of the stock of social capital that existed within the NPF community, it is a reasonable assumption that it would not be high. The transitory nature of tenants, the lack of a tenants' association (that was origi-nally established at NPF but fragmented and then disbanded), and the problems experi-enced within the NPF means that there would be little evidence of the attributes of social capital, such as norms and trust and a well-functioning network that would be a resource for shared knowledge and ideas and mutually beneficial endeavors (Coleman 1988).

With the benefit of hindsight, there was inadequate institutional support for the NPF community and project, given the context within which the computing room was located. There was insufficient support in fostering community involvement in ICTs and developing social capital and human support networks found by Sipior, Volonino, and Marzec (2001) to be essential elements in successful projects. A review of many community and ICT projects worldwide suggests that, for the establishment of successful ICT initiatives, a critical success factor is the existence of a high level of social capital (Otis and Johanson 2004; Pigg 2001; Simpson 2002).

6.2 Human Resources

Warschauer believes the human dimension to be one of the most important factors affecting social inclusion and exclusion. He offers a wide definition for human resources that includes issues such as literacy and education (as well as the particular types of literacy practices that are required for computer use and online communication).

Some users of the Fujitsu room benefitted from working through the self-paced learning program for applications, supported by the volunteer coordinator. There was no quantitative evaluation of the "rates of return to technology use" (DiMaggio and Hargittai 2001, p. 17) but the qualitative data, especially in the initial years of this project, indicate that there was a positive "rate of return" that varied over a range of issues. These related mainly to social benefits that include participation, emotional satisfaction, social capital, learning, and, in a few cases, economic benefit such as users who searched for, and sometimes found, jobs. Numerous tenants and members of the wider Newtown community learned basic computing and Internet skills, thus meeting a number of the objectives specified for the Smart Newtown Project. These included improving educational achievement and interest in participation in further education, development of ICT skill levels among disadvantaged groups, strengthening intra-family relationships and cooperation (especially through use of e-mail), improving opportunities for residents, and expression of cultural heritage.

In the early years of the hub's operation, communities of practice were established where people formed networks through being engaged in similar activities and, at the same time, learned from each other. This happened within the more formal context of the self-paced learning program for applications and in the informal groups such as families, similar ethnicities, and sometimes groups (such as an Indian church group) that used the center on a regular basis. The iterative nature of Warschauer's model was evident as some of the learners became volunteers, thus contributing to the sustainability of the hub in terms of reliable opening hours and responsibility for the safety of the room.

Another aspect of human resources which Pinkett and O'Bryant (2003) recommend for community technology and community building initiatives is the engagement of residents as active participants in the implementation process. They report that the process is not easy and requires relationship building, commitment, patience, and empathic listening on all sides. They believe these elements are fundamental to a project's success in order for residents to feel a sense of ownership and empowerment.

6.3 Digital Resources

This category refers to online resources: content, language, and overlaps with human resources. For community centers to be effective and useful, "asset mapping" is recommended so that the resources within a community can be leveraged, thus mobilizing them to "facilitate productive and meaningful connections (Pinkett and O'Bryant 2003, p. 192). An example is the immigrant English language classes at a nearby center where the teacher has integrated use of the computers, located in the adjoining classroom, with her lessons. Many of these students, having gained confidence from this blended learning experience, have gone on to attend application classes. Benefits from this include not only graduates with certificates and confidence with ICT but also the provision of a seamless introduction into a wider community, which is often difficult for new immigrants (Crump 2004).

6.4 Physical Resources

Of Warschauer's four resources essential for ICT access, the physical resources at the Fujitsu room were the most positive. Fujitsu NZ Ltd. signed memoranda of unerstanding with the council that defined their responsibilities in providing a network of personal computers and a server as well as on-going technical support. There were several equipment upgrades over the operational period.

7   RECOMMENDATIONS

What can be learned from this project? Most importantly, cognizance must be taken of the social context within which a community computing center is established.

Knowledge of the strength (or otherwise) of social capital existing within that community should guide the requirements and considerations needed to achieve sustainability of operation and financial sustainability. Key recommendations for implementing future projects are

- *Strategic, long-term planning that commits the provision and level of financial support from institutional bodies.* Financial sustainability is vital and requires planning and commitment. Just as the utilities of gas and electricity have become essential, so is knowledge and use of ICTs in this information age. Therefore funding community computing centers in council housing complexes should be viewed as an essential cost to be met by council or other organizations. Because funding is strongly contested across multiple council activities, restricting centers to areas of need and limiting funding to a finite time-frame may make such projects more likely to be accepted by the majority of ratepayers. During the funded period users interested in sustaining the center could be taught how to apply for grants and assisted with seeking funding beyond the set period.

  An alternative funding approach is for central government to take responsibility for establishing a national community computing program. The New Zealand digital strategy identifies community as one of the agents of change in becoming a world leader in using ICT. Such a strategy would be congruent with realizing this goal.

- *Build social capital.* When establishing a computing center in a community with poor networks and where people are disconnected from each other, priority must be given to building social capital. The closed social capital which is built within the community may begin by asset mapping, such as taking an inventory of skills and groups in the community. Bridging social capital could be assisted by working with tenants' associations from neighboring housing complexes and building relations among representatives of the partners involved in the project. New projects should be situated within an established community of activity such as a library or a community center where there are clubs and existing networks. The projects should have clearly stated, measurable goals, be targeted to users' needs (derived from a needs analysis), and, from the outset, have community participation.

- *Establish broad ownership.* A two-pronged approach needs to be adopted. First, establish multi-sector collaborations that include relationships with corporations, government agencies, nonprofit organizations, neighboring tenants' associations, and universities. Second, residents must be engaged as active participants in the implementation and sustainability process. The NPF community computing initiative may have had greater longevity and fewer resourcing problems had another nearby council housing complex, with an active tenants' association, been involved in the project from the outset.

- *Multilevel champions and strong communication.* Partnership models with multi-sector collaborators require relationship management. To facilitate communication and action among the different stakeholders, there needs to be appointment of a dedicated coordinator/champion. This person would have responsibility for project management, maintaining and developing community and institutional relationships, and be the central point of contact for the partners. Ideally there will be champions within each organization—a person who has responsibility, and enthusiasm, for the project.

• *Relevant content.* The relevance of ICT to people's lives must be clearly demonstrated. Once the basic skills of how to use a mouse and keyboard are achieved, a curriculum that is project-based and targeted to users' interests and needs would demonstrate relevancy and provide motivation.

• *On-going assessment.* A survey of potential users, designed with outcomes in mind, and conducted *before* implementation would provide valuable insight into the level of social capital already existing in the community and how technology can be made relevant to people's lives. Results of a further survey for comparative purposes would obtain useful data, which could be used to evaluate and measure outcomes and justify further projects.

8   CONCLUSION

The theoretical framework used in analyzing events leading to the closure of the NPF computer room has been useful in revealing the social embeddedness of technology. Examination of the use of Warschauer's four key resources shows that low social capital and the inadequate social resources of community and a supporting institution were key factors in the sustainability crisis experienced at the center.

Recent communication with a council employee, who has become involved with the project in latter years, indicates that the closure of this room is not permanent. Currently a strategy is being prepared which firmly places responsibility for funding sustainability with the council. The plan recommends commitment to new community computing initiatives to targeted disadvantaged Wellington communities. The strategy includes the appointment of a community ICT coordinator who will be responsible for the project management and on-going overview of community computing projects. This appointment, together with the employment of a paid on-site Fujitsu room coordinator, is considered crucial for the success of a reopening of the Fujitsu room and the opening of another council housing computing project. The strategy is clearly focused on social inclusion objectives, rather than economic development outcomes. It is "not the result of technological determinism but of the appropriate social construction of technology in a specific and localized context" (Williamson and Dekkers 2005, p. 5). Currently there is no commitment by Fujitsu New Zealand Ltd. to be involved with the reopening of the NPF Fujitsu room. However representatives have indicated a willingness to review the situation to decide if they wish to participate further.

Despite the difficulties experienced with the computing room, many of the project's social objectives have been met. There have been positive outcomes for the individuals who took advantage of the access and acquired skills in ICT—many of whom would otherwise not had the confidence or interest to participate. It remains to be seen whether reflection on lessons learned and the level of social capital at the NPF will be sufficient to ensure the sustainability of human and digital resources.

References

Bourdieu, P. "The Forms of Capital," in J. G. Richardson (ed.), *Handbook of Theory and Research for the Sociology of Education,* New York: Greenwood, 1986.

Coleman, J. S. "Social Capital in the Creation of Human Capital," *American Journal of Sociology, Supplement 94,* 1988, pp. S95-S120.

Crump, B. "Immigrants, Language and ICT: Factors for Success in Blended Learning," in *Proceedings of Informatics and Research on Women in ICT 2004 International Conference (Volume 2),* Kuala Lumpur, Malaysia, July 28-30, 2004, pp. 1175-1184.

Crump, B., and McIlroy, A. "The Digital Divide: Why the "Don't-Want-Tos" Won't Compute: Lessons from a New Zealand ICT Project," *FirstMonday* (8:12), 2003 (available online at http://www.firstmonday.org/issues/issue8_12/crump/).

DiMaggio, P. J., and Hargittai, E. "From the 'Digital Divide' to 'Digital Inequality': Studying Internet Use as Penetration Increases," Working Paper 19, Center for Arts and Cultural Policy Studies, Woodrow Wilson School, Princeton University, Princeton, NJ, 2001.

Hopkins, L. "What Is Social Capital?," Institute for Social Research Working Papers, No. 2, Swinburne University of Technology, Melbourne, Australia, 2002.

Liff, S., Steward, F., and Watts, P. "Gateways to the Virtual Society: Innovation for Social Inclusion," *Ikon,* undated (available online at http://users.wbs.ac.uk/group/ikon/research/gateways).

Lin, N. *Social Capital: A Theory of Social Structure and Action,* Cambridge, UK: Cambridge University Press, 2001.

McClenaghan, P. "Social Capital: Exploring the Theoretical Foundations of Community Development Education," *British Educational Research Journal* (26:5), 2000, pp. 565-82.

McGregor, J., McIlroy, A., and Crump, B. "Report on the Smart Newtown Project," Wellington, NZ: Wellington Regional Economic Development Agency, 2002.

Morino, M. "Policy and Philanthropy: Keys to Closing the Digital Divide," keynote address to the Networks for the People 2000 Conference, Technology Opportunities Program, October 30, 2000 (available online at Morino Institute, http://morino.org/closing_sp_dig.asp).

Oldenburg, R. *The Great Good Place, Cafes, Coffee Shops, Community Centers, Beauty Parlors, General Sstores, Bars, Hangouts, and How They Get You Through the Day,* New York: Paragon House, 1991.

Otis, N., and Johanson, G. "Community Sustainability and Information and Communications Technologies: Current Knowledge and Recent Cases," paper presented at the Australian Electronic Governance Conference, Center for Public Policy, University of Melbourne, April 14-15, 2004.

Pigg, K. "Applications of Community Informatics for Building Community and Enhancing Civic Society," *Information, Communication and Society* (4:4), 2001, pp. 507-527.

Pigg, K. E., and Crank, L. D. "Building Community Social Capital: The Potential and Promise of Information and Communications Technologies," *The Journal of Community Informatics* (1:1), 2004 (http://www.ci-journal.net/viewissue.php?id=3).

Pinkett, R., and O'Bryant, R. "Building Community, Empowerment and Self-Sufficiency," *Information, Communication and Society* (6:2), 2003, pp. 187-210.

Putnam, R. *Bowling Alone: The Collapse and Revival of American Community,* New York: Simon and Shuster, 2000.

Simpson, L. "Big Questions for Community Informatics Initiatives: A Social Capital Perspective," in *Proceedings of the Search Conference: Community and Information Technology:*

The Big Questions, Melbourne, Center for Community Networking Research, Monash University, October 16, 2002 (http://www.ccnr.net/searchconf/simpson.htm).

Sipior, J. C., Volonino, L., and Marzed, J. Z. "A Community Initiative that Diminished the Digital Divide," *Communications of the Association for Information Systems* (13), 2001, pp. 29-56.

Smart Newtown Project. *Submission by Wellington City Council, Fujitsu NZ Ltd., Wellington Regional 2020 Communications Trust, Positively Wellington Business and Smart Newtown*, Wellington: Positively Wellington Business, 2003.

Warschauer, M. *Technology and Social Inclusion: Rethinking the Digital Divide*, Cambridge, MA: The MIT Press, 2003.

Williamson, A., and Dekkers, J. "ICT as an Enabler in the Community and Voluntary Ssector in Aotearoa/New Zealand," in G. Irwin, W. Taylor, A. Bytheway, and C. Strumpfer (eds.), *Proceedings of the Community Informatics Research Network 2005 Conference*, Cape Town, South Africa: Community Informatics Research Network, 2005, pp. 408-429.

About the Author

Over the past six years **Barbara Crump** has been involved in evaluating the Smart Newtown Project, a community computing digital divide initiative in Wellington. She continued this interest when she was appointed Visiting Scholar at the University of Malaya, Kuala Lumpur, in 2004. Another focus of her research is investigating reasons for the low participation of women in tertiary computing programs and their involvement in the IT industry. This has led to a commissioned national study of women in the IT workforce that was replicated in Selangor State and Kuala Federal Territory, Malaysia. Barbara is a senior lecturer in the Department of Information Systems at Massey University, Wellington, and may be contacted at b.j.crump@massey.ac.nz.

23 HOW (CAN) NONUSERS ENGAGE WITH TECHNOLOGY: Bringing in the Digitally Excluded

Mike Cushman
Ela Klecun
London School of Economics and Political Science
London, U.K.

Abstract   This paper describes findings from the Penceil Project,[1] which aims to explore the experiences of nonusers and minimal users of ICTs, how nonuse affects their inclusion or exclusion from society, and how they can learn to use ICTs to meet their personal goals. The paper considers the applicability of the technology adoption model (TAM) to understanding the experiences of this group of people. By looking at theories of social exclusion and the project research findings, the paper argues that TAM is limited in the range of social conditions it anticipates and, thus, presumes a facility in formulating aspirations for use that people excluded from the use of ICTs cannot have. We argue that we need to consider engagement with technology rather than just adoption. We consider the implications of these findings for designing a revised basic ICT curriculum and describe the piloting of a new curriculum. We argue that, as ICTs in general—and Internet use in particular—are experienced technologies, perceived usefulness and perceived ease of use need to be reformulated to recognize limitations on people's ability to construct plans for future action since an actor's world is disclosed through action not given in advance.

Keywords   Digital exclusion, digital divide, e-literacy, engagement with technology, model of adoption of technology in households (MATH), social exclusion, technology adoption model (TAM), basic ICT curriculum

---

[1]The Penceil Project, "How People ENCounter E-ILiteracy," is funded by the UK Economic and Social Research Council under grant RES-341-25-0036 as part of its e-society program (http://penceil.lse.ac.uk/). The project partners are the London School of Economics and the National Institute of Adult and Continuing Education.

Please use the following format when citing this chapter:

Cushman, M., and Klecun, E., 2006, in IFIP International Federation for Information Processing, Volume 208, Social Inclusion: Societal and Organizational Implications for Information Systems, eds. Trauth, E., Howcroft, D., Butler, T., Fitzgerald, B., DeGross, J., (Boston: Springer), pp. 347-364.

1   INTRODUCTION

It is commonly stated that ICT is transforming every aspect of society: the way people learn, work, conduct business, spend leisure time, and organize their social lives. Recent figures show that 58 percent of UK households own a PC[2] and 60 percent use the Internet (Dutton et al. 2005).[3] Computer use and Internet access at home are supplemented by that at work or local e-gateway centers (such as libraries, Internet cafes, or local colleges). Yet, some people in the UK still do not own a computer nor do they (or can they) make use of one. Use is strongly linked to income: home access to the Internet ranges from 15 percent for the lowest income decile to 89 percent for the highest.[4] This describes a domestic, as opposed to an international, digital divide.

We suggest that the commonly used term, digital divide (see for example, Hubregtse 2005; Korupp and Szydlik 2005), is less helpful than *digital exclusion* (Devins et al. 2002). Divide implies a technological determinism, with the divide arising from the nature of the technology. Digital exclusion denotes a stronger sense of social process and, through the wording, provides a helpful association with other forms of social exclusion. We aim to add to the small, but growing, body of literature that considers different facets of digital exclusion: the barriers to and motivation for use of ICTs; and the implications of nonuse (Haddon 2000; Kvasny 2005; Liff et al. 2002; Selwyn et al. 2005; Wyatt et al. 2002)

A more sophisticated understanding of people's use and nonuse of ICT is developing, moving from a dichotomy of information "haves" and "have-nots" toward an acknowledgment of the complex nature of the processes taking place, (Cornford and Klecun-Dabrowska 2003; Silverstone and Haddon 1997, 1998). Despite increasingly sophisticated accounts of digital exclusion recently reflected in UK policy, academic understanding of who is making little or no use of ICT, and why, remains weak (Selwyn 2003a). Furthermore, the ability to use ICT is increasingly seen as a prerequisite to participating (living and working) in an e-society but there is limited understanding of how e-illiteracy and ICT nonuse affect people in their daily lives or of people's aspirations for their use.

This paper has a number of related aims. First, it seeks to challenge the focus of technology adoption literature on business people and students, and to highlight the importance of focusing on other sectors of the population. Second, it aims to indicate the shortcomings of the technology adoption model (TAM) and the model of adoption of technology in households (MATH). Third, it reviews key literature on social exclusion in order to interlink technology adoption and social exclusion. Fourth, it contributes to the understanding of nonuse of ICTs, and in particular it aims to identify barriers to use and people's perceptions of technology and their information needs. It further considers their understanding of what new technology can offer them, as well as

---

[2]National Statistics "Consumer Durables," 2005 (http://www.statistics.gov.uk/CCI/nugget.asp?ID=868&Pos=&ColRank=1&Rank=374).

[3]Broadly in line with other economically developed countries, as shown by the country reports gathered by the World Internet Project (http://www.worldinternetproject.net/).

[4]National Statistics, "Households with Home Access to the Internet by Gross Income Decile Group," 2004 (http://www.statistics.gov.uk/STATBASE/ssdataset.asp?vlnk=6937&More=Y).

the activities from which new ICTs exclude them. Finally, it outlines a curriculum for a course that would respond to those needs.

To achieve these aims, the paper starts by considering the dominant model in the IS literature on how people become users: TAM (Davis 1989, Davis et al. 1989) and MATH, its extension to households (Brown and Venkatesh 2005). It discusses to what extent TAM and MATH are appropriate theoretical constructs for gaining an understanding of why people who are socially excluded make no, or little, use of ICT, and how they might become users—in TAM's terms, their adoption intentions.

Our critique of TAM and MATH is multilevel. First, we consider the appropriateness of the research methods applied. Second, we question the theoretical assumptions behind such models and highlight their limitations. Finally, we query whether the popularity of these models in IS literature narrows the scope of reported research. Are the utilization of information systems in the workplace and home users' ICT purchasing intentions the only questions worth asking? We present an alternative approach to understanding nonuse and use of technology that draws on work on social exclusion. In the third section we describe our study, which investigates the experiences of those excluded by technology and outline its action research component, in which we designed and ran an innovative "Living with Computers" course.

We then outline the research findings in which attitudes of non- and minimal users of computers, their perceptions of technologies, and the uses they might make of it are described, arguing the need to construct alternative models of how wider use can be supported. Our conclusion highlights how e-literacy should be addressed and argues for giving socially excluded people's relationship to technology a more prominent place in information system research, including the research on technology adoption.

2 THE TECHNOLOGY ADOPTION MODEL

In considering how nonusers might become ICT users we start by exploring to what extent TAM (Davis 1989; Davis et al. 1989) might assist us. The model draws, amongst other approaches, on the theory of reasoned action. In his much-cited paper Davis (1989) proposes that two constructs, perceived usefulness (PU) and perceived ease of use (PEOU), are the fundamental determinants of user acceptance, and can be used to predict adoption. Davis concludes that PU is the better predictor of acceptance, "ease of use may be an antecedent to *usefulness*, rather than a parallel, direct determinant of usage" (p. 334), but subsequent studies have tended to regard the two concepts as more equal.

These two notions, particularly when translated into "is this any use to me" and "can I make this work easily," are a commonsensical way of approaching the issue but the way they have been applied fails to take account of how potential users come to the technology. We have reviewed recent studies published in *MIS Quarterly* to discover over what domains and with what assumptions TAM has been applied. Our concerns fall into three areas: the narrow domains explored; the assumptions about agency and choice which are removed from social context; and the view of people as users rather than actors.

Table 1. Subjects of TAM Studies

Subjects of Study	Number of Studies	Percentage
Knowledge workers	23	52
Administrative/clerical staff	2	5
Graduate Business and MBA students	10	23
Undergraduate Students	8	18
Students (unclassified)	1	2

The studies overwhelmingly concentrate on two groups—business professionals and university students—both of which have successful educational backgrounds and familiarity with environments where ICTs are pervasive.

Gefen and Straub's (2000) review of TAM studies between 1989 and 2000 details 44 investigations (see Table 1). They cover a strikingly narrow segment of the total population. The reason for the focus disclosed by these figures might be that TAM concentrated on IS in business. However, this limitation is not acknowledged. For example Gefen et al. (2003, p. 53) state, "Numerous empirical tests have shown that TAM is a parsimonious and robust model of technology acceptance behaviors in a wide variety of IT across... levels of expertise." They cite Taylor and Todd (1995) in support of this claim. However, Taylor and Todd studied use of a computer resource center by business school students, a somewhat restricted notion of "levels of expertise."

When Gefen and Straub (1997, p. 389) wished to address one possible dimension of exclusion, gender, they studied "groups of knowledge workers using e-mail systems in the airline industry in North America, Asia, and Europe." Again they concentrated on people who were, essentially, insiders.

The bias in a major study of adoption of home computers (Venkatesh and Brown 2001) is less obvious. However, the study is not interested in distinguishing between different population groups. It only reports the mean values for variables such as income for the sample and the whole population (p. 81); and it does not report on the employment status or qualification levels of the respondents. Furthermore its sample is skewed toward the suburbs and away from likely areas of social deprivation and exclusion.

TAM draws upon the theory of planned behavior (Ajzen 1991)—a rationalistic causal model—as does MATH. Critiques of such models point out that individuals act arationally, their ability to analyze their world and define and enact rational inten- tionalities is far more limited than bounded rationality concepts (Simon 1982) suggest. Introna (1997, Chapter 2) graphically describes Heidegger's notion of *thrownness*. We are always already within our world, constantly buffeted and disconcerted by events, never able to stand apart from the world and contemplate and plan. There is never the peace that Simon demands for making the best sense of the world we can, then planning accordingly within the bounds of our knowledge. We do not have stable intentions that we can project forward in time to know our PUs and our plans for our behavior. We are constantly engaged in bricolage (Ciborra 2002), forming and reforming our construc- tions in the flux of events. When we bring less experience to a situation, we are even less able to improvise a plan, to make sense of our situation (Weick 1993). The behavior of less experienced and skilled users of ICTs is consequently less amenable to analysis by TAM and MATH.

Lamb and Kling (2003) offer an important critique of these approaches in their explanation of engagement with technology: "the most common conception of the user in IS research is of an atomic individual with well-articulated preferences and the ability to exercise discretion in ICT choice and use, within certain cognitive limits" (p. 198). They argue for a view of individuals as social actors (networked beings) who have an engagement with technology, rather than simply as users: people who contribute to the construction and disposition of ICTs, not passive consumers, and who are co-constituted by the technologies with which they engage.

TAM, as a predictor of the behaviors of organizational members, is primarily concerned with whether staff will use the tools provided for them and aims to assist managers in deploying IT more effectively and extensively. MATH attempts to predict the likelihood of ICT purchase by individuals or households. Neither is concerned with the effects of ICTs on people—as workers, family members, or citizens—or their use of technologies, both see individuals as unchanged by the process of technology adoption. They see the learning of, say, Excel as the simple gaining of a skilled practice, excluding the existential dimension of becoming an Excel user. While we can predict, with lesser or greater accuracy, the use we may make of a new tool, there is a fundamental unknowableness about the change in our disposition toward, and engagement with, the world that possession of a new skill represents. PU is a moving target, changing as knowledge about, and facility with, the technology changes.

Furthermore, it is striking that none of the "sources for normative beliefs" presented by Brown and Venkatesh (2005) in MATH describe the influence of social status, social capital, ethnicity, or class except as they are seen as the influence of family and friends, nor are these seen as predictive factors for ICT use.

Some of the limitations of TAM can be explained through its intended focus on the business environment and, for MATH as well, on adoption of technology not its use, and people's experiences with it. Nor do they claim to be interested in social or digital exclusion. However, the problems with these models are more fundamental and stem from their theoretical assumptions. Our contention is that, because these models are dominant in IS research, they privilege the worldviews of the included and further marginalize the already excluded. Further, the worldviews that underlie these methodologies make the powerless, *the other*, even less of account in their suburban world of business men, women, and students, at work, at play, at shopping. If the questions we want to ask are about the excluded's engagement with, not acquisition of, technology and how the technology might mediate their engagement with the world, we need to go beyond TAM and MATH.

These are concerns we share with the critical research tradition in Information Systems which encourages us to identify the unconscious assumptions about the nature of organizations and society that lie behind such a narrowing of vision (Howcroft and Trauth 2005; Ngwenyama 1991).

3 SOCIAL EXCLUSION

We suggest that considering literature on social exclusion can deepen our understanding of why excluded people do not use ICT or make little use of it, and how they might become users. This will help us understand digital exclusion as both a result of, and constitutive of, social exclusion.

Social exclusion is a contested concept in the social policy literature (Hills et al. 2002). Its origin was in France in the 1960s and arose out of a concern with *les exclus*, those on the margins of society, with little connection, or commitment, to general social norms (Burchardt et al. 2002). The concept arises from a concern that poverty, while remaining a central element in exclusion, is not a sufficient descriptor. People's life chances are not solely determined by their wealth but are constituted by a range of resources that they can, or cannot, deploy—their educational, cultural and social capital (Bourdieu 1986).

Gordon et al. (2000, p. 73) in their study of poverty in Britain describe social exclusion as,

> A lack or denial of access to the kinds of social relations, social customs and activities in which the great majority of people in British society engage. In current usage, social exclusion is often regarded as a "process" rather than a "state" and this helps in being constructively precise in deciding its relationship to poverty.

Despite the attempt to provide a wider understanding through this term, Milbourne (2002, p. 328) argues

> these interpretations rest heavily on individual or household isolation; and the remedies on re-inclusion and membership of mainstream social institutions. Little change is therefore implied to the social institutions themselves, nor do such interpretations recognize the need to address the accumulation of wealth elsewhere, nor other dominant and powerful institutions which promote inequality and potentially exclude and define those outside as disadvantaged, whether by race, class, gender, age or disability. Social exclusion then fails to address equality in the wider sense.

Veit-Wilson (1998, p. 45) draws a distinction between strong and weak concepts of social exclusion. Weak is linked to deficiency notions and places responsibility on the individual for failing to succeed, while strong identifies the issues as structural, with the powerful elements in society responsible for the excluding. Relating this to nonuse of ICTs, we may either view the problem as individuals failing to take up opportunities to learn and use, or as structural, about the type and availability of access to equipment and to relevant education and support.

Concepts of social exclusion are holistic. They aim to see exclusion as a complex system with multiple elements and systemic properties of feedback and homeostasis. They describe a process that persists over time. Remedial actions are inevitably partial and reductionist. They may involve detailed multiagency intervention at an individual level, which changes the state of an individual or family without disturbing the phenomenon at a community or social level (Maguire et al. 2003). Alternatively, interventions are singular changes for a community: improved childcare provision; a free Internet café; housing renovation; or increased CCTV surveillance. While these interventions can, and do, ameliorate the living conditions of a few, or many, people, they cannot end social exclusion or even, it might be argued, lead to a significant diminution of exclusion. The structures of inequality are too mutually reinforcing and stable for that (Lupton 2003).

Social exclusion leads us away from a simplistic definition of poverty as the only and sufficient explanation of an individual's ability to participate in the social, cultural, and economic life of wider society. However, it should not be allowed to obscure the deep and continuing economic inequality that lies at its heart (Piachaud and Sutherland 2002).

Moreover, the reduction of exclusion experienced by those who can now participate more easily through e-channels, for example those whose mobility is restricted by disability or caring responsibilities, may be at the expense of further increasing exclusion of those furthest from participation. The e-walls of the city may now be extended, including and protecting greater numbers; but they are also higher and more difficult for those remaining outside to scale or enter.

4 SOCIAL EXCLUSION AND TECHNOLOGY NONUSE

This section briefly reviews the literature on nonuse of ICT. The focus is on work, considering reasons for nonuse rather than its consequences. Lack of access to suitable equipment was initially identified as the key reason for nonuse of ICT.[5] However, physical access to technology alone is not enough to promote a digitally inclusive society (Selwyn 2003b). Evaluation of UK online centers stated that learners considered any new ICT skill to be of "limited use" unless supplemented by home access. They pointed to inconvenience, perceived cost, and low interest as the key barriers to uptake, once issues of access had been resolved (Hall Aitken Associates 2004; Wyatt et al. 2003). The Digital Inclusion Panel (2004) additionally identified as barriers to the development of e-skills: lack of confidence, inaccessible content, and lack of physical access and adaptive technologies. However, these were coupled with less tangible factors such as lack of knowledge, awareness, skills, and social support. Georgiou (2004) also reported that many learners had concerns about content, lacked confidence in the security of the Internet for financial transactions, and often felt that technology was too complex for them to fix if it went wrong.

Selwyn (2004) argues that many adults seem to be creating a use for technology rather than the technology filling deficits in their lives, making learner motivation problematic. Similarly, a survey of lifelong learning centers (Wyatt et al. 2003) indicated that over 70 percent of users attended the centers to learn to use a computer. The second most common reason given was to learn to send e-mails to friends and family.

Longitudinal studies have discovered that meeting people, learning new skills, improving skills and confidence, improving employment prospects, reentering learning, and developing skills to help others were also motivating factors (Hall Aitken Associates

---

[5]Tony Blair, "Prime Minister's Speech at the Knowledge 2000 Conference," March 7, 2000 (http://www.number-10.gov.uk/output/page1521.asp).

2004), together with accessing information and improving health (Bradbrook and Fisher 2004). E-mail, shopping, and learning for personal interests were additional reasons for interest in the Internet by nonusers in the survey reported by Russell and Stafford (2002).

Selwyn (2003a) criticizes existing accounts of nonuse of technology for tending to assume that ICT use is inherently desirable and nonuse is seen as "abnormal." Nonuse is seen as arising from a deficit on the part of the nonuser: in cognition, personality, knowledge, resourcing, social situation, or personal ideology. Selwyn argues that to avoid such assumptions we should study the information needs of the individual rather than the perceived information needs of society. People can have legitimate and well thought-out reasons for not engaging with ICT; engagement depends upon individuals creating their own contextual framework and motivation for adoption, which is unlikely to occur without the encouragement of a compelling proposition. Woolgar (2002) suggests that the uptake and use of the technologies depend crucially on local social context.

In summary, our review reveals that the TAM and MATH models are unconcerned with socially excluded people's experiences with technology. On the other hand, the mainstream literature on social exclusion does not adequately account for the influence of ICTs. There is, however, a small but increasing body of literature on the digital divide, social exclusion and technology, and on nonuse of technology (Kvasny and Keil 2006). This review sets the context for our empirical study of nonusers of ICTs and their understanding of the technologies and their aspirations for use.

5   THE PENCEIL STUDY

In this section we briefly discuss our study design. Our aims included addressing the following question: What inhibits people who experience social exclusion from becoming competent and confident users and how can this be addressed? As Chatman (1996, p. 205) observes, "The process of understanding begins with research that *looks* at their [outsiders] social environment and that *defines* information from *their* perspective." Woolgar (2002, p. 7) also stresses the need to see how people interact with technologies: "We need to focus much more on bottom-up experiences, on the nitty-gritty of actually making the damn modem work." Thus, our research includes both an investigative element and action-research.

The field work for the study was conducted on and around a social housing estate in Lambeth, south London. The estate is typical of many in London, being characterized by high, but not extreme, levels of social deprivation; low income and qualification levels; and an ethnically and linguistically diverse population (Cushman 2004). Interviewees were recruited from users of a number of local agencies including a local community center, students attending local basic education and basic IT courses, parents at the local primary school, members of the estate's older people's club, and residents of an adjacent bail hostel.[6]

---

[6]A hostel for people recently released from prison, run by the probation service.

Our interviews covered both total nonusers of ICTs and people who were occasional and highly unconfident users. The interview extracts that follow are drawn from the 47 interviews conducted to date.

In setting the ethical policy for this research, which concerns people with little power, we identified a responsibility not to limit ourselves to studying but also striving to ameliorate the lives of people whom we investigate. For this reason action-research is a major component of our study. Based on the information collected during the interviews and drawing on the literature from the fields of education, social and digital exclusion, and information systems, we designed and ran an introductory IT course called "Living with Computers." Feedback from the participants and our experience of running the course is being used to revise the curriculum for future courses and to inform practice and policy in this area.

In designing the action-research element of our study, we sought not to set unrealistic goals. Reducing individual digital exclusion allows participants to achieve their life tasks more easily and maybe more cheaply, important for people on low incomes. Such interventions might, at the limit of their ambitions, allow excluded people to involve themselves, digitally and otherwise, in collective action aimed at changing the social conditions that define their life chances. Discovering better ways of teaching participants digital skills may also allow them to engage in the e-consumption of government services—to their benefit and to the benefit of service providers. This, however, is far from participating in an e-enabled democracy.

5.1 Motivations and Aspirations for Use

It was only among older interviewees that we met people with no contact with these technologies and no interest in using them. However it is important to acknowledge the warning by Selwyn et al. (2003) against identifying older people as a homogenous group. Through our field work we contacted a range of older people, from early 60s to 90s and from would-be enthusiasts to total "refusniks."

Most of the sample under retirement age had some, although often very restricted, experience with ICTs and all those with no experience expressed a wish to use them. Parents of school age children gave several reasons for wanting to know about computers. These included, having once purchased a computer for their children to use, wanting to know what their children were doing. As one parent explained,

AA:　*Sometimes they are on the computer, Internet, and you don't know what they are doing.* [Ghanaian female]

Others had acquired computers so that their children could use them for their homework and they wanted to be able to support them.

CM:　*She [my daughter] has been quite bad at IT at school, and she's struggled with it quite a bit, because she's not been able to practice. So I'm hoping that now we've got this, and when we get it up and running she will be on it quite a bit....And I want to be able to help her.* [English female]

Interestingly, even those who did not use computers nor have plans to use them in the near future expressed a belief that computer skills are becoming a necessity, even if they could not articulate activities for which they could potentially use computers.

DA: *Well, it makes you feel like, you know, I don't know if I am using the right words, but as if you are in the Dark Ages.* [Ghanaian female]

Most respondents envisaged some activities they could potentially perform using a computer. Communicating via e-mail was most commonly mentioned. Many respondents were born outside the UK and had identified e-mail as a way of keeping in touch with family and friends abroad, while avoiding high telephone bills.

Int: *What sort of things do you use it for?*
VR: *Just check my mail, and I send mail.*
Int: *Who to?*
VR: *My people in Africa, in the US, my friends in Canada.* [Nigerian female]
AH: *Oh, my brother says why you not get the e-mail and the computer for?* [Somali female]

Searching for information was sometimes mentioned spontaneously and frequently provoked an interested or even enthusiastic response, when prompted, but it was also an area of anxiety.

Int: *Why haven't you tried to look at the Web?*
AA: *Maybe I am a little bit scared. Not to do the wrong thing and maybe to affect her [daughter's] work or whatever it is. Just to leave it alone. Until I have more confidence.*
Int: *Would you like to look at Ghanaian newspapers and things like that?*
AA: *Oh yes. Yes. I would like to. I have a friend, just across, and the children go there and they go on Ghanaian web, and football and all that in the news. And it would be great to see what is going on.* [Ghanaian female]

Some interviewees expressed a wider list of aims.

DA: *There are so many things you can do with them, like shopping, research, and other things.* [Ghanaian female]

Nevertheless, common to the total nonusers of ICTs and the occasional users were their limited aspirations for the use of ICTs. Many interviewees knew about e-mail and were using it or wanted to use it for communicating with distant family and friends; none mentioned instant messaging as a way of achieving the same goal. VoIP (voice-over-Internet protocol), which had much media coverage during the later interviews, was not even recognized as a possibility.

Most respondents were familiar with the idea of e-shopping (surprisingly frequently identified as eBay) whether they wished to engage in it or not but eGovernment services were almost totally unknown. Only one or two were aware it was possible to use the

Internet to contact local or central government. Even when the possibilities were described, few people responded enthusiastically—most wished to continue to use the phone or visit offices in person. They appeared to mistrust the responsiveness of these services and believed it necessary to apply verbal or emotional pressure to gain their desired response, believing Internet messages would be ignored. The benefits of not hanging on the phone or waiting in an office, although recognized, would not compensate for the perceived loss of efficacy.

Int: *How about using it to sort out problems with the council and things like that?*

DB: *Um, I never thought of that, actually. I just get the local Lambeth News, and they send the thing to you, so you read it and you know the only thing you have really dealings with the council is to pay them the council tax.* [African-Caribbean female]

Int: *How about getting in touch with the council about home helps or social services or something like that?*

GR: *Can you do it online then? Does it cost you as much or not?*

Int: *You would rather use the telephone then to try to sort things out. Talk to people rather than send them messages.*

GR: *Yeah, because they might not be there.* [English female]

The local council tries to promote the use of the Internet for contacting services, and its newsletter, referred to by interviewee DB, carries many articles about, and advertisements for, these channels but they appear to have little impact on nonusers. It is only engagement with the technology that transforms these from unknown possibilities into appreciated opportunities.

At the beginning of the "Living with Computers" course, participants were asked about their experience of computers and their aims. Respondents mostly expressed their aims either in generalized terms, "to learn how to use a PC"; as a wish to perform some activity (mainly sending e-mail); or identified specific skills, like using a mouse (see Wyatt et al. 2003). Only four participants out of 13 gave different answers: "help me at work and use computer for football program," "advance in life and get a job in an office," "advance my business," and "help work on my finances."

5.2 Barriers to Use

Our research indicates the nature of the complex relation that people have with ICT. For the majority of our interviewees, ICTs appeared to offer a challenge that other domestic electronics did not. Most respondents described frequent use of mobile phones and many had surmounted the complex interface to send text messages. Most used VCRs for playing tapes and often for immediate recording of programs; however, few were able to program a VCR for deferred recording. Most also, occasionally or regularly, used ATMs to withdraw cash.

Physical access to computers did not represent the greatest barrier to use. Many have computers in their homes and there are free-to-use public computers locally. The barriers are skills and confidence.

> Int   *So, how much have you used computers in the past?*
> AT: *Never.*
> Int: *Have you ever wanted to?*
> AT: *I get as far as PlayStation games and that's about it. So it's not
> really computers. I just find them hard to work, hard to understand.
> I've tried. I just can't do.* [English male]

Another recurring theme from the interviews was anxiety about the technology itself. A number expressed the fear "I might break it." Some people did not use the computers they had at home because they feared destroying their children's or partner's work. This contrasts with the reaction of experienced users that the technology frustrates them because it breaks down on them. Respondents reported that they would ask a relative or a neighbor (or often their child) to fix a breakdown. There was little knowledge of commercial repairers or of manufacturer or supplier help lines. This indicated that social isolation was a factor enabling or preventing use of these technologies, distinct from social exclusion.

Many interviews revealed an amorphous fear that something might happen to their computer from out there—an ill-digested mixture of partly understood news items about viruses, phishing, and spam. Some perceived the Internet as a source of threat, particularly for children who might access inappropriate information or engage in chats with unsuitable people. E-shopping raised further anxieties.

> Int: *Why shop with the computer?*
> DA: *Oh, I think it is nice to go out and about shopping. But when you
> have got little ones sometimes it can be difficult. So to go online
> shopping ...*
> Int: *Right, you have credit cards and everything.*
> DA: *Yes, but I don't normally use them.*
> Int: *Would you be worried about security if you shopped online, do you
> think?*
> DA: *Yes, that's one thing.*
> Int: *What would you worry about?*
> DA: *About somebody getting to your details.* [Ghanaian female]

Use of the Internet for shopping requires possession of a credit or debit card and, further, a willingness to use it under unfamiliar conditions, against a background of media stories about Internet fraud and theft. The resulting issues of trust are important in understanding people's willingness or reluctance to use the Internet for transactions. Dutton and Shepherd (2003) describe the Internet as an *experience technology* and that it is only through use that people develop trust.

6   DISCUSSION

ICT nonuse in the domestic environment is a little researched topic. Research has been concentrated on the user rather than the nonuser. The work reported here allows us to start to understand the needs and demands of nonusers and to engage in strategies to address their needs.

Not surprisingly, our research supports claims in the literature that lack of confidence is an important barrier to computer use and that there is a link between personal circumstances (e.g. , parenthood, age, income) and computer ownership (Digital Inclusion Panel 2004; Dutton and Shepherd 2003). For example, it appears that people with school-age children are more motivated to buy a computer. However, not all parents actually use the computer they have purchased.

As in previous research (Georgiou 2004), our respondents expressed concerns about the Internet content and we have found that wishing to be able to supervise children motivated learning. They also worried about security of financial transactions and thus generally were not enthusiastic about e-shopping. They had little understanding of how to manage computers and relied heavily on social networks for support.

Our findings demonstrate that our respondents only imagined narrow uses for computers, largely shaped by popular media. The interviewees did not consider using the Internet to contact local or central government (actively encouraged in the UK). They did not envisage engaging in civil activities on the Internet nor building or joining any virtual communities. This implies that the UK government's vision of e-citizens is over-optimistic and excludes many groups of people, even in its very minimal form: picturing people as consumers of governments' e-services rather than active participants in e-democracy. The way that consumer ICTs are presented in the media—as black boxes to achieve pre-described ends—makes this imagining of potential more difficult and sets a challenge for educators.

However, it is clear that our interviewees valued the communication aspect of these technologies and wished to engage in communicative actions, not data management. They were also aware that communication entails risk, and new and unknown (and to them unknowable) risks are generated when the communication is mediated by ICTs. This demands assistance in explanation, management, and reduction of technology-amplified risk. The needs and aspirations revealed by our interviewees mapped very poorly onto existing basic ICT curricula. There has been considerable investment in basic IT skills training in the UK and courses are available at the community center and the local further education college. Our findings, however, call into question the curriculum offered.

UK basic IT curricula have remained essentially unchanged since they were first developed in the 1980s. They concentrate on learning to use applications, primarily MS Office, although courses in computer graphics, DTP, sound editing, etc. are also available. The office productivity courses rest on an assumption that students' over-whelming aspiration is to learn computing to gain an office job. While IT competencies are increasingly essential for employment, this is not the only reason to learn. Many of our interviewees were interested in gaining employment skills, but others—and not only those above retirement age—centered their aims on using computers for personal pur-poses. The conventional, highly skills-based curricula, do not promote discussion to explore possible uses nor the ways these technologies can be enrolled in changing forms of domestic life. Kvasny (2005) suggests that community technology centers should not only teach basic computing skills but also ways of using the Internet for consumption, civic engagement, communication, and self expression. To challenge social exclusion, an e-literacy curriculum must also respond to Livingstone's (2004, p. 5) demands to enable people "to access, analyze, evaluate and communicate messages in a variety of forms." The aspects of analyze and evaluate are frequently minimized or absent, and creation, which Livingstone sees as central, often marginalized.

Venkatesh and Brown (2001, p. 94) reported, "non-adopters were influenced strongly by the fear of obsolescence." Their emphasis on obsolescence as a barrier was not mirrored in our interviews and arguably represents the perception of people close to the technology and choosing not to purchase it, rather than the perceptions of people excluded by the technology.

Accordingly, the course syllabus[7] designed in our research places emphasis on discussion of different ways and reasons for engaging with ICT, analyzing and evaluating varied sources of information and their content, as well as communication and content creation (e.g., through blogging). It brings the activities, such as sending e-mail, that people have identified during interviews and in course entry questionnaires to the start of the program rather than relegated to the end. In addressing the fears of our respondents, the syllabus also outlines the key aspects of managing computers at home. This includes buying and setting up a computer for use at home, connecting to the Internet, security issues (fire walls, viruses, backups, etc.), and ways of dealing with breakdown.

7 CONCLUSION

Our findings argue that we should consider an approach to e-literacy needs as a negotiated set of understandings and competencies related to individually conceived tasks rather than as an externally imposed program. These skills sit within an individual's interaction with, and appropriation of, technologies not in abstract form to be banked for future application.

Our research has identified educational routes toward digital inclusion. The curriculum weaknesses identified in this research do not stand alone. They reflect a view of computer users as adjuncts to a controlling machine, not as active citizens mapping their own routes through this complex and contested terrain. Our new curriculum places learner aspirations at the center and sees engagement decisions as a dialogic and not an individualized process.

In contrast, TAM and MATH reflect a view of technologies as ends in themselves, to be adopted; not as intermediate steps in achieving ends or completing tasks, or enabling people to make progress through their life-worlds. This worldview is reflected in curricula which set targets of learning word-processing or spreadsheets. In contrast, our research identified learning aims, such as e-mailing or web searching, which are less application centered. However, achieving such tasks still masks the life experiences they are meant to enhance: maintaining contact with distant family and friends or doing the weekly shopping.

---

[7]The outline for the course is available at http://penceil.lse.ac.uk/documents/CoursePlan.pdf. We gratefully acknowledge the support of Lambeth Adult Learning Service in funding the course.

We identified respondents' inability to imagine the variety of uses to which they might put ICTs, coupled with a lack of knowledge about possible technologies or services, as a barrier to engagement and use. This indicates a conceptual problem in applying TAM and MATH in this setting. They presuppose a set of dispositions toward technology that require sufficient familiarity to allow users (not actors) to discriminate between alternative technologies on the basis of their anticipated usefulness and ease of use. Both approaches posit rational users, knowledgeable about their situation and the options that confront them, and thus able to review options and reach an optimal solution. One aspect of exclusion, both digital and social, is lack of knowledge about options, for which a conventional remedy is the provision of advice and advocacy services. Such advice on ICT selection is rarely formally provided. Our data suggests that this unknowingness makes nonusers' formulation of plans difficult and the support available to nurture their introduction to the technology—such as through education and training or accessible and trusted technical support— is a more important determinant of adoption than PU and PEOU.

Our concern is that research based on TAM and similar models further marginalize the excluded, seeing them as unsuitable subjects for technology adoption research. We worry that such studies give an impression of a cohesive consumer society, in which all can and do take advantage of e-services. The socially excluded should not be absent from technology adoption studies and correspondingly the literature on social exclusion must study the use and nonuse of technology.

Acknowledgments

We thank all our interviewees for their time, the ESRC for their funding and support, and our anonymous reviewers for their suggestions. We also thank Edgar Whitley, London School of Economics, and Linda Milbourne, King's College London, for their advice, and Eileen Trauth for her detailed and rigorous, but encouraging, comments.

References

Ajzen, I. "The Theory of Planned Behavior," *Organizational Behavior and Human Decision Processes* (50), March 1991, pp. 179-211.
Bourdieu, P. "The Forms of Capital" in S. Baron , J. Field, and T. Schuller (eds.), *Social Capital: Critical Perspectives*, Oxford, UK: Oxford University Press, 1986.
Bradbrook, G., and Fisher, J. "Digital Equality: Reviewing Digital Inclusion Activity and Mapping the Way Forwards," Citizens Online, Swindon UK, March 2004 (available online at http://www.citizensonline.org.uk/site/media/documents/939_DigitalEquality1.pdf)
Brown, S. A., and Venkatesh, V. "Model of Adoption of Technology in Households: A Baseline Model Test and Extension Incorporating Household Life Cycle," *MIS Quarterly* (29:3), 2005, pp. 399-426.
Burchardt, T., Le Grand, J., and Piachaud, D. "Introduction" in J. Hills, J. Le Grand, and D. Piachuad (eds.), *Understanding Social Exclusion*, Oxford, UK: Oxford University Press, 2002, p. xiv.
Chatman, E. A. "The Impoverished Life-World of Outsiders," *Journal of the American Society for Information Science* (47:3), 1996, pp. 193-206.
Ciborra, C. *The Labyrinths of Information: Challenging the Wisdom of Systems,* Oxford, UK: Oxford University Press, 2002.

Cornford, T., and Klecun-Dabrowska, E. "Social Exclusion and Information Systems in Community Healthcare" in M. Korpela, R. Montealegre, and A. Poulymenakou (eds.),*Organizational Information Systems in the Context of Globalization*, Boston: Kluwer Academic Publishers, 2003, pp 291-306,

Cushman, M. "St Martin's Estate—An Area Profile" Penceil Papers 1, Penceil Project, London School of Economics, 2004.

Davis, F. D. "Perceived Usefulness, Perceived Ease of Use, and User Acceptance of Information Technology," *MIS Quarterly* (13:3), 1989, pp. 319-340.

Davis, F. D., Bagozzi, R. P.,and Warshaw, P. R. "User Acceptance of Computer-Technology: A Comparison of Two Theoretical-Models," *Management Science* (35:8), 1989, pp. 982-1003.

Devins, D., Darlow, A., and Smith, V. "Lifelong Learning and Digital Exclusion: Lessons from the Evaluation of an ICT Learning Center and an Emerging Research Agenda," *Regional Studies* (36:8), 2002, pp. 941-945.

Digital Inclusion Panel. *Enabling a Digitally United Kingdom: A Framework for Action,* London: Cabinet Office, 2004.

Dutton, W. H., di Gennaro, C., and Hargrave, A. M. *Oxford Internet Survey (2005 Report): The Internet in Britain,* Oxford, UK: Oxford Internet Institute, 2005.

Dutton, W. H., and Shepherd, A. *Trust in the Internet: The Social Dynamics of an Experience Technology,* Oxford, UK: Oxford Internet Institute, 2003.

Gefen, D., Karahanna, E., and Straub, D. W. "Trust and TAM in Online Shopping: An Integrated Model," *MIS Quarterly* (27:1), 2003, pp. 51-90.

Gefen, D., and Straub, D. W. "Gender Differences in the Perception and Use of E-Mail: An Extension to the Technology Acceptance Model," *MIS Quarterly* (21:4), 1997, pp. 389-400.

Gefen, D., and Straub, D. W. "The Relative Importance of Perceived Ease of Use in IS Adoption: A Study of E-Commerce Adoption," *Journal of the Association for Information Systems* (1:8), 2000, pp. 1-30.

Georgiou, G. *General IT Literacy: A Research Report of a Survey of the British Population on Computer Usage,* London: The British Computer Society, 2004.

Gordon, D., Adelman, L., Ashworth, K., Bradshaw, J., Levitas, R., Middleton, S., Pantazsis, C., Patsios, D., Payne, S., Townsend, P., and Williams, J. *Poverty and Social Exclusion in Britain,* York, UK: Joseph Rowntree Foundation, 2000.

Haddon, L. "Social Exclusion and Information and Communication Technologies: Lessons from Studies of Single Parents and the Young Elderly," *New Media and Society* (2:4), 2000, pp. 387-406.

Hall Aitken Associates. *Community Access to Lifelong Learning Centers Evaluation: Interim Report on Survey Results,* Hall Aitken Associates, London, 2004.

Hills, J., Le Grand, J., and Piachaud, D. *Understanding Social Exclusion,* Oxford, UK: Oxford University Press, 2002

Howcroft, D., and Trauth, E. M. *Handbook of Critical Information Systems Research: Theory and Application,* Cheltenham, UK: Edward Elgar, 2005.

Hubregtse, S. "The Digital Divide Within the European Union," *New Library World* (106:3/4), 2005, pp. 164-172.

Introna, L. *Management, Information and Power,* Basingstoke, UK: Macmillan, 1997.

Korupp, S. E., and Szydlik, M. "Causes and Trends of the Digital Divide," *European Sociological Review* (21:4), 2005, pp. 409-422.

Kvasny, L. "The Role of the Habitus in Shaping Discourses About the Digital Divide," *Journal of Computer-Mediated Communication* (10:2), 2005 (available online at http://jcmc.indiana.edu/vol10/issue2/kvasny.html).

Kvasny, L., and Keil, M. "The Challenges of Redressing the Digital Divide: A Tale of Two US Cities," *Information Systems Journal* (16:1), 2006, pp. 23-53.

Lamb, R., and Kling, R. "Reconceptualizing Users as Social Actors in Information Systems Research," *MIS Quarterly* (27:2), 2003, pp. 197-235.

Liff, S., Steward, F., and Watts, P. "New Public Places for Internet Access: Networks for Practice-Based Learning and Social Inclusion" in S. Wolgar (ed.), *Virtual Society? Technology, Cyberbole, Reality*, Oxford, UK: Oxford University Press, 2002, pp. 99-114.

Livingstone, S. "Media Literacy and the Challenge of New Information and Communication Technologies," *The Communication Review* (7:1), 2004, pp. 3-14.

Lupton, R. *Poverty Street: Causes and Consequences of Neighbourhood Decline*, Bristol, UK: Policy Press, 2003.

Maguire, M., Macrae, S., and Milbourne, L. "Early Interventions: Preventing School Exclusions in the Primary Setting," *Westminster Journal of Studies in Education* (26:2), 2003, pp. 43-62.

Milbourne, L. "Life at the Margin: Education of Young People, Social Policy and the Meanings of Social Exclusion," *International Journal of Inclusive Education* (6:4), 2002, pp. 325-343.

Ngwenyama, O. K. "The Critical Social Theory Approach to Information Systems: Problems and Challenges" in H.-E. Nissen, H. K. Klein, and R. Hirschheim (eds.), *Information Systems Research: Contemporary Approaches and Emergent Traditions*, Amsterdam: North-Holland, 1991, pp. 267-280.

Piachaud, D., and Sutherland, H. "Changing Poverty Post-1997," CASE Oaper 63, Center for Analysis of Social Exclusion, London School of Economics, 2002.

Russell, N., and Stafford, N. "Trends in ICT Access and Use," Research Report No. 358, Department for Education and Skills, London, 2002.

Selwyn, N. "Apart from Technology: Understanding People's Non-Use of Information and Communication Technologies in Everyday Life," *Technology in Society* (25), 2003a, pp. 99-116.

Selwyn, N. "ICT for All? Access and Use of Public ICT Sites in the UK," *Information, Communication and Society* (6:3), 2003b, pp. 350-375.

Selwyn, N. "At Home to Adult Learning," *E-learning Age*, November 2004, pp. 20-21.

Selwyn, N., Gorard, S., and Furlong, J. "Whose Internet Is It Anyway? Exploring Adults' (Non)Use of the Internet in Everyday Life," *European Journal of Communication* (20:1), 2005, pp. 5-26.

Selwyn, N., Gorard, S., Furlong, J., and Madden, L. "Older Adults' Use of Information and Communications Technology in Everyday Life," *Ageing and Society* (23:5), 2003, pp. 561-582.

Silverstone, R., and Haddon, L. "The Role of Ac Services in Preventing Social Exclusion in the Emerging Information Society," Working Paper 28, Graduate Research Center for Culture and Communication, University of Sussex, 1997 (available online at http://www.databank.it/dbc/fair/download/fairform.asp?doc=wp_28.zip).

Silverstone, R., and Haddon, L. "New Dimension of Social Exclusion in a Telematic Society," Working Paper 45, Graduate Research Center for Culture and Communication (CULCOM), University of Sussex, 1998 (available onine at http://www.databank.it/).

Simon, H. A. *Models of Bounded Rationality,* Cambridge, MA: MIT Press, 1982.

Taylor, S., and Todd, P. A. "Understanding Information Technology Usage: A Test of Competing Models," *Information Systems Research* (6:2), 1995, pp. 144-176.

Veit-Wilson, J. *Setting Adequacy Standards: How Governments Define Minimum Incomes*, Bristol, UK: Polity Press, 1998.

Venkatesh, V., and Brown, S. A. "A Longitudinal Investigation of Personal Computers in Homes: Adoption Determinants and Emerging Challenges," *MIS Quarterly* (25:1), 2001, pp. 71-98.

Weick, K. E. "The Collapse of Sensemaking in Organizations: The Mann Gulch Disaster," *Administrative Science Quarterly* (38:4), 1993, pp. 628-652.

Woolgar, S. "Five Rules of Virtuality" in S. Woolgar (ed.), *Virtual Society?*, Oxford, UK: Oxford University Press, 2002, pp. 1-22.

Wyatt, J., Allison, S., Donoghue, D., Horton, P., and Kearney, K. "Evaluation of CMF Funded UK Online Centers," Hall Aitken Associates, London, 2003.

Wyatt, S., Thomas, G., and Terranova, T. "They Came, They Surfed, They Went Back to the Beach: Conceptualizing Use and Non-Use of the Internet," in S. Woolgar (ed.), *Virtual Society?*, Oxford, UK: Oxford University Press, 2002, pp. 23-40.

About the Authors

Mike Cushman is a research fellow in information systems at the London School of Economics working on the Penceil Project described in this paper. He has worked on projects on organizational learning and knowledge sharing in the construction industry. He also works on developing innovative uses of problem structuring methods. Prior to joining LSE, Mike worked in community education in inner London, where, in various capacities, he was responsible for developing programs for nonusers of the service and for individuals and communities who had been poorly served by the education service in the past. He finished his community education career as head of a large adult education service. Mike can be contacted at m.cushman@ lse.ac.uk.

Ela Klecun is a lecturer in information systems at the London School of Economics and Political Science (LSE). She holds a Ph.D. in information systems from the LSE. Her research interests include digital exclusion, e-literacy, health information systems, evaluation of information systems, and the application of critical theory and actor-network theory in the field of information systems. Ela can be reached by e-mail at e.klecun@lse.ac.uk or through her home page at http://personal.lse.ac.uk/klecun/.

Part 7

The Information Systems Profession

24 TO VANQUISH THE SOCIAL MONSTER: The Struggle for Social Inclusion among Peers in the Field of Systems Development

Thomas Elisberg
The IT University of Copenhagen
Copenhagen, Denmark

Richard Baskerville
Georgia State University
Atlanta, GA U.S.A.

Abstract   *The mechanisms of social inclusion and exclusion may operate among professionals within organizations and communities of practice. These mechanisms can be embedded into formal organizational structures, and exert powerful control over who the members of organizations and communities will deem to be acceptable and unacceptable within their society. Using capital theories as a theoretical lens, we analyze the texts of interviews with knowledge leaders in a software development organization. The analysis reveals how a threshold event operates to bring inclusion of newcomers to a collection of social communities. Until the threshold event, communities of newcomers are socially excluded. The existence of the threshold event, and the nature of the threshold event, is an unspoken and unacknowledged structure used in creating the social fabric of the organization or community. It is collectively, yet implicitly, decided when such an event occurs, and the social inclusion triggered without any explication otherwise.*

1 INTRODUCTION

Social inclusion and exclusion is often regarded from the perspective of large geographic communities. But these same phenomena can operate at an organizational level and consequently affect the design of information systems in software developing organizations because professional stakeholders are excluded from influence in the development process.

Please use the following format when citing this chapter:

Elisberg, T., and Baskerville, R., 2006, in IFIP International Federation for Information Processing, Volume 208, Social Inclusion: Societal and Organizational Implications for Information Systems, eds. Trauth, E., Howcroft, D., Butler, T., Fitzgerald, B., DeGross, J., (Boston: Springer), pp. 367-380.

The idea of social exclusion has conceptual connections to discussions about poverty and capability deprivation (O'Brien et al. 1997; Sen 2000; Silver 1994). Historically the term *social exclusion* has been associated with economic disadvantage, where the lack of income has been regarded as a root-cause for inequalities among actors at different levels in the society. However, adopting a capability perspective on poverty implies a multidimensional perspective on the phenomenon, since actors value distinct capabilities differently (Sen 2000). Since the introduction of the term social exclusion more than 30 years ago, the meaning of the concept has expanded widely and is today an unclear, imprecise concept (O'Brien et al. 1997) congested with economic, social, political, and cultural connotations (O'Reilly 2005). Social exclusion is, therefore, not only a result of lacking monetary capital, but can be attributed to lack of income over a wide range of different kinds of capital, including social, cultural, and symbolic capital. Acknowledging these aspects of social exclusion, this study is informed by Bourdieu and his idea of capital.

The term social exclusion has been interpreted in several ways (de Haan and Maxwell 1998). In this study we adopt the monopoly paradigm of social exclusion (Silver 1994), where social exclusion is seen as the consequence of group monopoly formation where certain groups are excluded from social closure. Within this paradigm, "the boundaries of exclusion may be drawn within or between nation-states, localities, firms or social groups" (Silver 1994, p. 543). Social exclusion is thus not only a phenomenon that operates at a societal level but also as a product of group dynamics in organizational settings. The focus on social exclusion in organizational groupings makes the characteristics of deprivation central in the analysis (de Haan 1998). Centralizing deprivation makes it possible to identify the criteria for inclusion and exclusion in organizational communities.

In this paper, we consider social inclusion and exclusion as related to communities of practice. It is generally accepted that communities of practice can be described as a group of people that share a basic interest or a passion for something (Lave and Wenger 1991; Wenger 1998). Communities of practice can be regarded as collectives with a high degree of shared capital. In one sense, gaining acceptance into the community means new members must to a large extent share the same capital as the other members of the community. Social inclusion and exclusion in terms of the community of practice is based on the degree to which people conform to the existing practice of that community. However, when these communities intersect within an organization, it raises the possibility of the social inclusion and exclusion of a community of practice as a whole. This might occur when the capital shared within the community has little importance or value among the other communities of practice within an organization. If a community's capital is undervalued outside of that community, all of its members may become excluded.

Using the notion of capital as a frame, we explore conflicts between social groups in a systems development organization. The research question we explore is: *How does social exclusion affect software development organizations?* We frame an interpretive analysis of the struggle of one professional group of developers to gain social inclusion within the remainder of the organization's software development communities. We show that software developers are not merely engaged in technical practice, but also in a social practice, in a constant struggle over scarce resources to position themselves in the organization to exert influence and consolidate their positions in the engagement of communities of practice.

2 CASE DESCRIPTION AND METHODOLOGY

This research engaged a company that may best be characterized as a software development organization specializing in mission critical applications over a wide range of business areas. The company (hereafter called Acme, a pseudonym) employs more than 300 people, most of whom hold academic degrees in systems engineering.

In the late 1990s, Acme settled on a strategic direction to concentrate focus on the capability maturity model paradigm (Humphrey 1989; Paulk et al. 1993) as a means to improve its systems development capabilities. Today Acme is certified level five according to the CMMI model (Chrissis et al. 2003). In its effort to implement the level five processes of the CMMI model, Acme has chosen to base the organizational implementation on the Microsoft Solution Framework (Microsoft 2003). Primarily, the team model presented in this framework has provided the inspiration for organizing Acme's knowledge network. Six disciplines are represented in the team model: Program Management, Development, Test, Release Management, User Experience, and Product Management.

Today each individual network is organized as something of an autonomous community of practice: a knowledge net consists of a number of members managed by a knowledge leadership group with typically four representatives. These representatives are considered to be professional experts within the discipline. The knowledge leadership is responsible for optimizing the process within the discipline and ensuring that state-of-the-art knowledge is continually evaluated and disseminated to the members of the network. The network also interacts with projects in the organization on a regular basis to ensure that this knowledge is applied in practice.

The decision to base the improvement effort on MSF was motivated by two factors. Apart from providing the organization with a framework for organizing the institutional tailoring of the high level processes of the CMMI model, this approach also addressed an emerging issue experienced in the projects: a lack of user involvement. Acme had recently been exposed to bad publicity regarding the user interfaces of its software products for a highly prestigious public project. This incident turned the attention to MSF, where the User Experience role is an integrated part of the framework. Top management agreed to adopt this framework, thus justifying the employment of people with skills in designing User Experience; a role that has not traditionally been represented in the systems development process. In this way, the justification for employing the User Experience people was motivated by an external demand for focus on the tangible design of the end product, not the internal architecture of the product that up to then had been a quality criteria in Acme.

The integration of technologies like CMMI and MSF into development practice produces increased perception of user and group empowerment (Adams et al. 2005). These models are in themselves loaded with certain values. In this study we acknowledge these technologies as structures that sustain the practice of the established community and thereby influence the criteria on which social exclusion and inclusion are determined (Adams et al. 2005).

2.1 Data Collection

This research is empirically grounded in an ongoing action research project. For the past 2 years, we as researchers have had regular access to the organization and engaged in work activities to collect data. This study is most accurately categorized as a case study within an action research project (Germonprez and Mathiassen 2004), although the study relies heavily on a thorough understanding of how Acme operates as an organization acquired through joint collaboration on action taking.

The practical problem that drove forward the case study design was centered on the disparate performance of the networks in the organization assessed on the basis of a general survey among members of the knowledge networks. The survey demonstrated that the User Experience network achieved the absolute lowest score, whereas the Test network was ranked as the overall best functioning network.

The specific data collection for this study involved 10 interviews. Subjects included two members of each network, two representatives from each network's knowledge leadership, and the knowledge leader in each network. The four interviews with the knowledge leaders serve as the primary data source used for the analysis in this study because of their central position in the networks. Subsequently the results of the study were presented to the knowledge leaders in Acme in order to triangulate the findings and to give the interviewees an opportunity to comment on the conclusions.

The interviews were conducted using a semi-structured interview guide, with six major categories. The six categories were focused on the respondents personal work in the organization, the application of knowledge in their work, their role in the knowledge network, their personal evaluation of the knowledge network they represented, changes, and, finally, current challenges and problems. Each interview was scheduled for 1 hour and was recorded with the respondents knowledge and permission. To protect the anonymity of the interviewees, they will be referenced as knowledge leader one through four (KL1–KL4) in the analysis. The interviews were all recorded and subsequently transcribed.

2.2 Interpretive Analysis

Our goal is the understanding of deeply held social and cultural beliefs of a community, rather than those of individuals. We approached the analysis using an interpretive frame (Walsham 1995) that regarded the interview transcripts as a collective text. Any such text can be interpreted using techniques from literary analysis (Johnson 1980; Norris 1982). Such analytical techniques are not only applied in literature and poetry, but have also been applied in marketing and advertising (Ahuvia 1998) as well as in information systems (Beath and Orlikowski 1994; Truex et al. 2000). Our analysis not only includes consideration for the message intended by the author (authorial intent), but also for multiple meanings that arise from the text itself in the context of the communities of practice.

3   ANALYTICAL FRAMEWORK

In the analysis, our interpretation is inhabited by a purpose of explicating social inclusion and exclusion. This study applies the work of the French sociologist Pierre

Bourdieu as an analytical framework to help guide the interpretation and help identify relevant passages in the empirical data. Bourdieu's theory is centered on three key elements that together seek to explain how social practice emerges. Bourdieu represents the logical relationships among the central concepts of his theory in an equation as [(Habitus) (Capital)] + Field = Practice (Bourdieu 1984, p. 101).

The *field* is defined as the social context in which social actors take part. The field is characterized by detached historical relations and structures anchored in certain forms of power or capital (Bourdieu and Wacquant 1992, p. 16). Within this arena, actors operate and fight for desirable resources. The field thus becomes a structured space of positions determined by the distribution of capital. Acceptance into a certain field can only be granted if the individual, who wants to enter, conforms to the governing social norms and displays an acceptable pattern of behavior (Kvasny 2002). Fields with a high degree of autonomy have high entry barriers for newcomers (Bourdieu and Wacquant 1992, p. 100), who must share the belief in the value of capital at stake in the field.

Habitus is defined as the existential setting that surrounds an actor. This includes internalized social norms and patterns of behavior. The habitus shapes the beliefs and character of individual actors. Habitus thus becomes the embodied practices that guide human agency. Bourdieu (1977) defines habitus as "a system of lasting, transportable dispositions which, integrating past experiences, functions at every moment as a matrix of perceptions, appreciations and actions and makes possible the achievements of infinitely diversified tasks."

Capital is a power resource that individuals can use to enter or change position in the field (Bourdieu and Wacquant 1992). Bourdieu defines four different kind of capital:

1. Economic: Monetary resources
2. Social: Group membership, relationships, networks of influence and support
3. Cultural: Knowledge, skills, competencies, education, and credentials
4. Symbol: Accumulated honor and prestige

The various forms of capital are means of power that can be used by actors to position themselves in the field. The relative importance of the various forms of capital is defined by the field.

4 THE STUDY

Our report below is structured according to the concepts in the theoretical framework. We attempt to expose the capital used by the interviewees in constructing the texts. Similarly, we explore the field that exists within the organization by exposing apparent structures that inhabit the interview texts. By revealing the field in the organization, we seek to understand the kinds of capital that are valued by actors in the field. To empirically ground the study, our interpretation of selected passages from the interviews will be presented in the analysis.

The analysis helps expose incoherence or contradiction in the social structures that inhabit the interview texts. Such incoherence or contradiction might explain the social inclusion or exclusion of various actors in the organization. Accordingly, this analysis is not intended to be a normative interpretation that evaluates conceptual schemas against a set of norms, but rather to more directly expose tensions and contradictions among the professional groupings in Acme. The aim is to identify naturally concealed aspects of practice in the software organization. In the following sections we seek to unveil the basic characteristics of the key elements central to Bourdieu's theory for actors in the two networks under investigation in Acme.

4.1 Defining the Habitus

It appears from the texts that the knowledge leaders in the User Experience group (KL1 and KL2) do not share common characteristics in their individual habitus. The two people come from different professional backgrounds and display different patterns of behavior. One of the knowledge leaders sees it as a prime objective to establish a well functioning network (words that provided key signs in the interpretation are underlined):

> _We_ have an _ambition_ in the network to also get the feeling that it is _fellowship_, but we do not feel this today, because the members do not _make any contributions_. (KL 1)

The use of the term fellowship has very thick connections, relationships of strongly held, closely shared values. The marginalized text is that KL1 wants to avoid being shunned or excommunicated from this community, or perhaps to shun others. An ambition to establish a User Experience fellowship, of course, is structured by the shared desire ("we") for the fellowship, but the lack of contribution by members. This clear contradiction could mean that "we" is really structured by "I." The text suggests the lack of shared values that would drive contributions, and KL1 believes his values should drive a powerful fellowship. KL1 is very focused on the process view, since a lot of his work effort is put here. KL1 surprisingly marginalizes the end-user in the interviews by not mentioning this group at all, although it is a prominent task for a knowledge leader in a User Experience network.

KL2 on the other hand marginalizes the process view that is central to the organization given its strategic interest for the CMMI model. Top management in Acme has emphasized the importance of the process view in the charter for the knowledge network mechanism. Yet KL2 does not refer to the process work that might be the most important part of the work in knowledge leadership. However, KL2 is very focused on the demonstration of the value of User Experience in the actual projects in the organization that develop software products.

> The only time that User Experience _succeeds_ is when you are out in the projects and get things to happen. Events and posters where everybody can see us including _processes are OK_, but there's got to be some _executive powers_. (KL2)

In this passage, success is connected with getting things to happen (real work). Processes are connected to executive powers ("where everybody can see us"). The framework of the text shows how KL2 values real work in the projects and the process work is some showpiece for the executives, perhaps disconnected from actual productive work.

The habitus of the User Experience knowledge leaders is quite divergent, especially in terms of the value of processes. In the Test network, on the other hand, it is apparent that the habitus of the knowledge leaders to a large extent is consistent and that they share characteristics. The actors espouse the same values and have a view of the knowledge network that is consistent with the official knowledge network charter.

The most important thing, when you are part of the leadership in a network,
is to be able to do leadership. That is, get the network to work! (KL3)

The process view is so strongly embodied in KL3 that the product view defers to this. Leadership gets the network to work. In the margins only do we find that it is the network that gets the product to work. In contrast to the User Experience network knowledge leaders, the Test network leaders see as their most prominent task to lead the network. There is no talk of fellowship or lack of contributions. The interview is constructed on the basis that members are actively involved in the work of the knowledge network, not in the construction of the knowledge network.

I see the knowledge network as an educational institution. It is all about
raising the knowledge level in house. (KL4)

Underlying this passage is the unit of analysis (the house and not the network). The network and its benefits are organization-wide, not located within a single group. This value reveals how the habitus of the knowledge leaders in the Test network is oriented toward the field in the organization. The values used to construct interviews with the User Experience network were different. The knowledge leaders of the Test network seamlessly fit the characteristics of the organization whereas the knowledge leaders of the User Experience network have difficulty in establishing an identity both internally and externally.

4.2 Valued Capital in the Field

Competing values and behavior prevent the knowledge leaders in the User Experience group from defining a common ground. More importantly, the actors fail to establish themselves by not sharing the valued capital in the governing field in the organization. Moving our analysis to focus more specifically on these values, the analysis reveals the specific forms of capital at stake in the field.

4.2.1 Social Capital

The field in organizations is heavily influenced by the structures in the organization. The determined adoption of the CMMI framework has influenced the design of the organization and has become a structure that guides practice. The concept of *process* has in this way become an influential source of valuable social capital, because these structures act as the focal point of all communication in the organization.

It is a classic question when you get introduced to the company. You are asked if you like processes. Little by little people become aligned, in the sense that they smile when you mention the word process....It is almost a question of religion. (KL3)

For actors to position themselves in the organizational field, they must believe in and value the process view. The religion metaphor used by KL3 contains the unspoken-of anathema that would characterize critiques of the process view. Indeed, the excommunication or shunning suggested earlier by KL1 is present in this text. If people do not support the process idea, they are considered nonbelievers. It becomes a central part of the social capital in the field, an important entry barrier for admission into the field and the social group. The presence of this value is also reflected by the frequent reference in all interviews to various processes in the organization.

I design processes. Right now I work intensely to get the User Experience part integrated into the common process definition of the organization. (KL1)

It cannot be the responsibility of the leadership e.g. to design new processes. This can be delegated out as a separate task. (KL4)

Do I follow any process? That's a good question. Well, I'm a part of a team where we follow a certain course of actions when reporting. But the work products that I deliver are not especially process controlled. KL2)

It is worth noting that the process concept is viewed in different ways across the two networks. The User Experience network is a fairly new discipline introduced by the organizational adoption of the Microsoft Solution Framework. The processes for User Experience are not yet defined and deployed in the organization. Perhaps this is why they lack processes that define the requirement of User Experience work products. The User Experience work in the organization is therefore coordinated through the use of common management processes. The interpretation of the interviews reveals that if "it" doesn't have a process, "it" doesn't exist, since the process is a fundamental structure in the field and a touchstone for all other aspects in the organization.

There is a big difference in the conception of the relationship between a process and a network. Where the Test network sees themselves as detached from their process, the User Experience network sees themselves as an internal part of their process. There are fundamentally conflicting views on processes and how processes are understood and valued differently by the two groups.

4.2.2   Cultural Capital

The cultural capital of value in the field seems to be based on a set of principles often associated with those of engineers. These values are openly expressed in the organization because of the overwhelming presence of engineers in the organization. These values may make it difficult for people from other disciplines, unindoctrinated in these values, to influence the shape of the capital in the field. Rather, people with competing beliefs must become assimilated into the governing cultural capital of the field.

> *It is really disreputable when we [User Experience people] are in the project. It is really an environment where the technical foundation has a high weight. When you sit as a UE representative among 50 others and argue that it is not supposed to be like that; then they will answer: But that's the way it is!* (KL2)

An unspoken concept inhabiting this passage is the source conflict KL2 has developed with others in the project. People don't explain to KL2 what is valued, they expect KL2 to understand (KL2 doesn't). User Experience people encounter the difficulty of penetrating the established ethos of the engineer. User Experience is a new discipline within systems development. KL2 earlier in the interview characterized this discipline as having a soft approach to systems development, safeguarding the interest of the end user based on a competing set of values. Such values contradict the principles of the engineer. KL3 characterizes the company as follows:

> *We are still an engineering company. This means that engineers to a great extend are very confident people who can work independently and who quickly can reach conclusions.* (KL3)

4.2.3 Symbolic Capital

In terms of symbolic capital, the interviews clearly demonstrate that a practical demonstration of expertise can change an actor's position in the field.

> *It is still a struggle being an unbalanced entity. For example, the User Experience network, they steadily fight for their acceptance. It has been a tough battle. In fact, Test has been through the same. It has actually arrived while I have been here. You must damn well prove you are worthy, before you will get a place at the table.* (KL3)

The value of practical demonstration of expertise is also revealed elsewhere in the analysis. All of the interviewees refer to previous or anticipated accomplishments in the organization, but there are unspoken differences between the User Experience group and the Test network. Both knowledge leaders in the Test network refer to accomplishments that are centered on processes. KL3 reports on an ongoing redesign of the existing process structure in the organization and KL4 concentrates on the development of an automatic unit test and GUI test to support the existing test process. Both actors are constructing the interviews in the context of anticipated savings in monetary capital that is particularly important in the field: cost reduction and time.

No such pattern seems to have been present in the construction of the interviews with the User Experience network. Nowhere do KL1 and KL2 refer to accomplishments that might be measured in any particular capital at all.

4.3 Defining the Field

During the process of analyzing the interview texts, certain themes emerged that prove valuable for achieving a deeper understanding of social exclusion in the software development process. In this section we will draw on selected parts of the texts to highlight these themes.

Organizational inclusion is of great importance for the User Experience people. This is not an issue in the Test network; they take it for granted that they are socially included in the organization. Recall KL3's earlier comment, "*You must damn well prove you are worthy, before you will get a place at the table.* By pointing out how the Test network has been through similar circumstances, KL3 marginalizes the issue of acceptance as an issue that is of importance to the Test network today; inclusion is taken for granted. Also the event or basis for the acceptance has been marginalized. It is not revealed how the Test network made the transition from being socially excluded to being included in the organization. This tacit achievement is left obscure and secret. Thirdly, the choice of the metaphor "get a place at the table"[1] implies a transition phase from being invisible to becoming visible in the organization. The text is constructed with the idea of a test where you get the opportunity to prove the value of your competencies. Finally the struggle is characterized as a steady fight, a tough battle. KL1, independent of KL3, makes use of the same battle metaphor to describe the current situation for the User Experience network.

4.4 The Battle Metaphor

For the last two years my main focus has been on the design of user interfaces. The User Experience network did not exist at this point in time. I fought a <u>*lonely battle*</u> *for more than ten months before the MSF roles were formally introduced.* (KL1)

...because a project can tailor its own process more or less as it pleases and because project managers possess a lot of power, then it doesn't by design ensure that User Experience will become a part of the project process....when a project manager is pressed for time they will drop processes that they do not know a lot about or processes that they believe will generate less value. It is an <u>*ongoing battle*</u>. (KL1)

These two extracts illustrate the context in which KL1 uses the battle metaphor. The interviewees repeatedly make reference to this combat metaphor. The texts show how KL1 sees himself as a champion; one that, given the singularity in values shown in the interpretation that revealed his habitus, perhaps has undertaken a heroic quest as a lonely champion. KL1 seeks to fight for the values in which he believes and that are not shared by other individuals in the organization. In the detailed accounting of the quest, KL1 never explicitly mentions the enemy that needs to be fought. The interpre-

---

[1]In Danish literally, "on the wall."

tation of this text reveals a champion with a cause but no clearly defined monster to battle. This is marginalized, a part of the story that was present for the interviews, but missing from the interview text itself.

I have simply got a sound beating and I was really low in the established hierarchy. (KL1)

The text makes reference to the "sound beating" of the champion. Yet, the monster that beat KL1 is marginalized. KL1 never names the monster that must be defeated to gain wide-spread acceptance in the organization. But the monster inhabits both networks. KL2 also fights this battle.

The purpose of User Experience network is to get more attention in house. There are two objectives: one is directed inwards, that is, we become better at what we are doing, and the second is directed outwards: that is, to render the User Experience part of the systems development visible to the organization. (KL2)

By emphasizing the importance of getting attention in house and rendering the User Experience network visible in the organization, KL2 marginalizes how the network is not visible in the house today. To become visible, the User Experience network must prove that they are worthy of their place at the table. Yet the battle that KL2 fights is not valued by peers.

This is still a discipline where we walk around—and I'm not the one to complain, because this is how it is in all organizations—and get into a context where there will be a natural resistance against what you represent. It corresponds to the job of internal police. (KL2)

KL2 uses the label "internal police" to characterize his own responsibility in the process. Internal police serves as a control function to verify that some unpronounced "law" is enforced. Present in this passage is a certain legalistic code that requires force to enact. This comparison indicates that KL2 is aware of the resistance among his peers for what he represents and the (unspoken) violence necessary to overcome it.

Common in the underlying premises of KL1 and KL2 is that neither has earned the right to be in the field. The monster that they are struggling to subdue is not necessarily the same monster recognized and valued in the field. The User Experience network may have indeed failed to demonstrate to the field that this is a worthy monster to subdue and that its conquest should earn the capital that would penetrate the barriers for newcomers to the field. To penetrate the entry barriers of the field, the User Experience monster must be great enough to gain professional acceptance among peers in the organization. At this point in time, the User Experience network seems to be socially excluded because they haven't earned the capital that comes from battling and vanquishing a significant monster that roams the field.

5   DISCUSSION AND CONCLUSION

The use of Bourdieu's theory of social practice as an analytical lens to understand the mechanisms of social exclusion has contributed new insight into how professional communities new to an organization must struggle for social inclusion among peers. We have highlighted the metaphors of monsters, champions, battles, and conquests because these enliven our descriptions of the interview texts and the interpretive analysis. Indeed these metaphors were present in the interview text, although unpronounced by the actors. The underlying mechanics of social exclusion described in these texts can be explained in general terms as follow.

Larger software development organizations provide a venue for the intersection of a variety of communities of practice. This intersection provides a social engagement that constitutes a field. In software development organizations, newcomers to such a cohesive social group of peers with distinct shared values (i.e., a field or a community of practice) will be excluded until they demonstrate socially acceptable behavior and accumulate the right kinds of capital as defined by the larger field. For the particular case of this software development firm, this admission is dependent on a threshold event. This threshold event wins social inclusion for the excluded group, in this case, one community of practice.

The threshold event for this organization appears to be the acquisition of ownership of a respectable process by the individuals awaiting admission. This threshold event is a struggle, akin to vanquishing some monster. But the quality of the monster is an issue. The field collectively decides whether the monster is of sufficient magnitude to warrant the capital needed to enter. In our case, the software development organization socially decides whether the User Experience group has gained sufficient ownership of a sufficiently respectable process to be socially included.

There are some very important social features in the case concerning this threshold event. First, there is no formally pronounced process of social inclusion or exclusion in the organization. The User Experience network is by definition part of the formal organization. But everyone, including the User Experience network members, understands very precisely that they are outsiders, socially excluded from the rest of the network because they have earned no capital in the social field within the formal organization.

Second, no one ever tells newcomers that there is a threshold event or that they must find it and complete it, and what makes the event valuable. It is an unspoken assumption, understood and shared by all of the actors in the field. It's sort of, "*We'll know it when we see it*." Even this vagary is never pronounced, but simply inhabits the social texts. Newcomers are socially excluded from the community of practice until the threshold event occurs. Discovery that such an event brings the capital necessary to win admittance to the field is all the more difficult when a complete community of practice has been excluded. Newcomers may be doing the "right things" from the viewpoint of their peers within their own community of practice, yet doing the "wrong things" from the viewpoint of the peers within a larger field.

Third, loss of valued capital can lead to loss of position in the field. A group can lose its social inclusion by not keeping up skills, know-how, and command over their process. In other words, groups that are not vigilant will degenerate and be excluded. In other words, new monsters grow and attack the careless.

How, then, does social exclusion affect software development organizations? We have demonstrated that within organizations or between certain communities of practice, despite implementations of formal structures to the contrary, newcomers may be socially excluded. Efficiency and effectiveness in the software development process may consequently be limited because the integration of some functions in practice is not recognized by peers. In our case, the professional community in User Experience is socially excluded from the larger field because peers do not recognize the qualifications held by these people. In practice, this means that the User Experience community fails to safeguard the interest of the end user—not because there is a lack of formal structures or management commitment, but because the User Experience people haven't accumulated the right kind of capital to enter the larger field and become socially included.

For some software development organizations and communities of practice, winning social inclusion involves a threshold event that is recognized by the actors in the field as winning sufficient capital to gain position in the field. The existence and nature of the threshold event may never be expressed, although it inhabits the social constructs of the organization with great strength. In one sense, the threshold event is something of a monster that must be discovered and vanquished by the newcomers, within the unspoken recognition and approbation of the other organizational or community of practice members. Only champions grow worthy of social inclusion.

References

Adams, A., Blandford, A., and Lunt, P. "Social Empowerment and Exclusion: A case Study on Digital Libraries," *ACM Transactions on Computer-Human Interaction* (12:2), 2005, pp. 174-200.

Ahuvia, A. C. "Social Criticism of Advertising: On the Role of Literary Theory and the Use of Data," *Journal of Advertising* (27:1), 1998, pp. 143-162

Beath, C. M., and Orlikowski, W. J. "The Contradictory Structure of Systems Development Methodologies: Deconstruction the IS-User Relationship in Information Engineering," *Information Systems Research* (5:4), 1994, pp. 350-377.

Bourdieu, P. *Distinction: A Social Critique of the Judgement of Taste*, Cambridge, MA: Harvard University Press, 1984.

Bourdieu, P. *Outline of a Theory of Practice*, Cambridge, UK: Cambridge University Press, 1977.

Bourdieu, P., and Wacquant, L. J. D. *An Invitation to Reflexive Sociology*, Chicago: The University of Chicago Press, 1992.

Chrissis, M. B., Konrad, M., and Shrum, S. *CMMI: Guidelines for Process Integration and Product Improvement*," Boston: Addison Wesley, 2003.

de Haan, A. "Social Exclusion: An Alternative Concept for the Study of Deprivation," *IDS Bulletin* (29:1), 1998, pp. 10-19.

de Haan, A., and Maxwell, S. "Poverty and Social Exclusion in North and South," *IDS Bulletin* (29:1), 1998.

Germonprez, M., and Mathiassen, L. "The Role of Conventional Research Methods in Information Systems Action Research" in *Information Systems Research: Relevant Theory and Informed Practice*, B. Kaplan, D. Truex, D. Wastell, A. T. Wood-Harper, and J. I. DeGross (eds.), Boston: Kluwer Academic Publishing, 2004, pp. 335-352.

Humphrey, W. *Managing the Software Process*, Reading, MA: Addison-Wesley Publishing Company, 1989.

Johnson, B. *Critical Difference: Essays in the Contemporary Rhetoric of Reading*, Baltimore, MD: Johns Hopkins University Press, 1980.

Kvasny, L. *Problematizing the Digital Divide: Cultural and Social Reproduction in a Community Technology Initiative*, unpublished doctoral dissertation, Georgia State University, Atlanta, GA, 2002.

Lave, J., and Wenger, E. *Situated Learning: Legitimate Peripheral Participation*, Cambridge, UK: Cambridge University Press, 1991.

Microsoft. *Microsoft Solution Framework v3.0 Overview*, Microsoft Corporation, Redmond, WA, 2003.

Norris, C. (1982). *"Deconstruction - Theory and Practice,"* London, Routledge.

O'Brien, D., Wilkes, J., de Haan, A., and Maxwell, S. "Poverty and Social Exclusion in North and South," Institute of Development Studies and Poverty Research Unit, University of Sussex, 1997.

O'Reilly, D. "Social Inclusion: A Philosophical Anthropology," *Politics* (25:2), 2005, pp. 80-88.

Paulk, M. C., Curtis, B., Chrissis, M. B., and Weber, C. "Capability Maturity Model for Software ver. 1.1," Technical Report CMU/SEI-93-TR-24, Software Engineering Institute, Carnegie Mellon University, Pittsburgh, PA, 1993.

Sen, A. "Social Exclusion: Concept, Application, and Scrutiny," Report to the Office of Environment and Social Development, Asian Development Bank, Manila, The Philippines, 2000.

Silver, H. "Social Exclusion and Social Solidarity: Three Paradigms," *International Labour Review* (133:5/6), 1994, pp. 531-578.

Truex, D., Baskerville, R., and Travis, J. "Amethodical Systems Development: The Deferred Meaning of Systems Development Methods," *Accounting Management and Information Technologies* (10:1), 2000, pp. 53-79.

Walsham, G. "Interpretive Case Studies in IS Research: Nature and Method," *European Journal of Information Systems* (4:1), 1995, pp. 74-81.

Wenger, E. *Communities of Practice: Learning, Meaning, and Identity*, Cambridge, UK: Cambridge University Press, 1998.

About the Authors

Richard L. Baskerville is professor and chairman of the CIS Department at Georgia State University. His research and authored works regard security of information systems, methods of information systems design and development, and the interaction of information systems and organizations. Richard is the author of *Designing Information Systems Security* (John Wiley & Sons) and more than 100 articles in scholarly journals, practitioner magazines, and edited books. He is an editor for *The European Journal of Information Systems,* and associated with the editorial boards of *The Information Systems Journal* and *The Journal of Database Management.* He is a Chartered Engineer, holds a B.S. *summa cum laude* from The University of Maryland, and the M.Sc. and Ph.D. degrees from The London School of Economics. Richard can be reached at baskerville@acm.org.

Thomas Elisberg is a Ph.D. student at the IT University of Copenhagen. His primary research interests regard information systems development and software process improvement focusing on organizational and managerial issues. He holds an M.Sc. in Computer Science and Business Administration from Copenhagen Business School. Thomas can be reached at elisberg@itu.dk.

25 VIEWING INFORMATION TECHNOLOGY OUTSOURCING ORGANIZATIONS THROUGH A POSTCOLONIAL LENS

Ravishankar Mayasandra
The Business School
Loughborough University
Leicestershire, UK

Shan L. Pan
School of Computing
National University of Singapore
Singapore

Michael D. Myers
Information Systems and Operations Management
University of Auckland
Auckland, New Zealand

Abstract   *This paper discusses some of the difficulties and challenges that an information technology (IT) firm in a developing country faces in its attempt to become a global player. In 1999, the firm KnowICT[1] embarked on a strategic project called Knowledge Management (KM), whose main purpose was to unify and integrate knowledge that resided in the various organizational business units into one strategic knowledge infrastructure. By combining the knowledge resources dispersed in the various organizational business units, KnowICT managers hoped that KnowICT could be transformed into a leading global IT consultancy firm, rather than be seen just as a provider of routine outsourcing jobs. Although at a basic operational level the KM project has been deemed a success, the attempt to combine the knowledge resources from the various organizational business units proved more difficult than anticipated. We use postcolonial theory to explain the difficulties and*

Please use the following format when citing this chapter:

Mayasandra, R., Pan, S.L., and Myers, M.D., 2006, in IFIP International Federation for Information Processing, Volume 208, Social Inclusion: Societal and Organizational Implications for Information Systems, eds. Trauth, E., Howcroft, D., Butler, T., Fitzgerald, B., DeGross, J., (Boston: Springer), pp. 381-396.

challenges that KnowICT faces. Postcolonial theory draws attention to issues of power, ownership, control, and identity. We suggest postcolonial theory can meaningfully enhance our understanding of the development and use of information and communication technologies in developing countries.

1 INTRODUCTION

The benefits and costs of outsourcing information technology services to developing countries such as India have been discussed quite extensively in the literature, with the promise of lower costs being one of the key drivers (DiRomualdo and Gurbaxani 1998; Earl 1996; Lacity and Hirschheim 1993; McFarlan and Nolan 1995). One notable feature of the research literature on global outsourcing, however, is that most authors discuss outsourcing only from the perspective of the organization that is seeking to outsource part of its business. That is, the benefits, costs, and risks of outsourcing have been considered mostly in relation to the concerns of organizations in the developed world. Almost all of the published case studies of outsourcing are from first world countries (e.g., Baldwin et al. 2001; Lacity and Willcocks 1998; Zviran et al. 2001). There have been a few exceptions in recent years with researchers drawing on theoretical lenses such as organizational politics, culture, and power (Heeks et al. 2001; Nicholson and Sahay 2001) to highlight important issues in the interactions between vendor organizations in the third world and their global clients. Also, in 2003, a special issue of *The Electronic Journal of Information Systems in Developimg Countries* was devoted to the growth of the IT software export industry in developing countries. However, on the whole, much less is known from the perspective of the outsourcing vendors (i.e., organizations that offer IT outsourcing services) in developing countries. The benefits, costs and risks of outsourcing for organizations in developing countries seem to have been largely ignored. One of the contributions of this paper is that it explicitly considers outsourcing from the other side of the fence (i.e., from the perspective of KnowICT,[1] one of the largest outsourcing vendors in India).

The main contribution of this paper is its application of postcolonial theory to the development and use of information and communication technologies (ICT) in developing countries. In doing so, it draws mainly from the application of this theory to one specific project at KnowICT called *Knowledge Management* (KM) whose purpose was to unify and integrate knowledge that resided in the various business units into one strategic knowledge infrastructure. This paper is organized as follows. The next section discusses postcolonial theory. The following section discusses the research method. Next, the case of the KM project within KnowICT is discussed, followed by an analysis and discussion of the KM project in the light of postcolonial theory and conclusion.

---

[1]KnowICT is a pseudonym.

2 THEORETICAL BACKGROUND

Most of the studies on the topic of ICT in developing countries focus on the issue of their impact and use on economic development or public administration (Avgerou 1990; Bhatnagar 2000; Fleming 2002). A few others focus on cross-cultural issues especially in relation to the subject of globalization (Gallupe and Tan 1999; Ives and Jarvenpaa 1991). In the latter category, Walsham (2001, 2002) discusses what globalization means in particular situations and contexts. He says that, for some, globalization and the spread of ICT throughout the world means the increasing homogenization of culture. For others, globalization is interpreted as a process whereby imported ideas, concepts, and artefacts are "indigenized."

While we agree wholeheartedly that cross-cultural issues are very important in attempting to understand the role of ICT in developing countries, the main contribution of postcolonial theory is that it enables us to see ICT developments in the developing countries in a much broader context—the long-standing historical relationship of colonialism, neocolonialism, and postcolonialism of the West to the developing world (Adam and Myers 2003). Loomba (1998, p. 2) defines the word *colonialism* as "The conquest and control of other people's land and goods," for example, British colonialism. Colonialism describes a system of political, economic, and social dominance over the colony by another country (Adam and Myers 2003).

2.1 Postcolonialism

Young (2001) says that postcolonialism can be defined as coming after colonialism and imperialism, in their original meaning of direct-rule domination. The postcolonial "marks the broad historical facts of decolonization and the determined achievement of sovereignty—but also the realities of nations and peoples emerging into a new imperialistic context of economic and sometimes political domination" (Young 2001, p.57). Loomba suggests that a country may be both postcolonial (in the sense of being formally independent) and neocolonial (in the sense of remaining economically and/or culturally dependent) at the same time. She says that postcolonialism is a word that is useful only if we use it with caution and qualifications. Postcolonial is a descriptive not an evaluative term, a point further emphasized by Prasad (2003, p. 7), who suggests that when using postcolonial theory or postcolonialism it should be noted that "Postcolonialism is not a narrowly systematized and unitary theory. Rather, postcolonial theory is a set of productively syncretic theoretical and political positions that creatively employ concepts and epistemological perspectives deriving from a range of scholarly studies."

According to Quayson (2000, p. 2), "A possible working definition for postcolonialism is that it involves a studied engagement with the experience of colonialism and its past and present effects, both at the local level of ex-colonial societies as well as at the level of more general global developments thought to be the after-effects of empire." Ashcroft (2001) focuses on the response of the colonized to the political and cultural dominance of Europe. In his view, the term *postcolonial* refers to all culture affected by the imperial process from the moment of colonization to the present day. "Post-colonial discourse is the discourse of the colonized, which begins with colonization and doesn't stop when the colonizers go home" (p. 12). Ashcroft argues that post-colonial theory is particularly relevant to the subject of globalization. He says "we cannot understand globalization without understanding the structure of global power relations which flourishes in the twenty-first century as an economic, cultural and political legacy of Western imperialism" (p. 208). In other words, although the term *postcolonialism* suggests an engagement purely with the original European colonial powers, as a theory, postcolonialism includes in its ambit discussions of the engagement of the once colonized with most of the developed world, including both North America and Europe. We agree with Ashcroft's assessment and suggest that postcolonial theory is a useful device for understanding globalization and the role of ICT in developing countries.

2.2 Postcolonial Theory and India

Postcolonial theory is particularly relevant to India. For close to 200 years, India was ruled as a British colony. The direct and indirect impacts of colonialism on India continue to be an area of scholarly interest and it is widely acknowledged that postcolonial theory offers important insights into the social, cultural, political, and industrial developments in the country over the last few decades of independent rule (Cohn 1996; Dirks 2001). Generally speaking, there are two distinct perspectives on colonialism and its impacts on India. The first and more traditional set of arguments focus on the excesses of colonial rule and its deleterious effects on the people and society at large. The reasoning behind this focus is well expressed by Raychaudhari (1999, p. 157), who writes, "It is difficult for the citizens of a former dependency which has gone through a prolonged struggle for independence to acknowledge any benefits of colonial rule." Some scholars have noted that the colonizers cleverly appropriated the understanding of local languages, customs, and traditions at which they arrived in order to impose a stronger colonial rule (Cohn 1996; Dirks 2001). The second perspective of colonialism in India, while acknowledging the negative aspects of colonialism, notes that it also had a positive impact insofar that it mobilized disparate constituencies to come together, giving the nation itself an identity. As Khilnani (1997, p. 21) writes,

> Foreign rulers brought with them to India a concept of the state—with its distinct, if often locally influenced, administrative and military technologies, its claim to rule over a precise territory, its determination to initiate social reforms, and its reorganization of the texture of the community—that drastically changed ideas about power in India.

Over the last decade and a half, the postcolonial era has seen the creation of a number of private enterprises in India, many of which have emerged as highly competitive players in the global market. These enterprises were mostly formed by entrepreneurs who wished to operate globally and overcome the effects of what some scholars refer to as subtle forms of postcolonialism or neocolonialism. KnowICT is one such company.

In short, it appears to us that postcolonial theory is particularly relevant to the study of globalization and the role of ICT in developing countries. We suggest that the contemporary phenomenon of IT outsourcing is yet the latest incarnation of the (post)colonial encounter, and hence, postcolonial theory or postcolonialism has much to offer in helping us to understand this global phenomenon. Postcolonial theory draws attention to issues of power, ownership, control, and identity, issues that were central to the particular information system project discussed in this paper.

3   RESEARCH METHODS

The research method used was that of interpretive case study (Klein and Myers 1999). One of the authors conducted intensive fieldwork at KnowICT Technologies in three phases, for a total period of 8 months. Multiple qualitative data sources were used including documents, e-mails, the Internet, field notes, and KM artifacts. One of the main sources of data was 52 in-depth interviews with informants from various business units including middle level managers, top management, and software developers. All of the interviews were conducted at the headquarters of KnowICT in India. Each interview lasted on an average about 90 minutes. All of the interviews were audio taped with prior permission and then transcribed. All of the interviews were direct face-to-face interactions, while follow-up discussions were conducted via telephone and/or e-mail.

At the end of the first two phases of data collection, we invited a member of the top management at KnowICT to visit the National University of Singapore (at the time, the location of both the first and second authors). We discussed and clarified with him our preliminary understanding of the case and the ideas we had formulated thus far. At the end of the two phases of field-work, we had acquired vast amounts of both primary and secondary empirical material, in the analysis of which we followed broadly the approaches outlined in Walsham and Sahay (1999). Interview threads that appeared particularly engaging and fruitful were highlighted during a long, drawn-out initial cyclic process of listening to the audio tapes, transcribing, and re-listening. This was followed by an open coding process involving a line-by-line analysis of all of the interview transcripts and the field-notes (Strauss and Corbin 1998). The open coding process in tandem with the highlighted interview threads and field-notes led to the identification and inductive placement of the main emerging issues into conceptual categories. Periodically throughout this process, we read and discussed a number of times the interview transcripts and the detailed notes made during field work in order to develop a better understanding of the various categories. Once the relationships between the categories became clearer, they were combined with the available secondary data to produce a written draft describing the case. The three authors then engaged the empirical material in an iterative interaction with the theoretical formulations underpinning the study leading to the theoretically abstracted discussion and conclusion sections.

4   CASE DESCRIPTION

KnowICT is one of the largest IT companies in India. KnowICT serves more than 450 global clients, has more than 35 software development centers and sales offices world-wide, and employs more than 45,000 people. KnowICT offers IT services, IT products, and consulting services that cut across a diverse range of industry segments such as manufacturing, retail, energy, financial services, health care, and telecommunications. KnowICT was founded in the early 1980s with a vision of creating a world-class organization. The founders had come around to the view that the answers to the major issues facing India such as unemployment, poverty, bad living conditions, and lack of accountability, to name a few, were not to be found in the "inward" looking models of economic development. Rather, they came to believe that only by creating a strong and independent profit-oriented organization that engaged in trade globally could a contribution be made toward improving the lot of the country's growing population. They believed that, indirectly at least, the benefits of running a globally profitable and successful organization would percolate down to the people and the society as a whole.

4.1 Initial Hurdles

In the 1980s, Indian government agencies controlled the availability and movement of even basic resources that were required to run entrepreneurial private companies. The bureaucratic functioning of these governmental agencies presented numerous hurdles for companies like KnowICT. For example, importing computers from abroad was a long process that necessitated the approval of a host of government departments, sometimes taking years. However, things started looking up for KnowICT in 1991, with the Indian government relaxing some of its earlier regulations. Foreign companies were allowed to invest freely in indigenous companies, multinational companies were allowed to set up offices in India, licensing restrictions on import of technology goods were removed, and the role of the government in the initial public offering process of all companies was minimized. KnowICT grew rapidly throughout the 1990s. During this period, KnowICT moved away from doing short-term, one-off projects to handling more complex software development, maintenance, testing, and package implementation projects.

4.2 The Knowledge Management (KM) Project

In late 1999, KnowICT embarked on a strategic project called *Knowledge Management* (KM). A KM implementation team (or KM group) was created in conjunction with the organization's research and training department. The main purpose of the project was to unify and integrate knowledge that resided in the various business units into one strategic knowledge infrastructure. By combining the knowledge resources dispersed in the various organizational business units, KnowICT managers hoped that KnowICT could take big steps toward transforming itself into a truly global firm.

The top management team sensed from their interactions with clients that they expected a lot more from KnowICT. Rather than KnowICT throwing a solution across the wall in response to the customer throwing across a requirement, it appeared that the customers now expected KnowICT to anticipate their business requirements and come out with solutions that added strategic value. The top management team, therefore, wanted to initiate a project to effectively harness the knowledge dispersed and embedded in the various business units, thereby enabling KnowICT to be a step ahead of customers and in a position to offer "strategic IT solutions." Another reason for the KM project was to create a stronger KnowICT identity amongst KnowICT employees. This started to be seen as a problem given the rapid growth of KnowICT as a company. In 1997, less than 2,000 people worked for KnowICT, but by 1999, there were close to 20,000 KnowICTians dispersed throughout the organization in various parts of the world. Most of these employees tended to work closely with various client organizations, and so their sense of affiliation with KnowICT was not as strong as it could be. The KM challenge was thus to ensure that employees and business units working for important global clients also strengthened the knowledge resources of KnowICT. The former head of the KM group under whose stewardship the KM project was launched explained:

> *With the business model we follow, the notion of belonging to a single organizational entity is not as strong as compared to other industries. Typically, the technologies that we work on are not proprietary to KnowICT and, therefore, the extent to which KnowICTians tap into organizational resources for their learning and troubleshooting needs is minimal. Therefore, we felt that the organizational apparatus that people access needed further strengthening.*

The KM project gained increased visibility and a common platform with the introduction of a central KM portal. Knowledge Market (KMarket), the internally developed knowledge portal, was rolled out in early 2000; it now represents the platform for KnowICT's KM project. With the launch of the central KM portal, a nine-member team called the central KM group was formed to drive the organization-wide KM project. The KM group is a blend of senior project managers, software engineers, research analysts, and marketing managers. The organization-wide KM project mainly revolves around voluntary submission of documents (also called knowledge assets) to KMarket, and the subsequent use of these assets by other KnowICTians.

5 ANALYZING THE CHALLENGES

Although at a basic operational level the KM project has been deemed a success, KnowICT currently faces a few important challenges. The heavily decentralized structure of KnowICT and the exclusive long-term relationships with client organizations pose interesting questions to the KM implementation team and the organization. The challenges posed by the organizational structure will be considered first.

5.1 Organizational Restructuring

The decentralized structure of KnowICT and long-term relationships with client organizations pose interesting challenges to the KM implementation team and the organization. KnowICT has recently restructured itself into a number of decentralized business units (DBU), which function as independent profit-centers. The DBU-based organization structure is a more decentralized version of the earlier organizational structure and aims at empowering each strategic unit to differentiate itself from the others. To some extent the movement toward greater decentralization, specifically the DBU-based structure, which encourages each business unit to differentiate itself from other DBUs, has moved KnowICT further away from the KM vision of having a centralized knowledge apparatus. At the same time, however, it has meant that the KM project is seen as being needed more now than ever.

5.2 Knowledge Ownership

Exclusive long-term relationships with client organizations pose more fundamental challenges to the KM project. To illustrate the key problem of knowledge ownership, we will analyze the case of one DBU in particular, KnowICT-1, a business unit that caters to global clients belonging to a particular industry segment. KnowICT-1 has steadfastly focused on this industry segment over the last 10 years and, apart from a few renaming exercises and minor realignments during organizational restructuring, has retained its essential structure throughout this period. Rather than participating in one-off projects, KnowICT-1 plays a bigger role in the functioning of the client organization, a strategically beneficial situation for KnowICT. KnowICT-1 has dedicated development centers to serve its clients and the teams typically handle projects involving the design, development, and testing of software vital for the customers' operations. A few project teams at KnowICT-1 are also involved in the long-term maintenance and troubleshooting of the customer IT infrastructure. At present, KnowICT-1 employs about 1,500 KnowICTians who work on various projects. A notable feature of KnowICT-1's clients is that they come from the same industry segment, and they compete with one another in the global market. This means that KnowICT-1 employees who do work for Company A are unable to share information with other KnowICT-1 employees who might be working for Company B. This inability to share knowledge was explained by a senior software engineer as follows:

> *Organization-wide management of knowledge is a strict no-no here. We [KnowICT-1] serve mutually competing firms and each firm is very strict about guarding its intellectual property rights. Even innocent exchange of information and benevolent use of shared knowledge with the rest of the organization may infringe upon the IP of another client. So I am afraid we don't—are not allowed to—really share anything useful with the rest of the organization.*

KnowICT has signed explicit nondisclosure agreements with all the client organizations that KnowICT-1 serves. A senior project manager explained that the nondisclosure agreements with the client organizations were worded very carefully. Taking the case of KnowICT-1's three main client organizations, Xena, Rena, and Cena,[2] he explains:

Our agreements have more to it than just safeguards against explicit knowledge transfer. The agreement with Xena for example, very clearly states that members of KnowICT-1 working for Xena cannot be relocated to any KnowICT-1 team that works for Rena or Cena, unless they have spent a year in-between at some other KnowICT unit. We also have clauses that protect KnowICT against possible poaching by client organizations. None of our client organizations can directly absorb any KnowICT employee into their organizations, except in cases where the employee has left KnowICT and has worked elsewhere at least for a year.

The elaborate and stringent agreements with the client organizations at KnowICT-1 in effect prevent knowledge sharing within KnowICT-1, let alone knowledge sharing across the whole KnowICT organization. A project team leader at KnowICT-1 believed that the participation of KnowICT-1 in the organization-wide KM project could be counterproductive to the client organization:

The projects that we work on at our development centers at KnowICT-1 involve design and development of software for clients' infrastructure. And with KMarket or organization-wide KM, there is a good chance that a few designs, feature implementations, processes, practices etc, [could] find their way out to places where the client may not want it to. Besides, some of our project managers hold key business and market information about the client organization's current and future software releases...safeguarding such information is critical from the client's perspective.

A senior software engineer explained:

I have realized that in the first place, our clients are very particular about the nature of work they outsource to us. They meticulously scrutinize each and every single detail of the coding we are required to do to make sure that we are handling less strategic aspects. So it's not as if we are working on big ideas and innovations that carry a great risk if shared. Having said that, I feel the knowledge sharing restrictions have made it difficult for others at KnowICT to tap into our expertise. Basically all this shows who has the control!

---

[2]The names of the client organizations have been disguised to protect their identities.

For the client organizations outsourcing to KnowICT, it is imperative that the dedicated KnowICT project teams working for them function purely as offshore extensions of the client facility. Managing and sharing knowledge for the clients is an important issue as long as it is *within* the KnowICT project teams that are working for them, and as long as such knowledge sharing favors the client organizations. According to a senior software engineer at KnowICT-1, client organizations tend to be very committed to the implementation of KM practices, but only when these are within the boundaries of the project teams working for them. We observe that KnowICT-1 appears to remain separate or is isolated from KnowICT and the organization-wide KM project at two levels: at a technology level and at a subcultural level.

5.3 Technology-Based Separation

Responding to the client organizations' requirement for knowledge hoarding within the KnowICT-1 project teams (and explicit restrictions on knowledge sharing outside of those teams), KnowICT-1 requires its project teams to remain suitably isolated from the organizational mainstream. Therefore, the IT infrastructure at the various KnowICT-1 development centers is cordoned off from the rest of the organization using firewalls. As a result of this fire walling, the servers and workstations within KnowICT-1 cannot be accessed from the rest of the organization. Any access to the servers located within KnowICT-1 from outside is possible only through access authentication, which is available to a select few in the organizational hierarchy.

5.4 Subcultural Separation from the Organizational KM Project

As KnowICT moves ahead with its decentralization-focused organizational structure, and emphasizes long-term project assignments, the organization-wide KM project also runs into deeply entrenched subcultural patterns within its business units. Employees who have worked for a specific customer for a long time are guided in their actions by their frequent interaction with the client and identify with the client organization more than they do with KnowICT. A software engineer from business unit KnowICT-2 and part of a team that serves a manufacturing company said:

> *To me any process that the organization emphasizes is an overhead and I consider KM to be an overhead. But if the same process is mandated as a requirement by the client organization, then I would definitely take part in it. It's just the way we have come up, we are ready to do anything for the client. But even though we know that we also have to contribute to the KM project at the organizational level, somehow we don't seem to do that.*

The client organizations consider their respective offshore KnowICT teams as part of their global operations. Conversely, the KnowICT project team members see themselves as almost a part of the client organization. The strong identification with the client means that many project team members do not see much benefit in creating an integrated central knowledge apparatus for KnowICT as a whole.

6 DISCUSSION

We will now proceed to discuss the KM project at KnowICT in the light of postcolonial theory. Gardner and Lewis (1996, p. 2) note that,

> while it is certainly important to analyze the structures which perpetuate under-development, we must also recognize the ways in which individuals and societies strategize to maximize opportunities, how they resist structures which subordinate them and, in some cases, how they successfully embrace capitalist development.

This is exactly what we have attempted to do in telling the story of the KM project at KnowICT. KnowICT executives have strategized to maximize their opportunities and, by and large, they have been remarkably successful. They have successfully embraced capitalist development and KnowICT has emerged as one of the largest IT firms in India.

Ashcroft (2001) says that the most contentious problems in postcolonial theory continue to be those hinging on the capacity of the colonized subjects to intervene in colonial discourse to contest it, change it, or generally make the voice of the colonized heard. He says that "the colonial subject may engage imperial culture by *using* it as a communicative medium or *consuming* it as cultural capital" (p. 45). To this particular point of Ashcroft's, we would add that the phenomenon of global outsourcing takes this one step further. KnowICT does not just use and/or consume Western or imperial knowledge and culture; rather, KnowICT actually *produces* it. KnowICT produces software applications, technology, and knowledge for companies in the developed world. But the paradox is that KnowICT does not own much of the knowledge or technology it produces. Loomba (1998) points out that colonialist knowledge was produced via negotiation with or an incorporation of indigenous ideas: "At a very practical level, colonialists were dependent upon natives for their access to the 'new' lands and their secrets" (p. 67). In a similar way, large companies in the developed world have become dependent upon KnowICT for the development of new software applications, maintenance services, implementation of new technologies, and network management. In the light of postcolonial theory, the global outsourcing phenomenon can be seen as a postcolonial extension of the appropriation or incorporation of indigenous ideas. One important difference from the colonial area, of course, is that KnowICT's role is to produce *new* software and *new* knowledge, not traditional indigenous knowledge. However, the outcome is still the same: the goods and resources that are produced are owned by companies in the developed world, not KnowICT. The intellectual property belongs entirely to client organizations such as IBM or Microsoft.

The problems of agency referred to earlier by Ashcroft—the extent the colonized can "intervene"—are central to the case of the KM project at KnowICT. On the one hand, KnowICT managers realized that "knowledge is power"—and they wanted more knowledge concentrated within their own company. The KM project at KnowICT was explicitly designed to unify and integrate knowledge that resided in the various business units into one strategic knowledge infrastructure. However, the KM project failed in its strategic objective to unify and integrate knowledge within the company. One of the main reasons for its failure was the nondisclosure agreements with clients. As it is the large companies in the developed world (the clients of KnowICT) that pay for the outsourcing work to be done, they are the ones that retain all of the intellectual property rights. Loomba says that "knowledge is not innocent but profoundly connected with the operation of power" (p. 43). In this particular case, then, KnowICT remained as "powerless" as before. It did not gain ownership of or even access to the knowledge it produces. The knowledge that it produced remained firmly locked up within the fire-walled enclosures of its business units.

On the other hand, we have seen that KnowICT managers and employees do not lack agency. For example, KnowICT executives restructured the company into decentralized business units; they themselves took this initiative, and no one forced them to do so. While this restructuring was done for sound business reasons, it had the effect of strengthening the independence and identity of each DBU at the expense of KnowICT as a whole. It moved KnowICT further away from the goal of having a shared KnowICT identity, which brings us to the issue of identity, an important concept in postcolonial theory. Like the issues of ownership and control, the issue of identity is central to understanding the failure of the KM project. An interesting feature of KnowICT is that many of its employees identify as much if not more with the client than they do with their own company. One reason is that KnowICT likes to have long-term relationships with its clients. Teams within KnowICT tend to be separated tech-nologically and subculturally from each other. In a sense, this separation is a post-colonial variant of the British strategy of "divide and rule"—although, of course, this effect today is largely unintended by KnowICT's clients. Further, the strong identi-fication with the client and the culture of knowledge sharing *within* teams meant that most KnowICT employees within the DBU had little interest in contributing to the organization-wide KM project. Our research reveals that the KM project was effectively doomed from the start (or at least it was doomed with respect to the achievement of its strategic objectives).

Finally, we note that it is important to compare KnowICT's case with other IT organizations (e.g., organizations operating in developed countries and global organi-zations having operations in developing countries) that face similar issues of knowledge ownership and confidentiality with client organizations. At first glance, the presence of similar issues in these other IT organizations suggests that these are simply indicators of tensions in all client-vendor relationships, rather than unique expressions of postcolonial asymmetries in KnowICT's case. However, we argue that a closer exami-nation of issues of power and control at the industry and governmental levels would still reveal that indigenous firms in developing countries are heavily constrained by their inability to intervene meaningfully in comparison with other IT organizations when furthering their global aspirations. In this paper, we have suggested that such constraints faced by indigenous organizations, in addition to being manifestations of organizational issues can also be viewed in the much larger context of postcolonialism. Further empirical work is required to investigate in greater detail the issues raised here.

7 CONCLUSION

KnowICT has been tremendously successful in the postcolonial era in India by offering outsourcing services to global clients in the developed world. However, it faces numerous challenges as it seeks to move away from routine outsourcing jobs and transform itself into a leading global IT consultancy firm. These challenges are vitally concerned with issues of power, ownership, control, and identity. We have suggested that postcolonial theory offers a useful perspective from which to understand the difficulties and challenges that KnowICT faces. It enables us to look at the development and use of ICT in developing countries within a broad context. From the perspective of postcolonial theory, the global outsourcing phenomenon can be seen as but the latest incarnation of colonialism. KnowICT produces knowledge, technology, and systems for clients in the developed world, but it does not own it. The lack of ownership and control over knowledge was brought into sharp relief by the KM project that was started in 1999. Although the main purpose of this project was to unify and integrate knowledge that resided in the various business units into one strategic knowledge infrastructure, the goal was never achieved. Intellectual property agreements with clients, the technology and subcultural separation of teams from one another, and a closer identification of KnowICT employees with the client organizations meant that any meaningful knowledge sharing was impossible.

One possible limitation of our study is the perspective of knowledge that we have taken in discussing the KM project. While we have viewed knowledge mostly as a commodity that the vendor organization gains or loses, taking a *practice* perspective of knowledge as some organization theorists have done (e.g., Blackler 1995) would require us to question the exact nature of organizational knowledge being gained or lost by the vendor. In conclusion, although KnowICT was started in response to the perceived postcolonial handicaps of India as a developing country, the company remains dependent upon companies in the developed world, albeit in a more subtle and sophisticated way. How KnowICT moves ahead from routine outsourcing and transforms itself into a leading IT consulting firm remains to be seen.

References

Adam, M. S., and Myers, M. D. "Have You Got Anything to Declare? Neo-colonialism, Information Systems, and the Imposition of Customs and Duties in a Third World Country," in M. Korpela, R. Montealegre, and A. Poulymenakou (eds.), *IS Perspectives and Challenges in the Context of Globalization,* Boston: Kluwer Academic Publishers, 2003, pp. 101-115.

Ashcroft, B. *Post-Colonial Transformation*, London: Routledge, 2001.

Avgerou, C. "Computer-Based Information Systems and Modernisation of Public Administration in Developing Countries," in S. C. Bhatnagar and N. Bjørn-Andersen (eds.), *Information Technology in Developing Countries,* Amsterdam: Elsevier Science Publishers, 1990, pp. 243-250.

Baldwin, L. P., Irani, Z., and Love, P. E. "Outsourcing Information Systems: Drawing Lessons from a Banking Case Study," *European Journal of Information Systems* (10:1), 2001, pp. 15-24.

Bhatnagar, S. "Social Implications of Information and Communication Technology in Developing Countries: Lessons from Asian Success Stories," *Electronic Journal on Information Systems in Developing Countries* (1:4), 2000, pp. 1-10.

Blackler, F. "Knowledge, Knowledge Work and Organizations: An Overview and Interpretation," *Organization Studies* (16:6), 1995, pp. 1020-1042.

Cohn, B. S. *Colonialism and its Forms of Knowledge*, Princeton, NJ: Princeton University Press, 1996.

Dirks, N. B. *Castes of Mind: Colonialism and the Making of Modern India*, Princeton, NJ: Princeton University Press, 2001.

DiRomualdo, A., and Gurbaxani, V. "Strategic Intent for IT Outsourcing," *Sloan Management Review* (39:4), 1998, pp. 67-80.

Earl, M. J. "The Risks of Outsourcing IT," *Sloan Management Review* (37:3), 1996, pp. 26-32.

Fleming, S. "Information and Communication Technologies (ICTs) and Democracy Development in the South: Potential and Current Reality," *Electronic Journal on Information Systems in Developing Countries* (10:3), 2002, pp. 1-10.

Gardner, K., and Lewis, D. *Anthropology, Development and the Post-Modern Challenge*, Chicago: Pluto Press, 1996.

Gallupe, R. B., and Tan, F. B. "A Research Manifesto for Global Information Management," *Journal of Global Information Management* (7:3), 1999, pp. 5-18.

Heeks, R., Krishna, S., Nicholson, B., and Sahay, S. "Synching or Sinking: Global Software Outsourcing Relationships," *IEEE Software* (18:2), 2001, pp. 54-60.

Ives, B., and Jarvenpaa, S. L. "Applications of Global Information Technology: Key Issues for Management," *MIS Quarterly* (15:1), 1991, pp. 32-49.

Khilnani, S. *The Idea of India*, London: Hamish Hamilton, 1997.

Klein, H. K., and Myers, M. D. "A Set of Principles for Conducting and Evaluating Interpretive Field Studies in Information Systems," *MIS Quarterly* (23:1), 1999, pp. 67-93.

Lacity, M. C., and Hirschheim, R. "The Information Systems Outsourcing Bandwagon," *Sloan Management Review* (35:1), 1993, pp. 73-86.

Lacity, M. C., and Willcocks, L. P. "An Empirical Investigation of Information Technology Sourcing Practices: Lessons from Experience," *MIS Quarterly* (22:3), 1998, pp. 363-408.

Loomba, A. *Colonialism/Postcolonialism*, London: Routledge, 1998.

McFarlan, F. W., and Nolan, R. L. "How to Manage an IT Outsourcing Alliance," *Sloan Management Review* (36:2), 1995, pp. 9-23.

Nicholson, B., and Sahay, S. "Some Political and Cultural Issues in the Globalization of Software Development: Case Experience from Britain and India," *Information and Organization* (11:1), 2001, pp. 25-43.

Prasad, A. (ed.). *Postcolonial Theory and Organizational Analysis: A Critical Engagement*, New York: Palgrave Macmillan, 2003.

Quayson, A. *Postcolonialism: Theory, Practice or Process?*, Cambridge, UK: Polity Press, 2000.

Raychaudhuri, T. *Perceptions, Emotions, Sensibilities*, Oxford, UK: Oxford University Press, 1999.

Strauss, A., and Corbin, J. *Basics of Qualitative Research*, Thousand Oaks, CA: Sage Publications, 1998.

Walsham, G. "Cross-Cultural Software Production and Use: A Structurational Analysis," *MIS Quarterly* (26:3), 2002, pp. 359-380.

Walsham, G. *Making a World of Difference: IT in a Global Context*, Chichester: Wiley, 2001.

Walsham, G., and Sahay, S. "GIS for District-Level Administration in India: Problems and Opportunities," *MIS Quarterly* (23:1) 1999, pp. 39-65.

Young, R. J. C. *Postcolonialism: An Historical Introduction*, Oxford, UK: Blackwell Publishers, 2001.

Zviran, M., Ahituv, N., and Armoni, A. "Building Outsourcing Relationships Across the Global Community: The UPS-Motorola Experience," *Journal of Strategic Information Systems* (10:4), 2001, pp. 313-333.

About the Authors

Ravishankar Mayasandra is a lecturer in Strategy and part of the International Business and Strategy (IBS) research group at The Business School, Loughborough University, UK. He completed his doctoral research at the Department of Information Systems, School of Computing, National University of Singapore, in 2005. Earlier, he received his Bachelor of Engineering degree in Electronics and Communication Engineering (1999) from Bangalore University, India, and spent close to two years in a business development position at an India-based IT start-up firm. His current research interests include strategic global IT outsourcing, IT in developing nations, KM solutions for the business process outsourcing (BPO) industry, and issues of identity in large organizations. Typically, in conducting and presenting his research, Ravi adopts qualitative research methods such as case studies and ethnographies. Ravi can be reached by e-mail at M.N.Ravishankar@lboro.ac.uk

Shan L Pan is an assistant professor and the coordinator of Knowledge Management Laboratory in the Department of Information Systems, School of Computing at the National University of Singapore. Shan has research interests in the socio-organizational processes that underlie the interaction between information systems and their human and organizational contexts. His primary research focuses on the recursive interaction of organizations and information communication and technology, with particular emphasis on organizational issues such as work practices, cultures, structures, decision-making, change, and strategy implementation that often require qualitative research methods. His research work has been published in *MIS Quarterly Executive*, *IEEE Transaction on Engineering Management*, *Journal of the American Society for Information Systems and Technology*, *IEEE Transactions on Systems, Man, and Cybernetics*, *IEEE Transactions on Information Technology in Biomedicine*, *European Journal of Operational Research*, *Communications of ACM*, *Information and Organization*, *Journal of Strategic Information Systems*, *Journal of Organizational Computing and Electronic Commerce*, *European Journal of Information Systems*, *Decision Support Systems*, and *DATA BASE for Advances in Information Systems*. Shan can be reached by e-mail at pansl@comp.nus.edu.sg.

Michael D. Myers is Professor of Information Systems and Associate Dean (Postgraduate and Research) at the University of Auckland Business School, New Zealand. He currently serves as Editor in Chief of the *University of Auckland Business Review* and Editor of the *ISWorld Section on Qualitative Research*. He previously served as Senior Editor of *MIS Quarterly* from

2001-2005, as Associate Editor of *Information Systems Research* from 2000-2005, and as Associate Editor of *Information Systems Journal* from 1995-2000. His research articles have been published in many journals and books. He won the Best Paper award (with Heinz Klein) for the most outstanding paper published in *MIS Quarterly* in 1999. He also won the Best Paper Award (with Lynda Harvey) for the best paper published in *Information Technology & People* in 1997. He currently serves as the President-Elect of the Association for Information Systems (AIS) and as Chair of the International Federation of Information Processing (IFIP) Working Group 8.2. Michael can be reached at m.myers@auckland.ac.nz.

26 METHODS AS THEORIES: Evidence and Arguments for Theorizing on Software Development

Steve Sawyer
Pennsylvania State University
University Park, PA U.S.A.

Hala Annabi
University of Washington
Seattle, WA U.S.A.

Abstract   *In this paper we argue that software development methods represent theories on how best to engage the impressively complex and inherently socio-technical activity of making software. To help illustrate our points we draw on examples of three software methods: the waterfall approach, packaged software development, and free/libre and open source software development, In doing this, we highlight that software development methods reflect—too often implicitly —theories of (1) how people should behave, (2) how groups of people should interact, (3) the tasks that people should do, (4) the order of these tasks, (5) the tools needed to achieve these tasks, (6) the proper outcomes of these tasks, (7) the means to make this all happen, and (8) that these relations among concepts are further set in specific social, cultural, economic, and industrial contexts. We conclude by highlighting three trends in conceptualizing these eight elements.*

1   INTRODUCTION

Through this paper we argue that software development methods are vehicles for theorizing on the impressively complex and inherently socio-technical activity of making software. We support this argument by comparing the systems development lifecycle with packaged software development and free/libre and open source methods of software development. In revealing the implicit theorizing on software development, we depict aspects of the software development process affecting social inclusion.

Please use the following format when citing this chapter:

Sawyer, S., and Annabi, H., 2006, in IFIP International Federation for Information Processing, Volume 208, Social Inclusion: Societal and Organizational Implications for Information Systems, eds. Trauth, E., Howcroft, D., Butler, T., Fitzgerald, B., DeGross, J., (Boston: Springer), pp. 397-411.

Framing software development as socio-technical is common (e.g., Sawyer 2004; Scacchi 2002b). A socio-technical lens demands we explicitly attend to the bound-up nature of people, particular technological elements, and the contexts of these nuanced interdependencies (Bijker 1995; Bijker et al. 1987; Law and Bijker 1992).[1] Social aspects of software development include how people interact, behave, and organize. Technological aspects of software development include the use of methods, techniques, and computing technologies. In practice it is difficult to disentangle the ways people do things from the methods, techniques, and computing technologies they use for this doing.

We further note that software development differs from information systems development methods in at least two ways (Sawyer 2001). First, software development is focused on the development of an artifact—some defined set of working code that reflects specifications. An IS development effort is further focused on ensuring that software is brought together with specific users in specific organizational settings.

Second, current trends in labor specialization are reflected in differences among skill sets of those that develop software and those that implement IS. Simply, software engineers do different work than information systems consultants. These two groups of people also tend to work for different organizations, separate from one another and from the consumer organization (that purchased the software but needs an IS). This division of labor is made more clear by considering the business analysts, trainers, technical specialists, usability staff, and others who serve to make an IS from software.

The range of new approaches to both software and IS development, the constant evolution in current approaches, and the ongoing attention suggest that our theorizing is still incomplete. Here we focus specifically on the underlying, and too-often implicit, elements of this theorizing. We begin by arguing that all software development methods have eight common elements. To support this argument we draw on a comparison of three software development approaches. We conclude with specific suggestions for improving our theorizing on methods.

2   SOFTWARE DEVELOPMENT AS THEORIZING

We contend that software development methods are a form of theory.[2] A theory is a relationship between (or among) two (or more) concepts (Merton 1967). The simplest form is causal: "A" leads to "B." An example would be to be born (A) leads to, at some point, dieing (B). Typically the goal of theory is to develop the relationships among the constructs to such a point that the theory is general, specific, and accurate. These three criteria, however, are not mutually attainable. The principle known as "Occam's razor" suggests that any theory can pursue two of three criteria, sacrificing the third. In our example, we pursued accuracy and generality, but could not pursue specificity.

---

[1]This conceptual perspective is increasingly known as *social informatics*. A simple summary of social informatics is presented in Sawyer (2005). More complete discussions can be found in Kling (1999, 2000) and Kling et al. (2005).

[2]In this paper we make the claim and illustrate our position, leaving to other papers the conceptual justification. The value of this paper is the support we can provide this premise.

Developing, testing, and using theory are central goals of contemporary scholarship. Variations in representation, notation, value of directionality, and centrality of theory are contentious topics in every academic discipline. We acknowledge the passion this topic engenders, leaving to others a more detailed engagement. Our point in raising theory as a scholarly goal is to aver that in software development, methods are forms of theory (they identify concepts and presuppose relations). Weick (1995) makes clear that this is a process, one he calls theorizing. He goes on to argue the importance of making theorizing more visible to scholars and others. We agree and in this paper do so by examining the common conceptual elements that make up software development methods-as-theory.[3]

2.1 Socio-Technical Theorizing

Our efforts to theorize software development as a socio-technical activity builds on the social-shaping of technology (SST) perspectives developed in Bijker (1995), Law and Bijker (1992), and Bijker, et al. (1987). The SST perspective highlights that the material characteristics and actions of any technology are shaped by the social actions of the designers, the specific uses of that technology, and the evolving patterns of use over time. This differs from the codesign approach that is prevalent in North America. As Scacchi (2005) notes, the codesign approach too often evolves into a benign neglect of the interaction between what is social and technical, leading to an evocation of the concepts without a concomitant analytical activity.

Bijker's four socio-technical principles frame our theorizing. The *seamless web* principle states that any socio-technical analysis should not *a priori* privilege technological or material explanations ahead of social explanations, and vice versa. The principle of *change and continuity* argues that socio-technical analyses must account for both change and continuity, not just one or the other. The *symmetry principle* states that the successful working of a technology must be explained as a process, rather than assumed to be the outcome of "superior technology." The *actor and structure principle* states that socio-technical analyses should address both the actor-oriented side of social behavior, with its actor strategies and micro interactions, and the structure-oriented side of social behavior, with its larger collective and institutionalized social norms and processes.

2.2 Software Development Methods as Socio-Technical Theories

Two elements of any software development method-as-theory are guidance on how people should behave and how groups of people should interact. For example, one might theorize that people are to share information selflessly and pursue egoless

---

[3]In this paper we take the first step of engaging the concepts that are part of software development methods as theory, leaving to future work the task of sorting through the relationships among these concepts.

programming. Another approach would be to theorize that people will have differences of opinion and that there will be interpersonal conflict among team members.

Software development methods also reflect a set of expectations relative to the tasks that people should do, the order of these tasks, and the tools needed to achieve these tasks. The details of conduct, input and output elements, sequencing, and resource needs of tasks are central elements of any software development method and the core of this discourse (e.g., Cubranic and Booth 1999; Egyedi 2004).

The proper outcomes of these tasks continue to be an active area of scholarship. One trend is a steady movement toward multiple measures and to focusing on measurement of use in addition to measures of the software artifact's structure, size, and technical performance (Melone 1990). The rise of open source development has elevated the attention to theorizing on the reasons why developers perform, and the incentives that encourage (and discourage) performance (e.g., Bergquist and Ljungberg 2001).

Software development methods also incorporate, explicitly or implicitly, relations to specific contexts. For example, clean-room, participatory, and packaged software development approaches demand separation, inclusion, or distance from various groups of users. The literature on virtual teams and distributed development make clear a second form of context (geography) (e.g., Moon and Sproull 2000). The differences among custom and packaged software further suggest that the industrial environment matters (e.g., Sawyer 2000).

In sum, as laid out in Table 1, software development methods are explicit representations of (1) how people should behave, (2) how groups of people should interact, (3) the tasks that people should do, (4) the order of these tasks, (5) the tools needed to achieve these tasks, (6) the proper outcomes of these tasks (including means and ways to evaluate these outcomes), and (7) the means to make this all happen. The relations among these concepts are further set in (8) specific contexts, implying that the exact nature of such relations are contingent to some degree on the larger social milieu.

Table 1. Concepts Important to Theorizing Software Development Methods

Element	Details
People's individual behavior	What is expected of people engaged in developing software
People's collective action	The interactions among people working together to develop software
Task selection	The particular tasks that need to be done to develop software
Task ordering	The ordering of the particular tasks to develop software
Tool support	The roles and featured of tools used to support tasks/ordering
Outcomes (measures)	The elements measured to assess both progress and completion
Incentives	The structures put in place to encourage positive, and discourage negative, behaviors and interactions
Contexts	The larger social, cultural, economic and industrial milieu in which software development takes place

3 COMPARING SDLC, PACKAGE AND FREE/LIBRE OPEN SOURCE SOFTWARE APPROACHES

To illustrate how these eight concepts underscore methods, we compare three approaches to developing software. We select the SDLC, packaged software development, and FLOSS methods, providing in this section a brief review of these three approaches before developing our comparison (this is summarized in Table 2).

3.1 Systems Development Life Cycle

The systems development life cycle (SDLC) or waterfall approach is well-known, oft-referenced, and rarely followed. In the SDLC, specific steps are linearly sequenced with some overlap between steps to allow for knowledge transfer. Specific skills and resources for each step, its inputs and outputs, and proper approaches to pursuing the transfer of inputs to outputs are documented.

The premise of the SDLC is that process drives outcomes. The measures for SDLC success typically include cost, quality, and user satisfaction as recognition of value to the larger corporate mission. Implicit in the SDLC are at least two relevant assumptions. First, it implies that software development takes place within one organization (or, at least, is totally controlled by that organization— i.e., when hiring a contractor or consultant to construct a custom product). This reflects vertical integration (a hierarchy). Second, the SDLC is focused on building, not buying, software. This is appropriate, for that was its purpose.

Staff costs should be minimized and typical SDLC-based efforts are characterized by team membership turnover, division of labor by both phase and function, and disbanding following the completion of the first release (Cusumano and Smith 1997). Thus, these are more like *ad hoc* work groups, not teams (Goodman et al. 1986).

3.2 Packaged Software Development

Packaged software—also known as shrink-wrapped, commercial-off-the-shelf (COTS), and commercial software—means the code is sold as a (licensed) product (purchased from a vendor, distributor or store) for all computer platforms including mainframes, work-stations, and microcomputers (Carmel 1997; Carmel and Sawyer 1998; Sawyer 2000).

In PSD, time pressures (not cost) drive development. Packaged software developers tend to have a product (not process) view of development (Carmel 1995; Carmel and Becker 1995; Cusumano and Smith 1997). A product focus means that the dominant goal of the software development effort is to ship a product. This product focus also implies that these products have distinct trajectories with the software evolving through a planned set of releases.

Table 2. Comparing SDLC, Package and FLOSS Development Approaches

Element	SDLC	Package	Open Source
People's individual behavior	Process-focused, specialized to particular roles, sequenced, ego-less, and sharing-oriented	Product-focused, competitive, skill-based, interdependent, time-pressured	Self interest, skill-focused and altruistic.
People's collective action	Collective, controlled and focused on error reduction	Conflictual, focused on delivery, and coding	Product focused, focused on personal goals *and* producing a public good
Task selection	Defined by system requirements and mostly inflexible	Group defined and mostly flexible	Driven by self interest and supported by a merit system
Task ordering	Prescribed by phase or function	Iterative	Fluid, flexible, often iterative
Tool support	Enforce control and process adherence	Support interactions and interdependencies	Support interaction and sharing code
Outcomes (measures)	Adoption, customer satisfaction, cost	Market share, user and industry reviews	Developer satisfaction, market share, reviews, portability
Incentives	Income, skill-development	Profit, recognition	Developer personal satisfaction, project and developer recognition, public good
Contexts	Organizational	Market driven	User-base
Notes	Users involved through intermediaries	Users involved through intermediaries	Users directly involved (developers are often users, and users test and fix bugs and contribute code)

In packaged software firms, developers hold line positions so their needs are central to the performance of the organization. In effect, they are the company's production mechanism as they generate revenue. Packaged software developers often have at best a distant relationship with their user population. This separation means that intermediaries—such as help desk personnel and consultants—link users to developers (Grudin 1991; Keil and Carmel 1995; Maiden and Ncube 1998).

Packaged software products are measured by criteria such as favorable product reviews in trade publications, the degree of "mind share"—the awareness of a product in the minds of the target population, developing a large installed base and/or creating new markets (Andersson and Nilsson 1996; Brynjolfsson 1994).

3.3 Free/Libre Open Source Software

FLOSS is a broad categorization used to describe software developed and released under various "open source" licenses. Licenses offer a range of features, all allowing inspection of the software's source code. We use the term FLOSS to encompass the free software movement, which also releases software along the same terms as the OSS movement, but with a distinction that derivative works must be made available under the same nonrestrictive license terms. FLOSS projects comprise of a varying number of developers ranging from a few to a hundred or more. FLOSS development groups are groups working in distributed computer-mediated networked form (Scacchi 2002b).

FLOSS members interact primarily or exclusively via computer-mediated communications (CMC). Project members coordinate their activities primarily through private e-mail, mailing lists, bulletin boards, and chat rooms and use compilers, bug tracking, and version control systems for their software development.

In general, FLOSS processes are fluid not, complying with any particular software engineering method (Raymond 1998; Scacchi 2002). One of the most commonly mentioned models used to explain the methods or practices of FLOSS development is Raymond's (1998) "The Cathedral and the Bazaar" metaphor. Raymond depicts FLOSS developers as autonomously deciding schedule and contribution modes for software development as merchants in a bazaar would, thereby dismissing the need for central coordination as the construction of a cathedral would in a master architect. The bazaar metaphor is limited as it diminishes aspects of the FLOSS development process, such as the role of the project leader or core group and the existence of *de facto* hierarchies (Bezroukov 1999).

In FLOSS, a mixture of self-serving and altruistic goals drive development. Developers join FLOSS projects for one or more of several reasons, some of which are employment (as some FLOSS developers are employed by formal organizations to develop software), to meet a personal need, to contribute to creating a public good, to gain satisfaction from the software development process, and/or for potential career gains (Moody 2001).

Members of any project move from peripheral roles to a core developer role in the project through a merit-based process (Cubranic and Booth 1999). An individual's technical expertise and participation in developing the product results in his/her inclusion in the core group of developers. However, to become one of the core developers means they must have a detailed understanding of the software and development processes. Since there is no separate documentation for system requirements or design, this poses a significant barrier to entry (Fielding 1997; Hecker 1999). Designs and requirements evolve over time and are implicitly articulated in public mailing lists as a result of individual developers' desired functionality and a developer's willingness to implement them (Scacchi 2002b). Tasks are accomplished based on developers' needs and interests and articulated in to-do lists as seen in Apache Web Server in the early years (Annabi 2005).

FLOSS software success is measured by a variety of criteria. User satisfaction, portability, favorable product reviews, learning opportunities, user-base, developer satisfaction and developer recognition are some of the measure of FLOSS success (Crowston et al. 2003). Portfolios of measures can be used to assess any particular project depending on project and members goals.

3.4 Methods as Theories: Comparing the Three Approaches

In Table 2 and below we highlight via comparisons how the eight elements of a software development method reflect theorizing. A complete analysis is beyond the scope of this paper; so, here we summarize the concepts. We note the presence of these concepts in each of the three approaches, leaving to other work attention to relationships among the concepts.

People's individual behavior. Each of the three approaches make clear expectations for a certain set of behaviors from people. In the SDLC, people are to attend to process, share information, suppress ego issues, and focus on developing role-specific technical and professional skills. The PSD approach conceives of people as product-focused, competitive, technically skilled, with limited need for social skills, willing to take risks, and time-pressured. In FLOSS, people are seen as pursuing a mix of altruistic and self-serving goals, constrained by social controls, and with high technical skill levels.

People's collective action. In the SDLC, people are expected to be oriented to the goals of the collective and consensus is expected. In PSD, people's interactions will be guided by product needs, time pressures, and profit, and conflict is expected. In FLOSS, people's collective behavior is guided by the twin goals of public good and personal needs, and interactions are driven by performance goals.

Task selection. In the SDLC, tasks are predefined by the method and system requirements—an engineering ethic. The task inputs, outputs and means of proceeding are specified and often inflexible. In the PSD approach, tasks are more flexible, although there are common templates or forms that must be met. In FLOSS, tasks are mostly left to the developers, with a few (such as version control) serving as central aspects of the effort. These tasks help to structure FLOSS.

Task ordering. In the SDLC, task ordering is typically fixed, linear, and prescribed. In PSD, the ordering of tasks is more fluid while particular inputs and outputs are less prescribed. It is difficult to develop a task ordering in FLOSS beyond observing that certain tasks (such as the use of a configuration management tool) serve as central and structuring elements of the approach.

Tool support. In the SDLC, software tools are used to enforce task ordering and task completion (a controlled production environment). These tools are often integrated, complex, and have limited flexibility. In both the PSD and FLOSS approaches, tools are engaged that support collaboration, coordination, and production support. These tools are more flexible, less integrated, and often quite simple.

Outcomes (measures). In the SDLC, process measures are used, and these measures focus on cost, quality, and user take-up/value. In PSD, product measures are used, and these measures focus on installed base/market share, sales, margin, and defect rates. In FLOSS, there is a combination of product and personal measures. This remains an active area of inquiry and continues to be poorly understood (see Crowston et al. 2003).

Incentives. In the SDLC, developers' behaviors are motivated by salary/income, since developers are employed, as well as opportunities to learn new skills from developing particular software. In PSD, incentives extend past salary to include stock options and shares of sales. In FLOSS, there are a variety of incentives depending on circumstances, but generally, developers are interested in developing a product for the common good while meeting their own needs, attaining satisfaction from engaging in the development process, and potentially gaining recognition for themselves and the project.

Contexts. In the SDLC, software development occurs in the context of organizational goals, needs, and capabilities. The main purpose is to meet organizational objectives within limited budgets while accommodating social, technological, and political factors. In the SDLC, risk mitigation is a central issue. In PSD, software is developed to meet a need present or forecasted in the market, and to pursue opportunities. In PSD, taking on risk is a central issue. In FLOSS, software is developed by users for users as ideas about the product evolve over time with user influence being the main driver. In FLOSS, risk is borne primarily by individuals.

We further note that the roles that users play shape development. And, this shaping has both a direct and an indirect component. For example, in the SDLC, users are the focus of one phase, and then kept distant from the development effort. However, a focus on meeting user's needs dominates the SDLC approach. In PSD, users are always distant, but there are extensive efforts to gather user needs and monitor their interests. These efforts, however, are one of several factors that influence design. In FLOSS, developers are often users and the blurry boundary between users and developers creates an interesting dynamic for development.

Table 3. Observations on Theorizing Software Development Methods

Element	Details
People's individual behavior	An increasingly richer view of people as having passion, engaging conflict and pursuing personal agendas (not just as error-producing and limited cognitive agents).
People's collective action	Interactions among people are central characteristics of methods and must be accounted for in the design of tasks, tools and outcome measures.
Task selection	Tasks are becoming more fluid and more flexible.
Task ordering	Task ordering is becoming less linear.
Tool support	Tool support moving towards supporting interaction and access to materials, not (just) code production and process enforcement.
Outcomes (measures)	Measures are expanding and evolving.
Incentives	Incentives are under-explored (though FLOSS approaches require engaging this directly).
Contexts	Contexts are under-explored (though evidence and awareness that a one-size-fits-all approach to software development is growing).
Notes	The number, needs, skills, social power and other resources of users have substantial and multiple, indirect, effects on how software is developed.

3.5 Observations

Drawing on this analysis, in Table 3 and below we summarize and discuss eight observations regarding software development methods as incipient theories.

People's individual behavior. We observe a trend toward a more complex view of people as having passion, engaging conflict, and pursuing personal agendas (not just as error-producing and limited cognitive agents). This is most evident in FLOSS development as one of the top reasons and features of the development process is "satisfying an itch" for developing and creating to meet needs (Crowston et al. 2003).

People's collective action. We note that there is a shift toward conceiving the interaction among people as central characteristics of methods that must be accounted for in the design of tasks, tools, and outcome measures. Both the PSD and FLOSS literature make clear that managing interactions are central issues to success (Annabi 2005; Crowston et al. 2003; Sawyer 2000).

Task selection. We observe that task structures are seen as more fluid and responsive. Tasks are defined and chosen through consensus and conflict and with user involvement. As in the cases of both PSD and FLOSS, developers define tasks through interactions categorized by both conflict and consensus.

Task ordering. We observe that task ordering is becoming more iterative, with expectations among developers and users that specific tasks are likely to have multiples passes. A second aspect of this iterative orientation is the increased flexibility in the order of tasks.

Tool support. We observe that the roles and uses of software development tools are moving toward supporting interaction and access to materials. In doing this, the tools are moving away from focusing solely on code production and process enforcement. The most vivid example of this is the FLOSS uses of version control software (Shaikh and Cornford 2004).

Measures. The number of measures being used to evaluate software development continues to expand. These measures can be seen as a suite and encompass developer behavior, development team processes, measures of use and value to customers, and measures of the artifacts size, quality, and resources.

Incentives. It appears that incentives (and disincentives) remain an under-explored area in SDLC and PSD. FLOSS development suggests that incentives are both intrinsic and extrinsic (Crowston et al. 2003), affecting developers' interactions with the product and others in the development group.

Contexts. We observe that the professional community of software developers, and many in the academic community studying software development, are aware that there is no one-size-fits-all approach to software development. There are, however, common elements that define software development (the point we are arguing here) and that the way these elements are engaged is driven in part by the context. This contingency perspective suggests that differences in software development methods are critical.

For more than 20 years, scholars have noted that the number, needs, skills, social power, and other resources of users have substantial and multiple effects on how software is developed (e.g., Keil and Carmel 1995; Kling and Iacona 1984; Markus 1983) and how it meets the needs of underserved groups. It appears this user pressure is influencing the recent work in software development methods. We further note that the variations among these concepts across the three examples suggests that while the concepts are common, the pattern of relationships among these concepts differs.

4 IMPLICATIONS

We have argued here that software development methods can be best understood as theories and posited that these engage eight concepts. Drawing on a comparison of three approaches, we have observed that social inclusion (e.g., users and uses) helps to shape software development in many direct and indirect ways. In Table 4 and below, we look beyond our current observations to speculate on how we might advance theorizing on software development methods.

4.1 More Complex Representations of People's Behaviors

We expect that future software development methods will have more nuanced and complex representations of people's behaviors. For example, we expect that developers will be increasingly construed as problem-solvers (and not error-prone code writers) (Mockus and Herbsleb 2002). In part this more complex view of software developers is driven by our increased understanding of their work. It may also, at least indirectly, draw on our increased understanding of knowledge-based work. That is, we see software developers as knowledge workers, and increasingly they are able to choose what projects to join (Annabi 2005; Drucker 1998). This more inclusive view of people's behaviors is likely to drive a resurgence of empirical studies on performance and process (such as is seen in the FLOSS literature).

A second trend we expect to see in future theorizing on software development is that the interactions among people, and among people and the various tools and repositors used in developing software, will be seen as a central activity (e.g., Mockus and Herbsleb 2002; Scacchi 2002a). As we note below, this will influence the design and uses of tools and incentives. This trend is likely to be instantiated in guidance for pair programming, team development, structured communication, shared work environments, and a more discourse-oriented approach to documenting decisions.

Table 4. Guidance for Continued Theorizing on Software Development Methods

Leverage Points:
1. More complex representations of people's behaviors
2. More fluid task elements supported with more flexible tools
3. Increased integration of incentives, measures and context

4.2 More Fluid Task Elements Supported with More Flexible Tools

We speculate that future theorizing on software development methods will build on the concepts of templates. A template-oriented view makes clear that these structures are a guide, to be interpreted, not followed. In contrast, the SDLC and other recipe-based views makes guidance more like scripts: inflexible and increasingly unwieldy (as exceptions and errors lead to expanded scripting). The move toward templates means a blurring of tasks and ordering (even though the focus on particular inputs and outputs will sharpen). So, even as the sequence of tasks becomes more fluid, and perhaps less linear, the specific needs at templated points will increasingly become clearer (and better understood). And, as noted above and in Sawyer (2004), we speculate that the tools used will better support people's collaboration and interaction—going beyond production and control functions (e.g, Vessey and Sravanapudi 1995).

4.3 Increased Integration of Incentives, Measures and Context

Future theorizing on software development methods will better align participant's incentives with tasks and in doing this, these incentives will reflect the more creative, problem-solving, collaborative nature of people (Halloran and Scherlis 2002; Mockus and Herbsleb 2005; Scacchi 2005). These incentives are likely to draw on multiple measures and a better understanding of tradeoffs (e.g., for FLOSS portfolios of measures suggested by Crowston et al. 2003). And, these methods will reflect contingencies such as contextual pressures and needs, including users' engagement issues. This is especially significant to the issue of social inclusion. The inclusion of underrepresented groups in the software development process produces software that is consistent with their needs leading to their inclusion.

Looking beyond these specific speculations regarding future theorizing on software development methods, we argue that such work will explicitly or implicitly engage the relationships among eight core concepts. More subtly, but perhaps more profoundly, we introduced three socio-technical principles as the basis of this theorizing. These principles engage us to consider people's actions as coequals with tasks, to focus on processes as flexible and contextual, and to highlight both the structural and agent-like nature of people and tools. If one takes seriously our position—that software development methods are incipient theories—then the socio-technical principles of theorizing provide the conceptual guidance for how to proceed.

References

Andersson, R., and Nilsson, A. "The Standard Application Package Market—An Industry in Transition?," in M. Lundeberg and B. Sundgren (eds.), *Advancing Your Business: People and Information Systems in Concert*, Stockholm: EFI, Stockholm School of Economics, 1996.

Annabi, H. *Moving from Individual Contribution to Group Learning: The Early Years of the Apache Web Server*, unpublished Ph.D. dissertation, Syracuse University, Syracuse, New York, 2005.

Bergquist, M., and Ljungberg, J. "The Power of Gifts: Organizing Social Rrelationships in Open Source Communities," *Information Systems Journal* (11:4), 2001, pp. 305-320.

Bezroukov, N. "A Second Look at the Cathedral and the Bazaar," *First Monday* (4:12), 1999.

Bijker, W. *Of Bicycles, Bakelites, and Bulbs: Toward a Theory of Socio-Technical Change*, Cambridge, MA: MIT Press, 1995.

Bijker, W., Hughes, T. , and Pinch, T. *The Social Construction of Technological Systems*, Cambridge, MA: MIT Press, 1987.

Brynjolfsson, E. "The Productivity Paradox of Information Technology," *Communications of the ACM* (36:12), 1994, pp. 67-77.

Carmel, E. "American Hegemony in Packaged Software Trade and the 'Culture of Software,'" *The Information Society* (13:1), 1997, pp. 125-142.

Carmel, E. "Cycle-Time in Packaged Software Firms," *Journal of Product Innovation Management* (12:2), 1995, pp. 110-123.

Carmel, E., and Becker, S. "A Process Model for Packaged Software Development," *IEEE Transactions on Engineering Management* (41:5), 1995, pp. 50-61

Carmel, E., and Sawyer, S. "Packaged Software Development Teams: What Makes Them Different?," *Information Technology & People* (11:1), 1998, pp. 7-19.

Crowston, K., Annabi, H., and Howison, J. "Defining Open Source Software Project Success," in S. T. March, A. Massey, and J. I. DeGross (eds.), *Proceedings of the 24th International Conference for Information Systems*, Seattle, WA, December 2003, pp. 327-340.

Cubranic, D., and Booth, K. S. "Coordinating Open-Source Software Development," paper presented at the Seventh IEEE Workshop on Enabling Technologies: Infrastructure for Collaborative Enterprises, 1999.

Cusumano, M., and Smith, S. "Beyond the Waterfall: Software Development at Microsoft," in D. Yoffie (ed.), *Competing in the Age of Digital Convergence*, Boston: Harvard Business School Press, 1997, pp. 371-411.

Drucker, P. F. "Management's New Paradigms," *Forbes* (162), 1998, pp. 152-177.

Egyedi, T. M. "Standardization and Other Coordination Mechanisms in Open Source oSftware," *International Journal of IT Standards & Standardization Research* (2:2), 2004, pp. 1-17.

Fielding, R. T. "The Apache Group: A Case Study of Internet Collaboration and Virtual Communities," UCI School of Social Sciences Seminar Series, University of California, Irvine, 1997 (available online at http://roy.gbiv.com/talks/ssapache/title.htm).

Goodman, P., Ravlin, E., and Argote, L. "Current Thinking About Groups: Setting the Stage for New Ideas," in P. Goodman and Associates (eds.), *Designing Effective Work Groups*, San Francisco: Jossey-Bass, 1986, pp. 1-33.

Grudin, J. "Interactive Systems: Bridging the Gap between Developers and Users," *IEEE Computer* (24:5), 1991, pp. 59-69.

Halloran, T. , and Scherlis, W. "High Quality and Open Source Software Practices," paper presented at the Second Workshop on Open Source Software Engineering, Orlando, FL, May 2002.

Hecker, F. "Mozilla at One: A Look Back and Ahead," Mozilla.org, April 2, 1999 (available online at http://www.mozilla.org/mozilla-at-one.html).

Keil, M., and Carmel, E. "Customer-Developer Links in Software Development," *Communications of the ACM* (38:5), 1995, pp. 33-44.

Kling, R. "Learning about Information Technologies and Social Change: The Contribution of Social Informatics," *The Information Society* (16:3), 2000, pp. 212-234.

Kling, R. "What Is Social Informatics and Why Does it Matter?," *D-Lib Magazine* (5:1), January 1999 (available online at http://www.dlib.org:80/dlib/january99/kling/01kling.html).

Kling, R., and Iacono, S. "The Control of Information Systems Developments After Implementation," *Communications of the ACM* (27:12), 1984, pp. 1218-1226.

Kling, R., Rosenbaum, H., and Sawyer, S. *Understanding and Communicating Social Informatics: A Framework for Studying and Teaching the Human Contexts of Information and Communication Technologies*, Medford, NJ: Information Today, 2005.

Law, J., and Bijker, W. "Technology, Stability and Social Theory," in W. Bijker (ed.), *Shaping Technology/Building Society*, Cambridge, MA: MIT Press, 1992, pp. 32-50.

Maiden, N., and Ncube, C. "Acquiring COTS Software Selection Requirements," *IEEE Software* (15:2), 1998, pp. 46-56.

Markus, M. "Power, Politics, and MIS Implementation," *Communications of the ACM* (26:6), 1983, pp. 430-444.

Melone, N. "A Theoretical Assessment of the User-Satisfaction Construct in Information Systems Research," *Management Science* (36:1), 1990, pp. 76-91.

Merton, R. *On Theoretical Sociology*, New York: The Free Press, 1967.

Mockus, A., and Herbsleb, J. "Why Not Improve Coordination in Distributed Software Development by Stealing Good Ideas from Open Source?," paper presented at the Second Workshop on Open Source Software Engineering, Orlando, FL, May 2002.

Moody, G. *Rebel Code—Inside Linux and the Open Source Movement*, Cambridge, MA: Perseus Publishing, 2001.

Moon, J. Y., and Sproull, L. "Essence of Distributed Work: The Case of Linux Kernel," *First Monday* (5:11), 2000 (available online at http://www.firstmonday.org/issues/issue5_11/moon/index.html).

Raymond, E. S. "The Cathedral and the Bazaar," *First Monday* (3:3), 1998 (available online at http://www.firstmonday.org/issues/issue3_3/raymond/index.html).

Sawyer, S. "Information Systems Development: A Market-Oriented Perspective," *Communications of the ACM* (44:11), 2001, pp. 97-102.

Sawyer, S. "Packaged Software: Implications of the Differences from Custom Approaches to Software Development," *European Journal of Information Systems* (9:1), 2001, pp. 47-58.

Sawyer, S. "Social Informatics: Principles and Opportunties," *Bulletin of the American Society for Information Science and Technology*, June 2005, pp. 2-6.

Sawyer, S. "Software Development Teams: Three Archetypes and Their Differences." *Communications of the ACM* (17:12), 2004, pp. 92-97.

Scacchi, W. "Process Models in Software Engineering," in J. Marciniak (ed.), *Encyclopedia of Software Engineering* (2nd ed.), New York: Wiley, 2002a, pp. 993-1005.

Scacchi, W. "Socio-Technical Interaction Networks in Free/Open Source Software Development Processes," in S. T. Acuña and N. Juristo (eds.), *Software Process Modeling*, New York: Springer Science+Business Media Inc., 2005, pp. 1-27.

Scacchi, W. "Understanding the Requirements for Developing Open Source Ssoftware Systems.," *IEE Proceedings-Software* (14:1), 2002b, pp. 24-39.

Shaikh, M., and Cornford, T. "Version Control Tools: A Collaborative Vehicle for Learning in F/OS," paper presented at the 26th International Conference on Software Engineering: Collaboration, Conflict and Control: The Fourth Workshop on Open Source Software Engineering, Edinburgh, Scotland., May 25, 2004.

Vessey, I., and Sravanapudi, P. "Case Tools as Collaborative Support Technologies," *Communications of the ACM* (38:1), 1995, pp. 83-95.

Weick, K. "What Theory Is Not: Theorizing Is," *Administrative Science Quarterly* (40), 1995, pp. 385-390.

About the Authors

Steve Sawyer conducts research on social and organizational informatics, studying how people work together and how they use information and communication technologies. His most recent research programs include investigating how software development can be improved through attending to the social aspects of working together; studying how people adapt to working with large-scale information systems implementations (such as enterprise resource packages); and understanding the changes to organizations (and organizational work) due to the increased distribution of computing. Corning, IBM, Sonoco, Xerox, the Lattanze Foundation, and the National Science Foundation have supported his research. Steve teaches information systems analysis and design, project management, and implementation; information-technology-enabled organizational change; social informatics; and field-based research methods. He can be reached at sawyer@ist.psu.edu.

Hala Annabi is an assistant professor at the Information School at the University of Washington. Her research addresses the effects of information technology on learning in both the work and educational settings. More specifically, she studies how the new forms of computer mediated work affect individual, group and organizational learning in distributed work settings. She is currently investigating group learning in Open Source Software development teams and organizational learning in distributed multinational engineering firm. Additionally, she is interested in the effects of asynchronous learning networks on learning in educational settings. She is currently investigating how asynchronous learning networks can be used to improve learning and student satisfaction in large lecture style courses. Her teaching interests are in the impact of information technology on organizations, organizational learning and knowledge management, and organizational behavior. For more information please contact Hala at hpannabi@u.washington.edu.

27 THE CORPORATE DIGITAL DIVIDE BETWEEN SMALLER AND LARGER FIRMS

Nava Pliskin
Ben-Gurion University of the Negev
Beer-Sheva, Israel

Margi Levy
Warwick Business School
Coventry, U.K.

Tsipi Heart
University College Cork
Cork, Ireland

Brian O'Flaherty
University College Cork
Cork, Ireland

Paul O'Dea
Select Strategies
Ireland

1 INTRODUCTION/BACKGROUND

Investments by large corporations in information and communication technologies (ICTs) is steadily growing, comprising on average 4 percent of corporate revenues, with about two-thirds of the ICT investment directed to operations and only about a third to strategic opportunities (META 2005). While true for larger organizations (these figures were calculated based on data gathered from 1,907 organizations with more than $1 billion in revenue), the picture is somewhat different for small or medium-sized enterprises (SMEs), with between 10 and 250 employees, most of which invest a much smaller proportion of their revenue in ICT. For example, Heart et al. (2001) found that hospitality SMEs invest only about 1 percent of revenue in ICT. In their constant struggle to reduce costs, SMEs invest in mandatory ICT operations and their utilization of ICT is often inefficient.

Please use the following format when citing this chapter:

Pliskin, N., Levy, M., Heart, T., O'Flaherty, B., and O'Dea, P., 2006, in IFIP International Federation for Information Processing, Volume 208, Social Inclusion: Societal and Organizational Implications for Information Systems, eds. Trauth, E., Howcroft, D., Butler, T., Fitzgerald, B., DeGross, J., (Boston: Springer), pp. 413-417.

Larger organizations can opt for outsourcing arrangements to reduce IT operational costs (IT outsourcing expenditure was up 5 percent from 2004 to 2005 for large companies). However, for many SMEs, outsourcing is not an option for at least three reasons. First, SMEs do not have the financial resources to pay outsourcing fees. Second, SMEs often do not recognize the need for continual refreshment of their ICT provision (Ballantine et al. 1998). Third, the relatively underdeveloped ICT accounts of SMEs are unattractive for the major ICT outsourcers. Earlier predictions that software might soon become a remotely accessed, cheap commodity are yet unfulfilled, with even SMEs unwilling to pioneer with remote access via application service providers (ASPs) to their mission-critical applications (Heart and Pliskin 2002).

Consequently, there is evidence about SMEs neither utilizing ICT strategically, to gain competitive edge, nor maximizing business value of IT (Levy et al. 2002). This puts SMEs at a strategic disadvantage relative to larger organizations. SMEs, with their focus on business survival, form an underprivileged sector in terms of ICT usage. It thus makes sense to note, and discuss in this panel, the corporate digital divide between larger (haves) and smaller (have-nots) enterprises, which resembles the digital divide at the individual level, where those underprivileged parts of the population have no access to the benefits acquired by ICT usage.

An additional element of the corporate digital divide is the lack of ICT training for employees (who represent 65 percent of the workforce). This is likely to limit the benefits at both the individual and firm level of ICT usage in SMEs. The panel has relevance for the conference theme not only because a corporate digital divide does exists but also because the two types of digital divide are closely linked.

2   PANEL CONTENT AND ORGANIZATION

Nava Pliskin will introduce the subject and moderate. It is now evident from both research and practice that information technology plays a critical role in the competitive position of firms. Effective and efficient IT utilization is required in order to achieve market visibility, marketing strength and customer intimacy, as well as cost-effective business processes. Whereas larger organizations have invested millions in implementing enterprise-wide ERP, CRM, SRM, and DW systems, smaller organizations can neither afford the cost nor the expertise required for acquiring ERP utilization competencies. Although both SAP and Oracle now offer cheaper packages for middle-sized firms, these packages still require an up-front investment of $300,000 to $500,000, plus a need to employ expensive internal experts. For a smaller firm struggling to win or at least survive in a competitive market, such an investment is still unachievable. Developing customized applications is likewise unaffordable, since such organizations cannot allocate the resources required to smoothly complete a software development project. Consequently, organizations such as national hotel chains or restaurants often end up with a fragmented, underutilized application suite, procured off-the-shelf based on affordability considerations, rather than on genuine strategic and business-oriented IT planning. This situation reflects a digital divide between the larger and smaller organizations, placing a serious barrier for the latter to successfully compete and thrive in turbulent markets.

Margi Levy will present the strategic struggle of SMEs in ICT adoption. Research suggests that there are distinct approaches to IS investment in SMEs depending on the relative dominance of customers and the strategic focus of the firm. Customer dominance is dependent on the firm's size and the competitiveness of the market. Smaller firms and firms with few customers have high dependence. As firms grow and the customer base declines, the dependency is reduced. Customer dependency can influence IS investment decisions in SMEs.

The owner is critical in determining the strategic focus of the firm. The owner's influence depends upon several factors: (1) knowledge about the potential for business value from information systems is a key influence on adoption of strategic IS; (2) the desire to grow the business; and (3) recognition that there is a need for a strategy to manage growth. The approach taken to strategic growth determines whether owners view IS investment as a cost to the business, a necessary evil that requires minimal resources, or as adding value to achieving strategic objectives.

This leads to the identification of four scenarios for strategic IS investment in SMEs and the identification of different strategic management perspectives. Research suggests that firm growth may change strategic IS investment while those SMEs that do not plan for growth are in danger of ossification.

Tsipi Heart will present the status of application hosting as a plausible, more affordable ICT source for SMEs. Research shows that firms invest on average 60 to 70 percent of their annual IT budget on maintenance and operations; thus only about a third of the budget is actually invested in enhancing IT to better cater to changing market requirements. Firms now strive to reduce IT expenses and total cost of ownership (TCO), outsourcing being the major solution adopted by many. While reliable and trustworthy multinational vendors, such as IBM and EDS would compete on such large accounts, they would often refrain from taking on IT operations of smaller firms, assuming it infeasible. Thus, smaller organizations either end up with lower-tier, less reliable vendors, usually outsourcing to multiple vendors, or keep their IT operation internal. IT remote hosting in various forms is recently emerging as a viable sourcing option for the smaller organization. Recent research shows that first-wave vendors did not exhibit the characteristics essential for adopting the ASP optino required by decision makers in SMEs. Although the first wave of application service providers (ASPs) did not succeed in establishing a stable and value-adding business model, second-generation ASPs are now emerging. The difference between the offerings of the second wave ASPs and their earlier counterparts will be discussed, leading to the assumption, supported by Carr (2005), that Web hosting might be a new, feasible IT sourcing option for SMEs, perhaps leading to bridging the digital divide between these firms and their larger competitors.

Brian O'Flaherty will speak about innovation in SMEs. In the current, turbulent international market, innovation is a common strategy adopted by SMEs in order to keep abreast of competition and enter new markets. These innovative approaches can involve new product, service or business model strategies and, if implemented successfully, smaller companies can disrupt larger incumbent market leaders. While studies show that smaller firms are less likely to adopt IT in supporting their business, research also indicates that smaller firms are more innovative than their larger counterparts, but they also adopt different innovation processes in pursuit of differentiation. This provides a contradiction and clear evidence of a digital divide, where SMEs are slow to adopt technology, but are required, by their nature, to innovate.

Paul O'Dea will describe the situation of IT adoption and IT selling by Irish SMEs. The continous state of rapid evolution and dynamic market conditions that are the hallmarks of high technology places severe stress on companies striving for survival, success, and ultimately hyper-growth. Clarity of purpose, a laser-like focus on execution, and an uncluttered vision of implementation strategies and tactics are essential ingredients in defining the recipe for achievement. If ambiguity or fuzziness exists, or if the correct offering is not being provided to the right customers through the optimum sales and marketing channels, failure is a certainty. Information technology is an enabler in monitoring essential activities leading start-ups to the required growth, yet these tools are often unaffordable or too complex for smaller start-ups. Paul, who is familiar with the Irish and global start-ups market, will describe how these emerging firms utilize IT as a tool leading to success.

3   ABOUT THE PANELISTS

Nava Pliskin (pliskinN@bgu.ac.il) is in charge of the Information Systems programs at the Department of Industrial Engineering and Management Ben-Gurion University in Israel. Previously she was a Thomas Henry Carroll Ford Foundation Visiting Associate Professor at the Harvard Business School. She received her Ph.D.and S.M.degrees from Harvard University. Her research, focused on longitudinal analysis of IS impacts at the global, national, organizational, and individual levels, has been published in such journals as *IEEE Transactions on Engineering Management, ACM Transactions on Information Systems, The Information Society, Communications of the ACM, Decision Support Systems, Information & Management,* and *Data Base.*

Margi Levy (Margi.Levy@wbs.ac.uk) is a senior lecturer and a member of the Operational Research and Information Systems Group at Warwick Business School. She has an M.Sc., B.Sc., and PGME degrees. Margi joined the Warwick Business School as a lecturer in 1992. Formerly she lectured on information systems at Curtin University of Technology in Western Australia. Before that, she worked as an IS consultant with Coopers and Lybrand in Western Australia, and also worked for various firms in London as a business systems analyst. Her research interests are e-business strategies for SMEs; IS strategy for SMEs; e-networks for SMEs; IS success; IT adoption in SMEs. She has published in such journals as *Information Resource Management, European Journal of Information Systems, Small Business Economics, Journal of Information Technology,* and *Information and Management.* She is the coauthor, with Philip Powell, of *Strategies for Growth in SMEs: The Role of Information and Information Systems,* recently published by Butterworth-Heinemann..

Tsipi Heart (t.heart@ucc.ie) is a lecturer in the Business Information Systems Department at University College Cork, Ireland, where she teaches IT management related courses. She has received her Ph.D. at the Department of Industrial Engineering and Management of Ben-Gurion University of the Negev in Israel,after serving as CIO and a consultant in Israeli organizations. Tsipi's research focuses on IT implementation in small and medium size enterprises, IT strategy and management, IT innovation and adoption, cultural differences in IT usage, and application service providers. Her work has been published in such journals as *Information Technology and Tourism, International Journal of Hospitality Information Technology, Communications of the AIS, INFOR,* and *Journal of Information Technology Theory and Application.*

Brian O'Flaherty (b.oflaherty@uccc.ie) is a member of faculty in the Department of Business Information Systems at University College Cork. Having initially worked in the software industry, he has been teaching in UCC for over 15 years. He recently completed his doctoral research in Management Science at the University of Strathclyde, Glasgow. He is actively involved in research commercialization training initiatives within UCC and has secured EI funding for an enterprise start-up program specifically for academic and research staff. In collaboration with colleagues in the Business Faculty, he initiated a research commercialization business module, which will be available to every doctoral student in the University in the next academic year. His areas of interest include information infrastructures, spatial data infrastructures, innovation and software. His work has been presented in conferences such as ECIS and PACIS.

Paul O'Dea (bpodea@selectstrategies.com) is CEO of Select Strategies, Ireland. He achieved extraordinary success as a founder of a leading international banking software company, prior to its acquisition by one of the world's largest application software companies. He has worked with, and mentored, sales organizations in the United States, Europe, Australia, and Asia. He has led numerous high technology companies through early market development, sales process and execution, and international growth. He is also a guest lecturer in international competitive strategy in the Smurfit Business School, Dublin, one of the world's leading business schools.

References

Ballantine, J., Levy, M., and Powell, P. "Evaluating Information Systems in SMEs: Issues and Evidence," *European Journal of Information Systems* (7), 1998, pp. 241-251.

Carr, N. "The End of Corporate Computing," *MIT Sloan Management Review* (46:3), 2005, pp. 66-73.

Heart, T., and Pliskin, N. "Business-to-Business eCommerce of Information Systems: Two Cases of ASP-to-SME eRental," *INFOR* (40:1), 2002, pp. 23-34

Heart, T., Pliskin, N., Shechtman, E., and Reichel, A. "Information Technology in the Hospitality Industry: The Israeli Scene and Beyond," *Information Technology & Tourism* (4:1), 2001, pp. 41-64.

Levy, M., Powell, P., and Yetton, P. "The Dynamics of SME Information Systems," *Small Business Economics* (19), 2002, pp. 341-354.

META Group. Worldwide IT Benchmark Report, 2005.

Index of Contributors